American Gothic

"This is the definitive anthology of American Gothic tales, the one that offers the most representative range of major authors and texts, in addition to excellent introductions and helpful annotations. All of this has only been enhanced in this second edition, since now there is an even wider range of important Gothic works for students and more advanced scholars to study and interpret. For reading and understanding the American Gothic short story, then, there is no better single volume anywhere." — *Jerrold E. Hogle, University of Arizona*

"This anthology is comprehensive and authoritative and will be an essential source for scholars and students for years to come. Professor Crow is to be congratulated for the meticulous care he has taken to introduce authors and for the extraordinary inclusiveness of the material selected." — *Andrew Smith, University of Sheffield*

"This new edition of Charles L. Crow's anthology presents a panoramic overview of the American Gothic tradition from its Puritan origins to the 1930s Weird tale. One of the main strengths of the collection lies in the fact that it places, alongside the intelligent selections from authors already rightly well associated with the genre (figures such as Hawthorne, Poe, Brown, Irving, and James), contributions from lesser known figures such as George Lippard, John Neal, Charles W. Chesnutt, and Cotton Mather, to name but a few. This edition also benefits from a much greater acknowledgment of the traditionally overlooked contributions to the genre made by female authors: Crow selects not just obvious authors and poets such as Emily Dickinson, Charlotte Perkins Gilman, Louisa May Alcott, and Edith Wharton, but also the likes of Rose Terry Cooke, Harriet Prescott Spofford, Gertrude Atherton, and Madeline Yale Wynne. It is a development which, as Crow acknowledges in his preface, reflects the considerable amount of scholarly work that has been done in this area since the first version of the book was published.

Academics and students will find helpful other new additions such as the chronology (which collates relevant literary events with historical ones) and the thematic table of contents, which helpfully groups extracts under suggestive headings such as 'Animals,' 'Children,' 'Cities,' and 'Feminist Themes,' thereby facilitating a rewarding cross-pollination of authors and texts that might not otherwise be considered alongside one another. The anthology's thoughtful selection of texts and authors, and practical scholarly apparatus, mean that it should be an immensely useful resource for anyone teaching on courses related to this ever-expanding and influential subsection of American literary studies." — *Bernice Murphy, Trinity College Dublin*

AMERICAN GOTHIC

FROM SALEM WITCHCRAFT TO
H. P. LOVECRAFT, AN ANTHOLOGY

Second Edition

EDITED BY CHARLES L. CROW

WILEY-BLACKWELL

A John Wiley & Sons, Ltd., Publication

This second edition first published 2013
Editorial material and organization © 2013 John Wiley & Sons, Ltd.

Edition history: Blackwell Publishers Ltd (1e, 1999)

Wiley-Blackwell is an imprint of John Wiley & Sons, formed by the merger of Wiley's global
Scientific, Technical and Medical business with Blackwell Publishing.

Registered Office
John Wiley & Sons, Ltd, The Atrium, Southern Gate, Chichester, West Sussex, PO19 8SQ, UK

Editorial Offices
350 Main Street, Malden, MA 02148-5020, USA
9600 Garsington Road, Oxford, OX4 2DQ, UK
The Atrium, Southern Gate, Chichester, West Sussex, PO19 8SQ, UK

For details of our global editorial offices, for customer services, and for information
about how to apply for permission to reuse the copyright material in this book please
see our website at www.wiley.com/wiley-blackwell.

The right of Charles L. Crow to be identified as the author of the editorial material in this
work has been asserted in accordance with the UK Copyright, Designs and Patents Act 1988.

Library of Congress Cataloging-in-Publication Data

American gothic : From Salem witchcraft to H. P. Lovecraft, An Anthology / edited by
Charles L. Crow. – Second edition.
      pages   cm
  Previous edition: American gothic : an anthology, 1787–1916. Malden, Mass. :
Blackwell, 1999.
  Includes bibliographical references and indexes.
  ISBN 978-0-470-65980-9 (cloth) – ISBN 978-0-470-65979-3 (pbk.)   1. American literature.
2. Gothic revival (Literature)–United States.   3. Supernatural–Literary collections.
4. Horror tales, American.   5. Fantasy literature, American.   6. Fear–Literary collections.
I. Crow, Charles L.
  PS507.A56 2013
  810.8–dc23

                                                2012016772

A catalogue record for this book is available from the British Library.

Cover image: Elihu Vedder, *Memory*, 1870. Los Angeles County Museum of Art, Mr and
Mrs William Preston Harrison Collection 33.11.1. © 2012 Digital image Museum Associates /
LACMA / Art Resource NY / Scala, Florence.
Cover design: Richard Boxall Design Associates
Ornament image © Keith Bishop / iStockphoto

Set in 10.5/12pt Dante by SPi Publisher Services, Pondicherry, India
Printed in Singapore by C.O.S. Printers Pte Ltd

2   2015

Contents

List of Authors

Louisa May Alcott (1832–1888)
Gertrude Atherton (1857–1948)
Ambrose Bierce (1842–1914?)
Charles Brockden Brown (1771–1810)
George Washington Cable (1844–1925)
Robert W. Chambers (1865–1933)
Charles W. Chesnutt (1858–1932)
Kate Chopin (1851–1904)
Rose Terry Cooke (1827–1892)
Stephen Crane (1871–1900)
J. Hector St. John de Crèvecoeur
    (1735–1813)
Emily Dickinson (1830–1886)
Paul Laurence Dunbar (1872–1906)
Mary E. Wilkins Freeman (1852–1930)
Charlotte Perkins Gilman (1860–1935)
Nathaniel Hawthorne (1804–1864)
Washington Irving (1783–1859)
Henry James (1843–1916)

Sarah Orne Jewett (1849–1909)
Henry Clay Lewis (1825–1850)
George Lippard (1822–1854)
Jack London (1876–1916)
Henry Wadsworth Longfellow (1807–1882)
H[oward] P[hillips] Lovecraft (1890–1937)
Edgar Lee Masters (1868–1950)
Cotton Mather (1663–1728)
Herman Melville (1819–1891)
John Neal (1793–1876)
Frank Norris (1870–1902)
"Abraham Panther" (?)
Elia Wilkinson Peattie (1862–1935)
Edgar Allan Poe (1809–1849)
Alexander Posey (1873–1908)
Edwin Arlington Robinson (1869–1935)
Harriet Prescott Spofford (1835–1921)
Edith Wharton (1862–1937)
Madeline Yale Wynne (1847–1918)

Chronology

Date	Literary Event	Historical Event
1663		Cotton Mather b.
1689	Mather, *Memorable Provinces, Relating to Witchcrafts and Possessions*	
1692		Salem Witch trials begin
1693	Mather, *The Wonders of the Invisible World*	
		Witch trials end
1702	Mather, *Magnalia Christi Americana*	
1728		Cotton Mather d.
1735		J. Hector St. John de Crèvecoeur b.
1771		Charles Brockden Brown b.
1776		United States Declaration of Independence
1787	Anon., "An Account of a Beautiful Young Lady"	
1794	William Godwin, *Caleb Williams*	
1798	Brown, *Wieland*	
1799	Brown, *Arthur Mervyn, Ormond, Edgar Huntly*	
1782	Crèvecoeur, *Letters from an American Farmer*	
1783		Washington Irving b.
1787		U.S. Constitution signed
1793		John Neal b.
1803		Louisiana Purchase
1804		Nathaniel Hawthorne b.
1807		Henry Wadsworth Longfellow b.
1809		Edgar Allan Poe b.
1810		Charles Brockden Brown d.
1812		War with Britain
1813		J. Hector St. John de Crèvecoeur d.
1818	Mary Shelley, *Frankenstein*	
1819	Irving, *The Sketch Book* begins serial publication	
		Herman Melville b.
1820		Missouri Compromise

Date	Literary Event	Historical Event
1822		George Lippard b.
1825		Henry Clay Lewis b.
1827		Rose Terry Cooke b.
1830		Indian Removal Act signed
		Emily Dickinson b.
1831	Poe, *Poems by Edgar A. Poe*	
1832		Louisa May Alcott b.
1835		Harriet Prescott Spofford b.
1836	Ralph Waldo Emerson, *Nature*	
1837	Hawthorne, *Twice-Told Tales*	
1838	Poe, *The Narrative of Arthur Gordon Pym*	
1840	Poe, *Tales of the Grotesque and Arabesque*	
1841	Longfellow, *Ballads and Other Poems*	
1842		Ambrose Bierce b.
1843		Henry James b.
1844	Lippard, *The Quaker City; or, the Monks of Monk Hall*	
		George Washington Cable b.
1845	Poe, *Tales*	
	Poe, *The Raven and Other Poems*	
1846	Hawthorne, *Mosses from an Old Manse*	
1847		Madeline Yale Wynne b.
1848		Gold discovered in California
1849		Edgar Allan Poe d.
		Sarah Orne Jewett b.
1850	Hawthorne, *The Scarlet Letter*	
	Harper's New Monthly Magazine founded	Henry Clay Lewis d.
	Lewis, *Odd Leaves from the Life of a Louisiana Swamp Doctor*	
1851	Melville, *Moby-Dick*	
	Hawthorne, *House of the Seven Gables*	Kate Chopin b.
1852	Hawthorne, *The Blithedale Romance*	
	Melville, *Pierre*	Mary E. Wilkins Freeman b.
1854		George Lippard d.
1856	Melville, *Piazza Tales*	
1857	Melville, *The Confidence Man*	Dred Scott decision by Supreme Court
	Atlantic Monthly founded	Gertrude Atherton b.
1858	Cooke, "My Visitation"	Charles W. Chesnutt b.
1859	Charles Darwin, *The Origin of Species*	John Brown's raid on Harper's Ferry
		Washington Irving d.
1860	Hawthorne, *The Marble Faun*	Abraham Lincoln elected
	Spofford, "Circumstance"	Charlotte Perkins Gilman b.
1861		Civil War begins
1862		Elia Wilkinson Peattie b.
		Edith Wharton b.
1863	Alcott, "A Whisper in the Dark"	
1864		Nathaniel Hawthorne d.
1865		Civil War ends
		Lincoln assassinated
		Robert W. Chambers b.
1868	Alcott, *Little Women*, v. 1	Edgar Lee Masters b.

Date	Literary Event	Historical Event
1868		Edwin Arlington Robinson b.
1869	Alcott, *Little Women*, v. 2	
1870		Frank Norris b.
1871		Stephen Crane b.
1872	Spofford, "Her Story"	Paul Laurence Dunbar b.
1873		Alexander Posey b.
1876		Jack London b.
		Battle of Little Big Horn
		Philadelphia Exposition
		John Neal d.
1877		President Hayes ends Southern Reconstruction
1879	G. W. Cable, *Old Creole Days*	
1880	Cable, *The Grandissimes*	
1882		Henry Wadsworth Longfellow d.
1884	Mark Twain, *Adventures of Huckleberry Finn*	
1886	Bierce, "An Inhabitant of Carcosa"	Haymarket Riot in Chicago
		Emily Dickinson d.
1888		Louisa May Alcott d.
1890		H[oward] P[hillips] Lovecraft b.
1891	Bierce, "The Death of Halpin Frayser"	Herman Melville d.
	Gilman, "The Giant Wisteria"	
1892	Bierce, *Black Beetles in Amber*	Rose Terry Cooke d.
	Gilman, "The Yellow Wallpaper"	
1893	Fran Norris, "Lauth"	Major Depression begins
		Columbian Exposition in Chicago
1894	Twain, *The Tragedy of Pudd'nhead Wilson*	
1895	Chambers, *The King in Yellow*	
	Wynne, "The Little Room"	
1896	Jewett, *The Country of the Pointed Firs*	
1897	E. A. Robinson, *Children of the Night*	
	Bram Stoker, *Dracula*	
1898	James, *The Turn of the Screw*	Spanish–American War
	Peattie, "The House That Was Not"	
1899	Bierce, *Fantastic Fables*	
	Chesnutt, *The Conjure Woman*, *The Wife of His Youth*	
	Crane, "The Monster"	
	Norris, *McTeague*	
1900	Chesnutt, *The House Behind the Cedars*	Stephen Crane d.
1901	Chesnutt, *The Marrow of Tradition*	McKinley assassinated
		T. Roosevelt president
1902	Chesnutt, *The Colonel's Dream*	
		Frank Norris d.
1904	Dunbar, *The Heart of Happy Hollow*	Kate Chopin d.
1905	Atherton, *The Bell in the Fog and Other Stories*	
1906		Paul Laurence Dunbar d.
1908		Alexander Posey d.
1909		Sarah Orne Jewett d.
1910	Wharton, "The Eyes"	Mexican Revolution begins

Chronology

Date	Literary Event	Historical Event
1911	Wharton, *Ethan Frome*	
1914	Norris, *Vandover and the Brute*	World War I begins
1915	Masters, *Spoon River Anthology*	
1916	Robinson, *The Man Against the Sky*	Henry James d.
		Jack London d.
		Ambrose Bierce d.?
1917		Russian Revolution begins
1918		World War I ends
		Madeline Yale Wynne d.
1920	Robinson, *The Three Taverns*	Mexican Revolution ends
1921		Harriet Prescott Spofford d.
1925	Robinson, *Dionysus in Doubt*	George Washington Cable d.
1926	Lovecraft, "The Outsider"	
1930		Mary E. Wilkins Freeman d.
1932		Charles W. Chesnutt d.
1933		Robert W. Chambers d.
1935		Charlotte Perkins Gilman d.
		Elia Wilkinson Peattie d.
		Edwin Arlington Robinson d.
1937		H. P. Lovecraft d.
		Edith Wharton d.
1948		Gertrude Atherton d.
1950		Edgar Lee Masters d.
1955	Thomas H. Johnson (ed.), *The Complete Poems of Emily Dickinson*	
1967	Richard M. Dorson (ed.), *American Negro Folktales*	

Thematic Table of Contents

Doubles

Dreams and Nightmares

Families (*see also* Children, Incest)

Folklore

Friendship and Same-Sex Love

Ghosts, Demons, and Vampires (see also Haunted Houses or Castles)

Haunted Houses or Castles (see also Ghosts, Demons, and Vampires)

Imprisonment (see also Lawyers and the Law)

Village Life

Wilderness, Frontier, and the Natural World

Witchcraft

Preface to the Second Edition

The first edition of this volume appeared in 1999. In the intervening period of more than a decade, Gothic studies has grown as an academic discipline, in large part due to work by members of the International Gothic Association, which celebrated the twentieth anniversary of its founding at its 2011 convention in Heidelberg.

In American Gothic specifically, classes and seminars in the field, once rare, now are found in universities throughout the United States and in many other countries.

In recent years, researchers have combed through periodicals of the nineteenth century and have uncovered a rich trove of Gothic texts, many by women authors. Many recent studies, as represented by this edition's bibliography, have sharpened our historical and critical understanding of American Gothic. This second edition reflects the growth of this scholarship and the experiences of students and teachers who have used the book, many of whom have made helpful suggestions.

Editorial Principles

Sources are given for each text. Wherever possible the exact spelling and punctuation of the original are retained, even (and especially) in the case of eccentric usage by writers like Emily Dickinson. Original spelling and punctuation are retained also for the oldest works, those by Cotton Mather. In a few instances obvious errors have been corrected, and this has been stated in the headnote.

Words that may be unfamiliar but can be checked in a desk dictionary usually are not footnoted. Words that are less accessible, potentially misleading to the contemporary reader, or in dialect or a foreign language are footnoted, as are literary and biblical allusions, where possible.

Acknowledgments

In the years since the first edition of this book, I have benefited from collegial discussions with members of the International Gothic Association, of whom I would like to mention especially Jerrold E. Hogle (who first suggested this anthology), David Punter, William Hughes, Andrew Smith, John Whatley, Zofia Kolbuszewska, and the late Allan Lloyd-Smith.

A number of scholars have made suggestions for this edition, or have helpfully answered my queries. Among them are Chad Rohman, Carol Siegel, Jeffrey Andrew Weinstock, Cynthia Kuhn, Matthew W. Sivils, Bernice M. Murphy, and Sherry Truffin. Wiley-Blackwell's reviewers for this revised edition made useful comments, most of which have been incorporated.

My graduate students at Bowling Green State University were among the first users of the 1999 edition. Though more than a decade has passed, those discussions are remembered and have influenced the evolution of our text. I would like to recognize the contributions particularly of Katherine Harper and Julia Shaw.

In my acknowledgments to the first edition, I thanked Cynthia, Jon, and Sarah Crow "for keeping the Editor from sinking too deeply into Gothic gloom." That gratitude needs to be repeated, and extended to new members of the family, Joan Lau and Raphael, Fiona and Jacob Goldman.

The following publishers have granted permission to reprint material under copyright:

Poems by Emily Dickinson reprinted by permission of the publishers and the Trustees of Amherst College from *The Poems of Emily Dickinson: Variorum Edition*, edited by Ralph W. Franklin (Cambridge, MA: The Belknap Press of Harvard University Press), Copyright © 1998 by the President and Fellows of Harvard College. Copyright © 1951, 1955, 1979, 1983 by the President and Fellows of Harvard College.

Duke University Press for Charles Chesnutt, "The Dumb Witness," in *The Conjure Woman and Other Conjure Tales*, edited by Richard Broadhead, pp. 158–71. Copyright © 1993, Duke University Press. All rights reserved. Reprinted by permission of the publisher. www.dukeupress.edu.

Alexander Posey's "Chinnubbie and the Owl" reprinted with permission from the Alexander Posey Collection, Gilcrease Museum Archives, University of Tulsa. Flat Storage. Registration #4627.33.

H. P. Lovecraft's "The Outsider" Copyright 1926 and renewed © 1963 by August Derleth and Donald Wandrei. Reprinted by permission of Arkham House Publishers, Inc., and Arkham's agents, JABerwocky Literary Agency, Inc., PO Box 4558, Sunnyside NY 11104-0558.

Introduction

The Gothic is a larger and more important part of the literature of the United States than is generally thought. It has been so since colonial days, and has been used to explore serious issues. And much of the country's literature is Gothic: it is not an obscure area, but includes some of its best-known works and authors. *Moby-Dick* is Gothic; so are many of the poems of Emily Dickinson; so are *The Sea Wolf, Absalom, Absalom!, Native Son*, and *Beloved*. So are films as diverse as *Alien, Lone Star, Sling Blade*, and *Winter's Bone*.

Clearly some definitions are needed to support these claims. We begin with a distinction. The supernatural is permitted but not essential to the Gothic. Mysterious events and shadowy beings have had a continuous presence in this tradition, from early English Gothic romances to the latest thriller by Stephen King or the last installment in Anne Rice's vampire saga; but they are not essential. Nor is there any particular setting required by the Gothic, in spite of the prevalence of big old houses, claustrophobic rooms, and dark forests. A whaling ship can be a suitable Gothic site as well as a castle. Poe observed that "terror is not of Germany, but of the soul," and his observation points us in the right direction, and away from the stage props.

What, then, are the qualities of the Gothic? Most definitions divide into two approaches, and either address the response of the reader or the characters and events within the work. Certainly most readers understand that the Gothic generates fear, or something like fear. We feel a certain chill at some point, as we encounter a Gothic work. This emotional response – what takes place in the soul, as Poe terms it – is in some way the *point* of the Gothic experience, and is, paradoxically, a source of pleasure. "'Tis so appalling – it exhilarates," as Emily Dickinson puts it. The thrill can be mindless, like that of riding a roller-coaster, and can be satisfied by manipulation of formulas by skilled popular authors or film makers. Yet moments of fear can also be moments of imaginative liberation, and of recognition. In the Gothic, taboos are often broken, forbidden secrets are spoken, and barriers are crossed. The key moment in a Gothic work will occur at the point of boundary crossing or revelation, when something hidden or unexpressed is revealed, and we experience the shock of an encounter which is both unexpected and expected. If we think, and perhaps scream, *No!* then another part of our mind may be acknowledging: *Yes, that is it!*

Within a Gothic work, there is usually a confusion of good and evil, as conventionally defined. We may be asked to suspend our usual patterns of judgment. A frequently

American Gothic: From Salem Witchcraft to H. P. Lovecraft, An Anthology, Second Edition. Edited by Charles L. Crow.
Editorial material and organization © 2013 John Wiley & Sons, Ltd. Published 2013 by John Wiley & Sons, Ltd.

encountered character combines and blurs the roles of hero and villain. Captain Ahab, the "grand ungodly godlike man," is a model of the Gothic villain-hero. But Gothic characters occur in small and private worlds as well. In our collection, Old Woman Magoun is both a kindly, nurturing grandmother and a child murderer. The governess of Henry James's famously ambiguous novella *The Turn of the Screw* may be a heroic defender of her pupils or a lunatic.

American writers understood, quite early, that the Gothic offered a way to explore areas otherwise denied them. The Gothic is a literature of opposition. If the national story of the United States has been one of faith in progress and success and in opportunity for the individual, Gothic literature can tell the story of those who are rejected, oppressed, or who have failed. The Gothic has provided a forum for long-standing national concerns about race, that great and continuing issue that challenges the national myth. In this collection, for example, a number of stories about monsters objectify racial fear and hatred, and the largely forbidden topic of miscegenation is explored by several authors. If the national myth was of equality, a society in which class (like race) does not matter, the Gothic could expose, in stories about brutes, the real class anxiety present in periods of emigration and economic flux. Similarly, in an age when gender roles were shifting, sexual difference could be a source of fear. This anxiety was further heightened by an epidemic of sexually transmitted disease, another forbidden topic of the age. Scholar Elaine Showalter has suggested that this issue underlies the popularity of vampires in Victorian fiction. In any case, the Gothic has been especially congenial to women authors, who found in it ways to explore alternative visions of female life, power, and even revenge. Similarly, homophobia and homoeroticism could be approached within the Gothic when overt discussion was impossible. If the dominant national story was about progress, and a part of this set of values was faith in science and technology to improve everyone's life, then the Gothic can expose anxiety about what the scientist might create, and what threats might be posed by machines, if they escape our control. While we want to believe in wholesome families, the Gothic can expose what many may know about, and never acknowledge: the hatred that can exist alongside of love, the reality of child abuse, even incest.

In all of these areas, then, Gothic explores frontiers: between races, genders, and classes; people and machines; health and disease; the living and the dead; and the boundary of the closed door. It has enabled a dialog to exist instead of a single story, and has given a voice to people, and fears, otherwise left silent.

This volume attempts to show the breadth of the American Gothic tradition. Authors long understood to practice the Gothic, like Poe and Hawthorne, are of course represented. But the reader will find familiar authors who are seldom defined as Gothic, such as Stephen Crane and Jack London. Little-known authors – some of them unjustly obscure – are represented as well as familiar and famous names. Moreover, since it is our intention to stretch the definition of the Gothic, the reader will encounter works which are subtly Gothic; that is, which reveal their Gothic elements slowly, or upon reflection, or in hybrid form with other modes of discourse.

We begin with the Puritan divine and historian Cotton Mather. Mather certainly did not consider himself a Gothic writer. Indeed, the term would have been meaningless to him. Nonetheless, the two selections from Mather represent two of the foundations of American Gothic: the "Matter of Salem" (the witch trials of 1692–3) so important to later writers like Hawthorne; and the Indian captivity narrative, a distinctive American form that shaped the Gothic of American wilderness.

Our collection ends, more than two hundred years later, with stories and poems that carry American Gothic into the modern age.

Cotton Mather (1663–1728)

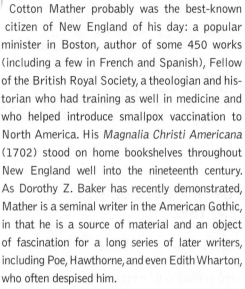

Cotton Mather probably was the best-known citizen of New England of his day: a popular minister in Boston, author of some 450 works (including a few in French and Spanish), Fellow of the British Royal Society, a theologian and historian who had training as well in medicine and who helped introduce smallpox vaccination to North America. His *Magnalia Christi Americana* (1702) stood on home bookshelves throughout New England well into the nineteenth century. As Dorothy Z. Baker has recently demonstrated, Mather is a seminal writer in the American Gothic, in that he is a source of material and an object of fascination for a long series of later writers, including Poe, Hawthorne, and even Edith Wharton, who often despised him.

Today Cotton Mather's name is most often connected with the Salem witchcraft trials of 1692, events with which he was only marginally involved. Had his advice to the trial judges been followed, that they not accept "specter" evidence (testimony that an image of an accused witch, not the actual person, had appeared to a victim), the trials would not have become the legal horror that still haunts America's memory. Laws about witchcraft in New England were the most rational in the Christian world, and (unlike in Britain and continental Europe) it was possible for an accused witch to mount a successful legal defense, be acquitted, and even sue for damages. But how to defend against the charge that one's specter has committed a crime? Despite Mather's misgivings about the legal direction of the trials, he notoriously intervened to prevent citizens from stopping the execution of five condemned witches on August 19, 1692 – an event that Hawthorne

savagely retells in "Alice Doan's Appeal." In *Wonders of the Invisible World* (1693), Mather defends the judges and the outcomes of the trials at a time when public opinion was swinging against them. By the time the trials had ended, nineteen men and women, and two dogs, had been executed, and one man pressed to death under stones because he refused to enter a plea. (According to legend, the last words of this man, Giles Corey, were "more weight.")

Martha Carrier and George Burroughs (whom Mather calls only by his initials) were two of the "witches" executed on August 19. The others were John Willard, George Jacobs, Sr., and John Proctor, about whom Arthur Miller would write a play, *The Crucible*, in 1953. Before his hanging, Burroughs led the witnesses in reciting the Lord's Prayer, which in popular belief was impossible for a witch to do. It was this performance that moved spectators to try to stop the execution. Mather rode his horse in front of them and ordered them to obey the law.

As in witchcraft trials everywhere, unpopular members of the community were the first accused. Burroughs was a minister who had lost his congregation in Salem. He was abusive of his first two wives, and apparently intimidated his neighbors with displays of physical strength as well as claims of magical powers. Martha Carrier was quarrelsome and suspected of poisoning her neighbors' cattle. In both trials we see the "afflicted" girls, presumed victims of witchcraft, screaming in pain when confronted with the accused. (In later years several of these girls would recant their testimony.) In both trials specter evidence was used to convict.

American Gothic: From Salem Witchcraft to H. P. Lovecraft, An Anthology, Second Edition. Edited by Charles L. Crow. Editorial material and organization © 2013 John Wiley & Sons, Ltd. Published 2013 by John Wiley & Sons, Ltd.

The other selection from Mather's writing is a "providence tale" from *Magnalia Christi Americana* (the great deeds of Christ in America). Providence tales were intended as examples of God's protection of his chosen people in New England. This tale, that of Hannah Dustan, is also an Indian captivity narrative, a popular form considered to be an original American genre. Mather constructed his account from Dustan's own transcribed oral testimony. She was from the beginning a controversial figure, and her story was retold by several later American authors, including Hawthorne and Whittier. Her bloody and profitable vengeance against her Indian captors stands near the beginning of the Gothic of the American wilderness and frontier.

Texts: The trials of Martha Carrier and G[eorge] B[urrows] are from *The Wonders of the Invisible World: Being an Account of the Tryals of Several Witches Lately Excuted [sic] in New England...* (London: John Dunton, 1693). The Dustan Narrative is from *Magnalia Christi Americana; or, the Ecclesiastical History of New-England* (London: Thomas Parkhurst, 1702).

The Tryal of G. B. at a Court of OYER AND TERMINER, HELD IN SALEM, 1692

GLAD should I have been, if I had never known the Name of this Man; or never had this occasion to mention so much as the first Letters of his Name. But the Government requiring some Account of his Trial to be inserted in this Book, it becomes me with all Obedience to submit unto the Order.

1. This *G. B.* Was Indicted for Witch-craft, and in the prosecution of the Charge against him, he was Accused by five or six of the Bewitched, as the Author of their Miseries; he was Accused by Eight of the Confessing Witches, as being an head Actor at some of their Hellish Randezvouzes, and one who had the promise of being a King in Satan's Kingdom, now going to be Erected: He was accused by Nine Persons for extraordinary Lifting, and such feats of Strength as could not be done without a Diabolical Assistance. And for other such things he was Accused, until about thirty Testimonies were brought in against him; nor were these judg'd the half of what might have been considered for his Conviction: However they were enough to fix the Character of a Witch upon him according to the Rules of Reasoning, by the Judicious *Gaule*,[1] in that Case directed.

2. The Court being sensible, that the Testimonies of the Parties Bewitched, use to have a Room among the *Suspicions* or *Presumptions*, brought in against one Indicted for Witchcraft; there were now heard the Testimonies of several Persons, who were most notoriously Bewitched, and every day Tortured by Invisible Hands, and these now all charged the Spectres of *G. B.* to have a share in their Torments. At the Examination of this *G. B.* the Bewitched People were grievously harrassed with Preternatural Mischiefs, which could not possibly be Dissembled; and they still ascribed it unto the endeavours of *G. B.* to Kill them. And now upon the Tryal of one of the Bewitched Persons, testified, that in her Agonies, a little black Hair'd Man came to her, saying his Name was *B.* and bidding her set her hand to a Book which he shewed unto her; and bragging that he was a *Conjurer*, above the ordinary Rank of Witches; That he often Persecuted her with the

Notes

THE TRYAL OF G. B.

[1] John Gaule, *Select Cases of Conscience Touching Witches and Witchcrafts* (London, 1646).

offer of that Book, saying, *She should be well, and need fear nobody, if she would but Sign it*; But he inflicted cruel Pains and Hurts upon her, because of her denying so to do. The Testimonies of the other Sufferers concurred with these; and it was remarkable that whereas *Biting* was one of the ways which the Witches used for the vexing of the Sufferers; when they cry'd out of G. B. Biting them, the print of the Teeth would be seen on the Flesh of the Complainers, and just such a Set of Teeth as G. B.'s would then appear upon them, which could be distinguished from those of some other Mens. Others of them testified, That in their Torments, G. B. tempted them to go unto a Sacrament, unto which they perceived him with a Sound of Trumpet, Summoning of other Witches, who quickly after the Sound, would come from all Quarters unto the Rendezvouz. One of them falling into a kind of Trance, affirmed, that G. B. had carried her away into a very high Mountain, where he shewed her mighty and glorious Kingdoms, and said, *He would give them all to her, if she would write in his Book*; But she told him, *They were none of his to give*; and refused the Motions; enduring of much Misery for that refusal.

It cost the Court a wonderful deal of Trouble, to hear the Testimonies of the Sufferers; for when they were going to give in their Depositions, they would for a long time be taken with Fits, that made them uncapable of saying any thing. The Chief Judg asked the Prisoner, who he thought hindered these Witnesses from giving their *Testimonies*? And he answered, *He supposed it was the Devil.* That Honourable Person replied, *How comes the Devil then to be so loath to have any Testimony born against you?* Which cast him into very great Confusion.

3. It has been a frequent thing for the Bewitched People to be entertained with Apparitions of *Ghosts* of Murdered People, at the same time that the *Spectres* of the Witches trouble them. These Ghosts do always affright the Beholders more than all the other spectral Representations; and when they exhibit themselves, they cry out, of being Murthered by the Witch-crafts or other Violences of the Persons who are then in Spectre present. It is further considered, that once or twice, these *Apparitions* have been seen by others, at the very same time they have shewn themselves to the Bewitched; and seldom have there been these *Apparitions*, but when something unusual or suspected, have attended the Death of the Party thus Appearing. Some that have been accused by these *Apparitions* accosting of the Bewitched People, who had never heard a word of any such Person ever being in the World, have upon a fair Examination, freely and fully confessed the Murthers of those very Persons, altho' these also did not know how the Apparitions had complained of them. Accordingly several of the Bewitched, had given in their Testimony, that they had been troubled with the Apparitions of two Women, who said, that they were G. B.'s two Wives, and that he had been the Death of them; and that the Magistrates must be told of it, before whom if B. upon his Tryal denied it, they did not know but that they should appear again in Court. Now, G. B. had been Infamous for the Barbarous usage of his two late Wives, all the Country over. Moreover, it was testified, the Spectre of G. B. threatning of the Sufferers, told them, he had Killed (besides others) Mrs. *Lawson* and her Daughter *Ann*. And it was noted, that these were the Vertuous Wife and Daughter of one at whom this G. B. might have a prejudice for his being serviceable at *Salem Village*, from whence himself had in ill Terms removed some Years before: And that when they dy'd, which was long since, there were some odd Circumstances about them, which made some of the Attendents there suspect something of Witch-craft, tho none Imagined from what Quarter it should come.

Well, G. B. being now upon his Tryal, one of the Bewitched Persons was cast into Horror at the Ghost of B's two Deceased Wives then appearing before him, and crying for *Vengeance* against him. Hereupon several of the Bewitched Persons were successively called in, who all not knowing what the former had seen and said, concurred in their Horror of the Apparition, which they affirmed that he had before him. But he, tho much appalled, utterly deny'd that he discerned any thing of it; nor was it any part of his *Conviction*.

4. Judicious Writers have assigned it a great place in the Conviction of *Witches, when Persons are Impeached by other notorious Witches, to be as ill as themselves; especially, if the Persons have been much noted for neglecting the Worship of God.* Now, as there might have been Testimonies enough of *G. B's* Antipathy to *Prayer,* and the other Ordinances of God, tho by his Profession, singularly Obliged thereunto; so, there now came in against the Prisoner, the Testimonies of several Persons, who confessed their own having been horrible *Witches,* and ever since their Confessions, had been themselves terribly Tortured by the Devils and other Witches, even like the other Sufferers; and therein undergone the Pains of many *Deaths* for their Confessions.

These now testified, that *G. B.* had been at Witch-meetings with them; and that he was the Person who had Seduc'd, and Compell'd them into the snares of Witchcraft: That he promised them *Fine Cloaths,* for doing it; that he brought Poppets to them, and Thorns to stick into those Poppets, for the Afflicting of other People; and that he exhorted them with the rest of the Crew, to Bewitch all *Salem Village,* but be sure to do it Gradually, if they would prevail in what they did.

When the *Lancashire Witches* were Condemm'd, I don't remember that there was any considerable further Evidence, than that of the Bewitched, and than that of some that confessed. We see so much already against *G. B.* But this being indeed not enough, there were other things to render what had been already produced *credible.*

5. A famous Divine recites this among the Convictions of a Witch; *The Testimony of the party Bewitched, whether Pining or Dying; together with the joint Oaths of sufficient Persons that have seen certain Prodigious Pranks or Feats wrought by the Party Accused.* Now, God had been pleased so to leave this *G. B.* that he had ensnared himself by several Instances, which he had formerly given of a Preternatural Strength, and which were now produced against him. He was a very Puny Man, yet he had often done things beyond the strength of a Giant. A Gun of about seven foot Barrel, and so heavy that strong Men could not steadily hold it out with both hands; there were several Testimonies, given in by Persons of Credit and Honor, that he made nothing of taking up such a Gun behind the Lock, with but one hand, and holding it out like a Pistol, at Arms-end. *G. B.* in his Vindication, was so foolish as to say, *That an* Indian *was there, and held it out at the same time:* Whereas none of the Spectators ever saw any such *Indian;* but they supposed, the *Black Man,* (as the Witches call the Devil; and they generally say he resembles an *Indian*) might give him that Assistance. There was Evidence likewise brought in, that he made nothing of taking up whole Barrels fill'd with *Molasses* or *Cider,* in very disadvantageous Postures, and Carrying of them through the difficultest Places out of a Canoo to the Shore.

Yea, there were two Testimonies, that *G. B.* with only putting the Fore Finger of his Right Hand into the Muzzle of an heavy Gun, a Fowling-piece of about six or seven foot Barrel, did lift up the Gun, and hold it out at Arms-end; a Gun which the Deponents thought strong Men could not with both hands lift Up, and hold out at the But-end, as is usual. Indeed, one of these Witnesses was over-perswaded by some Persons, to be out of the way upon *G. B's* Tryal, but he came afterwards with Sorrow for his withdraw, and gave in his Testimony: Nor were either of these Witnesses made use of as Evidences in the Trial.

6. There came in several Testimonies relating to the Domestick Affairs of *G. B.* which had a very hard Aspect upon him; and not only prov'd him a very ill Man; but also confirmed the belief of the Character, which had been already fastned on him.

'Twas testified, that keeping his two Successive Wives in a strange kind of Slavery, he would when he came home from abroad, pretend to tell the Talk which any had with them; That he has brought them to the point of Death, by his harsh Dealings with his Wives, and then made the people about him, to promise that in case Death should happen, they would say nothing of it; That he used all means to make his Wives Write, Sign, Seal, and Swear a Covenant, never to reveal any of his Secrets; That his Wives had privately complained unto the Neighbours about frightful Apparitions of Evil Spirits, with which their House was sometimes infested; and that many such things have been whispered among the Neighbourhood. There were also some other Testimonies relating to the Death of People whereby the Consciences of an Impartial Jury were convinced that G. B. had Bewitched the Persons mentioned in the Complaints. But I am forced to omit several passages, in this, as well as in all the succeeding Tryals, because the Scribes who took notice of them, have not supplyed me.

7. One Mr. *Ruck*, Brother-in-Law to this G. B. testified, that G. B. and himself, and his Sister, who was *G. B's* Wife, going out for two or three Miles to gather Straw-berries, *Ruck* with his Sister, the Wife of G. B. Rode home very Softly, with G. B. on Foot in their Company, G. B. stept aside a little into the Bushes; whereupon they halted and Halloo'd for him. He not answering, they went away homewards, with a quickened pace, without expectation of seeing him in a considerable while; and yet when they were got near home, to their Astonishment, they found him on foot with them, having a Basket of Strawberries. G. B. immediately then fell to Chiding his Wife, on the account of what she had been speaking to her Brother, of him, on the Road: which when they wondred at, he said, *He knew their thoughts*. *Ruck* being startled at that, made some Reply, intimating, that the Devil himself did not know so far; but G. B. answered, *My God makes known your thoughts unto me*. The Prisoner now at the Bar had nothing to answer, unto what was thus witnessed against him, that was worth considering. Only he said, *Ruck, and his Wife left a Man with him, when they left him*. Which *Ruck* now affirm'd to be false; and when the court asked G. B. *What the Man's Name was?* his Countenance was much altered; nor could he say, who 'twas. But the Court began to think, that he then step'd aside, only that by the assistance of the *Black Man*, he might put on his *Invisibility*, and in that *Fascinating Mist*, gratifie his own Jealous Humour, to hear what they said of him. Which trick of rendring themselves *Invisible*, our Witches do in their Confessions pretend, that they sometimes are Masters of; and it is the more credible, because there is Demonstration, that they often render many other things utterly *Invisible*.

8. *Faltring, faulty, unconstant, and contrary Answers upon judicial and deliberate Examination*, are counted some unlucky Symptoms of Guilt, in all Crimes, especially in Witchcrafts. Now there never was a Prisoner more eminent for them, than G. B. both at his Examination and on his Trial. His *Tergiversations, Contradictions, and Falshoods* were very sensible: he had little to say, but that he had heard some things that he could not prove, Reflecting upon the Reputation of some of the Witnesses. Only he gave in a Paper to the Jury; wherein, altho' he had many times before, granted, not only that there are *Witches*, but also, that the present Sufferings of the Country are the effects of *horrible Witchcrafts*, yet he now goes to evince it, *That there neither are, nor ever were Witches, that having made a Compact with the Devil, can send a Devil to Torment other people at a distance*. This Paper was Transcribed out of *Ady;*[2] which the Court presently knew, as soon as they heard it. But he said, he had taken none of it out of any Book; for which, his Evasion afterwards, was, That a Gentleman gave him the Discourse in a Manuscript, from whence he Transcribed it.

Notes

[2] Thomas Ady, *A Candle in the Dark* (London, 1656).

9. The Jury brought him in *guilty*: But when he came to Die, he utterly deni'd the Fact, whereof he had been thus convicted.

The Trial of Martha Carrier, at the COURT OF OYER AND TERMINER, HELD BY ADJOURNMENT AT SALEM, AUGUST 2, 1692

MARTHA CARRIER was Indicted for the bewitching certain Persons, according to the Form usual in such Cases, pleading *Not Guilty*, to her Indictment; there were first brought in a considerable number of the bewitched Persons; who not only made the Court sensible of an horrid Witchcraft committed upon them, but also deposed, That it was *Martha Carrier*, or her Shape, that grievously tormented them, by Biting, Pricking, Pinching and Choaking of them. It was further deposed, That while this *Carrier* was on her Examination, before the Magistrates, the Poor People were so tortured that everyone expected their Death upon the very spot, but that upon the binding of *Carrier* they were eased. Moreover the Look of *Carrier* then laid the Afflicted People for dead; and her Touch, if her Eye at the same time were off them, raised them again: Which Things were also now seen upon her Tryal. And it was testified, That upon the mention of some having their Necks twisted almost round, by the Shape of this *Carrier*, she replyed, *Its no matter though their Necks had been twisted quite off.*

II. Before the Tryal of this Prisoner, several of her own children had frankly and fully confessed, not only that they were Witches themselves, but that this their Mother had made them so. This Confession they made with great Shews of Repentance, and with much Demonstration of Truth. They related Place, Time, Occasion; they gave an account of Journeys, Meetings and Mischiefs by them performed, and were very credible in what they said. Nevertheless, this Evidence was not produced against the Prisoner at the Bar, inasmuch as there was other Evidence enough to proceed upon.

III. *Benjamin Abbot* gave his Testimony, That last *March* was a twelvemonth, this *Carrier* was very angry with him, upon laying out some Land, near her Husband's: Her Expressions in this Anger, were, *That she would stick as close* to Abbot *as the Bark stuck to the Tree; and that he should repent of it afore seven years came to an End,* so as *Doctor* Prescot *should never cure him. These* Words were heard by others besides *Abbot* himself; who also heard her say, *She would hold his Nose as close to the grindstone as ever it was held since his Name was* Abbot. Presently after this, he was taken with a Swelling in his Foot, and then with a Pain in his Side, and exceedingly tormented. It bred into a Sore, which was launced by Doctor *Prescot*, and several Gallons of Corruption ran out of it. For six Weeks it continued very bad, and then another Sore bred in the Groin, which was also lanced by Doctor *Prescot*. Another Sore then bred in his Groin, which was likewise cut, and put him to very great Misery: He was brought unto Death's Door, and so remained until *Carrier* was taken, and carried away by the Constable, from which very Day he began to mend, and so grew better every Day, and is well ever since.

Sarah Abbot also, his Wife, testified, That her Husband was not only all this while Afflicted in his Body, but also that strange extraordinary and unaccountable Calamities befel his Cattel; their Death being such as they could guess at no Natural Reason for.

IV. *Allin Toothaker* testify'd, That *Richard*, the son of *Martha Carrier*, having some difference with him, pull'd him down by the Hair of the Head. When he Rose again, he was going to strike at *Richard Carrier*; but fell down flat on his Back to the ground, and had not power to stir hand or foot, until he told *Carrier* he yielded; and then he saw the shape of *Martha Carrier*, go off his breast.

This *Toothaker*, had Received a wound in the *Wars*; and he now testify'd, that *Martha Carrier* told him, *He should never be Cured*. Just afore the Apprehending of *Carrier*, he could thrust a knitting Needle into his wound, four inches deep; but presently after her being seized, he was thoroughly healed. He further testify'd, that when *Carrier* and he sometimes were at variance, she would clap her hands at him, and say, *He should get nothing by it*; whereupon he several times lost his Cattle, by strange Deaths, whereof no natural causes could be given.

V. *John Rogger* also testifyed, That upon the threatning words of this malicious *Carrier*, his Cattle would be strangely bewitched; as was more particularly then described.

VI. *Samuel Preston* testify'd, that about two years ago, having some difference with *Martha Carrier*, he lost a *Cow* in a strange Preternatural unusual manner; and about a month after this, the said *Carrier*, having again some difference with him, she told him, *He had lately lost a Cow, and it should not be long before he lost another*; which accordingly came to pass; for he had a thriving and well-kept *Cow*, which without any known cause quickly fell down and dy'd.

VII. *Phebe Chandler* testify'd, that about a Fortnight before the apprehension of *Martha Carrier*, on a Lords-day while the Psalm was singing in the *Church*, this *Carrier* then took her by the shoulder and shaking her, asked her, *where she lived*: she made her no Answer, although as *Carrier*, who lived next door to her Fathers House, could not in reason but know who she was.

Quickly after this, as she was at several times crossing the Fields, she heard a voice, that she took to be *Martha Carriers*, and it seem'd as if it was over her head. The voice told her, *she should within two or three days be poisoned*. Accordingly, within such a little time, one half of her right hand, became greatly swollen, and very painful; as also part of her Face: whereof she can give no account how it came. It continued very bad for some dayes, and several times since, she has had a great pain in her breast; and been so seized on her leggs, that she has hardly been able to go. She added, that lately, going well to the House of God, *Richard*, the son of *Martha Carrier*, look'd very earnestly upon her, and immediately her hand, which had formerly been poisoned, as is above-said, began to pain her greatly, and she had a strange Burning at her stomach; but was then struck deaf, so that she could not hear any of the prayer, or singing, till the two or three last words of the Psalm.

VIII. One *Foster*, who confessed her own share in the Witchcraft for which the Prisoner stood indicted, affirm'd, that she had seen the prisoner at some of their *Witch-meetings*, and that it was this *Carrier*, who perswaded her to be a Witch. She confessed, that the Devil carry'd them on a pole, to a Witch-meeting; but the pole broke, and she hanging about *Carriers neck*, they both fell down, and she then received an hurt by the Fall, whereof she was not at this very time recovered.

IX. One *Lacy*, who likewise confessed her share in this Witchcraft, now testify'd, that she and the prisoner were once Bodily present at a *Witch-meeting* in *Salem Village*; and that she knew the prisoner to be a Witch, and to have been at a Diabolical sacrament, and that the prisoner was the undoing of her, and her Children, by enticing them into the snare of the Devil.

X. Another *Lacy*, who also confessed her share in this Witchcraft, now testify'd, that the prisoner was at the *Witch-meeting*, in *Salem Village*, where they had Bread and Wine Administred unto them.

XI. In the time of this prisoners Trial, one *Susanna Sheldon*, in open Court had her hands Unaccountably ty'd together with a wheel-band, so fast that without cutting, it could not be loosed: It was done by a *Spectre*; and the Sufferer affirm'd, it was the *Prisoners*.

Memorandum. This rampant Hag, *Martha Carrier*, was the person, of whom the Confessions of the Witches, and of her own children among the rest, agreed, That the Devil had promised her, she should be *Queen of Hell*.

A Notable Exploit; wherein, Dux Faemina Facti[1] [The Narrative of Hannah Dustan]

ON *March* 15. 1697, the *Salvages* made a Descent upon the Skirts of *Haverhil*, Murdering and Captiving about Thirty-nine Persons, and Burning about half a Dozen Houses. In this Broil, one *Hannah Dustan* having lain-in about a Week,[2] attended with her Nurse, *Mary Neff*, a Widow, a Body of terrible *Indians* drew near unto the House where she lay, with Designs to carry on their Bloody Devastations. Her Husband hastened from his Employments abroad unto the relief of his Distressed Family; and first bidding *Seven* of his *Eight* Children (which were from *Two* to *Seventeen* Years of Age) to get away as fast as they could unto some Garrison in the Town, he went in to inform his Wife of the horrible Distress come upon them. E'er she could get up, the fierce *Indians* were got so near, that utterly despairing to do her any Service, he ran out after his Children; resolving that on the Horse which he had with him, he would Ride away with *That* which he should in this Extremity find his Affections to pitch most upon, and leave the rest unto the Care of the Divine Providence. He over-took his Children about Forty Rod from his Door; but then such was the *Agony* of his Parental Affections, that he found it impossible for him to distinguish anyone of them from the rest; wherefore he took up a Courageous Resolution to Live and Die with them all. A Party *of Indians* came up with him; and now though they Fired at him, and he Fired at them, yet he Manfully kept at the Reer of his *Little Army* of Unarmed Children, while they Marched off with the Pace of a Child of Five Years Old; until, by the Singular Providence of God, he arrived safe with them all unto a Place of Safety about a Mile or two from his House. But his House must in the mean time have more dismal *Tragedies* acted at it. The *Nurse* trying to escape with the New-born Infant, fell into the Hands of the Formidable *Salvages*; and those furious Tawnies coming into the House, bid poor *Dustan* to rise immediately. Full of Astonishment she did so; and sitting down in the Chimney with an Heart full of most fearful *Expectation*, she saw the raging Dragons rifle all that they could carry away, and set the House on Fire. About Nineteen or Twenty *Indians* now led these away, with about half a Score other *English Captives*; but e'er they had gone many Steps, they dash'd out the Brains of the *Infant* against a Tree; and several of the other *Captives*, as they began to Tire in their sad *Journey*, were Soon sent unto their *Long Home;*[3] the *Salvages* would presently Bury their Hatchets in their Brains, and leave their Carcasses on the Ground for Birds and Beasts to Feed upon. However, *Dustan* (with her Nurse) notwithstanding her present Condition, Travelled that Night about a Dozen Miles, and then kept up with their New Masters in a long Travel of an Hundred and Fifty Miles, more or less, within a few Days Ensuing, without any sensible Damage in

Notes

A NOTABLE EXPLOIT
[1] A woman was the leader of the action (approximately).

[2] That is, she had given birth about a week before.
[3] They were killed.

their Health, from the Hardships of their *Travel,* their *Lodging,* their *Diet,* and their many other Difficulties. These Two poor Women were now in the Hands of those whose *Tender Mercies are Cruelties;* but the good God, who hath all *Hearts in his own Hands,* heard the Sighs of these *Prisoners,* and gave them to find unexpected Favour from the *Master* who laid claim unto them. That *Indian Family* consisted of Twelve Persons; Two Stout Men, Three Women, and Seven Children; and for the Shame of many an *English Family,* that has the Character of *Prayerless* upon it, I must now Publish what these poor Women assure me: 'Tis this, in Obedience to the Instructions which the *French* have given them, they would have *Prayers* in their Family no less than Thrice every Day; in the *Morning,* at *Noon,* and in the *Evening;* nor would they ordinarily let their Children *Eat or Sleep* without first saying their *Prayers.*[4] Indeed these *Idolaters* were like the rest of their whiter Brethren *Persecutors,* and would not endure that these poor Women should retire to their *English Prayers,* if they could hinder them. Nevertheless, the poor Women had nothing but Fervent Prayers to make their Lives Comfortable or Tolerable; and by being daily sent out upon Business, they had Opportunities together and asunder to do like another *Hannah,* in *Pouring out their Souls before the Lord:*[5] Nor did their praying Friends among our selves forbear to *Pour out* Supplications for them. Now they could not observe it without some Wonder, that their *Indian* Master sometimes when he saw them dejected would say unto them, *What need you Trouble your self? If your God will have you delivered, you shall be so!* And it seems our God would have it so to be. This *Indian Family* was now Travelling with these Two Captive Women, (and an *English* Youth taken from *Worcester* a Year and half before,) unto a Rendezvouz of *Salvages,* which they call a *Town* somewhere beyond *Penacook;* and they still told these poor Women, that when they came to this Town they must be Stript, and Scourg'd, and Run the *Gantlet* through the whole Army of *Indians.* They said this was the *Fashion* when the Captives first came to a Town; and they derided some of the Faint-hearted *English,* which they said, fainted and swoon'd away under the *Torments* of this Discipline. But on *April* 30, while they were yet, it may be, about an Hundred and Fifty Miles from the *Indian* Town, a little before break of Day, when the whole Crew was in a *Dead Sleep,* (Reader, see if it prove not so!) one of these Women took up a Resolution to imitate the Action of *Jael* upon *Sisera;*[6] and being where she had not her own *Life* secured by any *Law* unto her, she thought she was not forbidden by any *Law* to take away the *Life* of the *Murderers,* by whom her *Child* had been Butchered. She heartened the *Nurse* and the *Youth* to assist her in this Enterprize; and all furnishing themselves with *Hatchets* for the purpose, they struck such home Blows upon the Heads of their *Sleeping Oppressors,* that e'er they could any of them struggle into any effectual resistance, *at the Feet* of those poor Prisoners, *they bow'd, they fell, they lay down; at their Feet they bowed, they fell; where they bowed, there they fell down Dead.* Only one *Squaw* escaped sorely Wounded from them in the Dark; and one *Boy,* whom they reserved asleep, intending to bring him away with them, suddenly wak'd and Scuttled away from this Desolation. But cutting off the *Scalps* of the *Ten Wretches,* they came off, and received *Fifty Pounds* from the General Assembly of the Province, as a Recompence of their Action; besides which, they received many *Presents of Congratulation* from their more private Friends; but none gave 'em a greater Taste of Bounty than Colonel *Nicholson,* the Governour of *Maryland,* who hearing of their Action, sent 'em a very generous Token of his Favour.

Notes

[4] These Indians had been converted to Catholicism by the French.

[5] See 1 Samuel 1: 5.

[6] See Judges 5.

"Abraham Panther"

Nothing is known of the author who used the pseudonym "Abraham Panther." The narrative appeared in pamphlet form in Middletown, Connecticut, in 1787, and was reprinted in various places, with abridgments, in New England and New York, for several years.

While presenting itself as a factual account, the Panther narrative clearly is a piece of fiction. It fashions itself on the perennially popular "Indian captivity" narrative, of which Mary Rowlandson's is the best-known example. Other models may have been present in the author's mind, such as the story of Judith and Holofernes from the apocryphal "Book of Judith."

Abraham Panther, whoever he or she may have been, introduces a number of patterns to be seen again in American Gothic. The setting is not a haunted castle but the wilderness, that repository of so many complex and contradictory American values. The Lady journeys into the forest and encounters a horrifying and self-altering series of challenges, culminating in her defeat of the giant and occupation of his den. She returns, transformed, to find wealth and reconciliation in the settlement she had fled nine years before. Though very compressed, with the simplicity of a folk tale, the Panther narrative suggests many of the issues of race and gender which later writers in this collection will revisit.

Text: Abraham Panther, *A Surprising Account of the Discovery of a Lady Who Was Taken by the Indians in the Year 1777, and After Making Her Escape, She Retired to a Lonely Cave, Where She Lived Nine Years*. In *Bickerstaff's Almanac, for ...* 1788 (Norwich, CT: John Trumbull, 1787). A few distracting spellings have been silently corrected.

A surprising account of the Discovery of a Lady who was taken by the Indians in the year 1777, and after making her escape, she retired to a lonely Cave, where she lived nine years

SIR,

Having returned from the Westward, I now sit down agreeable to your request to give you an account of my journey. Two days after you left my house Mr. Isaac Camber and myself, after providing ourselves with provisions, begun our journey; determining to penetrate the Western wilderness as far as prudence and safety would permit. We travelled for thirteen days in a westerly direction, without meeting any thing uncommon or worthy description, except the very great variety of birds and wild beasts, which would frequently start before us, and as we had our muskets contributed not a little to our amusement and support. The land we found exceeding rich and fertile, every where well watered, and the variety of berries, nuts, ground-nuts, &c. afforded us very comfortable living.

On the 14th day of our travels, while we were observing a high hill, at the foot of which ran a beautiful stream, which passing through a small plain, after a few windings lost itself in a thicket, and observing the agreeable picturesque prospect which presented itself on all sides, we were surprised at the sound of a voice which seemed at no great distance. At first we were uncertain whether the voice was a human one, or that of some bird as many extraordinary ones inhabited these wilds. After listening some time the voice ceased, and we then determined to proceed up the hill, from whence we judged the sound to come, that we might if possible discover what voice it was that had so much astonished us. Accordingly crossing the brook we proceeded up the hill, and having arrived near the summit we again distinctly heard a voice singing in our own language a mournful song. When the voice ceased we observed a small foot path which we followed, and arriving at the top of the hill, passed round a large rock, then through a thicket of bushes at the end of which was a large opening; upon our arrival here, to our inexpressible amazement, we beheld a most beautiful young LADY sitting near the mouth of a cave. She not observing us begun again to sing. We now attempted to approach her, when a dog which we had not before observed, sprung up and began to bark at us, at which she started up and seeing us, gave a scream and swooned away. We ran to her assistance and having lifted her up, she soon recovered; and looking wildly at us exclaimed, Heavens! Where am I? and who, and from whence are you? We desired her to be under no uneasiness, told her we were travellers, that we came only to view the country but that in all our travels we had not met with any thing that had surprised us so much as her extraordinary appearance, in a place which we imagined totally unfrequented.

After a little conversation, having convinced her of our peaceable dispositions, she invited us into the cave where she refreshed us with some ground nuts, a kind of apples, some Indian cake and excellent water. We found her to be an agreeable, sensible lady, and after some conversation we requested to know who she was and how she came to this place, she very readily complied with this request and begun her story as follows. "Strangers, your appearance and conversation intitle you to my confidence, and though my story cannot be very interesting or entertaining, yet it may possibly excite your pity, while it gratifies your curiosity. I was born near Albany – in the year 1760. My father was a man of some consequence and of considerable estate in the place where he lived, I was his only child. In the 15th year of my age my father received into his family a young gentleman of education as his clerk – he had not been long with us before he conceived an unfortunate passion for me, and as he had frequent opportunities of conversing with me, his insinuating address, added to his sensible, engaging conversation, soon found way to my heart. After this we spent together many happy evenings, vowing unalterable love, and fondly anticipating future happiness. We were however obliged to conceal our attachment from my father, who as he was excessively eager in pursuit of riches, we had no reason to suppose he would countenance our loves or consent to my marriage with a man destitute of fortune. It happened one evening while we were discoursing by ourselves in a little garden adjoining our house, that we were overheard by my father. Next morning my father with an angry countenance upbraided my lover with treacherously engaging his daughter[']s affections, and after calling him many hard names, dismissed him with peremptory order never again to enter his house. By means however of an old servant, long attached to my lover, we found means to carry on a correspondence, and in about a month after we so contrived matters that I had an interview with my lover: I then agreed to quit my father's house and retire into the country, to a little hut, my father enraged at my elopement, had hired several men to search the country in pursuit of us, that he threatened vengeance to us both, and declared that he would be the death of the man who had carried off his daughter. In order to elude the search of those who were in pursuit of us, we proposed to move further back into the country, and there to wait till time should calm my father's rage, or effectually cool his resentment.

We accordingly left the hut and travelled at an easy rate for four days, determining to avoid being taken. But O! how shall I relate the horrid scene that followed? – Towards the evening of the fourth day we were surrounded and made prisoners by a party of Indians, who led us about two miles and then barbarously murdered my lover, cutting and mangling him in a most inhuman manner after tying him to a stake they kindled a fire round him, and while he burnt they run round singing and dancing, rejoicing in their brutal cruelty. I was at a few rods' distance during this transaction, and this scene had well nigh deprived me of life. I fainted away and lay some time motionless on the ground, when I recovered my senses, I perceived that my guard had joined his companions, some of whom were seated round in rings, and others continued singing and dancing. Seeing them all engaged I withdrew by degrees into the bushes, and being out of their sight I got up and run for about an hour: I then sat down by the side of a tree and being overcome by fatigue and the sight I had seen, I either fainted or fell asleep, and knew nothing till next morning about 7 o'clock. 'Tis impossible for me to describe my feelings – or for you to conceive a situation more wretched than mine, at this time. Surrounded, as I supposed, on all sides by danger – I knew not what to do, without a guide to direct, or friend to protect me.

At length I got up, and after walking some time I resolved to seek some place of shelter where I might be secure from storms by day and from beasts by night, where I might dwell till a period should be put to my miserable existence. – With this view I wandered about for 14 days without knowing whither I went. By day the spontaneous produce of the earth supplied me with food, by night the ground was my couch, and the canopy of heaven my only covering. In the afternoon of the fifteenth day I was surprized at seeing a man of a gigantic figure walking towards me – to run I knew would be vain, and no less vain to attempt to hide. He soon came up with me and accosted me in a language I did not understand, and after surveying me for some time he took me by the hand and led me to this cave, having entered he pointed to a stone seat on which I sat down, he then gave me to eat some nuts and some Indian cake, after which he stretched himself out upon a long stone covered with skins which he used as a bed, and several times motioned to me to lay myself beside him; I declined his offer, and at length he rose in a passion and went into another apartment of the cave and brought forth a sword and hatchet. He then motioned to me that I must either accept of his bed or expect death for my obstinacy; I still declined his offer, and was resolved to die rather than comply with his desire. He then brought a walnut bark, and having bound me pointed to the east, intimating that he left me till next morning to consider his proposal, he then returned to his bed and happily for me soon fell asleep. Having the liberty of my mouth I soon made out to bite the bark in two with which he bound me, by which I found means to liberate myself while he continued sleeping. As I considered this as the only opportunity I should have of freeing myself from him, – as I expected that he would use violence when he awaked, to make me partake of his bed, and as I knew I could not escape him by flight I did not long deliberate, but took up the hatchet he had brought, and summoning resolution I with three blows effectually put an end to his existence. I then cut off his head, and next day having cut him into quarters drew him out of the cave about half a mile distance, when after covering him with leaves and bushes I returned to this place. I now found myself alone in possession of this cave in which are several apartments. I found here a kind of Indian corn which I planted, and have yearly raised a small quantity, here I contented myself as well as my wretched situation would permit – here have I existed for nine long years, in all which time this faithful dog which I found in the cave has been my only companion, and you are the only human beings who ever heard me tell my tale." Here she finished her narration, and after shedding a plentiful shower of tears and a little conversation she requested us to take rest, which request we willingly complied with.

Next morning she conducted us through the cave, in which were four appartments, one of which appeared to be dug pretty deep in the earth, in which was a spring of excellent water – in the other three were nothing remarkable, except four skulls, which we supposed were of persons murdered by the owner of the cave, or of his former companions. We found also three hatchets, four bows and several arrows, one large tinder box, one sword, one old gun and a number of skins of dead beasts, and a few clothes. The bows, some arrows, the sword and one hatchet we brought away, which are now in my possession. After continuing in the cave five days we proposed returning home, and requested the lady to accompany us – at first she refused to quit her cave; but after some persuasion she consented. We together left the cave on the morning of the sixth day after our arrival in it, and travelling the way we went, arrived at my house in 17 days. After resting about a week we accompanied the Lady, agreeable to her desire, to her father's house: the old man did not at first recognize his daughter, but being told who she was – he looked at her for some time and then tenderly embraced her crying, O! my child, my long lost child, do I once more fold thee in my arms – He then fainted away. We with difficulty brought him to life; but the scene had overcome him; he opened his eyes and being recovered, a little requested to know where she had lived so long, and what had happened to her since her leaving his house. We desired him to wait till he should be better recovered – but he begged to be satisfied immediately, observing that he had but a few moments to live. She then briefly related what had happened to her and the tragical death of her lover – he seemed much affected, and when she had finished, he took her by the hand and affectionately squeezed it, acknowledged he had been unjustly cruel to her, asked her forgiveness and attempted to say something more, but immediately fainted – all our endeavours to recover him were in vain. – he lay about seven hours and then expired. He left a handsome fortune to his daughter, who, notwithstanding his cruelty, was deeply affected at his sudden death. This adventure, the most singular and extraordinary of my life, I have communicated agreeable to your desire, as it really happened, without addition or diminition, and am Sir, yours, &c.

ABRAHAM PANTHER.

J. Hector St. John de Crèvecoeur (1735–1813)

Crèvecoeur was a French aristocrat who adopted the persona of a simple American farmer named John. His *Letters from an American Farmer* (1782) is a classic statement of American exceptionalism. In answering the rhetorical question "What is an American?" Crèvecoeur produces a still evocative picture of simple pastoral life under lenient laws, and a new kind of person formed in a melting pot, in which the mutual hostilities of European nations are dissolved. But this vision of perfection, offered especially in the often anthologized Letter III, is disrupted by Letter IX. As Teresa A. Goddu persuasively argues in *Gothic America*, Letter IX demonstrates a basic pattern of American Gothic by subverting the narrative of the earlier letters, and revealing what they must conceal. John's horrifying encounter with the caged slave is a true Gothic moment, and exposes the key issue of race and American culture.

Text: J. Hector St. John de Crèvecoeur, *Letters From an American Farmer, reprinted from the original ed.* (New York: Fox, Duffield, 1904). A small number of obvious misprints have been silently corrected, and present-day conventions for quotation marks applied.

Letters from an American Farmer
LETTER IX.
DESCRIPTION OF CHARLES-TOWN; THOUGHTS ON SLAVERY; ON PHYSICAL EVIL; A MELANCHOLY SCENE

CHARLES-TOWN is, in the north, what Lima is in the south; both are Capitals of the richest provinces of their respective hemispheres: you may therefore conjecture, that both cities must exhibit the appearances necessarily resulting from riches. Peru abounding in gold, Lima is filled with inhabitants who enjoy all those gradations of pleasure, refinement, and luxury, which proceed from wealth. Carolina produces commodities, more valuable perhaps than gold, because they are gained by greater industry; it exhibits also on our northern stage, a display of riches and luxury, inferior indeed to the former, but far superior to what are to be seen in our northern towns. Its situation is admirable, being built at the confluence of two large rivers, which receive in their course a great number of inferior streams; all navigable in the spring, for flat boats. Here the produce of this extensive territory concentres; here therefore is the seat of the most valuable exportation; their wharfs, their docks, their magazines, are extremely convenient to facilitate this great commercial business. The inhabitants are the gayest in America; it is called the centre of our beau monde, and is always filled with the richest planters of the province, who resort hither in quest of health and pleasure. Here are always to be seen a great number of valetudinarians from the West-Indies, seeking for the renovation of health, exhausted by the debilitating nature of their sun, air, and modes of living. Many of these West-Indians have I seen, at thirty, loaded with the infirmities of old age; for nothing is more common in those countries of wealth, than for persons to lose the abilities of enjoying the comforts of life, at a time when we northern men just begin to taste the fruits of our labour and prudence. The round of pleasure, and the expenses of those citizens' tables, are much superior to what you would imagine: indeed the growth of this town and province has been aston-ishingly rapid. It is pity that the narrowness of the neck on which it stands prevents it from increasing; and which is the reason why houses are so dear. The heat of the cli-mate, which is sometimes very great in the interior parts of the country, is always temperate in Charles-Town; though sometimes when they have no sea breezes the sun is too powerful. The climate renders excesses of all kinds very dangerous, particularly those of the table; and yet, insensible or fearless of danger, they live on, and enjoy a short and a merry life: the rays of their sun seem to urge them irresistibly to dissipa-tion and pleasure: on the contrary, the women, from being abstemious, reach to a longer period of life, and seldom die without having had several husbands. An European at his first arrival must be greatly surprised when he sees the elegance of their houses, their sumptuous furniture, as well as the magnificence of their tables. Can he imagine himself in a country, the establishment of which is so recent?

The three principal classes of inhabitants are, lawyers, planters, and merchants; this is the province which has afforded to the first the richest spoils, for nothing can exceed their wealth, their power, and their influence. They have reached the *ne plus ultra* of worldly felicity; no plantation is secured, no title is good, no will is valid, but what they dictate, regulate, and approve. The whole mass of provincial property is become tributary to this society; which, far above priests and bishops, disdain to be satisfied with the poor Mosaical portion of the tenth. I appeal to the many inhabitants, who, while contending perhaps for their right to a few hundred acres, have lost by the mazes of the law their whole patrimony. These men are more properly law givers than interpreters of the law; and have united here, as well as in most other provinces, the skill and dexterity of the scribe with the power and ambition of the prince: who can tell where this may lead in a future day? The nature of our laws, and the spirit of freedom, which often tends to make us litigious, must necessarily throw the greatest part of the property of the colonies into the hands of these gentlemen. In another century, the law will possess in the north, what now the church possesses in Peru and Mexico.

While all is joy, festivity, and happiness in Charles-Town, would you imagine that scenes of misery overspread in the country? Their ears by habit are become deaf, their hearts are hardened; they neither see, hear, nor feel for the woes of their poor slaves, from whose painful labours all their wealth proceeds. Here the horrors of slavery, the hardship of incessant toils, are unseen; and no one thinks with compassion of those showers of sweat and of tears which from the bodies of Africans daily drop, and moisten the ground they till. The cracks of the whip urging these miserable beings to excessive labour, are far too distant from the gay Capital to be heard. The chosen race eat, drink, and live happy, while the unfortunate one grubs up the ground, raises indigo, or husks the rice; exposed to a sun full as scorching as their native one; without the support of good food, without the cordials of any cheering liquor. This great contrast has often afforded me subjects of the most conflicting meditation. On the one side, behold a people enjoying all that life affords most bewitching and pleasurable, without labour, without fatigue, hardly subjected to the trouble of wishing. With gold, dug from Peruvian mountains, they order vessels to the coasts of Guinea; by virtue of that gold, wars, murders, and devastations are committed in some harmless, peaceable African neighbourhood, where dwelt innocent people, who even knew not but that all men were black. The daughter torn from her weeping mother, the child from the wretched parents, the wife from the loving husband; whole families swept away and brought through storms and tempests to this rich metropolis! There, arranged like horses at a fair, they are branded like cattle, and then driven to toil, to starve, and to languish for a few years on the different plantations of these citizens. And for whom must they work? For persons they know not, and who have no other power over them than that of violence, no other right than what this accursed metal has given them! Strange order of things! Oh, Nature, where art thou? – Are not these blacks thy children as well as we? On the other side, nothing is to be seen but the most diffusive misery and wretchedness, unrelieved even in thought or wish! Day after day they drudge on without any prospect of ever reaping for themselves; they are obliged to devote their lives, their limbs, their will, and every vital exertion to swell the wealth of masters; who look not upon them with half the kindness and affection with which they consider their dogs and horses. Kindness and affection are not the portion of those who till the earth, who carry the burdens, who convert the logs into useful boards. This reward, simple and natural as one would conceive it, would border on humanity; and planters must have none of it!

If negroes are permitted to become fathers, this fatal indulgence only tends to increase their misery: the poor companions of their scanty pleasures are likewise the companions of their labours; and when at some critical seasons they could wish to see them relieved, with tears in their eyes they behold them perhaps doubly oppressed, obliged to bear the burden of nature – a fatal present – as well as that of unabated tasks. How many have I seen cursing the irresistible propensity, and regretting, that by having tasted of those harmless joys, they had become the authors of double misery to their wives. Like their masters, they are not permitted to partake of those ineffable sensations with which nature inspires the hearts of fathers and mothers; they must repel them all, and become callous and passive. This unnatural state often occasions the most acute, the most pungent of their afflictions; they have no time, like us, tenderly to rear their helpless offspring, to nurse them on their knees, to enjoy the delight of being parents. Their paternal fondness is embittered by considering, that if their children live, they must live to be slaves like themselves; no time is allowed them to exercise their pious office, the mothers must fasten them on their backs, and, with this double load, follow their husbands in the fields, where they too often hear no other sound than that of the voice or whip of the task-master, and the cries of their infants, broiling in the sun. These unfortunate creatures cry and weep like their parents, without a possibility of relief; the very instinct of the brute, so laudable, so irresistible, runs counter here to their master's interest; and to that god, all the laws of nature must give way. Thus planters get rich; so raw, so unexperienced am I in this mode of life, that were I to be possessed of a plantation, and my slaves treated as in general they are here, never could I rest in peace; my sleep would be perpetually disturbed by a retrospect of the frauds committed in Africa, in order to entrap them; frauds surpassing in enormity everything which a common mind can possibly conceive. I should be thinking of the barbarous treatment they meet with on ship-board; of their anguish, of the despair necessarily inspired by their situation, when torn from their friends and relations; when delivered into the hands of a people differently coloured, whom they cannot understand; carried in a strange machine over an ever agitated element, which they had never seen before; and finally delivered over to the severities of the whippers, and the excessive labours of the field. Can it be possible that the force of custom should ever make me deaf to all these reflections, and as insensible to the injustice of that trade, and to their miseries, as the rich inhabitants of this town seem to be? What then is man; this being who boasts so much of the excellence and dignity of his nature, among that variety of unscrutable mysteries, of unsolvable problems, with which he is surrounded? The reason why man has been thus created, is not the least astonishing! It is said, I know that they are much happier here than in the West-Indies; because land being cheaper upon this continent than in those islands, the fields allowed them to raise their subsistence from, are in general more extensive. The only possible chance of any alleviation depends on the humour of the planters, who, bred in the midst of slaves, learn from the example of their parents to despise them; and seldom conceive either from religion or philosophy, any ideas that tend to make their fate less calamitous; except some strong native tenderness of heart, some rays of philanthropy, overcome the obduracy contracted by habit.

I have not resided here long enough to become insensible of pain for the objects which I every day behold. In the choice of my friends and acquaintance, I always endeavour to find out those whose dispositions are somewhat congenial with my own. We have slaves likewise in our northern provinces; I hope the time draws near when they will be all emancipated: but how different their lot, how different their situation, in every possible respect! They enjoy as much liberty as their masters, they are as well clad, and as well fed; in health and sickness they are tenderly taken care of; they live under the same roof, and are, truly speaking, a part of our families. Many of them are taught to read and write, and are well instructed in the principles of religion; they are the companions of our labours, and treated as such; they enjoy many perquisites, many established holidays, and are not obliged to work more than white people. They marry where inclination leads them; visit their wives every week; are as decently clad as the common people; they are indulged in educating, cherishing, and chastising their children, who are taught subordination to them as to their lawful parents: in short, they participate in many of the benefits of our society, without being obliged to bear any of its burdens. They are fat, healthy, and hearty, and far from repining at their fate; they think themselves happier than many of the lower class whites: they share with their masters the wheat and meat provision they help to raise; many of those whom the good Quakers have emancipated have received that great benefit with tears of regret, and have never quitted, though free, their former masters and benefactors.

But is it really true, as I have heard it asserted here, that those blacks are incapable of feeling the spurs of emulation, and the cheerful sound of encouragement? By no means; there are a thousand proofs existing of their gratitude and fidelity: those hearts in which such noble dispositions can grow, are then like ours, they are susceptible of every generous sentiment, of every useful motive of action; they are capable of receiving lights, of imbibing ideas that would greatly alleviate the weight of their miseries. But what methods have in general been made use of to obtain so desirable an end? None; the day in which they arrive and are sold, is the first of their labours; labours, which from that hour admit of no respite; for though indulged by law with relaxation on Sundays, they are obliged to employ that time which is intended for rest, to till their little plantations. What can be expected from wretches in such circumstances? Forced from their native country, cruelly treated when on board, and not less so on the plantations to which they are driven; is there anything in this treatment but what must kindle all the passions, sow the seeds of inveterate resentment, and nourish a wish of perpetual revenge? They are left to the irresistible effects of those strong and natural propensities; the blows they receive, are they conducive to extinguish them, or to win their affections? They are neither soothed by the hopes that their slavery will ever terminate but with their lives; or yet encouraged by the goodness of their food, or the mildness of their treatment. The very hopes held out to mankind by religion, that consolatory system, so useful to the miserable, are never presented to them; neither moral nor physical means are made use of to soften their chains; they are left in their original and untutored state; that very state wherein the natural propensities of revenge and warm passions are so soon kindled. Cheered by no one single motive that can impel the will, or excite their efforts; nothing but terrors and punishments are presented to them; death is denounced if they run away; horrid delaceration if they speak with their native freedom; perpetually awed by the terrible cracks of whips, or by the fear of capital punishments, while even those punishments often fail of their purpose.

A clergyman settled a few years ago at George-Town, and feeling as I do now, warmly recommended to the planters, from the pulpit, a relaxation of severity; he introduced the benignity of Christianity, and pathetically made use of the admirable precepts of that system to melt the hearts of his congregation into a greater degree of compassion toward their slaves than had been hitherto customary; "Sir," said one of his hearers, "we pay you a genteel salary to read to us the prayers of the liturgy, and to explain to us such parts of the Gospel as the rule of the church directs; but we do not want you to teach us what we are to do with our blacks." The clergyman found it prudent to with-hold any farther admonition. Whence this astonishing right, or rather this barbarous custom, for most certainly we have no kind of right beyond that of force? We are told, it is true, that slavery cannot be so repugnant to human nature as we at first imagine, because it has been practised in all ages, and in all nations: the Lacedemonians themselves, those great assertors of liberty, conquered the Helotes with the design of making them their slaves; the Romans, whom we consider as our masters in civil and military policy, lived in the exercise of the most horrid oppression; they conquered to plunder and to enslave. What a hideous aspect the face of the earth must then have exhibited! Provinces, towns, districts, often depopulated! their inhabitants driven to Rome, the greatest market in the world, and there sold by thousands! The Roman dominions were tilled by the hands of unfortunate people, who had once been, like their victors, free, rich, and possessed of every benefit society can confer; until they became subject to the cruel right of war, and to lawless force. Is there then no superintending power who conducts the moral operations of the world, as well as the physical? The same sublime hand which guides the planets round the sun with so much exactness, which preserves the arrangement of the whole with such exalted wisdom and paternal care, and prevents the vast system from falling into confusion; doth it abandon mankind to all the errors, the follies, and the miseries, which their most frantic rage, and their most dangerous vices and passions can produce?

The history of the earth! doth it present anything but crimes of the most heinous nature, committed from one end of the world to the other? We observe avarice, rapine, and murder, equally prevailing in all parts. History perpetually tells us of millions of people abandoned to the caprice of the maddest princes, and of whole nations devoted to the blind fury of tyrants. Countries destroyed; nations alternately buried in ruins by other nations; some parts of the world beautifully cultivated, returned again to the pristine state; the fruits of ages of industry, the toil of thousands in a short time destroyed by a few! If one corner breathes in peace for a few years, it is, in turn subjected, torn, and levelled; one would almost believe the principles of action in man, considered as the first agent of this planet, to be poisoned in their most essential parts. We certainly are not that class of beings which we vainly think ourselves to be; man an animal of prey, seems to have rapine and the love of bloodshed implanted in his heart; nay, to hold it the most honourable occupation in society: we never speak of a hero of mathematics, a hero of knowledge of humanity; no, this illustrious appellation is reserved for the most successful butchers of the world. If Nature has given us a fruitful soil to inhabit, she has refused us such inclinations and propensities as would afford us the full enjoyment of it. Extensive as the surface of this planet is, not one half of it is yet cultivated, not half replenished; she created man, and placed him either in the woods or plains, and provided him with passions which must for ever oppose his happiness; everything is submitted to the power of the strongest; men, like the elements, are always at war; the weakest yield to the most potent; force, subtlety, and malice, always triumph over unguarded honesty and simplicity. Benignity, moderation, and justice, are virtues adapted only to the humble paths of life: we love to talk of virtue and to admire its beauty, while in the shade of solitude and retirement; but when we step forth into active life, if it happen to be in competition with any passion or desire, do we observe it to prevail? Hence so many religious impostors have triumphed over the credulity of mankind, and have rendered their frauds the creeds of succeeding generations, during the course of many ages; until worn away by time, they have been replaced by new ones. Hence the most unjust war, if supported by the greatest force, always succeeds; hence the most just ones, when supported only by their justice, as often fail. Such is the ascendancy of power; the supreme arbiter of all the revolutions which we observe in this planet: so irresistible is power, that it often thwarts the tendency of the most forcible causes, and prevents their subsequent salutary effects, though ordained for the good of man by the Governor of the universe. Such is the perverseness of human nature; who can describe it in all its latitude?

In the moments of our philanthropy we often talk of an indulgent nature, a kind parent, who for the benefit of mankind has taken singular pains to vary the genera of plants, fruits, grain, and the different productions of the earth; and has spread peculiar blessings in each climate. This is undoubtedly an object of contemplation which calls forth our warmest gratitude; for so singularly benevolent have those parental intentions been, that where barrenness of soil or severity of climate prevail, there she has implanted in the heart of man, sentiments which overbalance every misery, and supply the place of every want. She has given to the inhabitants of these regions, an attachment to their savage rocks and wild shores, unknown to those who inhabit the fertile fields of the temperate zone. Yet if we attentively view this globe, will it not appear rather a place of punishment, than of delight? And what misfortune! that those punishments should fall on the innocent, and its few delights be enjoyed by the most unworthy. Famine, diseases, elementary convulsions, human feuds, dissensions, etc., are the produce of every climate; each climate produces besides, vices, and miseries peculiar to its latitude. View the frigid sterility of the north, whose famished inhabitants hardly acquainted with the sun, live and fare worse than the bears they hunt: and to which they are superior only in the faculty of speaking. View the arctic and antarctic regions, those huge voids, where nothing lives; regions of eternal snow: where winter in all his horrors has established his throne, and arrested every creative power of nature. Will you call the miserable stragglers in these countries by the name of men? Now contrast this frigid power of the north and south with that of the sun; examine the parched lands of the torrid zone, replete with sulphureous exhalations; view those countries of Asia subject to pestilential infections which lay nature waste; view this globe often convulsed both from within and without; pouring forth from several mouths, rivers of boiling matter, which are imperceptibly leaving immense subterranean graves, wherein millions will one day perish! Look at the poisonous soil of the equator, at those putrid slimy tracks, teeming with horrid monsters, the enemies of the human race; look next at the sandy continent, scorched perhaps by the fatal approach of some ancient comet, now the abode of desolation. Examine the rains, the convulsive storms of those climates, where masses of sulphur, bitumen, and electrical fire, combining their dreadful powers, are incessantly hovering and bursting over a globe threatened with dissolution. On this little shell, how very few are the spots where man can live and flourish? even under those mild climates which seem to breathe peace and happiness, the poison of slavery, the fury of despotism, and the rage of superstition, are all combined against man! There only the few live and rule, whilst the many starve and utter ineffectual complaints: there, human nature appears more debased, perhaps than in the less favoured climates. The fertile plains of Asia, the rich low lands of Egypt and of Diarbeck, the fruitful fields bordering on the Tigris and the Euphrates, the extensive country of the East Indies in all its separate districts; all these must to the geographical eye, seem as if intended for terrestrial paradises: but though surrounded with the spontaneous riches of nature, though her kindest favours seem to be shed on those beautiful regions with the most profuse hand; yet there in general we find the most wretched people in the world. Almost everywhere, liberty so natural to mankind is refused, or rather enjoyed but by their tyrants; the word slave, is the appellation of every rank, who adore as a divinity, a being worse than themselves; subject to every caprice, and to every lawless rage which unrestrained power can give. Tears are shed, perpetual groans are heard, where only the accents of peace, alacrity, and gratitude should resound. There the very delirium of tyranny tramples on the best gifts of nature, and sports with the fate, the happiness, the lives of millions: there the extreme fertility of the ground always indicates the extreme misery of the inhabitants!

Every where one part of the human species are taught the art of shedding the blood of the other; of setting fire to their dwellings; of levelling the works of their industry: half of the existence of nations regularly employed in destroying other nations. What little political felicity is to be met with here and there, has cost oceans of blood to purchase; as if good was never to be the portion of unhappy man. Republics, kingdoms, monarchies, founded either on fraud or successful violence, increase by pursuing the steps of the same policy, until they are destroyed in their turn, either by the influence of their own crimes, or by more successful but equally criminal enemies.

If from this general review of human nature, we descend to the examination of what is called civilised society; there the combination of every natural and artificial want, makes us pay very dear for what little share of political felicity we enjoy. It is a strange heterogeneous assemblage of vices and virtues, and of a variety of other principles, for ever at war, for ever jarring, for ever producing some dangerous, some distressing extreme. Where do you conceive then that nature intended we should be happy? Would you prefer the state of men in the woods, to that of men in a more improved situation? Evil preponderates in both; in the first they often eat each other for want of food, and in the other they often starve each other for want of room. For my part, I think the vices and miseries to be found in the latter, exceed those of the former; in which real evil is more scarce, more supportable, and less enormous. Yet we wish to see the earth peopled; to accomplish the happiness of kingdoms, which is said to consist in numbers. Gracious God! to what end is the introduction of so many beings into a mode of existence in which they must grope amidst as many errors, commit as many crimes, and meet with as many diseases, wants, and sufferings!

The following scene will I hope account for these melancholy reflections, and apologize for the gloomy thoughts with which I have filled this letter: my mind is, and always has been, oppressed since I became a witness to it. I was not long since invited to dine with a planter who lived three miles from ——, where he then resided. In order to avoid the heat of the sun, I resolved to go on foot, sheltered in a small path, leading through a pleasant wood. I was leisurely travelling along, attentively examining some peculiar plants which I had collected, when all at once I felt the air strongly agitated, though the day was perfectly calm and sultry. I immediately cast my eyes toward the cleared ground, from which I was but at a small distance, in order to see whether it was not occasioned by a sudden shower; when at that instant a sound resembling a deep rough voice, uttered, as I thought, a few inarticulate monosyllables. Alarmed and surprised, I precipitately looked all round, when I perceived at about six rods distance something resembling a cage, suspended to the limbs of a tree; all the branches of which appeared covered with large birds of prey, fluttering about, and anxiously endeavouring to perch on the cage. Actuated by an involuntary motion of my hands, more than by any design of my mind, I fired at them; they all flew to a short distance, with a most hideous noise: when, horrid to think and painful to repeat, I perceived a negro, suspended in the cage, and left there to expire! I shudder when I recollect that the birds had already picked out his eyes, his cheek bones were bare; his arms had been attacked in several places, and his body seemed covered with a multitude of wounds. From the edges of the hollow sockets and from the lacerations with which he was disfigured, the blood slowly dropped, and tinged the ground beneath. No sooner were the birds flown, than swarms of insects covered the whole body of this unfortunate wretch, eager to feed on his mangled flesh and to drink his blood. I found myself suddenly arrested by the power of affright and terror; my nerves were convulsed; I trembled, I stood motionless, involuntarily contemplating the fate of this negro, in all its dismal latitude. The living spectre, though deprived of his eyes, could still distinctly hear, and in his uncouth dialect begged me to give him some water to allay his thirst. Humanity herself would have recoiled back with horror; she would have balanced whether to lessen such reliefless distress, or mercifully with one blow to end this dreadful scene of agonising torture! Had I had a ball in my gun, I certainly should have despatched him; but finding myself unable to perform so kind an office, I sought, though trembling, to relieve him as well as I could. A shell ready fixed to a pole, which had been used by some negroes, presented itself to me; filled it with water, and with trembling hands I guided it to the quivering lips of the wretched sufferer. Urged by the irresistible power of thirst, he endeavoured to meet it, as he instinctively guessed its approach by the noise it made in passing through the bars of the cage. "Tankè, you whitè man, tankè you, putè somè poison and givè me." "How long have you been hanging there?" I asked him. "Two days, and me no die; the birds, the birds; aaah me!" Oppressed with the reflections which this shocking spectacle afforded me, I mustered strength enough to walk away, and soon reached the house at which I intended to dine. There I heard that the reason for this slave being thus punished, was on account of his having killed the overseer of the plantation. They told me that the laws of self-preservation rendered such executions necessary; and supported the doctrine of slavery with the arguments generally made use of to justify the practice; with the repetition of which I shall not trouble you at present.

Adieu.

Charles Brockden Brown
(1771–1810)

Charles Brockden Brown's career was short, and, like all American writers of fiction before Irving, he failed to make a commercial success from his talent. Nonetheless, many readers would now agree that his is the best American fiction of his era, and his novels would not be matched for decades after his death. Brown was deeply interested in psychology, and had a strong sense of the evil that is latent in human nature.

His finest novels are *Wieland, Arthur Mervyn*, and *Edgar Huntly*. In them we often encounter situations like that of "Somnambulism": a night scene in which several individuals or groups act at cross purposes, confusion and misunderstanding abound, and violence always threatens. In "Somnambulism" we enter a region called Norwood, where travelers are menaced and led astray by the trickster-monster Nick Handyside. From the beginning, however, Brown suggests that the narrator, Althorpe, not Nick Handyside, may be responsible for the night's violence. The problem posed for Althorpe, and for the reader, is one visited repeatedly in Brown's fiction: is it possible to discover truth if we cannot trust the evidence of our senses?

Text: *Literary Magazine* (May 1805), 335–47.

Somnambulism: A Fragment

[The following fragment will require no other preface or commentary than an extract from the *Vienna Gazette* of June 14, 1784. "At Great Glogau, in Silesia, the attention of physicians, and of the people, has been excited by the case of a young man, whose behaviour indicates perfect health in all respects but one. He has a habit of rising in his sleep, and performing a great many actions with as much order and exactness as when awake. This habit for a long time showed itself in freaks and achievements merely innocent, or, at least, only troublesome and inconvenient, till about six weeks ago. At that period a shocking event took place about three leagues from the town, and in the neighbourhood where the youth's family resides. A young lady, travelling with her father by night, was shot dead upon the road, by some person unknown. The officers of justice took a good deal of pains to trace the author of the crime, and at length, by carefully comparing circumstances, a suspicion was fixed upon this youth. After an accurate scrutiny, by the tribunal of the circle, he has been declared author of the murder: but what renders the case truly extraordinary is, that there are good reasons for believing that the deed was perpetrated by the youth while asleep, and was entirely unknown to himself. The young woman was the object of his affection, and the journey in which she had engaged had given him the utmost anxiety for her safety."]

– Our guests were preparing to retire for the night, when somebody knocked loudly at the gate. The person was immediately admitted, and presented a letter to Mr. Davis. This letter was from a friend, in which he informed our guest of certain concerns of great importance, on which the letter-writer was extremely anxious to have a personal conference with his friend; but knowing that he intended to set out from _____ four days previous to his writing, he was hindered from setting out by the apprehension of missing him upon the way. Meanwhile, he had deemed it best to send a special message to quicken his motions, should he be able to find him.

The importance of this interview was such, that Mr. Davis declared his intention of setting out immediately. No solicitations could induce him to delay a moment. His daughter, convinced of the urgency of his motives, readily consented to brave the perils and discomforts of a nocturnal journey.

This event had not been anticipated by me. The shock that it produced in me was, to my own apprehension, a subject of surprise. I could not help perceiving that it was greater than the occasion would justify. The pleasures of this intercourse were, in a moment, to be ravished from me. I was to part from my new friend, and when we should again meet it was impossible to foresee. It was then that I recollected her expressions, that assured me that her choice was fixed upon another. If I saw her again, it would probably be as a wife. The claims of friendship, as well as those of love, would then be swallowed up by a superior and hateful obligation.

But, though betrothed, she was not wedded. That was yet to come; but why should it be considered as inevitable? Our dispositions and views must change with circum-stances. Who was he that Constantia Davis had chosen? Was he born to outstrip all competitors in ardour and fidelity? We cannot fail of chusing that which appears to us most worthy of choice. He had hitherto been unrivalled; but was not this day destined to introduce to her one, to whose merits every competitor must yield? He that would resign this prize, without an arduous struggle, would, indeed, be of all wretches the most pusillanimous and feeble.

Why, said I, do I cavil at her present choice? I will maintain that it does honour to her discernment. She would not be that accomplished being which she seems, if she had acted otherwise. It would be sacrilege to question the rectitude of her conduct. The object of her choice was worthy. The engagement of her heart in his favour was unavoidable, because her experience had not hitherto produced one deserving to be placed in competition with him. As soon as his superior is found, his claims will be annihilated. Has not this propitious accident supplied the defects of her former obser-vation? But soft! is she not betrothed? If she be, what have I to dread? The engagement is accompanied with certain conditions. Whether they be openly expressed or not, they necessarily limit it. Her vows are binding on condition that the present situation continues, and that another does not arise, previously to marriage, by whose claims those of the present lover will be justly superseded.

But how shall I contend with this unknown admirer? She is going whither it will not be possible for me to follow her. An interview of a few hours is not sufficient to accomplish the important purpose that I meditate; but even this is now at an end. I shall speedily be forgotten by her. I have done nothing that entitles me to a place in her remembrance. While my rival will be left at liberty to prosecute his suit, I shall be abandoned to solitude, and have no other employment than to ruminate on the bliss that has eluded my grasp. If scope were allowed to my exertions, I might hope that they would ultimately be crowned with success; but, as it is, I am manacled and powerless. The good would easily be reached, if my hands were at freedom: now that they are fettered, the attainment is impossible.

But is it true that such is my forlorn condition? What is it that irrecoverably binds me to this spot? There are seasons of respite from my present occupations, in which I commonly indulge myself in journeys. This lady's habitation is not at an immeasurable distance from mine. It may be easily comprised within the sphere of my excursions. Shall I want a motive or excuse for paying her a visit? Her father has claimed to be better acquainted with my uncle. The lady has intimated, that the sight of me, at any future period, will give her pleasure. This will furnish ample apology for visiting their house. But why should I delay my visit? Why not immediately attend them on their way? If not on their whole journey, at least for a part of it? A journey in darkness is not unaccompanied with peril. Whatever be the caution or knowledge of their guide, they cannot be supposed to surpass mine, who have trodden this part of the way so often, that my chamber floor is scarcely more familiar to me. Besides, there is danger, from which, I am persuaded, my attendance would be a sufficient, an indispensable safeguard.

I am unable to explain why I conceived this journey to be attended with uncommon danger. My mind was, at first, occupied with the remoter consequences of this untimely departure, but my thoughts gradually returned to the contemplation of its immediate effects. There were twenty miles to a ferry, by which the travellers designed to cross the river, and at which they expected to arrive at sun-rise the next morning. I have said that the intermediate way was plain and direct. Their guide professed to be thoroughly acquainted with it. – From what quarter, then, could danger be expected to arise? It was easy to enumerate and magnify possibilities; that a tree, or ridge, or stone unobserved might overturn the carriage; that their horse might fail, or be urged, by some accident, to flight, were far from being impossible. Still they were such as justified caution. My vigilance would, at least, contribute to their security. But I could not for a moment divest myself of the belief, that my aid was indispensable. As I pondered on this image my emotions arose to terror.

All men are, at times, influenced by inexplicable sentiments. Ideas haunt them in spite of all their efforts to discard them. Prepossessions are entertained, for which their reason is unable to discover any adequate cause. The strength of a belief, when it is destitute of any rational foundation, seems, of itself, to furnish a new ground for credulity. We first admit a powerful persuasion, and then, from reflecting on the insufficiency of the ground on which it is built, instead of being prompted to dismiss it, we become more forcibly attached to it.

I had received little of the education of design. I owed the formation of my character chiefly to accident. I shall not pretend to determine in what degree I was credulous or superstitious. A belief, for which I could not rationally account, I was sufficiently prone to consider as the work of some invisible agent; as an intimation from the great source of existence and knowledge. My imagination was vivid. My passions, when I allowed them sway, were incontroulable. My conduct, as my feelings, was characterised by precipitation and headlong energy.

On this occasion I was eloquent in my remonstrances. I could not suppress my opinion, that unseen danger lurked in their way. When called upon to state the reasons of my apprehensions, I could only enumerate possibilities of which they were already apprised, but which they regarded in their true light. I made bold enquiries into the importance of the motives that should induce them to expose themselves to the least hazard. They could not urge their horse beyond his real strength. They would be compelled to suspend their journey for some time the next day. A few hours were all that they could hope to save by their utmost expedition. Were a few hours of such infinite moment?

In these representations I was sensible that I had over-leaped the bounds of rigid decorum. It was not my place to weigh his motives and inducements. My age and situation, in this family, rendered silence and submission my peculiar province. I had hitherto confined myself within bounds of scrupulous propriety, but now I had suddenly lost sight of all regards but those which related to the safety of the travellers.

Mr. Davis regarded my vehemence with suspicion. He eyed me with more attention than I had hitherto received from him. The impression which this unexpected interference made upon him, I was, at the time, too much absorbed in other considerations to notice. It was afterwards plain that he suspected my zeal to originate in a passion for his daughter, which it was by no means proper for him to encourage. If this idea occurred to him, his humanity would not suffer it to generate indignation or resentment in his bosom. On the contrary, he treated my arguments with mildness, and assured me that I had over-rated the inconveniences and perils of the journey. Some regard was to be paid to his daughter's ease and health. He did not believe them to be materially endangered. They should make suitable provision of cloaks and caps against the inclemency of the air. Had not the occasion been extremely urgent, and of that urgency he alone could be the proper judge, he should certainly not consent to endure even these trivial inconveniences. "But you seem," continued he, "chiefly anxious for my daughter's sake. There is, without doubt, a large portion of gallantry in your fears. It is natural and venial in a young man to take infinite pains for the service of the ladies; but, my dear, what say you? I will refer this important question to your decision. Shall we go, or wait till the morning?"

"Go, by all means," replied she. "I confess the fears that have been expressed appear to be groundless. I am bound to our young friend for the concern he takes in our welfare, but certainly his imagination misleads him. I am not so much a girl as to be scared merely because it is dark."

I might have foreseen this decision; but what could I say? My fears and my repugnance were strong as ever.

The evil that was menaced was terrible. By remaining where they were till the next day they would escape it. Was no other method sufficient for their preservation? My attendance would effectually obviate the danger.

This scheme possessed irresistible attractions. I was thankful to the danger for suggesting it. In the fervour of my conceptions, I was willing to run to the world's end to show my devotion to the lady. I could sustain with alacrity, the fatigue of many nights of travelling and watchfulness, should unspeakably prefer them to warmth and ease, if I could thereby extort from this lady a single phrase of gratitude or approbation.

I proposed to them to bear them company, at least till the morning light. They would not listen to it. Half my purpose was indeed answered by the glistening eyes and affectionate looks of Miss Davis, but the remainder I was pertinaciously bent on likewise accomplishing. If Mr. Davis had not suspected my motives, he would probably have been less indisposed to compliance. As it was, however, his objections were insuperable. They earnestly insisted on my relinquishing my design. My uncle, also, not seeing any thing that justified extraordinary precautions, added his injunctions. I was conscious of my inability to show any sufficient grounds for my fears. As long as their representations rung in my ears, I allowed myself to be ashamed of my weakness, and conjured up a temporary persuasion that my attendance was, indeed, superfluous, and that I should show most wisdom in suffering them to depart alone.

But this persuasion was transient. They had no sooner placed themselves in their carriage, and exchanged the parting adieus, but my apprehensions returned upon me as forcibly as ever. No doubt part of my despondency flowed from the idea of separation, which, however auspicious it might prove to the lady, portended unspeakable discomforts to me. But this was not all. I was breathless with fear of some unknown and terrible disaster that awaited them. A hundred times I resolved to disregard their remonstrances, and hover near them till the morning. This might be done without exciting their displeasure. It was easy to keep aloof and be unseen by them. I should doubtless have pursued this method if my fears had assumed any definite an consistent form; if, in reality, I had been able distinctly to tell what it was that I feared. My guardianship would be of no use against the obvious sources of danger in the ruggedness and obscurity of the way. For that end I must have tendered them my services, which I knew would be refused, and, if pertinaciously obtruded on them, might justly excite displeasure. I was not insensible, too, of the obedience that was due to my uncle. My absence would be remarked. Some anger and much disquietude would have been the consequences with respect to him. And after all, what was this groundless and ridiculous persuasion that governed me? Had I profited nothing by experience of the effects of similar follies? Was I never to attend to the lessons of sobriety and truth? How ignominious to be thus the slave of a fortuitous and inexplicable impulse! To be the victim of terrors more chimerical than those which haunt the dreams of idiots and children! They can describe clearly, and attribute a real existence to the object of their terrors. Not so can I.

Influenced by these considerations, I shut the gate at which I had been standing, and turned towards the house. After a few steps I paused, turned and listened to the distant sounds of the carriage. My courage was again on the point of yielding, and new efforts were requisite before I could resume my first resolutions.

I spent a drooping and melancholy evening. My imagination continually hovered over our departed guests. I recalled every circumstance of the road. I reflected by what means they were to pass that bridge, or extricate themselves from this slough. I imagined the possibility of their guide's forgetting the position of a certain oak that grew in the road. It was an ancient tree, whose boughs extended, on all sides, to an extraordinary distance. They seemed disposed by nature in that way in which they would produce the most ample circumference of shade. I could not recollect any other obstruction from which much was to be feared. This indeed was several miles distant, and its appearance was too remarkable not to have excited attention.

The family retired to sleep. My mind had been too powerfully excited to permit me to imitate their example. The incidents of the last two days passed over my fancy like a vision. The revolution was almost incredible which my mind had undergone, in consequence of these incidents. It was so abrupt and entire that my soul seemed to have passed into a new form. I pondered on every incident till the surrounding scenes disappeared, and I forgot my real situation. I mused upon the image of Miss Davis till my whole soul was dissolved in tenderness, and my eyes overflowed with tears. There insensibly arose a sort of persuasion that destiny had irreversibly decreed that I should never see her more.

While engaged in this melancholy occupation, of which I cannot say how long it lasted, sleep overtook me as I sat. Scarcely a minute had elapsed during this period without conceiving the design, more or less strenuously of sallying forth, with a view to overtake and guard the travellers; but this design was embarrassed with invincible objections, and was alternately formed and laid aside. At length, as I have said, I sunk into profound slumber, if that slumber can be termed profound, in which my fancy was incessantly employed in calling up the forms, into new combinations, which had constituted my waking reveries. – The images were fleeting and transient, but the events of the morrow recalled them to my remembrance with sufficient distinctness. The terrors which I had so deeply and unaccountably imbibed could not fail of retaining some portion of their influence, in spite of sleep.

In my dreams, the design which I could not bring myself to execute while awake I embraced without hesitation. I was summoned, methought, to defend this lady from the attacks of an assassin. My ideas were full of confusion and inaccuracy. All that I can recollect is, that my efforts had been unsuccessful to avert the stroke of the murderer. This, however, was not accomplished without drawing on his head a bloody retribution. I imagined myself engaged, for a long time, in pursuit of the guilty, and, at last, to have detected him in an artful disguise. I did not employ the usual preliminaries which honour prescribes, but, stimulated by rage, attacked him with a pistol, and terminated his career by a mortal wound.

I should not have described these phantoms had there not been a remarkable coincidence between them and the real events of that night. In the morning, my uncle, whose custom it was to rise first in the family, found me quietly reposing in the chair in which I had fallen asleep. His summons roused and startled me. This posture was so unusual that I did not readily recover my recollection, and perceive in what circumstances I was placed.

I shook off the dreams of the night. Sleep had refreshed and invigorated my frame, as well as tranquillized my thoughts. I still mused on yesterday's adventures, but my reveries were more cheerful and benign. My fears and bodements were dispersed with the dark, and I went into the fields, not merely to perform the duties of the day, but to ruminate on plans for the future.

My golden visions, however, were soon converted into visions of despair. A messenger arrived before noon, intreating my presence, and that of my uncle, at the house of Dr. Inglefield, a gentleman who resided at the distance of three miles from our house. The messenger explained the intention of this request. It appeared that the terrors of the preceding evening had some mysterious connection with truth. By some deplorable accident, Miss Davis had been shot on the road, and was still lingering in dreadful agonies at the house of this physician. I was in a field near the road when the messenger approached the house. On observing me, he called me. His tale was meagre and imperfect, but the substance of it was easy to gather. I stood for a moment motionless and aghast. As soon as I recovered my thoughts I set off full speed, and made not a moment's pause till I reached the house of Inglefield.

The circumstances of this mournful event, as I was able to collect them at different times, from the witnesses, were these. After they had parted from us, they proceeded on their way for some time without molestation. The clouds disappearing, the starlight enabled them with less difficulty to discern their path. They met not a human being till they came within less than three miles of the oak which I have before described. Here Miss Davis looked forward with some curiosity and said to her father, "Do you not see some one in the road before us? I saw him this moment move across from the fence on the right hand and stand still in the middle of the road."

"I see nothing, I must confess," said the father: "but that is no subject of wonder; your young eyes will of course see farther than my old ones."

"I see him clearly at this moment," rejoined the lady. "If he remain a short time where he is, or seems to be, we shall be able to ascertain his properties. Our horse's head will determine whether his substance be impassive or not."

The carriage slowly advancing, and the form remaining in the same spot, Mr. Davis at length perceived it, but was not allowed a clearer examination, for the person, having, as it seemed, ascertained the nature of the cavalcade, shot across the road, and disappeared. The behaviour of this unknown person furnished the travellers with a topic of abundant speculation.

Few possessed a firmer mind than Miss Davis; but whether she was assailed, on this occasion, with a mysterious foreboding of her destiny; whether the eloquence of my fears had not, in spite of resolution, infected her; or whether she imagined evils that my incautious temper might draw upon me, and which might originate in our late interview, certain it was that her spirits were visibly depressed. This accident made no sensible alteration in her. She was still disconsolate and incommunicative. All the efforts of her father were insufficient to inspire her with cheerfulness. He repeatedly questioned her as to the cause of this unwonted despondency. Her answer was, that her spirits were indeed depressed, but she believed that the circumstance was casual. She knew of nothing that could justify despondency. But such is humanity. Cheerfulness and dejection will take their turns in the best regulated bosoms, and come and go when they will, and not at the command of reason. This observation was succeeded by a pause. At length Mr. Davis said, "A thought has just occurred to me. The person whom we just now saw is young Althorpe."

Miss Davis was startled: "Why, my dear father, should you think so? It is too dark to judge, at this distance, by resemblance of figure. Ardent and rash as he appears to be, I should scarcely suspect him on this occasion. With all the fiery qualities of youth, unchastised by experience, untamed by adversity, he is capable no doubt of extravagant adventures, but what could induce him to act in this manner?"

"You know the fears that he expressed concerning the issue of this night's journey. We know not what foundation he might have had for these fears. He told us of no danger that ought to deter us, but it is hard to conceive that he should have been thus vehement without cause. We know not what motives might have induced him to conceal from us the sources of his terror. And since he could not obtain our consent to his attending us, he has taken these means, perhaps, of effecting his purpose. The darkness might easily conceal him from our observation. He might have passed us without our noticing him, or he might have made a circuit in the woods we have just passed, and come out before us."

"That I own," replied the daughter, "is not improbable. If it be true, I shall be sorry for his own sake, but if there be any danger from which his attendance can secure us, I shall be well pleased for all our sakes. He will reflect with some satisfaction, perhaps, that he has done or intended us a service. It would be cruel to deny him a satisfaction so innocent."

"Pray, my dear, what think you of this young man? Does his ardour to serve us flow from a right source?"

"It flows, I have no doubt, from a double source. He has a kind heart, and delights to oblige others: but this is not all. He is likewise in love and imagines that he cannot do too much for the object of his passion."

"Indeed!" exclaimed Mr. Davis, in some surprise. "You speak very positively. That is no more than I suspected; but how came you to know it with so much certainty?"

"The information came to me in the directest manner. He told me so himself."

"So ho! why, the impertinent young rogue!"

"Nay, my dear father, his behaviour did not merit that epithet. He is rash and inconsiderate. That is the utmost amount of his guilt. A short absence will show him the true state of his feelings. It was unavoidable, in one of his character, to fall in love with the first woman whose appearance was in any degree auspicious. But attachments like these will be extinguished as easily as they are formed. I do not fear for him on this account."

"Have you reason to fear for him on any account?"

"Yes. The period of youth will soon pass away. Overweening and fickle, he will go on committing one mistake after another, incapable of repairing his errors, or of profiting by the daily lessons of experience. His genius will be merely an implement of mischief. His greater capacity will be evinced merely by the greater portion of unhappiness that, by means of it, will accrue to others or rebound upon himself."

"I see, my dear, that your spirits are low. Nothing else, surely, could suggest such melancholy presages. For my part, I question not, but he will one day be a fine fellow and a happy one. I like him exceedingly. I shall take pains to be acquainted with his future adventures, and do him all the good that I can."

"That intention," said his daughter, "is worthy of the goodness of your heart. He is no less an object of regard to me than to you. I trust I shall want neither the power nor inclination to contribute to his welfare. At present, however, his welfare will be best promoted by forgetting me. Hereafter, I shall solicit a renewal of intercourse."

"Speak lower," said the father. "If I mistake not, there is the same person again." He pointed to the field that skirted the road on the left hand. The young lady's better eyes enabled her to detect his mistake. It was the trunk of a cherry-tree that he had observed.

They proceeded in silence. Contrary to custom, the lady was buried in musing. Her father, whose temper and inclinations were moulded by those of his child, insensibly subsided into the same state.

The re-appearance of the same figure that had already excited their attention diverted them anew from their contemplations. "As I live," exclaimed Mr. Davis, "that thing, whatever it be, haunts us. I do not like it. This is strange conduct for young Althorpe to adopt. Instead of being our protector, the danger, against which he so pathetically warned us, may be, in some inscrutable way, connected with this person-age. It is best to be upon our guard."

"Nay, my father," said the lady, "be not disturbed. What danger can be dreaded by two persons from one? This thing, I dare say, means us no harm. What is at present inexplicable might be obvious enough if we were better acquainted with this neigh-bourhood. It is not worth a thought. You see it is now gone." Mr. Davis looked again, but it was no longer discernible.

They were now approaching a wood. Mr. Davis called to the guide to stop. His daughter enquired the reason of this command. She found it arose from his uncer-tainty as to the propriety of proceeding.

"I know not how it is," said he, "but I begin to be affected with the fears of young Althorpe. I am half resolved not to enter this wood. That light yonder informs that a house is near. It may not be unadvisable to stop. I cannot think of delaying our journey till morning; but, by stopping a few minutes, we may possibly collect some useful infor-mation. Perhaps it will be expedient and practicable to procure the attendance of another person. I am not well pleased with myself for declining our young friend's offer."

To this proposal Miss Davis objected the inconveniences that calling at a farmer's house, at this time of night, when all were retired to rest, would probably occasion. "Besides," continued she, "the light which you saw is gone: a sufficient proof that it was nothing but a meteor."

At this moment they heard a noise, at a small distance behind them, as of shutting a gate. They called. Speedily an answer was returned in a tone of mildness. The person approached the chaise, and enquired who they were, whence they came, whither they were going, and, lastly, what they wanted.

Mr. Davis explained to this inquisitive person, in a few words, the nature of their situation, mentioned the appearance on the road, and questioned him, in his turn, as to what inconveniences were to be feared from prosecuting his journey. Satisfactory answers were returned to these enquiries.

"As to what you seed in the road," continued he, "I reckon it was nothing but a sheep or a cow. I am not more scary than some folks, but I never goes out a' nights without I sees some *sich* thing as that, that I takes for a man or woman, and am scared a little oftentimes, but not much. I'm sure after to find that it's not nothing but a cow, or hog, or tree, or something. If it wasn't some sich thing you seed, I reckon it was *Nick Handyside*."

"Nick Handyside! who was he?"

"It was a fellow that went about the country a' nights. A shocking fool to be sure, that loved to plague and frighten people. Yes. Yes. It couldn't be nobody, he reckoned, but Nick. Nick was a droll thing. He wondered they'd never heard of Nick. He reck-oned they were strangers in these here parts."

"Very true, my friend. But who is Nick? Is he a reptile to be shunned, or trampled on?"

"Why I don't know how as that Nick is an odd soul to be sure; but he don't do nobody no harm, as ever I heard, except by scaring them. He is easily skeart though, for that matter, himself. He loves to frighten folks, but he's shocking apt to be frightened himself. I reckon you took Nick for a ghost. That's a shocking good story, I declare. Yet it's happened hundreds and hundreds of times, I guess, and more."

When this circumstance was mentioned, my uncle, as well as myself, was astonished at our own negligence. While enumerating, on the preceding evening, the obstacles and inconveniences which the travellers were likely to encounter, we entirely and unaccountably overlooked one circumstance, from which inquietude might reasonably have been expected. Near the spot where they now were, lived a Mr. Handyside, whose only son was an idiot. He also merited the name of monster, if a projecting breast, a misshapen head, features horrid and distorted, and a voice that resembled nothing that was ever before heard, could entitle him to that appellation. This being, besides the natural deformity of his frame, wore looks and practiced gesticulations that were, in an inconceivable degree, uncouth and hideous. He was mischievous, but his freaks were subjects of little apprehension to those who were accustomed to them, though they were frequently occasions of alarm to strangers. He particularly delighted in imposing on the ignorance of strangers and the timidity of women. He was a perpetual rover. Entirely bereft of reason, his sole employment consisted in sleeping, and eating, and roaming. He would frequently escape at night, and a thousand anecdotes could have been detailed respecting the tricks which Nick Handyside had played upon way-farers.

Other considerations, however, had, in this instance, so much engrossed our minds, that Nick Handyside had never been once thought or mentioned. This was the more remarkable, as there had very lately happened an adventure, in which this person had acted a principal part. He had wandered from home, and got bewildered in a desolate tract, known by the name of Norwood. It was a region, rude, sterile, and lonely, bestrewn with rocks, and embarrassed with bushes.

He had remained for some days in this wilderness. Unable to extricate himself, and, at length, tormented with hunger, he manifested his distress by the most doleful shrieks. These were uttered with most vehemence, and heard at greatest distance, by night. At first, those who heard them were panic-struck; but, at length, they furnished a clue by which those who were in search of him were guided to the spot. Notwithstanding the recentness and singularity of this adventure, and the probability that our guests would suffer molestation from this cause, so strangely forgetful had we been, that no caution on this head had been given. This caution, indeed, as the event testified, would have been superfluous, and yet I cannot enough wonder that in hunting for some reason, by which I might justify my fears to them or to myself, I had totally overlooked this mischief-loving idiot.

After listening to an ample description of Nick, being warned to proceed with particular caution in a part of the road that was near at hand, and being assured that they had nothing to dread from human interference, they resumed their journey with new confidence.

Their attention was frequently excited by rustling leaves or stumbling footsteps, and the figure which they doubted not to belong to Nick Handyside, occasionally hovered in their sight. This appearance no longer inspired them with apprehension. They had been assured that a stern voice was sufficient to repulse him, when most importunate. This antic being treated all others as children. He took pleasure in the effects which the sight of his own deformity produced, and betokened his satisfaction by a laugh, which might have served as a model to the poet who has depicted the ghastly risibilities of Death. On this occasion, however, the monster behaved with unusual moderation.

He never came near enough for his peculiarities to be distinguished by star-light. There was nothing fantastic in his motions, nor any thing surprising, but the celerity of his transitions. They were unaccompanied by those howls, which reminded you at one time of a troop of hungry wolves, and had, at another, something in them inexpressibly wild and melancholy. This monster possessed a certain species of dexterity. His talents, differently applied, would have excited rational admiration. He was fleet as a deer. He was patient, to an incredible degree, of watchfulness, and cold, and hunger. He had improved the flexibility of his voice, till his cries, always loud and rueful, were capable of being diversified without end. Instances had been known, in which the stoutest heart was appalled by them; and some, particularly in the case of women, in which they had been productive of consequences truly deplorable.

When the travellers had arrived at that part of the wood where, as they had been informed, it was needful to be particularly cautious, Mr. Davis, for their greater security, proposed to his daughter to alight. The exercise of walking, he thought, after so much time spent in a close carriage, would be salutary and pleasant. The young lady readily embraced the proposal. They forthwith alighted, and walked at a small distance before the chaise, which was now conducted by the servant. From this moment the spectre, which, till now, had been occasionally visible, entirely disappeared. This incident naturally led the conversation to this topic. So singular a specimen of the forms which human nature is found to assume could not fail of suggesting a variety of remarks.

They pictured to themselves many combinations of circumstances in which Handyside might be the agent, and in which the most momentous effects might flow from his agency, without its being possible for others to conjecture the true nature of the agent. The propensities of this being might contribute to realize, on an American road, many of those imaginary tokens and perils which abound in the wildest romance. He would be an admirable machine, in a plan whose purpose was to generate or foster, in a given subject, the frenzy of quixotism. – No theatre was better adapted than Norwood to such an exhibition. This part of the country had long been deserted by beasts of prey. Bears might still, perhaps, be found during a very rigorous season, but wolves which, when the country was a desert, were extremely numerous, had now, in consequence of increasing population, withdrawn to more savage haunts. Yet the choice of Handyside, varied with the force and skill of which he was known to be capable, would fill these shades with outcries as ferocious as those which are to be heard in Siamese or Abyssinian forests. The tale of his recent elopement[1] had been told by the man with whom they had just parted, in a rustic but picturesque style.

"But why," said the lady, "did not our kind host inform us of this circumstance? He must surely have been well acquainted with the existence and habits of this Handyside. He must have perceived to how many groundless alarms our ignorance, in this respect, was likely to expose us. It is strange that he did not afford us the slightest intimation of it."

Mr. Davis was no less surprised at this omission. He was at a loss to conceive how this should be forgotten in the midst of those minute directions, in which every cause had been laboriously recollected from which he might incur danger or suffer obstruction.

This person, being no longer an object of terror, began to be regarded with a very lively curiosity. They even wished for his appearance and near approach, that they might carry away with them more definite conceptions of his figure. The lady declared she should be highly pleased by hearing his outcries, and consoled herself with the belief, that he would not allow them to pass the limits which he had prescribed to his

Notes

SOMNAMBULISM: A FRAGMENT
[1] Running away; the time Nick was lost in Norwood.

wanderings, without greeting them with a strain or two. This wish had scarcely been uttered, when it was completely gratified.

The lady involuntarily started, and caught hold of her father's arm. Mr. Davis himself was disconcerted. A scream, dismally loud, and piercingly shrill, was uttered by one at less than twenty paces from them.

The monster had shown some skill in the choice of a spot suitable to his design. Neighbouring precipices, and a thick umbrage of oaks, on either side, contributed to prolong and to heighten his terrible notes. They were rendered more awful by the profound stillness that preceded and followed them. They were able speedily to quiet the trepidations which this hideous outcry, in spite of preparation and foresight, had produced, but they had not foreseen one of its unhappy consequences.

In a moment Mr. Davis was alarmed by the rapid sound of footsteps behind him. His presence of mind, on this occasion, probably saved himself and his daughter from instant destruction. He leaped out of the path, and, by a sudden exertion, at the same moment, threw the lady to some distance from the tract. The horse that drew the chaise rushed by them with the celerity of lightning. Affrighted at the sounds which had been uttered at a still less distance from the horse than from Mr. Davis, possibly with a malicious design to produce this very effect, he jerked the bridle from the hands that held it, and rushed forward with headlong speed. The man, before he could provide for his own safety, was beaten to the earth. He was considerably bruised by the fall, but presently recovered his feet, and went in pursuit of the horse.

This accident happened at about a hundred yards from the *oak*, against which so many cautions had been given. It was not possible, at any time, without considerable caution, to avoid it. It was not to be wondered at, therefore, that, in a few seconds, the carriage was shocked against the trunk, overturned, and dashed into a thousand fragments. The noise of the crash sufficiently informed them of this event. Had the horse been inclined to stop, a repetition, for the space of some minutes, of the same savage and terrible shrieks would have added tenfold to his consternation and to the speed of his flight. After this dismal strain had ended, Mr. Davis raised his daughter from the ground. She had suffered no material injury. As soon as they recovered from the confusion into which this accident had thrown them, they began to consult upon the measures proper to be taken upon this emergency. They were left alone. The servant had gone in pursuit of the flying horse. Whether he would be able to retake him was extremely dubious. Meanwhile they were surrounded by darkness. What was the distance of the next house could not be known. At that hour of the night they could not hope to be directed, by the far-seen taper,[2] to any hospitable roof. The only alternative, therefore, was to remain where they were, uncertain of the fate of their companion, or to go forward with the utmost expedition.

They could not hesitate to embrace the latter. In a few minutes they arrived at the oak. The chaise appeared to have been dashed against a knotty projecture of the trunk, which was large enough for a person to be conveniently seated on it. Here they again paused. – Miss Davis desired to remain here a few minutes to recruit her exhausted strength. She proposed to her father to leave her here, and go forward in quest of the horse and the servant. He might return as speedily as he thought proper. She did not fear to be alone. The voice was still. Having accomplished his malicious purposes, the spectre had probably taken his final leave of them. At all events, if the report of the rustic was true, she had no personal injury to fear from him.

Through some deplorable infatuation, as he afterwards deemed it, Mr. Davis complied with her intreaties, and went in search of the missing. He had engaged in a

Notes ———
[2] Candle.

most unpromising undertaking. The man and horse were by this time at a considerable distance. The former would, no doubt, shortly return. Whether his pursuit succeeded or miscarried, he would surely see the propriety of hastening his return with what tidings he could obtain, and to ascertain his master's situation. Add to this, the impropriety of leaving a woman, single and unarmed, to the machinations of this demoniac. He had scarcely parted with her when these reflections occurred to him. His resolution was changed. He turned back with the intention of immediately seeking her. At the same moment, he saw the flash and heard the discharge of a pistol. The light proceeded from the foot of the oak. His imagination was filled with horrible forebodings. He ran with all his speed to the spot. He called aloud upon the name of his daughter, but, alas! she was unable to answer him. He found her stretched at the foot of the tree, senseless, and weltering in her blood. He lifted her in his arms, and seated her against the trunk. He found himself stained with blood, flowing from a wound, which either the darkness of the night, or the confusion of his thoughts, hindered him from tracing. Overwhelmed with a catastrophe so dreadful and unexpected, he was divested of all presence of mind. The author of his calamity had vanished. No human being was at hand to succour him in his uttermost distress. He beat his head against the ground, tore away his venerable locks, and rent the air with his cries.

Fortunately there was a dwelling at no great distance from this scene. The discharge of a pistol produces a sound too loud not to be heard far and wide, in this lonely region. This house belonged to a physician. He was a man noted for his humanity and sympathy. He was roused, as well as most of his family, by a sound so uncommon. He rose instantly, and calling up his people, proceeded with lights to the road. The lamentations of Mr. Davis directed them to the place. To the physician the scene was inexplicable. Who was the author of this distress; by whom the pistol was discharged; whether through some untoward chance or with design, he was as yet uninformed, nor could he gain any information from the incoherent despair of Mr. Davis.

Every measure that humanity and professional skill could suggest were employed on this occasion. The dying lady was removed to the house. The ball had lodged in her brain, and to extract it was impossible. Why should I dwell on the remaining incidents of this tale? She languished till the next morning, and then expired. –

Washington Irving (1783–1859)

Irving was the first American fiction writer to achieve international fame, and the first to become financially successful through his work. His influence on later short fiction was immense, surpassed only by Poe's.

"The Legend of Sleepy Hollow" is a genial comic work, like most of Irving's fiction. It is not a Gothic tale. The gently ironic tone keeps the reader at an amused distance from the action. We understand from Irving's many hints and winks the true identity of Ichabod Crane's pursuing enemy, and smile at the description of Ichabod and his steed Gunpowder, so easily turned into animated figures by Walt Disney in the twentieth century.

But if "The Legend of Sleepy Hollow" is not a Gothic tale, it is a sophisticated story *about* Gothic storytelling. Characters repeatedly tell each other ghostly tales, and we observe the social context of the storytelling, and its effect on its audience, especially on Ichabod. The various sources for the storytelling include fantastic legends of regional and European origin, and local history such as that of the "unfortunate" John André (1750–80), the handsome and popular British intelligence officer who was captured in civilian clothing after a meeting with Benedict Arnold, and executed as a spy.

Like Hawthorne's "Alice Doan's Appeal," "The Legend of Sleepy Hollow" may be considered a study in the materials of American Gothic, and like Hawthorne, Irving turns inevitably to the matter of Salem. Ichabod Crane finds his most frightening material in the cases of witchcraft recounted by Cotton Mather.

An understated but important dimension to the story is the presence of African American characters around its margins. New York was, after all, a slave state at the time Irving's story takes place. The riches of the Van Tassel farm were produced by slave labor. An enslaved servant brings Ichabod the invitation to the party, while another, a locally famous musician, plays his fiddle for the dancers, while ambiguously smiling black faces watch Ichabod's frenetic dancing through doors and windows. We may speculate that among the ghostly tales told by the Dutch farmers on the Van Tassel veranda may be some that had passed through the imaginations of black storytellers.

Text: Washington Irving, *The Sketch-Book of Geoffrey Crayon, Gent.* (New York: William L. Allison, 1840). The punctuation and spelling of this edition have been preserved. A small number of obvious typographical errors have been corrected.

The Legend of Sleepy Hollow.
Found Among the Papers of the Late Diedrich Knickerbocker.

A pleasing land of drowsy head it was,
Of dreams that wave before the half-shut eye;

And of gay castles in the clouds that pass,
Forever flushing round a summer sky.
CASTLE OF INDOLENCE.[1]

IN the bosom of one of those spacious coves which indent the eastern shore of the
Hudson, at that broad expansion of the river denominated by the ancient Dutch navi-
gators the Tappan Zee, and where they always prudently shortened sail and implored
the protection of St. Nicholas when they crossed, there lies a small market-town or
rural port, which by some is called Greensburgh, but which is more generally and
properly known by the name of Tarry Town. This name was given, we are told, in
former days, by the good housewives of the adjacent country, from the inveterate pro-
pensity of their husbands to linger about the village tavern on market days. Be that as
it may, I do not vouch for the fact, but merely advert to it, for the sake of being precise
and authentic. Not far from this village, perhaps about two miles, there is a little valley,
or rather lap of land, among high hills, which is one of the quietest places in the whole
world. A small brook glides through it, with just murmur enough to lull one to repose;
and the occasional whistle of a quail, or tapping of a woodpecker, is almost the only
sound that ever breaks in upon the uniform tranquillity.

I recollect that, when a stripling, my first exploit in squirrel-shooting was in a grove
of tall walnut-trees that shades one side of the valley. I had wandered into it at noon
time, when all nature is peculiarly quiet, and was startled by the roar of my own gun,
as it broke the Sabbath stillness around, and was prolonged and reverberated by the
angry echoes. If ever I should wish for a retreat, whither I might steal from the world
and its distractions, and dream quietly away the remnant of a troubled life, I know of
none more promising than this little valley.

From the listless repose of the place, and the peculiar character of its inhabitants,
who are descendants from the original Dutch settlers, this sequestered glen has long
been known by the name of SLEEPY HOLLOW, and its rustic lads are called the
Sleepy Hollow Boys throughout all the neighboring country. A drowsy, dreamy influ-
ence seems to hang over the land, and to pervade the very atmosphere. Some say that
the place was bewitched by a High German doctor, during the early days of the set-
tlement; others, that an old Indian chief, the prophet or wizard of his tribe, held his
powwows there before the country was discovered by Master Hendrick Hudson.
Certain it is, the place still continues under the sway of some witching power, that
holds a spell over the minds of the good people, causing them to walk in a continual
reverie. They are given to all kinds of marvelous beliefs; are subject to trances and
visions; and frequently see strange sights, and hear music and voices in the air. The
whole neighborhood abounds with local tales, haunted spots, and twilight supersti-
tions; stars shoot and meteors glare oftener across the valley than in any other part of
the country, and the nightmare, with her whole nine fold,[2] seems to make it the
favorite scene of her gambols.

The dominant spirit, however, that haunts this enchanted region, and seems to be
commander-in-chief of all the powers of the air, is the apparition of a figure on horse-
back, without a head. It is said by some to be the ghost of a Hessian trooper, whose
head had been carried away by a cannon-ball, in some nameless battle during the revo-
lutionary war; and who is ever and anon seen by the country folk, hurrying along in

Notes

THE LEGEND OF SLEEPY HOLLOW
[1] A long poem published in 1748 by James Thompson (1700–48).

[2] Irving's witty wordplay: ninefold nightmares, the night *mare's*
nine *foals.*

the gloom of night, as if on the wings of the wind. His haunts are not confined to the valley, but extend at times to the adjacent roads, and especially to the vicinity of a church at no great distance. Indeed, certain of the most authentic historians of those parts, who have been careful in collecting and collating the floating facts concerning this spectre, allege that the body of the trooper, having been buried in the church-yard, the ghost rides forth to the scene of battle in nightly quest of his head; and that the rushing speed with which he sometimes passes along the Hollow, like a midnight blast, is owing to his being belated, and in a hurry to get back to the church-yard before daybreak.

Such is the general purport of this legendary superstition, which has furnished materials for many a wild story in that region of shadows; and the spectre is known, at all the country firesides, by the name of the Headless Horseman of Sleepy Hollow.

It is remarkable that the visionary propensity I have mentioned is not confined to the native inhabitants of the valley, but is unconsciously imbibed by every one who resides there for a time. However wide awake they may have been before they entered that sleepy region, they are sure, in a little time, to inhale the witching influence of the air, and begin to grow imaginative – to dream dreams, and see apparitions.

I mention this peaceful spot with all possible laud; for it is in such little retired Dutch valleys, found here and there embosomed in the great State of New-York, that population, manners, and customs remain fixed; while the great torrent of migration and improvement, which is making such incessant changes in other parts of this restless country, sweeps by them unobserved. They are like those little nooks of still water which border a rapid stream; where we may see the straw and bubble riding quietly at anchor, or slowly revolving in their mimic harbor, undisturbed by the rush of the passing current. Though many years have elapsed since I trod the drowsy shades of Sleepy Hollow, yet I question whether I should not still find the same trees and the same families vegetating in its sheltered bosom.

In this by-place of nature, there abode, in a remote period of American history, that is to say, some thirty years since, a worthy wight of the name of Ichabod Crane; who sojourned, or, as he expressed it "tarried," in Sleepy Hollow, for the purpose of instructing the children of the vicinity. He was a native of Connecticut; a State which supplies the Union with pioneers for the mind as well as for the forest, and sends forth yearly its legions of frontier woodmen and country schoolmasters. The cognomen of Crane was not inapplicable to his person. He was tall, but exceedingly lank, with narrow shoulders, long arms and legs, hands that dangled a mile out of his sleeves, feet that might have served for shovels, and his whole frame most loosely hung together. His head was small and flat at top, with huge ears, large, green, glassy eyes, and a long snipe nose, so that it looked like a weather-cock perched, upon his spindle neck, to tell which way the wind blew. To see him striding along the profile of a hill on a windy day, with his clothes bagging and fluttering about him, one might have mistaken him for the genius of famine descending upon the earth, or some scarecrow eloped from a cornfield.

His school-house was a low building of one large room, rudely constructed of logs; the windows partly glazed, and partly patched with leaves of old copy-books. It was most ingeniously secured at vacant hours, by a withe twisted in the handle of the door, and stakes set against the window shutters; so that though a thief might get in with perfect ease, he would find some embarrassment in getting out; an idea most probably borrowed by the architect, Yost Van Houten, from the mystery of an eel-pot. The school-house stood in a rather lonely but pleasant situation, just at the foot of a woody hill, with a brook running close by, and a formidable birch tree growing at one end of it. From hence the low murmur of his pupils' voices, conning over their lessons, might be heard in a drowsy summer's day, like the hum of a beehive; interrupted now and then by the authoritative voice of the master, in the tone of menace or command; or, peradventure, by the appalling sound of the birch, as he urged some tardy loiterer along the flowery path of knowledge. Truth to say, he was a conscientious man, and ever bore in mind the golden maxim, "Spare the rod and spoil the child." Ichabod Crane's scholars certainly were not spoiled.

I would not have it imagined, however, that he was one of those cruel potentates of the school who joy in the smart of their subjects; on the contrary, he administered justice with discrimination rather than severity; taking the burden off the backs of the weak, and laying it on those of the strong. Your mere puny stripling, that winced at the least flourish of the rod, was passed by with indulgence; but the claims of justice were satisfied by inflicting a double portion on some little, tough, wrong-headed, broad-skirted Dutch urchin, who sulked and swelled and grew dogged and sullen beneath the birch. All this he called "doing his duty by their parents;" and he never inflicted a chastisement without following it by the assurance, so consolatory to the smarting urchin, that "he would remember it, and thank him for it the longest day he had to live."

When school hours were over he was even the companion and playmate of the larger boys; and on holiday afternoons would convoy some of the smaller ones home, who happened to have pretty sisters, or good housewives for mothers, noted for the comforts of the cupboard. Indeed, it behooved him to keep on good terms with his pupils. The revenue arising from his school was small, and would have been scarcely sufficient to furnish him with daily bread, for he was a huge feeder, and though lank, had the dilating powers of an anaconda; but to help out his maintenance, he was, according to country custom in those parts, boarded and lodged at the houses of the farmers whose children he instructed. With these he lived successively a week at a time; thus going the rounds of the neighborhood, with all his worldly effects tied up in a cotton handkerchief.

That all this might not be too onerous on the purses of his rustic patrons, who are apt to consider the costs of schooling a grievous burden, and schoolmasters as mere drones, he had various ways of rendering himself both useful and agreeable. He assisted the farmers occasionally in the lighter labors of their farms; helped to make hay; mended the fences; took the horses to water; drove the cows from pasture; and cut wood for the winter fire. He laid aside, too, all the dominant dignity and absolute sway with which he lorded it in his little empire, the school, and became wonderfully gentle and ingratiating. He found favor in the eyes of the mothers, by petting the children, particularly the youngest; and like the lion bold, which whilom so magnanimously the lamb did hold, he would sit with a child on one knee, and rock a cradle with his foot for whole hours together.

In addition to his other vocations, he was the singing-master of the neighborhood, and picked up many bright shillings by instructing the young folks in psalmody. It was a matter of no little vanity to him on Sundays, to take his station in front of the church gallery, with a band of chosen singers; where, in his own mind, he completely carried away the palm from the parson. Certain it is, his voice resounded far above all the rest of the congregation; and there are peculiar quavers still to be heard in that church, and which may even be heard half a mile off, quite to the opposite side of the millpond, on a still Sunday morning, which are said to be legitimately descended from the nose of Ichabod Crane. Thus, by divers little make-shifts in that ingenious way which is commonly denominated "by hook and by crook," the worthy pedagogue got on tolerably enough, and was thought, by all who understood nothing of the labor of headwork, to have a wonderfully easy life of it.

The schoolmaster is generally a man of some importance in the female circle of a rural neighborhood; being considered a kind of idle, gentlemanlike personage, of vastly superior taste and accomplishments to the rough country swains, and, indeed, inferior in learning only to the parson. His appearance, therefore, is apt to occasion some little stir at the tea-table of a farmhouse, and the addition of a supernumerary dish of cakes or sweetmeats, or, peradventure, the parade of a silver tea-pot. Our man of letters, therefore, was peculiarly happy in the smiles of all the country damsels. How he would figure among them in the church-yard, between services on Sundays! gathering grapes for them from the wild vines that overran the surrounding trees; reciting for their amusement all the epitaphs on the tombstones; or sauntering with a whole bevy of them along the banks of the adjacent millpond; while the more bashful country bumpkins hung sheepishly back, envying his superior elegance and address.

From his half itinerant life, also, he was a kind of travelling gazette, carrying the whole budget of local gossip from house to house; so that his appearance was always greeted with satisfaction. He was, moreover, esteemed by the women as a man of great erudition, for he had read several books quite through, and was a perfect master of Cotton Mather's history of New England Witchcraft, in which, by the way, he most firmly and potently believed.

He was, in fact, an odd mixture of small shrewdness and simple credulity. His appetite for the marvelous, and his powers of digesting it, were equally extraordinary; and both had been increased by his residence in this spell-bound region. No tale was too gross or monstrous for his capacious swallow. It was often his delight, after his school was dismissed in the afternoon, to stretch himself on the rich bed of clover bordering the little brook that whimpered by his school-house, and there con over old Mather's direful tales, until the gathering dusk of evening made the printed page a mere mist before his eyes. Then, as he wended his way, by swamp and stream and awful woodland, to the farmhouse where he happened to be quartered, every sound of nature, at that witching hour, fluttered his excited imagination: the moan of the whip-poor-will* from the hillside; the boding cry of the tree-toad, that harbinger of storm; the dreary hooting of the screech owl, or the sudden rustling in the thicket of birds frightened from their roost. The fire-flies, too, which sparkled most vividly in the darkest places, now and then startled him, as one of uncommon brightness would stream across his path; and if, by chance, a huge blockhead of a beetle came winging his blundering flight against him, the poor varlet was ready to give up the ghost, with the idea that he was struck with a witch's token. His only resource on such occasions, either to drown thought, or drive away evil spirits, was to sing psalm tunes; – and the good people of Sleepy Hollow, as they sat by their doors of an evening, were often filled with awe, at hearing his nasal melody, "in linked sweetness long drawn out,"[3] floating from the distant hill, or along the dusky road.

Another of his sources of fearful pleasure was to pass long winter evenings with the old Dutch wives, as they sat spinning by the fire with a row of apples roasting and spluttering along the hearth, and listen to their marvelous tales of ghosts and goblins, and haunted fields, and haunted brooks, and haunted bridges, and haunted houses, and particularly of the headless horseman, or galloping Hessian of the Hollow, as they sometimes called him. He would delight them equally by his anecdotes of witchcraft, and of the direful omens and portentous sights and sounds in the air, which prevailed

Notes

* The whip-poor-will is a bird which is only heard at night. It receives its name from its note, which is thought to resemble these words. [Irving's note.]

[3] From John Milton's "L'Allegro," published 1646.

in the earlier times of Connecticut; and would frighten them woefully with speculations upon comets and shooting stars; and with the alarming fact that the world did absolutely turn round, and that they were half the time topsy-turvy!

But if there was a pleasure in all this, while snugly cuddling in the chimney corner of a chamber that was all of a ruddy glow from the crackling wood fire, and where, of course, no spectre dared to show its face, it was dearly purchased by the terrors of his subsequent walk homewards. What fearful shapes and shadows beset his path amidst the dim and ghastly glare of a snowy night! With what wistful look did he eye every trembling ray of light streaming across the waste fields from some distant window! How often was he appalled by some shrub covered with snow, which, like a sheeted spectre, beset his very path! How often did he shrink with curdling awe at the sound of his own steps on the frosty crust beneath his feet; and dread to look over his shoulder, lest he should behold some uncouth being tramping close behind him! – and how often was he thrown into complete dismay by some rushing blast, howling among the trees, in the idea that it was the Galloping Hessian on one of his nightly scourings!

All these, however, were mere terrors of the night, phantoms of the mind that walk in darkness; and though he had seen many spectres in his time, and been more than once beset by Satan in divers shapes in his lonely perambulations, yet daylight put an end to all these evils; and he would have passed a pleasant life of it, in despite of the devil and all his works, if his path had not been crossed by a being that causes more perplexity to mortal man than ghosts, goblins, and the whole race of witches put together, and that was – a woman.

Among the musical disciples who assembled, one evening in each week, to receive his instructions in psalmody, was Katrina Van Tassel, the daughter and only child of a substantial Dutch farmer. She was a blooming lass of fresh eighteen; plump as a partridge; ripe and melting and rosy cheeked as one of her father's peaches, and universally famed, not merely for her beauty, but her vast expectations. She was withal a little of a coquette, as might be perceived even in her dress, which was a mixture of ancient and modern fashions, as most suited to set off her charms. She wore the ornaments of pure yellow gold which her great-great-grandmother had brought over from Saardam; the tempting stomacher of the olden time; and withal a provokingly short petticoat, to display the prettiest foot and ankle in the country round.

Ichabod Crane had a soft and foolish heart towards the sex; and it is not to be wondered at that so tempting a morsel soon found favor in his eyes; more especially after he had visited her in her paternal mansion. Old Baltus Van Tassel was a perfect picture of a thriving, contented, liberal-hearted farmer. He seldom, it is true, sent either his eyes or his thoughts beyond the boundaries of his own farm; but within those everything was snug, happy and well-conditioned. He was satisfied with his wealth, but not proud of it; and piqued himself upon the hearty abundance, rather than the style in which he lived. His stronghold was situated on the banks of the Hudson, in one of those green, sheltered, fertile nooks, in which the Dutch farmers are so fond of nestling. A great elm-tree spread its broad branches over it; at the foot of which bubbled up a spring of the softest and sweetest water, in a little well, formed of a barrel; and then stole sparkling away through the grass, to a neighboring brook, that babbled along among alders and dwarf willows. Hard by the farm-house was a vast barn that might have served for a church; every window and crevice of which seemed bursting forth with the treasures of the farm; the flail was busily resounding within it from morning to night; swallows and martins skimmed twittering about the eaves; and rows of pigeons, some with one eye turned up, as if watching the weather, some with their heads under their wings, or buried in their bosoms, and others swelling, and cooing, and bowing about their dames, were enjoying the sunshine on the roof. Sleek, unwieldy porkers were grunting in the repose and abundance of their pens; from whence sallied forth, now and then, troops of sucking pigs, as if to snuff the air. A stately squadron of snowy geese were riding in an adjoining pond, convoying whole fleets of ducks; regiments of turkeys were gobbling through the farmyard, and guinea fowls fretting about it, like ill-tempered housewives, with their peevish, discontented cry. Before the barn door strutted the gallant cock, that pattern of a husband, a warrior and a fine gentleman, clapping his burnished wings, and crowing in the pride and gladness of his heart – sometimes tearing up the earth with his feet, and then generously calling his ever-hungry family of wives and children to enjoy the rich morsel which he had discovered.

The pedagogue's mouth watered as he looked upon this sumptuous promise of luxurious winter fare. In his devouring mind's eye, he pictured to himself every roasting-pig running about with a pudding in his belly, and an apple in his mouth; the pigeons were snugly put to bed in a comfortable pie, and tucked in with a coverlet of crust; the geese were swimming in their own gravy; and the ducks pairing cosily in dishes, like snug married couples, with a decent competency of onion sauce. In the porkers he saw carved out the future sleek side of bacon, and juicy relishing ham; not a turkey but he beheld daintily trussed up, with its gizzard under its wing, and, peradventure, a necklace of savory sausages; and even bright chanticleer himself lay sprawling on his back, in a side-dish, with uplifted claws, as if craving that quarter which his chivalrous spirit disdained to ask while living.

As the enraptured Ichabod fancied all this, and as he rolled his great green eyes over the fat meadow-lands, the rich fields of wheat, of rye, of buckwheat, and Indian corn, and the orchards burdened with ruddy fruit, which surrounded the warm tenement of Van Tassel, his heart yearned after the damsel who was to inherit these domains, and his imagination expanded with the idea, how they might be readily turned into cash, and the money invested in immense tracts of wild land, and shingle palaces in the wilderness. Nay, his busy fancy already realized his hopes, and presented to him the blooming Katrina, with a whole family of children, mounted on the top of a wagon loaded with household trumpery, with pots and kettles dangling beneath; and he beheld himself bestriding a pacing mare, with a colt at her heels, setting out for Kentucky, Tennessee, or the Lord knows where.

When he entered the house the conquest of his heart was complete. It was one of those spacious farmhouses, with high-ridged, but lowly-sloping roofs, built in the style handed down from the first Dutch settlers; the low, projecting eaves forming a piazza along the front, capable of being closed up in bad weather. Under this were hung flails, harness, various utensils of husbandry, and nets for fishing in the neighboring river. Benches were built along the sides for summer use; and a great spinning-wheel at one end, and a churn at the other, showed the various uses to which this important porch might be devoted. From this piazza the wondering Ichabod entered the hall, which formed the centre of the mansion, and the place of usual residence. Here, rows of resplendent pewter, ranged on a long dresser, dazzled his eyes. In one corner stood a huge bag of wool, ready to be spun; in another a quantity of linsey-woolsey just from the loom; ears of Indian corn, and strings of dried apples and peaches, hung in gay festoons along the walls, mingled with the gaud of red peppers; and a door left ajar gave him a peep into the best parlor, where the claw-footed chairs, and dark, mahogany tables, shone like mirrors; andirons, with their accompanying shovel and tongs, glistened from their covert of asparagus tops; mock-oranges and conch-shells decorated the mantel-piece; strings of various-colored birds' eggs were suspended above it: a great ostrich egg was hung from the centre of the room, and a corner cupboard, knowingly left open, displayed immense treasures of old silver and well-mended china.

From the moment Ichabod laid his eyes upon these regions of delight, the peace of his mind was at an end, and his only study was how to gain the affections of the peerless daughter of Van Tassel. In this enterprise, however, he had more real difficulties than generally fell to the lot of a knight-errant of yore, who seldom had anything but giants, enchanters, fiery dragons, and such like easily-conquered adversaries, to contend with; and had to make his way merely through gates of iron and brass, and walls of adamant, to the castle keep, where the lady of his heart was confined; all which he achieved as easily as a man would carve his way to the centre of a Christmas pie; and then the lady gave him her hand as a matter of course. Ichabod, on the contrary, had to win his way to the heart of a country coquette, beset with a labyrinth of whims and caprices, which were forever presenting new difficulties and impediments; and he had to encounter a host of fearful adversaries of real flesh and blood, the numerous rustic admirers, who beset every portal to her heart; keeping a watchful and angry eye upon each other, but ready to fly out in the common cause against any new competitor.

Among these, the most formidable was a burly, roaring, roystering blade, of the name of Abraham, or, according to the Dutch abbreviation, Brom Van Brunt, the hero of the country round, which rang with his feats of strength and hardihood. He was broad-shouldered and double-jointed, with short curly black hair, and a bluff, but not unpleasant countenance, having a mingled air of fun and arrogance. From his Herculean frame and great powers of limb, he had received the nickname of BROM BONES, by which he was universally known. He was famed for great knowledge and skill in horsemanship, being as dexterous on horseback as a Tartar. He was foremost at all races and cock-fights; and, with the ascendancy which bodily strength acquires in rustic life, was the umpire in all disputes, setting his hat on one side, and giving his decisions with an air and tone that admitted of no gainsay or appeal. He was always ready for either a fight or a frolic; but had more mischief than ill-will in his composition; and, with all his overbearing roughness, there was a strong dash of waggish good humor at bottom. He had three or four boon companions, who regarded him as their model, and at the head of whom he scoured the country, attending every scene of feud or merriment for miles round. In cold weather he was distinguished by a fur cap, surmounted with a flaunting fox's tail; and when the folks at a country gathering descried this well-known crest at a distance, whisking about among a squad of hard riders, they always stood by for a squall. Sometimes his crew would be heard dashing along past the farmhouses at midnight, with whoop and halloo, like a troop of Don Cossacks; and the old dames, startled out of their sleep, would listen for a moment till the hurry-scurry had clattered by, and then exclaim, "Ay, there goes Brom Bones and his gang!" The neighbors looked upon him with a mixture of awe, admiration, and good-will; and when any madcap prank, or rustic brawl, occurred in the vicinity, always shook their heads, and warranted Brom Bones was at the bottom of it.

This rantipole[4] hero had for some time singled out the blooming Katrina for the object of his uncouth gallantries, and though his amorous toyings were something like the gentle caresses and endearments of a bear, yet it was whispered that she did not altogether discourage his hopes. Certain it is, his advances were signals for rival candidates to retire, who felt no inclination to cross a lion in his amours; insomuch that when his horse was seen tied to Van Tassel's paling, on a Sunday night, a sure sign that his master was courting, or, as it is termed, "sparking," within, all other suitors passed by in despair, and carried the war into other quarters.

Notes
4 Wild, reckless.

Such was the formidable rival with whom Ichabod Crane had to contend, and, considering all things, a stouter man than he would have shrunk from the competition, and a wiser man would have despaired. He had, however, a happy mixture of pliability and perseverance in his nature; he was in form and spirit like a supple-jack[5] – yielding, but tough; though he bent, he never broke; and though he bowed beneath the slightest pressure, yet, the moment it was away – jerk! – he was as erect, and carried his head as high as ever.

To have taken the field openly against his rival would have been madness; for he was not a man to be thwarted in his amours, any more than that stormy lover, Achilles. Ichabod, therefore, made his advances in a quiet and gently-insinuating manner. Under cover of his character of singing-master, he made frequent visits at the farmhouse; not that he had anything to apprehend from the meddlesome interference of parents, which is so often a stumbling-block in the path of lovers. Balt Van Tassel was an easy, indulgent soul; he loved his daughter better even than his pipe, and, like a reasonable man and an excellent father, let her have her way in everything. His notable little wife, too, had enough to do to attend to her housekeeping and manage her poultry; for, as she sagely observed, ducks and geese are foolish things, and must be looked after, but girls can take care of themselves. Thus, while the busy dame bustled about the house, or plied her spinning-wheel at one end of the piazza, honest Balt would sit smoking his evening pipe at the other, watching the achievements of a little wooden warrior, who, armed with a sword in each hand, was most valiantly fighting the wind on the pinnacle of the barn. In the mean time, Ichabod would carry on his suit with the daughter by the side of the spring under the great elm, or sauntering along in the twilight, that hour so favorable to the lover's eloquence.

I profess not to know how women's hearts are wooed and won. To me they have always been matters of riddle and admiration. Some seem to have but one vulnerable point, or door of access; while others have a thousand avenues, and may be captured in a thousand different ways. It is a great triumph of skill to gain the former, but a still greater proof of generalship to maintain possession of the latter, for the man must battle for his fortress at every door and window. He who wins a thousand common hearts is, therefore, entitled to some renown; but he who keeps undisputed sway over the heart of a coquette, is, indeed, a hero. Certain it is, this was not the case with the redoubtable Brom Bones; and from the moment Ichabod Crane made his advances, the interests of the former evidently declined; his horse was no longer seen tied at the palings on Sunday nights, and a deadly feud gradually arose between him and the preceptor of Sleepy Hollow.

Brom, who had a degree of rough chivalry in his nature, would fain have carried matters to open warfare, and have settled their pretensions to the lady, according to the mode of those most concise and simple reasoners, the knights-errant of yore – by single combat; but Ichabod was too conscious of the superior might of his adversary to enter the lists against him; he had overheard a boast of Bones, that he would "double the schoolmaster up and lay him on a shelf of his own school-house;" and he was too wary to give him an opportunity. There was something extremely provoking in this obstinately pacific system; it left Brom no alternative but to draw upon the funds of rustic waggery in his disposition, and to play off boorish practical jokes upon his rival. Ichabod became the object of whimsical persecution to Bones and his gang of rough riders. They harried his hitherto peaceful domains; smoked out his singing school by stopping up the chimney; broke into the school-house at night, in spite of its formidable fastenings of withe and window stakes, and turned everything topsy-turvy:

Notes

[5] A shrub.

so that the poor schoolmaster began to think all the witches in the country held their meetings there. But what was still more annoying, Brom took all opportunities of turning him into ridicule in presence of his mistress, and had a scoundrel dog whom he taught to whine in the most ludicrous manner, and introduced as a rival of Ichabod's, to instruct her in psalmody.

In this way matters went on for some time, without producing any material effect on the relative situations of the contending powers. On a fine, autumnal afternoon, Ichabod, in his pensive mood, sat enthroned on the lofty stool whence he usually watched all the concerns of his little literary realm. In his hand he swayed a ferule, that sceptre of despotic power; the birch of justice reposed on three nails behind the throne, a constant terror to evil doers; while on the desk before him might be seen sundry contraband articles and prohibited weapons, detected upon the persons of idle urchins; such as half-munched apples, popguns, whirligigs, fly-cages, and whole legions of rampant little paper game-cocks. Apparently there had been some appalling act of justice recently inflicted, for his scholars were all busily intent upon their books, or slyly whispering behind them with one eye kept upon the master; and a kind of buzzing stillness reigned throughout the school-room. It was suddenly interrupted by the appearance of a negro, in tow-cloth jacket and trousers, a round-crowned fragment of a hat, like the cap of Mercury, and mounted on the back of a ragged, wild, half-broken colt, which he managed with a rope by way of halter. He came clattering up to the school door with an invitation to Ichabod to attend a merry-making or "quilting frolic," to be held that evening at Mynheer Van Tassel's; and having delivered his message with that air of importance, and effort at fine language, which a negro is apt to display on petty embassies of the kind, he dashed over the brook, and was seen scampering away up the hollow, full of the importance and hurry of his mission.

All was now bustle and hubbub in the late quiet school-room. The scholars were hurried through their lessons, without stopping at trifles; those who were nimble skipped over half with impunity, and those who were tardy, had a smart application now and then in the rear, to quicken their speed, or help them over a tall word. Books were flung aside without being put away on the shelves, inkstands were overturned, benches thrown down, and the whole school was turned loose an hour before the usual time, bursting forth like a legion of young imps, yelping and racketing about the green, in joy at their early emancipation.

The gallant Ichabod now spent at least an extra half hour at his toilet, brushing and furbishing up his best, and, indeed, only suit of rusty black, and arranging his locks by a bit of broken looking-glass that hung up in the school-house. That he might make his appearance before his mistress in the true style of a cavalier, he borrowed a horse from the farmer with whom he was domiciliated, a choleric old Dutchman of the name of Hans Van Ripper, and, thus gallantly mounted, issued forth, like a knight-errant in quest of adventures. But it is meet I should, in the true spirit of romantic history, give some account of the looks and equipments of my hero and his steed. The animal he bestrode was a broken-down plow-horse, that had outlived almost everything but its viciousness. He was gaunt and shagged, with a ewe neck and a head like a hammer; his rusty mane and tail were tangled and knotted with burs; one eye had lost its pupil, and was glaring and spectral; but the other had the gleam of a genuine devil in it. Still he must have had fire and mettle in his day, if we may judge from the name he bore of Gunpowder. He had, in fact, been a favorite steed of his master's, the choleric Van Ripper, who was a furious rider, and had infused, very probably, some of his own spirit into the animal; for, old and broken-down as he looked, there was more of the lurking devil in him than in any young filly in the country.

Ichabod was a suitable figure for such a steed. He rode with short stirrups, which brought his knees nearly up to the pommel of the saddle; his sharp elbows stuck out like grasshoppers'; he carried his whip perpendicularly in his hand, like a sceptre, and, as his horse jogged on, the motion of his arms was not unlike the flapping of a pair of wings. A small wool hat rested on the top of his nose, for so his scanty strip of forehead might be called; and the skirts of his black coat fluttered out almost to the horse's tail. Such was the appearance of Ichabod and his steed as they shambled out of the gate of Hans Van Ripper, and it was altogether such an apparition as is seldom to be met with in broad daylight.

It was, as I have said, a fine autumnal day; the sky was clear and serene, and nature wore that rich and golden livery which we always associate with the idea of abundance. The forests had put on their sober brown and yellow, while some trees of the tenderer kind had been nipped by the frosts into brilliant dyes of orange, purple, and scarlet. Streaming files of wild ducks began to make their appearance high in the air; the bark of the squirrel might be heard from the groves of beech and hickory nuts, and the pensive whistle of the quail at intervals from the neighboring stubble-field.

The small birds were taking their farewell banquets. In the fullness of their revelry, they fluttered, chirping and frolicking, from bush to bush, and tree to tree, capricious from the very profusion and variety around them. There was the honest cock-robin, the favorite game of stripling sportsmen, with its loud, querulous note; and the twittering blackbirds flying in sable clouds; and the golden-winged wood-pecker with his crimson crest, his broad, black gorget, and splendid plumage; and the cedar bird, with its red-tipt wings and yellow-tipt tail and its little monteiro cap[6] of feathers; and the blue jay, that noisy coxcomb, in his gay, light-blue coat and white under-clothes, screaming and chattering, nodding and bobbing and bowing, and pretending to be on good terms with every songster of the grove.

As Ichabod jogged slowly on his way, his eye, ever open to every symptom of culinary abundance, ranged with delight over the treasures of jolly autumn. On all sides he beheld vast store of apples; some hanging in oppressive opulence on the trees; some gathered into baskets and barrels for the market; others heaped up in rich piles for the cider-press. Farther on he beheld great fields of Indian corn, with its golden ears peeping from their leafy coverts, and holding out the promise of cakes and hasty pudding; and the yellow pumpkins lying beneath them, turning up their fair, round bellies to the sun, and giving ample prospects of the most luxurious of pies; and anon he passed the fragrant buckwheat fields, breathing the odor of the bee-hive, and as he beheld them, soft anticipations stole over his mind of dainty slapjacks, well buttered, and garnished with honey or treacle, by the delicate little dimpled hand of Katrina Van Tassel.

Thus feeding his mind with many sweet thoughts and "sugared suppositions," he journeyed along the sides of a range of hills which look out upon some of the goodliest scenes of the mighty Hudson. The sun gradually wheeled his broad disk down in the west. The wide bosom of the Tappan Zee lay motionless and glassy, excepting that here and there a gentle undulation waved and prolonged the blue shadow of the distant mountain. A few amber clouds floated in the sky, without a breath of air to move them. The horizon was of a fine, golden tint, changing gradually into a pure apple green, and from that into the deep blue of the mid-heaven. A slanting ray lingered on the woody crests of the precipices that overhung some parts of the river, giving greater depth to the dark gray and purple of their rocky sides. A sloop was loitering in the distance, dropping slowly down with the tide, her sail hanging uselessly

Notes ————————————————————————————————————

[6] Presumably montero cap, a Spanish hunter's cap.

against the mast; and as the reflection of the sky gleamed along the still water, it seemed as if the vessel was suspended in the air.

It was toward evening that Ichabod arrived at the castle of the Heer Van Tassel, which he found thronged with the pride and flower of the adjacent country. Old farmers, a spare leathern-faced race, in homespun coats and breeches, blue stockings, huge shoes, and magnificent pewter buckles. Their brisk, withered little dames, in close crimped caps, long-waisted short gowns, homespun petticoats, with scissors and pincushions, and gay, calico pockets hanging on the outside. Buxom lasses, almost as antiquated as their mothers, excepting where a straw hat, a fine ribbon, or, perhaps a white frock, gave symptoms of city innovation. The sons, in short, square-skirted coats, with rows of stupendous brass buttons, and their hair generally queued in the fashion of the times, especially if they could procure an eel skin for the purpose, it being esteemed, throughout the country, as a potent nourisher and strengthener of the hair.

Brom Bones, however, was the hero of the scene, having come to the gathering on his favorite steed Daredevil, a creature, like himself, full of mettle and mischief, and which no one but himself could manage. He was, in fact, noted for preferring vicious animals, given to all kinds of tricks, which kept the rider in constant risk of his neck, for he held a tractable, well-broken horse as unworthy of a lad of spirit.

Fain would I pause to dwell upon the world of charms that burst upon the enraptured gaze of my hero, as he entered the state parlor of Van Tassel's mansion. Not those of the bevy of buxom lasses, with their luxurious display of red and white; but the ample charms of a genuine Dutch country tea-table, in the sumptuous time of autumn. Such heaped-up platters of cakes of various and almost indescribable kinds, known only to experienced Dutch housewives! There was the doughty doughnut, the tender oly koek, and the crisp and crumbling cruller; sweet cakes and short cakes, ginger cakes and honey cakes, and the whole family of cakes. And then there were apple pies and peach pies and pumpkin pies; besides slices of ham and smoked beef; and, moreover, delectable dishes of preserved plums, and peaches, and pears, and quinces; not to mention broiled shad and roasted chickens; together with bowls of milk and cream, all mingled higgledy-piggledy, pretty much as I have enumerated them, with the motherly tea-pot sending up its clouds of vapor from the midst – Heaven bless the mark! I want breath and time to discuss this banquet as it deserves, and am too eager to get on with my story. Happily, Ichabod Crane was not in so great a hurry as his historian, but did ample justice to every dainty.

He was a kind and thankful creature, whose heart dilated in proportion as his skin was filled with good cheer, and whose spirits rose with eating, as some men's do with drink. He could not help, too, rolling his large eyes round him as he ate, and chuckling with the possibility that he might one day be lord of all this scene of almost unimaginable luxury and splendor. Then, he thought, how soon he'd turn his back upon the old school-house; snap his fingers in the face of Hans Van Ripper, and every other niggardly patron, and kick any itinerant pedagogue out of doors that should dare to call him comrade!

Old Baltus Van Tassel moved about among his guests with a face dilated with content and good humor, round and jolly as the harvest moon. His hospitable attentions were brief, but expressive, being confined to a shake of the hand, a slap on the shoulder, a loud laugh, and a pressing invitation to "fall to, and help themselves."

And now the sound of the music from the common room, or hall, summoned to the dance. The musician was an old gray-headed negro, who had been the itinerant orchestra of the neighborhood for more than half a century. His instrument was as old and battered as himself. The greater part of the time he scraped on two or three strings, accompanying every movement of the bow with a motion of the head; bowing almost to the ground, and stamping with his foot whenever a fresh couple were to start.

Ichabod prided himself upon his dancing as much as upon his vocal powers. Not a limb, not a fibre about him was idle; and to have seen his loosely hung frame in full motion, and clattering about the room, you would have thought St. Vitus himself, that blessed patron of the dance, was figuring before you in person. He was the admiration of all the negroes; who, having gathered, of all ages and sizes, from the farm and the neighborhood, stood forming a pyramid of shining black faces at every door and window, gazing with delight at the scene, rolling their white eye-balls, and showing grinning rows of ivory from ear to ear. How could the flogger of urchins be otherwise than animated and joyous? The lady of his heart was his partner in the dance, and smiling graciously in reply to all his amorous oglings; while Brom Bones, sorely smitten with love and jealousy, sat brooding by himself in one corner.

When the dance was at an end, Ichabod was attracted to a knot of the sager folks, who, with Old Van Tassel, sat smoking at one end of the piazza, gossiping over former times, and drawing out long stories about the war.

This neighborhood, at the time of which I am speaking, was one of those highly-favored places which abound with chronicle and great men. The British and American line had run near it during the war; it had, therefore, been the scene of marauding, and infested with refugees, cow-boys, and all kinds of border chivalry. Just sufficient time had elapsed to enable each story-teller to dress up his tale with a little becoming fiction, and, in the indistinctness of his recollection, to make himself the hero of every exploit.

There was the story of Doffue Martling, a large, blue-bearded Dutchman, who had nearly taken a British frigate with an old iron nine-pounder from a mud breastwork, only that his gun burst at the sixth discharge. And there was an old gentleman who shall be nameless, being too rich a mynheer to be lightly mentioned, who, in the battle of Whiteplains, being an excellent master of defence, parried a musket-ball with a small sword, insomuch that he absolutely felt it whiz round the blade, and glance off at the hilt: in proof of which he was ready at any time to show the sword, with the hilt a little bent. There were several more that had been equally great in the field, not one of whom but was persuaded that he had a considerable hand in bringing the war to a happy termination.

But all these were nothing to the tales of ghosts and apparitions that succeeded. The neighborhood is rich in legendary treasures of the kind. Local tales and superstitions thrive best in these sheltered, long-settled retreats; but are trampled under foot by the shifting throng that forms the population of most of our country places. Besides, there is no encouragement for ghosts in most of our villages, for they have scarcely had time to finish their first nap, and turn themselves in their graves, before their surviving friends have travelled away from the neighborhood; so that when they turn out at night to walk their rounds, they have no acquaintance left to call upon. This is, perhaps, the reason why we so seldom hear of ghosts except in our long-established Dutch communities.

The immediate cause, however, of the prevalence of supernatural stories in these parts, was, doubtless, owing to the vicinity of Sleepy Hollow. There was a contagion in the very air that blew from that haunted region; it breathed forth an atmosphere of dreams and fancies infecting all the land. Several of the Sleepy Hollow people were present at Van Tassel's, and, as usual, were doling out their wild and wonderful legends. Many dismal tales were told about funeral trains, and mourning cries and wailings heard and seen about the great tree where the unfortunate Major André was taken, and which stood in the neighborhood. Some mention was made also of the woman in white that haunted the dark glen at Raven Rock, and was often heard to shriek on winter nights before a storm, having perished there in the snow. The chief part of the stories, however, turned upon the favorite spectre of Sleepy Hollow, the headless horseman, who had been heard several times of late, patrolling the country; and, it was said, tethered his horse nightly among the graves in the church-yard.

The sequestered situation of this church seems always to have made it a favorite haunt of troubled spirits. It stands on a knoll, surrounded by locust-trees and lofty elms, from among which its decent, whitewashed walls shine modestly forth, like Christian purity beaming through the shades of retirement. A gentle slope descends from it to a silver sheet of water, bordered by high trees, between which peeps may be caught at the blue hills of the Hudson. To look upon its grass-grown yard, where the sunbeams seem to sleep so quietly, one would think that there, at least, the dead might rest in peace. On one side of the church extends a wide, woody dell, along which raves a large brook among broken rocks and trunks of fallen trees. Over a deep black part of the stream, not far from the church, was formerly thrown a wooden bridge; the road that led to it, and the bridge itself, were thickly shaded by overhanging trees, which cast a gloom about it, even in the daytime; but occasioned a fearful darkness at night. Such was one of the favorite haunts of the headless horseman; and the place where he was most frequently encountered. The tale was told of old Brouwer, a most heretical disbeliever in ghosts, how he met the horseman returning from his foray into Sleepy Hollow, and was obliged to get up behind him; how they galloped over bush and brake, over hill and swamp, until they reached the bridge; when the Horseman suddenly turned into a skeleton, threw old Brouwer into the brook, and sprang away over the tree-tops with a clap of thunder.

This story was immediately matched by a thrice marvelous adventure of Brom Bones, who made light of the galloping Hessian as an arrant jockey. He affirmed that, on returning one night from the neighboring village of Sing Sing, he had been overtaken by this midnight trooper; that he had offered to race with him for a bowl of punch, and should have won it, too, for Daredevil beat the goblin horse all hollow, but just as they came to the church-bridge, the Hessian bolted, and vanished in a flash of fire.

All these tales, told in that drowsy undertone with which men talk in the dark, the countenances of the listeners only now and then receiving a casual gleam from the glare of a pipe, sank deep in the mind of Ichabod. He repaid them in kind with large extracts from his invaluable author Cotton Mather, and added many marvelous events that had taken place in his native State of Connecticut, and fearful sights which he had seen in his nightly walks about Sleepy Hollow.

The revel now gradually broke up. The old farmers gathered together their families in their wagons, and were heard for some time rattling along the hollow roads, and over the distant hills. Some of the damsels mounted on pillions behind their favorite swains, and their light-hearted laughter, mingling with the clatter of hoofs, echoed along the silent woodlands, sounding fainter and fainter until they gradually died away – and the late scene of noise and frolic was all silent and deserted. Ichabod only lingered behind, according to the custom of country lovers, to have a tête-à-tête with the heiress, fully convinced that he was now on the high road to success. What passed at this interview I will not pretend to say, for in fact I do not know. Something, however, I fear me, must have gone wrong, for he certainly sallied forth, after no very great interval, with an air quite desolate and chop-fallen. – Oh, these women! these women! Could that girl have been playing off any of her coquettish tricks? Was her encouragement of the poor pedagogue all a mere sham to secure her conquest of his rival? Heaven only knows, not I! Let it suffice to say, Ichabod stole forth with the air of one who had been sacking a hen-roost, rather than a fair lady's heart. Without looking to the right or left to notice the scene of rural wealth on which he had so often gloated, he went straight to the stable, and with several hearty cuffs and kicks, roused his steed most uncourteously from the comfortable quarters in which he was soundly sleeping, dreaming of mountains of corn and oats, and whole valleys of timothy and clover.

It was the very witching time of night that Ichabod, heavy-hearted and crest-fallen, pursued his travels homewards, along the sides of the lofty hills which rise above Tarry Town, and which he had traversed so cheerily in the afternoon. The hour was as dismal as himself. Far below him the Tappan Zee spread its dusky and indistinct waste of waters, with here and there the tall mast of a sloop riding quietly at anchor under the land. In the dead hush of midnight, he could even hear the barking of the watchdog from the opposite shore of the Hudson; but it was so vague and faint as only to give an idea of his distance from this faithful companion of man. Now and then, too, the long-drawn crowing of a cock, accidentally awakened, would sound far, far off, from some farmhouse away among the hills – but it was like a dreaming sound in his ear. No signs of life occurred near him, but occasionally the melancholy chirp of a cricket, or, perhaps, the guttural twang of a bull-frog from a neighboring marsh, as if sleeping uncomfortably, and turning suddenly in his bed.

All the stories of ghosts and goblins that he had heard in the afternoon, now came crowding upon his recollection. The night grew darker and darker; the stars seemed to sink deeper in the sky, and driving clouds occasionally hid them from his sight. He had never felt so lonely and dismal. He was, moreover, approaching the very place where many of the scenes of the ghost stories had been laid. In the centre of the road stood an enormous tulip-tree, which towered like a giant above all the other trees of the neighborhood, and formed a kind of landmark. Its limbs were gnarled and fantastic, large enough to form trunks for ordinary trees, twisting down almost to the earth, and rising again into the air. It was connected with the tragical story of the unfortunate André, who had been taken prisoner hard by; and was universally known by the name of Major André's tree. The common people regarded it with a mixture of respect and superstition, partly out of sympathy for the fate of its ill-starred namesake, and partly from the tales of strange sights and doleful lamentations, told concerning it.

As Ichabod approached this fearful tree, he began to whistle: he thought his whistle was answered – it was but a blast sweeping sharply through the dry branches. As he approached a little nearer, he thought he saw something white, hanging in the midst of the tree – he paused and ceased whistling; but on looking more narrowly, perceived that it was a place where the tree had been scathed by lightning, and the white wood laid bare. Suddenly he heard a groan – his teeth chattered and his knees smote against the saddle: it was but the rubbing of one huge bough upon another, as they were swayed about by the breeze. He passed the tree in safety, but new perils lay before him.

About two hundred yards from the tree, a small brook crossed the road, and ran into a marshy and thickly-wooded glen, known by the name of Wiley's Swamp. A few rough logs, laid side by side, served for a bridge over this stream. On that side of the road where the brook entered the wood, a group of oaks and chestnuts, matted thick with wild grape-vines, threw a cavernous gloom over it. To pass this bridge was the severest trial. It was at this identical spot that the unfortunate André was captured, and under the covert of those chestnuts and vines were the sturdy yeomen concealed who surprised him. This has ever since been considered a haunted stream, and fearful are the feelings of the schoolboy who has to pass it alone after dark.

As he approached the stream his heart began to thump; he summoned up, however, all his resolution, gave his horse half a score of kicks in the ribs, and attempted to dash briskly across the bridge; but instead of starting forward, the perverse old animal made a lateral movement, and ran broadside against the fence. Ichabod, whose fears increased with the delay, jerked the reins on the other side, and kicked lustily with the contrary foot: it was all in vain; his steed started, it is true, but it was only to plunge to the opposite side of the road into a thicket of brambles and alder bushes. The schoolmaster now bestowed both whip and heel upon the starveling ribs of old Gunpowder, who dashed forward, snuffling and snorting, but came to a stand just by the bridge, with a suddenness that had nearly sent his rider sprawling over his head. Just at this moment a plashy tramp by the side of the bridge caught the sensitive ear of Ichabod. In the dark shadow of the grove, on the margin of the brook, he beheld something huge, misshapen, black and towering. It stirred not, but seemed gathered up in the gloom, like some gigantic monster ready to spring upon the traveller.

The hair of the affrighted pedagogue rose upon his head with terror. What was to be done? To turn and fly was now too late; and besides, what chance was there of escaping ghost or goblin, if such it was, which could ride upon the wings of the wind? Summoning up, therefore, a show of courage, he demanded in stammering accents – "Who are you?" He received no reply. He repeated his demand in a still more agitated voice. Still there was no answer. Once more he cudgelled the sides of the inflexible Gunpowder, and, shutting his eyes, broke forth with involuntary fervor into a psalm tune. Just then the shadowy object of alarm put itself in motion, and, with a scramble and a bound stood at once in the middle of the road. Though the night was dark and dismal, yet the form of the unknown might now in some degree be ascertained. He appeared to be a horseman of large dimensions, and mounted on a black horse of powerful frame. He made no offer of molestation or sociability, but kept aloof on one side of the road, jogging along on the blind side of old Gunpowder, who had now got over his fright and waywardness.

Ichabod, who had no relish for this strange midnight companion, and bethought himself of the adventure of Brom Bones with the galloping Hessian, now quickened his steed in hopes of leaving him behind. The stranger, however, quickened his horse to an equal pace. Ichabod pulled up, and fell into a walk, thinking to lag behind – the other did the same. His heart began to sink within him; he endeavored to resume his psalm tune, but his parched tongue clove to the roof of his mouth, and he could not utter a stave. There was something in the moody and dogged silence of this pertinacious companion that was mysterious and appalling. It was soon fearfully accounted for. On mounting a rising ground, which brought the figure of his fellow-traveller in relief against the sky, gigantic in height, and muffled in a cloak, Ichabod was horror-struck on perceiving that he was headless! – but his horror was still more increased on observing that the head, which should have rested on his shoulders, was carried before him on the pommel of his saddle: his terror rose to desperation; he rained a shower of kicks and blows upon Gunpowder, hoping, by a sudden movement to give his companion the slip – but the spectre started full jump with him. Away then they dashed, through thick and thin; stones flying, and sparks flashing at every bound. Ichabod's flimsy garments fluttered in the air, as he stretched his long, lank body away over his horse's head, in the eagerness of his flight.

They had now reached the road which turns off to Sleepy Hollow; but Gunpowder, who seemed possessed with a demon, instead of keeping up it, made an opposite turn, and plunged headlong down hill to the left. This road leads through a sandy hollow, shaded by trees for about a quarter of a mile, where it crosses the bridge famous in goblin story, and just beyond swells the green knoll on which stands the whitewashed church.

As yet the panic of the steed had given his unskilful rider an apparent advantage in the chase; but just as he had got half way through the hollow, the girths of the saddle gave way, and he felt it slipping from under him. He seized it by the pommel, and endeavored to hold it firm, but in vain; and had just time to save himself by clasping old Gunpowder round the neck, when the saddle fell to the earth, and he heard it trampled under foot by his pursuer. For a moment the terror of Hans Van Ripper's wrath passed across his mind – for it was his Sunday saddle; but this was no time for petty fears; the goblin was hard on his haunches; and (unskilful rider that he was!) he had much ado to maintain his seat; sometimes slipping on one side, sometimes on another, and sometimes jolted on the high ridge of his horse's back-bone, with a violence that he verily feared would cleave him asunder.

An opening in the trees now cheered him with the hopes that the church bridge was at hand. The wavering reflection of a silver star in the bosom of the brook told him that he was not mistaken. He saw the walls of the church dimly glaring under the trees beyond. He recollected the place where Brom Bones' ghostly competitor had disappeared. "If I can but reach that bridge," thought Ichabod, "I am safe." Just then he heard the black steed panting and blowing close behind him; he even fancied that he felt his hot breath. Another convulsive kick in the ribs, and old Gunpowder sprang upon the bridge; he thundered over the resounding planks; he gained the opposite side; and now Ichabod cast a look behind to see if his pursuer should vanish, according to rule, in a flash of fire and brimstone. Just then he saw the goblin rising in his stirrups, and in the very act of hurling his head at him. Ichabod endeavored to dodge the horrible missile, but too late. It encountered his cranium with a tremendous crash – he was tumbled headlong into the dust, and Gunpowder, the black steed, and the goblin rider, passed by like a whirlwind.

The next morning the old horse was found without his saddle, and with the bridle under his feet, soberly cropping the grass at his master's gate. Ichabod did not make his appearance at breakfast – dinner-hour came, but no Ichabod. The boys assembled at the school-house, and strolled idly about the banks of the brook; but no schoolmaster. Hans Van Ripper now began to feel some uneasiness about the fate of poor Ichabod, and his saddle. An inquiry was set on foot, and after diligent investigation they came upon his traces. In one part of the road leading to the church was found the saddle trampled in the dirt; the tracks of horses' hoofs deeply dented in the road, and evidently at furious speed, were traced to the bridge, beyond which, on the bank of a broad part of the brook, where the water ran deep and black, was found the hat of the unfortunate Ichabod, and close beside it a shattered pumpkin.

The brook was searched, but the body of the schoolmaster was not to be discovered. Hans Van Ripper, as executor of his estate, examined the bundle which contained all his worldly effects. They consisted of two shirts and a half; two stocks for the neck; a pair or two of worsted stockings; an old pair of corduroy small-clothes; a rusty razor; a book of psalm tunes full of dog's ears; and a broken pitchpipe. As to the books and furniture of the school-house, they belonged to the community, excepting Cotton Mather's History of Witchcraft, a New England Almanac, and a book of dreams and fortune-telling; in which last was a sheet of foolscap much scribbled and blotted in several fruitless attempts to make a copy of verses in honor of the heiress of Van Tassel. These magic books and the poetic scrawl were forthwith consigned to the flames by Hans Van Ripper; who from that time forward determined to send his children no more to school; observing, that he never knew any good come of this same reading and writing. Whatever money the schoolmaster possessed, and he had received his quarter's pay but a day or two before, he must have had about his person at the time of his disappearance.

The mysterious event caused much speculation at the church on the following Sunday. Knots of gazers and gossips were collected in the church-yard, at the bridge, and at the spot where the hat and pumpkin had been found. The stories of Brouwer, of Bones, and a whole budget of others were called to mind; and when they had diligently considered them all, and compared them with the symptoms of the present case, they shook their heads, and came to the conclusion that Ichabod had been carried off by the galloping Hessian. As he was a bachelor, and in nobody's debt, nobody troubled his head any more about him. The school was removed to a different quarter of the hollow, and another pedagogue reigned in his stead.

It is true, an old farmer, who had been down to New York on a visit several years after, and from whom this account of the ghostly adventure was received, brought home the intelligence that Ichabod Crane was still alive; that he had left the neighborhood, partly through fear of the goblin and Hans Van Ripper, and partly in mortification at having been suddenly dismissed by the heiress; that he had changed his quarters to a distant part of the country; had kept school and studied law at the same time, had been admitted to the bar, turned politician, electioneered, written for the newspapers; and finally had been made a justice of the Ten Pound Court. Brom Bones, too, who shortly after his rival's disappearance conducted the blooming Katrina in triumph to the altar, was observed to look exceedingly knowing whenever the story of Ichabod was related, and always burst into a hearty laugh at the mention of the pumpkin; which led some to suspect that he knew more about the matter than he chose to tell.

The old country wives, however, who are the best judges of these matters, maintain to this day that Ichabod was spirited away by supernatural means; and it is a favorite story often told about the neighborhood round the winter evening fire. The bridge became more than ever an object of superstitious awe, and that may be the reason why the road has been altered of late years, so as to approach the church by the border of the mill-pond. The school-house being deserted soon fell to decay, and was reported to be haunted by the ghost of the unfortunate pedagogue; and the plow-boy, loitering homeward of a still summer evening, has often fancied his voice at a distance, chanting a melancholy psalm tune among the tranquil solitudes of Sleepy Hollow.

POSTSCRIPT.
FOUND IN THE HANDWRITING OF MR. KNICKERBOCKER

The preceding Tale is given almost in the precise words in which I heard it related at a Corporation meeting at the ancient city of Manhattoes, at which were present many of its sagest and most illustrious burghers. The narrator was a pleasant, shabby, gentlemanly old fellow, in pepper-and-salt clothes, with a sadly humourous face; and one whom I strongly suspected of being poor, – he made such efforts to be entertaining. When his story was concluded, there was much laughter and approbation, particularly from two or three deputy aldermen, who had been asleep the greater part of the time. There was, however, one tall, dry-looking old gentleman, with beetling eyebrows, who maintained a grave and rather severe face throughout: now and then folding his arms, inclining his head, and looking down upon the floor, as if turning a doubt over in his mind. He was one of your wary men, who never laugh but upon good grounds – when they have reason and law on their side. When the mirth of the rest of the company had subsided, and silence was restored, he leaned one arm on the elbow of his chair, and sticking the other akimbo, demanded, with a slight, but exceedingly sage motion of the head and contraction of the brow, what was the moral of the story, and what it went to prove?

The story-teller, who was just putting a glass of wine to his lips, as a refreshment after his toils, paused for a moment, looked at his inquirer with an air of infinite deference, and, lowering the glass slowly to the table, observed that the story was intended most logically to prove: –

"That there is no situation in life but has its advantages and pleasures – provided we will but take a joke as we find it:

"That, therefore, he that runs races with goblin troopers is likely to have rough riding of it.

"Ergo, for a country schoolmaster to be refused the hand of a Dutch heiress, is a certain step to high preferment in the state."

The cautious old gentleman knit his brows tenfold closer after this explanation, being sorely puzzled by the ratiocination of the syllogism; while, methought, the one in pepper-and-salt eyed him with something of a triumphant leer. At length he observed that all this was very well, but still he thought the story a little on the extravagant – there were one or two points on which he had his doubts.

"Faith, sir," replied the story-teller, "as to that matter, I don't believe one-half of it myself."

D. K.

John Neal (1793–1876)

John Neal, a Maine-born author, had a strong reputation in his lifetime as a critic and novelist – a reputation of which, at present, little remains. However, among his short stories are fine works like "Idiosyncrasies," a master-piece of what might be called "domestic Gothic." Like his younger contemporary Poe, Neal excels at placing a story in the mouth of a madman who protests that he is not mad. The story told by William Southard Lee reveals considerable psychological insight into quirks of character – closely linked to the patriarchal patterns of his society – which lead him to destroy his family and his own happiness.

Text: John Neal, "Idiosyncrasies," *Brother Jonathan,* 5 (May–Sept. 1843), 25, 274–80.

Idiosyncrasies

An Introductory Chapter

And what the plague are Idiosyncrasies? Why not tell us in good wholesome English what your meaning is? A learned man, to be sure; but what of that? Of what value to the multitude is that learning which the multitude cannot understand? You might as well preach in Hebrew, as employ the language of books, in the familiar business of life. Away with all this parade of learning, if you have to do with people. Would you ask for bread and butter in blank verse? or begin – as most people do – with the most difficult part of a language – its poetry – Telemachus, for example, if you wanted your children to talk French? No, no, my friend; if you are to tell your story to any good purpose, it should be in that household speech, whereof we hear so much and read so little. That you are unlike other men, I know; but I do not know in what particulars. I see you won-dered at – reverenced – reviled, and as I believe, shamefully misunderstood, not to say misrepresented; but whose fault is it? You came before the world as a Prophet and a Teacher. You foretell the inevitable consequences of our doings, and thus far, had you been gifted with the spirit of ancient prophecy, you could not have been more trium-phantly happy in your soothsaying. You go about doing good. You venture to rebuke, in language that no man is able to withstand, the mighty of our earth, no matter who they are, nor how they are looked upon by the rest of mankind, nor where they dwell. As if commissioned from on High, you lift up your voice from the midst of the great cozen-ing patient multitude, while they are prostrating themselves by thousands and tens of thousands, before the feet of their Idol, and say to him in a language that thrills the blood – *thou art the man!* And yet, if we are to believe you, you are a byword and a reproach, powerless and aimless; alike unfeared, unsought, unhoped for.

That you are unhappy, all can see. That you have made others happy – *very* happy – that to do so has been the great business of your life, so far as they know or believe, all are ready to acknowledge. Doing so much for others, can you do nothing for yourself?

Wake up, my friend! Be a man! Shake off the unworthy load that crushes you to the earth; and be a man – altogether a man, once more! Are you weary of the world, tired of life: or is there indeed nothing worth living for?

Stop. I see what you want, said the other. Stop. You shall have my story. Having heard it, you will judge for yourself. I hate babbling – and eaves-dropping – but you have prevailed. Overmastered by circumstances, I give up.

Look at this hand. A month ago – not more – it was the hand of a strong man. Lift your eyes to mine. You see how pale they are; how they tremble when you try to look into their mysterious depths. Yet only a month ago, they would allow me to gaze upon the sun, at noonday, without winking. They would allow me to see an angel sitting there, as plainly as I now see you; and after gazing at her for a little time, her counte-nance haunted me – till, look where I would, there it was, glowing and smiling for ever and ever, and looking – as I live my young friend, I tell you nothing but the truth – the simple truth – looking as if it had a message for me, and would if it might, comfort me. Do you wonder that I grew blind with gazing? that people began to persuade themselves – not me, sir but themselves – they were never able to persuade me into such a preposterous belief – that I wanted looking after. Sir! – would you believe it! at the very moment, while I was lecturing under one name, to a large class of scientific men, upon a subject of transcendent importance, my *friends* were upon the watch for me, under another, as a wretched lunatic, who needed the guardianship of a toothless old nurse and chattering driveller, like the man they have built into the hospital where you found me. I say *built* in, because no other language would so well express the rela-tion he bears to the whole building, inside and out, which he has had the spoiling of. Blockheads! – do they not know, can they not be made to know, that, however mad a man may be north-north-west, as our friend Hamlet the Dane has it, he may still know a hawk from a handsaw – hanshaw, some people say[1] – but I don't care a snap for their opinions, do you? – when the wind is easterly? Ah – you think I am wandering; I can see. You need not shake your head – were you put upon oath now, you would be will-ing to swear that you once had a long talk with me, and that I kept wandering from the subject; wouldn't you now? – there's a good fellow. And yet, as sure as you are alive, I am no more of a mad man than you are. Try me: question me: probe my understand-ing to the quick. See if I cannot repeat all I have been saying to you, and all you have said to me, and precisely in the same order. Can I be out of my senses then? are mad men able to do these things? If so – who would not be a mad man?

A poser, by Jupiter!

Oh, you smile; and you are not more than half-persuaded of my sanity; not-withstanding what I foresee you will be pleased to call hereafter, if questioned by the court, my craft and cunning, or mayhap my eloquence. What say you sir? As a man, I ask you; and as a man I charge you to speak the simple truth. Should you or not be willing to testify, if called to the stand, that I had acted very strangely in your presence; that I had talked incoherently, and kept wandering from the subject? And if you did, and others like you should do the same, what should hinder me from cutting the throat of any person I might take a fancy to – your own, for example? – there, there, don't be frightened; I am only putting the case. And yet, mark me – you would swear to a false-hood, and so would they. I am not now – I never have been beside myself. That I have counterfeited madness heretofore, that I could do it now, so as to deceive you, and half

Notes

IDIOSYNCRASIES

[1] The speaker, William Southard Lee, displays his awareness of the famous scholarly quibble over the reading of a line in *Hamlet*, Act II, scene 2, and by implication compares himself to the Prince.

the physicians of the country, is very true; and that – if I were so disposed, I could satisfy any jury upon earth, impannelled for the purpose, that I had gone mad before their faces, and that, let me tell you, without rolling my eyes or making faces, or screaming or staring. You might feel my pulse – or watch my breathing – and still you would be satisfied. You might examine the palms of my hands – my tongue – the moisture upon my forehead – or myself; and the result would be alike satisfactory to the bar and the bench – to the jury and the mob. Have you ever happened to see drunkenness well represented – by such a player as Matthews,[2] for example? Which would be the easier, think you, to counterfeit a loss of appetite, a devouring thirst, watchfulness, and a wandering or flighty speech; or to play the drunkard to the life?

No sir, I am not mad. I never was mad. And though I should cut the throat of my best friend to-morrow – or blow out the brains of my worst enemy – it matters little which, for the more unprovoked and atrocious the crime, the stronger the argument, you know, in favor of my insanity – and if you, yourself, were disposed to go into court and testify to this very conversation, with a view to punish a murderer, the very acknowledgment I have now made to you, would ensure my acquittal. Once get possessed of the notion that a man is mad – and every thing he does or says, will count for proof. Let the public sympathy be engaged in favor of a man – and you cannot punish him, do what he may, in this country: *provided* nevertheless and notwithstanding, that he is able to engage lawyers enough – the "indiscriminate defenders of right and wrong." For ten thousand dollars, I would undertake for the acquittal of any man, under any circumstances – the more aggravated the better. You have but to engage the newspapers – bespeak the sympathy of people, whose sympathy is always in the market – and have half a dozen decent members of the bar, and your business is done.

Goodness me! – what are we coming to, if what you say is the truth! whispered the little man, at our elbow.

To business, I hope. Don't I know what I say to be true? Haven't I tried it? – You shudder! – poh! – You shall have the story at length, when we meet again. See if I don't show you how to bamboozle a jury, to say nothing of judges, by the help of lawyers and the newspapers.

Chapter II

Be seated. You shall have the story. There's a storm brewing off yonder; the waves are tumbling over the rocks, very much as they did, when I – but no matter; I'm in the humor, I tell you, and come what may, you shall have the facts, just as they happened, without disguise or palliation.

Did you ever hear of a father being jealous of his own child? Look at me – poh, poh – don't be frightened; don't make a fool of yourself – I am that man. But that you may understand the origin, the growth, and the strange history, of what must appear unnatural to you, coldblooded as you are; I shall go back to the time when I was first acquainted with her mother.

Men have loved children, and little children, grown men, heretofore, with a purity and a strength, beyond all comparison – greater and holier, than you of the North can have an idea of. Talk about the love of men and women! I tell you sir, that between the mature and fully grown of equal age, there is no such thing as love – high-hearted, strong, and pure, unconquerable love. Men and women have other and very different feelings toward each other, and wholly mistake the diviner impulses, and the deeper

Notes

[2] Possibly the English actor Charles Mathews.

and warmer sensibilities, that belong to the pure of heart, the faithful by nature, and the *wholly inexperienced*. Well, well; I was a man – a full grown, serious-looking man, I had gone by forever, and almost forgotten, forever, the feelings and allurements of youth. I had loved the society of women, believing it to be a safeguard against every sort of debasing and soiling temptation. That I found them weak, changeable, frivolous – and everything but faithless, and heartless, and treacherous, I acknowledge. But, with all their faults, I always found them better than men, better-hearted, more trustworthy, and altogether more self-sacrificing – more unselfish. And so, I began to look about me, and tried for a long while to understand *why* it was, that women were so change-able, and weak, and frivolous; and having found it in the *Institutions of Society*, as we men call them, *we*, the founders, framers, and supporters of those very institutions, which imprison the soul of woman, and set a seal upon her faculties – and seven seals upon the fountain of her thoughts; forbidding her to reason for herself, to enquire for herself, to judge for herself – nay even to believe for herself; and allowing her no share whatever in the glorious birthright we claim, of governing ourselves: Having found the cause, I say, in these institutions, the handy-work of Man, and believing in my heart, as I hope to be believed hereafter, that where the evil was, there the remedy must be sought for, I went to work, with a determination to help the first women I should meet with, having the courage and steadfastness of purpose, needed for such a struggle, up – up – and into the place she had been created for – that of entire compan-ionship with Man.

Think not I meant to make her the less a woman – a loveable and loving women – by uplifting her from the degradation she had grown so familiar with. She was to be only the better wife, the better mother, and the better housekeeper, for being the better and truer woman. I saw – I still see – no harm in giving to Women healthy minds; no mis-chief in strengthening their faculties, their reasoning powers, and their self-dependence: and not much, in teaching them to breathe freely, to walk freely, to think boldly, to judge for themselves, and to take care of themselves, without Man's help.

Well, it so happened, that one day, as I sat near a young and lovely women, reasoning with her upon her duties to herself; wondering at her beauty, and gazing into her serene eyes, with a look, I am sure, of unearthly admiration – for I saw nothing, and felt nothing, as my look wandered over her divine countenance and richly-moulded person – but a magnificent flower: a spirituality in blossom; a creature whose wings, if they were let alone, would grow visible before she left the earth. I had just finished a care-fully considered answer to a question which she had put to me, touching the equality of the sexes; having satisfied her, as I supposed, that *equality* was one thing, *identity* another, in the mind as well as in the body; that although I held Women to be fully equal to Men, take all their properties together, of mind and body, I did not hold them to be *equal* in every thing, nor *alike* in anything – woman being inferior to Man in some things, *if you take man for the standard*; man inferior to Woman in others, *if you take woman for the standard*; while if you allow Woman to have a standard of her own, as you allow Man to have a standard of his own, she is no more inferior to him, than he is inferior to her. I had just endeavored to maintain, that you cannot if you would, and ought not if you could – compare two beings created for such different purposes: How would you compare fruit with blossoming herbage? – rivers with seas? – or clouds with autumnal foliage? – a bird of prey, with a nightingale? how would you do so, I mean, if your object were to show which of any two were *superior* to the other, not of the same sex, nor of the same species? My eyes had been turned away for a few minutes, not more than five, at the most, I should think, and I was comforting my self with the idea that I had made a profound impression; that I had been listened to as I deserved – in short, that I had been helping a woman to reason for herself – when – would you believe it! – a slight giggle at my ear, followed by a pinch, made me look up, and there was the fair girl I had been talking to, fast asleep on the sofa; a little imp I had upon my knee, enjoying my confusion, as if she understood the whole drift of what I had been saying, and almost pitied me. Before I well knew what I was about, I had risen from the chair – how I got rid of the child in my lap, I never knew – but as I reached for my hat – I felt her little warm hand stealing into mine; and when I looked down upon her, I started, for tears were in her eyes and her sweet mouth trembled, as if I had been rough with her. God help me – I cannot go on – I see that child before me now: I hear the delicate chiming of her low clear voice! I see her soft eyes changing color, as I stoop to kiss her forehead – not her lips – but her forehead, for the first time in all my life. Again I sit by her, watching the growth of her mind – the first flowering of her affections – the first signs of a womanly nature. Need I say more? That child understood me; and after a few years, we were married, and she became the mother of a child, so like herself, when I first saw her – Or she had been in my lap forty times I dare say; and I had kissed her a thousand times, and romped with her by the hour – and yet I can truly say that I never *saw* her; that I never looked into her eyes, till I was about to steal away on tip-toe, from the presence of a woman I had just put to sleep, while reasoning with her of temperance and righteousness, and a life to come; and found a little hand comforting and soothing me – Yes, of another child! so like herself when I first saw her, that I never could bear the thought of her loving anybody on earth but me. You are amazed – and so am I, that I should take the trouble to open my heart to you in this way; that I should be fool enough to acknowledge – and to a stranger – that I have been made miserable, by the love that my own child felt for another of her own age. – But mark you, she was my only child, and, as I live, the only thing I had on earth to care for, after the death of her blessed mother, who died –

> "I dare not tell thee *how*,
> But look, 'tis *written in my brow*."[3]

Stay! Before you can be fully prepared to understand me, I must tell you something about her mother's death, and of the narrow escape I had from the hands of a jury, before I knew what juries were made of.

Chapter III – The Story

Well, sir, since you have made up your mind for the worst, you shall have the story. Enough to say that I married the child. I pass over the season of courtship, and the season of trial that followed our marriage. We were happy. I loved her as no man ever loved woman – I know what I say and mean it – for I loved her, not because of her womanhood, but because of something yet holier; because, happen what might, I knew well that I could depend upon her. Whether she loved me, I cannot take upon myself to say. If she did, her love was unlike that of any other woman, I ever saw, or heard of. You may believe me, when I tell you that she seldom spoke to me above her breath, when we were alone; that even, up to the birth of our second child, if I but touched her hand, she would tremble and quake, and her eyes would fill and she would lean upon me as if her heart were brimming over with unutterable emotion. She thought she loved me – poor girl – she persisted in that belief all her life long, though I labored mightily to undeceive her, and she died at last to prove that I was mistaken.

God help me! Here he stopped and turned away his head for a moment, and flung up the window – and walked to and fro, the whole length of the room, five or six

Notes ───────────────────────────────────

[3] From Lord Byron's *The Giaour* (1813).

times; but he neither drew out his pocket handkerchief, nor wiped his eyes with his hand, as they do upon the stage.

Yes, *sir – God help me!* I know what I'm saying and I mean it for a prayer. It is long since I gave up the habit of using words lightly, and without reference to their significa-tion. "She died – I dare not tell thee how – but *look! 'tis written on my brow!*" May be I've said that before – I think I have?

I nodded.

No matter if I have. The lines have a meaning, and so have I. She died – that's the simple fact –. She died; and left me to quarrel with mankind for having allowed such a creature to belong to me. Much as I loved her, I knew nothing, absolutely nothing of her real worth, 'till I had lost her – and was tried for my life, *because* I had lost her, when I would rather have lost myself. In a word – I did not deserve such a Woman – I, altogether a Man; and therefore it is, that I deserved her not.

Well, sir – not to waste your time, nor my own breath, which is getting to be very dear to me – now that I have nothing else to care for, let us come to the period of our first and mightiest trial, after we had linked ourselves with the cherubim. Two children sprung from our loins – a boy and girl – a man child and a seraph. The boy was a large, handsome, resolute fellow whom his mother found it impossible to manage, even by kindness. And therefore it was, that I, his father – an iron-hearted man, if God ever made anything so frightful – used to try him as with fire and water, almost every day of his life. My purpose, I acknowledge to you. I wanted to make a great and good man of him without help. I said to myself, without lifting my eyes to my father, and to his father, sufficient for the boy are the wisdom and strength of the man who begat him – and the mother that bore him. Have I not toiled and triumphed? – and am I not quali-fied to teach? Are not our offspring a part of ourselves? And may we not do what we will with our own? My wife sinned with me. So – we forgot God, and called the child *ours*. And now, mark the consequence.

But first, let me tell you of the girl. She was of the second blossom and the dearest, the truest, the most loveable child you ever saw. Everybody *took* to her: everybody remembered her; and all the little children she had ever played with, used to cry for her. How often have I heard strangers, who had forgotten her name, ask after her as that child with the soft eyes – and the sweet mouth. Well, sir – she lived and blossomed up to her tenth year; and we so yearned after her, when she was away, though for a single hour, that when she reached her tenth birth day, I doubt if she had ever been out of our sight for a single month put it all together.

Well, sir. It was in the dead of winter. We were travelling. And it so happened that we stopped one night, within a few miles of a mountain covered with snow. My wife mentioned to me, as we were standing at the window – with our eyes fixed upon the top, all red with the watch fires of a setting sun, that she had often heard of mountain scenery, in the depth of winter; but had never seen anything to be compared with this. One thing led to another, till our boy, who had come in to bid us good night unper-ceived by his mother, put up his mouth to kiss her; and in doing so, I heard him whisper something – and then say, *now – don't tell father*.

And pray, sir, said I – what is it you would not have her tell father?

My wife smiled, and the boy – poor Willy – looked up as if he could bear anything better than a *smile* from his mother at such a time.

Remember your promise mother.

I have made no promise, my dear. Go to bed, and your father and I will talk the matter over, and you shall know in the morning.

The boy growled –

Go to bed Sir! said I, and to bed he went, without kissing me.

Whereupon I called after him, saying, hark ye Sir! you are not to kiss me for a month. Remember what I told you – this is the third time – and was turning away from the window, when I felt something at my side, and looking down, saw little Biddy in her night-gown, bare-footed, and half-asleep, standing by her mother, and pulling at her apron and trying to engage her attention, without being seen by me.

Ah Biddy! is that you? said I – what are you up for at this time of night, hey?

She looked at me, and her soft eyes filled – and her sweet voice trembled – and then she whispered half sobbing – for a whole month father?

Yes my dear for a whole month. I have warned your brother about this time and again.

Yes father.

And I will not be trifled with?

No father – but a whole month, father.

Whereupon her mother caught her up to her bosom, and half smothered her with kisses.

Go to bed, my child, said I, somewhat seriously; for I felt that I had a duty to perform.

Yes, Father – and then she put up her little damp mouth to kiss me – but *do* forgive Willy, this time father – *do* now!

I was obliged to turn away my face, while I answered. No, my dear – Willy must learn to command his temper.

Yes father, but –

But *what!* said I, somewhat peevishly I fear.

My wife turned away; and the child whispered *good night father!* and *good night mother!* and we were alone once more.

Well, wife –

Well, my dear. The mystery you are waiting to have cleared up, is only this. Willy wants to go up the mountain to-morrow morning, and see the sun rise!

And what said you in reply? I hope you didn't encourage the simpleton.

Encourage him! no indeed – not I! on the contrary, I said everything I could to *discourage* him.

And why so?

Because I thought it a foolish, and to say the truth, a somewhat dangerous undertaking.

But how *dangerous*, my dear?

Indeed – I wish I could tell – wouldn't the snow be very deep?

Undoubtedly – but what then? There is a fine strong crust over it, all the way up – you may see it glitter now, in the starlight like frozen water running aslant from the skies.

And wouldn't the crust be dangerous, *my dear?* And then what if he should break through!

Dangerous *my love!* – poh! Break through indeed; pshaw! I hope you didn't discourage the boy.

Well! upon my word, Mr. Lee! – it was always *my dear* with her, except on very serious occasions, when she called me Mr. Lee, as if I were an elderly gentleman she had just got acquainted with. There's no understanding you to day. One moment you blame me for *encouraging* the boy – she had never said so much to me in all her life before – and the next you *hope* I haven't *discouraged* him!

There was but one answer for this – on the part of a husband, (who knew his rights, and knowing, must maintain them.) So, I went to the door, and called Willy to get up, and come down to his mother directly.

He had been listening, I fancy – at any rate, he was wide awake – for I heard his step on the floor, almost as soon as the words were out of my mouth; and, the next moment, he was standing before me in his night-gown with shut lips, and eyes that looked as if their color had changed to that of glittering steel, since we parted.

My son, said I – I like to be impressive at such times – my son, said I, – I am about to ask you a question. Let me have the simple truth in reply. Take your time – don't be in a hurry – and answer me, as you would, in a matter of life and death. Are you ready?

Yes, father.

Do you really want to go up the mountain, to-morrow morning, before day light?

Yes father.

But why before day light, Mr. Lee? said my wife, growing rather pale.

That he may see the sun rise, my dear.

Oh – true said she. And will there be no danger? I saw her tremble, and it vexed me.

Willy, said I – are you afraid?

No, father.

Would you like to go up alone?

Alone, father! – *no*; not unless you desire it.

Well done, my boy! I shall go with you.

Oh, I am so glad! whispered my wife; and then laying her hand quietly on my shoulder, she added: if the crust is strong enough to bear *you*, my dear – of course, it will bear *me*.

I kissed her, and was just on the point of bidding her mind her own business – or go to bed and not make a fool of herself, when all at once a strange fancy seized me; and I thought I should like to see how she would behave; and how far the courage of a woman's heart would carry her, in spite of all her quailing and shivering; and I said – yes, my love; and if you feel strong enough tomorrow morning, we will go together.

God bless you for *that*, said my wife: Yes – for *that*. Surely she must have meant something; me too, father! me too father! sung out little Biddy, from the top of the stairs, where she had kept watch. I verily believe, from the first moment I had called her brother up; thinking I meant to forgive him, perhaps, or wishing to be ready, for another appeal, whatever might happen.

Yes, my love, and you too, said I.

Heaven and earth! whispered my wife – that child!

That was enough. Wasn't I a husband and a father? And why not? said I. Hasn't that child walked off a dozen miles upon the stretch, without stopping or complaining? and if her strength and courage are *ever* to be tried on *earth*, can we hope for a better opportunity? – Would you believe it! – instead of shutting up, after what she knew I meant for a – *that's enough, my dear*, – *the thing is settled* – she came out with – But if anything *should* happen! – and you know how frightfully cold it must be up there. Of course you have made all the proper inquiries about the best path?

I was nettled at this. The question itself implied a doubt, and a reproach – for I had never thought of making the inquiries; so, husband-like, I answered her as she deserved – the blessed woman! – very much as if it was none of her business.

Here he turned to the window, and flung it up, and thrust his head out into the open air, and drew a long breath, and looked up and down the river, as if he saw something in its depths – and whispered to himself "you scarce would start to meet a spirit there!" – and it was a good while before he got a going again. At last, after a hurried remark about the weather, and the expression of a fear that he was tiring me to death – to which I answered, by no means – on the contrary! – though I hardly knew what I said – he continued as follows:

No, my dear, said I – I have not inquired, nor do I mean to inquire. I am well acquainted with this neighborhood – my father used to live within a hundred miles of it. I have Greenleaf's Map and the Gazeteer. I should no more think of troubling the landlord or anybody else with questions about the best way of getting to the top of that hill yonder, than I should about the best way to my bedroom.

Hill! said my wife – wouldn't you rather call it a *mountain?*

At another time he would, mother, whispered the young rascal at her elbow; and how would he ever find the bedroom, if he didn't ask the way? – whereupon I ordered him off to bed, and repeated, with considerable emphasis, I acknowledge, the word *hill.*

Her mouth was finely stopped, hey? Didn't I make her know her place! And then, having indicated the authority of a husband, I proceeded to give my directions for the morrow.

Then we're all a-goin', father! cried Biddy, clapping her little hands at the top of the stairs, and half-screaming for joy – all a-goin', father! Pompey and all, father!

Yes, baby – Pompey and all. Here, Pomp, here! up sprang the dog from under the bed, and away he went up stairs; and the next moment there was a loud scream – and a laugh – and both came down stairs together, tumbling head over heels. But Biddy was safe, and the first thing we saw, Poor Pomp was limping away, with one foot held up, and Biddy after him, rubbing her shoulder with one hand, while she was trying to pat him on the head with the other. *Ah!* you are getting impatient, I see – no wonder – you are not married? I bowed. Never had any children of your own, hey?

None to speak of.

Well, well – I pity you – and you must bear with me. I dwell upon the incidents of this evening, and upon the innocent prattle of that child, and the bold, manly bearing of her brother, and the language of my dear, *dear wife* – poor Jenny! – for a reason you will understand after we get through, if you don't before.

I began to feel strangely. I foresaw by his manner that something was to happen; and I almost held my breath as he continued. But we may as well break off here, and begin tomorrow with a new chapter.

Chapter IV

Well, sir, continued he. Well, sir, I waked the landlord, who stared at me with his pale, sleepy eyes, when I told him what I wanted, as if he thought me beside myself, and hinted that I had better be careful, though for his part he didn't think there was any danger – the crust being strong enough to bear a loaded ox-team below; and if we did happen to break through, why, we couldn't go far – sink very deep; and being together, it would be the easiest thing in the world for one to pull the others out. Half ashamed of the littleness of the undertaking, after what he told me, I verily believe I should have abandoned it, hadn't I caught my wife saying something with her eyes to Willy, who appeared to understand her as I did – for he looked sheepish and dissatisfied. But what business had she to anticipate her husband? So I said nothing more – and there was an end to consultation. Wrap yourselves in the warmest and snuggest clothing you have, said I – and put on thick shoes – and be ready when you are called.

By five the next morning we were afoot, well prepared for whatever we were likely to meet with – hard fare, deep snow, high winds or rough weather. You look at me with amazement. I understand you – but hear me through, and then judge for yourself. Aware that such a thing might be useful if we found it slippery, I took with me part of a bedcord which happened to lie in my way, and slipped it into one of my outside pockets, without saying a word to my wife or anybody else – for if the truth must be told, I was half ashamed of myself – and took it I hardly knew why, till after the day was over – and wouldn't for the world have had even the youngest know that I had thought it worth my while to make any sort of serious preparation for a thing I spoke so lightly of.

Here he stopped for a moment as if to take breath; and when I looked up, I saw large drops of sweat standing upon his forehead, and a dampness about his mouth never to be mistaken. His deep eyes grew deeper and larger and clearer – and there was a sort of swarthy flame – a deep inward burning, like the half-smothered fire of a carbuncle, within their innermost depths. As the man himself said many times in the progress of the story, I know what I mean, and I know of no other language that can express what I desire to say. Within the deep of his eyes there was a lower deep – glowing with fire. At times I declare to you they were like live coals – and I have trembled to think of them since, when I have been sitting alone by the river-side, or the sea; and have more than once persuaded myself, on waking suddenly, at midnight, that I could see them in the darkness fastened upon me, and shining like fire.

Well, sir – bear with me for a few minutes longer, and you shall have the truth and the whole truth – and that is what no mortal man ever had before. I only wish you were a father – his voice trembled – you never *will* understand the feelings of a father till you are; nor ever, till you have undertaken to help forward your other self – the image and superscription of a man – along the dreariest and most dangerous paths of life. You must have a man-child born of your highest hope, in the flower and majesty of your strength, while the woman you love is altogether a woman, coating, trusting, overflowing with hope and joy, and ready to die with you, or for you.

The eloquent man! How I gazed upon him, and listened to him, as he broke out upon me in flashes like these, every half hour, while going on with the story.

Well, sir – we reached the top of the mountain. We saw the great sun leave his bridal chamber, and come forth rejoicing in his strength. And all had happened as we wished, and we were on our way back, wondering at ourselves that we had been able to endure so much: for I had carried little Biddy, and dragged my wife, more than half the way up, knowing they would both find it easy enough to get back; and leaving the boy to take care of himself. We had been three hours and a half on the way, when happening to turn my head, I saw Biddy's fur cap flying over the snow, and Pompey after it, and Willy trying to overtake Pompey, and Biddy screaming and clapping her hands like mad, and her mother pale and speechless with terror – which always vexed me. Suddenly the dog stopped – . Have you read that poem by Longfellow, where he speaks – of

> "The half-frozen sound,
> Which the poor whimpering hound
> Trembled to walk on"?[4]

I started, and looked again into the man's eyes, wondering which of the two were the maddest, he or I? – he, to be opening his heart before a stranger, – and I, listening to such talk in such a place, and at such a time of night, beyond the reach of human help, if he should happen to be what I had good reason to believe – a mono-maniac, and perhaps a murderer.

After wiping his forehead, he went on to say – Well, well – you have never met with it, perhaps – but I have; or you may have forgotten it, but I never shall – *never*, to my dying day. It is only a month ago that I saw it, and if the apparition of my dear boy had

Notes ───

4 See "The Skeleton in Armor" in this anthology.

started up before me, I couldn't have been more taken by surprise. *The poor whimpering hound!* He stopped short, and the cap lodged within a few feet of him just on the verge of what appeared to be a large overhanging snow-drift. Willy kept on, laughing and shouting to the dog. Afraid he might slip, I called to him, but he did not hear me; and I should have repeated the call, hadn't his mother, like a simpleton, caught me by the arm, and whispered, for God's sake, don't let him go any further! Encouraged by the cries of little Biddy, who was running about hither and thither, and screaming for Pompey, – and lured by the cheerful sound of the rattling crust we had disengaged a long way above us, now slipping past them by cartloads, – the boy kept on till he seemed almost near enough to touch the dog, and then he stopped, and both stood stock still and seemed frightened.

My wife could hardly stand, – poor Biddy called out *they're slumping, father!* and seemed just ready to drop. What I might have done at another time I hardly know; but now – having satisfied myself at a single glance that even if the boy and dog did slump through there would be no danger, – and that if the whole body of snow gave way and carried them with it, a little steadiness and self-possession would save them both – while a too hurried interference might be fatal – I called for Biddy to come to her mother. She obeyed, trembling from head to foot, pale as death, and sinking at every step.

Stay where you are, my brave boy, said I. There is no danger – only don't be frightened. Lie down at your whole length, and keep still.

Yes, father – and then he said something else, which I couldn't make out; but his mother told me afterwards that he wanted me to call off Pompey, for the snow was slipping away from under them. I remembered then that I saw it move, though I didn't think of it at the time – God forgive me! Aware that the boy was beyond my reach, and vexed to see the dog whimpering as if afraid to move, I had begun to fumble in my pockets for the bedcord which I had so providentially brought with me, when my wife interfered again – Oh, for the love of God, save him! save him! she cried. This frightened the boy, and vexed me more than anything she ever did in her life.

Nonsense! I said – and put the line back into my pocket. And then, to punish her for such untimely interference, I called out to Willy to send Pompey for the cap, and *make him fetch it.*

Yes, father.

But the dog wouldn't stir an inch. He would neither go for the cap, nor leave his young master.

What ails the dog? said I.

He's frightened, father.

Well, and what if he is? – and are you frightened, my boy?

Yes, father.

Well, then, fetch me that cap!

Yes, father. And the brave boy stood up, and looked over, and pushed forward one foot, and the dog whimpered again, and my wife shut her eyes and fell back upon the snow, and I stood up "alone – all – *all* alone – *alone* on that wide, *wide* sea," awaiting the consummation! Twice, nay three time, I had it upon my lips to cry out – come back, my dear boy! – come back to your father! – but the enemy of man stopped me, and smothered my voice, – I tell you nothing but the truth – don't I know? – haven't I felt his gripe *here!* – so that I couldn't have made the child hear me if I *had* called to him. At last, while I was watching him, and his hand was actually outstretched, and in another moment he would have seized the cap – his mother woke and screamed – and then – oh, Lord God of the childless, be merciful to me! – I heard him say, *father! father!* – and he was gone!

For a few moments, or minutes, perhaps, I was so completely stupefied with amazement and horror, that I lost my self possession, and was about rushing after my poor boy to the very brink of the precipice where he had vanished so unaccountably, – and over into the abyss below, perhaps, – when something in the appearance of the dog brought me to my senses. He had withdrawn but a very little way from the spot, and now stood there leaning forward, like a pointer, as if listening to sounds afar off. The idea instantly struck me, that he might hear my poor Willy struggling in the snow – and I was the more convinced of this, from the fact that every now and then he would give a short, quick help, as if he saw something he was afraid to go near. Finding my wife insensible, and poor Biddy cuddled up to her, with her face buried in her lap, I determined to know the worst, before they could possibly interfere; and fetching a turn round some bushes, the tops of which were just visible above the snow, with one end of the line, I took the other in my hand and slid to the spot – aye, sir, to the very spot where my dear boy had vanished. In fact, I couldn't well do otherwise after I had got a going, for I couldn't stop myself, though the line blistered my hands. Judge of my horror when I had reached the place, and on looking down could see nothing but a vast and gloomy hollow, as if the whole broadside of the mountain had given way at once underneath our feet. I stooped and listened, and after a few moments I persuaded myself that I saw something move – nay, that I heard a voice calling *father! father!* – and the dog must have heard it too, for he ran about yelping over the snow for joy, so that he roused my wife. She started up, and before I had time to speak, or lift my finger, I saw her coming towards me. I shouted to her to stop, – I flung myself athwart her path, – but all in vain. Before she could stay herself, and before I could put forth a hand to save her, she was hurrying past me, as if swept along by a whirlwind. My mind was instantly made up – we would perish together! – and I started to my feet, took another wide sweep, and flung myself towards her with so much strength, and with so hearty a will, keeping hold of the rope as I did so, that I swept by the utmost verge of the great gulf like a weaver's shuttle; and before she had quite lost her breath, I held her clutched to my bosom, with my feet planted upon the living rock – the rock of ages! My wife! my dear wife! I cried – be thou my companion – my equal – forever and ever! Awake! and stand upon thy strength, oh woman! – Awake! and help me to save thy child! Awake! the boy lives – I have heard his voice! – I have almost seen him! Bear up – yet a little while and with God's help, he may be restored to us like one from the dead!

Whereupon, O, stranger! all the woman awoke within her at my bidding! – all the mother! – and she stood listening, with lips apart, and eyes brimful of awakened strength and unquailing hope. They were the eyes of a mother gazing devoutly upon her first-born, for the first time. The gulf cannot be very deep, said I, finding her prepared to labor with me to the last. It appears to be the bed of a torrent, which has long been undermining the snow. Here – watch me – you see how I fasten this end of the rope to the tree. The other end I take in my hand, that I may avail myself of its whole length. Instead of answering me, she clutched at my arm, and pointing to the spot where she had left Biddy, screamed, or rather tried to scream – it was only a loud gasping for breath; and when I looked up, there was the baby – (we used to call her the baby then, and I always called her the baby after the death of her mother, and up to the time when she took it into her head to leave her old doating father for a stranger of yesterday, who happened to ask her to marry him) – there she was, trying to come down backwards, on her hands and knees, to the help of her mother! Stop! I cried – stop, my dear, – not another step for your life! – and well it was that I did, for she was but just able to stop herself, with Pompey's help, upon the outer edge of the very drift along which her mother had been swept with such fearful swiftness a few minutes before.

My dear Jenny, said I – I believe I told you what my wife's name was? – Well, well, no matter if I didn't – others called her Jane, but nothing would do for me but Jenny, though I never could persuade her to call me William, or Southard – for I had a sweeter-sounding middle name as heart could wish – or *husband* – she never could make up her mouth for that – she used to say, no! that isn't it. Poor Jenny! – it was too much of a mouthful, she used to say – that's it – ! Stop! – where am I – ?

You were speaking to Mrs. Lee, I believe.

To Mrs. Lee! – poh! poh! – to my wife, you mean, – to poor little Jenny. Well, said I to her – beginning to breathe freely, now that Pompey was quiet, and the baby safe – we must depend upon ourselves, my dear, and upon ourselves alone. She shook her head, and looked up at the overhanging skies. I knew what she meant, but continued – There is no human help within our reach. Now, hear me! Everything depends upon you. I shall take the other end of the rope, and let myself down into the gulf with it, as far as it will let me go.

My wife shuddered. Can it be strong enough, dear? Hadn't you better double it?

Give yourself no uneasiness about the strength of the rope – a fishing-line will bear double the weight of a man, if made of good material. When I touch the snow, or get a good foothold, or see a chance for dropping – .

For dropping!

Just hear me through, if you please, my dear. When I want the whole rope – no matter for what reason – I will give it a twitch, and then you must promise me to unfasten it. All you have to do, you see, is to cast off one turn, and let me drop.

And let you drop – you! my husband! – into that unfathomable gulf!

To be sure, said I. Upon no other terms can I answer for the boy.

Never! – never! – I never should have the strength to do it.

You will need no strength, my dear. Stay – I will fix it so, that when you feel the rope shake, or hear my voice, you will only have to let go.

To let go! she screamed, covering her face with her hands, and shaking all over.

Hear me, Jenny! said I. There is no sort of danger, if you will only do as I wish.

But how are you to get back? If you fail to reach the bottom, or find it deeper than you now suppose – or if you should want to get back, no matter for what reason, – my strength would be of no use to you.

Well thought of, my dear. I can climb up.

But your hands are already blistered, and you might be unable to climb so far – and then – oh God! what would become of me!

Faith, but the woman was right after all, and at another time, perhaps, I might have acknowledged it, as I always did when she was wrong – but there was no time for it now.

Couldn't you tie knots in the rope? and wouldn't they keep you, my dear? – and wouldn't it be well to secure it round your waist, in such a way that if your hand slipped you would still be safe.

A plague on the counsels of a woman! If she had let me alone, I should have thought of all these things myself.

No, no, said I – don't you see that would shorten the rope?

That's true – and you want every inch of it, don't you? Stay – and she fell upon her knees. Oh, my dear husband! (It was the first time she had ever called me husband in all her life) – oh, my dear, *dear* husband! you are strong, – I am weak; – you are heavy, – I am light. You can draw me up with ease. Nay, nay, I beseech you to hear me! – let me go down for the child. Fasten the rope to me, and let me go down first, and look about me; and then if I fail, something else may be thought of.

Was the woman mad? I determined to try her. Will you promise to shut your eyes, and not scream? said I.

Yes, yes – growing very pale.

But if you should faint, or grow dizzy?

That you must provide for by fastening the rope to me in such a way that I cannot fall, even if I should let go; and oh, I beseech you to be quick!

And you are serious, are you, my dear?

Serious! – try me – and she took the rope and passing it twice round her waist, and saying, now, my dear, tie such a knot as you think will be safe, and one, that upon a pinch I may be able to untie – and let me show you whether I am serious, or not.

Oh, father! father! what are you going to do to mother! screamed Biddy, when she saw me tying the rope; and down she came – at full speed, followed by Pompey, at such a distance, however, from the edge of the gulf, that we had nothing to fear.

Instantly a thought struck me. The lamb had offered itself for the sacrifice. The hand of the High Priest had been lifted as with a bloody knife – and lo! an offering had leaped forth from the midst of the snows and rocks.[5]

I told the sweet child what her mother was going to do. She turned deadly pale, and running up to her mother, clasped her round the knees, and began to cry, Oh, mother! Oh, father! Oh, dear Willy! and then her mother having loosened her arms, kneeled down by her in the snow, and kissed, and kissed her, as if she never expected to see her again alive, and undertook to tell her what the reasons were. Having heard her through, the little creature jumped up – she *did!* as you're a living man – she *did*, as I hope for mercy! – and said to me, growing paler and paler, at every breath – let me go down, please; but, O, father! do tie the rope strong – won't you, dear father? and then she began to tremble so, she could hardly stand. It would be easy for you and mother to pull me up – wouldn't it? – and then, you know, there's no danger, is there father?

Not much, dear – you might be a little bruised.

Oh, I shouldn't mind that father; and I'm all ready now – you're sure you heard brother Willy – just call to him, father, and say, I'm coming down to see him, will you?

The thought was happy, and I shouted at the top of my lungs for him to keep a good heart, and we would soon have him out. His mother followed – and then the baby – but, alas, alas! we could hear no answer.

Now father, now! said the dear child; growing impatient, and trying to fasten the rope, with her own little trembling fingers. You won't let me slip, will you father? said she, just as we were about to swing her off.

Are you very much afraid, my love?

Yes, father – I suppose I am; but then, I am all ready and willing to go – kiss me mother – kiss me again, dear father – I want to kiss you both, more than ever – and then! Oh, Willy, Willy! and here she fell a sobbing, as if her heart would break – oh brother Willy! – If I shouldn't find him after all! Come, come, father – let me go – I must go – stop a moment – and she dropped upon her knees and said over that little prayer; now I lay me down to sleep.

Wishing to have her entirely prepared, I said to her, while taking a double turn about her waist, and making a loop for her feet, and another for her dear little hands. It is very dark down there, Biddy.

Yes father; but I am not much afraid in the dark, though I do want the blinds open after I'm asleep; but Willy always goes to bed in the dark you know; and he isn't afraid of anything; is he mother?

Notes

[5] See Abraham's sacrifice, Genesis 22, a biblical episode which has considerable resonance with this story.

I looked at my wife – and she at me – and then we took up the dear child in our arms and kissed her again and again, and breathing a prayer over her, such as none but a father and mother could breathe; and finding her unterrified and firm, though she shuddered when I trod with her on my arms, upon the slippery verge of the abyss, we wrapped her about with shawls and a fur cape, so that she couldn't be chafed, and bidding her shut her eyes, I let her down slowly and steadily from a rock, into what seemed the bed of a torrent, and very near the place where Willy had vanished. Not a word – not a single moan or cry escaped her; but the dog whimpered, and when he saw her shut her eyes, as she went swinging to and fro in the darkness, it seemed as if he could bear it no longer; for after a short struggle with himself, he leaped after her headlong into the abyss. For a moment, all my strength was gone – I felt as if there was no hope; and but for the timely interference of my dear wife I don't know but I might have let the rope go, or tumbled in myself, it grew dark so suddenly, and my knees trembled so, when the dog leaped yelling past our child: but the next! O, merciful Father! We heard the yelping of the dog underneath our very feet, as it seemed to me, and the cry was full of comfort and assurance.

The dog had not fallen far – and it was clear that he couldn't be much hurt, and if so, the chances were – God! how I tremble, when I call to mind, the first thought I had of his being buried alive in the snow! In the midst of the strange, sickening terror that followed, depriving me of all strength for a moment, we heard a noise from below, as of two children whispering together – no, no! we could not be mistaken! and a moment afterwards, there came up a cry of joy from poor Biddy, saying – there's Willy, father! I see him, father!

I fell upon my knees, and my wife came staggering to my side – before either of us knew whether the child were living or dead.

All right father! shouted Biddy – he knows me; and he's trying to get up – and he wants you!

I crept to the edge of the precipice, and looked over; and finding the rope loose, called out to Biddy to know what she was standing on.

I'm in the snow father – up to my middle! and every time I move or speak, down comes more snow tumbling upon me from the roof; and there's brother Willy, just down there, father – and he wants you – and he wants you – and he wants me to ask you if he has been a good boy; and he says he's got the cap, and he's very sorry the snow fell before he could get away – and hopes mother isn't much frightened.

Poor Willy!

But I'm growing dizzy father – and I can't see Willy, now; and now, oh, dear! oh dear, what's that! oh father! father! here it comes! and then there was a furious barking, and a loud scream, followed by a tremendous avalanche.

Not another word, my love – I'm going to draw you up now! cried I, beginning to pull; but to my unspeakable horror and amazement, I found the rope fast! with all my strength, I could but stretch it a few inches – and every time I did, I fancied I heard a low growl.

An idea of the truth instantly flashed through my brain like a thunderbolt. Having ascertained that more than half the rope was left, I took a turn round the stump, and clutching a knife that never failed me – here it is now – down I went, determined not to be spoiled of both children at one swoop, though I had to battle with the she-bear, among the holes of the rock, for them.

On reaching the great bed of snow, into which the child had partly sunk, I found her lying upon her face, and literally buried alive in it. – I soon liberated her; and the first words she spoke – poor thing! – were, I knew you would help me out father; and I felt safe, when I saw it a coming.

Saw what coming dear?

I don't know father – maybe 'twas the snow. Pompey was frightened too – and, O dear father, where's Willy! I don't see him now! Brother Willy! brother Willy!

Where did you see him last – show me dear.

The child pointed to a place twenty feet lower; a sort of ledge covered with rubbish, drift wood, and loose earth.

Will you be a good girl, and stay here – just here, under this overhanging rock, while I go for your brother? You mustn't cry nor be frightened.

No father – yes father – but I'm very cold.

Courage wife! courage! mind the rope, and be of good cheer! I shouted.

A scream of joy followed from above; and choosing my way, along by the rough edges of the rocks, I soon reached the place where Willy had been lying a few minutes before. It was very dark, and while I was straining my eyes to see further down the bed of the torrent, something moved so near me, as to make my very blood curdle. I grasped my knife and shouted with all my strength – and instantly there was a loud windy rush – a furious barking, a hundred feet below it seemed to me, and another avalanche, vast, and heavy enough to overwhelm a city. For a few moments, I was nearly stunned; but as the barking continued, and I knew little Biddy was safe, I determined to follow it. And well it was that I did so; for after a few plunges, I saw light below, and feeling my way along, came to a place where I found my poor boy, lying stiff and stark upon the snow, speechless with cold and terror – but otherwise unharmed.

The dog was lying over him; and when I lifted him up, and began to rub him and speak to him, he knew me, and saying may I kiss you now, father? I knew you wouldn't leave me here! – laid his cheek to mine, and began to sob with a violence that frightened me – he was only twelve, you must know.

I tried to soothe him, and calling out to Biddy that I had found him, was waiting to hear the voice of her mother in reply – when he whispered I couldn't help it father! I am very sorry – but some how or other I've lost the cap.

God bless the poor fellow! – what cared I for a cap – or for ten thousand caps, filled with diamonds – when I had him once more safely in my arms!

At this moment, I heard the voice of my wife. Our arrangements were soon made. On going a little further, I found we could creep out on the side of the mountain, and make our way down without much difficulty through the trees. Having satisfied myself upon this point, I returned to Biddy, and lifting her in my arms, called out to her mother to make her way down by the path we came up – as Biddy, and Willy, and Pompey and I were all safe, and would go by another way. In short sir – here he drew out his watch – it is not yet my hour, and perhaps, I may as well finish the story.

If you please.

Well then, the boy was saved; but he died within a twelvemonth afterwards, poor fellow! – perhaps of fright, and perhaps of something else, but however that may be – I never could bring myself to forgive his mother.

To forgive his mother! what had his mother done, I should like to know?

Why, don't you see, that she was the death of the boy? But for that confounded scream, just as he had his hand upon the cap, the boy would have got back safely enough, and all would have been well.

I rose to go.

Stop sir! I have not done with you yet. You know, I suppose, that I put my wife to death for that very scream.

Sir! said I, and my very blood ran cold, as I looked into his eyes.

Yes, but I did though – much as I loved her, and while I was ready to lay down my life at any hour to make her happy.

Pity you didn't! I was just on the point of saying: but I forbore – anxious to hear the end of the story.

Let me tell you how it was. We had often talked about our brave boy – sitting side by side, and holding each other by the hand, till our eyes were streaming with tears – but I never could make her believe that she was to blame. I could see, though she never said so, that in *her* opinion, his death lay at my door. Well, it so happened after many years, that we were walking together one day, near Wentworth falls, and the subject of our boy's death came up – and the behavior of poor little Biddy, just then flowering into womanhood – and I happened to say something like this – I do in my heart believe, that if I had commanded either of those children to leap into the whirlpool yonder, I should have been obeyed instantly.

And if you were – what then? said she.

Why then, said I, somewhat nettled, I acknowledge, at the strange propriety of the question; and the difficulty I found in answering it: Why then said I, with a biting emphasis, and looking into her large clear eyes, as if I could see into the very depths of her heart – I wish to Heaven I could find any other living creature capable of such obedience.

You would! – said my wife.

Yes – *I would*.

And it would really make you happier?

It would indeed, I replied.

We were walking together, a few feet from the bank. She stopped and kissed me – and whispering, *Be happier then!* Sprang into the whirlpool.

I started up from my chair. And what did you do, said I.

I! – – Oh, I followed her.

You did! – give us your hand!

Yes – and with what advantage to myself think you?

To yourself! – to her, you mean?

No, but I don't though.

And you saved her?

No – but I didn't. She was drowned – and I had the narrowest escape you ever heard of – only to be tried for my life.

Tried for your life!

Yes – they charged me with pushing her in. Fools! when I would rather have been pushed in forty times myself. Poor Jenny! what a simpleton she was, to be sure! but then, lord help you, what business had she to drown herself without my leave! what a fool to do so at the bidding of a husband! and such a husband! I declare to you, my heart bleeds for her. She has been dead a good while now; but if I live these dozen years, I never shall forget my poor dear Jenny. But the best of the joke after all is – the narrow escape I had afterwards, at the hands of the law – I came very near swinging for it: and how do you think I got clear?

Can't imagine. The circumstances were all against you – and we have only your own story to explain the matter; and that never goes for much, you know.

That's it – that's the very thing! I told my own story, instead of employing a lawyer to spout it for me; and the jury, bless their hearts, and the bench and the bar took it for granted that I was mad, from that circumstance alone, I verily believe. Wholly innocent, I should have been hanged beyond a doubt, because appearances were against me. Guilty – I had nothing to fear. Stop! hold on! I haven't quite finished. I told you, if I do not mistake, that I was a jealous father, – jealous of my own daughter. So I am. That very child, Bridget – I have done calling her *Biddy* now, and for all this world wouldn't call her *Baby* now that she has forsaken and forgotten her father – that very child, what do you think she has been guilty of?

Cannot guess for the life of me.

You can't! Well, then, she has fallen in love, as they call it, the simpleton! without consulting her father; and now she wants to be married. To be married! d'ye hear! – that *child*, – a little wee bit of a thing but the other day, wholly dependent upon me, after the death of her poor mother, for every moment of happiness in life, – that child, over whose bed I have passed a hundred sleepless nights, – a creature who, till within a few months at furthest, would have laid down her life for me without a murmur, – even she wants to be married, and to a man – –.

Bless me! would you have her marry a woman?

A man, sir, old enough to be her father.

Horrible!

Yes, sir, to a man. Did you ever see a man in your life you would be fool enough to marry, if you were a woman? I never did. They are all alike, selfish and heartless and exacting. No, sir – no! – nothing would serve that child's turn but a husband. It was not enough that she had a father, a fond, faithful, doating old father, who never could bear her out of his sight! No, no – what are fathers good for when husbands are wanted? "How sharper than a serpent's tooth it is to have a thankless child!"[6] Poor thing! a father would not do, though he had nursed her with his heart's blood! – though he had worshipped her as the image of a beloved wife! She must have a man to herself, – a man of her own, – that *child!* Of course, I could have nothing more to say to her! That's *one* of my idiosyncrasies – and *you're another!*

God bless me! I cried, jumping up, and making for the door, – the gentleman after me, as if he had not quite finished the job he had in view. Happily for me I escaped; and the next day I satisfied myself that his strange story was true – substantially true, that is; that he had been charged with the murder of his wife, a most beautiful woman, and actually tried for his life upon that charge; and that he had been lately put under guardianship; and finally locked up in a madhouse for life, by his only child – the dear little Biddy he had been telling me of. That broke his heart, and crazed him, poor fellow! beyond all hope; and now he spends most of his time in making speeches to the jury, and telling over the story you have just read, to every stranger that falls his way.

Notes ———————

[6] *King Lear*, Act I, scene iv.

Nathaniel Hawthorne
(1804–1864)

In his four published novels (which he called "romances"), and his short fiction, Hawthorne developed a literature of shadows and moonlight. In Hawthorne's world "the Actual and the Imaginary may meet," as he said in his introduction to *The Scarlet Letter*. Psychological and often historical realism are thus tempered by the author's symbolic vision. Since he saw evil as a real force in the world, the Gothic mode was natural to him, as it was for his friend Melville – and for Poe. In this view of "the power of blackness" (Melville's term) Hawthorne differed sharply from his other literary friends, Emerson and Thoreau.

"Alice Doan's Appeal" (1835) is a curious, self-aware, almost postmodern work, which is at the same time a Gothic tale (or two tales) and an inquiry into the nature of the Gothic. In it Hawthorne records his failure in telling an overextended Gothic story set in the era of the Salem witchcraft trials; then he describes his success in moving his audience with a historical account of the executions of five condemned witches on August 19, 1692. (In condemning Cotton Mather for the executions, Hawthorne does not mention, however, the role played by his own ancestors in the trials.)

"Young Goodman Brown" (1835), the most often reprinted of Hawthorne's stories, may be considered the fruition of his meditation on American Gothic. Discarding the horrendous incest, revenge, and murder plot of "Alice Doan's Appeal," Hawthorne grounds his story in the experience of a single imagined Puritan Everyman just before the outbreak of the witchcraft scare. While the events, if they occur rather than being dreamed, are supernatural, the psychology of the era is sharply and realistically recreated. The questions with which Brown struggles are in fact those of the witchcraft trials: did these events really happen, or are we deceived by hallucinations? Readers who may be tempted to dismiss these questions as historical curiosities might look at late twentieth-century trials in the United States over alleged Satanic child-abuse cults, and over the alleged recovery of repressed memories of childhood sexual abuse: episodes in which modern juries struggled on the frontiers between medicine, psychology, and law, exactly as did the judges in Salem in the 1690s.

Texts: "Alice Doan's Appeal," from *The Token: A Christmas and New Year's Present* (Boston: D. H. Williams, 1835). Hawthorne never collected "Alice Doan's Appeal." "Young Goodman Brown," from *Mosses from an Old Manse* (New York: Macmillan, 1916).

Alice Doane's Appeal

On a pleasant afternoon of June, it was my good fortune to be the companion of two young ladies in a walk. The direction of our course being left to me, I led them neither to Legge's Hill, nor to the Cold Spring, nor to the rude shores and old batteries of the Neck, nor yet to Paradise; though if the latter place were rightly named, my fair friends would have been at home there. We reached the outskirts of the town, and turning aside from a street of tanners and curriers, began to ascend a hill, which at a distance, by its dark slope and the even line of its summit, resembled a green rampart along the road. It was less steep than its aspect threatened. The eminence formed part of an extensive tract of pasture land, and was traversed by cow paths in various directions; but, strange to tell, though the whole slope and summit were of a peculiarly deep green, scarce a blade of grass was visible from the base upward. This deceitful verdure was occasioned by a plentiful crop of "wood-wax," which wears the same dark and glossy green throughout the summer, except at one short period, when it puts forth a profusion of yellow blossoms. At that season to a distant spectator, the hill appears absolutely overlaid with gold, or covered with a glory of sunshine, even beneath a clouded sky. But the curious wanderer on the hill will perceive that all the grass, and every thing that should nourish man or beast, has been destroyed by this vile and ineradicable weed: its tufted roots make the soil their own, and permit nothing else to vegetate among them; so that a physical curse may be said to have blasted the spot, where guilt and phrenzy consummated the most execrable scene, that our history blushes to record. For this was the field where superstition won her darkest triumph; the high place where our fathers set up their shame, to the mournful gaze of generations far remote. The dust of martyrs was beneath our feet. We stood on Gallows Hill.

For my own part, I have often courted the historic influence of the spot. But it is singular, how few come on pilgrimage to this famous hill; how many spend their lives almost at its base, and never once obey the summons of the shadowy past, as it beckons them to the summit. Till a year or two since, this portion of our history had been very imperfectly written, and, as we are not a people of legend or tradition, it was not every citizen of our ancient town that could tell, within half a century, so much as the date of the witchcraft delusion. Recently, indeed, an historian has treated the subject in a manner that will keep his name alive, in the only desirable connection with the errors of our ancestry, by converting the hill of their disgrace into an honorable monument of his own antiquarian lore, and of that better wisdom, which draws the moral while it tells the tale. But we are a people of the present and have no heartfelt interest in the olden time. Every fifth of November, in commemoration of they know not what, or rather without an idea beyond the momentary blaze, the young men scare the town with bonfires on his haunted height, but never dream of paying funeral honors to those who died so wrongfully, and without a coffin or a prayer, were buried here.

Though with feminine susceptibility, my companions caught all the melancholy associations of the scene, yet these could but imperfectly overcome the gayety of girlish spirits. Their emotions came and went with quick vicissitude, and sometimes combined to form a peculiar and delicious excitement, the mirth brightening the gloom into a sunny shower of feeling, and a rainbow in the mind. My own more sombre mood was tinged by theirs. With now a merry word are next a sad one, we trod among the tangled weeds, and almost hoped that our feet would sink into the hollow of a witch's grave. Such vestiges were to be found within the memory of man, but have vanished now, and with them, I believe, all traces of the precise spot of the executions. On the long and broad ridge of the eminence, there is no very decided elevation of any one point, nor other prominent marks, except the decayed stumps of two trees, standing near each other, and here and there the rocky substance of the hill, peeping just above the wood-wax.

There are few such prospects of town and village, woodland and cultivated field, steeples and country seats, as we beheld from this unhappy spot. No blight had fallen on old Essex; all was prosperity and riches, healthfully distributed. Before us lay our native town, extending from the foot of the hill to the harbor, level as a chess board, embraced by two arms of the sea, and filling the whole peninsula with a close assemblage of wooden roofs, overtopt by many a spire, and intermixed with frequent heaps of verdure, where trees threw up their shade from unseen trunks. Beyond, was the bay and its islands, almost the only objects, in a country unmarked by strong natural features, on which time and human toil had produced no change. Retaining these portions of the scene, and also the peaceful glory and tender gloom of the declining sun, we threw, in imagination, a veil of deep forest over the land, and pictured a few scattered villages, and this old town itself a village, as when the prince of hell bore sway there. The idea thus gained, of its former aspect, its quaint edifices standing far apart, with peaked roofs and projecting stories, and its single meeting house pointing up a tall spire in the midst, the vision, in short, of the town in 1692, served to introduce a wondrous tale of those old times.

I had brought the manuscript in my pocket. It was one of a series written years ago, when my pen, now sluggish and perhaps feeble, because I have not much to hope or fear, was driven by stronger external motives, and a more passionate impulse within, than I am fated to feel again. Three or four of these tales had appeared in the Token,[1] after a long time and various adventures, but had incumbered me with no troublesome notoriety, even in my birth place. One great heap had met a brighter destiny: they had fed the flames; thoughts meant to delight the world and endure for ages, had perished in a moment, and stirred not a single heart but mine.[2] The story now to be introduced, and another, chanced to be in kinder custody at the time, and thus by no conspicuous merits of their own, escaped destruction.

The ladies, in consideration that I had never before intruded my performances on them, by any but the legitimate medium, through the press, consented to hear me read. I made them sit down on a moss-grown rock, close by the spot where we chose to believe that the death-tree had stood. After a little hesitation on my part, caused by a dread of renewing my acquaintance with fantasies that had lost their charm, in the ceaseless flux of mind, I began the tale, which opened darkly with the discovery of a murder.

A hundred years, and nearly half that time, have elapsed since the body of a murdered man was found, at about the distance of three miles, on the old road to Boston. He lay in a solitary spot, on the bank of a small lake, which the severe frost of December had covered with a sheet of ice. Beneath this, it seemed to have been the intention of the murderer to conceal his victim in a chill and watery grave, the ice being deeply hacked, perhaps with the weapon that had slain him, though its solidity was too stubborn for the patience of a man with blood upon his hand. The corpse therefore reclined on the earth, but was separated from the road by a thick growth of dwarf pines. There had been a slight fall of snow during the night, and as if Nature were shocked at the

Notes

ALICE DOANE'S APPEAL

[1] "Gift books" such as *The Token*, a popular form of publication in the decades before the Civil War, were annual volumes, often richly bound and illustrated, intended to be purchased and given as Christmas or New Year gifts. *The Token* was published by S. G. Goodwin in Boston (1827–42), and included many of Hawthorne's early stories.

[2] Hawthorne burned five manuscripts from a never-to-be-published collection of apprentice work he called *Seven Tales of My Native Land*.

deed, and strove to hide it with her frozen tears, a little drifted heap had partly buried the body, and lay deepest over the pale dead face. An early traveller, whose dog had led him to the spot, ventured to uncover the features, but was affrighted by their expression. A look of evil and scornful triumph had hardened on them, and made death so life-like and so terrible, that the beholder at once took flight, as swiftly as if the stiffened corpse would rise up and follow.

I read on, and identified the body as that of a young man, a stranger in the country, but resident during several preceding months in the town which lay at our feet. The story described, at some length, the excitement caused by the murder, the unavailing quest after the perpetrator, the funeral ceremonies, and other common place matters, in the course of which, I brought forward the personages who were to move among the succeeding events. They were but three. A young man and his sister; the former characterized by a diseased imagination and morbid feelings; the latter, beautiful and virtuous, and instilling something of her own excellence into the wild heart of her brother, but not enough to cure the deep taint of his nature. The third person was a wizard; a small gray, withered man, with fiendish ingenuity in devising evil and superhuman power to execute it, but senseless as an idiot and feebler than a child, to all better purposes. The central scene of the story was an interview between this wretch and Leonard Doane, in the wizard's hut, situated beneath a range of rocks at some distance from the town. They sat beside a mouldering fire, while a tempest of wintry rain was beating on the roof. The young man spoke of the closeness of the tie which united him and Alice, the concentrated fervor of their affection from childhood upwards, their sense of lonely sufficiency to each other, because they only of their race had escaped death, in a night attack by the Indians. He related his discovery, or suspicion of a secret sympathy between his sister and Walter Brome, and told how a distempered jealousy had maddened him. In the following passage, I threw a glimmering light on the mystery of the tale.

"Searching," continued Leonard, "into the breast of Walter Brome, I at length found a cause why Alice must inevitably love him. For he was my very counterpart! I compared his mind by each individual portion, and as a whole, with mine. There was a resemblance from which I shrank with sickness, and loathing, and horror, as if my own features had come and stared upon me in a solitary place, or had met me in struggling through a crowd. Nay! the very same thoughts would often express themselves in the same words from our lips, proving a hateful sympathy in our secret souls. His education, indeed, in the cities of the old world, and mine in this rude wilderness, had wrought a superficial difference. The evil of his character, also, had been strengthened and rendered prominent by a reckless and ungoverned life, while mine had been softened and purified by the gentle and holy nature of Alice. But my soul had been conscious of the germ of all the fierce and deep passions, and of all the many varieties of wickedness, which accident had brought to their full maturity in him. Nor will I deny, that in the accursed one, I could see the withered blossom of every virtue, which by a happier culture, had been made to bring forth fruit in me. Now, here was a man, whom Alice might love with all the strength of sisterly affection, added to that impure passion which alone engrosses all the heart. The stranger would have more than the love which had been gathered to me from the many graves of our household – and I be desolate!"

Leonard Doane went on to describe the insane hatred that had kindled his heart into a volume of hellish flame. It appeared, indeed, that his jealousy had grounds, so far as that Walter Brome had actually sought the love of Alice, who also had betrayed an undefinable, but powerful interest in the unknown youth. The latter, in spite of his passion for Alice, seemed to return the loathful antipathy of her brother; that similarity of their dispositions made them like joint possessors of an individual nature, which could not become wholly the property of one, unless by the extinction of the other. At last, with the same devil in each bosom, they chanced to meet, they two on a lonely road. While Leonard spoke, the wizard had sat listening to what he already knew, yet with tokens of pleasurable interest, manifested by flashes of expression across his vacant features, by grisly smiles and by a word here and there, mysteriously filling up some void in the narrative. But when the young man told, how Walter Brome had taunted him with indubitable proofs of the shame of Alice, and before the triumphant sneer could vanish from his face, had died by her brother's hand, the wizard laughed aloud. Leonard started, but just then a gust of wind came down the chimney, forming itself into a close resemblance of the slow, unvaried laughter, by which he had been interrupted. "I was deceived," thought he; and thus pursued his fearful story.

"I trod out his accursed soul, and knew that he was dead; for my spirit bounded as if a chain had fallen from it and left me free. But the burst of exulting certainty soon fled, and was succeeded by a torpor over my brain and a dimness before my eyes, with the sensation of one who struggles through a dream. So I bent down over the body of Walter Brome, gazing into his face, and striving to make my soul glad with the thought, that he, in very truth, lay dead before me. I know not what space of time I had thus stood, nor how the vision came. But it seemed to me that the irrevocable years, since childhood had rolled back, and a scene, that had long been confused and broken in my memory, arrayed itself with all its first distinctness. Methought I stood a weeping infant by my father's hearth; by the cold and blood-stained hearth where he lay dead. I heard the childish wail of Alice, and my own cry arose with hers, as we beheld the features of our parent, fierce with the strife and distorted with the pain, in which his spirit had passed away. As I gazed, a cold wind whistled by, and waved my father's hair. Immediately, I stood again in the lonesome road, no more a sinless child, but a man of blood, whose tears were falling fast over the face of his dead enemy. But the delusion was not wholly gone; that face still wore a likeness of my father; and because my soul shrank from the fixed glare of the eyes, I bore the body to the lake, and would have buried it there. But before his icy sepulchre was hewn, I heard the voices of two travellers and fled."

Such was the dreadful confession of Leonard Doane. And now tortured by the idea of his sister's guilt, yet sometimes yielding to a conviction of her purity; stung with remorse for the death of Walter Brome, and shuddering with a deeper sense of some unutterable crime, perpetrated, as he imagined, in madness or a dream; moved also by dark impulses, as if a fiend were whispering him to meditate violence against the life of Alice; he had sought this interview with the wizard, who, on certain conditions, had no power to withhold his aid in unravelling the mystery. The tale drew near its close.

The moon was bright on high; the blue firmament appeared to glow with an inherent brightness; the greater stars were burning in their spheres; the northern lights threw their mysterious glare far over the horizon; the few small clouds aloft were burthened with radiance; but the sky with all its variety of light, was scarcely so brilliant as the earth. The rain of the preceding night had frozen as it fell, and, by that simple magic, had wrought wonders. The trees were hung with diamonds and many-colored gems; the houses were overlaid with silver, and the streets paved with slippery brightness; a frigid glory was flung over all familiar things, from the cottage chimney to the steeple of the meeting house, that gleamed upward to the sky. This living world, where we sit by our firesides, or go forth to meet beings like ourselves, seemed rather the creation of wizard power, with so much of resemblance to known objects, that a man might shudder at the ghostly shape of his old beloved dwelling, and the shadow of a ghostly tree before his door. One looked to behold inhabitants suited to such a town, glittering in icy garments, with motionless features, cold, sparkling eyes, and just sensation enough in their frozen hearts to shiver at each other's presence.

By this fantastic piece of description, and more in the same style, I intended to throw a ghostly glimmer round the reader, so that his imagination might view the town through a medium that should take off its every day aspect, and make it a proper theatre for so wild a scene as the final one. Amid this unearthly show, the wretched brother and sister were represented as setting forth, at midnight, through the gleaming streets, and directing their steps to a grave yard, where all the dead had been laid, from the first corpse in that ancient town, to the murdered man who was buried three days before. As they went, they seemed to see the wizard gliding by their sides, or walking dimly on the path before them. But here I paused, and gazed into the faces of my two fair auditors, to judge whether, even on the hill where so many had been brought to death by wilder tales than this, I might venture to proceed. Their bright eyes were fixed on me; their lips apart. I took courage, and led the fated pair to a new made grave, where for a few moments, in the bright and silent midnight, they stood alone. But suddenly, there was a multitude of people among the graves.

Each family tomb had given up its inhabitants, who, one by one, through distant years, had been borne to its dark chamber, but now came forth and stood in a pale group together. There was the gray ancestor, the aged mother, and all their descendants, some withered and full of years, like themselves, and others in their prime; there, too, were the children who went prattling to the tomb, and there the maiden who yielded her early beauty to death's embrace, before passion had polluted it. Husbands and wives arose, who had lain many years side by side, and young mothers who had forgotten to kiss their first babes, though pillowed so long on their bosoms. Many had been buried in the habiliments of life, and still wore their ancient garb; some were old defenders of the infant colony, and gleamed forth in their steel caps and bright breast-plates, as if starting up at an Indian war-cry; other venerable shapes had been pastors of the church, famous among the New England clergy, and now leaned with hands clasped over their grave stones, ready to call the congregation to prayer. There stood the early settlers, those old illustrious ones, the heroes of tradition and fireside legends, the men of history whose features had been so long beneath the sod, that few alive could have remembered them. There, too, were faces of former townspeople, dimly recollected from childhood, and others, whom Leonard and Alice had wept in later years, but who now were most terrible of all, by their ghastly smile of recognition. All, in short, were there; the dead of other generations, whose moss-grown names could scarce be read upon their tomb stones, and their successors, whose graves were not yet green; all whom black funerals had followed slowly thither, now reappeared where the mourners left them. Yet none but souls accursed were there, and fiends counterfeiting the likeness of departed saints.

The countenances of those venerable men, whose very features had been hallowed by lives of piety, were contorted now by intolerable pain or hellish passion, and now by an unearthly and derisive merriment. Had the pastors prayed, all saintlike as they seemed, it had been blasphemy. The chaste matrons, too, and the maidens with untasted lips, who had slept in their virgin graves apart from all other dust, now wore a look from which the two trembling mortals shrank, as if the unimaginable sin of twenty worlds were collected there. The faces of fond lovers, even of such as had pined into the tomb, because there their treasure was, were bent on one another with glances of hatred and smiles of bitter scorn, passions that are to devils, what love is to the blest. At times, the features of those, who had passed from a holy life to heaven, would vary to and fro, between their assumed aspect and the fiendish lineaments whence they had been transformed. The whole miserable multitude, both sinful souls and false spectres of good men, groaned horribly and gnashed their teeth, as they looked upward to the calm loveliness of the midnight sky, and beheld those homes of bliss where they must never dwell. Such was the apparition, though too shadowy for language to portray; for here would be the moonbeams on the ice, glittering through a warrior's breast-plate, and there the letters of a tomb stone, on the form that stood before it; and whenever a breeze went by, it swept the old men's hoary heads, the women's fearful beauty, and all the unreal throng into one indistinguishable cloud together.

I dare not give the remainder of the scene, except in a very brief epitome. This company of devils and condemned souls had come on a holiday, to revel in the discovery of a complicated crime; as foul a one as ever was imagined in their dreadful abode. In the course of the tale, the reader had been permitted to discover, that all the incidents were results of the machinations of the wizard, who had cunningly devised that Walter Brome should tempt his unknown sister to guilt and shame, and himself perish by the hand of his twin-brother. I described the glee of the fiends, at this hideous conception and their eagerness to know if it were consummated. The story concluded with the Appeal of Alice to the spectre of Walter Brome; his reply, absolving her from every stain; and the trembling awe with which ghost and devil fled, as from the sinless presence of an angel.

The sun had gone down. While I held my page of wonders in the fading light, and read how Alice and her brother were left alone among the graves, my voice mingled with the sigh of a summer wind, which passed over the hill top with the broad and hollow sound, as of the flight of unseen spirits. Not a word was spoken, till I added, that the wizard's grave was close beside us, and that the wood-wax had sprouted originally from his unhallowed bones. The ladies started; perhaps their cheeks might have grown pale, had not the crimson west been blushing on them; but after a moment they began to laugh, while the breeze took a livelier motion, as if responsive to their mirth. I kept an awful solemnity of visage, being indeed a little piqued, that a narrative which had good authority in our ancient superstitions, and would have brought even a church deacon to Gallows Hill, in old witch times, should now be considered too grotesque and extravagant, for timid maids to tremble at. Though it was past supper time, I detained them a while longer on the hill, and made a trial whether truth were more powerful than fiction.

We looked again towards the town, no longer arrayed in that icy splendor of earth, tree and edifice, beneath the glow of a wintry midnight, which, shining afar through the gloom of a century, had made it appear the very home of visions in visionary streets. An indistinctness had begun to creep over the mass of buildings and blend them with the intermingled tree tops, except where the roof of a statelier mansion, and the steeples and brick towers of churches, caught the brightness of some cloud that yet floated in the sunshine. Twilight over the landscape was congenial to the obscurity of time. With such eloquence as my share of feeling and fancy could supply, I called back hoar antiquity, and bade my companions imagine an ancient multitude of people, congregated on the hill side, spreading far below, clustering on the steep old roofs, and climbing the adjacent heights, wherever a glimpse of this spot might be obtained. I strove to realize and faintly communicate, the deep, unutterable loathing and horror, the indignation, the affrighted wonder, that wrinkled on every brow, and filled the universal heart. See! the whole crowd turns pale and shrinks within itself, as the virtuous emerge from yonder street. Keeping pace with that devoted company, I described them one by one; here tottered a woman in her dotage, knowing neither the crime imputed her, nor its punishment; there another, distracted by the universal madness, till feverish dreams were remembered as realities, and she almost believed her guilt. One, a proud man once, was so broken down by the intolerable hatred heaped upon him, that he seemed to hasten his steps, eager to hide himself in the grave hastily dug, at the foot of the gallows. As they went slowly on, a mother looked behind, and beheld her peaceful dwelling; she cast her eyes elsewhere, and groaned inwardly, yet with bitterest anguish; for there was her little son among the accusers. I watched the face of an ordained pastor, who walked onward to the same death; his lips moved in prayer, no narrow petition for himself alone, but embracing all, his fellow sufferers and the frenzied multitude; he looked to heaven and trod lightly up the hill.

Behind their victims came the afflicted, a guilty and miserable band; villains who had thus avenged themselves on their enemies, and viler wretches, whose cowardice had destroyed their friends; lunatics, whose ravings had chimed in with the madness of the land; and children, who had played a game that the imps of darkness might have envied them, since it disgraced an age, and dipped a people's hands in blood. In the rear of the procession rode a figure on horseback, so darkly conspicuous, so sternly triumphant, that my hearers mistook him for the visible presence of the fiend himself, but it was only his good friend, Cotton Mather, proud of his well won dignity, as the representative of all the hateful features of his time; the one bloodthirsty man, in whom were concentrated those vices of spirit and errors of opinion, that sufficed to madden the whole surrounding multitude. And thus I marshalled them onward, the innocent who were to die, and the guilty who were to grow old in long remorse – tracing their every step, by rock, and shrub, and broken track, till their shadowy visages had circled round the hill-top, where we stood. I plunged into my imagination for a blacker horror, and a deeper woe, and pictured the scaffold –

But here my companions seized an arm on each side; their nerves were trembling; and sweeter victory still, I had reached the seldom trodden places of their hearts, and found the wellspring of their tears. And now the past had done all it could. We slowly descended, watching the lights as they twinkled gradually through the town, and listening to the distant mirth of boys at play, and to the voice of a young girl, warbling somewhere in the dusk, a pleasant sound to wanderers from old witch times. Yet ere we left the hill, we could not but regret, that there is nothing on its barren summit, no relic of old, nor lettered stone of later days, to assist the imagination in appealing to the heart. We build the memorial column on the height which our fathers made sacred with their blood, poured out in a holy cause. And here in dark, funereal stone, should rise another monument, sadly commemorative of the errors of an earlier race, and not to be cast down, while the human heart has one infirmity that may result in crime.

Young Goodman Brown

Young Goodman Brown came forth, at sunset, into the street of Salem village, but put his head back, after crossing the threshold, to exchange a parting kiss with his young wife. And Faith, as the wife was aptly named, thrust her own pretty head into the street, letting the wind play with the pink ribbons of her cap, while she called to Goodman Brown.

"Dearest heart," whispered she, softly and rather sadly, when her lips were close to his ear, "pr'y thee, put off your journey until sunrise, and sleep in your own bed to-night. A lone woman is troubled with such dreams and such thoughts, that she's afeard of herself, sometimes. Pray, tarry with me this night, dear husband, of all nights in the year!"

"My love and my Faith," replied young Goodman Brown, "of all nights in the year, this one night must I tarry away from thee. My journey, as thou callest it, forth and back again, must needs be done 'twixt now and sunrise. What, my sweet, pretty wife, dost thou doubt me already, and we but three months married!"

"Then, God bless you!" and Faith, with the pink ribbons, "and may you find all well, when you come back."

"Amen!" cried Goodman Brown. "Say thy prayers, dear Faith, and go to bed at dusk, and no harm will come to thee."

So they parted; and the young man pursued his way, until, being about to turn the corner by the meeting-house, he looked back, and saw the head of Faith still peeping after him, with a melancholy air, in spite of her pink ribbons.

"Poor little Faith!" thought he, for his heart smote him. "What a wretch am I, to leave her on such an errand! She talks of dreams, too. Methought, as she spoke, there was trouble in her face, as if a dream had warned her what work is to be done to-night. But, no, no! 'twould kill her to think it. Well; she's a blessed angel on earth; and after this one night, I'll cling to her skirts and follow her to Heaven."

With this excellent resolve for the future, Goodman Brown felt himself justified in making more haste on his present evil purpose. He had taken a dreary road, darkened by all the gloomiest trees of the forest, which barely stood aside to let the narrow path creep through, and closed immediately behind. It was all as lonely as could be; and there is this peculiarity in such a solitude, that the traveller knows not who may be concealed by the innumerable trunks and the thick boughs overhead; so that, with lonely footsteps, he may yet be passing through an unseen multitude.

"There may be a devilish Indian behind every tree," said Goodman Brown, to himself; and he glanced fearfully behind him, as he added, "What if the devil himself should be at my very elbow!"

His head being turned back, he passed a crook of the road, and looking forward again, beheld the figure of a man, in grave and decent attire, seated at the foot of an old tree. He arose, at Goodman Brown's approach, and walked onward, side by side with him.

"You are late, Goodman Brown," said he. "The clock of the Old South was striking as I came through Boston; and that is full fifteen minutes agone."[1]

"Faith kept me back awhile," replied the young man, with a tremor in his voice, caused by the sudden appearance of his companion, though not wholly unexpected.

It was now deep dusk in the forest, and deepest in that part of it where these two were journeying. As nearly as could be discerned, the second traveller was about fifty years old, apparently in the same rank of life as Goodman Brown, and bearing a considerable resemblance to him, though perhaps more in expression than features. Still, they might have been taken for father and son. And yet, though the elder person was as simply clad as the younger, and as simple in manner too, he had an indescribable air of one who knew the world, and would not have felt abashed at the governor's dinner-table, or in King William's court, were it possible that his affairs should call him thither. But the only thing about him, that could be fixed upon as remarkable, was his staff, which bore the likeness of a great black snake, so curiously wrought, that it might almost be seen to twist and wriggle itself, like a living serpent. This, of course, must have been an ocular deception, assisted by the uncertain light.

"Come, Goodman Brown!" cried his fellow-traveller, "this is a dull pace for the beginning of a journey. Take my staff, if you are so soon weary."

Notes

Young Goodman Brown

[1] This distance, of course, could not have been accomplished by natural means.

"Friend," said the other, exchanging his slow pace for a full stop, "having kept covenant by meeting thee here, it is my purpose now to return whence I came. I have scruples, touching the matter thou wot'st of."

"Sayest thou so?" replied he of the serpent, smiling apart. "Let us walk on, nevertheless, reasoning as we go, and if I convince thee not, thou shalt turn back. We are but a little way in the forest, yet."

"Too far, too far!" exclaimed the goodman, unconsciously resuming his walk. "My father never went into the woods on such an errand, nor his father before him. We have been a race of honest men and good Christians, since the days of the martyrs. And shall I be the first of the name of Brown, that ever took this path, and kept – "

"Such company, thou wouldst say," observed the elder person, interpreting his pause. "Well said, Goodman Brown! I have been as well acquainted with your family as with ever a one among the Puritans; and that's no trifle to say. I helped your grandfather, the constable, when he lashed the Quaker woman so smartly through the streets of Salem. And it was I that brought your father a pitch-pine knot, kindled at my own hearth, to set fire to an Indian village, in King Philip's war. They were my good friends, both; and many a pleasant walk have we had along this path, and returned merrily after midnight. I would fain be friends with you, for their sake."

"If it be as thou sayest," replied Goodman Brown, "I marvel they never spoke of these matters. Or, verily, I marvel not, seeing that the least rumor of the sort would have driven them from New-England. We are a people of prayer, and good works, to boot, and abide no such wickedness."

"Wickedness or not," said the traveller with the twisted staff, "I have a very general acquaintance here in New-England. The deacons of many a church have drunk the communion wine with me; the selectmen, of divers towns, make me their chairman; and a majority of the Great and General Court are firm supporters of my interest. The governor and I, too – but these are state-secrets."

"Can this be so!" cried Goodman Brown, with a stare of amazement at his undisturbed companion. "Howbeit, I have nothing to do with the governor and council; they have their own ways, and are no rule for a simple husbandman, like me. But, were I to go on with thee, how should I meet the eye of that good old man, our minister, at Salem village? Oh, his voice would make me tremble, both Sabbath-day and lecture-day!"

Thus far, the elder traveller had listened with due gravity, but now burst into a fit of irrepressible mirth, shaking himself so violently, that his snake-like staff actually seemed to wriggle in sympathy.

"Ha! ha! ha!" shouted he, again and again; then composing himself, "Well, go on, Goodman Brown, go on; but, pr'y thee, don't kill me with laughing!"

"Well, then, to end the matter at once," said Goodman Brown, considerably nettled, "there is my wife, Faith. It would break her dear little heart; and I'd rather break my own!"

"Nay, if that be the case," answered the other, "e'en go thy ways, Goodman Brown. I would not, for twenty old women like the one hobbling before us, that Faith should come to any harm."

As he spoke, he pointed his staff at a female figure on the path, in whom Goodman Brown recognized a very pious and exemplary dame, who had taught him his catechism, in youth, and was still his moral and spiritual adviser, jointly with the minister and Deacon Gookin.

"A marvel, truly, that Goody Cloyse should be so far in the wilderness, at night-fall!" said he. "But, with your leave, friend, I shall take a cut through the woods, until we have left this Christian woman behind. Being a stranger to you, she might ask whom I was consorting with, and whither I was going."

"Be it so," said his fellow-traveller. "Betake you to the woods, and let me keep the path."

Accordingly, the young man turned aside, but took care to watch his companion, who advanced softly along the road, until he had come within a staff's length of the old dame. She, meanwhile, was making the best of her way, with singular speed for so aged a woman, and mumbling some indistinct words, a prayer, doubtless, as she went. The traveller put forth his staff, and touched her withered neck with what seemed the serpent's tail.

"The devil!" screamed the pious old lady.

"Then Goody Cloyse knows her old friend?" observed the traveller, confronting her, and leaning on his writhing stick.

"Ah, forsooth, and is it your worship, indeed?" cried the good dame. "Yea, truly is it, and in the very image of my old gossip, Goodman Brown, the grandfather of the silly fellow that now is. But – would your worship believe it? – my broomstick hath strangely disappeared, stolen, as I suspect, by that unhanged witch, Goody Cory,[2] and that, too, when I was all anointed with the juice of smallage and cinque-foil and wolf's-bane – "

"Mingled with fine wheat and the fat of a new-born babe," said the shape of old Goodman Brown.

"Ah, your worship knows the receipt," cried the old lady, cackling aloud. "So, as I was saying, being all ready for the meeting, and no horse to ride on, I made up my mind to foot it; for they tell me, there is a nice young man to be taken into communion to-night. But now your good worship will lend me your arm, and we shall be there in a twinkling."

"That can hardly be," answered her friend. "I may not spare you my arm, Goody Cloyse, but here is my staff, if you will."

So saying, he threw it down at her feet, where, perhaps, it assumed life, being one of the rods which its owner had formerly lent to the Egyptian Magi. Of this fact, however, Goodman Brown could not take cognizance. He had cast up his eyes in astonishment, and looking down again, beheld neither Goody Cloyse nor the serpentine staff, but his fellow-traveller alone, who waited for him as calmly as if nothing had happened.

"That old woman taught me my catechism!" said the young man; and there was a world of meaning in this simple comment.

They continued to walk onward, while the elder traveller exhorted his companion to make good speed and persevere in the path, discoursing so aptly, that his arguments seemed rather to spring up in the bosom of his auditor, than to be suggested by himself. As they went, he plucked a branch of maple, to serve for a walking-stick, and began to strip it of the twigs and little boughs, which were wet with evening dew. The moment his fingers touched them, they became strangely withered and dried up, as with a week's sunshine. Thus the pair proceeded, at a good free pace, until suddenly, in a gloomy hollow of the road, Goodman Brown sat himself down on the stump of a tree, and refused to go any farther.

"Friend," said he, stubbornly, "my mind is made up. Not another step will I budge on this errand. What if a wretched old woman do choose to go to the devil, when I thought she was going to Heaven! Is that any reason why I should quit my dear Faith, and go after her?"

Notes

2 Martha Corey would be executed on September 22, 1692. Sarah Cloyse was convicted of witchcraft but ultimately escaped hanging.

"You will think better of this, by-and-by," said his acquaintance, composedly. "Sit here and rest yourself awhile; and when you feel like moving again, there is my staff to help you along."

Without more words, he threw his companion the maple stick, and was as speedily out of sight, as if he had vanished into the deepening gloom. The young man sat a few moments, by the road-side, applauding himself greatly, and thinking with how clear a conscience he should meet the minister, in his morning-walk, nor shrink from the eye of good old Deacon Gookin. And what calm sleep would be his, that very night, which was to have been spent so wickedly, but purely and sweetly now, in the arms of Faith! Amidst these pleasant and praiseworthy meditations, Goodman Brown heard the tramp of horses along the road, and deemed it advisable to conceal himself within the verge of the forest, conscious of the guilty purpose that had brought him thither, though now so happily turned from it.

On came the hoof-tramps and the voices of the riders, two grave old voices, conversing soberly as they drew near. These mingled sounds appeared to pass along the road, within a few yards of the young man's hiding-place; but owing, doubtless, to the depth of the gloom, at that particular spot, neither the travellers nor their steeds were visible. Though their figures brushed the small boughs by the way-side, it could not be seen that they intercepted, even for a moment, the faint gleam from the strip of bright sky, athwart which they must have passed. Goodman Brown alternately crouched and stood on tip-toe, pulling aside the branches, and thrusting forth his head as far as he durst, without discerning so much as a shadow. It vexed him the more, because he could have sworn, were such a thing possible, that he recognized the voices of the minister and Deacon Gookin, jogging along quietly, as they were wont to do, when bound to some ordination or ecclesiastical council. While yet within hearing, one of the riders stopped to pluck a switch.

"Of the two, reverend Sir," said the voice like the deacon's, "I had rather miss an ordination-dinner than to-night's meeting. They tell me that some of our community are to be here from Falmouth and beyond, and others from Connecticut and Rhode-Island; besides several of the Indian powows, who after their fashion, know almost as much deviltry as the best of us. Moreover, there is a goodly young woman to be taken into communion."

"Mighty well, Deacon Gookin!" replied the solemn old tones of the minister. "Spur up, or we shall be late. Nothing can be done, you know, until I get on the ground."

The hoofs clattered again, and the voices, talking so strangely in the empty air, passed on through the forest, where no church had ever been gathered, nor solitary Christian prayed. Whither, then, could these holy men be journeying, so deep into the heathen wilderness? Young Goodman Brown caught hold of a tree, for support, being ready to sink down on the ground, faint and overburthened with the heavy sickness of his heart. He looked up to the sky, doubting whether there really was a Heaven above him. Yet, there was the blue arch, and the stars brightening in it.

"With Heaven above, and Faith below, I will yet stand firm against the devil!" cried Goodman Brown.

While he still gazed upward, into the deep arch of the firmament, and had lifted his hands to pray, a cloud, though no wind was stirring, hurried across the zenith, and hid the brightening stars. The blue sky was still visible, except directly overhead, where this black mass of cloud was sweeping swiftly northward. Aloft in the air, as if from the depths of the cloud, came a confused and doubtful sound of voices. Once, the listener fancied that he could distinguish the accents of town's-people of his own, men and women, both pious and ungodly, many of whom he had met at the communion-table, and had seen others rioting at the tavern. The next moment, so indistinct were the sounds, he doubted whether he had heard aught but the murmur of the old forest, whispering without a wind. Then came a stronger swell of those familiar tones, heard daily in the sunshine, at Salem village, but never, until now, from a cloud of night. There was one voice, of a young woman, uttering lamentations, yet with an uncertain sorrow, and entreating for some favor, which, perhaps, it would grieve her to obtain. And all the unseen multitude, both saints and sinners, seemed to encourage her onward.

"Faith!" shouted Goodman Brown, in a voice of agony and desperation; and the echoes of the forest mocked him, crying – "Faith! Faith!" as if bewildered wretches were seeking her, all through the wilderness.

The cry of grief, rage, and terror, was yet piercing the night, when the unhappy husband held his breath for a response. There was a scream, drowned immediately in a louder murmur of voices, fading into far-off laughter, as the dark cloud swept away, leaving the clear and silent sky above Goodman Brown. But something fluttered lightly down through the air, and caught on the branch of a tree. The young man seized it, and beheld a pink ribbon.

"My Faith is gone!" cried he, after one stupefied moment. "There is no good on earth; and sin is but a name. Come, devil! for to thee is this world given."

And maddened with despair, so that he laughed loud and long, did Goodman Brown grasp his staff and set forth again, at such a rate, that he seemed to fly along the forest-path, rather than to walk or run. The road grew wilder and drearier, and more faintly traced, and vanished at length, leaving him in the heart of the dark wilderness, still rushing onward, with the instinct that guides mortal man to evil. The whole forest was peopled with frightful sounds; the creaking of the trees, the howling of wild beasts, and the yell of Indians; while, sometimes, the wind tolled like a distant church-bell, and sometimes gave a broad roar around the traveller, as if all Nature were laughing him to scorn. But he was himself the chief horror of the scene, and shrank not from its other horrors.

"Ha! ha! ha!" roared Goodman Brown, when the wind laughed at him. "Let us hear which will laugh loudest! Think not to frighten me with your deviltry! Come witch, come wizard, come Indian powow, come devil himself! and here comes Goodman Brown. You may as well fear him as he fear you!"

In truth, all through the haunted forest, there could be nothing more frightful than the figure of Goodman Brown. On he flew, among the black pines, brandishing his staff with frenzied gestures, now giving vent to an inspiration of horrid blasphemy, and now shouting forth such laughter, as set all the echoes of the forest laughing like demons around him. The fiend in his own shape is less hideous, than when he rages in the breast of man. Thus sped the demoniac on his course, until, quivering among the trees, he saw a red light before him, as when the felled trunks and branches of a clearing have been set on fire, and throw up their lurid blaze against the sky, at the hour of midnight. He paused, in a lull of the tempest that had driven him onward, and heard the swell of what seemed a hymn, rolling solemnly from a distance, with the weight of many voices. He knew the tune; it was a familiar one in the choir of the village meeting-house. The verse died heavily away, and was lengthened by a chorus, not of human voices, but of all the sounds of the benighted wilderness, pealing in awful harmony together. Goodman Brown cried out; and his cry was lost to his own ear, by its unison with the cry of the desert.

In the interval of silence, he stole forward, until the light glared full upon his eyes. At one extremity of an open space, hemmed in by the dark wall of the forest, arose a rock, bearing some rude, natural resemblance either to an altar or a pulpit, and surrounded by four blazing pines, their tops a flame, their stems untouched, like candles at an evening meeting. The mass of foliage, that had overgrown the summit of the rock, was all on fire, blazing high into the night, and fitfully illuminating the whole field. Each pendent twig and leafy festoon was in a blaze. As the red light arose and fell, a numerous congregation alternately shone forth, then disappeared in shadow, and again grew, as it were, out of the darkness, peopling the heart of the solitary woods at once.

"A grave and dark-clad company!" quoth Goodman Brown.

In truth, they were such. Among them, quivering to-and-fro, between gloom and splendor, appeared faces that would be seen, next day, at the council-board of the province, and others which, Sabbath after Sabbath, looked devoutly heavenward, and benignantly over the crowded pews, from the holiest pulpits in the land. Some affirm, that the lady of the governor was there. At least, there were high dames well known to her, and wives of honored husbands, and widows, a great multitude, and ancient maidens, all of excellent repute, and fair young girls, who trembled, lest their mothers should espy them. Either the sudden gleams of light, flashing over the obscure field, bedazzled Goodman Brown, or he recognized a score of the church-members of Salem village, famous for their especial sanctity. Good old Deacon Gookin had arrived, and waited at the skirts of that venerable saint, his revered pastor. But, irreverently consorting with these grave, reputable, and pious people, these elders of the church, these chaste dames and dewy virgins, there were men of dissolute lives and women of spotted fame, wretches given over to all mean and filthy vice, and suspected even of horrid crimes. It was strange to see, that the good shrank not from the wicked, nor were the sinners abashed by the saints. Scattered, also, among their pale-faced enemies, were the Indian priests, or powows, who had often scared their native forest with more hideous incantations than any known to English witchcraft.

"But, where is Faith?" thought Goodman Brown; and, as hope came into his heart, he trembled.

Another verse of the hymn arose, a slow and solemn strain, such as the pious love, but joined to words which expressed all that our nature can conceive of sin, and darkly hinted at far more. Unfathomable to mere mortals is the lore of fiends. Verse after verse was sung, and still the chorus of the desert swelled between, like the deepest tone of a mighty organ. And, with the final peal of that dreadful anthem, there came a sound, as if the roaring wind, the rushing streams, the howling beasts, and every other voice of the unconverted wilderness, were mingling and according with the voice of guilty man, in homage to the prince of all. The four blazing pines threw up a loftier flame, and obscurely discovered shapes and visages of horror on the smoke-wreaths, above the impious assembly. At the same moment, the fire on the rock shot redly forth, and formed a glowing arch above its base, where now appeared a figure. With reverence be it spoken, the apparition bore no slight similitude, both in garb and manner, to some grave divine of the New-England churches.

"Bring forth the converts!" cried a voice, that echoed through the field and rolled into the forest.

At the word, Goodman Brown stept forth from the shadow of the trees, and approached the congregation, with whom he felt a loathful brotherhood, by the sympathy of all that was wicked in his heart. He could have well nigh sworn, that the shape of his own dead father beckoned him to advance, looking downward from a smoke-wreath, while a woman, with dim features of despair, threw out her hand to warn him back. Was it his mother? But he had no power to retreat one step, nor to resist, even in thought, when the minister and good old Deacon Gookin, seized his arms, and led him to the blazing rock. Thither came also the slender form of a veiled female, led between Goody Cloyse, that pious teacher of the catechism, and Martha Carrier, who had received the devil's promise to be queen of hell. A rampant hag was she! And there stood the proselytes, beneath the canopy of fire.

"Welcome, my children," said the dark figure, "to the communion of your race! Ye have found, thus young, your nature and your destiny. My children, look behind you!"

They turned; and flashing forth, as it were, in a sheet of flame, the fiend-worshippers were seen; the smile of welcome gleamed darkly on every visage.

"There," resumed the sable form, "are all whom ye have reverenced from youth. Ye deemed them holier than yourselves, and shrank from your own sin, contrasting it with their lives of righteousness, and prayerful aspirations heavenward. Yet, here are they all, in my worshipping assembly! This night it shall be granted you to know their secret deeds; how hoary-bearded elders of the church have whispered wanton words to the young maids of their households; how many a woman, eager for widow's weeds, has given her husband a drink at bed-time, and let him sleep his last sleep in her bosom; how beardless youths have made haste to inherit their fathers' wealth; and how fair damsels – blush not, sweet ones! – have dug little graves in the garden, and bidden me, the sole guest, to an infant's funeral. By the sympathy of your human hearts for sin, ye shall scent out all the places – whether in church, bed-chamber, street, field, or forest – where crime has been committed, and shall exult to behold the whole earth one stain of guilt, one mighty blood-spot. Far more than this! It shall be yours to penetrate, in every bosom, the deep mystery of sin, the fountain of all wicked arts, and which inexhaustibly supplies more evil impulses than human power – than my power, at its utmost! – can make manifest in deeds. And now, my children, look upon each other."

They did so; and, by the blaze of the hell-kindled torches, the wretched man beheld his Faith, and the wife her husband, trembling before that unhallowed altar.

"Lo! there ye stand, my children," said the figure, in a deep and solemn tone, almost sad, with its despairing awfulness, as if his once angelic nature could yet mourn for our miserable race. "Depending upon one another's hearts, ye had still hoped, that virtue were not all a dream. Now are ye undeceived! Evil is the nature of mankind. Evil must be your only happiness. Welcome, again, my children, to the communion of your race!"

"Welcome!" repeated the fiend-worshippers, in one cry of despair and triumph.

And there they stood, the only pair, as it seemed, who were yet hesitating on the verge of wickedness, in this dark world. A basin was hollowed, naturally, in the rock. Did it contain water, reddened by the lurid light? or was it blood? or, perchance, a liquid flame? Herein did the Shape of Evil dip his hand, and prepare to lay the mark of baptism upon their foreheads, that they might be partakers of the mystery of sin, more conscious of the secret guilt of others, both in deed and thought, than they could now be of their own. The husband cast one look at his pale wife, and Faith at him. What polluted wretches would the next glance shew them to each other, shuddering alike at what they disclosed and what they saw!

"Faith! Faith!" cried the husband. "Look up to Heaven, and resist the Wicked One!"

Whether Faith obeyed, he knew not. Hardly had he spoken, when he found himself amid calm night and solitude, listening to a roar of the wind, which died heavily away through the forest. He staggered against the rock and felt it chill and damp, while a hanging twig, that had been all on fire, besprinkled his cheek with the coldest dew.

The next morning, young Goodman Brown came slowly into the street of Salem village, staring around him like a bewildered man. The good old minister was taking a walk along the graveyard to get an appetite for breakfast and meditate his sermon, and bestowed a blessing, as he passed, on Goodman Brown. He shrank from the venerable saint, as if to avoid an anathema. Old Deacon Gookin was at domestic worship, and the holy words of his prayer were heard through the open window. "What God doth the wizard pray to?" quoth Goodman Brown. Goody Cloyse, that excellent old Christian, stood in the early sunshine, at her own lattice, catechizing a little girl, who had brought her a pint of morning's milk. Goodman Brown snatched away the child, as from the grasp of the fiend himself. Turning the corner by the meeting-house, he spied the head of Faith, with the pink ribbons, gazing anxiously forth, and bursting into such joy at sight of him, that she skipt along the street, and almost kissed her husband before the whole village. But Goodman Brown looked sternly and sadly into her face, and passed on without a greeting.

Had Goodman Brown fallen asleep in the forest, and only dreamed a wild dream of a witch-meeting?

Be it so, if you will. But, alas! it was a dream of evil omen for young Goodman Brown. A stern, a sad, a darkly meditative, a distrustful, if not a desperate man, did he become, from the night of that fearful dream. On the Sabbath-day, when the congregation were singing a holy psalm, he could not listen, because an anthem of sin rushed loudly upon his ear, and drowned all the blessed strain. When the minister spoke from the pulpit, with power and fervid eloquence, and, with his hand on the open Bible, of the sacred truths of our religion, and of saintlike lives and triumphant deaths, and of future bliss or misery unutterable, then did Goodman Brown turn pale, dreading, lest the roof should thunder down upon the gray blasphemer and his hearers. Often, awakening suddenly at midnight, he shrank from the bosom of Faith, and at morning or eventide, when the family knelt down at prayer, he scowled, and muttered to himself, and gazed sternly at his wife, and turned away. And when he had lived long, and was borne to his grave, a hoary corpse, followed by Faith, an aged woman, and children and grandchildren, a goodly procession, besides neighbors, not a few, they carved no hopeful verse upon his tombstone; for his dying hour was gloom.

Henry Wadsworth Longfellow (1807–1882)

Longfellow, a Bowdoin College classmate of Hawthorne, became for a time the most popular and venerated poet in English. His work was memorized by generations of American students. "The Skeleton in Armor," a favorite in the nineteenth century, is from *Ballads and Other Poems* (1841). In a prose headnote, Longfellow links the poem to the ruined "Round Tower" of Newport, Rhode Island, which was believed to be of Viking origin. Many sites around New England had such legends attached to them, examples of what critic Faye Ringel has called "fantastic archeology": legends fulfilling, perhaps, the desire of European settlers for connection with this raw and new (to them) landscape. Longfellow, like Irving, felt, and met, similar need by adapting European legends and folk tales to the American scene.

Approached in the right mood, Longfellow's ghost-narrator (one of several in this collection) can still generate a sympathetic chill.

Text: *The Complete Poetical Works of Henry Wadsworth Longfellow* (Boston and New York: Houghton, Mifflin, [1900]).

The Skeleton in Armor

"Speak! speak! thou fearful guest,
Who, with thy hollow breast
Still in rude armor drest,
    Comest to daunt me!
Wrapt not in Eastern balms,
But with thy fleshless palms
Stretched, as if asking alms,
    Why dost thou haunt me?"

Then, from those cavernous eyes
Pale flashes seemed to rise,
As when the Northern skies
    Gleam in December;
And, like the water's flow
Under December's snow,
Came a dull voice of woe
    From the heart's chamber.

"I was a Viking old!
My deeds, though manifold,

No Skald[1] in song has told,
   No Saga taught thee!
Take heed, that in thy verse
Thou dost the tale rehearse,
Else dread a dead man's curse;
   For this I sought thee.

"Far in the Northern Land,
By the wild Baltic's strand,
I, with my childish hand,
   Tamed the gerfalcon;
And, with my skates fast-bound,
Skimmed the half-frozen Sound,
That the poor whimpering hound
   Trembled to walk on.

"Oft to his frozen lair
Tracked I the grisly bear,
While from my path the hare
   Fled like a shadow;
Oft through the forest dark
Followed the were-wolf's bark,
Until the soaring lark
   Sang from the meadow.

"But when I older grew,
Joining a corsair's crew,
O'er the dark sea I flew
   With the marauders.
Wild was the life we led;
Many the souls that sped,
Many the hearts that bled
   By our stern orders.

"Many a wassail-bout
Wore the long Winter out;
Often our midnight shout
   Set the cocks crowing,
As we the Berserk's tale
Measured in cups of ale,
Draining the oaken pail,
   Filled to o'erflowing.

"Once as I told in glee
Tales of the stormy sea,
Soft eyes did gaze on me,
   Burning yet tender;

Notes

The Skeleton in Armor
[1] A singer or bard.

And as the white stars shine
On the dark Norway pine,
On that dark heart of mine
   Fell their soft splendor.

"I wooed the blue-eyed maid,
Yielding, yet half afraid,
And in the forest's shade
   Our vows were plighted.
Under its loosened vest
Fluttered her little breast,
Like birds within their nest
   By the hawk frighted.

"Bright in her father's hall
Shields gleamed upon the wall,
Loud sang the minstrels all,
   Chanting his glory;
When of old Hildebrand
I asked his daughter's hand,
Mute did the minstrels stand
   To hear my story.

"While the brown ale he quaffed,
Loud then the champion laughed.
And as the wind-gusts waft
   The sea-foam brightly,
So the loud laugh of scorn,
Out of those lips unshorn,
From the deep drinking-horn
   Blew the foam lightly.

"She was a Prince's child,
I but a Viking wild,
And though she blushed and smiled,
   I was discarded!
Should not the dove so white
Follow the sea-mew's flight,
Why did they leave that night
   Her nest unguarded?

"Scarce had I put to sea,
Bearing the maid with me, –
Fairest of all was she
   Among the Norsemen! –
When on the white sea-strand,
Waving his armèd hand,
Saw we old Hildebrand,
   With twenty horsemen.

"Then launched they to the blast,
Bent like a reed each mast,
Yet we were gaining fast,
    When the wind failed us,
And with a sudden flaw
Came round the gusty Skaw,
So that our foe we saw
    Laugh as he hailed us.

"And as to catch the gale
Round veered the flapping sail,
Death! was the helmsman's hail,
    Death without quarter!
Mid-ships with iron keel
Struck we her ribs of steel;
Down her black hulk did reel
    Through the black water!

"As with his wings aslant,
    Sails the fierce cormorant,
Seeking some rocky haunt,
    With his prey laden, —
So toward the open main,
Beating to sea again,
Through the wild hurricane,
    Bore I the maiden.

"Three weeks we westward bore,
And when the storm was o'er,
Cloud-like we saw the shore
    Stretching to lee-ward;
There for my lady's bower
Built I the lofty tower,
Which, to this very hour,
    Stands looking seaward.

"There lived we many years;
Time dried the maiden's tears;
She had forgot her fears,
    She was a mother;
Death closed her mild blue eyes,
Under that tower she lies;
Ne'er shall the sun arise
    On such another!

"Still grew my bosom then,
Still as a stagnant fen!
Hateful to me were men,
    The sunlight hateful!
In the vast forest here,

Clad in my warlike gear,
Fell I upon my spear,
   Oh, death was grateful!

"Thus, seamed with many scars,
Bursting these prison bars,
Up to its native stars
   My soul ascended!
There from the flowing bowl
Deep drinks the warrior's soul,
   Skoal! to the Northland! *Skoal!*"

– Thus the tale ended.

Edgar Allan Poe (1809–1849)

Poe is among the most familiar of American authors, and most readers know something of the classic legend of the doomed artist: his early loss of parents, his adoption by a wealthy Richmond businessman, John Allan, who ultimately disinherited him; his marriage to his 13-year-old cousin, Virginia Clemm; his struggles with poverty and alcoholism; Virginia's death; and his own death under mysterious circumstances in Baltimore. All this is true, though incomplete, and recent biographers, as a corrective, have stressed other elements of this complicated man, such as his athletic skill as a youth (he was a champion swimmer), his short but successful career in the army, and his considerable practical abilities as a magazine editor. There is no evidence, his first biographer to the contrary, that he used drugs other than alcohol.

Poe's influence – one is tempted to say his shadow – is immense. No American poet of the nineteenth century, with the possible exception of Walt Whitman, did as much to shape the direction of later poetry. He had an especially profound influence on French verse. He defined the genre of the modern detective story. And, of course, he was a master of the Gothic tradition, in poetry and prose.

Readers inevitably find autobiographical details in his work, but it is probably best to read these selections as deliberate experiments in achieving the Gothic effects Poe valued. We encounter a range of Poe settings and characters: nightmare landscapes, claustrophobic interiors, bereaved lovers, madmen, victims or imagined victims pursuing their revenge. Throughout Poe's work we find the contrast between an imperfect world with mutable (often decaying) flesh, and an imagined world of perfect forms. The awareness of this contrast is sometimes termed "Romantic Agony." A related theme, which Poe shared with Hawthorne and Melville, is a sense of pervasive evil, evil as an active and real presence. These concerns are not always abstract, divorced from Poe's times. "Hop-Frog," for example, can be seen as a fable with several applications to the 1840s, including the potential eruption of that volcano feared by all Southern slave-owners, a slave rebellion.

Texts: Stories from *The Works of the Late Edgar Allan Poe*, ed. Rufus Wilmot Griswold, 4 vols. (New York: Redfield, 1857). "The Raven" from the *Richmond Weekly Examiner*, September 25, 1849. "The City in the Sea" from Poe, *The Raven and Other Poems* (New York: Wiley & Putnam, 1845). "Ulalume – A Ballad" from *The Poets and Poetry of America*, 10th edn., ed. Rufus Wilmot Griswold (Philadelphia: Carey & Hart, 1850). "Annabel Lee" from the *Southern Literary Messenger*, November 1849. "Dreamland" from the *Richmond Weekly Examiner*, October 23, 1849.

Hop-Frog

I never knew any one so keenly alive to a joke as the king was. He seemed to live only for joking. To tell a good story of the joke kind, and to tell it well, was the surest road to his favor. Thus it happened that his seven ministers were all noted for their

American Gothic: From Salem Witchcraft to H. P. Lovecraft, An Anthology, Second Edition. Edited by Charles L. Crow.
Editorial material and organization © 2013 John Wiley & Sons, Ltd. Published 2013 by John Wiley & Sons, Ltd.

accomplishments as jokers. They all took after the king, too, in being large, corpulent, oily men, as well as inimitable jokers. Whether people grow fat by joking, or whether there is something in fat itself which predisposes to a joke, I have never been quite able to determine; but certain it is that a lean joker is a *rara avis in terris*.[1]

About the refinements, or, as he called them, the "ghosts" of wit, the king troubled himself very little. He had an especial admiration for *breadth* in a jest, and would often put up with *length*, for the sake of it. Over-niceties wearied him. He would have preferred Rabelais's "Gargantua," to the "Zadig" of Voltaire:[2] and, upon the whole, practical jokes suited his taste far better than verbal ones.

At the date of my narrative, professing jesters had not altogether gone out of fashion at court. Several of the great continental "powers" still retained their "fools," who wore motley, with caps and bells, and who were expected to be always ready with sharp witticisms, at a moment's notice, in consideration of the crumbs that fell from the royal table.

Our king, as a matter of course, retained his "fool." The fact is, he *required* something in the way of folly – if only to counterbalance the heavy wisdom of the seven wise men who were his ministers – not to mention himself.

His fool, or professional jester, was not *only* a fool, however. His value was trebled in the eyes of the king, by the fact of his being also a dwarf and a cripple. Dwarfs were as common at court, in those days, as fools; and many monarchs would have found it difficult to get through their days (days are rather longer at court than elsewhere) without both a jester to laugh *with*, and a dwarf to laugh *at*. But, as I have already observed, your jesters, in ninety-nine cases out of a hundred, are fat, round, and unwieldy – so that it was no small source of self-gratulation with our king that, in Hop-Frog (this was the fool's name), he possessed a triplicate treasure in one person.

I believe the name "Hop-Frog" was *not* that given to the dwarf by his sponsors at baptism, but it was conferred upon him, by general consent of the seven ministers, on account of his inability to walk as other men do. In fact, Hop-Frog could only get along by a sort of interjectional gait – something between a leap and a wriggle – a movement that afforded illimitable amusement, and of course consolation, to the king, for (notwithstanding the protuberance of his stomach and a constitutional swelling of the head) the king, by his whole court, was accounted a capital figure.

But although Hop-Frog, through the distortion of his legs, could move only with great pain and difficulty along a road or floor, the prodigious muscular power which nature seemed to have bestowed upon his arms, by way of compensation for deficiency in the lower limbs, enabled him to perform many feats of wonderful dexterity, where trees or ropes were in question, or anything else to climb. At such exercises he certainly much more resembled a squirrel, or a small monkey, than a frog.

I am not able to say, with precision, from what country Hop-Frog originally came. It was from some barbarous region, however, that no person ever heard of – a vast distance from the court of our king. Hop-Frog, and a young girl very little less dwarfish than himself (although of exquisite proportions, and a marvellous dancer), had been forcibly carried off from their respective homes in adjoining provinces, and sent as presents to the king, by one of his ever-victorious generals.

Notes

HOP-FROG
[1] Latin: a rare bird in the world.

[2] That is, he preferred broad, earthy humor to intellectual satire.

Under these circumstances, it is not to be wondered at that a close intimacy arose between the two little captives. Indeed, they soon became sworn friends. Hop-Frog, who, although he made a great deal of sport, was by no means popular, had it not in his power to render Trippetta many services; but she, on account of her grace and exquisite beauty (although a dwarf) was universally admired and petted: so she possessed much influence; and never failed to use it, whenever she could, for the benefit of Hop-Frog.

On some grand state occasion – I forget what – the king determined to have a masquerade; and whenever a masquerade, or anything of that kind, occurred at our court, then the talents both of Hop-Frog and Trippetta were sure to be called into play. Hop-Frog, in especial, was so inventive in the way of getting up pageants, suggesting novel characters, and arranging costume, for masked balls, that nothing could be done, it seems, without his assistance.

The night appointed for the *fête* had arrived. A gorgeous hall had been fitted up, under Trippetta's eye, with every kind of device which could possibly give *éclât* to a masquerade. The whole court was in a fever of expectation. As for costumes and characters, it might well be supposed that everybody had come to a decision on such points. Many had made up their minds (as to what *rôles* they should assume) a week, or even a month, in advance; and, in fact, there was not a particle of indecision anywhere – except in the case of the king and his seven ministers. Why *they* hesitated I never could tell, unless they did it by way of a joke. More probably, they found it difficult, on account of being so fat, to make up their minds. At all events, time flew; and, as a last resort, they sent for Trippetta and Hop-Frog.

When the two little friends obeyed the summons of the king, they found him sitting at his wine with the seven members of his cabinet council; but the monarch appeared to be in a very ill humor. He knew that Hop-Frog was not fond of wine; for it excited the poor cripple almost to madness; and madness is no comfortable feeling. But the king loved his practical jokes, and took pleasure in forcing Hop-Frog to drink and (as the king called it) "to be merry."

"Come here, Hop-Frog," said he, as the jester and his friend entered the room; "swallow this bumper to the health of your absent friends [here Hop-Frog sighed,] and then let us have the benefit of your invention. We want characters – *characters*, man, – something novel – out of the way. We are wearied with this everlasting sameness. Come, drink! the wine will brighten your wits."

Hop-Frog endeavored, as usual, to get up a jest in reply to these advances from the king; but the effort was too much. It happened to be the poor dwarf's birthday, and the command to drink to his "absent friends" forced the tears to his eyes. Many large, bitter drops fell into the goblet as he took it, humbly, from the hand of the tyrant.

"Ah! ha! ha! ha!" roared the latter, as the dwarf reluctantly drained the beaker. "See what a glass of good wine can do! Why, your eyes are shining already!"

Poor fellow! his large eyes *gleamed*, rather than shone; for the effect of wine on his excitable brain was not more powerful than instantaneous. He placed the goblet nervously on the table, and looked round upon the company with a half-insane stare. They all seemed highly amused at the success of the king's "joke."

"And now to business," said the prime minister, a *very* fat man.

"Yes," said the king. "Come, Hop-Frog, lend us your assistance. Characters, my fine fellow; we stand in need of characters – all of us – ha! ha! ha!" and as this was seriously meant for a joke, his laugh was chorused by the seven.

Hop-Frog also laughed, although feebly and somewhat vacantly.

"Come, come," said the king, impatiently, "have you nothing to suggest?"

"I am endeavoring to think of something *novel*," replied the dwarf, abstractedly, for he was quite bewildered by the wine.

"Endeavoring!" cried the tyrant, fiercely; "what do you mean by *that*? Ah, I perceive. You are sulky, and want more wine. Here, drink this!" and he poured out another goblet full and offered it to the cripple, who merely gazed at it, gasping for breath.

"Drink, I say!" shouted the monster, "or by the fiends – "

The dwarf hesitated. The king grew purple with rage. The courtiers smirked. Trippetta, pale as a corpse, advanced to the monarch's seat, and, falling on her knees before him, implored him to spare her friend.

The tyrant regarded her, for some moments, in evident wonder at her audacity. He seemed quite at a loss what to do or say – how most becomingly to express his indignation. At last, without uttering a syllable, he pushed her violently from him, and threw the contents of the brimming goblet in her face.

The poor girl got up as best she could, and, not daring even to sigh, resumed her position at the foot of the table.

There was a dead silence for about half a minute, during which the falling of a leaf, or of a feather, might have been heard. It was interrupted by a low, but harsh and protracted *grating* sound which seemed to come at once from every corner of the room.

"What – what – *what* are you making that noise for?" demanded the king, turning furiously to the dwarf.

The latter seemed to have recovered, in great measure, from his intoxication, and looking fixedly but quietly into the tyrant's face, merely ejaculated:

"I – I? How could it have been me?"

"The sound appeared to come from without," observed one of the courtiers. "I fancy it was the parrot at the window, whetting his bill upon his cage-wires."

"True," replied the monarch, as if much relieved by the suggestion; "but, on the honor of a knight, I could have sworn that it was the gritting of this vagabond's teeth."

Hereupon the dwarf laughed (the king was too confirmed a joker to object to any one's laughing), and displayed a set of large, powerful and very repulsive teeth. Moreover, he avowed his perfect willingness to swallow as much wine as desired. The monarch was pacified; and having drained another bumper with no very perceptible ill effect, Hop-Frog entered at once, and with spirit, into the plans for the masquerade.

"I cannot tell what was the association of ideas," observed he, very tranquilly, and as if he had never tasted wine in his life, "but *just after* your majesty had struck the girl and thrown the wine in her face – *just after* your majesty had done this, and while the parrot was making that odd noise outside the window, there came into my mind a capital diversion – one of my own country frolics – often enacted among us, at our masquerades: but here it will be new altogether. Unfortunately, however, it requires a company of eight persons, and – "

"Here we *are*!" cried the king, laughing at his acute discovery of the coincidence; "eight to a fraction – I and my seven ministers. Come! what is the diversion?"

"We call it," replied the cripple, "the Eight Chained Ourang-Outangs, and it really is excellent sport if well enacted."

"*We* will enact it," remarked the king, drawing himself up, and lowering his eyelids.

"The beauty of the game," continued Hop-Frog, "lies in the fright it occasions among the women."

"Capital!" roared in chorus the monarch and his ministry.

"*I* will equip you as ourang-outangs," proceeded the dwarf; "leave all that to me. The resemblance shall be so striking, that the company of masqueraders will take you for real beasts – and of course, they will be as much terrified as astonished."

"Oh, this is exquisite!" exclaimed the king. "Hop-Frog! I will make a man of you."

"The chains are for the purpose of increasing the confusion by their jangling. You are supposed to have escaped, *en masse*, from your keepers. Your majesty cannot conceive the *effect* produced, at a masquerade, by eight chained ourang-outangs, imagined to be real ones by most of the company; and rushing in with savage cries, among the crowd of delicately and gorgeously habited men and women. The *contrast* is inimitable."

"It must be," said the king: and the council arose hurriedly (as it was growing late), to put in execution the scheme of Hop-Frog.

His mode of equipping the party as ourang-outangs was very simple, but effective enough for his purposes. The animals in question had, at the epoch of my story, very rarely been seen in any part of the civilized world; and as the imitations made by the dwarf were sufficiently beast-like and more than sufficiently hideous, their truthfulness to nature was thus thought to be secured.

The king and his ministers were first encased in tight-fitting stockinet shirts and drawers. They were then saturated with tar. At this stage of the process, some one of the party suggested feathers; but the suggestion was at once overruled by the dwarf, who soon convinced the eight, by ocular demonstration, that the hair of such a brute as the ourang-outang was much more efficiently represented by *flax*. A thick coating of the latter was accordingly plastered upon the coating of tar. A long chain was now procured. First, it was passed about the waist of the king, *and tied*; then about another of the party, and also tied; then about all successively, in the same manner. When this chaining arrangement was complete, and the party stood as far apart from each other as possible, they formed a circle; and to make all things appear natural, Hop-Frog passed the residue of the chain, in two diameters, at right angles, across the circle, after the fashion adopted, at the present day, by those who capture Chimpanzees, or other large apes, in Borneo.

The grand saloon in which the masquerade was to take place, was a circular room, very lofty, and receiving the light of the sun only through a single window at top. At night (the season for which the apartment was especially designed,) it was illuminated principally by a large chandelier, depending by a chain from the centre of the sky-light, and lowered, or elevated, by means of a counter-balance as usual; but (in order not to look unsightly) this latter passed outside the cupola and over the roof.

The arrangements of the room had been left to Trippetta's superintendence; but, in some particulars, it seems, she had been guided by the calmer judgment of her friend the dwarf. At his suggestion it was that, on this occasion, the chandelier was removed. Its waxen drippings (which, in weather so warm, it was quite impossible to prevent) would have been seriously detrimental to the rich dresses of the guests, who, on account of the crowded state of the saloon, could not *all* be expected to keep from out its centre – that is to say, from under the chandelier. Additional sconces were set in various parts of the hall, out of the way; and a flambeau, emitting sweet odor, was placed in the right hand of each of the Caryatides[3] that stood against the wall – some fifty or sixty all together.

The eight ourang-outangs, taking Hop-Frog's advice, waited patiently until midnight (when the room was thoroughly filled with masqueraders) before making their appearance. No sooner had the clock ceased striking, however, than they rushed, or rather rolled in, all together – for the impediments of their chains caused most of the party to fall, and all to stumble as they entered.

Notes

[3] A supporting column which is also a statue of a woman.

The excitement among the masqueraders was prodigious, and filled the heart of the king with glee. As had been anticipated, there were not a few of the guests who supposed the ferocious-looking creatures to be beasts of *some* kind in reality, if not precisely ourang-outangs. Many of the women swooned with affright; and had not the king taken the precaution to exclude all weapons from the saloon, his party might soon have expiated their frolic in their blood. As it was, a general rush was made for the doors; but the king had ordered them to be locked immediately upon his entrance; and, at the dwarf's suggestion, the keys had been deposited with *him*.

While the tumult was at its height, and each masquerader attentive only to his own safety (for, in fact, there was much *real* danger from the pressure of the excited crowd), the chain by which the chandelier ordinarily hung, and which had been drawn up on its removal, might have been seen very gradually to descend, until its hooked extremity came within three feet of the floor.

Soon after this, the king and his seven friends having reeled about the hall in all directions, found themselves, at length, in its centre, and, of course, in immediate contact with the chain. While they were thus situated, the dwarf, who had followed noiselessly at their heels, inciting them to keep up the commotion, took hold of their own chain at the intersection of the two portions which crossed the circle diametrically and at right angles. Here, with the rapidity of thought, he inserted the hook from which the chandelier had been wont to depend; and, in an instant, by some unseen agency, the chandelier-chain was drawn so far upward as to take the hook out of reach, and, as an inevitable consequence, to drag the ourang-outangs together in close connection, and face to face.

The masqueraders, by this time, had recovered, in some measure, from their alarm; and, beginning to regard the whole matter as a well-contrived pleasantry, set up a loud shout of laughter at the predicament of the apes.

"Leave them to *me*!" now screamed Hop-Frog, his shrill voice making itself easily heard through all the din. "Leave them to *me*. I fancy I know them. If I can only get a good look at them, I can soon tell who they are."

Here, scrambling over the heads of the crowd, he managed to get to the wall; when, seizing a flambeau from one of the Caryatides, he returned, as he went, to the centre of the room – leaped, with the agility of a monkey, upon the king's head – and thence clambered a few feet up the chain – holding down the torch to examine the group of ourang-outangs, and still screaming: "I shall soon find out who they are!"

And now, while the whole assembly (the apes included) were convulsed with laughter, the jester suddenly uttered a shrill whistle; when the chain flew violently up for about thirty feet – dragging with it the dismayed and struggling ourang-outangs, and leaving them suspended in mid-air between the sky-light and the floor. Hop-Frog, clinging to the chain as it rose, still maintained his relative position in respect to the eight maskers, and still (as if nothing were the matter) continued to thrust his torch down toward them, as though endeavoring to discover who they were.

So thoroughly astonished was the whole company at this ascent, that a dead silence, of about a minute's duration, ensued. It was broken by just such a low, harsh, *grating* sound, as had before attracted the attention of the king and his councillors when the former threw the wine in the face of Trippetta. But, on the present occasion, there could be no question as to *whence* the sound issued. It came from the fang-like teeth of the dwarf, who ground them and gnashed them as he foamed at the mouth, and glared, with an expression of maniacal rage, into the upturned countenances of the king and his seven companions.

"Ah, ha!" said at length the infuriated jester. "Ah, ha! I begin to see who these people *are*, now!" Here, pretending to scrutinize the king more closely, he held the flambeau to the flaxen coat which enveloped him, and which instantly burst into a sheet of vivid flame. In less than half a minute the whole eight ourang-outangs were blazing fiercely, amid the shrieks of the multitude who gazed at them from below, horror-stricken, and without the power to render them the slightest assistance.

At length the flames, suddenly increasing in virulence, forced the jester to climb higher up the chain, to be out of their reach; and, as he made this movement, the crowd again sank, for a brief instant, into silence. The dwarf seized his opportunity, and once more spoke:

"I now see *distinctly*," he said, "what manner of people these maskers are. They are a great king and his seven privy-councillors – a king who does not scruple to strike a defenceless girl, and his seven councillors who abet him in the outrage. As for myself, I am simply Hop-Frog, the jester – and *this is my last jest.*"

Owing to the high combustibility of both the flax and the tar to which it adhered, the dwarf had scarcely made an end of his brief speech before the work of vengeance was complete. The eight corpses swung in their chains, a fetid, blackened, hideous, and indistinguishable mass. The cripple hurled his torch at them, clambered leisurely to the ceiling, and disappeared through the sky-light.

It is supposed that Trippetta, stationed on the roof of the saloon, had been the accomplice of her friend in his fiery revenge, and that, together, they effected their escape to their own country; for neither was seen again.

The Cask of Amontillado

The thousand injuries of Fortunato I had borne as I best could; but when he ventured upon insult, I vowed revenge. You, who so well know the nature of my soul, will not suppose, however, that I gave utterance to a threat. *At length* I would be avenged; this was a point definitively settled – but the very definitiveness with which it was resolved, precluded the idea of risk. I must not only punish, but punish with impunity. A wrong is unredressed when retribution overtakes its redresser. It is equally unredressed when the avenger fails to make himself felt as such to him who has done the wrong.

It must be understood, that neither by word nor deed had I given Fortunato cause to doubt my good will. I continued, as was my wont, to smile in his face, and he did not perceive that my smile *now* was at the thought of his immolation.

He had a weak point – this Fortunato – although in other regards he was a man to be respected and even feared. He prided himself on his connoisseurship in wine. Few Italians have the true virtuoso spirit. For the most part their enthusiasm is adopted to suit the time and opportunity – to practise imposture upon the British and Austrian *millionnaires*. In painting and gemmary Fortunato, like his countrymen, was a quack – but in the matter of old wines he was sincere. In this respect I did not differ from him materially: I was skilful in the Italian vintages myself, and bought largely whenever I could.

It was about dusk, one evening during the supreme madness of the carnival season, that I encountered my friend. He accosted me with excessive warmth, for he had been drinking much. The man wore motley. He had on a tight-fitting parti-striped dress, and his head was surmounted by the conical cap and bells. I was so pleased to see him, that I thought I should never have done wringing his hand.

I said to him – "My dear Fortunato, you are luckily met. How remarkably well you are looking to-day! But I have received a pipe of what passes for Amontillado,[1] and I have my doubts."

Notes _____

THE CASK OF AMONTILLADO
[1] Fortified wine, drier and lighter than ordinary sherry.

"How?" said he. "Amontillado? A pipe? Impossible! And in the middle of the carnival!"

"I have my doubts," I replied; "and I was silly enough to pay the full Amontillado price without consulting you in the matter. You were not to be found, and I was fearful of losing a bargain."

"Amontillado!"

"I have my doubts."

"Amontillado!"

"And I must satisfy them."

"Amontillado!"

"As you are engaged, I am on my way to Luchesi. If any one has a critical turn, it is he. He will tell me – "

"Luchesi cannot tell Amontillado from Sherry."

"And yet some fools will have it that his taste is a match for your own."

"Come, let us go."

"Whither?"

"To your vaults."

"My friend, no; I will not impose upon your good nature. I perceive you have an engagement. Luchesi – "

"I have no engagement; – come."

"My friend, no. It is not the engagement, but the severe cold with which I perceive you are afflicted. The vaults are insufferably damp. They are encrusted with nitre."

"Let us go, nevertheless. The cold is merely nothing. Amontillado! You have been imposed upon. And as for Luchesi, he cannot distinguish Sherry from Amontillado."

Thus speaking, Fortunato possessed himself of my arm. Putting on a mask of black silk, and drawing a *roquelaire* closely about my person, I suffered him to hurry me to my palazzo.

There were no attendants at home; they had absconded to make merry in honor of the time. I had told them that I should not return until the morning, and had given them explicit orders not to stir from the house. These orders were sufficient, I well knew, to insure their immediate disappearance, one and all, as soon as my back was turned.

I took from their sconces two flambeaux, and giving one to Fortunato, bowed him through several suites of rooms to the archway that led into the vaults. I passed down a long and winding staircase, requesting him to be cautious as he followed. We came at length to the foot of the descent, and stood together on the damp ground of the catacombs of the Montresors.

The gait of my friend was unsteady, and the bells upon his cap jingled as he strode.

"The pipe," said he.

"It is farther on," said I; "but observe the white web-work which gleams from these cavern walls."

He turned toward me, and looked into my eyes with two filmy orbs that distilled the rheum of intoxication.

"Nitre?" he asked, at length.

"Nitre," I replied. "How long have you had that cough?"

"Ugh! ugh! ugh! – ugh! ugh! ugh! – ugh! ugh! ugh! – ugh! ugh! ugh! – ugh! ugh! ugh!"

My poor friend found it impossible to reply for many minutes.

"It is nothing," he said, at last.

"Come," I said, with decision, "we will go back; your health is precious. You are rich, respected, admired, beloved; you are happy, as once I was. You are a man to be missed. For me it is no matter. We will go back; you will be ill, and I cannot be responsible. Besides, there is Luchesi – "

"Enough," he said; "the cough is a mere nothing; it will not kill me. I shall not die of a cough."

"True – true," I replied; "and, indeed, I had no intention of alarming you unnecessarily; but you should use all proper caution. A draught of this Medoc will defend us from the damps."

Here I knocked off the neck of a bottle which I drew from a long row of its fellows that lay upon the mould.

"Drink," I said, presenting him the wine.

He raised it to his lips with a leer. He paused and nodded to me familiarly, while his bells jingled.

"I drink," he said, "to the buried that repose around us."

"And I to your long life."

He again took my arm, and we proceeded.

"These vaults," he said, "are extensive."

"The Montresors," I replied, "were a great and numerous family."

"I forget your arms."

"A huge human foot d'or, in a field azure; the foot crushes a serpent rampant whose fangs are imbedded in the heel."

"And the motto?"

"Nemo me impune lacessit."[2]

"Good!" he said.

The wine sparkled in his eyes and the bells jingled. My own fancy grew warm with the Medoc. We had passed through walls of piled bones, with casks and puncheons intermingling, into the inmost recesses of the catacombs. I paused again, and this time I made bold to seize Fortunato by an arm above the elbow.

"The nitre!" I said; "see, it increases. It hangs like moss upon the vaults. We are below the river's bed. The drops of moisture trickle among the bones. Come, we will go back ere it is too late. Your cough – "

"It is nothing," he said; "let us go on. But first, another draught of the Medoc."

I broke and reached him a flaçon of De Grâve. He emptied it at a breath. His eyes flashed with a fierce light. He laughed and threw the bottle upward with a gesticulation I did not understand.

I looked at him in surprise. He repeated the movement – a grotesque one.

"You do not comprehend?" he said.

"Not I," I replied.

"Then you are not of the brotherhood."

"How?"

"You are not of the masons."

"Yes, yes," I said, "yes, yes."

"You? Impossible! A mason?"

"A mason," I replied.

"A sign," he said.

"It is this," I answered, producing a trowel from beneath the folds of my *roquelaire*.

"You jest," he exclaimed, recoiling a few paces. "But let us proceed to the Amontillado."

"Be it so," I said, replacing the tool beneath the cloak, and again offering him my arm. He leaned upon it heavily. We continued our route in search of the Amontillado.

Notes

[2] Latin: no one provokes me with impunity.

We passed through a range of low arches, descended, passed on, and descending again, arrived at a deep crypt, in which the foulness of the air caused our flambeaux rather to glow than flame.

At the most remote end of the crypt there appeared another less spacious. Its walls had been lined with human remains, piled to the vault overhead, in the fashion of the great catacombs of Paris. Three sides of this interior crypt were still ornamented in this manner. From the fourth the bones had been thrown down, and lay promiscuously upon the earth, forming at one point a mound of some size. Within the wall thus exposed by the displacing of the bones, we perceived a still interior recess, in depth about four feet, in width three, in height six or seven. It seemed to have been constructed for no special use within itself, but formed merely the interval between two of the colossal supports of the roof of the catacombs, and was backed by one of their circumscribing walls of solid granite.

It was in vain that Fortunato, uplifting his dull torch, endeavored to pry into the depth of the recess. Its termination the feeble light did not enable us to see.

"Proceed," I said; "herein is the Amontillado. As for Luchesi – "

"He is an ignoramus," interrupted my friend, as he stepped unsteadily forward, while I followed immediately at his heels. In an instant he had reached the extremity of the niche, and finding his progress arrested by the rock, stood stupidly bewildered. A moment more and I had fettered him to the granite. In its surface were two iron staples, distant from each other about two feet, horizontally. From one of these depended a short chain, from the other a padlock. Throwing the links about his waist, it was but the work of a few seconds to secure it. He was too much astounded to resist. Withdrawing the key I stepped back from the recess.

"Pass your hand," I said, "over the wall; you cannot help feeling the nitre. Indeed it is *very* damp. Once more let me *implore* you to return. No? Then I must positively leave you. But I must first render you all the little attentions in my power."

"The Amontillado!" ejaculated my friend, not yet recovered from his astonishment.

"True," I replied; "the Amontillado."

As I said these words I busied myself among the pile of bones of which I have before spoken. Throwing them aside, I soon uncovered a quantity of building stone and mortar. With these materials and with the aid of my trowel, I began vigorously to wall up the entrance of the niche.

I had scarcely laid the first tier of the masonry when I discovered that the intoxication of Fortunato had in a great measure worn off. The earliest indication I had of this was a low moaning cry from the depth of the recess. It was *not* the cry of a drunken man. There was then a long and obstinate silence. I laid the second tier, and the third, and the fourth; and then I heard the furious vibrations of the chain. The noise lasted for several minutes, during which, that I might hearken to it with the more satisfaction, I ceased my labors and sat down upon the bones. When at last the clanking subsided, I resumed the trowel, and finished without interruption the fifth, the sixth, and the seventh tier. The wall was now nearly upon a level with my breast. I again paused, and holding the flambeaux over the mason-work, threw a few feeble rays upon the figure within.

A succession of loud and shrill screams, bursting suddenly from the throat of the chained form, seemed to thrust me violently back. For a brief moment I hesitated – I trembled. Unsheathing my rapier, I began to grope with it about the recess: but the thought of an instant reassured me. I placed my hand upon the solid fabric of the catacombs, and felt satisfied. I reapproached the wall. I replied to the yells of him who clamored. I re-echoed – I aided – I surpassed them in volume and in strength. I did this, and the clamorer grew still.

It was now midnight, and my task was drawing to a close. I had completed the eighth, the ninth, and the tenth tier. I had finished a portion of the last and the eleventh; there remained but a single stone to be fitted and plastered in. I struggled with its weight; I placed it partially in its destined position. But now there came from out the niche a low laugh that erected the hairs upon my head. It was succeeded by a sad voice, which I had difficulty in recognizing as that of the noble Fortunato. The voice said –

"Ha! ha! ha! – he! he! – a very good joke indeed – an excellent jest. We will have many a rich laugh about it at the palazzo – he! he! he! – over our wine – he! he! he!"

"The Amontillado!" I said.

"He! he! he! – he! he! he! – yes, the Amontillado. But is it not getting late? Will not they be awaiting us at the palazzo, the Lady Fortunato and the rest? Let us be gone."

"Yes," I said, "let us be gone."

"For the love of God, Montresor!"

"Yes," I said, "for the love of God!"

But to these words I hearkened in vain for a reply. I grew impatient. I called aloud –

"Fortunato!"

No answer. I called again –

"Fortunato!"

No answer still. I thrust a torch through the remaining aperture and let it fall within. There came forth in return only a jingling of the bells. My heart grew sick – on account of the dampness of the catacombs. I hastened to make an end of my labor. I forced the last stone into its position; I plastered it up. Against the new masonry I re-erected the old rampart of bones. For half of a century no mortal has disturbed them. *In pace requiescat!*[3]

The Facts in the Case of M. Valdemar

Of course I shall not pretend to consider it any matter for wonder, that the extraordinary case of M. Valdemar has excited discussion. It would have been a miracle had it not – especially under the circumstances. Through the desire of all parties concerned, to keep the affair from the public, at least for the present, or until we had farther opportunities for investigation – through our endeavors to effect this – a garbled or exaggerated account made its way into society, and became the source of many unpleasant misrepresentations, and, very naturally, of a great deal of disbelief.

It is now rendered necessary that I give the *facts* – as far as I comprehend them myself. They are, succinctly, these:

My attention, for the last three years, had been repeatedly drawn to the subject of Mesmerism;[1] and, about nine months ago, it occurred to me, quite suddenly, that in the series of experiments made hitherto there had been a very remarkable and most unaccountable omission: – no person had as yet been mesmerized in *articulo mortis.*[2] It remained to be seen, first, whether, in such condition, there existed in the patient any susceptibility to the magnetic influence; secondly, whether, if any existed, it was

Notes

[3] Latin: may he rest in peace.

THE FACTS IN THE CASE OF M. VALDEMAR
[1] Hypnotism was popularized in Europe by the Austrian physician Anton Mesmer (1734–1815), and was called mesmerism or animal magnetism in Poe's time.

[2] At the moment of death.

impaired or increased by the condition; thirdly, to what extent, or for how long a period, the encroachments of Death might be arrested by the process. There were other points to be ascertained, but these most excited my curiosity – the last in especial, from the immensely important character of its consequences.

In looking around me for some subject by whose means I might test these particulars, I was brought to think of my friend, M. Ernest Valdemar, the well-known compiler of the "Bibliotheca Forensica," and author (under the *nom de plume* of Issachar Marx) of the Polish versions of "Wallenstein" and "Gargantua." M. Valdemar, who has resided principally at Harlem, N.Y., since the year 1839, is (or was) particularly noticeable for the extreme spareness of his person – his lower limbs much resembling those of John Randolph; and, also, for the whiteness of his whiskers, in violent contrast to the blackness of his hair – the latter, in consequence, being very generally mistaken for a wig. His temperament was markedly nervous, and rendered him a good subject for mesmeric experiment. On two or three occasions I had put him to sleep with little difficulty, but was disappointed in other results which his peculiar constitution had naturally led me to anticipate. His will was at no period positively, or thoroughly, under my control, and in regard to *clairvoyance*, I could accomplish with him nothing to be relied upon. I always attributed my failure at these points to the disordered state of his health. For some months previous to my becoming acquainted with him, his physicians had declared him in a confirmed phthisis. It was his custom, indeed, to speak calmly of his approaching dissolution, as of a matter neither to be avoided nor regretted.

When the ideas to which I have alluded first occurred to me, it was of course very natural that I should think of M. Valdemar. I knew the steady philosophy of the man too well to apprehend any scruples from *him*; and he had no relatives in America who would be likely to interfere. I spoke to him frankly upon the subject; and, to my surprise, his interest seemed vividly excited. I say to my surprise; for, although he had always yielded his person freely to my experiments, he had never before given me any tokens of sympathy with what I did. His disease was of that character which would admit of exact calculation in respect to the epoch of its termination in death; and it was finally arranged between us that he would send for me about twenty-four hours before the period announced by his physicians as that of his decease.

It is now rather more than seven months since I received, from M. Valdemar himself, the subjoined note:

"My Dear P—,

"You may as well come *now*. D— and F— are agreed that I cannot hold out beyond tomorrow midnight; and I think they have hit the time very nearly.

Valdemar."

I received this note within half an hour after it was written, and in fifteen minutes more I was in the dying man's chamber. I had not seen him for ten days, and was appalled by the fearful alteration which the brief interval had wrought in him. His face wore a leaden hue; the eyes were utterly lustreless; and the emaciation was so extreme that the skin had been broken through by the cheek-bones. His expectoration was excessive. The pulse was barely perceptible. He retained, nevertheless, in a very remarkable manner, both his mental power and a certain degree of physical strength. He spoke with distinctness – took some palliative medicines without aid – and, when I entered the room, was occupied in penciling memoranda in a pocket-book. He was propped up in the bed by pillows. Doctors D— and F— were in attendance.

After pressing Valdemar's hand, I took these gentlemen aside, and obtained from them a minute account of the patient's condition. The left lung had been for eighteen months in a semi-osseous or cartilaginous state, and was, of course, entirely useless for all purposes of vitality. The right, in its upper portion, was also partially, if not thoroughly, ossified, while the lower region was merely a mass of purulent tubercles, running one into another. Several extensive perforations existed; and, at one point, permanent adhesion to the ribs had taken place. These appearances in the right lobe were of comparatively recent date. The ossification had proceeded with very unusual rapidity; no sign of it had been discovered a month before, and the adhesion had only been observed during the three previous days. Independently of the phthisis, the patient was suspected of aneurism of the aorta; but on this point the osseous symptoms rendered an exact diagnosis impossible. It was the opinion of both physicians that M. Valdemar would die about midnight on the morrow (Sunday). It was then seven o'clock on Saturday evening.

On quitting the invalid's bed-side to hold conversation with myself, Doctors D— and F— had bidden him a final farewell. It had not been their intention to return; but, at my request, they agreed to look in upon the patient about ten the next night.

When they had gone, I spoke freely with M. Valdemar on the subject of his approaching dissolution, as well as, more particularly, of the experiment proposed. He still professed himself quite willing and even anxious to have it made, and urged me to commence it at once. A male and a female nurse were in attendance; but I did not feel myself altogether at liberty to engage in a task of this character with no more reliable witnesses than these people, in case of sudden accident, might prove. I therefore postponed operations until about eight the next night, when the arrival of a medical student with whom I had some acquaintance, (Mr. Theodore L—l,) relieved me from farther embarrassment. It had been my design, originally, to wait for the physicians; but I was induced to proceed, first, by the urgent entreaties of M. Valdemar, and secondly, by my conviction that I had not a moment to lose, as he was evidently sinking fast.

Mr. L—l was so kind as to accede to my desire that he would take notes of all that occurred; and it is from his memoranda that what I now have to relate is, for the most part, either condensed or copied *verbatim*.

It wanted about five minutes of eight when, taking the patient's hand, I begged him to state, as distinctly as he could, to Mr. L—l, whether he (M. Valdemar) was entirely willing that I should make the experiment of mesmerizing him in his then condition.

He replied feebly, yet quite audibly, "Yes, I wish to be mesmerized" – adding immediately afterwards, "I fear you have deferred it too long."

While he spoke thus, I commenced the passes which I had already found most effectual in subduing him. He was evidently influenced with the first lateral stroke of my hand across his forehead; but although I exerted all my powers, no farther perceptible effect was induced until some minutes after ten o'clock, when Doctors D— and F— called, according to appointment. I explained to them, in a few words, what I designed, and as they opposed no objection, saying that the patient was already in the death agony, I proceeded without hesitation – exchanging, however, the lateral passes for downward ones, and directing my gaze entirely into the right eye of the sufferer.

By this time his pulse was imperceptible and his breathing was stertorous, and at intervals of half a minute.

This condition was nearly unaltered for a quarter of an hour. At the expiration of this period, however, a natural although a very deep sigh escaped the bosom of the dying man, and the stertorous breathing ceased – that is to say, its stertorousness was no longer apparent; the intervals were undiminished. The patient's extremities were of an icy coldness.

At five minutes before eleven I perceived unequivocal signs of the mesmeric influence. The glassy roll of the eye was changed for that expression of uneasy *inward* examination which is never seen except in cases of sleep-waking, and which it is quite impossible to mistake. With a few rapid lateral passes I made the lids quiver, as in incipient sleep, and with a few more I closed them altogether. I was not satisfied, however, with this, but continued the manipulations vigorously, and with the fullest exertion of the will, until I had completely stiffened the limbs of the slumberer, after placing them in a seemingly easy position. The legs were at full length; the arms were nearly so, and reposed on the bed at a moderate distance from the loins. The head was very slightly elevated.

When I had accomplished this, it was fully midnight, and I requested the gentlemen present to examine M. Valdemar's condition. After a few experiments, they admitted him to be in an unusually perfect state of mesmeric trance. The curiosity of both the physicians was greatly excited. Dr. D— resolved at once to remain with the patient all night, while Dr. F— took leave with a promise to return at daybreak. Mr. L—l and the nurses remained.

We left M. Valdemar entirely undisturbed until about three o'clock in the morning, when I approached him and found him in precisely the same condition as when Dr. F— went away – that is to say, he lay in the same position; the pulse was imperceptible; the breathing was gentle (scarcely noticeable, unless through the application of a mirror to the lips); the eyes were closed naturally; and the limbs were as rigid and as cold as marble. Still, the general appearance was certainly not that of death.

As I approached M. Valdemar I made a kind of half effort to influence his right arm into pursuit of my own, as I passed the latter gently to and fro above his person. In such experiments with this patient I had never perfectly succeeded before, and assuredly I had little thought of succeeding now; but to my astonishment, his arm very readily, although feebly, followed every direction I assigned it with mine. I determined to hazard a few words of conversation.

"M. Valdemar," I said, "are you asleep?" He made no answer, but I perceived a tremor about the lips, and was thus induced to repeat the question, again and again. At its third repetition, his whole frame was agitated by a very slight shivering; the eyelids unclosed themselves so far as to display a white line of the ball; the lips moved sluggishly, and from between them, in a barely audible whisper, issued the words:

"Yes; – asleep now. Do not wake me! – let me die so!"

I here felt the limbs and found them as rigid as ever. The right arm, as before, obeyed the direction of my hand. I questioned the sleep-waker again:

"Do you still feel pain in the breast, M. Valdemar?"

The answer now was immediate, but even less audible than before:

"No pain – I am dying."

I did not think it advisable to disturb him farther just then, and nothing more was said or done until the arrival of Dr. F—, who came a little before sunrise, and expressed unbounded astonishment at finding the patient still alive. After feeling the pulse and applying a mirror to the lips, he requested me to speak to the sleep-waker again. I did so, saying:

"M. Valdemar, do you still sleep?"

As before, some minutes elapsed ere a reply was made; and during the interval the dying man seemed to be collecting his energies to speak. At my fourth repetition of the question, he said very faintly, almost inaudibly:

"Yes; still asleep – dying."

It was now the opinion, or rather the wish, of the physicians, that M. Valdemar should be suffered to remain undisturbed in his present apparently tranquil condition, until death should supervene – and this, it was generally agreed, must now take place within a few minutes. I concluded, however, to speak to him once more, and merely repeated my previous question.

While I spoke, there came a marked change over the countenance of the sleep-waker. The eyes rolled themselves slowly open, the pupils disappearing upwardly; the skin generally assumed a cadaverous hue, resembling not so much parchment as white paper; and the circular hectic spots which, hitherto, had been strongly defined in the centre of each cheek, *went out* at once. I use this expression, because the suddenness of their departure put me in mind of nothing so much as the extinguishment of a candle by a puff of the breath. The upper lip, at the same time, writhed itself away from the teeth, which it had previously covered completely; while the lower jaw fell with an audible jerk, leaving the mouth widely extended, and disclosing in full view the swollen and blackened tongue. I presume that no member of the party then present had been unaccustomed to death-bed horrors; but so hideous beyond conception was the appearance of M. Valdemar at this moment, that there was a general shrinking back from the region of the bed.

I now feel that I have reached a point of this narrative at which every reader will be startled into positive disbelief. It is my business, however, simply to proceed.

There was no longer the faintest sign of vitality in M. Valdemar; and concluding him to be dead, we were consigning him to the charge of the nurses, when a strong vibratory motion was observable in the tongue. This continued for perhaps a minute. At the expiration of this period, there issued from the distended and motionless jaws a voice – such as it would be madness in me to attempt describing. There are, indeed, two or three epithets which might be considered as applicable to it in part; I might say, for example, that the sound was harsh, and broken and hollow; but the hideous whole is indescribable, for the simple reason that no similar sounds have ever jarred upon the ear of humanity. There were two particulars, nevertheless, which I thought then, and still think, might fairly be stated as characteristic of the intonation – as well adapted to convey some idea of its unearthly peculiarity. In the first place, the voice seemed to reach our ears – at least mine – from a vast distance, or from some deep cavern within the earth. In the second place, it impressed me (I fear, indeed, that it will be impossible to make myself comprehended) as gelatinous or glutinous matters impress the sense of touch.

I have spoken both of "sound" and of "voice." I mean to say that the sound was one of distinct – of even wonderfully, thrillingly distinct – syllabification. M. Valdemar *spoke* – obviously in reply to the question I had propounded to him a few minutes before. I had asked him, it will be remembered, if he still slept. He now said:

"Yes; – no; – I *have been* sleeping – and now – now – *I am dead*."

No person present even affected to deny, or attempted to repress, the unutterable, shuddering horror which these few words, thus uttered, were so well calculated to convey. Mr. L—l (the student) swooned. The nurses immediately left the chamber, and could not be induced to return. My own impressions I would not pretend to render intelligible to the reader. For nearly an hour, we busied ourselves, silently – without the utterance of a word – in endeavors to revive Mr. L—l. When he came to himself, we addressed ourselves again to an investigation of M. Valdemar's condition.

It remained in all respects as I have last described it, with the exception that the mirror no longer afforded evidence of respiration. An attempt to draw blood from the arm failed. I should mention, too, that this limb was no farther subject to my will. I endeavored in vain to make it follow the direction of my hand. The only real indication, indeed, of the mesmeric influence, was now found in the vibratory movement of the tongue, whenever I addressed M. Valdemar a question. He seemed to be making an effort to reply, but had no longer sufficient volition. To queries put to him by any other person than myself he seemed utterly insensible – although I endeavored to place each member of the company in mesmeric *rapport* with him. I believe that I have now related all that is necessary to an understanding of the sleep-waker's state at this epoch. Other nurses were procured; and at ten o'clock I left the house in company with the two physicians and Mr. L—l.

In the afternoon we all called again to see the patient. His condition remained precisely the same. We had now some discussion as to the propriety and feasibility of awakening him; but we had little difficulty in agreeing that no good purpose would be served by so doing. It was evident that, so far, death (or what is usually termed death) had been arrested by the mesmeric process. It seemed clear to us all that to awaken M. Valdemar would be merely to insure his instant, or at least his speedy dissolution.

From this period until the close of last week – *an interval of nearly seven months* – we continued to make daily calls at M. Valdemar's house, accompanied, now and then, by medical and other friends. All this time the sleeper-waker remained *exactly* as I have last described him. The nurses' attentions were continual.

It was on Friday last that we finally resolved to make the experiment of awakening, or attempting to awaken him; and it is the (perhaps) unfortunate result of this latter experiment which has given rise to so much discussion in private circles – to so much of what I cannot help thinking unwarranted popular feeling.

For the purpose of relieving M. Valdemar from the mesmeric trance, I made use of the customary passes. These, for a time, were unsuccessful. The first indication of revival was afforded by a partial descent of the iris. It was observed, as especially remarkable, that this lowering of the pupil was accompanied by the profuse out-flowing of a yellowish ichor (from beneath the lids) of a pungent and highly offensive odor.

It was now suggested that I should attempt to influence the patient's arm, as heretofore. I made the attempt and failed. Dr. F— then intimated a desire to have me put a question. I did so, as follows:

"M. Valdemar, can you explain to us what are your feelings or wishes now?"

There was an instant return of the hectic circles on the cheeks; the tongue quivered, or rather rolled violently in the mouth (although the jaws and lips remained rigid as before;) and at length the same hideous voice which I have already described, broke forth:

"For God's sake! – quick! – quick! – put me to sleep – or, quick! – waken me! – quick! – *I say to you that I am dead!*"

I was thoroughly unnerved, and for an instant remained undecided what to do. At first I made an endeavor to re-compose the patient; but, failing in this through total abeyance of the will, I retraced my steps and as earnestly struggled to awaken him. In this attempt I soon saw that I should be successful – or at least I soon fancied that my success would be complete – and I am sure that all in the room were prepared to see the patient awaken.

For what really occurred, however, it is quite impossible that any human being could have been prepared.

As I rapidly made the mesmeric passes, amid ejaculations of "dead! dead!" absolutely *bursting* from the tongue and not from the lips of the sufferer, his whole frame at once – within the space of a single minute, or even less, shrunk – crumbled – absolutely *rotted* away beneath my hands. Upon the bed, before that whole company, there lay a nearly liquid mass of loathsome – of detestable putrescence.

The Fall of the House of Usher

Son cœur est un luth suspendu;
Sitôt qu'on le touche il résonne.[1]
De Béranger

During the whole of a dull, dark, and soundless day in the autumn of the year, when the clouds hung oppressively low in the heavens, I had been passing alone, on horseback, through a singularly dreary tract of country; and at length found myself, as the shades of the evening drew on, within view of the melancholy House of Usher. I know not how it was – but, with the first glimpse of the building, a sense of insufferable gloom pervaded my spirit. I say insufferable; for the feeling was unrelieved by any of that half-pleasurable, because poetic, sentiment with which the mind usually receives even the sternest natural images of the desolate or terrible. I looked upon the scene before me – upon the mere house, and the simple landscape features of the domain – upon the bleak walls – upon the vacant eye-like windows – upon a few rank sedges – and upon a few white trunks of decayed trees – with an utter depression of soul which I can compare to no earthly sensation more properly than to the after-dream of the reveller upon opium – the bitter lapse into every-day life – the hideous dropping off of the veil. There was an iciness, a sinking, a sickening of the heart – an unredeemed dreariness of thought which no goading of the imagination could torture into aught of the sublime. What was it – I paused to think – what was it that so unnerved me in the contemplation of the House of Usher? It was a mystery all insoluble; nor could I grapple with the shadowy fancies that crowded upon me as I pondered. I was forced to fall back upon the unsatisfactory conclusion, that while, beyond doubt, there *are* combinations of very simple natural objects which have the power of thus affecting us, still the analysis of this power lies among considerations beyond our depth. It was possible, I reflected, that a mere different arrangement of the particulars of the scene, of the details of the picture, would be sufficient to modify, or perhaps to annihilate its capacity for sorrowful impression; and, acting upon this idea, I reined my horse to the precipitous brink of a black and lurid tarn that lay in unruffled lustre by the dwelling, and gazed down – but with a shudder even more thrilling than before – upon the remodelled and inverted images of the gray sedge, and the ghastly tree-stems, and the vacant and eye-like windows.

Nevertheless, in this mansion of gloom I now proposed to myself a sojourn of some weeks. Its proprietor, Roderick Usher, had been one of my boon companions in boyhood; but many years had elapsed since our last meeting. A letter, however, had lately reached me in a distant part of the country – a letter from him – which, in its wildly importunate nature, had admitted of no other than a personal reply. The MS. gave evidence of nervous agitation. The writer spoke of acute bodily illness – of a mental disorder which oppressed him – and of an earnest desire to see me, as his best, and indeed his only personal friend, with a view of attempting, by the cheerfulness of my society, some alleviation of his malady. It was the manner in which all this, and much more, was said – it was the apparent *heart* that went with his request – which allowed me no room for hesitation; and I accordingly obeyed forthwith what I still considered a very singular summons.

Notes ────────────────────────────────

THE FALL OF THE HOUSE OF USHER
[1] French: His heart is a suspended lute; touch it, and it resonates.

Although, as boys, we had been even intimate associates, yet I really knew little of my friend. His reserve had been always excessive and habitual. I was aware, however, that his very ancient family had been noted, time out of mind, for a peculiar sensibility of temperament, displaying itself, through long ages, in many works of exalted art, and manifested, of late, in repeated deeds of munificent yet unobtrusive charity, as well as in a passionate devotion to the intricacies, perhaps even more than to the ortho-dox and easily recognizable beauties, of musical science. I had learned, too, the very remarkable fact, that the stem of the Usher race, all time-honored as it was, had put forth, at no period, any enduring branch; in other words, that the entire family lay in the direct line of descent, and had always, with very trifling and very temporary varia-tion, so lain. It was this deficiency, I considered, while running over in thought the perfect keeping of the character of the premises with the accredited character of the people, and while speculating upon the possible influence which the one, in the long lapse of centuries, might have exercised upon the other – it was this deficiency, per-haps, of collateral issue, and the consequent undeviating transmission, from sire to son, of the patrimony with the name, which had, at length, so identified the two as to merge the original title of the estate in the quaint and equivocal appellation of the "House of Usher" – an appellation which seemed to include, in the minds of the peas-antry who used it, both the family and the family mansion.

I have said that the sole effect of my somewhat childish experiment – that of looking down within the tarn – had been to deepen the first singular impression. There can be no doubt that the consciousness of the rapid increase of my superstition – for why should I not so term it? – served mainly to accelerate the increase itself. Such, I have long known, is the paradoxical law of all sentiments having terror as a basis. And it might have been for this reason only, that, when I again uplifted my eyes to the house itself, from its image in the pool, there grew in my mind a strange fancy – a fancy so ridiculous, indeed, that I but mention it to show the vivid force of the sensations which oppressed me. I had so worked upon my imagination as really to believe that about the whole mansion and domain there hung an atmosphere peculiar to themselves and their immediate vicinity – an atmosphere which had no affinity with the air of heaven, but which had reeked up from the decayed trees, and the gray wall, and the silent tarn – a pestilent and mystic vapor, dull, sluggish, faintly discernible, and leaden-hued.

Shaking off from my spirit what *must* have been a dream, I scanned more narrowly the real aspect of the building. Its principal feature seemed to be that of an excessive antiquity. The discoloration of ages had been great. Minute fungi overspread the whole exterior, hanging in a fine tangled web-work from the eaves. Yet all this was apart from any extraordinary dilapidation. No portion of the masonry had fallen; and there appeared to be a wild inconsistency between its still perfect adaptation of parts, and the crumbling condition of the individual stones. In this there was much that reminded me of the specious totality of old wood-work which has rotted for long years in some neglected vault, with no disturbance from the breath of the external air. Beyond this indication of extensive decay, however, the fabric gave little token of instability. Perhaps the eye of a scrutinizing observer might have discovered a barely perceptible fissure, which, extending from the roof of the building in front, made its way down the wall in a zig-zag direction, until it became lost in the sullen waters of the tarn.

Noticing these things, I rode over a short causeway to the house. A servant in wait-ing took my horse, and I entered the Gothic archway of the hall. A valet, of stealthy step, thence conducted me, in silence, through many dark and intricate passages in my progress to the *studio* of his master. Much that I encountered on the way contributed, I know not how, to heighten the vague sentiments of which I have already spoken. While the objects around me – while the carvings of the ceilings, the sombre tapestries of the walls, the ebon blackness of the floors, and the phantasmagoric armorial trophies which rattled as I strode, were but matters to which, or to such as which, I had been accustomed from my infancy – while I hesitated not to acknowledge how familiar was all this – I still wondered to find how unfamiliar were the fancies which ordinary images were stirring up. On one of the staircases, I met the physician of the family. His countenance, I thought, wore a mingled expression of low cunning and perplexity. He accosted me with trepidation and passed on. The valet now threw open a door and ushered me into the presence of his master.

The room in which I found myself was very large and lofty. The windows were long, narrow, and pointed, and at so vast a distance from the black oaken floor as to be altogether inaccessible from within. Feeble gleams of encrimsoned light made their way through the trellissed panes, and served to render sufficiently distinct the more prominent objects around; the eye, however, struggled in vain to reach the remoter angles of the chamber, or the recesses of the vaulted and fretted ceiling. Dark draperies hung upon the walls. The general furniture was profuse, comfortless, antique, and tattered. Many books and musical instruments lay scattered about, but failed to give any vitality to the scene. I felt that I breathed an atmosphere of sorrow. An air of stern, deep, and irredeemable gloom hung over and pervaded all.

Upon my entrance, Usher arose from a sofa on which he had been lying at full length, and greeted me with a vivacious warmth which had much in it, I at first thought, of an overdone cordiality – of the constrained effort of the *ennuyé* man of the world. A glance, however, at his countenance convinced me of his perfect sincerity. We sat down; and for some moments, while he spoke not, I gazed upon him with a feeling half of pity, half of awe. Surely, man had never before so terribly altered, in so brief a period, as had Roderick Usher! It was with difficulty that I could bring myself to admit the identity of the wan being before me with the companion of my early boyhood. Yet the character of his face had been at all times remarkable. A cadaverousness of complexion; an eye large, liquid, and luminous beyond comparison; lips somewhat thin and very pallid, but of a surpassingly beautiful curve; a nose of a delicate Hebrew model, but with a breadth of nostril unusual in similar formations; a finely moulded chin, speaking, in its want of prominence, of a want of moral energy; hair of a more than weblike softness and tenuity; these features, with an inordinate expansion above the regions of the temple, made up altogether a countenance not easily to be forgotten. And now in the mere exaggeration of the prevailing character of these features, and of the expression they were wont to convey, lay so much of change that I doubted to whom I spoke. The now ghastly pallor of the skin, and the now miraculous lustre of the eye, above all things startled and even awed me. The silken hair, too, had been suffered to grow all unheeded, and as, in its wild gossamer texture, it floated rather than fell about the face, I could not, even with effort, connect its Arabesque expression with any idea of simple humanity.

In the manner of my friend I was at once struck with an incoherence – an inconsistency; and I soon found this to arise from a series of feeble and futile struggles to overcome an habitual trepidancy – an excessive nervous agitation. For something of this nature I had indeed been prepared, no less by his letter, than by reminiscences of certain boyish traits, and by conclusions deduced from his peculiar physical conformation and temperament. His action was alternately vivacious and sullen. His voice varied rapidly from a tremulous indecision (when the animal spirits seemed utterly in abeyance) to that species of energetic concision – that abrupt, weighty unhurried, and hollow-sounding enunciation – that leaden, self-balanced, and perfectly modulated guttural utterance, which may be observed in the lost drunkard, or the irreclaimable eater of opium, during the periods of his most intense excitement.

It was thus that he spoke of the object of my visit, of his earnest desire to see me, and of the solace he expected me to afford him. He entered, at some length, into what he conceived to be the nature of his malady. It was, he said, a constitutional and a family evil, and one for which he despaired to find a remedy – a mere nervous affection, he immediately added, which would undoubtedly soon pass off. It displayed itself in a host of unnatural sensations. Some of these, as he detailed them, interested and bewildered me; although, perhaps, the terms, and the general manner of their narration had their weight. He suffered much from a morbid acuteness of the senses; the most insipid food was alone endurable; he could wear only garments of certain texture; the odors of all flowers were oppressive; his eyes were tortured by even a faint light; and there were but peculiar sounds, and these from stringed instruments, which did not inspire him with horror.

To an anomalous species of terror I found him a bounden slave. "I shall perish," said he, "I *must* perish in this deplorable folly. Thus, thus, and not otherwise, shall I be lost. I dread the events of the future, not in themselves, but in their results. I shudder at the thought of any, even the most trivial, incident, which may operate upon this intolerable agitation of soul. I have, indeed, no abhorrence of danger, except in its absolute effect – in terror. In this unnerved, in this pitiable, condition I feel that the period will sooner or later arrive when I must abandon life and reason together, in some struggle with the grim phantasm, FEAR."

I learned, moreover, at intervals, and through broken and equivocal hints, another singular feature of his mental condition. He was enchained by certain superstitious impressions in regard to the dwelling which he tenanted, and whence, for many years, he had never ventured forth – in regard to an influence whose supposititious force was conveyed in terms too shadowy here to be re-stated – an influence which some peculiarities in the mere form and substance of his family mansion had, by dint of long sufferance, he said, obtained over his spirit – an effect which the *physique* of the gray walls and turrets, and of the dim tarn into which they all looked down, had, at length, brought about upon the *morale* of his existence.

He admitted, however, although with hesitation, that much of the peculiar gloom which thus afflicted him could be traced to a more natural and far more palpable origin – to the severe and long-continued illness – indeed to the evidently approaching dissolution – of a tenderly beloved sister, his sole companion for long years, his last and only relative on earth. "Her decease," he said, with a bitterness which I can never forget, "would leave him (him, the hopeless and the frail) the last of the ancient race of the Ushers." While he spoke, the lady Madeline (for so was she called) passed through a remote portion of the apartment, and, without having noticed my presence, disappeared. I regarded her with an utter astonishment not unmingled with dread; and yet I found it impossible to account for such feelings. A sensation of stupor oppressed me as my eyes followed her retreating steps. When a door, at length, closed upon her, my glance sought instinctively and eagerly the countenance of the brother – but he had buried his face in his hands, and I could only perceive that a far more than ordinary wanness had overspread the emaciated fingers through which trickled many passionate tears.

The disease of the lady Madeline had long baffled the skill of her physicians. A settled apathy, a gradual wasting away of the person, and frequent although transient affections of a partially cataleptical character were the unusual diagnosis. Hitherto she had steadily borne up against the pressure of her malady, and had not betaken herself finally to bed; but on the closing in of the evening of my arrival at the house, she succumbed (as her brother told me at night with inexpressible agitation) to the prostrating power of the destroyer; and I learned that the glimpse I had obtained of her person would thus probably be the last I should obtain – that the lady, at least while living, would be seen by me no more.

For several days ensuing, her name was unmentioned by either Usher or myself: and during this period I was busied in earnest endeavors to alleviate the melancholy of my friend. We painted and read together; or I listened, as if in a dream, to the wild improvisations of his speaking guitar. And thus, as a closer and still closer intimacy admitted me more unreservedly into the recesses of his spirit, the more bitterly did I perceive the futility of all attempts at cheering a mind from which darkness, as if an inherent positive quality, poured forth upon all objects of the moral and physical universe in one unceasing radiation of gloom.

I shall ever bear about me a memory of the many solemn hours I thus spent alone with the master of the House of Usher. Yet I should fail in any attempt to convey an idea of the exact character of the studies, or of the occupations, in which he involved me, or led me the way. An excited and highly distempered ideality threw a sulphureous lustre over all. His long improvised dirges will ring forever in my ears. Among other things, I hold painfully in mind a certain singular perversion and amplification of the wild air of the last waltz of Von Weber. From the paintings over which his elaborate fancy brooded, and which grew, touch by touch, into vaguenesses at which I shuddered the more thrillingly, because I shuddered knowing not why; – from these paintings (vivid as their images now are before me) I would in vain endeavor to educe more than a small portion which should lie within the compass of merely written words. By the utter simplicity, by the nakedness of his designs, he arrested and overawed attention. If ever mortal painted an idea, that mortal was Roderick Usher. For me at least, in the circumstances then surrounding me, there arose out of the pure abstractions which the hypochondriac contrived to throw upon his canvas, an intensity of intolerable awe, no shadow of which felt I ever yet in the contemplation of the certainly glowing yet too concrete reveries of Fuseli.

One of the phantasmagoric conceptions of my friend, partaking not so rigidly of the spirit of abstraction, may be shadowed forth, although feebly, in words. A small picture presented the interior of an immensely long and rectangular vault or tunnel, with low walls, smooth, white, and without interruption or device. Certain accessory points of the design served well to convey the idea that this excavation lay at an exceeding depth below the surface of the earth. No outlet was observed in any portion of its vast extent, and no torch or other artificial source of light was discernible; yet a flood of intense rays rolled throughout, and bathed the whole in a ghastly and inappropriate splendor.

I have just spoken of that morbid condition of the auditory nerve which rendered all music intolerable to the sufferer, with the exception of certain effects of stringed instruments. It was, perhaps, the narrow limits to which he thus confined himself upon the guitar which gave birth, in great measure, to the fantastic character of his performances. But the fervid *facility* of his *impromptus* could not be so accounted for. They must have been, and were, in the notes, as well as in the words of his wild fantasias (for he not unfrequently accompanied himself with rhymed verbal improvisations), the result of that intense mental collectedness and concentration to which I have previously alluded as observable only in particular moments of the highest artificial excitement. The words of one of these rhapsodies I have easily remembered. I was, perhaps, the more forcibly impressed with it as he gave it, because, in the under or mystic current of its meaning, I fancied that I perceived, and for the first time, a full consciousness on the part of Usher of the tottering of his lofty reason upon her throne. The verses, which were entitled "The Haunted Palace," ran very nearly, if not accurately, thus:

I.

In the greenest of our valleys,
    By good angels tenanted,
Once a fair and stately palace –
    Radiant palace – reared its head.
In the monarch Thought's dominion –
    It stood there!
Never seraph spread a pinion
    Over fabric half so fair.

II.

Banners yellow, glorious, golden,
    On its roof did float and flow;
(This – all this – was in the olden
    Time long ago)
And every gentle air that dallied,
    In that sweet day,
Along the ramparts plumed and pallid,
    A winged odor went away.

III.

Wanderers in that happy valley
    Through two luminous windows saw
Spirits moving musically
    To a lute's well-tunèd law;
Round about a throne, where sitting
    (Porphyrogene!)[2]
In state his glory well befitting,
    The ruler of the realm was seen.

IV.

And all with pearl and ruby glowing
    Was the fair palace door,
Through which came flowing, flowing, flowing
    And sparkling evermore,
A troop of Echoes whose sweet duty
    Was but to sing,
In voices of surpassing beauty,
    The wit and wisdom of their king.

V.

But evil things, in robes of sorrow,
    Assailed the monarch's high estate;
(Ah, let us mourn, for never morrow
    Shall dawn upon him, desolate!)
And, round about his home, the glory
    That blushed and bloomed

Notes

[2] A word Poe invented, which means "born to the purple,"
i.e. royal.

Is but a dim-remembered story
Of the old time entombed.

VI.
And travellers now within that valley,
    Through the red-litten windows see
Vast forms that move fantastically
    To a discordant melody;
While, like a rapid ghastly river,
    Through the pale door;
A hideous throng rush out forever,
    And laugh – but smile no more.

I well remember that suggestions arising from this ballad led us into a train of thought wherein there became manifest an opinion of Usher's which I mention not so much on account of its novelty (for other men* have thought thus), as on account of the pertinacity with which he maintained it. This opinion, in its general form, was that of the sentience of all vegetable things. But, in his disordered fancy, the idea had assumed a more daring character, and trespassed, under certain conditions, upon the kingdom of inorganization. I lack words to express the full extent, or the earnest *abandon* of his persuasion. The belief, however, was connected (as I have previously hinted) with the gray stones of the home of his forefathers. The conditions of the sentience had been here, he imagined, fulfilled in the method of collocation of these stones – in the order of their arrangement, as well as in that of the many *fungi* which overspread them, and of the decayed trees which stood around – above all, in the long undisturbed endurance of this arrangement, and in its reduplication in the still waters of the tarn. Its evidence – the evidence of the sentience – was to be seen, he said (and I here started as he spoke), in the gradual yet certain condensation of an atmosphere of their own about the waters and the walls. The result was discoverable, he added, in that silent yet importunate and terrible influence which for centuries had moulded the destinies of his family, and which made him what I now saw him – what he was. Such opinions need no comment, and I will make none.

Our books – the books which, for years, had formed no small portion of the mental existence of the invalid – were, as might be supposed, in strict keeping with this character of phantasm. We pored together over such works as the Ververt et Chartreuse of Gresset; the Belphegor of Machiavelli; the Heaven and Hell of Swedenborg; the Subterranean Voyage of Nicholas Klimm by Holberg; the Chiromancy of Robert Flud, of Jean D'Indaginé, and of Dela Chambre; the Journey into the Blue Distance of Tieck; and the City of the Sun of Campanella. One favorite volume was a small octavo edition of the *Directorium Inquisitorium*, by the Dominican Eymeric de Gironne; and there were passages in Pomponius Mela, about the old African Satyrs and Œgipans, over which Usher would sit dreaming for hours. His chief delight, however, was found in the perusal of an exceedingly rare and curious book in quarto Gothic – the manual of a forgotten church – the *Vigiliae Mortuorum secundum Chorum Ecclesiae Maguntinae*.

I could not help thinking of the wild ritual of this work, and of its probable influence upon the hypochondriac, when, one evening, having informed me abruptly that the lady Madeline was no more, he stated his intention of preserving her corpse for a

Notes

* Watson, Dr. Percival, Spallanzani, and especially the Bishop
of Landaff. – See "Chemical Essays," vol. v. [Poe's note.]

fortnight (previously to its final interment,) in one of the numerous vaults within the main walls of the building. The worldly reason, however, assigned for this singular proceeding, was one which I did not feel at liberty to dispute. The brother had been led to his resolution (so he told me) by consideration of the unusual character of the malady of the deceased, of certain obtrusive and eager inquiries on the part of her medical men, and of the remote and exposed situation of the burial-ground of the family. I will not deny that when I called to mind the sinister countenance of the person whom I met upon the staircase, on the day of my arrival at the house, I had no desire to oppose what I regarded as at best but a harmless, and by no means an unnatural, precaution.

At the request of Usher, I personally aided him in the arrangements for the temporary entombment. The body having been encoffined, we two alone bore it to its rest. The vault in which we placed it (and which had been so long unopened that our torches, half smothered in its oppressive atmosphere, gave us little opportunity for investigation) was small, damp, and entirely without means of admission for light; lying, at great depth, immediately beneath that portion of the building in which was my own sleeping apartment. It had been used, apparently, in remote feudal times, for the worst purposes of a donjon-keep, and, in later days, as a place of deposit for powder, or some other highly combustible substance, as a portion of its floor, and the whole interior of a long archway through which we reached it, were carefully sheathed with copper. The door, of massive iron, had been, also, similarly protected. Its immense weight caused an unusually sharp, grating sound, as it moved upon its hinges.

Having deposited our mournful burden upon tressels within this region of horror, we partially turned aside the yet unscrewed lid of the coffin, and looked upon the face of the tenant. A striking similitude between the brother and sister now first arrested my attention; and Usher, divining, perhaps, my thoughts, murmured out some few words from which I learned that the deceased and himself had been twins, and that sympathies of a scarcely intelligible nature had always existed between them. Our glances, however, rested not long upon the dead – for we could not regard her unawed. The disease which had thus entombed the lady in the maturity of youth, had left, as usual in all maladies of a strictly cataleptical character, the mockery of a faint blush upon the bosom and the face, and that suspiciously lingering smile upon the lip which is so terrible in death. We replaced and screwed down the lid, and, having secured the door of iron, made our way, with toil, into the scarcely less gloomy apartments of the upper portion of the house.

And now, some days of bitter grief having elapsed, an observable change came over the features of the mental disorder of my friend. His ordinary manner had vanished. His ordinary occupations were neglected or forgotten. He roamed from chamber to chamber with hurried, unequal, and objectless step. The pallor of his countenance had assumed, if possible, a more ghastly hue – but the luminousness of his eye had utterly gone out. The once occasional huskiness of his tone was heard no more; and a tremendous quaver, as if of extreme terror, habitually characterized his utterance. There were times, indeed, when I thought his unceasingly agitated mind was laboring with some oppressive secret, to divulge which he struggled for the necessary courage. At times, again, I was obliged to resolve all into the mere inexplicable vagaries of madness, for I beheld him gazing upon vacancy for long hours, in an attitude of the profoundest attention, as if listening to some imaginary sound. It was no wonder that his condition terrified – that it infected me. I felt creeping upon me, by slow yet certain degrees, the wild influences of his own fantastic yet impressive superstitions.

It was, especially, upon retiring to bed late in the night of the seventh or eighth day after the placing of the lady Madeline within the donjon, that I experienced the full power of such feelings. Sleep came not near my couch – while the hours waned and waned away. I struggled to reason off the nervousness which had dominion over me. I endeavored to believe that much, if not all of what I felt, was due to the bewildering influence of the gloomy furniture of the room – of the dark and tattered draperies, which, tortured into motion by the breath of a rising tempest, swayed fitfully to and fro upon the walls, and rustled uneasily about the decorations of the bed. But my efforts were fruitless. An irrepressible tremor gradually pervaded my frame; and, at length, there sat upon my very heart an incubus of utterly causeless alarm. Shaking this off with a gasp and a struggle, I uplifted myself upon the pillows, and, peering earnestly within the intense darkness of the chamber, hearkened – I know not why, except that an instinctive spirit prompted me – to certain low and indefinite sounds which came, through the pauses of the storm, at long intervals, I knew not whence. Overpowered by an intense sentiment of horror, unaccountable yet unendurable, I threw on my clothes with haste (for I felt that I should sleep no more during the night), and endeavored to arouse myself from the pitiable condition into which I had fallen, by pacing rapidly to and fro through the apartment.

I had taken but few turns in this manner, when a light step on an adjoining staircase arrested my attention. I presently recognized it as that of Usher. In an instant afterward he rapped, with a gentle touch, at my door, and entered, bearing a lamp. His countenance was, as usual, cadaverously wan – but, moreover, there was a species of mad hilarity in his eyes an evidently restrained *hysteria* in his whole demeanor. His air appalled me – but any thing was preferable to the solitude which I had so long endured, and I even welcomed his presence as a relief.

"And you have not seen it?" he said abruptly, after having stared about him for some moments in silence – "you have not then seen it? – but, stay! you shall." Thus speaking, and having carefully shaded his lamp, he hurried to one of the casements, and threw it freely open to the storm.

The impetuous fury of the entering gust nearly lifted us from our feet. It was, indeed, a tempestuous yet sternly beautiful night, and one wildly singular in its terror and its beauty. A whirlwind had apparently collected its force in our vicinity; for there were frequent and violent alterations in the direction of the wind; and the exceeding density of the clouds (which hung so low as to press upon the turrets of the house) did not prevent our perceiving the lifelike velocity with which they flew careering from all points against each other, without passing away into the distance. I say that even their exceeding density did not prevent our perceiving this – yet we had no glimpse of the moon or stars, nor was there any flashing forth of the lightning. But the under surfaces of the huge masses of agitated vapor, as well as all terrestrial objects immediately around us, were glowing in the unnatural light of a faintly luminous and distinctly visible gaseous exhalation which hung about and enshrouded the mansion.

"You must not – you shall not behold this!" said I, shuddering, to Usher, as I led him, with a gentle violence, from the window to a seat. "These appearances, which bewilder you, are merely electrical phenomena not uncommon – or it may be that they have their ghastly origin in the rank miasma of the tarn. Let us close this casement; – the air is chilling and dangerous to your frame. Here is one of your favorite romances. I will read, and you shall listen; – and so we will pass away this terrible night together."

The antique volume which I had taken up was the "Mad Trist" of Sir Launcelot Canning; but I had called it a favorite of Usher's more in sad jest than in earnest; for, in truth, there is little in its uncouth and unimaginative prolixity which could have had interest for the lofty and spiritual ideality of my friend. It was, however, the only book immediately at hand; and I indulged a vague hope that the excitement which now agitated the hypochondriac, might find relief (for the history of mental disorder is full of similar anomalies) even in the extremeness of the folly which I should read. Could I have judged, indeed, by the wild overstrained air of vivacity with which he hearkened, or apparently hearkened, to the words of the tale, I might well have congratulated myself upon the success of my design.

I had arrived at that well-known portion of the story where Ethelred, the hero of the Trist, having sought in vain for peaceable admission into the dwelling of the hermit, proceeds to make good an entrance by force. Here, it will be remembered, the words of the narrative run thus:

"And Ethelred, who was by nature of a doughty heart, and who was now mighty withal, on account of the powerfulness of the wine which he had drunken, waited no longer to hold parley with the hermit, who, in sooth, was of an obstinate and maliceful turn, but, feeling the rain upon his shoulders, and fearing the rising of the tempest, uplifted his mace outright, and, with blows, made quickly room in the plankings of the door for his gauntleted hand; and now pulling therewith sturdily, he so cracked, and ripped, and tore all asunder, that the noise of the dry and hollow-sounding wood alarummed and reverberated throughout the forest."

At the termination of this sentence I started and, for a moment, paused; for it appeared to me (although I at once concluded that my excited fancy had deceived me) – it appeared to me that, from some very remote portion of the mansion, there came, indistinctly, to my ears, what might have been, in its exact similarity of character, the echo (but a stifled and dull one certainly) of the very cracking and ripping sound which Sir Launcelot had so particularly described. It was, beyond doubt, the coincidence alone which had arrested my attention; for, amid the rattling of the sashes of the casements, and the ordinary commingled noises of the still increasing storm, the sound, in itself, had nothing, surely, which should have interested or disturbed me. I continued the story:

"But the good champion Ethelred, now entering within the door, was sore enraged and amazed to perceive no signal of the maliceful hermit; but, in the stead thereof, a dragon of a scaly and prodigious demeanor, and of a fiery tongue, which sate in guard before a palace of gold, with a floor of silver; and upon the wall there hung a shield of shining brass with this legend enwritten –

> Who entereth herein, a conqueror hath bin;
> Who slayeth the dragon, the shield he shall win.

And Ethelred uplifted his mace, and struck upon the head of the dragon, which fell before him, and gave up his pesty breath, with a shriek so horrid and harsh, and withal so piercing, that Ethelred had fain to close his ears with his hands against the dreadful noise of it, the like whereof was never before heard."

Here again I paused abruptly, and now with a feeling of wild amazement – for there could be no doubt whatever that, in this instance, I did actually hear (although from what direction it proceeded I found it impossible to say) a low and apparently distant, but harsh, protracted, and most unusual screaming or grating sound – the exact counterpart of what my fancy had already conjured up for the dragon's unnatural shriek as described by the romancer.

Oppressed, as I certainly was, upon the occurrence of this second and most extraordinary coincidence, by a thousand conflicting sensations, in which wonder and extreme terror were predominant, I still retained sufficient presence of mind to avoid exciting, by any observation, the sensitive nervousness of my companion. I was by no means certain that he had noticed the sounds in question; although, assuredly, a strange alteration had, during the last few minutes, taken place in his demeanor. From a position fronting my own, he had gradually brought round his chair, so as to sit with his face to the door of the chamber; and thus I could but partially perceive his features, although I saw that his lips trembled as if he were murmuring inaudibly. His head had dropped upon his breast – yet I knew that he was not asleep, from the wide and rigid opening of the eye as I caught a glance of it in profile. The motion of his body, too, was at variance with this idea – for he rocked from side to side with a gentle yet constant and uniform sway. Having rapidly taken notice of all this, I resumed the narrative of Sir Launcelot, which thus proceeded:

"And now, the champion, having escaped from the terrible fury of the dragon, bethinking himself of the brazen shield, and of the breaking up of the enchantment which was upon it, removed the carcass from out of the way before him, and approached valorously over the silver pavement of the castle to where the shield was upon the wall; which in sooth tarried not for his full coming, but fell down at his feet upon the silver floor, with a mighty great and terrible ringing sound."

No sooner had these syllables passed my lips, than – as if a shield of brass had indeed, at the moment, fallen heavily upon a floor of silver – I became aware of a distinct, hollow, metallic, and clangorous, yet apparently muffled, reverberation. Completely unnerved, I leaped to my feet; but the measured rocking movement of Usher was undisturbed. I rushed to the chair in which he sat. His eyes were bent fixedly before him, and throughout his whole countenance there reigned a stony rigidity. But, as I placed my hand upon his shoulder, there came a strong shudder over his whole person; a sickly smile quivered about his lips; and I saw that he spoke in a low, hurried, and gibbering murmur, as if unconscious of my presence. Bending closely over him, I at length drank in the hideous import of his words.

"Not hear it? – yes, I hear it, and *have* heard it. Long – long – long – many minutes, many hours, many days, have I heard it – yet I dared not – oh, pity me, miserable wretch that I am! – I dared not – I *dared* not speak! *We have put her living in the tomb!* Said I not that my senses were acute? I now tell you that I heard her first feeble movements in the hollow coffin. I heard them – many, many days ago – yet I dared not – *I dared not speak!* And now – to-night – Ethelred – ha! ha! – the breaking of the hermit's door, and the death-cry of the dragon, and the clangor of the shield – say, rather, the rending of her coffin, and the grating of the iron hinges of her prison, and her struggles within the coppered archway of the vault! Oh whither shall I fly? Will she not be here anon? Is she not hurrying to upbraid me for my haste? Have I not heard her footstep on the stair? Do I not distinguish that heavy and horrible beating of her heart? Madman!" – here he sprang furiously to his feet, and shrieked out his syllables, as if in the effort he were giving up his soul – "*Madman! I tell you that she now stands without the door!*"

As if in the superhuman energy of his utterance there had been found the potency of a spell – the huge antique pannels to which the speaker pointed, threw slowly back, upon the instant, their ponderous and ebony jaws. It was the work of the rushing gust – but then without those doors there *did* stand the lofty and enshrouded figure of the lady Madeline of Usher. There was blood upon her white robes, and the evidence of some bitter struggle upon every portion of her emaciated frame. For a moment she remained trembling and reeling to and fro upon the threshold – then, with a low moaning cry fell heavily inward upon the person of her brother, and in her violent and now final death-agonies, bore him to the floor a corpse, and a victim to the terrors he had anticipated.

From that chamber, and from that mansion, I fled aghast. The storm was still abroad in all its wrath as I found myself crossing the old causeway. Suddenly there shot along the path a wild light, and I turned to see whence a gleam so unusual could have issued; for the vast house and its shadows were alone behind me. The radiance was that of the full, setting and blood-red moon, which now shone vividly through that once barely discernible fissure, of which I have before spoken as extending from the roof of the building, in a zig-zag direction, to the base. While I gazed, this fissure rapidly widened – there came a fierce breath of the whirlwind – the entire orb of the satellite burst at once upon my sight – my brain reeled as I saw the mighty walls rushing asunder – there was a long tumultuous shouting sound like the voice of a thousand waters – and the deep and dank tarn at my feet closed sullenly and silently over the fragments of the *"House of Usher."*

Five Poems

The Raven

Once upon a midnight dreary, while I pondered, weak and weary,
Over many a quaint and curious volume of forgotten lore –
While I nodded, nearly napping, suddenly there came a tapping,
As of some one gently rapping, rapping at my chamber door.
"'Tis some visiter," I muttered, "tapping at my chamber door –
    Only this and nothing more."

Ah, distinctly I remember it was in the bleak December;
And each separate dying ember wrought its ghost upon the floor.
Eagerly I wished the morrow; – vainly I had sought to borrow
From my books surcease of sorrow – sorrow for the lost Lenore –
For the rare and radiant maiden whom the angels name Lenore –
    Nameless *here* for evermore.

And the silken, sad, uncertain rustling of each purple curtain
Thrilled me – filled me with fantastic terrors never felt before;
So that now, to still the beating of my heart, I stood repeating
Some late visiter entreating entrance at my chamber door; –
"'Tis some visiter entreating entrance at my chamber door; –
    This it is and nothing more."

Presently my soul grew stronger; hesitating then no longer,
"Sir," said I, "or Madam, truly your forgiveness I implore;
But the fact is I was napping, and so gently you came rapping,
And so faintly you came tapping, tapping at my chamber door,
That I scarce was sure I heard you" – here I opened wide the door; – –
    Darkness there and nothing more.

Deep into that darkness peering, long I stood there wondering, fearing,
Doubting, dreaming dreams no mortals ever dared to dream before;
But the silence was unbroken, and the stillness gave no token,
And the only word there spoken was the whispered word, "Lenore?"
This I whispered, and an echo murmured back the word, "Lenore!" –
    Merely this and nothing more.

Back into the chamber turning, all my soul within me burning,
Soon again I heard a tapping something louder than before.
"Surely" said I, "surely that is something at my window lattice;
Let me see, then, what thereat is, and this mystery explore –
Let my heart be still a moment, and this mystery explore; –
　　　'Tis the wind and nothing more!"

Open here I flung the shutter, when, with many a flirt and flutter,
In there stepped a stately Raven of the saintly days of yore;
Not the least obeisance made he; not a minute stopped or stayed he;
But, with mien[1] of lord or lady, perched above my chamber door –
Perched upon a bust of Pallas[2] just above my chamber door –
　　　Perched, and sat, and nothing more.

Then this ebony bird beguiling my sad fancy into smiling,
By the grave and stern decorum of the countenance it wore,
"Though thy crest be shorn and shaven, thou," I said, "art sure no craven,
Ghastly grim and ancient Raven wandering from the Nightly shore –
Tell me what thy lordly name is on the Night's Plutonian[3] shore!"
　　　Quoth the Raven, "Nevermore."

Much I marvelled this ungainly fowl to hear discourse so plainly,
Though its answer little meaning – little relevancy bore;
For we cannot help agreeing that no living human being
Ever yet was blessed with seeing bird above his chamber door –
Bird or beast upon the sculptured bust above his chamber door,
　　　With such name as "Nevermore."

But the Raven, sitting lonely on that placid bust, spoke only
That one word, as if his soul in that one word he did outpour.
Nothing farther then he uttered – not a feather then he fluttered –
Till I scarcely more than muttered "Other friends have flown before –
On the morrow *he* will leave me as my Hopes have flown before."
　　　Then the bird said, "Nevermore."

Startled at the stillness broken by reply so aptly spoken,
"Doubtless," said I, "what it utters is its only stock and store
Caught from some unhappy master whom unmerciful Disaster
Followed fast and followed faster till his songs one burden bore –
Till the dirges of his Hope that melancholy burden bore
　　　Of 'Never – nevermore'."

But the Raven still beguiling my sad fancy into smiling,
Straight I wheeled a cushioned seat in front of bird, and bust and door;

Notes

THE RAVEN
[1] Manner or expression.
[2] Pallas Athena, Greek goddess of wisdom.
[3] Pluto was god of the underworld in Greek mythology; thus "Plutonian shore" means the underworld or hell.

Then, upon the velvet sinking, I betook myself to linking
Fancy unto fancy, thinking what this ominous bird of yore –
What this grim, ungainly, ghastly, gaunt, and ominous bird of yore
Meant in croaking "Nevermore."

This I sat engaged in guessing, but no syllable expressing
To the fowl whose fiery eyes now burned into my bosom's core;
This and more I sat divining, with my head at ease reclining
On the cushion's velvet lining that the lamp-light gloated o'er,
But whose velvet-violet lining with the lamp-light gloating o'er
She shall press, ah, nevermore!

Then, methought, the air grew denser, perfumed from an unseen censer
Swung by Seraphim whose foot-falls tinkled on the tufted floor.
"Wretch," I cried, "thy God hath lent thee – by these angels he hath sent thee
Respite – respite and nepenthe[4] from thy memories of Lenore;
Quaff, oh quaff this kind nepenthe and forget this lost Lenore!"
Quoth the Raven, "Nevermore."

"Prophet!" said I, "thing of evil! – prophet still, if bird or devil! –
Whether Tempter sent, or whether tempest tossed thee here ashore,
Desolate yet all undaunted, on this desert land enchanted –
On this home by Horror haunted – tell me truly, I implore –
Is there – *is* there balm in Gilead?[5] – tell me – tell me, I implore!"
Quoth the Raven, "Nevermore."

"Prophet!" said I, "thing of evil! – prophet still, if bird or devil!
By that heaven that bends above us – by that God we both adore –
Tell this soul with sorrow laden if, within the distant Aidenn,[6]
It shall clasp a sainted maiden whom the angels name Lenore –
Clasp a rare and radiant maiden whom the angels name Lenore."
Quoth the Raven, "Nevermore."

"Be that word our sign of parting, bird or fiend!" I shrieked, upstarting –
"Get thee back into the tempest and the Night's Plutonian shore!
Leave no black plume as a token of that lie thy soul hath spoken!
Leave my loneliness unbroken! quit the bust above my door!
Take thy beak from out my heart, and take thy form from off my door!"
Quoth the Raven, "Nevermore."

And the Raven, never flitting, still is sitting, *still* is sitting
On the pallid bust of Pallas just above my chamber door;
And his eyes have all the seeming of a demon's that is dreaming,
And the lamp-light o'er him streaming throws his shadow on the floor;
And my soul from out that shadow that lies floating on the floor
Shall be lifted – nevermore!

Notes

4 Fabled drink causing forgetfulness.
5 Approximately: Is there relief in heaven?
6 Distant Aidenne (Eden): heaven.

The City in the Sea

Lo! Death has reared himself a throne
In a strange city lying alone
Far down within the dim West,
Where the good and the bad and the worst and the best
Have gone to their eternal rest.
There shrines and palaces and towers
(Time-eaten towers that tremble not!)
Resemble nothing that is ours.
Around, by lifting winds forgot,
Resignedly beneath the sky
The melancholy waters lie.

No rays from the holy heaven come down
On the long night-time of that town;
But light from out the lurid sea
Streams up the turrets silently –
Gleams up the pinnacles far and free –
Up domes – up spires – up kingly halls –
Up fanes – up Babylon-like walls –
Up shadowy long-forgotten bowers
Of sculptured ivy and stone flowers –
Up many and many a marvellous shrine
Whose wreathéd friezes intertwine
The viol, the violet, and the vine.

Resignedly beneath the sky
The melancholy waters lie.
So blend the turrets and shadows there
That all seem pendulous in air,
While from a proud tower in the town
Death looks gigantically down.

There open fanes and gaping graves
Yawn level with the luminous waves;
But not the riches there that lie
In each idol's diamond eye –
Not the gaily-jewelled dead
Tempt the waters from their bed;
For no ripples curl, alas!
Along that wilderness of glass –
No swellings tell that winds may be
Upon some far-off happier sea –
No heavings hint that winds have been
On seas less hideously serene.

But lo, a stir is in the air!
The wave – there is a movement there!
As if the towers had thrown aside,

In slightly sinking, the dull tide –
As if their tops had feebly given
A void within the filmy Heaven.
The waves have now a redder glow –
The hours are breathing faint and low –
And when, amid no earthly moans,
Down, down that town shall settle hence,
Hell, rising from a thousand thrones,
Shall do it reverence.

Ulalume: A Ballad

THE skies they were ashen and sober;
    The leaves they were crispéd and sere –
    The leaves they were withering and sere;
It was night in the lonesome October
    Of my most immemorial year;
It was hard by the dim lake of Auber,
    In the misty mid region of Weir –
It was down by the dank tarn of Auber,
    In the ghoul-haunted woodland of Weir.

Here once, through an alley Titanic,
    Of cypress, I roamed with my soul –
    Of cypress, with Psyché, my soul.
These were days when my heart was volcanic
    As the scoriac[1] rivers that roll –
    As the lavas that restlessly roll
Their sulphurous currents down Yaanek
    In the ultimate climes of the pole –
That groan as they roll down Mount Yaanek
    In the realms of the boreal pole.[2]

Our talk had been serious and sober,
    But our thoughts they were palsied and sere –
    Our memories were treacherous and sere –
For we knew not the month was October,
    And we marked not the night of the year –
    (Ah, night of all nights in the year!)
We noted not the dim lake of Auber,
    (Though once we had journeyed down here) –
Remember'd not the dank tarn of Auber,
    Nor the ghoul-haunted woodland of Weir.

And now, as the night was senescent,
    And star-dials pointed to morn –
    As the star-dials hinted of morn –

Notes

ULALUME: A BALLAD
[1] Full of scoria, rough fragments of lava.

[2] The North Pole.

At the end of our path a liquescent
   And nebulous lustre was born,
Out of which a miraculous crescent
   Arose with a duplicate horn –
Astarte's[3] bediamonded crescent
   Distinct with its duplicate horn.

And I said – "She is warmer than Dian:[4]
   She rolls through an ether of sighs –
   She revels in a region of sighs:
She has seen that the tears are not dry on
   These cheeks, where the worm never dies,
And has come past the stars of the Lion[5]
   To point us the path to the skies –
   To the Lethean[6] peace of the skies –
Come up, in despite of the Lion,
   To shine on us with her bright eyes –
Come up through the lair of the Lion,
   With love in her luminous eyes."

But Psyché, uplifting her finger,
   Said – "Sadly this star I mistrust –
   Her pallor I strangely mistrust:
Oh, hasten! – oh, let us not linger!
   Oh, fly! – let us fly! – for we must."
In terror she spoke, letting sink her
   Wings till they trailed in the dust –
In agony sobbed letting sink her
   Plumes till they trailed in the dust –
   Till they sorrowfully trailed in the dust.

I replied – "This is nothing but dreaming:
   Let us on by this tremulous light –
   Let us bathe in this crystalline light!
Its sybilic[7] splendor is beaming
   With hope and in beauty to-night:
   See, it flickers up the sky through the night!
Ah, we safely may trust to its gleaming,
   And be sure it will lead us aright –
We safely may trust to a gleaming
   That cannot but guide us aright,
   Since it flickers up to heaven through the night."

Notes

[3] Phoenician goddess of love and fertility, here associated with the planet Venus.
[4] Diana, Roman goddess of the moon.
[5] The constellation Leo.
[6] In Greek mythology, drinking from the waters of the River Lethe, in the underworld, would bring forgetfulness.
[7] The Sibyls were women who were regarded as prophets by the Greeks and Romans. "Sybilic" may mean "mysterious" in this context.

Thus I pacified Psyché and kissed her,
    And tempted her out of her gloom –
    And conquered her scruples and gloom;
And we passed to the end of the vista,
    But were stopped by the door of a tomb –
    By the door of a legended tomb;
And I said, "What is written, sweet sister,
    On the door of this legended tomb?"
    She replied, "Ulalume – Ulalume –
    'Tis the vault of thy lost Ulalume!"

Then my heart it grew ashen and sober
    As the leaves that were crispéd and sere –
    As the leaves that were withering and sere,
And I cried, "It was surely October
    On *this* very night of last year,
    That I journeyed – I journeyed down here –
    That I brought a dread burden down here –
    On this night of all nights in the year
    Oh, what demon has tempted me here?
Well I know, now, this dim lake of Auber,
    This misty mid region of Weir –
Well I know, now, this dank tarn of Auber,
    In the ghoul-haunted woodland of Weir."

Said *we* then – the two, then – "Ah, can it
    Have been that the woodlandish ghouls –
    The pitiful, the merciful ghouls –
To bar up our way and to ban it
    From the secret that lies in these wolds[8] –
    From the thing that lies hidden in these wolds –
Have drawn up the spectre of a planet
    From the limbo of lunary souls –
This sinfully scintillant planet
    From the hell of the planetary souls?"

Annabel Lee

It was many and many a year ago,
    In a kingdom by the sea,
That a maiden there lived whom you may know
    By the name of Annabel Lee; –
And this maiden she lived with no other thought
    Than to love and be loved by me.

She was a child and *I* was a child,
    In this kingdom by the sea,

Notes ───────────────────────────

[8] Moors: open, swampy land.

But we loved with a love that was more than love –
    I and my Annabel Lee –
With a love that the wingéd seraphs of Heaven
    Coveted her and me.

And this was the reason that, long ago,
    In this kingdom by the sea,
A wind blew out of a cloud by night
    Chilling my Annabel Lee;
So that her high-born kinsmen came
    And bore her away from me,
To shut her up in a sepulchre
    In this kingdom by the sea.

The angels, not half so happy in Heaven,
    Went envying her and me;
Yes! – that was the reason (as all men know,
    In this kingdom by the sea)
That the wind came out of the cloud, chilling
    And killing my Annabel Lee.

But our love it was stronger by far than the love
    Of those who were older than we –
    Of many far wiser than we –
And neither the angels in Heaven above
    Nor the demons down under the sea,
Can ever dissever my soul from the soul
    Of the beautiful Annabel Lee: –
For the moon never beams without bringing me dreams
    Of the beautiful Annabel Lee;

And the stars never rise but I feel the bright eyes
    Of the beautiful Annabel Lee;
And so, all the night-tide, I lie down by the side
Of my darling, my darling, my life and my bride
    In her sepulchre there by the sea –
    In her tomb by the side of the sea.

Dream-Land

By a route obscure and lonely,
Haunted by ill angels only,
Where an Eidolon,[1] named NIGHT,
On a black throne reigns upright,
I have reached these lands but newly

Notes

DREAM-LAND
[1] A phantom.

From an ultimate dim Thule[2] –
From a wild weird clime that lieth, sublime,
　　Out of SPACE – out of TIME.

Bottomless vales and boundless floods,
And chasms, and caves, and Titan woods,
With forms that no man can discover
For the tears that drip all over;
Mountains toppling evermore
Into seas without a shore;
Seas that restlessly aspire,
Surging, unto skies of fire;
Lakes that endlessly outspread
Their lone waters – lone and dead, –
Their still waters – still and chilly
With the snows of the lolling lily.

By the lakes that thus outspread
Their lone waters, lone and dead, –
Their sad waters, sad and chilly
With the snows of the lolling lily, –
By the mountains – near the river
Murmuring lowly, murmuring ever, –
By the gray woods, – by the swamp
Where the toad and the newt encamp, –
By the dismal tarns and pools
　　Where dwell the Ghouls, –
By each spot the most unholy –
In each nook most melancholy, –
There the traveller meets, aghast,
Sheeted Memories of the Past –
Shrouded forms that start and sigh
As they pass the wanderer by –
White-robed forms of friends long given,
In agony, to the Earth – and Heaven.

For the heart whose woes are legion
'Tis a peaceful, soothing region –
For the spirit that walks in shadow
O! it is an Eldorado!
But the traveller, travelling through it,
May not – dare not openly view it;
Never its mysteries are exposed
To the weak human eye unclosed;
So wills its King, who hath forbid
The uplifting of the fringed lid;
And thus the sad Soul that here passes
Beholds it but through darkened glasses.

Notes

[2] Ultimate Thule is proverbial for a place beyond all maps.

By a route obscure and lonely,
Haunted by ill angels only,
Where an Eidolon, named NIGHT,
On a black throne reigns upright,
I have wandered home but newly
From this ultimate dim Thule.

Herman Melville (1819–1891)

Melville was born to prosperity in New York City, but, following his father's bankruptcy and death (when Herman was 12), the family slid into genteel poverty. Denied the college education he once expected, Melville went to sea. He later said that a whaling ship was his Harvard and Yale. Most of his early tales of sailing and south sea adventures, based on his own experiences, were commercially successful. Friendship with Hawthorne, and discovery of the older writer's symbolic style, emboldened him to a series of experiments, beginning with *Moby-Dick* (1851), which pushed him into new artistic territory but ultimately cost him his audience. In his last decades he was nearly forgotten, publishing occasional verse and working on *Billy Budd* (1924), the novella that would be discovered and published years after his death.

Melville coined the phrase "the power of blackness" to describe the quality he most admired in Hawthorne's fiction; of course, Melville was naming his own values as well. With his strong belief in the reality of evil, a sense that reality is slippery and ambiguous, and an oppositional stance toward many conventional American values, the Gothic mode was natural, perhaps inevitable, for Melville.

Though not usually described in such terms, *Moby-Dick* is a Gothic novel, and Ahab, that "grand ungodly godlike man," one of the greatest of Gothic villain-heroes. *Pierre* (1852), the novel which followed his whale-and-truth hunting masterpiece, is explicitly in the Gothic mode. The novella *Benito Cereno* (1856) is a profound Gothic meditation on race in the Americas.

"The Bell-Tower" (1856) pays homage to Hawthorne in many ways, including an Italian setting which recalls such stories as "The Birthmark" and "Rappaccini's Daughter." Melville's tale is complex and many-layered. A series of biblical and historical allusions operate: to the Tower of Babel, the story of Sisera and Jael, Esther and Haman, and others. The allusions are linked by common themes of dominance and rebellion. Taken together, Melville implies a criticism of modern western society's attempt to dominate women, nature, machines, and other peoples: a quality of western civilization that is ultimately self-destructive. There were few Americans of the time who were capable of making this observation, which was true of the Renaissance and of Melville's era, and which still has validity.

Text: *The Piazza Tales* (New York: Dix & Edwards, 1856).

The Bell-Tower

"*Like negroes, these powers own man sullenly; mindful of their higher master; while serving, plot revenge.*"

"*The world is apoplectic with the high-living of ambition; and apoplexy has its fall.*"

"*Seeking to conquer a larger liberty, man but extends the empire of necessity.*"

From a Private MS

In the south of Europe, nigh a once-frescoed capital, now with dank mould cankering its bloom, central in a plain, stands what, at a distance, seems the black mossed stump of some immeasurable pine, fallen, in forgotten days, with Anak and the Titan.[1]

As all along where the pine tree falls, its dissolution leaves a mossy mound – last-flung shadow of the perished trunk; never lengthening, never lessening; unsubject to the fleet falsities of the sun; shade immutable and true gauge which cometh by prostration – so westward from what seems the stump, one steadfast spear of lichened ruin veins the plain.

From that tree-top, what birded chimes of silver throats had rung. A stone pine; a metallic aviary in its crown: the Bell-Tower, built by the great mechanician, the unblest foundling, Bannadonna.

Like Babel's, its base was laid in a high hour of renovated earth, following the second deluge, when the waters of the Dark Ages had dried up, and once more the green appeared. No wonder that, after so long and deep submersion, the jubilant expectation of the race should, as with Noah's sons, soar into Shinar[2] aspiration.

In firm resolve, no man in Europe at that period went beyond Bannadonna. Enriched through commerce with the Levant,[3] the state in which he lived voted to have the noblest Bell-Tower in Italy. His repute assigned him to be architect.

Stone by stone, month by month, the tower rose. Higher, higher; snail-like in pace, but torch or rocket in its pride.

After the masons would depart, the builder, standing alone upon its ever-ascending summit, at close of every day saw that he overtopped still higher walls and trees. He would tarry till a late hour there, wrapped in schemes of other and still loftier piles. Those who of saints' days thronged the spot – hanging to the rude poles of scaffolding, like sailors on yards, or bees on boughs, unmindful of lime and dust, and falling chips of stone – their homage not the less inspirited him to self-esteem.

At length the holiday of the Tower came. To the sound of viols, the climax-stone slowly rose in air, and, amid the firing of ordinance, was laid by Bannadonna's hands upon the final course. Then mounting it, he stood erect, alone, with folded arms; gazing upon the white summits of blue inland Alps, and whiter crests of bluer Alps off-shore – sights invisible from the plain. Invisible, too, from thence was that eye he turned below, when, like the cannon booms, came up to him the people's combustions of applause.

That which stirred them so was, seeing with what serenity the builder stood three hundred feet in air, upon an unrailed perch. This none but he durst do. But his periodic standing upon the pile, in each stage of its growth – such discipline had its last result.

Little remained now but the bells. These, in all respects, must correspond with their receptacle.

The minor ones were prosperously cast. A highly enriched one followed, of a singular make, intended for suspension in a manner before unknown. The purpose of this bell, its rotary motion, and connection with the clock-work, also executed at the time, will, in the sequel, receive mention.

In the one erection, bell-tower and clock-tower were united, though, before that period, such structures had commonly been built distinct; as the Campanile and the Torre dell' Orologio of St. Mark[4] to this day attest.

But it was upon the great state-bell that the founder lavished his more daring skill. In vain did some of the less elated magistrates here caution him; saying that

Notes

THE BELL-TOWER
[1] That is, a time even before the Greek Olympian gods.
[2] The Tower of Babel was built in the plain of Shinar. See Genesis 11.
[3] The eastern Mediterranean.
[4] In Venice.

though truly the tower was Titanic, yet limit should be set to the dependent weight of its swaying masses. But undeterred, he prepared his mammoth mould, dented with mythological devices; kindled his fires of balsamic firs; melted his tin and copper; and throwing in much plate, contributed by the public spirit of the nobles, let loose the tide.

The unleashed metals bayed like hounds. The workmen shrunk. Through their fright, fatal harm to the bell was dreaded. Fearless as Shadrach,[5] Bannadonna, rushing through the glow, smote the chief culprit with his ponderous ladle. From the smitten part, a splinter was dashed into the seething mass, and at once was melted in.

Next day a portion of the work was heedfully uncovered. All seemed right. Upon the third morning, with equal satisfaction, it was bared still lower. At length, like some old Theban king, the whole cooled casting was disinterred. All was fair except in one strange spot. But as he suffered no one to attend him in these inspections, he concealed the blemish by some preparation which none knew better to devise.

The casting of such a mass was deemed no small triumph for the caster; one, too, in which the state might not scorn to share. The homicide was overlooked. By the charitable that deed was but imputed to sudden transports of esthetic passion, not to any flagitious quality. A kick from an Arabian charger; not sign of vice, but blood.

His felony remitted by the judge, absolution given him by the priest, what more could even a sickly conscience have desired!

Honoring the tower and its builder with another holiday, the republic witnessed the hoisting of the bells and clockwork amid shows and pomps superior to the former.

Some months of more than usual solitude on Bannadonna's part ensued. It was not unknown that he was engaged upon something for the belfry, intended to complete it, and surpass all that had gone before. Most people imagined that the design would involve a casting like the bells. But those who thought they had some further insight, would shake their heads, with hints, that not for nothing did the mechanician keep so secret. Meantime, his seclusion failed not to invest his work with more or less of that sort of mystery pertaining to the forbidden.

Ere long he had a heavy object hoisted to the belfry, wrapped in a dark sack or cloak; a procedure sometimes had in the case of an elaborate piece of sculpture, or statue, which, being intended to grace the front of a new edifice, the architect does not desire exposed to critical eyes, till set up, finished, in its appointed place. Such was the impression now. But, as the object rose, a statuary[6] present observed, or thought he did, that it was not entirely rigid, but was, in a manner, pliant. At last, when the hidden thing had attained its final height, and, obscurely seen from below, seemed almost of itself to step into the belfry, as if with little assistance from the crane, a shrewd old blacksmith present ventured the suspicion that it was but a living man. This surmise was thought a foolish one, while the general interest failed not to augment.

Not without demur from Bannadonna, the chief-magistrate of the town, with an associate – both elderly men – followed what seemed the image up the tower. But, arrived at the belfry, they had little recompense. Plausibly entrenching himself behind the conceded mysteries of his art, the mechanician withheld present explanation. The magistrates glanced toward the cloaked object, which, to their surprise, seemed now to have changed its attitude, or else had before been more perplexingly concealed by the violent muffling action of the wind without. It now seemed seated upon some sort of frame, or chair, contained within the domino.[7] They observed

Notes

5 In Daniel 3, Shadrach is one of three men who survive being thrown into the "fiery furnace" by King Nebuchadnezzar.   6 Sculptor.

that nigh the top, in a sort of square, the web of the cloth, either from accident or design, had its warp partly withdrawn, and the cross-threads plucked out here and there, so as to form a sort of woven grating. Whether it were the low wind or no, stealing through the stone lattice-work, or only their own perturbed imaginations, is uncertain, but they thought they discerned a slight sort of fitful, spring-like motion, in the domino. Nothing, however incidental or insignificant, escaped their uneasy eyes. Among other things, they pried out, in a corner, an earthen cup, partly corroded and partly encrusted, and one whispered to the other, that this cup was just such a one as might, in mockery, be offered to the lips of some brazen statue, or, perhaps, still worse.

But, being questioned, the mechanician said, that the cup was simply used in his founder's business, and described the purpose; in short, a cup to test the condition of metals in fusion. He added, that it had got into the belfry by the merest chance.

Again, and again, they gazed at the domino, as at some suspicious incognito – at a Venetian mask. All sorts of vague apprehensions stirred them. They even dreaded lest, when they should descend, the mechanician, though without a flesh and blood companion, for all that, would not be left alone.

Affecting some merriment at their disquietude, he begged to relieve them, by extending a coarse sheet of workman's canvas between them and the object.

Meantime he sought to interest them in his other work; nor, now that the domino was out of sight, did they long remain insensible to the artistic wonders lying round them; wonders hitherto beheld but in their unfinished state; because, since hoisting the bells, none but the caster had entered within the belfry. It was one trait of his, that, even in details, he would not let another do what he could, without too great loss of time, accomplish himself. So, for several preceding weeks, whatever hours were unemployed in his secret design, had been devoted to elaborating the figures on the bells.

The clock-bell, in particular, now drew attention. Under a patient chisel, the latent beauty of its enrichments, before obscured by the cloudings incident to casting that beauty in its shyest grace, was now revealed. Round and round the bell, twelve figures of gay girls, garlanded, hand-in-hand, danced in a choral ring – the embodied hours.

"Bannadonna," said the chief, "this bell excels all else. No added touch could here improve. Hark!" hearing a sound, "was that the wind?"

"The wind, Eccellenza," was the light response. "But the figures, they are not yet without their faults. They need some touches yet. When those are given, and the – block yonder," pointed toward the canvas screen, "when Haman[8] there, as I merrily call him, – him? it, I mean – when Haman is fixed on this, his lofty tree, then, gentlemen, will I be most happy to receive you here again."

The equivocal reference to the object caused some return of restlessness. However, on their part, the visitors forbore further allusion to it, unwilling, perhaps, to let the foundling see how easily it lay within his plebeian art to stir the placid dignity of nobles.

"Well, Bannadonna," said the chief, "how long ere you are ready to set the clock going, so that the hour shall be sounded? Our interest in you, not less than in the work itself, makes us anxious to be assured of your success. The people, too, – why, they are shouting now. Say the exact hour when you will be ready."

"To-morrow, Eccellenza, if you listen for it, – or should you not, all the same – strange music will be heard. The stroke of one shall be the first from yonder bell," pointing to

Notes

[7] Cloak. But later in the passage "domino" refers to the figure within the cloak.

[8] In the book of Esther, the evil Haman builds a gallows on which to hang Mordecai, but is hanged on it himself. See Esther 5 and 7.

the bell adorned with girls and garlands, "that stroke shall fall there, where the hand of Una clasps Dua's. The stroke of one shall sever that loved clasp. To-morrow, then, at one o'clock, as struck here, precisely here," advancing and placing his finger upon the clasp, "the poor mechanic will be most happy once more to give you liege audience, in this his littered shop. Farewell till then, illustrious magnificoes, and hark ye for your vassal's stroke."

His still, Vulcanic[9] face hiding its burning brightness like a forge, he moved with ostentatious deference towards the scuttle, as if so far to escort their exit. But the junior magistrate, a kind hearted man, troubled at what seemed to him a certain sardonical disdain, lurking beneath the foundling's humble mien, and in Christian sympathy more distressed at it on his account than on his own, dimly surmising what might be the final fate of such a cynic solitaire, nor perhaps uninfluenced by the general strangeness of surrounding things, this good magistrate had glanced sadly, sideways from the speaker, and thereupon his foreboding eye had started at the expression of the unchanging face of the Hour Una.

"How is this, Bannadonna?" he lowly asked, "Una looks unlike her sisters."

"In Christ's name, Bannadonna," impulsively broke in the chief, his attention, for the first time, attracted to the figure, by his associate's remark, "Una's face looks just like that of Deborah, the prophetess, as painted by the Florentine, Del Fonca."[10]

"Surely, Bannadonna," lowly resumed the milder magistrate, "you meant the twelve should wear the same jocundly abandoned air. But see, the smile of Una seems a fatal one. 'Tis different."

While his mild associate was speaking, the chief glanced, inquiringly, from him to the caster, as if anxious to mark how the discrepancy would be accounted for. As the chief stood, his advanced foot was on the scuttle's curb.

Bannadonna spoke.

"Eccellenza, now that, following your keener eye, I glance upon the face of Una, I do, indeed perceive some little variance. But look all round the bell, and you will find no two faces entirely correspond. Because there is a law in art – – – but the cold wind is rising more; these lattices are but a poor defense. Suffer me, magnificoes, to conduct you, at least, partly on your way. Those in whose well-being is a public stake, should be heedfully attended."

"Touching the look of Una, you were saying, Bannadonna, that there was a certain law in art," observed the chief, as the three now descended the stone shaft, "pray, tell me, then –."

"Pardon; another time, Eccellenza; – the tower is damp."

"Nay, I must rest, and hear it now. Here, – here is a wide landing, and through this leeward slit, no wind, but ample light. Tell us of your law; and at large."

"Since, Eccellenza, you insist, know that there is a law in art, which bars the possibility of duplicates. Some years ago, you may remember, I graved a small seal for your republic, bearing, for its chief device, the head of your own ancestor, its illustrious founder. It becoming necessary, for the customs' use, to have innumerable impressions for bales and boxes, I graved an entire plate, containing one hundred of the seals. Now, though, indeed, my object was to have those hundred heads identical, and though, I dare say, people think them so, yet, upon closely scanning an uncut impression from

Notes

[9] In classical mythology, Vulcan was the blacksmith of the gods.
[10] In Judges 4, Deborah's prophecy is that a much larger enemy force would be defeated by the Israelite army, but a woman would receive the glory. The enemy general, Sisera, flees the battlefield and seeks refuge in the tent of Jael. After he falls asleep, Jael drives a tent peg through his skull. The painter Del Fonca is apparently Melville's invention, but the story was often the subject of paintings.

the plate, no two of those five-score faces, side by side, will be found alike. Gravity is the air of all; but, diversified in all. In some, benevolent; in some, ambiguous; in two or three, to a close scrutiny, all but incipiently malign, the variation of less than a hair's breadth in the linear shadings round the mouth sufficing to all this. Now, Eccellenza, transmute that general gravity into joyousness, and subject it to twelve of those variations I have described, and tell me, will you not have my hours here, and Una one of them? But I like –."

"Hark! is that – a footfall above?"

"Mortar, Eccellenza; sometimes it drops to the belfry-floor from the arch where the stone-work was left undressed. I must have it seen to. As I was about to say: for one, I like this law forbidding duplicates. It evokes fine personalities. Yes, Eccellenza, that strange, and – to you – uncertain smile, and those fore-looking eyes of Una, suit Bannadonna very well."

"Hark! – sure we left no soul above?"

"No soul, Eccellenza; rest assured, no soul. – Again the mortar."

"It fell not while we were there."

"Ah, in your presence, it better knew its place, Eccellenza," blandly bowed Bannadonna.

"But, Una," said the milder magistrate, "she seemed intently gazing on you; one would have almost sworn that she picked you out from among us three."

"If she did, possibly, it might have been her finer apprehension, Eccellenza."

"How, Bannadonna? I do not understand you."

"No consequence, no consequence, Eccellenza – but the shifted wind is blowing through the slit. Suffer me to escort you on; and then, pardon, but the toiler must to his tools."

"It may be foolish, Signore," said the milder magistrate, as, from the third landing, the two now went down unescorted, "but somehow, our great mechanician moves me strangely. Why, just now, when he so superciliously replied, his walk seemed Sisera's, God's vain foe, in Del Fonca's painting. – And that young, sculptured Deborah, too. Aye, and that – "

"Tush, tush, Signore!" returned the chief. "A passing whim. Deborah? – Where's Jael, pray?"

"Ah," said the other, as they now stepped upon the sod, "Ah, Signore, I see you leave your fears behind you with the chill and gloom; but mine, even in this sunny air, remain. Hark!"

It was a sound from just within the tower door, whence they had emerged. Turning, they saw it closed.

"He has slipped down and barred us out," smiled the chief; "but it is his custom."

Proclamation was now made, that the next day, at one hour after meridian, the clock would strike, and – thanks to the mechanician's powerful art – with unusual accompaniments. But what those should be, none as yet could say. The announcement was received with cheers.

By the looser sort, who encamped about the tower all night, lights were seen gleaming through the topmost blindwork, only disappearing with the morning sun. Strange sounds, too, were heard, or were thought to be, by those whom anxious watching might not have left mentally undisturbed, sounds, not only of some ringing implement, but also – so they said – half-suppressed screams and plainings, such as might have issued from some ghostly engine, over-plied.

Slowly the day drew on; part of the concourse chasing the weary time with songs and games, till, at last, the great blurred sun rolled, like a football, against the plain.

At noon, the nobility and principal citizens came from the town in cavalcade; a guard of soldiers, also, with music, the more to honor the occasion.

Only one hour more. Impatience grew. Watches were held in hands of feverish men, who stood, now scrutinizing their small dial-plates, and then, with neck thrown back, gazing toward the belfry, as if the eye might foretell that which could only be made sensible to the ear; for, as yet, there was no dial to the tower-clock.

The hour-hands of a thousand watches now verged within a hair's breadth of the figure 1. A silence, as of the expectation of some Shiloh,[11] pervaded the swarming plain. Suddenly a dull, mangled sound – naught ringing in it; scarcely audible, indeed, to the outer circles of the people – that dull sound dropped heavily from the belfry. At the same moment, each man stared at his neighbor blankly. All watches were upheld. All hour-hands were at – had passed – the figure 1. No bell-stroke from the tower. The multitude became tumultuous.

Waiting a few moments, the chief magistrate, commanding silence, hailed the belfry, to know what thing unforeseen had happened there.

No response.

He hailed again and yet again.

All continued hushed.

By his order the soldiers burst in the tower-door; when, stationing guards to defend it from the now surging mob, the chief, accompanied by his former associate, climbed the winding stairs. Half-way up, they stopped to listen. No sound. Mounting faster, they reached the belfry; but, at the threshold, startled at the spectacle disclosed. A spaniel which, unbeknown to them, had followed them thus far, stood shivering as before some unknown monster in a brake: or, rather, as if it snuffed foot-steps leading to some other world.

Bannadonna lay prostrate and bleeding at the base of the bell which was adorned with girls and garlands. He lay at the feet of the hour Una; his head coinciding, in a vertical line, with her left hand, clasped by the hour Dua. With downcast face impending over him, like Jael over nailed Sisera in the tent, was the domino; now no more becloaked.

It had limbs, and seemed clad in a scaly mail, lustrous as a dragon-beetle's. It was manacled, and its clubbed arms were uplifted, as if, with its manacles, once more to smite its already smitten victim. One advanced foot of it was inserted beneath the dead body, as if in the act of spurning it.

Uncertainty falls on what now followed.

It were but natural to suppose that the magistrates would at first shrink from immediate personal contact with what they saw. At the least, for a time, they would stand in involuntary doubt; it may be, in more or less of horrified alarm. Certain it is, that an arquebuss[12] was called for from below. And some add, that its report, followed by a fierce whiz, as of the sudden snapping of a main-spring, with a steely din, as if a stack of sword-blades should be dashed upon a pavement, these blended sounds came ringing to the plain, attracting every eye far upward to the belfry, whence, through the lattice-work, thin wreaths of smoke were curling.

Some averred that it was the spaniel, gone mad by fear, which was shot. This, others, denied. True it was, the spaniel never more was seen; and, probably, for some unknown reason, it shared the burial now to be related of the domino. For, whatever the preceding circumstances might have been, the first instinctive panic over, or else all ground of reasonable fear removed, the two magistrates, by themselves, quickly rehooded the figure in the dropped cloak wherein it had been hoisted. The same night, it was secretly lowered to the ground, smuggled to the beach, pulled far out to sea, and sunk. Nor to

Notes

11 The Lord appears to Samuel at a place called Shiloh (1 Samuel 3:21); thus Shiloh has come to mean a site of revelation.

12 Also called a harquebus: a primitive musket.

any after urgency, even in free convivial hours, would the twain ever disclose the full secrets of the belfry.

From the mystery unavoidably investing it, the popular solution of the foundling's fate involved more or less of supernatural agency. But some few less unscientific minds pretended to find little difficulty in otherwise accounting for it. In the chain of circumstancial inferences drawn, there may, or may not, have been some absent or defective links. But, as the explanation in question is the only one which tradition has explicitly preserved, in dearth of better, it will here be given. But, in the first place, it is requisite to present the supposition entertained as to the entire motive and mode, with their origin, of the secret design of Bannadonna; the minds above-mentioned assuming to penetrate as well into his soul as into the event. The disclosure will indirectly involve reference to peculiar matters, none of the clearest, beyond the immediate subject.

At that period, no large bell was made to sound otherwise than as at present, by agitation of a tongue within, by means of ropes, or percussion from without, either from cumbrous machinery, or stalwart watchmen, armed with heavy hammers, stationed in the belfry, or in sentry-boxes on the open roof, according as the bell was sheltered or exposed.

It was from observing these exposed bells, with their watchmen, that the foundling, as was opined, derived the first suggestion of his scheme. Perched on a great mast or spire, the human figure, viewed from below, undergoes such a reduction of its apparent size, as to obliterate its intelligent features. It evinces no personality. Instead of bespeaking volition, its gestures rather resemble the automatic ones of the arms of a telegraph.

Musing, therefore, upon the purely Punchinello[13] aspect of the human figure thus beheld, it had indirectly occurred to Bannadonna to devise some metallic agent, which should strike the hour with its metallic hand, with even greater precision than the vital one. And, moreover, as the vital watchman on the roof, sallying from his retreat at the given periods, walked to the bell with uplifted mace, to smite it, Bannadonna had resolved that his invention should likewise possess the power of locomotion, and, along with that, the appearance, at least, of intelligence and will.

If the conjectures of those who claimed acquaintance with the intent of Bannadonna be thus far correct, no unenterprising spirit could have been his. But they stopped not here; intimating that though, indeed, his design had, in the first place, been prompted by the sight of the watchman, and confined to the devising of a subtle substitute for him; yet, as is not seldom the case with projectors, by insensible gradations, proceeding from comparatively pigmy aims to Titanic ones, the original scheme had, in its anticipated eventualities, at last, attained to an unheard of degree of daring. He still bent his efforts upon the locomotive figure for the belfry, but only as a partial type of an ulterior creature, a sort of elephantine Helot,[14] adapted to further, in a degree scarcely to be imagined, the universal conveniences and glories of humanity; supplying nothing less than a supplement to the Six Days' Work; stocking the earth with a new serf, more useful than the ox, swifter than the dolphin, stronger than the lion, more cunning than the ape, for industry an ant, more fiery than serpents, and yet, in patience, another ass. All excellences of all God-made creatures, which served man, were here to receive advancement, and then to be combined in one. Talus was to have been the all-accomplished Helot's name. Talus,[15] iron slave to Bannadonna, and, through him, to man.

Notes

[13] Punchinello is a short, fat character in traditional Italian puppet shows.

[14] The Helots were a people enslaved by the Spartans.

[15] In mythology, a bronze giant in Crete; in Spenser's *The Faerie Queene*, an iron man armed with an iron flail.

Here, it might well be thought that, were these last conjectures to the foundling's secrets not erroneous, then must he have been hopelessly infected with the craziest chimeras of his age; far outgoing Albert Magnus and Cornelius Agrippa.[16] But the contrary was averred. However marvelous his design, however apparently transcending not alone the bounds of human invention, but those of divine creation, yet the proposed means to be employed were alleged to have been confined within the sober forms of sober reason. It was affirmed that, to a degree of more than skeptic scorn, Bannadonna had been without sympathy for any of the vain-glorious irrationalities of his time. For example, he had not concluded, with the visionaries among the meta-physicians, that between the finer mechanic forces and the ruder animal vitality, some germ of correspondence might prove discoverable. As little did his scheme partake of the enthusiasm of some natural philosophers, who hoped, by physiological and chemical inductions, to arrive at a knowledge of the source of life, and so qualify themselves to manufacture and improve upon it. Much less had he aught in common with the tribe of alchemists, who sought, by a species of incantations, to evoke some surprising vitality from the laboratory. Neither had he imagined with certain san-guine theosophists, that, by faithful adoration of the Highest, unheard-of powers would be vouchsafed to man. A practical materialist, what Bannadonna had aimed at was to have been reached, not by logic, not by crucible, not by altars; but by plain vice-bench and hammer. In short, to solve nature, to steal into her, to intrigue beyond her, to procure some one else to bind her to his hand; – these, one and all, had not been his objects; but, asking no favors from any element or any being, of himself, to rival her, outstrip her, and rule her. He stooped to conquer. With him, common sense was theurgy; machinery, miracle; Prometheus,[17] the heroic name for machinist; man, the true God.

Nevertheless, in his initial step, so far as the experimental automation for the belfry was concerned, he allowed fancy some little play; or perhaps, what seemed his fanci-fulness was but his utilitarian ambition collaterally extended. In figure, the creature for the belfry should not be likened after the human pattern, nor any animal one, nor after the ideals, however wild, of ancient fable, but equally in aspect as in organism be an original production; the more terrible to behold, the better.

Such, then, were the suppositions as to the present scheme, and the reserved intent. How, at the very threshold, so unlooked for a catastrophe overturned all, or rather, what was the conjecture here, is now to be set forth.

It was thought that on the day preceding the fatality, his visitors having left him, Bannadonna had unpacked the belfry image, adjusted it, and placed it in the retreat provided, – a sort of sentry-box in one corner of the belfry; in short, throughout the night, and for some part of the ensuing morning, he had been engaged in arranging every thing connected with the domino: the issuing from the sentry-box each sixty minutes; sliding along a grooved way, like a railway; advancing to the clock-bell, with uplifted manacles; striking it at one of the twelve junctions of the four-and-twenty hands: then wheeling, circling the bell, and retiring to the post, there to bide for another sixty minutes when the same process was to be repeated; the bell, by a cunning mechanism, meantime turning on its vertical axis, so as to present, to the descending mace, the clasped hands of the next two figures, when it would strike two, three, and so on to the end. The musical metal in this time-bell being so managed in the fusion,

Notes

[16] Albertus Magnus (?1206–80), scholastic philosopher, teacher of Thomas Aquinas; Henry Cornelius Agrippa von Nettesheim (1486–1535), German writer, solider, physician, and magician.

[17] Greek demigod who stole fire from the gods and gave it to humans.

by some art perishing with its originator, that each of the clasps of the four-and-twenty hands should give forth its own peculiar resonance when parted.

But on the magic metal, the magic and metallic stranger never struck but that one stroke, drove but that one nail, severed but that one clasp, by which Bannadonna clung to his ambitious life. For, after winding up the creature in the sentry-box, so that, for the present, skipping the intervening hours, it should not emerge till the hour of one, but should then infallibly emerge, and, after deftly oiling the grooves whereon it was to slide, it was surmised that the mechanician must then have hurried to the bell, to give his final touches to its sculpture. True artist, he here became absorbed; and absorption still further intensified, it may be, by his striving to abate that strange look of Una; which, though, before others, he had treated with such unconcern, might not, in secret, have been without its thorn.

And so, for the interval, he was oblivious of his creature; which, not oblivious of him, and true to its creation, and true to its heedful winding up, left its post precisely at the given moment; along its well-oiled route, slid noiselessly towards its mark; and aiming at the hand of Una, to ring one clangorous note, dully smote the intervening brain of Bannadonna, turned backwards to it; the manacled arms then instantly upspringing to their hovering poise. The falling body clogged the thing's return; so there it stood, still impending over Bannadonna, as if whispering some post-mortem terror. The chisel lay dropped from the hand, but beside the hand; the oil-cask spilled across the iron track.

In this unhappy end, not unmindful of the rare genius of the mechanician, the republic decreed him a stately funeral. It was resolved that the great bell – the one whose casting had been jeopardized through the timidity of the ill-starred workman – should be rung upon the entrance of the bier into the cathedral. The most robust man of the country round was assigned the office of bell-ringer.

But as the pall-bearers entered the cathedral porch, naught but a broken and disastrous sound, like that of some lone Alpine land-slide, fell from the tower upon their ears. And then, all was hushed.

Glancing backwards, they saw the groined belfry crashed sideways in. It afterwards appeared that the powerful peasant who had the bell-rope in his charge, wishing to test at once the full glory of the bell, had swayed down upon the rope with one concentrate jerk. The mass of quaking metal, too ponderous for its frame, and strangely feeble somewhere at its top, loosed from its fastening, tore sideways down, and tumbling in one sheer fall, three hundred feet to the soft sward below, buried itself inverted and half out of sight.

Upon its disinterment, the main fracture was found to have started from a small spot in the ear; which, being scraped, revealed a defect, deceptively minute, in the casting; which defect must subsequently have been pasted over with some unknown compound.

The remolten metal soon reässumed its place in the tower's repaired super-structure. For one year the metallic choir of birds sang musically in its belfry-bough-work of sculptured blinds and traceries. But on the first anniversary of the tower's completion – at early dawn, before the concourse had surrounded it – an earthquake came; one loud crash was heard. The stone-pine, with all its bower of songsters, lay overthrown upon the plain.

So the blind slave obeyed its blinder lord; but in obedience, slew him. So the creator was killed by the creature. So the bell was too heavy for its tower. So that bell's main weakness was where man's blood had flawed it. And so pride went before the fall.*

Notes

* It was not necessary to adhere to the peculiar notation of Italian time. Adherence to it would have impaired the familiar comprehension of the story. Kindred remarks might be offered touching an anachronism or two that occur. [Melville's note.]

George Lippard (1822–1854)

George Lippard was a flamboyant Philadelphia author and editor and political reformer. David S. Reynolds, the scholar most responsible for his recent rediscovery, notes parallels between Lippard's work and a number of the best-known American authors, and possible influences on them, including Poe (a friend of Lippard), Hawthorne, Melville, Whitman, and Mark Twain. *The Quaker City; or, The Monks of Monk Hall* (1845) sold more copies than any American novel before *Uncle Tom's Cabin*.

This seminal, if long-forgotten, Gothic novel, seems stylistically undisciplined, but has a carefully designed structure. A number of lurid plots, many involving seduction or rape and revenge, take place over a few days; all pass through Monk Hall, the decaying mansion used as a gambling club and brothel by Philadelphia's elite, and as a hide-out by the city's criminals. Thus the sprawling mansion, with its secret chambers, trap doors, and burial vaults, is both an emblem of the corrupt structure of the city and of the complex, many-layered novel itself. Presiding over Monk Hall is a deformed, one-eyed monster named "Devil-Bug," whom Reynolds calls "perhaps the most gleefully evil, sadistic character in American literature."

The following selection is a kind of intermission from the novel's several plots. The setting is underground chamber of Monk Hall, strewn about with torture implements and bones of victims. Devil-Bug and some thirty criminals have been captured by police. (Devil-Bug, of course, will escape.) While awaiting transport to prison, Devil-Bug tells this story of serving as a hangman, a particularly pleasant episode of his life, as he recalls it. The story he tells provides a chilling insight into the mind of this character, and at the same time reveals Lippard's moral outrage at a corrupt society.

In this excerpt, Lippard's haphazard use of quotation marks has been regularized for clarity, but his eccentric spelling and punctuation are otherwise retained.

Text: George Lippard, *The Quaker City; or The Monks of Monk Hall: A Romance of Philadelphia Life, Mystery, and Crime* (Philadelphia: T. B. Peterson & Brothers, [1845]).

from *The Quaker City; or, The Monks of Monk Hall*

The Hangman's Glee*

"Hurray for hangin' say I! It's only a kick an' a jerk, and a feller goes like a shot, right slap into kingdom come. It does wons heart good to look upon them two

Notes

FROM *THE QUAKER CITY; OR, THE MONKS OF MONK HALL*
* The main incidents of this episode are strictly true. The Hangman, of course, is alone, responsible for the language and opinions of the story. [Lippard's note.]

pieces o' timber, with a beam fixed cross-wise, and a rope danglin' down – hurray for hangin'!

"It war'n't more nor five years since, that I hung a man. Talk o' hangin' a dog or a cat, wot is it to hangin' a man? When I was quite a little shaver I used to hang a puppy or a pussy-cat, and I used to think it quite refreshin'. But hangin' a man? Ho-hoo! That's the ticket!

"It was a fine June morning, and I walks along one o' them dark entries in the Eastern Pennytensherry, and I walks into a cell. It was purty dark I tell you. A bit of light came through the narrer winder, an' in one corner o' the cell I sees a young man, with a white face, and curly dark hair. He was settin' in a corner, with his knees drawed up to his chin.

"'Get up' ses I, 'get up young man. There's business for you.' He raises his head, an he gives a kind o' start. You see I'm not werry han'some, at any time, but just then, I looked pertiklerly dev'lish. The Marshal had giv' me a yard or two of black crepe, and I'd put it round my face, with a hole cut, for my eye, to look thro' and –

"'Come my feller,' ses I, 'There's business for you.'

"'I did'n't murder the Capt'n,' ses he. 'Before God, if it was my last word I did'n't –'

"Yo' see he'd been condemned for murderin' the Capt'in of a wessel at sea, an' there wos considerable doubt about it, but as he was a poor devil, and a stranger, the Judge and the jury, thought the best thing they could do for him was to hang him, for *fear you* know he might'n't be able to get work the next winter.

"'Come my chap,' ses I, a-bindin' his hands. 'I'm an ugly devil, but you need'n't be frightened, for I'm sent here by the LAW,' pronouncin' the word big you know? 'THE LAW, wot takes care ov everybody and can't never be bribed. Come feller.'

"I bound his hands, and led him from the cell. The poor fool was mutterin' nonsense about his mother and sister all the while. In a minnit we stood under the archway o' the prissin gate. It wos werry cold and damp. A kind of chill, went thro' me when I looked at the pitiful face of the boy, for he wasn't more nor ninenteen, but that was only the cold you know? It only tuk a minnit to rig him out in a white roundabout,[1] and then I led him out of the prissin gate.

"Hurray, wot a sight! Soldiers in gay coats and spangles, all standin around a cart, with a pine box, an' a parson in it!

"'Wot's that?' says Charley – for that wos his name – 'Wot's that?'

"'Oh' ses I, 'that's the blue sky, and yander's Bush Hill, an' yander' Fairmount Water Works, and them things wot yo' hear singin' is birds and –'

"'But that thing in the cart,' ses he.

"'That's a black bird, or rather a crow come to pray over yer dead body, boy. It's a parson, Charley. For you're to be *hung*, to day hung, *hung*, d'ye hear, and these soldiers and the parson and me, is to be chief mourners at yer funeral.'

"I never saw sich a feller in my life! His lip was like iron, and his dark eye, firm as rivet.

"'But that,' ses he, pintin' to th' cart, 'That box –'

"'That's yer coffin,' ses I, helpin' him into the cart, 'Sit down an' take a cheer.' He sit down on the coffin, mutterin' about his mother and sisters in some far away land, an' I seized the reins and giv' the horse a lick, and the soldiers began to march, and the wheels o' th' cart to rumble, and the parson to look solemn – hurray!

Notes ———————————————————————

[1] A short jacket.

"Trum-te-trum-te-tum-tum, went the drums a-beatin' the dead march, rattle, rattle, went the wheels of the cart, and away we goes, down Schuylkill Sixth Street, toward Bush Hill.

"Charley, the poor devil, wot was a-goin' to be hung, set on th' cart a-groanin'. 'My mother, my mother!' he cries, 'and my sister Annie – oh God! Oh God!'

"'Don't swear,' ses the parson, 'My werry dear young friend, don't you know its wrong to swear, and them wot does it, 'ill be burnt in th' burnin' lake –'

"'Parson,' ses I, turning suddenly round, 'What 'ill you have for dinner to day?'

"'Roast lamb with mint sauce,' ses he, and then he blushed, for I'd took him all aback. I know'd he was thinkin' on his dinner all the while, and I thought I'd expose the old genelman.

"'Hurray,' ses I, as the cart reached the top of a little hill in the middle of the dusty street. 'Hurray' ses I, 'look yander my boy!'

"Charley looks up, and gives a groan. What d'ye think he saw? A great big, black, mass of people, reaching over Bush Hill, fur as the eye could see, with a gibbet rising in the middle of the crowd. The hot sun, was shinin' down upon us, and the drums went trum-te-trum, and the cart wheels went rumble rumble, and on we went, the poor devil that wos to be hung, the Parson that wos to pray over him, and *me* that wos to hang him!

"The mob seed us, and like a shot they rushed toward the cart. 'There he is,' ses a woman with a baby in her arms; 'Where, where!' roars a man who come sixty miles a-foot to see him hung, 'By G–d he'll die game,' screams a gambler with a sweat cloth in one hand and a table in the tother.

"You never see'd sich a mob in all your life. All over Bush Hill, from the old Hospital, where the people used to die of yeller fever, away towards Fairmount, that crowd was scattered, hooting, yelling, swearing and screaming like devils, as they see'd the cart and the soldiers, movin' toward the gibbet.

"'Keep up your spirits Charley,' ses I, 'The Law –' pronouncin' it big – 'The LAW is a merciful old codger, is the law! There's a strong rope for you yonder, and a good stout piece o' timber –'

"As I said this, whether it was from the heat or the dust, or whether the poor crittur was ashamed to be seen in sich work, I never could 'xactly tell, but the horse fell down like *that*, and lay in the middle o' th' road, dead as a stone.

"The mob giv' a yell! I puts the coffin on my shoulder, and hooks Charlie's arm in mine, and beckons to the Parson, and the Captain giv's the word to the soldiers, and away we tramps toward the gallows.

"'The Lord is merciful,' whispered the Parson. 'His word is peace and good will to men –'

"'Then why do they hang me?' cries Charley, as he went boldly for'ard, 'Oh my God – my mother, and my sister!' and then the feller begins to moan, and talk of his mammy and sister sittin' at the cottage door in England, expectin' their Charley to come back and, 'Here,' ses he, 'Here am I goin' to be hung like a dog, like a dog,' yes ses he repeatin' it, *Like a dog!*

"As he sed this, a white pidgeon fluttered over his head. The boy looks up, and a tear stands in his eye.

"'Look here my chap,' ses he to me, as I went trampin' on with the coffin on my shoulder, 'Jist sich a pidgeon as that, white as snow, I gave to Annie afore I left home –'

"Would you believe it? The words was n't out o' his lips when the pidgeon fell dead at his feet, in the hot dust of the road.

"The mob yelled agin! What they yelled about, I never could tell, but there's some-thin' so jolly in seein' a live man, walking to a gallows, that I could'nt help joinin' in with 'em; 'Hurray,' ses I, 'Hurray for the gibbet! The good old gallows law for ever an' Amen!'*

"Charley did n't say a word arter that, but went up the gallow's steps without so much as a start. Wasn't it a grand sight for us fellers on the platform? There was the Marshall, a fine fat faced feller; there was the Parson, in his white cravat and black clothes, there was I, Devil-Bug, the Hangman, with the crepe over my face, and there was the poor devil, as wos to be hung, standin' in the midst of us all, dressed in a white roundabout, with a face like a cloth, and curly hair, dark as jet.

"'Hurray,' ses I, 'wot a sight! Keep up yer spirits Charley. Jist look at the people, come to see yo' hung! Look at the Soldiers with their feathers and bagnets,² jist look at the women, with babies in their arms, look at the gamblers, playin' thimble rig, look at the rum, my boy, in the tents yonder, and then, hurray! Look at the folks scattered all over Bush Hill, on the house tops away off yonder, and far down the streets! Hurray, my boy, there's a big crowd come to see you die, and so wot's the use o' grumblin' about yer mother and sister, and a cussed white pidgeon?'

"The mob giv' a howl! It was near twelve o'clock, and they wanted their show.

"'It wants ten minnits o' th' time,' ses the Marshall, an' the Parson, comes up to Charley, and taps him on the shoulder, and ses he, 'Look up, my friend. God is merci-ful. Let us pray!'

"And then we all kneeled down, and the Parson made a short prayer about the Mercy o' God and the widders and orphans, and them deluded devils as had n't sich a good Gospel an' sich a stout Gallows. While he was prayin' I saw two gentlemen, with knowin' faces, slyly creepin' up the ladder, and lookin' over the edge o' th' platform. I know'd 'em well. I'd stole dead bodies for 'em a hundred times. They were doctors, a-waitin' for the dead body o' Charley the English boy.³

"The Parson cuts his prayer off short, and we all gits on our feet ag'in.

"'Come Charley' ses I, don't be frightened, an' I fixes the knot behind his ear. A delicate knot, it was! You know it was tied right behind the ear, so that his fall, would break his neck, like *that!* Then I felt his smooth neck, and ses I, 'it 'ill soon be over Charley, and you wont think anything more of yer mother, or yer sister, or that cussed white pidgeon.'

"'Feller,' ses he, 'yer honest. Here's all I have to giv' yo'. Keep it for my sake.'

"An' he giv' me the striped handkercher from his neck. It was purty hot, I tell yo', but a shiver ran over me, when he did this.

"'Time's up,' ses the Marshall. The mob giv' a yell. The doctors waitin' for the body, comes up a step higher on the ladder, and the Parson, smacked his lips, as tho' he felt uncommon hungry.

"'A glass o' water,' ses Charley, in a faint way, but still as firm as a rock. A boy with blue eyes an' yeller hair, was hoisted on a man's shoulder's, from among the mob, till he was even with the platform.

"'God bless yo' my boy,' ses Charley, 'An' may yo' never have a mother an' a sister, a-sittin' at the cottage door, a-waitin' fur yo' to come home, when yer a-hangin' in some far off land, hangin' like a dog!'

"He takes the glass o' water; he looks at it for a minnit; and then at the sky, and the sun, and the great big crowd, and the roofs of the houses filled with people. I'll never

Notes

* "The good old gallows law, for ever, and ever, A-men!" [Lippard's note]
² Possibly Devil-Bug's pronunciation of "burgonets," a type of helmet.

³ The insatiable desire of physicians for corpses to dissect is a commonplace of fiction of this period.

forgit that look! His eyes looked as if they was set afire, and his lower lip, worked like a bit o' twisted rope.

" 'I am innocent,' ses he, and then, cool as you please, he pours the tumbler o' water, right down on the platform floor.

" 'That water will dry up, but my blood, will never dry up, from your soil, while yonder sun shines!'

" 'Time's up,' ses the Marshall. I stuck the white cap on his forehead. I draw'd it over his eyes! Hurray! What a look he giv' as the cap, came down over his forehead. He stood in the centre o' th' platform, with the cap over his eyes an' the rope around his neck. The mob held their breath. In that big crowd, you could n't hear the sound of a human voice.

"With one kick o' my foot, I pushed away the trap. For a minnit the sun seemed dark, and the next minnit – ho, hoo! There quiverin' strugglin', twistin', was the body of a man, plungin' at the end of a rope, with his tongue – black as a hat – stickin' out from under the edge o' th' white cap – hurray!

"There was a noise like water pourin' from a jug turned up-side down, there was a plunge and a jerk and then the body o' the poor devil quivered like a leaf. The mob gave one yell, which sounded as tho' Fairmount Dam had broke loose, with a devil shoutin' from every wave! You could see a quiverin' run over the body of the boy, from head to foot. May-be he heered that yell, may-be he see'd strange sights in 'tother world! Who knows?

"For thirty minutes we kept him hanging, for thirty minutes the mob yelled and cursed and swore and hurrahed!

"But when I cut the dead body down – that was the time for fun! To see the Doctors huddle the carcase into the pine coffin, to see the Parson hurry one way, the Marshall another, to see the soldiers march off, with old Devil-Bug in their midst, guardin' him from danger!

"Ho-hoo! This individooal felt like a king, about that time!

"And then to look back and see the mob tearing the gibbet to pieces, and bearin' splinter's away in their fingers, that they might take 'em home to their families, and brag of seein' a man hung! Ho-hoo!

"That night I see'd the poor devil's dead body cut and slashed on a dissectin' table, with old doctors prowlin' about like wolves, with bits o' flesh between their fingers!

"One of 'em scraped his skull, and cleaned it like a bowl, an' put it in a case, with a label, 'This is the skull of Charles – the Pirate.'

"Hurray for the gallows, say I! It's only a kick an' a jerk, and a feller goes straight to kingdom come!"

Henry Clay Lewis (1825–1850)

Henry Clay Lewis's only book, *Odd Leaves from the Life of a Louisiana Swamp Doctor* (1850), purported to be the memoirs of an elderly physician named Madison Tensas. Lewis was, in fact, a backwoods doctor, but he drowned while crossing a swamp at age 25. The sketches in *Odd Leaves* fall broadly into a tradition inadequately called "Old Southwest Humor": a rough-hewn literature practiced in this region by lawyers, doctors, journalists, and other professionals, who often wrote under pseudonyms and published much of their material in a New York men's magazine called *The Spirit of the Times*. Stories in this tradition are often crude, almost always violent, sometimes macabre and even Gothic. Even – and especially! – the most talented practitioners of this form (George Washington Harris, for example), were far too raw for general magazine audiences at the time. Certainly many of these tales are not funny, even by frontier standards. But this tradition had an energy which influenced many writers, from Melville to Mark Twain and even William Faulkner in the twentieth century.

"A Struggle for Life" is another example of the night journey into the wilderness, cumulating in a transforming encounter. As is usual with this pattern, the "other" encountered in the woods is a version of the traveler himself: for what is the violent dwarf but an incarnation of the evil racist fantasies of Madison Tensas? This threatening figure – compounded of white guilt, fear of slave rebellion, repressed sexuality (the reader can complete the list) – is familiar in the American Gothic. It is familiar as well to black authors, who well knew what stereotypes were projected by the collective imagination of the dominant group. Chesnutt, Dunbar, and Richard Wright, more recently, would produce their versions of the black man transformed into a monster.

Text: *Henry Clay Lewis, Odd Leaves from the Life of a Louisiana Swamp Doctor, by Madison Tensas* (Philadelphia: A. Hart, 1850).

A Struggle for Life

It was the spring of 183–, the water from the Mississippi had commenced overflowing the low swamps, and rendering travelling on horseback very disagreeable. The water had got to that troublesome height, when it was rather too high for a horse, and not high enough for a canoe or skiff to pass easily over the submerged grounds.

I was sitting out under my favourite oak, congratulating myself that I had no travelling to do just then, – it was very healthy – when my joy was suddenly nipped in the bud by a loud hello from the opposite side of the bayou. Looking over, and answering the hail, I discerned first a mule, and then something which so closely resembled an ape or an ourang outang, that I was in doubt whether the voice had proceeded from it, until a repetition of the hail, this time coming unmistakeably from it, assured me that it was a human.

"Massa doctor at home?" yelled the voice.

"Yes, I am the doctor; what do you want?"

"Massa sent me with a letter to you."

Jumping in the skiff, a few vigorous strokes sent me to the opposite shore, where the singular being awaited my coming.

He was a negro dwarf of the most frightful appearance; his diminutive body was garnished with legs and arms of enormously disproportionate length; his face was hideous: a pair of tushes[1] projected from either side of a double hare-lip; and taking him altogether, he was the nearest resemblance to the ourang outang mixed with the devil that human eyes ever dwelt upon. I could not look at him without feeling disgust.

"Massa Bill sent me with a letter," was his reply to my asking him his business.

Opening it, I found a summons to see a patient, the mother of a man named Disney, living some twenty miles distant by the usual road. It was in no good humour that I told the dwarf to wait until I could swim my horse over, and I would accompany him.

By the time I had concluded my preparations, and put a large bottle of brandy in my pocket, my steed was awaiting me upon the opposite shore.

"Massa tole me to tell you ef you didn't mine swimming a little you had better kum de nere way."

"Do you have to swim much?"

"Oh no, massa, onely swim Plurisy Lake, and wade de back water a few mile, you'll save haf de way at leste."

I looked at the sun. It was only about two hours high, and the roads were in such miserable condition that six miles an hour would be making fine speed, so I determined to go the near way, and swim "Pleurisy Slough."

"You are certain you know the road, boy?"

"Oh, yes, massa, me know um ebery inch ob de groun'; hunted possum an' coon ober him many a night. Massa, you ain't got any 'baccy, is you?"

"There's a chaw – and here's a drink of brandy. I'll give you another if you pilot me safe through, and a good pounding if you get lost."

"Dank you, Massa, um's good. No fere I lose you, know ebery inch of de groun'."

I had poured him out a dram, not considering his diminutive stature, sufficient to unsettle the nerves of a stout man, but he drank it off with great apparent relish; and by this time, everything being ready, we commenced ploughing our way through the muddy roads.

We made but slow progress. I would dash on, and then have to wait for the dwarf, who, belabouring his mule with a cudgel almost as large as himself, strove in vain to keep up.

The road was directly down the bayou, for some miles. There were few settlers on it then, and the extent of their clearing consisted of a corn-patch. They were the pre-emptioners or squatters; men who settled upon government land before its survey, and awaited the incoming of planters with several negroes to buy their claims, themselves to be bought out by more affluent emigrants. To one of the first-mentioned class – the pre-emptioners – my visit was directed, or rather to his mother, who occupied an intermediate grade between the squatter and the small planter, inasmuch as she possessed one negro, the delectable morsel for whom I was waiting every few hundred yards.

Notes

A STRUGGLE FOR LIFE

[1] Tusks.

It wanted but an hour to sundown when we reached the place where it was optional with me, either to go the longer route by the bayou, or save several miles by cutting across the bend of the stream, having, however, to swim "Pleurisy Slough" if I did so.

The path across was quite obscure, and it would be dark by the time we crossed; but the negro declared he knew every inch of the way, and as saving distance was a serious consideration, I determined to try it and "Pleurisy Slough."

Taking a drink to warm me, for the dew that had commenced to fall was quite chilling, I gave one to the negro, not noticing the wild sparkle of his eye or the exhilaration of his manner.

We pressed on eagerly, I ahead as long as the path lasted; but it giving out at the edge of the back water, it became necessary for the negro to precede and pilot the way.

I followed him mechanically for some distance, relying on his intimate knowledge of the swamp, our steeds making but slow progress through the mud and water.

When we entered the swamp I had remarked that the sun was in our faces; and great was my astonishment, when we had travelled some time, on glancing my eye upwards to see if it had left the tree-tops, to perceive its last beams directly at my back, the very reverse of what it should have been. Thinking perhaps that it was some optical illusion, I consulted the moss on the trees, and its indication was that we were taking the back track. I addressed the negro very sharply for having misled me, when, instead of excusing himself, he turned on me his hideous countenance and chuckled the low laugh of drunkenness. I saw that I had given him too much brandy for his weak brain, and that he was too far gone to be of any assistance to me in finding the way.

Mine was a pleasant situation truly. To return home would be as bad as to endeavour to go on; it would be night at any rate before I could get out of the swamp; and after it fell, as there was no moon, it would be dangerous to travel, as the whole country was full of lakes and sloughs, and we might be precipitated suddenly into one of them, losing our animals if not being drowned ourselves.

It was evident that I would have to pass the night in the swamp, my only companion the drunken dwarf. I had nothing to eat, and no weapons to protect myself if assailed by wild beasts; but the swamp was high enough to preclude the attack of anything but an alligator, and their bellow was resounding in too close proximity to be agreeable.

Fortunately, being a cigar-smoker, I had a box of matches in my pocket, so I would have a fire at least. My next care was to find a ridge sufficiently above the water to furnish a dry place for building a fire and camp. After considerable search, just at night-fall the welcome prospect of a cane ridge above the overflow met my gaze; hurrying up the negro, who by this time was maudlin drunk, I reached the cane, and forcing my way with considerable difficulty through it until I got out of the reach of the water, dismounted, and tying my horse, took the negro down and performed the same office for his mule.

My next care was to gather materials for a fire before impenetrable darkness closed over the swamp; fortunately for me, a fallen oak presented itself not ten steps from where I stood. To have a cheerful blazing fire was the work of a few minutes. Breaking off sufficient cane-tops to last the steeds till morning, I stripped my horse – the mule had nothing on but a bridle – and with the saddle and cane-leaves made me a couch that a monarch, had he been as tired as I was, would have found no fault with. As the negro was perfectly helpless, and nearly naked, I gave him my saddle blanket, and making him a bed at a respectful distance, bade him go to sleep.

Replenishing the fire with sufficient fuel to last till morning, I lit a cigar, and throwing myself down upon my fragrant couch, gave myself up to reflections upon the peculiarity of my situation. Had it been a voluntary bivouac with a set of chosen companions, it would not have awakened half the interest in my mind that it did, for the attending circumstances imparted to it much of the romantic.

There, far from human habitation, my only companion a hideous dwarf, surrounded with water, the night draperied darkly around, I lay, the cane-leaves for my bed, the saddle for my pillow; the huge fire lighting up the darkness for a space around, and giving natural objects a strange, distorted appearance, bringing the two steeds into high relief against the dark background of waving cane, which nodded over, discoursing a wild, peculiar melody of its own. Occasionally a loud explosion would be heard as the fire communicated with a green reed; the wild hoot of an owl was heard, and directly I almost felt the sweep of his wings as he went sailing by, and alighted upon an old tree just where the light sank mingling with the darkness. I followed him with my eye, and as he settled himself, he turned his gaze towards me; I moved one of the logs, and his huge eyes fairly glistened with light, as the flames shot up with increased vigour; the swamp moss was flowing around him in long, tangled masses, and as a more vivid gleam uprose, I gazed and started involuntarily. Had I not known it was an owl surrounded with moss that sat upon that stricken tree, I would have sworn it was the form of an old man, clad in a sombre flowing mantle, his arm raised in an attitude of warning, that I gazed upon. A cane exploding, startled the owl, and with a loud "tu whit, tu whoo," he went sailing away in the darkness. The unmelodious bellow of the alligator, and the jarring cry of the heron, arose from a lake on the opposite side of the cane; whilst the voices of a myriad of frogs, and the many undistinguishable sounds of the swamp, made the night vocal with discordancy.

My cigar being by this time exhausted, I took the bottle from my pocket, and taking a hearty drink to keep the night air from chilling me when asleep, was about to restore it to its place, and commend myself to slumber, when, glancing at the dwarf, I saw his eyes fixed upon me with a demoniac expression that I shall never forget.

"Give me a dram," he said very abruptly, not prefacing the request by those deferential words never omitted by the slave when in his proper mind.

"No, sir, you have already taken too much; I will give you no more," I replied.

"Give me a dram," he again said, more fiercely than before.

Breaking off a cane, I told him that if he spoke to me in that manner again I would give him a severe flogging.

But to my surprise he retorted, "D—n you, white man, I will kill you ef you don't give me more brandy!" his eyes flashing and sparkling with electric light.

I rose to correct him, but a comparison of my well developed frame with his stunted deformed proportions, and the reflection that his drunkenness was attributable to my giving him the brandy, deterred me.

"I will kill you," he again screamed, his fangs clashing, and the foam flying from his mouth, his long arms extended as if to clutch me, and the fingers quivering nervously.

I took a hasty glance of my condition. I was lost in the midst of the swamp, an unknown watery expanse surrounding me; remote from any possible assistance; the swamps were rapidly filling with water, and if we did not get out to-morrow or next day, we would in all probability be starved or drowned; the negro was my only dependence, to pilot me to the settlements, and he was threatening my life if I did not give him more brandy; should I do it or not? Judging from the effects of the two drinks I had given him, if he got possession of the bottle it might destroy him, or at least render him incapable of travelling, until starvation and exposure would destroy us. My mind was resolved upon that subject; I would give him no more. There was no alternative, I would have to stand his assault; considering I was three times his size, a fearful adventure, truly, thought I, not doubting a moment but that my greater size would give me proportionate strength; I must not hurt him, but will tie him until he recovers.

The dwarf, now aroused to maniacal fury by the persistance in my refusal, slowly approached me to carry his threat into execution. The idea of such a diminutive object destroying without weapons a man of my size, presented something ludicrous, and I laughingly awaited his attack, ready to tie his hands before he could bite or scratch me. Wofully I underrated his powers!

With a yell like a wild beast's, he precipitated himself upon me; evading my blow, he clutched with his long fingers at my throat, burying his talons in my flesh, and writhing his little body around mine, strove to bear me to earth.

I summoned my whole strength, and endeavoured to shake him off; but, possessing the proverbial power of the dwarf, increased by his drunken mania to an immense degree, I found all my efforts unavailing, and, oh God! horrors of horrors, what awful anguish was mine, when I found him bearing me slowly to earth, and his piercing talons buried in my throat, cutting off my breath! My eyes met his with a more horrid gleam than that he glared upon me: his was the fire of brutal nature, aroused by desire to intense malignancy; and mine the gaze of despair and death. Closer and firmer his grip closed upon my throat, barring out the sweet life's breath. I strove to shriek for help, but could not. How shall I describe the racking agony that tortured me? A mountain, heavier than any earth's bosom holds, was pressing upon my breast, slowly crushing me to fragments. All kinds of colours first floated before my eyes, and then everything wore a settled, intensely fiery red. I felt my jaw slowly dropping, and my tongue protruding, till it rested on the hellish fangs that encircled my throat. I could hear distinctly every pulsation of even the minutest artery in my frame. Its wild singing was in my ears like the ocean wave playing over the shell-clad shore. I remember it all perfectly, for the mind, through all this awful struggle, still remained full of thought and clearness. Closer grew the gripe of those talons around my throat, and I knew that I could live but a few moments more. I did not pray. I did not commend my soul to God. I had not a fear of death. But oh! awful were my thoughts at dying in such a way – suffocated by a hellish negro in the midst of the noisome swamp, my flesh to be devoured by the carrion crow, my bones to whiten where they lay for long years, and then startle the settler, when civilization had strode into the wilderness, and the cane that would conceal my bones would be falling before the knife of the cane-cutter. I ceased to breathe. I was dead. I had suffered the last pangs of that awful hour, and either it was the soul not yet resigned to leave its human tenement, or else immortal mind triumphing over death, but I still retained the sentient principle within my corpse. I remember distinctly when the demon relaxed his clutch, and shaking me to see if I were really dead, broke into a hellish laugh. I remember distinctly when tearing the bottle from me, he pulled my limber body off my couch, and stretched himself upon it. And what were my thoughts? I was dead, yet am living now. Ay, dead as human ever becomes. My lungs had ceased to play; my heart was still; my muscles were inactive; even my skin had the dead clammy touch. Had men been there, they would have placed me in a coffin, and buried me deep in the ground, and the worm would have eaten me, and the death-rats made nests in my heart, and what was lately a strong man would have become a loathsome mass. But still in that coffin amidst those writhing worms, would have been the immortal mind, and still would it have thought and pondered on till the last day was come. For such is the course of soul and death, as my interpretation has it. I was dead, all but my mind, and that still thought on as vividly, as ramblingly, as during life. My body lay dead in that murderer's swamp, my mind roamed far away in thought, reviewing my carnal life. I stood, as when a boy, by my mother's grave. The tall grass was waving over it, the green sod smiled at my feet. "Mother," I whispered, "your child is weary – the world looks harsh upon him – coldness comes from those who should shelter the orphan. Mother, open your large black eyes and smile upon your child." Again, I stood upon the steamer, a childish fugitive, giving a last look upon my fleeing home, and mingling my tears with the foaming wave beneath. I dragged my exhausted frame through the cotton-fields of the south. My back was wearied with stooping – we were picking the first opening – and as dreams of future distinction would break upon my soul, the strap of the cotton-sack, galling my shoulder, recalled me to myself. All the phases of my life were repeated, until they ended where I lay dead! – dead as mortal ever becomes. I thought, What will my friends say when they hear that on a visit to the sick, I disappeared in the swamp, and was never heard of more? – drowned or starved to death? Will they weep for me? for me? – Not many, I ween, will be the tears that will be shed for me. Then, after the lapse of long years, my bones will be found. I wonder who will get my skull? Perhaps an humble doctor like myself, who, meditating upon it, will not think that it holds the mind of a creature of his own ambition – his own lofty instincts. He will deem it but an empty skull, and little dream that it held a sentient principle. But I know that the mind will still tenant it. Ha, ha! how that foul ape is gurgling his blood-bought pleasure. I would move if I could, and wrench the bottle from him; but mine is thought, not action. Hark! there is a storm arising. I hear with my ear, that is pressed on the earth, the thunder of the hurricane. How the trees crash beneath it! Will it prostrate those above me? Hark! what awful thunder! Ah me! what fierce pang is that piercing my very vitals? There is a glimmering of light before my eyes. Can it be that I the dead am being restored to human life? Another thunder peal! 'tis the second stroke of my heart – my blood is red-hot – it comes with fire through my veins – the earth quakes – the mountain is rolling off my chest – I live! – I breathe! – I see! – I hear! – Where am I? Who brought me here? I hear other sounds, but cannot my own voice. Where am I? Ah! I remember the dwarf strangled me. Hark! where is he? Is that the sunbeam playing over the trees? What noisome odour like consuming flesh is that which poisons the gale? Great God! can that disfigured half-consumed mass be my evil genius?"

I rose up, and staggering, fell again; my strength was nearly gone. I lay until I thought myself sufficiently recruited to stand, and then got up and surveyed the scene. The animals were tied as I left them, and were eating their cane unconcernedly; but fearfully my well-nigh murderer had paid for his crime, and awful was the retribution. Maddened by the spirits, he had rushed into the flames, and, in the charred and loathsome mass, nothing of the human remained; he had died the murderer's death and been buried in his grave, – a tomb of fire.

To remain longer in the horrid place was impossible; my throat pained me excessively where the talons had penetrated the flesh, and I could not speak above a whisper. I turned the mule loose, thinking that it would return home, and conduct me out of the swamp. I was not incorrect in my supposition; the creature led me to his owner's cabin. The patient had died during the night.

My account of the dwarf's attack did not surprise the family; he had once, when in a similar condition, made an attack upon his mistress, and would have strangled her, had assistance not been near.

His bones were left to bleach where they lay. I would not for the universe have looked again upon the place; and his mistress being dead, there were none to care for giving him the rites of sepulture.

THE END.

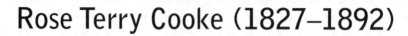

Rose Terry Cooke (1827–1892)

Rose Terry Cooke enjoyed popularity and critical esteem during a career of fifty year. A poet and short story writer, Cooke was important to the American tradition of women's regional realism, and stands near its beginning. She was one of two women to appear in the first number of the *Atlantic Monthly*.

The narrator of "My Visitation," like many of Poe's, immediately announces her unreliability. The tale she tells is remarkable for its account of same-sex love. In a story built on competing courtships, the affair of the narrator and Eleanor ends indeed in a bedroom, though its passion is deflected into a ghostly quasi-religious consummation.

Text: Rose Terry Cooke, "My Visitation," *Harper's New Monthly Magazine*, 17 (July 1858), 232–9.

My Visitation

"Is not this she of whom,
When first she came, all flushed you said to me,

*   *   *   *   *   *   *

Now could you share your thought; now should men see
Two women faster welded in one love
Than pairs of wedlock?"

– The Princess[1]

If this story is incoherent – arranged rather for the writer's thought than for the reader's eye – it is because the brain which dictated it reeled with the sharp assaults of memory, that living anguish that abides while earth passes away into silence; and because the hand that wrote it trembled with electric thrills from a past that can not die, forever fresh in the soul it tested and tortured – powerful after the flight of years as in its first agony, to fill the dim eye with tears, and throb the languid pulses with fresh fever and passion.

Take, then, the record as it stands, and ask not from a cry of mortal pain the liquid cadence and accurate noting of an operatic bravura.

The first time *It* came was in broad day. I was ill, unable to rise; the day was cold; autumnal sunshine, pure and still, streamed through the house and came in at both the south windows of my room, the curtains drawn side to receive it, for the ague of sickness is worse to me than its pain, and not yet had my preparations for winter enabled me to have a fire. Every thing was clear and chill; Aunt Mary, down stairs in the parlor, sat and knitted, as it was her custom to do of an afternoon; Uncle Seth was not at

Notes

My Visitation

[1] From *The Princess*, by Alfred, Lord Tennyson (1809–92).

home; the servant had gone to mass, for it was some feast-day of her Church – no sound or echo disturbed the solitude.

There is something peculiar in a silent day of autumn; melancholy pierces its fine sting through the rays of sunshine; sadness cries in the cricket's monotonous voice; separation and death symbolize in the slow leaves that quit the bough reluctantly, and lie down in dust to be over-trodden – to rot. I can endure any silence better than this hush of decay; it fills me with preternatural horror; it is as if a tomb opened and breathed out its dank, morbid breath across the murmur of life, to paralyze and to chill.

But that day I had taken refuge from the awe and foreboding, the ticking of the clock, the dust-motes floating on light, the startling crack that now and then a springing board or an ill-hung window made. I had taken a book. I was deep in *Shirley*; it excited, it affected me; it is always to me like a brief and voluntary brain-fever to read that book. *Jane Eyre* is insanity for the time. *Villette* is like the scarlet fever; it possesses, it chokes, flushes, racks you; it leaves you weak and in vague pain, apprehensive of some bad result; but it was *Shirley* I read, so forgetting every thing.[2] I am not lonely usually, yet I know when I am alone; there is an indescribable freedom in the sense of solitude, no alien sphere crosses and disturbs mine, no intrusive influence distorts the orbit; I am myself – or I was, then. Presently, as I lay there, the clock struck three. I was to take some potion at that hour. I must rise and get it. I set one foot on the floor, and was putting a shoe upon the other cautiously, when it occurred to me, why was I so careful? and I remembered that it had seemed to me something was on the bed when I moved – my kitten perhaps. I looked, there was nothing there; but I was not alone in the room – there was something else I could not see, I did not hear, but I knew it.

A horror of flesh and sense crept over me; but I was ashamed; I treated it with contempt. Shivering, I walked to the shelf, reached the cup, swallowed my nauseous dose – now tasteless – and went back to bed. It is not worth denying that I trembled. I am a coward. I am always afraid, even when I face the fear; so, shaking, I lay down. My throat was parched, my lips beaded with a sweat of terror, but the consciousness of solitude returned in time to save me from faintness. *It* had gone. And that was the first time.

Here, perhaps, it is best to interpolate my own story, as much of it as is needful to the understanding of this visitation.

I was an orphan, living in the family of my guardian and uncle by marriage, Mr. Van Alstyne. I was not an orphan till fifteen years of happy life at home had fitted me to feel the whole force of such a bereavement. My parents had died within a year of each other, and at the time my story begins I had been ten years under my uncle's roof, He was kind, gentle, generous, and good; all that he could be, not being my father.

It is not necessary to say that I grieved long and deeply over my loss; my nature is intense as well as excitable, and I had no mother. What that brief sentence expresses many will feel; many, more blessed, can not imagine. It is to all meaning enough to define my longing for what I had not, my solitude in all that I had, my eager effort to escape from both longing and solitude.

After I had been a year under my guardian's care, Eleanor Wyse, a far-off cousin of Mr. Van Alstyne, came to board at the house and go to school with me. She was fifteen, I sixteen, but she was far the oldest. In the same family as we were, in the same classes, there were but two ways for us to take, either rivalry or friendship; between two girls of so much individuality there was no neutral ground, and within a month I had decided the matter by falling passionately in love with Eleanor Wyse.

Notes ————————————————————————————————

[2] *Shirley* (1849), *Jane Eyre* (1847), *Villette* (1853): novels by Charlotte Brontë (1818–48).

I speak advisedly in the use of that term; no other phrase expresses the blind, irrational, all-enduring devotion I gave to her; no less vivid word belongs to that madness. If I had not been in love with her I should have seen her as I can now – as what she really was; for I believe in physiognomy. I believe that God writes the inner man upon the outer as a restraint upon society; what the moulding of feature lacks, expression, subtle traitor, supplies; and it is only years of repression, of training, of diplomacy, that put the flesh totally in the power of the spirit, and enable man or woman to seem what they are not, what they would be thought.

Eleanor's face was very beautiful; its Greek outline, straight and clear, cut to a perfect contour; the white brow; the long, melancholy eye, with curved, inky lashes; the statuesque head, its undulant, glittering hair bound in a knot of classic severity; the proud, serene mouth, full of carved beauty, opening its scarlet lips to reveal tiny pearl-grains of teeth of that rare delicacy and brilliance that carry a fatal warning; the soft, oval cheek, colorless but not pale, opaque and smooth, betraying Southern blood; the delicate throat, shown whiter under the sweeping shadow and coil of her black-brown tresses; the erect, stately, perfect figure, slight as became her years, but full of strength and promise; all these captivated my intense adoration of beauty. I did not see the label of the sculptor; I did not perceive in that cold, strict chiseling the assertion that its material was marble. I believed the interpretation of its hieroglyphic legend would have run thus: "This is the head of young Pallas; power, intellect, purity are her ægis; the daughter of Jove has not yet tasted passion; virgin, stainless, strong for sacrifice and victory, let the ardent and restless hearts of women seek her to be calmed and taught. *Evoe Athena!*"[3] Nor did I like to see the goddess moved; expression did not become her; the soul that pierced those deep eyes was eager, unquiet, despotic; nothing divine, indeed, yet, in my eyes, it was the unresting, hasting meteor that flashed and faded through mists of earth toward its rest – where I knew not, but its flickering seemed to me atmospheric, not intrinsic.

I looked up to Eleanor with respect as well as fervor. She was full of noble theories. To hear her speak you would have been inwardly shamed by the great and pure thoughts she expressed, the high standard by which she measured all. Truth, disinterestedness, honor, purity, humility, found in her a priestess garmented in candor. If I thought an evil thought, I was thereafter ashamed to see her; if I was indolent or selfish, her presence reproached me; her will, irresistible and mighty, awoke me; if she was kind in speech or act – if she spoke to me caressingly – if she put her warm lips upon my cheek – I was thrilled with joy; her presence affected me, as sunshine does, with a sense of warm life and delight; when we rode, walked, or talked together, I wished the hour eternal; and when she fell into some passion, and burned me with bitter words, stinging me into retort by their injustice, their hard cruelty, it was I who repented – I who humiliated myself – I who, with abundant tears, asked her pardon, worked, plead, prayed to obtain it; and if some spasmodic conscientiousness roused her to excuse herself – to say she had been wrong – my hand closed her lips: I could not hear that: the fault was mine, mine only. I was glad to be clay as long as she was queen and deity.

I do not think this passion of mine moved Eleanor much. She liked to talk with me; our minds mated, our tastes were alike. I had no need to explain my phrases to her, or to do more than indicate my thoughts; she was receptive and appreciative of thought, not of emotion. Me she never knew. I had no reserve in my nature – none of what is

Notes

[3] *Evoe Athena! Evoe* (Latinized version of Greek *euoi*) was a mystical word usually used to evoke Dionysius, not Athena.

commonly called pride; what I felt I said, to the startling of good usual persons; and- because I said it, Eleanor did not think I felt it. To her organization utterance and sim- plicity were denied; she could not speak her emotions if she would; she would not if she could; and she had no faith in words from others. My demonstrations annoyed her; she could not return them; they could not be ignored; there was a certain spice of life and passion in them that asserted itself poignantly and disturbed her. My services she liked better; yet there was in her the masculine contempt for spaniels; she despised a creature that would endure a blow, mental or physical, without revenging itself; and from her I endured almost any repulse, and forgot it.

She was with us in the house three years, and in that time she learned to love me after a fashion of her own, and I, still blind, adored her more. She found in me a recep- tivity that suited her, and a useful power of patient endurance. Her will made me a potent instrument. What she wanted she must have, and her want was my law. No time, no pains, no patience were wanting in me to fulfill her ends. I served her truly, and I look back upon it with no regret; futile or fertile, such devotion widens and ripens the soul that it inhabits. No aftershock of anguish can contract the space or undo the maturity; and even in my deepest humiliation before her sublime theories and superhuman ideals I unconsciously grew better myself. A capacity for worship implies much, and results in much.

Yet I think I loved her without much selfishness. I desired nothing better than to see her appreciated and admired. It was inexplicable to me when she was not; and I charged the coolness with which she was spoken of, and the want of enthusiasm for her person and character in general society, to her own starry height above common people, and their infinite distance from her nature.

So these years passed by. We went to school; we finished our school-days; we came out into the world; for, in the mean time, her mother had died, and her father removed to Bangor. She liked the place as a residence, and it had become home to her of late. I hoped it was pleasanter for her to be near me. When Eleanor was about twenty a nephew of Uncle Van Alstyne's came to make us a visit; he was no new acquaintance; he had come often in his boyhood, but since we grew up he had been in college, at the seminary, last in Germany for two years' study, and we did not know him well in his maturer character until this time. Herman Van Alstyne was quiet and plain, but of great capacity; I saw him much, and liked him. Love did not look at us. I was absorbed in Eleanor; so was he; but to her he was of no interest. I think she respected him, but her manner was careless and cold, even neglectful. Herman perceived the repulsion. At first he had taken pains to interest her – to mould her traits – to develop some inner nature in which he had faith; but the stone was intractable; neither ductile nor docile was Pallas; her soul yielded no more to him than the strong sea yields place or submis- sion to the winged wind that smites it in passing.

He was with us three months waiting for a call he said, but stricter chains held him till he broke them with one blow and went to a Western parish.

He had not offered himself to Eleanor and been refused. Wisely he refrained from bringing the matter to a foreknown crisis: he spared himself the pain and Eleanor the regret of a refusal that he regarded truly as certain. I was sorry for the whole affair, for I believed she would scarcely know a better man, but it passed away; I promised to write him when his mother found the correspondence wearying, and we interchanged a few letters at irregular intervals till we met again, letters into which Eleanor's name found no entrance.

Three years after he left I went, early in July, to spend some weeks at the sea-side, for I was not strong; in the last few years my health had failed slowly, but progressively, till I was alarmingly weak and ordered to breathe salt air and use sea-bathing as the best hope of restoration. I do not know why I should reserve the cause of this long languor and sinking: it was nothing wrong in me that I owed it to the breaking of a brief engagement. A young girl, totally inexperienced, I had loved a man and been taught by himself to despise him – a tragedy both trite and sharp; one that is daily reacted, noted, and forgotten by observers, to find a cold record in marble or the catalogues of insane asylums, another perhaps in the eternal calendar of the heavens above. I was too strong in nature to grace either of these mortal lists, and I loved Eleanor too well. I had always loved her more than that man; and when the episode was over, I discovered in myself that I never could have loved any man as I did her, and I went out into the world in this conviction, finding that life had not lost all its charms – that so long as she lived for me I should neither die nor craze. But the shock and excitement of the affair shattered my nervous system and undermined my health, and the listless, aimless life of a young lady offered no reactive agency to help me: so I went from home to new scenes and fresh atmosphere.

The air of Gloucester Beach strengthened me day by day. The exquisite scenery was a pleasure endless and pure. I asked nothing better than to sit upon some tide-washed rock and watch the creeping waves slide back in half-articulate murmur from the repelling shore, or, eager with the strength of flood, fling themselves, in mock anger, against cliff and crag, only to break in wreaths of silver spray and foam-bells – to glitter and fall in a leap of futile mirth, then rustling in the shingle and sea-weed with vague whispers, that

> "Song half asleep or speech half awake,"[4]

which has lulled so many restless hearts to a momentary quiet, singing them the long lullaby that preludes a longer slumber.

It was excitement enough to walk alone upon the beach when a hot cloudy night drooped over land and sea; when the soft trance and enchantment of summer lulled cloud and wave into stillness absolute and cherishing, when the sole guide I had in that warm gloom was the white edge of surf, and the only sound that smote the quiet, the still-recurring, apprehensive dash, as wave after wave raced, leaped, panted, and hissed after its forerunner.

The Beach House was almost empty at that early season, and I enjoyed all this alone, not without constant yearnings for Eleanor; wanting her, even this scenery lost a charm, and I gave it but faint admiration since I could not see it with her eyes. It must be a very pure love of nature that can exist alone, and without flaw, in the absence of association. The austere soul of the great mother offers no sympathy to the petulant passion or irrational grief of her children. It is only to the heart that has proved itself strong and lofty that her potent and life-giving traits reveal themselves. In this love, as in all others, save only the love of God, the return that is yielded is measured by the power of the adorer, not his want. Truly,

> "Nature never did betray
> The heart that loved her;"[5]

but she has many and many a time betrayed the partial love – scoffed at the divided worship.

After I had been a fortnight at the Beach, I was joined by Herman Van Alstyne. He had come on from the West to recruit his own health, suffering from a long intermittent

Notes

[4] From "Garden Fancies: The Flower's Name," a poem by Robert Browning (1812–89).

[5] From "Lines Composed a Few Miles above Tintern Abbey," by William Wordsworth (1770–1850).

fever, by sea-air; and hearing I was at Gloucester, had come there, and asked my leave to remain, gladly accorded to him. We had always been good friends, and my unspoken sympathy with his liking for, and loss of, Eleanor had established a permanent bond between us. In the constant association into which we were now thrown I learned daily to like him better. He was very weak indeed, quite unable to walk or drive far, and the connection of our families was a sufficient excuse to others for our intimacy. I delighted to offer him any kindness or service in my power, and he repaid me well by the charm of his society.

We spent our mornings always together in some niche of the lofty cliff that towered from the tide below in bare grandeur, reflecting the sun from its abrupt brown crags till every fibre of grass rooted in their crevices grew blanched, and the solitary streamer of bramble or wild creeper became crisp long ere autumn. But this heat was my element; the slow blood quickened in my veins under its vital glow; I felt life stealing back to its deserted and chilly conduits; I basked like a cactus or a lizard into brighter tints and a gayer existence.

There we often sat till noon, talking or silent as we would; for though there was a peculiar charm in the appreciative, thoughtful conversation of Herman Van Alstyne, a better and a rarer trait he possessed in full measure – the power of "a thousand silences."[6]

Or, perhaps, under the old cedars that shed aromatic scents upon the sun-thrilled air, and strewed bits of dry, sturdy leaves upon the short grass that carpeted the summit of the cliff, we preferred shadow to sunshine; and while I rested against some ragged bole, and inhaled all odor and health, he read to me some quaint German story, some incredibly exquisite bit of Tennyson, some sensitively musical passage of Kingsley, or, better and more apt, a song or a poem of Shelley's – vivid, spiritual, supernatural; the ideal of poetry; the leaping flame-tongue of lonely genius hanging in mid-air, self-poised, self-containing, glorious, and unattainable.

I have never known so delicate an apprehension as Mr. Van Alstyne possessed; his nobler traits I was afterward to know – to feel; but now it suited me thoroughly to be so well understood – to feel that I might utter the wildest imagination, or the most unexpected peculiarity of opinion, and never once be asked to explain what I meant – to reduce into social formulas that which was not social but my own. If there is one rest above another to a weary mind it is this freedom from shackles, this consciousness of true response. Never did I perceive a charm in the landscape that he had not noticed before or simultaneously with me; the same felicity of diction or of thought in what we read struck us as with one stroke; we liked the same people, read the same books, agreed in opinion so far as to disagree on and discuss many points without a shadow of impatience or an uncandid expression. We talked together as few men talk – perhaps no women –

> "Talked at large of worldly fate,
> And drew truly every trait"[7]

– but we never spoke of Eleanor.

And so the summer wore on. I perceived a gradual change creep over Herman's manner in its process; he watched me continually. I felt his eyes fixed on me whenever I sat sewing or reading; I never looked up without meeting them. He grew absent and fitful. I did not know what had happened. I accused myself of having pained him. I feared he was ill. I never once thought of the true trouble; and one day it came – he asked me to marry him.

Notes

6 From "Merops," by Ralph Waldo Emerson (1803–82).   7 From "Hermione," by Emerson.

Never was any woman more surprised. I had not thought of the thing. I could not speak at first. I drew from him the hand he attempted to grasp. I did not collect my stricken and ashamed thoughts till, looking up, I saw him perfectly pale, his eyes dark with emotion, waiting, in rigid self-control, for my answer.

I could not, in justice to him or to myself, be less than utterly candid.

I told him how much I liked him; how grieved I was that I could have mistaken his feeling for me so entirely; and then I said what I then believed – that I could not marry him – for I had but the lesser part of a heart to give any man. I loved a woman too well to love or to marry. A deep flush of relief crossed his brow.

"Is that the only objection you offer to me?" asked he, calmly.

"It is enough," said I. "If you think that past misery of mine interferes against you, you are in the wrong. I know now that I never loved that man as a woman should love the man she marries, and had I done so, the utter want of respect or trust I feel for him now would have silenced the love forever."

"I did not think of that," said he. "I needed but one assurance – that, except for Miss Wyse, you might have loved me; is it so?"

I could not tell him – I did not know. The one present and all-absorbing passion of my soul was Eleanor; beside her, no rival could enter. I shuddered at the possibility of loving a man so utterly, and then placing myself at his mercy for life, I felt that my safety lay in my freedom from any such tie to Eleanor. She made me miserable often enough as it was; what might she not do were I in her power always? Yet this face of the subject I did not suggest to Mr. Van Alstyne; it was painful enough to be kept to myself. I told him plainly that I could not love another as I did her; that I would not if I could.

He looked at me, not all unmoved, though silently; a gentle shading of something like pity stole across his regard, fixed and keen at first. He neither implored nor deprecated, but lifted my hand reverently to his lips, and said, in a tone of supreme calmness, "I can wait."

I should have combated the hope implied in those words. I was afterward angry with myself for enduring them; but at the moment uncertainty, shaped out of instinct and apprehension, closed my lips; I could not speak, and he left me. I went to my room more moved than I liked to acknowledge; and when he went away the next morning, though I felt the natural relief from embarrassment – knowing that I should not meet him as before – I still missed him, as a part of my daily life.

A month longer at the Beach protracted my stay into autumn; and then, with refreshed health and new strength, I returned home – home! whose chief charm lay in the prospect of seeing Eleanor.

It is true that this hope was not unalloyed. I am possessed of a nature singularly instinctive, and for some weeks past a certain shadow had crept into her letters that pained me. No word or phrase denoted change; but I perceived the uncertain aura, and was irrationally harassed by a trouble too vague for expression.

When I reached Bangor it lay waiting for me sufficiently tangible and legible in the shape of a note from Eleanor.

* * * * * *

And here must I leave a blank. The forgiveness which stirs me to this record refuses to define for alien eyes what that trouble was. All that I can say to justify the extreme and piteous result which followed is, that Eleanor Wyse had utterly, cruelly, and deliberately deceived me; and when it was no longer possible to do so, had been obliged by circumstances to show me what she had done.

Of that day it is best to say but little: the world cracked and reeled under me; I returned from a brief stupor into one bitter, blind tempest of contempt; and in its strength I answered her note concisely and coldly. An hour's time brought me a rejoinder not worth answering, simply perfidious – a regret, "deep and true," that she had been compelled to grieve me, to "reserve" from me any thing.

True! I had believed in truth, in goodness, in disinterested love, in principle; where now were such faiths swept? Verily, over the cliff into the sea! I was morally destroyed; I made shipwreck of myself and my life; my whole soul was a salt raging wave, tideless and foaming, without rest, without intent, without faith or hope in God – for he who loses faith in man loses faith in man's Maker – and this had Eleanor Wyse done for me.

Doubtless, to many, this emotion of mine will seem exaggerated. Let them remember that it was the loss of all that bound to life a lonely, morbid, intense, and excitable woman. Need I say more? If, after many years, with the kind help of nobler men and women, and the great patience of God, I have worn my way, inch by inch, back to some foothold of belief, I feel even yet – in some recoils of memory, some recurring habit of my soul – the reflex influence of those wretched days, months, years, when I suspected every one – "hateful, and hating," of a truth.

Death is hard to bear when its angel breathes upon the face we love, and extinguishes therein the fiery spark of life; but what is death compared to such dissolution as treachery brings? If Eleanor Wyse had died when I loved her and trusted her, I should have gone mourning softly all my days, but not in pain; to find her untrue admitted no remedy, no palliation. Truth was the ruling passion of my mind; that, and nothing else, contented me. Its absence or its loss were the loss and absence of all in those whom I loved; and it was only within a brief time, as years go, that I had grown into the discovery that men are liars in spite of education or policy; what was it, then, to know this of my ideal – Eleanor?

But let those helpless, miserable weeks go by. If I detail so much as I have, it is to show the reason of my righteous indignation – of my tenacious memory. After a time I supposed that I forgave Eleanor. I thought myself good, most Pharisaically[8] good, to have forgiven such an injury. I made some little comedy of friendship for visible use; I visited her, though not as often as I had done before. I saw her try to supply, with the love of others, the lavish devotion and service I had given her; I saw her fail and suffer in the consciousness of want and dissatisfaction, and, self-righteously, I forgave again! Senseless that I was! – as if forgiveness rankled and grew bitter in one's heart – as if pardon, full and pure, rejoiced in the retributions of this life – fed itself with salt recollections of the past, and evil foreshadowings of the future; as if it could exist without love, without forgetfulness; as if good deeds were its pledge, or good words its seal!

No! I never forgave her. I never forgot one pang she inflicted on me, one untruth she uttered; I never trusted her word or her smile again. I gathered up every circumstance of the past, and hunted it to its source; I discovered that she had not simply deceived but deluded me, and laughed at me in the process.

How my blood boiled over these revelations! how my flesh failed with my heart! Slow, persistent fever gnawed me; my nights were without sleep or rest; my days laggard and delirious. Why I did not go crazy is yet unexplained to myself. I think I did, only that there was a method in my madness that won for it the milder name of nervousness. I was ill – I tottered on the very tempting brink of death, without awe or regret; I made no effort to live, nor any to die, except to pray that I might – the only

Notes

[8] Self-righteously, in the manner of the strict Jewish sect of the Pharisees.

prayer that ever passed my seared lips. I was sent away from home again; and while I was gone Eleanor married a certain Mr. Mason, of Bangor, and they removed to Illinois – in time, still further West. I was no better for this absence; and, impatient of strangers and intrusive acquaintance, I came home, and, strange as it may seem, I missed Eleanor! Habit is the anchor of half the love in this world, and my habit of loving her survived the love – or held it, perhaps – for I missed her sorrowfully.

I found Herman Van Alstyne at my uncle's when I came, and I was glad – glad of any thing to break the desperate monotony of sorrow. He knew nothing more than everyone knew of this affair, except that he knew me, and from that gathered intuitively a part of the truth; and, by long patience, unwearied and delicate care – watching, waiting, forbearing, and enduring – he brought me nearer a certain degree of calm than I had believed possible, when a sudden summons called him away from Bangor; and it was during his absence that It began to come; as I said in the beginning, more than two years after I had lost Eleanor.

I lay still in my bed on that day of which I had spoken; the long stress of misery that I had undergone in the past years resulted in so much physical exhaustion as to have brought on the exquisite tortures of neuralgia, and it was a sudden access of this chronic rack that to-day held me prisoner. The draught I had taken was an anodyne, and under its influence I fell asleep. I must have slept an hour, when I woke abruptly with a renewed sense of something in the dusk beside me, at my pillow. I screamed as I woke into this terror, and instantly Aunt Mary came in. A cold sigh crossed my cheek; I shivered with a horror strange and unearthly. Aunt Mary asked if I had been asleep? I said yes. If I had been dreaming painfully? I did not answer that. I asked for some water, and getting it she forgot her question; but I could not bear to be alone. I begged her to sit beside me and to sleep with me, for I could not endure solitude; perpetual apprehension made me cringe in every nerve and fibre. I started at the slightest stir of leaf or insect upon the pane, and the repining autumn wind seemed to come over mile on mile of graves, bringing thence no mealy scent of white daisies – no infant-breathing violet odors – no frutescent perfume of sweet-briar, nor funereal smells of cypress, and plaintive whispers of fir and pine; but wave after wave of cries from half-free souls; sobbing with dull pain, and moans of deprecating anguish; a cry that neither heaven nor earth answered, but which crept – a live desolation – into the ear attent, and the brain morbidly excited.

Yet gradually this left me. I kept by some kindly human presence all day, and feared night no more till –

Let me say that all this time I was imperceptibly growing better than I had been. Hope, the very ministrant of Heaven, was by tiny crevice and unguarded postern stealing into my heart, though I knew it not, and softening all my hard thoughts of Eleanor, for I am moved to the outer world rather by my own moods than theirs; sorrow and pain make me selfish and unkind; peace, joy, even unconscious hope, expand my love for all mankind. I am better, more tender, more benevolent to others, when I receive some light and life within.

One night I was all alone; the low, unearthly glimmer of a waning moon lit the naked earth, a few leaves rustled on the fitful wind that lulled, and rose, and lulled again, with almost articulate meaning. I lay listening; a long pause came, of most significant quiet – a faint sigh crossed my brow. It was there beside me! – unseen, unheard, but felt in the secretest recesses of life and consciousness; a spirit, whereat my marrow curdled, my heart was constricted, my blood refused to run, my breath failed – fluttered – was it death? I sprung from my pillow; the presence drew farther away. I could see nothing, but I felt that something yearning, restless, pained, and sad regarded me. I began to gather courage. I began to pity a soul that had cast off life yet could not die to life; and now it drew nearer, as if some magnetism, born of my kindlier sympathies, melted the barrier between us, close – closer – till something rustled like a light touch the cover of my bed, stirred at my ear! Good Heaven! could I bear that? I could not shriek or cry, I fell forward upon my face. It went, and the wind began its wail; now reproachful sobs filled it: the moon sank, rain gathered overhead, and dripped with sullen persistence all night upon the roof, for all night I heard it.

It is tedious to recount each instance of this visitation. For weeks it staid beside me. I felt it on my bed at night; I felt it by my chair in the day; it swept past me in the garden paths, a cold waft of air; it watched me through the window-blinds; it hung over me sleeping; yet never was I wonted to the presence; every day thrilled me with fresh surprise, and daily it grew, for daily it became more perceivable.

At first I felt only a sense of alien life in a room otherwise solitary; then a breath of air, air from some other sphere than this, penetrative, dark, chilling; then a sound, not of voice, or pulse, but of motion in some inanimate thing, the motion of contact; then came a touch, the gentlest, faintest approach of lips or fingers, I knew not which, to my brow; and last, a growing, gathering, flickering into sight. I saw nothing at first, directly; from the oblique glance that fear impelled I drew an impression of quivering air beside me; then of a shadow, frail and variant; then a shapeless shape of mist, a cloud, dark and portentous and significant; and next those sidelong glances revealed to me an expression; no face, no feature, but, believe it who can, an expression, earnest, melancholy, beseeching; a look that pierced me, that pleaded with my soul's depth, that entreated shelter, succor, consolation, which even in my terror I longed to give.

I might perhaps have suffered physically more than I did from this visiting, but the winged hope of which I spoke before upheld me still, daily, with stronger hands.

Herman had returned to Bangor after a brief absence, and was there still. I could not see him so constantly as I did and refuse my admiration to those traits that ever rule and satisfy me. Mr. Van Alstyne passed with some people for a philosopher, with some for a reformer: there were those who called him singular and self-opinionated; there were others who revered him for his devout nature and stainless life. He was more than any of these, he was a true man: and even in his plain exterior the eye that knew him found a charm peculiar and salient; the deep-sunken, clear, earnest eyes, kindled with a spark of profound depth and meaning; the thin, sharply cut, aquiline outline; the flexible, pure, refined mouth; the bronzed coloring; the overhanging brow – all these wore beauty indefinable, fired by the sweet and vivid smile of the irradiate soul within. In his presence, calm, restful, and strengthening, no subterfuge or evasion could live. He was just, direct, and tenderly strong; it was to him, to him it is, that I owed and owe a new and higher life than I had known before; he saw my sinking and lonely soul, but he saw its self-recuperative power, and with the most delicate and careful tenderness beguiled that motive force into action. He did far more than that; he recalled to me the higher motives that anguish had well-nigh scourged out from my horizon; he taught me as a father teaches his little child a newer trust in the Father of us all. I returned to those divine consolations that he laid before me with a pierced and penitent heart; and in knowing that I was prayed and cared for on earth, I learned anew that God is more tender and more patient than his creatures, and the logic of strong emotion made the truth living and potent. In all this was I drawn toward Herman by the strongest tie that can bind one heart to another – a tie that overarches and outlasts all the fleeting passions of time, for it is the adamantine link of eternity; and had I lost him then, I should have felt for all my life that there was a relation between us, undying and sure, to be renewed and acknowledged at length where such relations respire their native air, where there is neither marrying nor giving in marriage.

But it pleased God that I should live to receive my heart's desire; what began in gratitude ended in love. I might have shrunk from admitting so potent a guest again into my soul, had any other soul sent the messenger thither; but I trusted him when I disbelieved every other creature, and with this trust had crept back to me my faith in God, in good, in life and its ends. Truly, so far as man can do it, he saved my soul alive!

Now it was the early part of December. It was still haunting me. I could see more – eyes, deep and pleading, the outline of a head, pure lineaments, seemed hovering beside me, but if I turned for a direct look they were gone. I did not fear it; my happy faith and Herman shielded me.

The year drew on. The day before Christmas came, still, crisp, but yet warm for its season; no snow shrouded the earth; the far-off sun beamed out benign and pale; the few dry leaves lay quiet as they fell; the firs upon the lawn with curved boughs waited for their ermine, stately and dark. Herman asked me to walk with him. I cloaked and hooded myself, and we went away, away into the deep woods. What we said in that sweet silence of a leafless, sunny forest is known to us two: it is not for you, reader, friendly though you be; it is enough to tell you that I had promised to be his wife, that I was homesick no more.

It was well for me that this happened that day – should I not rather say God ordered it? – for as ever in this life sorrow tramples upon the foregoing footsteps of joy, so I found upon my return a household in tears. Mr. Mason, Eleanor's husband, had written, at last, two months after it happened, and another month had the letter been in coming – ah! how ever shall I say it? Eleanor was dead! her latest breath had gasped out a cry for me!

If Death is the Spoiler, so is he the Restorer; who shall dare to soil the shroud with any thing but tears? I could do no more but weep; but I mourned for Eleanor again as I had never thought to do; evil, treachery, anguish, and distrust vanished – I remembered only love.

For hours I could not see or speak with Herman, the flood of misery overpowered me; and he too sorrowed, deeply, but serenely. It was late in the evening before I recovered any sort of composure. He sent to my chamber a brief penciled request, and I went down; worn out with weeping, I obeyed like a child. I ate the food he brought me; I drank the restorative draught; quiet, but languid, I laid my head upon his breast, and, held by the firm grasp of his arm, I rested, and he consoled me; a deep and vital draught of peace slaked my soul's feverish thirst. Such peace had I never known, for it was the daughter of experience and trust.

You who, full of youth and its intact passion, give a careless hour to these pages, wonder not that I could find it just to give so noble a man a heart once given and wasted! Know that it is not the flower of any tropic palm that is fit to feed and sustain man, but the ripened clusters of its fruitage – the result of time, and sun, and storm. The first blush, the earliest kiss, the tender and timid glance are sweet indeed; but the true household fire, deep and abiding, is oftenest kindled in the heart matured by passion and by pain, tested in the stress of life, deepened and strengthened by manifold experience; and such a heart receives no unworthy guest, lights its altar-fire for no idol of wood or clay. I felt that I rendered Herman Van Alstyne far nobler and higher homage, that I did him purer justice in loving him now than it had ever been in my power to do before.

First love is a honeyed and dewy romance, fit for novels and schoolgirls; but of the myriad women who have lived to curse their marriage-day nine-tenths have been those who married in their ignorant girlhood, and married boys.

I have digressed to honor Herman, to vindicate myself. That Christmas-eve I lay sheltered and at rest on his arm, till the toll of midnight rang clear upon my ear. I could forever sing the angels' song now, that for years had been a blank repetition to my wretched and ungodly soul.

"Peace on earth!" was no more a chimera; I knew it at heart. "Good will to men!" that was spontaneous; I loved all in and for one. "Glory to God in the highest!" What did that ask to utter it but a full thankfulness that bore me upward like the flood-tide of a summer sea?

Blessed as I was, my common sense reminded me that it was far into the night, that I ought to sleep; so I said good-night to Herman, and crept with weak steps to my room. I fell asleep to dream of him, of Eleanor, of peace, and I woke into the deep silence that always preceded – It.

I woke knowing what stood beside me. Keen starlight pierced the pane, and shed a dim, obscure perception of place and outline over my room. A long, restful, sobbing sigh parted my lips; I perceived It was at hand; fear fled; terror died out; I turned my eyes – oh God! it was Eleanor!

Wan – frail – a flowing outline of shadow, but the face in every faultless line and vivid expression; now an expression of intense longing, of wistful prayer, of pleading that would never be denied.

I lifted my heavy arms toward the vision; it swayed and bent above me: the white lips parted; no murmur nor sound clave them, yet they spoke – "Forgive! forgive!"

"Eleanor! Yes love, darling! yes, forever, as I hope to be forgiven!" I cried out aloud. A gleam of rapture and rest relaxed the brow, the sad eyes; love ineffable glowed along each lineament, and transfused to splendor the frigid moulding of snow.

I closed my eyes to crush inward the painful tears, and a touch of lips sealed them with sacred and unearthly repose. I looked again; It had gone forever. The Christmas bells pealed loud and clear for dawn, and my thoughts rung their own joy bells beside the steeple chimes. Herman and Eleanor both loved me – I had forgiven; I was forgiven.

Yet must day and space echo that word once more. Hear me, Eleanor! hear me, from that mystic country where thou hast fled before!

I repeat that forgiveness again. So may Heaven pardon me in the hour of need; so may God look upon me with strong affection in the parting of soul and body, even as I pardon and love thee, Eleanor, with a truth and faith eternal! Thee, forever loved, but, ah! not now forever lost?

Emily Dickinson (1830–1886)

The outline of Emily Dickinson's career has become a legend: she lived as a recluse in the upstairs room of her parents' home, dressed in white, published only a handful of works in her lifetime, and left nearly 1,800 poems, neatly hand-stitched into little volumes, to be found after her death. Whatever else one may say of her fabled eccentricities, they allowed this extraordinarily talented artist the privacy in which to create some of the most innovative poetry of the nineteenth century, works she knew her contemporaries were not prepared to understand.

Poe observed that "terror is not of Germany, but of the soul." Many of Emily Dickinson's poems confront the terrors of ordinary life: nightmares, repressed thoughts, the strangeness behind familiar nature.

Text: *The Poems of Emily Dickinson: Reading Edition,* ed. R. W. Franklin (Cambridge, MA: The Belknap Press of Harvard University Press, 1998). Copyright © 1998 by the President and Fellows of Harvard College. Copyright © 1951, 1955, 1979, 1983 by the President and Fellows of Harvard College. Reprinted by permission of the publishers and the Trustees of Amherst College.

Eight Poems

F 43

Through lane it lay – thro' bramble –
Through clearing and thro' wood –
Banditti often passed us
Opon the lonely road.

The wolf came peering curious –
The Owl looked puzzled down –
The serpent's satin figure
Glid stealthily along,

The tempests touched our garments –
The lightning's poniards gleamed –
Fierce from the Crag above us
The hungry Vulture screamed –

The Satyrs fingers beckoned –
The Valley murmured "Come" –
These were the mates –
This was the road
These Children fluttered home.

F 340

I felt a Funeral, in my Brain,
And Mourners to and fro
Kept treading – treading – till it seemed
That Sense was breaking through –

And when they all were seated,
A Service, like a Drum –
Kept beating – beating – till I thought
My mind was going numb –

And then I heard them lift a Box
And creak across my Soul
With those same Boots of Lead, again,
Then Space – began to toll,

As all the Heavens were a Bell,
And Being, but an Ear,
And I, and Silence, some strange Race
Wrecked, solitary, here –

And then a Plank in Reason, broke,
And I dropped down, and down –
And hit a World, at every plunge,
And Finished knowing – then –

F 341

'Tis so appalling – it exhilarates –
So over Horror, it half captivates –
The Soul stares after it, secure –
To know the worst, leaves no dread more –

To scan a Ghost, is faint –
But grappling, conquers it –
How easy, Torment, now –
Suspense kept sawing so –

The Truth, is Bald – and Cold –
But that will hold –
If any are not sure –
We show them – prayer –
But we, who know,
Stop hoping, now –

Looking at Death, is Dying –
Just let go the Breath –
And not the pillow at your cheek
So slumbereth –

Others, can wrestle –
Your's, is done –
And so of Wo, bleak dreaded – come,
It sets the Fright at liberty –
And Terror's free –
Gay, Ghastly, Holiday!

F 360

The Soul has Bandaged moments –
When too appalled to stir –
She feels some ghastly Fright come up
And stop to look at her –

Salute her, with long fingers –
Caress her freezing hair –
Sip, Goblin, from the very lips
The Lover – hovered – o'er –
Unworthy, that a thought so mean
Accost a Theme – so – fair –

The soul has moments of escape –
When bursting all the doors –
She dances like a Bomb, abroad,
And swings opon the Hours,

As do the Bee – delirious borne –
Long Dungeoned from his Rose –
Touch Liberty – then know no more –
But Noon, and Paradise –

The Soul's retaken moments –
When, Felon led along,
With shackles on the plumed feet,
And staples, in the song,

The Horror welcomes her, again,
These, are not brayed of Tongue –

F 407

One need not be a Chamber – to be Haunted –
One need not be a House –
The Brain has Corridors – surpassing
Material Place –

Far safer, of a midnight meeting
External Ghost
Than it's interior confronting –
That cooler Host –

Far safer, through an Abbey gallop,
The Stones a'chase –
Than unarmed, one's a'self encounter –
In lonesome Place –

Ourself behind ourself, concealed –
Should startle most –
Assassin hid in our Apartment
Be Horror's least –

The Body – borrows a Revolver –
He bolts the Door –
O'erlooking a superior spectre –
Or More –

F 425

'Twas like a Maelstrom, with a notch,
That nearer, every Day,
Kept narrowing it's boiling Wheel
Until the Agony

Toyed coolly with the final inch
Of your delirious Hem –
And you dropt, lost,
When something broke –
And let you from a Dream –

As if a Goblin with a Guage –
Kept measuring the Hours –
Until you felt your Second
Weigh, helpless, in his Paws –

And not a Sinew – stirred could help,
And Sense was setting numb
When God – remembered – and the Fiend
Let go, then, Overcome –

As if your Sentence stood – pronounced –
And you were frozen led
From Dungeon's luxury of Doubt
To Gibbets, and the Dead –

And when the Film had stitched your eyes
A Creature gasped "Reprieve"!
Which Anguish was the utterest – then –
To perish, or to live?

F 431

If I may have it, when it's dead,
I'll be contented – so –

If just as soon as Breath is out
It shall belong to me –

Until they lock it in the Grave,
'Tis Bliss I cannot weigh –
For tho' they lock Thee in the Grave,
Myself – can own the key –

Think of it Lover! I and Thee
Permitted – face to face to be –
After a Life – a Death – we'll say –
For Death was That –
And this – is Thee –

I'll tell Thee All – how Bald it grew –
How Midnight felt, at first – to me –
How all the Clocks stopped in the World –
And Sunshine pinched me – 'Twas so cold –

Then how the Grief got sleepy – some –
As if my soul were deaf and dumb –
Just making signs – across – to Thee –
That this way – thou could'st notice me –

I'll tell you how I tried to keep
A smile, to show you, when this Deep
All Waded – We look back for Play,
At those Old Times – in Calvary,

Forgive me, if the Grave come slow –
For Coveting to look at Thee –
Forgive me, if to stroke thy frost
Outvisions Paradise!

F 1433

What mystery pervades a well!
The water lives so far –
A neighbor from another world
Residing in a jar

Whose limit none have ever seen,
But just his lid of glass –
Like looking every time you please
In an abyss's face!

The grass does not appear afraid,
I often wonder he
Can stand so close and look so bold
At what is awe to me.

Related somehow they may be,
The sedge stands next the sea
Where he is floorless
And does no timidity betray –

But nature is a stranger yet;
The ones that cite her most
Have never passed her haunted house,
Nor simplified her ghost.

To pity those that know her not
Is helped by the regret
That those who know her, know her less
The nearer her they get.

Louisa May Alcott (1832–1888)

Louisa May Alcott was the daughter of Bronson Alcott, a leading member of the New England transcendentalist movement. Distinguished connections and friendship with such luminaries as Emerson and Thoreau (who tutored the young Louisa) did not keep the family from poverty, and at one point in her adolescence the future author of *Little Women* worked as a domestic servant.

Before the story of the March sisters brought her fame and wealth, Alcott published a series of thrillers, some anonymously, others under the pseudonym A. M. Barnard. Her thrillers, while written for a quick dollar, are solidly competent productions, and reveal her pleasure in the energetic if raw conventions of the popular literature of her era. They also show her immersion in Gothic fiction, up and down the scale of seriousness,

including that of her countrymen Hawthorne (at times a Concord neighbor) and Poe. Most of these stories and novellas were uncollected and were only discovered in the twentieth century by scholar Madeline Stern. However, "A Whisper in the Dark," first published anonymously in *Frank Leslie's Illustrated Magazine* in 1863, was published under Alcott's name with "A Modern Mephistopheles" in 1899.

"A Whisper in the Dark" is a Gothic tale in the tradition of Charlotte Brontë's *Jane Eyre*, with a strong feminist theme. The use of law and medicine to oppress and control women will be seen again in Gilman's "The Yellow Wallpaper."

Text: Louisa May Alcott, *A Modern Mephistopheles and A Whisper in the Dark* (Boston: Little, Brown, 1914).

A Whisper in the Dark

As we rolled along, I scanned my companion covertly, and saw much to interest a girl of seventeen. My uncle was a handsome man, with all the polish of foreign life fresh upon him; yet it was neither comeliness nor graceful ease which most attracted me; for even my inexperienced eye caught glimpses of something stern and somber below these external charms, and my long scrutiny showed me the keenest eye, the hardest mouth, the subtlest smile I ever saw, – a face which in repose wore the look that comes to those who have led lives of pleasure and learned their emptiness. He seemed intent on some thought that absorbed him, and for a time rendered him forgetful of my presence, as he sat with folded arms, fixed eyes, and restless lips. While I looked, my own mind was full of deeper thought than it had ever been before; for I was recalling, word for word, a paragraph in that half-read letter: –

"At eighteen Sybil is to marry her cousin, the compact having been made between my brother and myself in their childhood. My son is with me now, and I wish them to be together during the next few months, therefore my niece must leave you sooner than I at first intended. Oblige me by preparing her for an immediate and final separation, but leave all disclosures to me, as I prefer the girl to remain ignorant of the matter for the present."

That displeased me. Why was I to remain ignorant of so important an affair? Then I smiled to myself, remembering that I did know, thanks to the willful curiosity that prompted me to steal a peep into the letter that Mme. Bernard had pored over with such an anxious face. I saw only a single paragraph, for my own name arrested my eye; and, though wild to read all, I had scarcely time to whisk the paper back into the reticule the forgetful old soul had left hanging on the arm of her chair. It was enough, however, to set my girlish brain in a ferment, and keep me gazing wistfully at my uncle, conscious that my future now lay in his hands; for I was an orphan and he my guardian, though I had seen him but seldom since I was confided to madame a six years' child.

Presently my uncle became cognizant of my steady stare, and returned it with one as steady for a moment, then said, in a low, smooth tone, that ill accorded with the satirical smile that touched his lips, –

"I am a dull companion for my little niece. How shall I provide her with pleasanter amusement than counting my wrinkles or guessing my thoughts?"

I was a frank, fearless creature, quick to feel, speak, and act, so I answered readily, –

"Tell me about my cousin Guy. Is he as handsome, brave, and clever as madame says his father was when a boy?"

My uncle laughed a short laugh, touched with scorn, whether for madame, himself, or me I could not tell, for his countenance was hard to read.

"A girl's question and artfully put; nevertheless I shall not answer it, but let you judge for yourself."

"But, sir, it will amuse me and beguile the way. I feel a little strange and forlorn at leaving madame, and talking of my new home and friends will help me to know and love them sooner. Please tell me, for I've had my own way all my life, and can't bear to be crossed."

My petulance seemed to amuse him, and I became aware that he was observing me with a scrutiny as keen as my own had been; but I smilingly sustained it, for my vanity was pleased by the approbation his eye betrayed. The evident interest he now took in all I said and did was sufficient flattery for a young thing, who felt her charms and longed to try their power.

"I, too, have had my own way all my life; and as the life is double the length, the will is double the strength of yours, and again I say no. What next, mademoiselle?"

He was blander than ever as he spoke, but I was piqued, and resolved to try coaxing, eager to gain my point, lest a too early submission now should mar my freedom in the future.

"But that is ungallant, uncle, and I still have hopes of a kinder answer, both because you are too generous to refuse so small a favor to your 'little niece,' and because she can be charmingly wheedlesome when she likes. Won't you say yes now, uncle?" And pleased with the daring of the thing, I put my arm about his neck, kissed him daintily, and perched myself upon his knee with most audacious ease.

He regarded me mutely for an instant, then, holding me fast, deliberately returned my salute on lips, cheeks, and forehead, with such warmth that I turned scarlet and struggled to free myself, while he laughed that mirthless laugh of his till my shame turned to anger, and I imperiously commanded him to let me go.

"Not yet, young lady. You came here for your own pleasure, but shall stay for mine, till I tame you as I see you must be tamed. It is a short process with me, and I possess experience in the work; for Guy, though by nature as wild as a hawk, has learned to come at my call as meekly as a dove. Chut! What a little fury it is!"

I was just then; for exasperated at his coolness, and quite beside myself, I had suddenly stooped and bitten the shapely white hand that held both my own. I had better have submitted; for slight as the foolish action was, it had an influence on my afterlife as many another such has had. My uncle stopped laughing, his hand tightened its grasp, for a moment his cold eye glittered and a grim look settled round the mouth, giving to his whole face a ruthless expression that entirely altered it. I felt perfectly powerless. All my little arts had failed, and for the first time I was mastered. Yet only physically; my spirit was rebellious still. He saw it in the glance that met his own, as I sat erect and pale, with something more than childish anger. I think it pleased him, for swiftly as it had come the dark look passed, and quietly, as if we were the best of friends, he began to relate certain exciting adventures he had known abroad, lending to the picturesque narration the charm of that peculiarly melodious voice, which soothed and won me in spite of myself, holding me intent till I forgot the past; and when he paused I found that I was leaning confidentially on his shoulder, asking for more, yet conscious of an instinctive distrust of this man whom I had so soon learned to fear yet fancy.

As I was recalled to myself, I endeavored to leave him; but he still detained me, and, with a curious expression, produced a case so quaintly fashioned that I cried out in admiration, while he selected two cigarettes, mildly aromatic with the herbs they were composed of, lit them, offered me one, dropped the window, and leaning back surveyed me with an air of extreme enjoyment, as I sat meekly puffing and wondering what prank I should play a part in next. Slowly the narcotic influence of the herbs diffused itself like a pleasant haze over all my senses; sleep, the most grateful, fell upon my eyelids, and the last thing I remember was my uncle's face dreamily regarding me through a cloud of fragrant smoke. Twilight wrapped us in its shadows when I woke, with the night wind blowing on my forehead, the muffled roll of wheels sounding in my ear, and my cheek pillowed upon my uncle's arm. He was humming a French *chanson* about "love and wine, and the Seine tomorrow!" I listened till I caught the air, and presently joined him, mingling my girlish treble with his flutelike tenor. He stopped at once and, in the coolly courteous tone I had always heard in our few interviews, asked if I was ready for lights and home.

"Are we there?" I cried; and looking out saw that we were ascending an avenue which swept up to a pile of buildings that rose tall and dark against the sky, with here and there a gleam along its gray front.

"Home at last, thank heaven!" And springing out with the agility of a young man, my uncle led me over a terrace into a long hail, light and warm, and odorous with the breath of flowers blossoming here and there in graceful groups. A civil, middle-aged maid received and took me to my room, a bijou of a place, which increased my wonder when told that my uncle had chosen all its decorations and superintended their arrangement. "He understands women," I thought, handling the toilet ornaments, trying luxurious chair and lounge, and ending by slipping my feet into the scarlet-and-white Turkish slippers, coquettishly turning up their toes before the fire. A few moments I gave to examination, and, having expressed my satisfaction, was asked by my maid if I would be pleased to dress, as "the master" never allowed dinner to wait for anyone. This recalled to me the fact that I was doubtless to meet my future husband at that meal, and in a moment every faculty was intent upon achieving a grand toilette for this first interview. The maid possessed skill and taste, and I a wardrobe lately embellished with Parisian gifts from my uncle which I was eager to display in his honor.

When ready, I surveyed myself in the long mirror as I had never done before, and saw there a little figure, slender, yet stately, in a dress of foreign fashion, ornamented with lace and carnation ribbons which enhanced the fairness of neck and arms, while blond hair, wavy and golden, was gathered into an antique knot of curls behind, with a carnation fillet, and below a blooming dark-eyed face, just then radiant with girlish vanity and eagerness and hope.

"I'm glad I'm pretty!"

"So am I, Sybil."

I had unconsciously spoken aloud, and the echo came from the doorway where stood my uncle, carefully dressed, looking comelier and cooler than ever. The disagreeable smile flitted over his lips as he spoke, and I started, then stood abashed, till beckoning, he added in his most courtly manner, –

"You were so absorbed in the contemplation of your charming self that Janet answered my tap and took herself away unheard. You are mistress of my table now. It waits; will you come down?"

With a last touch to that unruly hair of mine, a last, comprehensive glance and shake, I took the offered arm and rustled down the wide staircase, feeling that the romance of my life was about to begin. Three covers were laid, three chairs set, but only two were occupied, for no Guy appeared. I asked no questions, showed no surprise, but tried to devour my chagrin with my dinner, and exerted myself to charm my uncle into the belief that I had forgotten my cousin. It was a failure, however, for that empty seat had an irresistible fascination for me, and more than once, as my eye returned from its furtive scrutiny of napkin, plate, and trio of colored glasses, it met my uncle's and fell before his penetrative glance. When I gladly rose to leave him to his wine – for he did not ask me to remain – he also rose, and, as he held the door for me, he said, –

"You asked me to describe your cousin. You have seen one trait of his character tonight; does it please you?"

I knew he was as much vexed as I at Guy's absence, so quoting his own words, I answered saucily, –

"Yes, for I'd rather see the hawk free than coming tamely at your call, Uncle."

He frowned slightly, as if unused to such liberty of speech, yet bowed when I swept him a stately little curtsy and sailed away to the drawing room, wondering if my uncle was as angry with me as I was with my cousin. In solitary grandeur I amused myself by strolling through the suite of handsome rooms henceforth to be my realm, looked at myself in the long mirrors, as every woman is apt to do when alone and in costume, danced over the mossy carpets, touched the grand piano, smelled the flowers, fingered the ornaments on étagère and table, and was just giving my handkerchief a second drench of some refreshing perfume from a filigree flask that had captivated me when the hall door was flung wide, a quick step went running upstairs, boots tramped overhead, drawers seemed hastily opened and shut, and a bold, blithe voice broke out into a hunting song in a tone so like my uncle's that I involuntarily flew to the door, crying, –

"Guy is come!"

Fortunately for my dignity, no one heard me, and hurrying back I stood ready to skim into a chair and assume propriety at a minute's notice, conscious, meanwhile, of the new influence which seemed suddenly to gift the silent house with vitality, and add the one charm it needed – that of cheerful companionship. "How will he meet me? And how shall I meet him?" I thought, looking up at the bright-faced boy, whose portrait looked back at me with a mirthful light in the painted eyes and a trace of his father's disdainful smile in the curves of the firm-set lips. Presently the quick steps came flying down again, past the door, straight to the dining room opposite, and, as I stood listening with a strange flutter at my heart, I heard an imperious young voice say rapidly, –

"Beg pardon, sir, unavoidably detained. Has she come? Is she bearable?"

"I find her so. Dinner is over, and I can offer you nothing but a glass of wine."

My uncle's voice was frostily polite, making a curious contrast to the other, so impetuous and frank, as if used to command or win all but one.

"Never mind the dinner! I'm glad to be rid of it; so I'll drink your health, Father, and then inspect our new ornament."

"Impertinent boy!" I muttered, yet at the same moment resolved to deserve his appellation, and immediately grouped myself as effectively as possible, laughing at my folly as I did so. I possessed a pretty foot, therefore one little slipper appeared quite naturally below the last flounce of my dress; a bracelet glittered on my arm as it emerged from among the lace and carnation knots; that arm supported my head. My profile was well cut, my eyelashes long, therefore I read with face half averted from the door. The light showered down, turning my hair to gold; so I smoothed my curls, retied my snood, and, after a satisfied survey, composed myself with an absorbed aspect and a quickened pulse to await the arrival of the gentlemen.

Soon they came. I knew they paused on the threshold, but never stirred till an irrepressible "You are right, sir!" escaped the younger. Then I rose prepared to give him the coldest greeting, yet I did not. I had almost expected to meet the boyish face and figure of the picture; I saw instead a man comely and tall. A dark moustache half hid the proud mouth; the vivacious eyes were far kinder, though quite as keen as his father's; and the freshness of unspoiled youth lent a charm which the older man had lost forever. Guy's glance of pleased surprise was flatteringly frank, his smile so cordial, his "Welcome, cousin!" such a hearty sound that my coldness melted in a breath, my dignity was all forgotten, and before I could restrain myself I had offered both hands with the impulsive exclamation, –

"Cousin Guy, I know I shall be very happy here! Are you glad I have come?"

"Glad as I am to see the sun after a November fog."

And bending his tall head, he kissed my hand in the graceful foreign fashion he had learned abroad. It pleased me mightily, for it was both affectionate and respectful. Involuntarily I contrasted it with my uncle's manner, and flashed a significant glance at him as I did so. He understood it, but only nodded with the satirical look I hated, shook out his paper, and began to read. I sat down again, careless of myself now; and Guy stood on the rug, surveying me with an expression of surprise that rather nettled my pride.

"He is only a boy, after all; so I need not be daunted by his inches or his airs. I wonder if he knows I am to be his wife, and likes it."

The thought sent the color to my forehead, my eyes fell, and despite my valiant resolution I sat like any bashful child before my handsome cousin. Guy laughed a boyish laugh as he sat down on his father's footstool, saying, while he warmed his slender brown hands, –

"I beg your pardon, Sybil. (We won't be formal, will we?) But I haven't seen a lady for a month, so I stare like a boor at sight of a silk gown and highbred face. Are those people coming, sir?"

"If Sybil likes, ask her."

"Shall we have a flock of people here to make it gay for you, Cousin, or do you prefer our quiet style better; just riding, driving, lounging, and enjoying life, each in his own wave. Henceforth it is to be as you command in such matters."

"Let things go on as they have done then. I don't care for society, and strangers wouldn't make it gay to me, for I like freedom; so do you, I think."

"Ah, don't I!"

A cloud flitted over his smiling face, and he punched the fire, as if some vent were necessary for the sudden gust of petulance that knit his black brows into a frown, and caused his father to tap him on the shoulder with the bland request, as he rose to leave the room, –

"Bring the portfolios and entertain your cousin; I have letters to write, and Sybil is too tired to care for music to-night."

Guy obeyed with a shrug of the shoulder his father touched, but lingered in the recess till my uncle, having made his apologies to me, had left the room; then my cousin rejoined me, wearing the same cordial aspect I first beheld. Some restraint was evidently removed, and his natural self appeared. A very winsome self it was, courteous, gay, and frank, with an undertone of deeper feeling than I thought to find. I watched him covertly, and soon owned to myself that he was all I most admired in the ideal hero every girl creates in her romantic fancy; for I no longer looked upon this young man as my cousin, but my lover, and through all our future intercourse this thought was always uppermost, full of a charm that never lost its power.

Before the evening ended Guy was kneeling on the rug beside me, our two heads close together, while he turned the contents of the great portfolio spread before us, looking each other freely in the face, as I listened and he described, both breaking into frequent peals of laughter at some odd adventure or comical mishap in his own travels, suggested by the pictured scenes before us. Guy was very charming, I my blithest, sweetest self, and when we parted late, my cousin watched me up the stairs with still another "Good night, Sybil," as if both sight and sound were pleasant to him.

"Is that your horse Sultan?" I called from my window next morning, as I looked down upon my cousin, who was coming up the drive from an early gallop on the moors.

"Yes, bonny Sybil; come and admire him," he called back, hat in hand, and a quick smile rippling over his face.

I went, and standing on the terrace, caressed the handsome creature, while Guy said, glancing up at his father's undrawn curtains, –

"If your saddle had come, we would take a turn before 'my lord' is ready for breakfast. This autumn air is the wine you women need."

I yearned to go, and when I willed the way soon appeared; so careless of bonnetless head and cambric gown, I stretched my hands to him, saying boldly, –

"Play young Lochinvar, Guy; I am little and light; take me up before you and show me the sea."

He liked the daring feat, held out his hand, I stepped on his boot toe, sprang up, and away we went over the wide moor, where the sun shone in a cloudless heaven, the lark soared singing from the green grass at our feet, and the September wind blew freshly from the sea. As we paused on the upland slope, that gave us a free view of the country for miles, Guy dismounted, and standing with his arm about the saddle to steady me in my precarious seat, began to talk.

"Do you like your new home, Cousin?"

"More than I can tell you!"

"And my father, Sybil?"

"Both yes and no to that question, Guy; I hardly know him yet."

True, but you must not expect to find him as indulgent and fond as many guardians would be to such as you. It's not his nature. Yet you can win his heart by obedience, and soon grow quite at ease with him."

"Bless you! I'm that already, for I fear no one. Why, I sat on his knee yesterday and smoked a cigarette of his own offering, though madame would have fainted if she had seen me; then I slept on his arm an hour, and he was fatherly kind, though I teased him like a gnat."

"The deuce he was!" with which energetic expression Guy frowned at the landscape and harshly checked Sultan's attempt to browse, while I wondered what was amiss between father and son, and resolved to discover; but finding the conversation at an end, started it afresh by asking, –

"Is any of my property in this part of the country, Guy? Do you know I am as ignorant as a baby about my own affairs; for, as long as every whim was gratified and my purse full, I left the rest to madame and uncle, though the first hadn't a bit of judgment, and the last I scarcely knew. I never cared to ask questions before, but now I am intensely curious to know how matters stand."

"All you see is yours, Sybil" was the brief answer.

"What, that great house, the lovely gardens, these moors, and the forest stretching to the sea? I'm glad! I'm glad! But where, then, is your home, Guy?"

"Nowhere."

At this I looked so amazed that his gloom vanished in a laugh, as he explained, but briefly, as if this subject were no pleasanter than the first, –

"By your father's will you were desired to take possession of the old place at eighteen. You will be that soon; therefore, as your guardian, my father has prepared things for you, and is to share your home until you marry."

"When will that be, I wonder?" And I stole a glance from under my lashes, wild to discover if Guy knew of the compact and was a willing party to it. His face was half averted, but over his dark cheek I saw a deep flush rise, as he answered, stooping to pull a bit of heather, –

"Soon, I hope, or the gentleman sleeping there below will be tempted to remain a fixture with you on his knee as madame my wife. He is not your own uncle, you know."

I smiled at the idea, but Guy did not see it; and seized with a whim to try my skill with the hawk that seemed inclined to peck at its master, I said demurely, –

"Well, why not? I might be very happy if I learned to love him, as I should, if he were always in that kindest mood of his. Would you like me for a little mamma, Guy?"

"No!" short and sharp as a pistol shot.

"Then you must marry and have a home of your own, my son."

"Don't, Sybil! I'd rather you didn't see me in a rage, for I'm not a pleasant sight, I assure you; and I'm afraid I shall be in one if you go on. I early lost my mother, but I love her tenderly, because my father is not much to me, and I know if she had lived I should not be what I am."

Bitter was his voice, moody his mien, and all the sunshine gone at once. I looked down and touched his black hair with a shy caress, feeling both penitent and pitiful.

"Dear Guy, forgive me if I pained you. I'm a thoughtless creature, but I'm not malicious, and a word will restrain me if kindly spoken. My home is always yours, and when my fortune is mine you shall never want, if you are not too proud to accept help from your own kin. You are a little proud, aren't you?"

"As Lucifer, to most people. I think I should not be to you, for you understand me, Sybil, and with you I hope to grow a better man."

He turned then, and through the lineaments his father had bequeathed him I saw a look that must have been his mother's, for it was womanly, sweet, and soft, and lent new beauty to the dark eyes, always kind, and just then very tender. He had checked his words suddenly, like one who has gone too far, and with that hasty look into my face had bent his own upon the ground, as if to hide the unwonted feeling that had mastered him. It lasted but a moment, then his old manner returned, as he said gaily, –

"There drops your slipper. I've been wondering what kept it on. Pretty thing! They say it is a foot like this that oftenest tramples on men's hearts. Are you cruel to your lovers, Sybil?"

"I never had one, for madame guarded me like a dragon, and I led the life of a nun; but when I do find one I shall try his mettle well before I give up my liberty."

"Poets say it is sweet to give up liberty for love, and they ought to know," answered Guy, with a sidelong glance.

I liked that little speech, and recollecting the wistful look he had given me, the significant words that had escaped him, and the variations of tone and manner constantly succeeding one another, I felt assured that my cousin was cognizant of the family league, and accepted it, yet with the shyness of a young lover, knew not how to woo. This pleased me, and quite satisfied with my morning's work, I mentally resolved to charm my cousin slowly, and enjoy the romance of a genuine wooing, without which no woman's life seems complete, – in her own eyes at least. He had gathered me a knot of purple heather, and as he gave it I smiled my sweetest on him, saying, –

"I commission you to supply me with nosegays, for you have taste, and I love wild flowers. I shall wear this at dinner in honor of its giver. Now take me home; for moors, though beautiful, are chilly, and I have no wrapper but this microscopic handkerchief."

Off went his riding jacket, and I was half smothered in it. The hat followed next, and as he sprang up behind I took the reins, and felt a thrill of delight in sweeping down the slope with that mettlesome creature tugging at the bit, that strong arm around me, and the happy hope that the heart I leaned on might yet learn to love me.

The day so began passed pleasantly, spent in roving over house and grounds with my cousin, setting my possessions in order, and writing to dear old madame. Twilight found me in my bravest attire, with Guy's heather in my hair, listening for his step, and longing to run and meet him when he came. Punctual to the instant he appeared, and this dinner was a far different one from that of yesterday, for both father and son seemed in their gayest and most gallant mood, and I enjoyed the hour heartily. The world seemed all in tune now, and when I went to the drawing room I was moved to play my most stirring marches, sing my blithest songs, hoping to bring one at least of the gentlemen to join me. It brought both, and my first glance showed me a curious change in each. My uncle looked harassed and yet amused; Guy looked sullen and eyed his father with covert glances.

The morning's chat flashed into my mind, and I asked myself, "Is Guy jealous so soon?" It looked a little like it, for he threw himself upon a couch and lay there silent and morose; while my uncle paced to and fro, thinking deeply, while apparently listening to the song he bade me finish. I did so, then followed the whim that now possessed me, for I wanted to try my power over them both, to see if I could restore that gentler mood of my uncle's, and assure myself that Guy cared whether I was friendliest with him or not.

"Uncle, come and sing with me; I like that voice of yours."

"Tut, I am too old for that; take this indolent lad instead. His voice is fresh and young, and will chord well with yours."

"Do you know that pretty *chanson* about 'love and wine, and the Seine tomorrow,' cousin Guy?" I asked, stealing a sly glance at my uncle.

"Who taught you that?" And Guy eyed me over the top of the couch with an astonished expression which greatly amused me.

"No one; uncle sang a bit of it in the carriage yesterday. I like the air, so come and teach me the rest."

"It is no song for you, Sybil. You choose strange entertainment for a lady, sir."

A look of unmistakable contempt was in the son's eye, of momentary annoyance in the father's, yet his voice betrayed none as he answered, still pacing placidly along the room, –

"I thought she was asleep, and unconsciously began it to beguile a silent drive. Sing on Sybil; that Bacchanalian snatch will do you no harm."

But I was tired of music now they had come, so I went to him, and passing my arm through his, walked beside him, saying with my most persuasive aspect, –

"Tell me about Paris, uncle; I intend to go there as soon as I'm of age, if you will let me. Does your guardianship extend beyond that time?"

"Only till you marry."

"I shall be in no haste, then, for I begin to feel quite homelike and happy here with you, and shall be content without other society; only you'll soon tire of me, and leave me to some dismal governess, while you and Guy go pleasuring."

"No fear of that, Sybil; I shall hold you fast till some younger guardian comes to rob me of my merry ward."

As he spoke, he took the hand that lay upon his arm into a grasp so firm, and turned on me a look so keen, that I involuntarily dropped my eyes lest he should read my secret there. Eager to turn the conversation, I asked, pointing to a little miniature hanging underneath the portrait of his son, before which he had paused, –

"Was that Guy's mother, sir?"

"No, your own."

I looked again, and saw a face delicate yet spirited, with dark eyes, a passionate mouth, and a head crowned with hair as plenteous and golden as my own; but the whole seemed dimmed by age, the ivory was stained, the glass cracked, and a faded ribbon fastened it. My eyes filled as I looked, and a strong desire seized me to know what had defaced this little picture of the mother whom I never knew.

"Tell me about her, uncle; I know so little, and often long for her so much. Am I like her, sir?"

Why did my uncle avert his eyes as he answered, –

"You are a youthful image of her, Sybil"?

"Go on, please, tell me more; tell me why this is so stained and worn; you know all, and surely I am old enough now to hear any history of pain and loss."

Something caused my uncle to knit his brows, but his bland voice never varied a tone as he placed the picture in my hand and gave me this brief explanation: –

"Just before your birth your father was obliged to cross the Channel, to receive the last wishes of a dying friend. There was an accident; the vessel foundered, and many lives were lost. He escaped, but by some mistake his name appeared in the list of missing passengers; your mother saw it, the shock destroyed her, and when your father returned he found only a motherless little daughter to welcome him. This miniature, which he always carried with him, was saved with his papers at the last moment; but though the seawater ruined it he would never have it copied or retouched, and gave it to me when he died in memory of the woman I had loved for his sake. It is yours now, my child; keep it, and never feel that you are fatherless or motherless while I remain."

Kind as was both act and speech, neither touched me, for something seemed wanting. I felt yet could not define it, for then I believed in the sincerity of all I met.

"Where was she buried, uncle? It may be foolish, but I should like to see my mother's grave."

"You shall someday, Sybil," and a curious change came over my uncle's face as he averted it.

"I have made him melancholy, talking of Guy's mother and my own; now I'll make him gay again if possible, and pique that negligent boy," I thought, and drew my uncle to a lounging chair, established myself on the arm thereof, and kept him laughing with my merriest gossip, both of us apparently unconscious of the long dark figure stretched just opposite, feigning sleep, but watching us through half-closed lids, and never stirring except to bow silently to my careless "Good night."

As I reached the stairhead, I remembered that my letter to madame, full of the frankest criticisms upon people and things, was lying unsealed on the table in the little room my uncle had set apart for my boudoir; fearing servants' eyes and tongues, I slipped down again to get it. The room adjoined the parlors, and just then was lit only by a ray from the hall lamp. I had secured the letter, and was turning to retreat, when I heard Guy say petulantly, as if thwarted yet submissive, –

"I *am* civil when you leave me alone; I *do* agree to marry her, but I won't be hurried or go a-wooing except in my own way. You know I never liked the bargain, for it's nothing else; yet I can reconcile myself to being sold, if it relieves you and gives us both a home. But, Father, mind this, if you tie me to that girl's sash too tightly I shall break away entirely, and then where are we?"

"I should be in prison and you a houseless vagabond. Trust me, my boy, and take the good fortune which I secured for you in your cradle. Look in pretty Sybil's face, and resignation will grow easy; but remember time presses, that this is our forlorn hope, and for God's sake be cautious, for she is a headstrong creature, and may refuse to fulfill her part if she learns that the contract is not binding against her will."

"I think she'll not refuse, sir; she likes me already. I see it in her eyes; she has never had a lover, she says, and according to your account a girl's first sweetheart is apt to fare the best. Besides, she likes the place, for I told her it was hers, as you bade me, and she said she could be very happy here, if my father was always kind."

"She said that, did she? Little hypocrite! For your father, read yourself, and tell me what else she babbled about in that early *tete-a-tete* of yours."

"You are as curious as a woman, sir, and always make me tell you all I do and say, yet never tell me anything in return, except this business, which I hate, because my liberty is the price, and my poor little cousin is kept in the dark. I'll tell her all, before I marry her, Father."

"As you please, hot-head. I am waiting for an account of the first love passage, so leave blushing to Sybil and begin."

I knew what was coming and stayed no longer, but caught one glimpse of the pair. Guy in his favorite place, erect upon the rug, half-laughing, half-frowning as he delayed to speak, my uncle serenely smoking on the couch; then I sped away to my own room, thinking, as I sat down in a towering passion, –

"So he does know of the baby betrothal and hates it, yet submits to please his father, who covets my fortune – mercenary creatures! I can annul the contract, can I? I'm glad to know that, for it makes me mistress of them both. I like you already, do I, and you see it in my eyes? Coxcomb! I'll be the thornier for that. Yet I do like him; I do wish he cared for me, I'm so lonely in the world, and he can be so kind."

So I cried a little, brushed my hair a good deal, and went to bed, resolving to learn all I could when, where, and how I pleased, to render myself as charming and valuable as possible, to make Guy love me in spite of himself, and then say yes or no, as my heart prompted me.

That day was a sample of those that followed, for my cousin was by turns attracted or repelled by the capricious moods that ruled me. Though conscious of a secret distrust of my uncle, I could not resist the fascination of his manner when he chose to exert its influence over me; this made my little plot easier of execution, for jealousy seemed the most effectual means to bring my wayward cousin to subjection. Full of this fancy, I seemed to tire of his society, grew thorny as a brier rose to him, affectionate as a daughter to my uncle, who surveyed us both with that inscrutable glance of his, and slowly yielded to my dominion as if he had divined my purpose and desired to aid it. Guy turned cold and gloomy, yet still lingered near me as if ready for a relenting look or word. I liked that, and took a wanton pleasure in prolonging the humiliation of the warm heart I had learned to love, yet not to value as I ought, until it was too late.

One dull November evening as I went wandering up and down the hall, pretending to enjoy the flowers, yet in reality waiting for Guy, who had left me alone all day, my uncle came from his room, where he had sat for many hours with the harassed and anxious look he always wore when certain foreign letters came.

Louisa May Alcott

"Sybil, I have something to show and tell you," he said, as I garnished his buttonhole with a spray of heliotrope,[1] meant for the laggard, who would understand its significance, I hoped. Leading me to the drawing room, my uncle put a paper into my hands, with the request, –

"This is a copy of your father's will; oblige me by reading it."

He stood watching my face as I read, no doubt wondering at my composure while I waded through the dry details of the will, curbing my impatience to reach the one important passage. There it was, but no word concerning my power to dissolve the engagement if I pleased; and, as I realized the fact, a sudden bewilderment and sense of helplessness came over me, for the strange law terms seemed to make inexorable the paternal decree which I had not seen before. I forgot my studied calmness, and asked several questions eagerly.

"Uncle, did my father really command that I should marry Guy, whether we loved each other or not?"

"You see what he there set down as his desire; and I have taken measures that you *should* love one another, knowing that few cousins, young, comely, and congenial, could live three months together without finding themselves ready to mate for their own sakes, if not for the sake of the dead and living fathers to whom they owe obedience."

"You said I need not, if I didn't choose; why is it not here?"

"I said that? Never, Sybil!" and I met a look of such entire surprise and incredulity it staggered my belief in my own senses, yet also roused my spirit, and, and, careless of consequences, I spoke out at once, –

"I heard you say it myself the night after I came, when you told Guy to be cautious, because I could refuse to fulfill the engagement, if I knew that it was not binding against my will."

This discovery evidently destroyed some plan, and for a moment threw him off his guard; for, crumpling the paper in his hand, he sternly demanded, –

"You turned eavesdropper early; how often since?"

"Never, uncle; I did not mean it then, but going for a letter in the dark, I heard your voices, and listened for an instant. It was dishonorable, but irresistible; and if you force Guy's confidence, why should not I steal yours? All is fair in war, sir, and I forgive as I hope to be forgiven."

"You have a quick wit and a reticence I did not expect to find under that frank manner. So you have known your future destiny all these months then, and have a purpose in your treatment of your cousin and myself?"

"Yes, uncle."

"May I ask what?"

I was ashamed to tell; and in the little pause before my answer came, my pique at Guy's desertion was augmented by anger at my uncle's denial of his own words the ungenerous hopes he cherished, and a strong desire to perplex and thwart him took possession of me, for I saw his anxiety concerning the success of this interview, though he endeavored to repress and conceal it. Assuming my coldest mien, I said, –

"No, sir, I think not; only I can assure you that my little plot has succeeded better than your own."

"But you intend to obey your father's wish, I hope, and fulfill your part of the compact, Sybil?"

Notes ────────────────────────────

A Whisper in the Dark

[1] The heliotrope is a symbol of love.

"Why should I? It is not binding, you know, and I'm too young to lose my liberty just yet; besides, such compacts are unjust, unwise. What right had my father to mate me in my cradle? How did he know what I should become, or Guy? How could he tell that I should not love someone else better? No! I'll not be bargained away like a piece of merchandise, but love and marry when I please!"

At this declaration of independence my uncle's face darkened ominously, some new suspicion lurked in his eye, some new anxiety beset him; but his manner was calm, his voice blander than ever as he asked, –

"Is there then someone whom you love? Confide in me, my girl."

"And if there were, what then?"

"All would be changed at once, Sybil. But who is it? Some young lover left behind at madame's?"

"No, sir."

"Who, then? You have led a recluse life here. Guy has no friends who visit him, and mine are all old, yet you say you love."

"With all my heart, uncle."

"Is this affection returned, Sybil?"

"I think so."

"And it is not Guy?"

I was wicked enough to enjoy the bitter disappointment he could not conceal at my decided words, for I thought he deserved that momentary pang; but I could not as decidedly answer that last question, for I would not lie, neither would I confess just yet; so, with a little gesture of impatience, I silently turned away, lest he should see the telltale color in my cheeks. My uncle stood an instant in deep thought, a slow smile crept to his lips, content returned to his mien, and something like a flash of triumph glittered for a moment in his eye, then vanished, leaving his countenance earnestly expectant. Much as this change surprised me, his words did more, for, taking both my hands in his, he gravely said, –

"Do you know that I am your uncle by adoption and not blood, Sybil?"

"Yes, sir; I heard so, but forgot about it," and I looked up at him, my anger quite lost in astonishment.

"Let me tell you then. Your grandfather was childless for many years, my mother was an early friend, and when her death left me an orphan, he took me for his son and heir. But two years from that time your father was born. I was too young to realize the entire change this might make in my life. The old man was too just and generous to let me feel it, and the two lads grew up together like brothers. Both married young, and when you were born a few years later than my son, your father said to me, 'Your boy shall have my girl, and the fortune I have innocently robbed you of shall make us happy in our children.' Then the family league was made, renewed at his death, and now destroyed by his daughter, unless – Sybil, I am forty-five, you not eighteen, yet you once said you could be very happy with me, if I were always kind to you. I can promise that I will be, for I love you. My darling, you reject the son, will you accept the Father?"

If he had struck me, it would scarcely have dismayed me more. I started up, and snatching away my hands, hid my face in them, for after the first tingle of surprise an almost irresistible desire to laugh came over me, but I dared not, and gravely, gently he went on, –

"I am a bold man to say this, yet I mean it most sincerely. I never meant to betray the affection I believed you never could return, and would only laugh at as a weakness; but your past acts, your present words, give me courage to confess that I desire to keep my ward mine forever. Shall it be so?"

He evidently mistook my surprise for maidenly emotion, and the suddenness of this unforeseen catastrophe seemed to deprive me of words. All thought of merriment or ridicule was forgotten in a sense of guilt, for if he feigned the love he offered it was well done, and I believed it then. I saw at once the natural impression conveyed by my conduct; my half confession and the folly of it all oppressed me with a regret and shame I could not master. My mind was in dire confusion, yet a decided "No" was rapidly emerging from the chaos, but was not uttered; for just at this crisis, as I stood with my uncle's arm about me, my hand again in his, and his head bent down to catch my answer, Guy swung himself gaily into the room.

A glance seemed to explain all, and in an instant his face assumed that expression of pale wrath so much more terrible to witness than the fiercest outbreak; his eye grew fiery, his voice bitterly sarcastic, as he said, –

"Ah, I see; the play goes on, but the actors change parts. I congratulate you, sir, on your success, and Sybil on her choice. Henceforth I am *de trop*. but before I go allow me to offer my wedding gift. You have taken the bride, let me supply the ring."

He threw a jewel box upon the table, adding, in that unnaturally calm tone that made my heart stand still:

"A little candor would have spared me much pain, Sybil; yet I hope you will enjoy your bonds as heartily as I shall my escape from them. A little confidence would have made me your ally, not your rival, Father. I have not your address; therefore I lose, you win. Let it be so. I had rather be the vagabond this makes me than sell myself, that you may gamble away that girl's fortune as you have your own and mine. You need not ask me to the wedding, I will not come. Oh, Sybil, I so loved, so trusted you!"

And with that broken exclamation he was gone.

The stormy scene had passed so rapidly, been so strange and sudden, Guy's anger so scornful and abrupt, I could not understand it, and felt like a puppet in the grasp of some power I could not resist; but as my lover left the room I broke out of the bewilderment that held me, imploring him to stay and hear me.

It was too late, he was gone, and Sultan's tramp was already tearing down the avenue. I listened till the sound died, then my hot temper rose past control, and womanlike asserted itself in vehement and voluble speech. I was angry with my uncle, my cousin, and myself, and for several minutes poured forth a torrent of explanations, reproaches, and regrets, such as only a passionate girl could utter.

My uncle stood where I had left him when I flew to the door with my vain cry; he now looked baffled, yet sternly resolved, and as I paused for breath his only answer was, –

"Sybil, you ask me to bring back that headstrong boy; I cannot; he will never come. This marriage was distasteful to him, yet he submitted for my sake, because I have been unfortunate, and we are poor. Let him go, forget the past, and be to me what I desire, for I loved your father and will be a faithful guardian to his daughter all my life. Child, it must be – come, I implore, I command you."

He beckoned imperiously as if to awe me, and held up the glittering betrothal ring as if to tempt me. The tone, the act, the look put me quite beside myself. I did go to him, did take the ring, but said as resolutely as himself, –

"Guy rejects me, and I have done with love. Uncle, you would have deceived me, used me as a means to your own selfish ends. I will accept neither yourself nor your gifts, for now I despise both you and your commands." And as the most energetic emphasis I could give to my defiance, I flung the ring, case and all, across the room; it struck the great mirror, shivered it just in the middle, and sent several loosened fragments crashing to the floor.

"Great heavens! Is the young lady mad?" exclaimed a voice behind us. Both turned and saw Dr. Karnac, a stealthy, sallow-faced Spaniard, for whom I had an invincible aversion. He was my uncle's physician, had been visiting a sick servant in the upper regions, and my adverse fate sent him to the door just at that moment with that unfortunate exclamation on his lips.

"What do you say?"

My uncle wheeled about and eyed the newcomer intently as he repeated his words. I have no doubt I looked like one demented, for I was desperately angry, pale and trembling with excitement, and as they fronted me with a curious expression of alarm on their faces, a sudden sense of the absurdity of the spectacle came over me; I laughed hysterically a moment, then broke into a passion of regretful tears, remembering that Guy was gone. As I sobbed behind my hands, I knew the gentlemen were whispering together and of me, but I never heeded them, for as I wept myself calmer a comforting thought occurred to me. Guy could not have gone far, for Sultan had been out all day, and though reckless of himself he was not of his horse, which he loved like a human being; therefore he was doubtless at the house of a humble friend nearby. If I could slip away unseen, I might undo my miserable work, or at least see him again before he went away into the world, perhaps never to return. This hope gave me courage for anything, and dashing away my tears, I took a covert survey. Dr. Karnac and my uncle still stood before the fire, deep in their low-toned conversation; their backs were toward me; and hushing the rustle of my dress, I stole away with noiseless steps into the hall, seized Guy's plaid, and, opening the great door unseen, darted down the avenue.

Not far, however; the wind buffeted me to and fro, the rain blinded me, the mud clogged my feet and soon robbed me of a slipper; groping for it in despair, I saw a light flash into the outer darkness; heard voices calling, and soon the swift tramp of steps behind me. Feeling like a hunted doe, I ran on, but before I had gained a dozen yards my shoeless foot struck a sharp stone, and I fell half stunned upon the wet grass of the wayside bank. Dr. Karnac reached me first, took me up as if I were a naughty child, and carried me back through a group of staring servants to the drawing room, my uncle following with breathless entreaties that I would be calm, and a most uncharacteristic display of bustle.

I was horribly ashamed; my head ached with the shock of the fall, my foot bled, my heart fluttered, and when the doctor put me down the crisis came, for as my uncle bent over me with the strange question "My poor girl, do you know me?" an irresistible impulse impelled me to push him from me, crying passionately, –

"Yes, I know and hate you; let me go! Let me go, or it will be too late!" Then, quite spent with the varying emotions of the last hour, for the first time in my life I swooned away.

Coming to myself, I found I was in my own room, with my uncle, the doctor, Janet, and Mrs. Best, the housekeeper, gathered about me, the latter saying, as she bathed my temples, –

"She's a sad sight, poor thing, so young, so bonny, and so unfortunate. Did you ever see her so before, Janet?"

"Bless you, no, ma'am; there was no signs of such a tantrum when I dressed her for dinner."

"What do they mean? Did they never see anyone angry before?" I dimly wondered, and presently, through the fast disappearing stupor that had held me, Dr. Karnac's deep voice came distinctly, saying, –

"If it continues, you are perfectly justified in doing so."

"Doing what?" I demanded sharply, for the sound both roused and irritated me, I disliked the man so intensely.

"Nothing, my dear, nothing," purred Mrs. Best, supporting me as I sat up, feeling weak and dazed, yet resolved to know what was going on. I was "a sad sight" indeed:

my drenched hair hung about my shoulders, my dress was streaked with mud, one shoeless foot was red with blood, the other splashed and stained, and a white, wild-eyed face completed the ruinous image the opposite mirror showed me. Everything looked blurred and strange, and a feverish unrest possessed me, for I was not one to subside easily after such a mental storm. Leaning on my arm, I scanned the room and its occupants with all the composure I could collect. The two women eyed me curiously yet pitifully; Dr. Karnac stood glancing at me furtively as he listened to my uncle, who spoke rapidly in Spanish as he showed the little scar upon his hand. That sight did more to restore me than the cordial just administered, and I rose erect, saying abruptly, –

"Please, everybody, go away; my head aches, and I want to be alone."

"Let Janet stay and help you, dear; you are not fit," began Mrs. Best; but I peremptorily stopped her.

"No, go yourself, and take her with you; I'm tired of so much stir about such foolish things as a broken glass and a girl in a pet."

"You will be good enough to take this quieting draft before I go, Miss Sybil."

"I shall do nothing of the sort, for I need only solitude and sleep to be perfectly well," and I emptied the glass the doctor offered into the fire.

He shrugged his shoulders with a disagreeable smile, and quietly began to prepare another draft, saying, –

"You are mistaken, my dear young lady; you need much care, and should obey, that your uncle may be spared further apprehension and anxiety."

My patience gave out at this assumption of authority; and I determined to earn matters with a high hand, for they all stood watching me in a way which seemed the height of impertinent curiosity.

"He is not my uncle! Never has been, and deserves neither respect nor obedience from me! I am the best judge of my own health, and you are not bettering it by contradiction and unnecessary fuss. This is my house, and you will oblige me by leaving it, Dr. Karnac; this is my room, and I insist on being left in peace immediately."

I pointed to the door as I spoke; the women hurried out with scared faces; the doctor bowed and followed, but paused on the threshold, while my uncle approached me, asking in a tone inaudible to those still hovering round the door, –

"Do you still persist in your refusal, Sybil?"

"How dare you ask me that again? I tell you I had rather die than marry you!"

"The Lord be merciful to us! Just hear how she's going on now about marrying Master. Ain't it awful, Jane?" ejaculated Mrs. Best, bobbing her head in for a last look.

"Hold your tongue, you impertinent creature!" I called out; and the fat old soul bundled away in such comical haste I laughed, in spite of languor and vexation.

My uncle left me, and I heard him say as he passed the doctor, –

"You see how it is."

"Nothing uncommon; but that virulence is a bad symptom," answered the Spaniard, and closing the door locked it, having dexterously removed the key from within.

I had never been subjected to restraint of any kind; it made me reckless at once, for this last indignity was not to be endured.

"Open this instantly!" I commanded, shaking the door. No one answered, and after a few ineffectual attempts to break the lock I left it, threw up the window and looked out; the ground was too far off for a leap, but the trellis where summer vines had clung was strong and high, a step would place me on it, a moment's agility bring me to the terrace below. I was now in just the state to attempt any rash exploit, for the cordial had both strengthened and excited me; my foot was bandaged, my clothes still wet, I could suffer no new damage, and have my own way at small cost. Out I crept, climbed safely down, and made my way to the lodge as I had at first intended. But Guy was not there; and returning, I boldly went in at the great door, straight to the room where my uncle and the doctor were still talking.

"I wish the key of my room" was my brief command.

Both started as if I had been a ghost, and my uncle exclaimed, "You here! How in heaven's name came you out?"

"By the window. I am no child to be confined for a fit of anger. I will not submit to it; tomorrow I shall go to madame; till then I will be mistress in my own house. Give me the key, sir."

"Shall I?" asked the doctor of my uncle, who nodded with a whispered, –

"Yes, yes; don't excite her again."

It was restored, and without another word I went loftily up to my room, locked myself in, and spent a restless, miserable night. When morning came, I breakfasted above stairs, and then busied myself packing trunks, burning papers, and collecting every trifle Guy had ever given me. No one annoyed me, and I saw only Janet, who had evidently received some order that kept her silent and respectful, though her face still betrayed the same curiosity and pitiful interest as the night before. Lunch was brought up, but I could not eat, and began to feel that the exposure, the fall, and excitement of the evening had left me weak and nervous, so I gave up the idea of going to madame till the morrow; and as the afternoon waned, tried to sleep, yet could not, for I had sent a note to several of Guy's haunts, imploring him to see me; but my messenger brought word that he was not to be found, and my heart was too heavy to rest.

When summoned to dinner, I still refused to go down; for I heard Dr. Karnac's voice, and would not meet him, so I sent word that I wished the carriage early the following morning, and to be left alone till then. In a few minutes, back came Janet with a glass of wine set forth on a silver salver, and a card with these words: –

"Forgive, forget, for your father's sake, and drink with me, 'Oblivion to the past.'"

It touched and softened me. I knew my uncle's pride, and saw in this an entire relinquishment of the hopes I had so thoughtlessly fostered in his mind. I was passionate, but not vindictive. He had been kind, I very willful. His mistake was natural, my resentment ungenerous. Though my resolution to go remained unchanged, I was sorry for my part in the affair; and remembering that through me his son was lost to him, I accepted his apology, drank his toast, and sent him back a dutiful "Good night."

I was unused to wine. The draft I had taken was powerful with age, and, though warm and racy to the palate, proved too potent for me. Still sitting before my fire, I slowly fell into a restless drowse, haunted by a dim dream that I was seeking Guy in a ship, whose motion gradually lulled me into perfect unconsciousness.

Waking at length, I was surprised to find myself in bed, with a shimmer of daylight peeping through the curtains. Recollecting that I was to leave early, I sprang up, took one step, and remained transfixed with dismay, for the room was not my own! Utterly unfamiliar was every object on which my eyes fell. The place was small, plainly furnished, and close, as if long unused. My trunks stood against the wall, my clothes lay on a chair, and on the bed I had left trailed a fur-lined cloak I had often seen on my uncle's shoulders. A moment I stared about me bewildered, then hurried to the window, – it was grated!

A lawn, sere and sodden, lay without, and a line of somber firs hid the landscape beyond the high wall which encompassed the dreary plot. More and more alarmed, I flew to the door and found it locked. No bell was visible, no sound audible, no human presence near me, and an ominous foreboding thrilled cold through nerves and blood, as, for the first time, I felt the paralyzing touch of fear. Not long, however. My native courage soon returned, indignation took the place of terror, and excitement gave me strength. My temples throbbed with a dull pain, my eyes were heavy, my limbs weighed down by an unwonted lassitude, and my memory seemed strangely confused; but one thing was clear to me: I must see somebody, ask questions, demand explanations, and get away to madame without delay.

With trembling hands I dressed, stopping suddenly with a cry; for lifting my hands to my head, I discovered that my hair, my beautiful, abundant hair, was gone! There was no mirror in the room, but I could feel that it had been shorn away close about face and neck. This outrage was more than I could bear, and the first tears I shed fell for my lost charm. It was weak, perhaps, but I felt better for it, clearer in mind and readier to confront whatever lay before me. I knocked and called. Then, losing patience, shook and screamed; but no one came or answered me; and wearied out at last, I sat down and cried again in impotent despair.

An hour passed, then a step approached, the key turned, and a hard-faced woman entered with a tray in her hand. I had resolved to be patient, if possible, and controlled myself to ask quietly, though my eyes kindled, and my voice trembled with resentment, –

"Where am I, and why am I here against my will?"

"This is your breakfast, miss; you must be sadly hungry" was the only reply I got.

"I will never eat till you tell me what I ask."

"Will you be quiet, and mind me if I do, miss?"

"You have no right to exact obedience from me, but I'll try."

"That's right. Now all I know is that you are twenty miles from the Moors, and came because you are ill. Do you like sugar in your coffee?"

"When did I come? I don't remember it."

"Early this morning; you don't remember because you were put to sleep before being fetched, to save trouble."

"Ah, that wine! Who brought me here?"

"Dr. Karnac, miss."

"Alone?"

"Yes, miss; you were easier to manage asleep than awake, he said."

I shook with anger, yet still restrained myself, hoping to fathom the mystery of this nocturnal journey.

"What is your name, please?" I meekly asked.

"You can call me Hannah."

"Well, Hannah, there is a strange mistake somewhere. I am not ill – you see I am not – and I wish to go away at once to the friend I was to meet today. Get me a carriage and have my baggage taken out."

"It can't be done, miss. We are a mile from town, and have no carriages here; besides, you couldn't go if I had a dozen. I have my orders, and shall obey 'em."

"But Dr. Karnac has no right to bring or keep me here."

"Your uncle sent you. The doctor has the care of you, and that is all I know about it. Now I have kept my promise, do you keep yours, miss, and eat your breakfast, else I can't trust you again."

"But what is the matter with me? How can I be ill and not know or feel it?" I demanded, more and more bewildered.

"You look it, and that's enough for them as is wise in such matters. You'd have had a fever, if it hadn't been seen to in time."

"Who cut my hair off?"

"I did; the doctor ordered it."

"How dared he? I hate that man, and never will obey him."

"Hush, miss, don't clench your hands and look in that way, for I shall have to report everything you say and do to him, and it won't be pleasant to tell that sort of thing."

The woman was civil, but grim and cool. Her eye was unsympathetic, her manner businesslike, her tone such as one uses to a refractory child, half soothing, half commanding. I conceived a dislike to her at once, and resolved to escape at all hazards, for my uncle's inexplicable movements filled me with alarm. Hannah had left my door open, a quick glance showed me another door also ajar at the end of a wide hall, a glimpse of green, and a gate. My plan was desperately simple, and I executed it without delay. Affecting to eat, I presently asked the woman for my handkerchief from the bed. She crossed the room to get it. I darted out, down the passage, along the walk, and tugged vigorously at the great bolt of the gate, but it was also locked. In despair I flew into the garden, but a high wall enclosed it on every side; and as I ran round and round vainly looking for some outlet, I saw Hannah, accompanied by a man as gray and grim as herself, coming leisurely toward me, with no appearance of excitement or displeasure. Back I would not go; and inspired with a sudden hope, swung myself into one of the firs that grew close against the wall. The branches snapped under me, the slender tree swayed perilously, but up I struggled, till the wide coping of the wall was gained. There I paused and looked back. The woman was hurrying through the gate to intercept my descent on the other side, and close behind me the man, sternly calling me to stop. I looked down, a stony ditch was below, but I would rather risk my life than tamely lose my liberty, and with a flying leap tried to reach the bank; failed, fell heavily among the stones, felt an awful crash, and then came an utter blank.

For many weeks I lay burning in a fever, fitfully conscious of Dr. Karnac and the woman's presence; once I fancied I saw my uncle, but was never sure, and rose at last a shadow of my former self, feeling pitifully broken, both mentally and physically. I was in a better room now, wintry winds howled without, but a generous fire glowed behind the high closed fender, and books lay on my table.

I saw no one but Hannah, yet could wring no intelligence from her beyond what she had already told, and no sign of interest reached me from the outer world. I seemed utterly deserted and forlorn, my spirit was crushed, my strength gone, my freedom lost, and for a time I succumbed to despair, letting one day follow another without energy or hope. It is hard to live with no object to give zest to life, especially for those still blessed with youth, and even in my prison house I soon found one quite in keeping with the mystery that surrounded me.

As I sat reading by day or lay awake at night, I became aware that the room above my own was occupied by some inmate whom I never saw. A peculiar person it seemed to be; for I heard steps going to and fro, hour after hour, in a tireless march that wore upon my nerves, as many a harsher sound would not have done. I could neither tease nor surprise Hannah into any explanation of the thing, and day after day I listened to it, till I longed to cover up my ears and implore the unknown walker to stop, for heaven's sake. Other sounds I heard and fretted over: a low monotonous murmur, as of someone singing a lullaby; a fitful tapping, like a cradle rocked on a carpetless floor; and at rare intervals cries of suffering, sharp but brief, as if forcibly suppressed. These sounds, combined with the solitude, the confinement, and the books I read, a collection of ghostly tales and weird fancies, soon wrought my nerves to a state of terrible irritability, and wore upon my health so visibly that I was allowed at last to leave my room.

The house was so well guarded that I soon relinquished all hope of escape, and listlessly amused myself by roaming through the unfurnished rooms and echoing halls, seldom venturing into Hannah's domain; for there her husband sat, surrounded by chemical apparatus, poring over crucibles and retorts. He never spoke to me, and I dreaded the glance of his cold eye, for it looked unsoftened by a ray of pity at the little figure that sometimes paused a moment on his threshold, wan and wasted as the ghost of departed hope.

The chief interest of these dreary walks centered in the door of the room above my own, for a great hound lay before it, eyeing me savagely as he rejected all advances, and uttering his deep bay if I approached too near. To me this room possessed an irresistible fascination. I could not keep away from it by day, I dreamed of it by night, it haunted me continually, and soon became a sort of monomania, which I condemned, yet could not control, till at length I found myself pacing to and fro as those invisible feet paced overhead. Hannah came and stopped me, and a few hours later Dr. Karnac appeared. I was so changed that I feared him with a deadly fear. He seemed to enjoy it; for in the pride of youth and beauty I had shown him contempt and defiance at my uncle's, and he took an ungenerous satisfaction in annoying me by a display of power. He never answered my questions or entreaties, regarded me as being without sense or will, insisted on my trying various mixtures and experiments in diet, gave me strange books to read, and weekly received Hannah's report of all that passed. That day he came, looked at me, said, "Let her walk," and went away, smiling that hateful smile of his.

Soon after this I took to walking in my sleep, and more than once woke to find myself roving lampless through that haunted house in the dead of night. I concealed these unconscious wanderings for a time, but an ominous event broke them up at last and betrayed them to Hannah.

I had followed the steps one day for several hours, walking below as they walked above; had peopled that mysterious room with every mournful shape my disordered fancy could conjure up; had woven tragical romances about it, and brooded over the one subject of interest my unnatural life possessed with the intensity of a mind upon which its uncanny influence was telling with perilous rapidity. At midnight I woke to find myself standing in a streak of moonlight, opposite the door whose threshold I had never crossed. The April night was warm, a single pane of glass high up in that closed door was drawn aside, as if for air; and as I stood dreamily collecting my sleep-drunken senses, I saw a ghostly hand emerge and beckon, as if to me. It startled me broad awake, with a faint exclamation and a shudder from head to foot. A cloud swept over the moon, and when it passed the hand was gone, but shrill through the keyhole came a whisper that chilled me to the marrow of my bones, so terribly distinct and imploring was it.

"Find it! For God's sake find it before it is too late!"

The hound sprang up with an angry growl; I heard Hannah leave her bed nearby; and with an inspiration strange as the moment, I paced slowly on with open eyes and lips apart, as I had seen *Amina* in the happy days when kind old madame took me to the theater, whose mimic horrors I had never thought to equal with such veritable ones.[2] Hannah appeared at her door with a light, but on I went in a trance of fear; for I was only kept from dropping in a swoon by the blind longing to fly from that spectral voice and hand. Past Hannah I went, she following; and as I slowly laid myself in bed, I heard her say to her husband, who just then came up, –

"Sleepwalking, John; it's getting worse and worse, as the doctor foretold; she'll settle down like the other presently, but she must be locked up at night, else the dog will do her a mischief."

The man yawned and grumbled; then they went, leaving me to spend hours of unspeakable suffering, which aged me more than years. What was I to find? Where was I to look? And when would it be too late? These questions tormented me; for I could find no answers to them, divine no meaning, see no course to pursue. Why was

Notes

[2] Sybil has seen a play or opera about the sixteenth-century African queen that included a sleepwalking scene.

I here? What motive induced my uncle to commit such an act? And when should I be liberated? were equally unanswerable, equally tormenting, and they haunted me like ghosts. I had no power to exorcise or forget. After that I walked no more, because I slept no more; sleep seemed scared away, and waking dreams harassed me with their terrors. Night after night I paced my room in utter darkness – for I was allowed no lamp – night after night I wept bitter tears wrung from me by anguish, for which I had no name; and night after night the steps kept time to mine, and the faint lullaby came down to me as if to soothe and comfort my distress. I felt that my health was going, my mind growing confused and weak; my thoughts wandered vaguely, memory began to fail, and idiocy or madness seemed my inevitable fate; but through it all my heart clung to Guy, yearning for him with a hunger that would not be appeased.

At rare intervals I was allowed to walk in the neglected garden, where no flowers doomed, no birds sang, no companion came to me but surly John, who followed with his book or pipe, stopping when I stopped, walking when I walked, keeping a vigilant eye upon me, yet seldom speaking except to decline answering my questions. These walks did me no good, for the air was damp and heavy with vapors from the marsh; for the house stood near a half-dried lake, and hills shut it in on every side. No fresh winds from upland moor or distant ocean ever blew across the narrow valley; no human creature visited the place, and nothing but a vague hope that my birthday might bring some change, some help, sustained me. It did bring help, but of such an unexpected sort that its effects remained through all my afterlife. My birthday came, and with it my uncle. I was in my room, walking restlessly – for the habit was a con-firmed one now – when the door opened, and Hannah, Dr. Karnac, my uncle, and a gentleman whom I knew to be his lawyer entered, and surveyed me as if I were a spectacle. I saw my uncle start and turn pale; I had never seen myself since I came, but if I had not suspected that I was a melancholy wreck of my former self, I should have known it then, such sudden pain and pity softened his ruthless countenance for a sin-gle instant. Dr. Karnac's eye had a magnetic power over me; I had always felt it, but in my present feeble state I dreaded, yet submitted to it with a helpless fear that should have touched his heart – it was on me then, I could not resist it, and paused fixed and fascinated by that repellent yet potent glance. Hannah pointed to the carpet worn to shreds by my weary march, to the walls which I had covered with weird, grotesque, or tragic figures to while away the heavy hours, lastly to myself mute, motionless, and scared, saying, as if in confirmation of some previous assertion, –

"You see, gentlemen, she is, as I said, quiet, but quite hopeless."

I thought she was interceding for me; and breaking from the bewilderment and fear that held me, I stretched my hands to them, crying with an imploring cry, –

"Yes, I *am* quiet! I *am* hopeless! Oh, have pity on me before this dreadful life kills me or drives me mad!"

Dr. Karnac came to me at once with a black frown, which I alone could see; I evaded him, and clung to Hannah, still crying frantically – for this seemed my last hope –

"Uncle, let me go! I will give you all I have, will never ask for Guy, will be obedient and meek if I may only go to madame and never hear the feet again, or see the sights that terrify me in this dreadful room. Take me out! For God's sake take me out!"

My uncle did not answer me, but covered up his face with a despairing gesture, and hurried from the room; the lawyer followed, muttering pitifully, "Poor thing! Poor thing!" and Dr. Karnac laughed the first laugh I had ever heard him utter as he wrenched Hannah from my grasp and locked me in alone. My one hope died then, and I resolved to kill myself rather than endure this life another month; for now it grew clear to me that they believed me mad, and death of the body was far more preferable than that of the mind. I think I *was* a little mad just then, but remember well the sense of peace that came to me as I tore strips from my clothing, braided them into a cord, hid it beneath my mattress, and serenely waited for the night. Sitting in the last twilight I thought to see in this unhappy world, I recollected that I had not heard the feet all day, and fell to pondering over the unusual omission. But if the steps had been silent in that room, voices had not, for I heard a continuous murmur at one time: the tones of one voice were abrupt and broken, the other low, yet resonant, and that, I felt assured, belonged to my uncle. Who was he speaking to? What were they saying? Should I ever know? And even then, with death before me, the intense desire to possess the secret filled me with its old unrest.

Night came at last; I heard the clock strike one, and listening to discover if John still lingered up, I heard through the deep hush a soft grating in the room above, a stealthy sound that would have escaped ears less preternaturally alert than mine. Like a flash came the thought, "Someone is filing bars or picking locks: will the unknown remember me and let me share her flight?" The fatal noose hung ready, but I no longer cared to use it, for hope had come to nerve me with the strength and courage I had lost. Breathlessly I listened; the sound went on, stopped; a dead silence reigned; then something brushed against my door, and with a suddenness that made me tingle from head to foot like an electric shock, through the keyhole came again that whisper, urgent, imploring, and mysterious, –

"Find it! For God's sake find it before it is too late!" Then fainter, as if breath failed, came the broken words, "The dog – a lock of hair – there is yet time."

Eagerness rendered me forgetful of the secrecy I should preserve, and I cried aloud, "What shall I find? Where shall I look?" My voice, sharpened by fear, rang shrilly through the house; Hannah's quick tread rushed down the hall; something fell; then loud and long rose a cry that made my heart stand still, so helpless, so hopeless was its wild lament. I had betrayed and I could not save or comfort the kind soul who had lost liberty through me. I was frantic to get out, and beat upon my door in a paroxysm of impatience, but no one came; and all night long those awful cries went on above, cries of mortal anguish, as if soul and body were being torn asunder. Till dawn I listened, pent in that room which now possessed an added terror; till dawn I called, wept, and prayed, with mingled pity, fear, and penitence; and till dawn the agony of that unknown sufferer continued unabated. I heard John hurry to and fro, heard Hannah issue orders with an accent of human sympathy in her hard voice; heard Dr. Karnac pass and repass my door; and all the sounds of confusion and alarm in that once quiet house. With daylight all was still, a stillness more terrible than the stir: for it fell so suddenly, remained so utterly unbroken, that there seemed no explanation of it but the dread word death.

At noon Hannah, a shade paler but grim as ever, brought me some food, saying she forgot my breakfast, and when I refused to eat, yet asked no questions, she bade me go into the garden and not fret myself over last night's flurry. I went, and passing down the corridor, glanced furtively at the door I never saw without a thrill; but experienced a new sensation then, for the hound was gone, the door was open, with an impulse past control, I crept in and looked about me. It was a room like mine, the carpet worn like mine, the windows barred like mine; there the resemblance ended, for an empty cradle stood beside the bed, and on that bed, below a sweeping cover, stark and still a lifeless body lay. I was inured to fear now, and an unwholesome craving for new terrors seemed to have grown by what it fed on: an irresistible desire led me close, nerved me to lift the cover and look below – a single glance, – then with a cry as panic-stricken as that which rent the silence of the night, I fled away, for the face I saw was a pale image of my own. Sharpened by suffering, pallid with death, the features were familiar as those I used to see; the hair, beautiful and blond as mine had been, streamed long over the pulseless breast, and on the hand, still clenched in that last struggle, shone the like-ness of a ring I wore, a ring bequeathed me by my father. An awesome fancy that it was myself assailed me; I had plotted death, and with the waywardness of a shattered mind, I recalled legends of spirits returning to behold the bodies they had left.

Glad now to seek the garden, I hurried down, but on the threshold of the great hall door was arrested by the sharp crack of a pistol; and as a little cloud of smoke dis-persed, I saw John drop the weapon and approach the hound, who lay writhing on the bloody grass. Moved by compassion for the faithful brute whose long vigilance was so cruelly repaid, I went to him, and kneeling there, caressed the great head that never yielded to my touch before. John assumed his watch at once, and leaning against a tree, cleaned the pistol, content that I should amuse myself with the dying creature, who looked into my face with eyes of almost human pathos and reproach. The brass collar seemed to choke him as he gasped for breath, and leaning nearer to undo it, I saw, half hidden in his own black hair, a golden lock wound tightly round the collar, and so near its color as to be unobservable, except upon a close inspection. No accident could have placed it there; no head but mine in that house wore hair of that sunny hue, – yes, one other, and my heart gave a sudden leap as I remembered the shining locks just seen on that still bosom.

"Find it – the dog – the lock of hair," rang in my ears, and swift as light came the conviction that the unknown help was found at last. The little band was woven close. I had no knife, delay was fatal. I bent my head as if lamenting over the poor beast and bit the knot apart, drew out a folded paper, hid it in my hand, and rising, strolled lei-surely back to my own room, saying I did not care to walk till it was warmer. With eager eyes I examined my strange treasure-trove. It consisted of two strips of thinnest paper, without address or signature, one almost illegible, worn at the edges and stained with the green rust of the collar; the other fresher, yet more feebly written, both abrupt and disjointed, but terribly significant to me. This was the first, –

"I have never seen you, never heard your name, yet I know that you are young, that you are suffering, and I try to help you in my poor way. I think you are not crazed yet, as I often am; for your voice is sane, your plaintive singing not like mine, your walking only caught from me, I hope. I sing to lull the baby whom I never saw; I walk to lessen the long journey that will bring me to the husband I have lost, – stop! I must not think of those things or I shall forget. If you are not already mad, you will be; I suspect you were sent here to be made so; for the air is poison, the solitude is fatal, and Karnac remorseless in his mania for plying into the mysteries of human minds. What devil sent you I may never know, but I long to warn you. I can devise no way but this; the dog comes into my room sometimes, you sometimes pause at my door and talk to him; you may find the paper I shall hide about his collar. Read, destroy, but obey it. I implore you to leave this house before it is too late."

The other paper was as follows:

"I have watched you, tried to tell you where to look, for you have not found my warning yet, though I often tie it there and hope. You fear the dog, perhaps, and my plot fails; yet I know by your altered step and voice that you are fast reaching my unhappy state; for I am fitfully mad, and shall be till I die. Today I have seen a famil-iar face; it seems to have calmed and strengthened me, and though he would not help you, I shall make one desperate attempt. I may not find you, so leave my warn-ing to the hound, yet hope to breathe a word into your sleepless ear that shall send you back into the world the happy thing you should be. Child! Woman! Whatever you are, leave this accursed house while you have power to do it."

That was all; I did not destroy the papers, but I obeyed them, and for a week watched and waited till the propitious instant came. I saw my uncle, the doctor, and two others follow the poor body to its grave beside the lake, saw all depart but Dr. Karnac, and felt redoubled hatred and contempt for the men who could repay my girlish slights with such a horrible revenge. On the seventh day, as I went down for my daily walk, I saw John and Dr. Karnac so deep in some uncanny experiment that I passed out unguarded. Hoping to profit by this unexpected chance, I sprang down the steps, but the next moment dropped half stunned upon the grass; for behind me rose a crash, a shriek, a sudden blaze that flashed up and spread, sending a noisome vapor rolling out with clouds of smoke and flame.

Aghast, I was just gathering myself up when Hannah fled out of the house, dragging her husband senseless and bleeding, while her own face was ashy with affright. She dropped her burden beside me, saying, with white lips and a vain look for help where help was not, –

"Something they were at has burst, killed the doctor, and fired the house! Watch John till I get help, and leave him at your peril!" then flinging open the gate she sped away.

"Now is my time," I thought, and only waiting till she vanished, I boldly followed her example, running rapidly along the road in an opposite direction, careless of bonnetless head and trembling limbs, intent only upon leaving that prison-house far behind me. For several hours, I hurried along that solitary road; the spring sun shone, birds sang in the blooming hedges, green nooks invited me to pause and rest; but I heeded none of them, steadily continuing my flight, till spent and footsore I was forced to stop a moment by a wayside spring. As I stooped to drink, I saw my face for the first time in many months, and started to see how like that dead one it had grown, in all but the eternal peace which made that beautiful in spite of suffering and age. Standing thus and wondering if Guy would know me, should we ever meet, the sound of wheels disturbed me. Believing them to be coming from the place I had left, I ran desperately down the hill, turned a sharp comer, and before I could check myself passed a carriage slowly ascending. A face sprang to the window, a voice cried "Stop!" but on I flew, hoping the traveler would let me go unpursued. Not so, however; soon I heard fleet steps following, gaining rapidly, then a hand seized me, a voice rang in my ears, and with a vain struggle I lay panting in my captor's hold, fearing to look up and meet a brutal glance. But the hand that had seized me tenderly drew me close, the voice that had alarmed cried joyfully, –

"Sybil, it is Guy! lie still, poor child, you are safe at last."

Then I knew that my surest refuge was gained, and too weak for words, clung to him in an agony of happiness, which brought to his kind eyes the tears I could not shed.

The carriage returned; Guy took me in, and for a time cared only to soothe and sustain my worn soul and body with the cordial of his presence, as we rolled homeward through a blooming world, whose beauty I had never truly felt before. When the first tumult of emotion had subsided, I told the story of my captivity and my escape, ending with a passionate entreaty not to be returned to my uncle's keeping, for henceforth there could be neither affection nor respect between us.

"Fear nothing, Sybil; madame is waiting for you at the Moors, and my father's unfaithful guardianship has ended with his life."

Then with averted face and broken voice Guy went on to tell his father's purposes, and what had caused this unexpected meeting. The facts were briefly these: The knowledge that my father had come between him and a princely fortune had always rankled in my uncle's heart, chilling the ambitious hopes he cherished even in his boyhood, and making life an eager search for pleasure in which to drown his vain regrets. This secret was suspected by my father, and the household league was formed as some atonement for the innocent offense. It seemed to soothe my uncle's resentful nature, and as years went on he lived freely, assured that ample means would be his through his son. Luxurious, self-indulgent, fond of all excitements, and reckless in their pursuit, he took no thought for the morrow till a few months before his return. A gay winter in Paris reduced him to those straits of which women know so little; creditors were oppressive, summer friends failed him, gambling debts harassed him, his son reproached him, and but one resource remained, Guy's speedy marriage with the half-forgotten heiress. The boy had been educated to regard this fate as a fixed fact, and submitted, believing the time to be far distant; but the sudden summons came, and he rebelled against it, preferring liberty to love. My uncle pacified the claimants by promises to be fulfilled at my expense, and hurried home to press on the marriage, which now seemed imperative. I was taken to my future home, approved by my uncle, beloved by my cousin, and, but for my own folly, might have been a happy wife on that May morning when I listened to the unveiling of the past. My mother had been melancholy mad since that unhappy rumor of my father's death; this affliction had been well concealed from me, lest the knowledge should prey upon my excitable nature and perhaps induce a like misfortune. I believed her dead, yet I had seen her, knew where her solitary grave was made, and still carried in my bosom the warning she had sent me, prompted by the unerring instinct of a mother's heart. In my father's will a clause was added just below the one confirming my betrothal, a clause decreeing that, if it should appear that I inherited my mother's malady, the fortune should revert to my cousin, with myself a mournful legacy, to be cherished by him whether his wife or not. This passage, and that relating to my freedom of choice, had been omitted in the copy shown me on the night when my seeming refusal of Guy had induced his father to believe that I loved him, to make a last attempt to keep the prize by offering himself, and, when that failed, to harbor a design that changed my little comedy into the tragical experience I have told.

Dr. Karnac's exclamation had caused the recollection of that clause respecting my insanity to flash into my uncle's mind – a mind as quick to conceive as fearless to execute. I unconsciously abetted the stratagem, and Dr. Karnac was an unscrupulous ally, for love of gain was as strong as love of science; both were amply gratified, and I, poor victim, was given up to be experimented upon, till by subtle means I was driven to the insanity which would give my uncle full control of my fortune and my fate. How the black plot prospered has been told; but retribution speedily overtook them both, for Dr. Karnac paid his penalty by the sudden death that left his ashes among the blackened ruins of that house of horrors, and my uncle had preceded him. For before the change of heirs could be effected my mother died, and the hours spent in that unhealthful spot insinuated the subtle poison of the marsh into his blood; years of pleasure left little vigor to withstand the fever, and a week of suffering ended a life of generous impulses perverted, fine endowments wasted, and opportunities forever lost. When death drew near, he sent for Guy (who, through the hard discipline of poverty and honest labor, was becoming a manlier man), confessed all, and implored him to save me before it was too late. He did, and when all was told, when each saw the other by the light of this strange and sad experience – Guy poor again, I free, the old bond still existing, the barrier of misunderstanding gone – it was easy to see our way, easy to submit, to forgive, forget, and begin anew the life these clouds had darkened for a time.

Home received me, kind madame welcomed me, Guy married me, and I was happy; but over all these years, serenely prosperous, still hangs for me the shadow of the past, still rises that dead image of my mother, still echoes that spectral whisper in the dark.

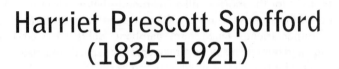

Harriet Prescott Spofford
(1835–1921)

Harriet Prescott Spofford had a long and successful career, often publishing in the august *Atlantic Monthly*. Her stories were admired by her New England contemporary, Emily Dickinson. With renewed interest in neglected women writers of the nineteenth century, Spofford's work has begun to find new readers, especially as a result of Alfred Bendixen's anthology, "*The Amber Gods" and Other Stories* (New Brunswick: Rutgers University Press, 1989).

Spofford was a romantic, and favored a lush, highly ornamented style filled with literary, biblical, and artistic allusions. In later years, however, responding to changing tastes in her audience, she developed a plainer style in the tradition of women's regional realism.

"Her Story" represents a favorite Spofford pattern, with two women dueling over the affections of a man. As in her story "The Amber Gods," one of the women is a beautiful witch or psychological vampire. Spofford's tale, like Alcott's "A Whisper in the Dark" and Gilman's "The Yellow Wallpaper," depicts a woman's descent into madness.

"Circumstance" allegedly was based on a story passed down within the author's family. It is a frontier Gothic story, an uncanny encounter in the wilderness, and has some of the qualities of a folk tale like "Little Red Riding Hood." A remarkable passage describes the horror of being eaten by an animal, and thus becoming a part of the savage life of the beast. The story can also be seen as representing the life of an artist whose craft is her only livelihood, and who must keep inventing and producing in order to survive.

Texts: "Circumstance," *The Atlantic Monthly*, 5 (May 1860), 558–65. "Her Story" was first published in *Lippincott's Magazine* in December 1872. Our text is taken from *Old Madame and Other Tragedies* (Boston: Richard G. Badger & Co., 1900), 205–49. One obviously wrong punctuation mark has been changed.

Her Story

WELLNIGH the worst of it all is the mystery.

If it were true, that accounts for my being here. If it were not true, then the best thing they could do with me was to bring me here. Then, too, if it were true, they would save themselves by hurrying me away; and if it were not true – You see, just as all roads lead to Rome, all roads led me to this Retreat. If it were true, it was enough to craze me; and if it were not true, I was already crazed. And there it is! I can't make out, sometimes, whether I am really beside myself or not; for it seems that whether I was crazed or sane, if it were true, they would naturally put me out of sight and hearing – bury me alive, as they have done, in this Retreat. They? Well, no — he. She stayed at home, I hear. If she had come with us, doubtless I should have found reason enough to say to the physician at once that she was the mad woman, not I – she, who, for the sake of her own brief pleasure, could make a whole after-life of misery for three of us. She – Oh no, don't rise, don't go. I am quite myself, I am perfectly calm. Mad! There was never a drop of crazy blood in the Ridgleys or the Bruces, or any of the generations behind them, and why should it suddenly break out like a smothered fire in me? That is one of the things that puzzle me – why should it come to light all at once in me if it were not true?

Now, I am not going to be incoherent. It was too kind in you to be at such trouble to come and see me in this prison, this grave. I will not cry out once: I will just tell you the story of it all exactly as it was, and you shall judge. If I can, that is – oh, if I can! For sometimes, when I think of it, it seems as if Heaven itself would fail to take my part if I did not lift my own voice. And I cry, and I tear my hair and my flesh, till I know my anguish weighs down their joy, and the little scale that holds that joy flies up under the scorching of the sun, and God sees the festering thing for what it is! Ah, it is not injured reason that cries out in that way: it is a breaking heart!

How cool your hand is, how pleasant your face is, how good it is to see you! Don't be afraid of me: I am as much myself, I tell you, as you are. What an absurdity! Certainly anyone who heard me make such a speech would think I was insane and without benefit of clergy. To ask you not to be afraid of me because I am myself. Isn't it what they call a vicious circle? And then to cap the climax by adding that I am as much myself as you are yourself! But no matter – you know better. Did you say it was ten years? Yes, I knew it was as much as that – oh, it seems a hundred years! But we hardly show it: your hair is still the same as when we were at school; and mine – Look at this lock – I cannot understand why it is only sprinkled here and there: it ought to be white as the driven snow. My babies are almost grown women, Elizabeth. How could he do without me all this time? Hush now! I am not going to be disturbed at all; only that the color of your hair puts me so in mind of his: perhaps there was just one trifle more of gold in his. Do you remember that lock that used to fall over his forehead and which he always tossed back so impatiently? I used to think that the golden Apollo of Rhodes had just such massive, splendid locks of hair as that; but I never told him; I never had the face to praise him; she had. She could exclaim how like ivory the forehead was – that great wide forehead – how that keen aquiline was to be found in the portrait of the Spencer of two hundred years ago. She could tell of the proud lip, of the fire burning in the hazel eye. She knew how, by a silent flattery, as she shrank away and looked up at him, to admire his haughty stature, and make him feel the strength and glory of his manhood and the delicacy of her womanhood.

She was a little thing – a little thing, but wondrous fair. Fair, did I say? No: she was dark as an Egyptian, but such perfect features, such rich and splendid color, such great soft eyes – so soft, so black – so superb a smile; and then such hair! When she let it down, the backward curling ends lay on the ground and she stood on them, or the children lifted them and carried them behind her as pages carry a queen's train. If I had my two hands twisted in that hair! Oh, how I hate that hair! It would make as good a bowstring as ever any Carthaginian woman's made.[1]

Ah, that is atrocious! I am sure you think so. But living all these lonesome years as I have done seems to double back one's sinfulness upon one's self. Because one is sane

Notes

HER STORY
[1] Supposedly the women of Carthage gave their hair for bowstrings during the siege of the city by the Romans in 146 BC.

it does not follow that one is a saint. And when I think of my innocent babies playing with the hair that once I saw him lift and pass across his lips! But I will not think of it!

Well, well! I was a pleasant thing to look at myself once on a time, you know, Elizabeth. He used to tell me so: those were his very words. I was tall and slender, and if my skin was pale it was clear with pearly clearness, and the lashes of my gray eyes were black as shadows; but now those eyes are only the color of tears.

I never told a syllable about it – I never could. It was so deep down in my heart, that love I had for him: it slept there so dark and still and full, for he was all I had in the world. I was alone, an orphan – if not friendless, yet quite dependent. I see you remember it all. I did not even sit in the pew with my cousin's family, – there were so many to fill it, – but down in one beneath the gallery, you know. And altogether life was a thing to me that hardly seemed worth the living. I went to church one Sunday, I recollect, idly and dreamingly as usual. I did not look off my book till a voice filled my ear – a strange new voice, a deep sweet voice, that invited you and yet commanded you – a voice whose sound divided the core of my heart, and sent thrills that were half joy, half pain, coursing through me. And then I looked up and saw him at the desk. He was reading the first lesson: "Fear not, for I have redeemed thee, I have called thee by thy name: thou art mine."[2] And I saw the bright hair, the bright upturned face, the white surplice, and I said to myself, It is a vision, it is an angel; and I cast down my eyes. But the voice went on, and when I looked again he was still there. Then I bethought me that it must be the one who was coming to take the place of our superannuated rector – the last of a fine line, they had been saying the day before, who, instead of finding his pleasure otherwise, had taken all his wealth and prestige into the Church.

Why will a trifle melt you so – a strain of music, a color in the sky, a perfume? Have you never leaned from the window at evening, and had the scent of a flower float by and fill you with as keen a sorrow as if it had been disaster touching you? Long ago, I mean – we never lean from the windows here. I don't know how, but it was in that same invisible way that this voice melted me; and when I heard it saying, "Behold, I will do a new thing; now it shall spring forth; shall ye not know it? I will even make a way in the wilderness and rivers in the desert,"[3] I was fairly crying. Oh, nervous tears, I dare say. The doctor here would tell you so, at any rate. And that that is what I complain of here: they give a physiological reason for every emotion – they could give you a chemical formula for your very soul, I have no doubt. Well, perhaps they were nervous tears, for certainly there was nothing to cry for, and the mood went as suddenly as it came – changed to a sort of exaltation, I suppose – and when they sang the psalm, and he had swept in, in his black gown, and had mounted the pulpit stairs, and was resting that fair head on the big Bible in his silent prayer, I too was singing – singing like one possessed:

> "Then, to thy courts when I repair,
> My soul shall rise on joyful wing,
> The wonders of thy love declare,
> And join the strain which angels sing."[4]

And as he rose I saw him searching for the voice unconsciously, and our eyes met. Oh, it was a fresh young voice, let it be mine or whose. I can hear it now as if it were someone else singing. Ah, ah, it has been silent so many years! Does it make you smile

Notes

[2] Isaiah 43:1.

[3] Isaiah 43:19.

[4] Hymn 37 in the Anglican Book of Common Prayer.

to hear me pity myself? It is not myself I am pitying: it is that fresh young girl that loved so. But it used to rejoice me to think that I loved him before I laid eyes on him.

He came to my cousin's in the week – not to see Sylvia or to see Laura: he talked of church-music with my cousin, and then crossed the room and sat down by me. I remember how I grew cold and trembled – how glad, how shy I was; and then he had me sing; and at first Sylvia sang with us, but by and by we sang alone – I sang alone. He brought me yellow old church music, written in quaint characters: he said those characters, those old square breves, were a text guarding secrets of enchantment as much as the text of Merlin's book did; and so we used to find it. Once he brought a copy of an old Roman hymn, written only in the Roman letters: he said it was a hymn which the ancients sang to Maia, the mother-earth, and which the Church fathers adopted, singing it stealthily in the hidden places of the Catacombs; and together we translated it into tones. A rude but majestic thing it was.

And once – The sunshine was falling all about us in the bright lonely room, and the shadows of the rose leaves at the window were dancing over us. I had been singing a Gloria while he walked up and down the room, and he came up behind me: he stooped and kissed me on the mouth. And after that there was no more singing, for, lovely as the singing was, the love was lovelier yet. Why do I complain of such a hell as this is now? I had my heaven once – oh, I had my heaven once! And as for the other, perhaps I deserve it all, for I saw God only through him: it was he that waked me to worship. I had no faith but Spencer's faith; if he had been a heathen, I should have been the same, and creeds and systems might have perished for me had he only been spared from the wreck. And he had loved me from the first moment that his eyes met mine. "When I looked at you," he said, "singing that simple hymn that first day, I felt as I do when I look at the evening star leaning out of the clear sunset lustre: there is something in your face as pure, as remote, as shining. It will always be there," he said, "though you should live a hundred years." He little knew, he little knew!

But he loved me then – oh yes, I never doubted that. There were no happier lovers trod the earth. We took our pleasure as lovers do: we walked in the fields; we sat on the river's side; together we visited the poor and sick; he read me the passages he liked best in his writing from week to week; he brought me the verse from which he meant to preach, and up in the organ-loft I improvised to him the thoughts that it inspired in me. I did that timidly indeed: I could not think my thoughts were worth his hearing till I forgot myself, and only thought of him and the glory I would have revealed to him, and then the great clustering chords and the full music of the diapason swept out beneath my hands – swept along the aisles and swelled up the raftered roof as if they would find the stars, and sunset and twilight stole around us there as we sat still in the succeeding silence. I was happy: I was humble too. I wondered why I had been chosen for such a blest and sacred lot. It was so blessed to be allowed to minister one delight to him. I had a little print of the angel of the Lord appearing to Mary with the lily of annunciation in his hand, and I thought – I dare not tell you what I thought. I made an idol of my piece of clay.

When the leaves had turned we were married, and he took me home. Ah, what a happy home it was! Luxury and beauty filled it. When I first went into it and left the chill October night without, fires blazed upon the hearths; flowers bloomed in every room; a marble Eros held a light up, searching for his Psyche. "*Our* love has found its soul," said he. He led me to the music-room – a temple in itself, for its rounded ceiling towered to the height of the house. There were golden organ-pipes and banks of keys fit for St. Cecilia's use; there were all the delightful outlines of violin and piccolo and harp and horn for any who would use them; there was a pianoforte near the door for me – one such as I had never touched before; and there were cases on all sides filled with the rarest musical works. The floor was bare and inlaid; the windows were latticed in stained glass, so that no common light of day ever filtered through, but light bluer than the sky, gold as the dawn, purple as the night; and then there were vast embowering chairs, in any of which he could hide himself away while I made my incantation, as he sometimes called it, of the great spirits of song. As I tried the piano that night he tuned the old Amati[5] which he himself now and then played upon, and together we improvised our own epithalamium. It was the violin that took the strong assuring part with strains of piercing sweetness, and music of the piano flowed along in a soft cantabile of undersong. It seemed to me as if his part was like the flight of some white and strong-winged bird above a sunny brook.

But he had hardly created this place for the love of me alone. He adored music as a regenerator; he meant to use it so among his people: here were to be pursued those labors which should work miracles when produced in the open church. For he was building a church with the half of his fortune – a church full of restoration of the old and creation of the new: the walls within were to be a frosty tracery of vines running to break into the gigantic passion-flower that formed the rose-window; the lectern a golden globe upon a tripod, clasped by a silver dove holding on outstretched wings the book.

I have feared, since I have been here, that Spencer's piety was less piety than partisanship: I have doubted if faith were so much alive in him as the love of a great perfect system, and the pride in it I know he always felt. But I never thought about it then: I believed in him as I would have believed in an apostle. So stone by stone the church went up, and stone by stone our lives followed it – lives of such peace, such bliss! Then fresh hopes came into it – sweet trembling hopes; and by and by our first child was born. And if I had been happy before, what was I then? There are some compensations in this world: such happiness could not come twice, such happiness as there was in that moment when I lay, painless and at peace, with the little I cheek nestled beside my own, while he bent above us both, proud and glad and tender. It was a dear little baby – so fair, so bright! and when she could walk she could sing. Her sister sang earlier yet; and what music their two shrill sweet voices made as they sat in their little chairs together at twilight before the fire, their curls glistening and their red shoes glistening, while they sang the evening hymn, Spencer on one side of the hearth and I upon the other! Sometimes we let the dear things sit up for a later hour in the music-room – for many a canticle we tried and practised there that hushed hearts and awed them when the choir gave them on succeeding Sundays – and always afterward I heard them singing in their sleep, just as a bird stirs in his nest and sings his stave in the night. Oh, we were happy then; and it was then she came.

She was the step-child of his uncle, had a small fortune of her own, and Spencer had been left her guardian; and so she was to live with us – at any rate, for a while. I dreaded her coming. I did not want the intrusion; I did not like the things I heard about her; I knew she would be a discord in our harmony. But Spencer, who had only seen her once in her childhood, had been told by some one who travelled in Europe with her that she was delightful and had a rare intelligence. She was one of those women often delightful to men indeed, but whom other women – by virtue of their own kindred instincts, it may be, perhaps by virtue of temptations overcome – see through and know for what they are. But she had her own way of charming: she was the being of infinite variety[6] – to-day glad, tomorrow sad, freakish, and always exciting you by curiosity as to her next caprice, and so moody that after a season of the lowering weather of one of her dull humors you were ready to sacrifice something for the

Notes

[5] Violin made by a 16th- and 17th-century family of Italian violin-makers.

[6] Compare the description of Cleopatra in Shakespeare's *Antony and Cleopatra* II. ii. 240–1.

sake of the sunshine that she knew how to make so vivid and so sweet. Then, too, she brought forward her forces by detachment. At first she was the soul of domestic life, sitting at night beneath the light and embossing on weblike muslin designs of flower and leaf which she had learned in her convent, listening to Spencer as he read, and taking from the little wallet of her work-basket apropos scraps which she had pre-served from the sermon of some Italian father of the Church or of some French divine. As for me, the only thing I knew was my poor music; and I used to burn with indignation when she interposed that unknown tongue between my husband and myself. Presently her horses came, and then, graceful in her dark riding-habit, she would spend a morning fearlessly subduing one of the fiery fellows, and dash away at last with plume and veil streaming behind her. In the early evening she would dance with the children – witch-dances they were – with her round arms linked above her head, and her feet weaving the measure in and out as deftly as any flashing-footed Bayadere[7] might do – only when Spencer was there to see: at other times I saw she pushed the little hindering things aside without a glance.

By and by she began to display a strange dramatic sort of power: she would rehearse to Spencer scenes that she had met with from day to day in the place, giving now the old churchwarden's voice and now the sexton's, their gestures and very faces; she could tell the ailments of half the old women in the parish who came to me with them, and in their own tone and manner to the life; she told us once of a street-scene, with the crier crying a lost child, the mother following with lamentations, the passing strangers questioning, the boys hooting, and the child's reappearance, followed by a tumult, with kisses and blows and cries, so that I thought I saw it all; and presently she had found the secret and vulnerable spot of every friend we had, and could personate them all as vividly as if she did it by necromancy.

One night she began to sketch our portraits in charcoal: the likenesses were not perfect; she exaggerated the careless elegance of Spencer's attitude; perhaps the primness of my own. But yet he saw there the ungraceful trait for the first time, I think. And so much led to more: she brought out her portfolios, and there were her pencil-sketches from the Rhine and from the Guadalquivir, rich water-colors of Venetian scenes, interiors of old churches, and sheet after sheet covered with details of church architecture. Spencer had been admiring all the others – in spite of some-thing that I thought I saw in them, a something that was not true, a trait of her own identity, for I had come to criticise her sharply – but when his eye rested on those sheets I saw it sparkle, and he caught them up and pored over them one by one.

"I see you have mastered the whole thing," he said: "you must instruct me here." And so she did. And there were hours, while I was busied with servants and accounts or with the children, when she was closeted with Spencer in the study, criticising, comparing, making drawings, hunting up authorities; other hours when they walked away together to the site of the new church that was building, and here an arch was destroyed, and, there an aisle was extended, and here a row of cloisters sketched into the plan, and there a row of windows, till the whole design was reversed and made over. And they had the thing between them, for, admire and sympathize as I might, I did not know. At first Spencer would repeat the day's achievement to me, but the contempt for my ignorance which she did not deign to hide soon put all end to it when she was present.

It was this interest that now unveiled a new phase of her character: she was devout. She had a little altar in her room; she knew all about albs and chasubles; she would

Notes

[7] In European convention, a Hindu dancing girl.

have persuaded Spencer to burn candles in the chancel; she talked of a hundred mysteries and symbols; she wanted to embroider a stole to lay across his shoulders. She was full of small church sentimentalities, and as one after another she uttered them, it seemed to me that her belief was no sound fruit of any system – if it were belief and not a mere bunch of fancies – but only, as you might say, a rotten windfall of the Romish Church: it had none of the round splendor of that Church's creed, none of the pure simplicity of ours: it would be no stay in trouble, no shield in temptation. I said as much to Spencer.

"You are prejudiced," said he: "her belief is the result of long observation abroad, I think. She has found the need of outward observances: they are, she has told me, a shrine to the body of her faith, like that commanded in the building of the tabernacle, where the ark of the covenant was enclosed in the holy of holies."

"And you didn't think it profane in her to speak so? But I don't believe it, Spencer," I said. "She has no faith: she has some sentimentalisms."

"You are prejudiced," he repeated. "She seems to me a wonderful and gifted being."

"Too gifted," I said. "Her very gifts are unnatural in their abundance. There must be scrofula there to keep such a fire in the blood and sting the brain to such action: she will die in a madhouse, depend upon it." Think of my saying such a thing as that!

"I have never heard you speak so before," he replied coldly. "I hope you do not envy her her powers."

"I envy her nothing," I cried. "For she is as false as she is beautiful!" But I did – oh I did!

"Beautiful?" said Spencer. "Is she beautiful? I never thought of that."

"You are very blind, then," I said with a glad smile.

Spencer smiled too. "It is not the kind of beauty I admire," said he.

"Then I must teach you, sir," said she. And we both started to see her in the doorway, and I, for one, did not know, till shortly before I found myself here, how much or how little she had learned of what we said.

"Then I must teach you, sir," said she again. And she came deliberately into the firelight and paused upon the rug, drew out the silver arrows and shook down all her hair about her, till the great snake-like coils unrolled upon the floor.

"Hyacinthine," said Spencer.[8]

"Indeed it is," said she. "The very color of the jacinth, with that red tint in its darkness that they call black in the shade and gold in the sun. Now look at me."

"Shut your eyes, Spencer," I cried, and laughed.

But he did not shut his eyes. The firelight flashed over her: the color in her cheeks and on her lips sprang ripe and red in it as she held the hair away from them with her rosy finger-tips; her throat curved small and cream-white from the bosom that the lace of her dinner-dress scarcely hid; and the dark eyes glowed with a great light as they lay full on his.

"You mustn't call it vanity," said she. "It is only that it is impossible, looking at the picture in the glass, not to see it as I see any other picture. But for all that, I know it is not every fool's beauty: it is no daub for the vulgar gaze, but a masterpiece that it needs the educated eye to find. I could tell you how this nostril is like that in a famous marble, how the curve of this cheek is that of a certain Venus, the line of this forehead like the line in the dreamy Antinous' forehead.[9] Are you taught? Is it – ?"

Notes

[8] Compare the "hyacinth hair" in Poe's "To Helen."

[9] Presumably the Antinous whom the Roman emperor Hadrian deified after the death of this court favorite, of whom many statues survive. The speaker's comparison of herself to a male, presumably homosexual, figure increases her strangeness.

Then she twisted her hair again and fastened the arrows, and laughed and turned away to look over the evening paper. But as for Spencer, as he lay back in his lordly way, surveying the vision from crown to toe, I saw him flush – I saw him flush and start and quiver, and then he closed his eyes and pressed his fingers on them, and lay back again and said not a word.

She began to read aloud something concerning services at the recent dedication of a church. I was called out as she read. When I came back, a half hour afterward, they were talking. I stopped at my work-table in the next room for a skein of floss that she had asked me for, and I heard her saying, "You cannot expect me to treat you with reverence. You are a married priest, and you know what opinion I necessarily must have of married priests." Then I came in and she was silent.

But I knew, I always knew, that if Spencer had not felt himself weak, had not found himself stirred, if he had not recognized that, when he flushed and quivered before her charm, it was the flesh and not the spirit that tempted him, he would not have listened to her subtle invitation to austerity. As it was, he did. He did – partly in shame, partly in punishment; but to my mind the listening was confession. She had set the wedge that was to sever our union – the little seed in a mere idle cleft that grows and grows and splits the rock asunder.

Well, I had my duties, you know. I never felt my husband's wealth a reason why I should neglect them any more than another wife should neglect her duties. I was wanted in the parish, sent for here and waited for there: the dying liked to see me comfort their living, the living liked to see me touch their dead; some wanted help, and others wanted consolation; and where I felt myself too young and unlearned to give advice, I could at least give sympathy. Perhaps I was the more called upon for such detail of duty because Spencer was busy with the greater things, the church-building and the sermons – sermons that once on a time lifted you and held you on their strong wings. But of late Spencer had been preaching old sermons. He had been moody and morose too: sometimes he seemed oppressed with melancholy. He had spoken to me strangely, had looked at me as if he pitied me, had kept away from me. But she had not regarded his moods: she had followed him in his solitary strolls, had sought him in his study; and she had ever a mystery or symbol to be interpreted, the picture of a private chapel that she had heard of when abroad, or the ground-plan of an ancient one, or some new temptation to his ambition, as I divine. And soon he was himself again.

I was wrong to leave him so to her, but what was there else for me to do? And as for those duties of mine, as I followed them I grew restive; I abridged them, I hastened home. I was impatient even with the detentions the children caused. I could not leave them to their nurses, for all that; but they kept me away from him and he was alone with her.

One day at last he told me that his mind was troubled by the suspicion that his marriage was a mistake; that on his part at least it had been wrong; that he had been thinking a priest should have the Church only for his bride, and should wait at the altar mortified in every affection; that it was not for hands that were full of caresses and lips that were covered with kisses to touch the sacrament, to offer praise. But for answer I brought my children and put them in his arms. I was white and cold and shaking, but I asked him if they were not justification enough. And I told him that he did his duty better abroad for the heartening of a wife at home, and that he knew better how to interpret God's love to men through his own love for his children. And I laid my head on his breast beside them, and he clasped us all and we cried together, he and I.

But that was not enough, I found. And when our good bishop came, who had always been like a father to Spencer, I led the conversation to that point one evening, and he discovered Spencer's trouble, and took him away and reasoned with him. The bishop was a power with Spencer, and I think that was the end of it.

The end of that, but only the beginning of the rest. For she had accustomed him to the idea of separation from me – the idea of doing without me. He had put me away from himself once in his mind: we had been one soul, and now we were two.

One day, as I stood in my sleeping room with the door ajar, she came in. She had never been there before, and I cannot tell you how insolently she looked about her. There was a bunch of flowers on a stand that Spencer himself placed there for me every morning. He had, always done so, and there had been no reason for breaking off the habit; and I had always worn one of them at my throat. She advanced a hand to pull out a blossom. "Do not touch them," I cried: "my husband puts them there."

"Suppose he does," said she lightly. "For how long?" Then she overlooked me with a long sweeping glance of search and contempt, shrugged her shoulders, and with a French sentence that I did not understand turned back and coolly broke off the blossom she had marked and hung it in her hair. I could not take her by the shoulders and put her from the room. I could not touch the flowers that she had desecrated. I left the room myself, and left her in it, and went down to dinner for the first time without the flower at my throat. I saw Spencer's eye note the omission: perhaps he took it as a release from me, for he never put the flowers in my room again after that day.

Nor did he ask me any more into his study, as he had been used, or read his sermons to me. There was no need of his talking over the church-building with me – he had her to talk it over with. And as for our music, that had been a rare thing since she arrived, for her conversation had been such as to leave but little time for it, and somehow when she came into the music-room and began to dictate to me the time in which I should take an Inflammatus and the spirit in which I should sing a ballad, I could not bear it. Then, too, to tell you the truth, my voice was hoarse and choked with tears full half the time.

It was some weeks after the flowers ceased that our youngest child fell ill. She was very ill – I don't think Spencer knew how ill. I dared not trust her with anyone, and Spencer said no one could take such care of her as her mother could; so, although we had nurses in plenty, I hardly left the room by night or day. I heard their voices down below, I saw them go, out for their walks. It was a hard fight, but I saved her.

But I was worn to a shadow when all was done – worn with anxiety for her, with alternate fevers of hope and fear, with the weight of my responsibility as to her life; and with anxiety for Spencer too, with a despairing sense that the end of peace had come, and with the total sleeplessness of many nights. Now, when the child was mending and gaining every day, I could not sleep if I would.

The doctor gave me anodynes, but to no purpose: they only nerved me wide awake. My eyes ached, and my brain ached, and my body ached, but it was of no use: I could not sleep. I counted the spots on the wall, the motes upon my eyes, the notes of all the sheets of music I could recall. I remembered the Eastern punishment of keeping the condemned awake till they die, and wondered what my crime was; I thought if I could but sleep I might forget my trouble, or take it up freshly and master it. But no, it was always there – a heavy cloud, a horror of foreboding. As I heard that woman's step go by the door I longed to rid the house of it, and I dinted my palms with my nails till she had passed.

I did not know what to do. It seemed to me that I was wicked in letting the thing go on, in suffering Spencer to be any longer exposed to her power; but then I feared to take a step lest I should thereby rivet the chains she was casting on him. And then I longed so for one hour of the old dear happiness – the days when I and the children had been all and enough. I did not know what to do; I had no one to counsel with; I was wild within myself, and all distraught. Once I thought if I could not rid the house of her I could rid it of myself; and as I went through a dark passage and chanced to look up where a bright-headed nail glittered, I questioned if it would bear my weight. For days the idea haunted me. I fancied that when I was gone perhaps he would love me again, and at any rate I might be asleep and at rest. But the thought of the children prevented me, and one other thought – I was not certain that even my sorrows would excuse me before God.

I went down to dinner again at last. How she glowed and abounded in her beauty as she sat there! And I – I must have been very thin and ghastly: perhaps I looked a little wild in all my bewilderment and hurt. His heart smote him, it may be, for he came round to where I sat by the fire afterward and smoothed my hair and kissed my fore-head. He could not tell all I was suffering then – all I was struggling with; for I thought I had better put him out of the world than let him, who was once so pure and good, stay in it to sin. I could have done it, you know. For though I still lay with the little girl, I could have stolen back into our own room with the chloroform, and he would never have known. I turned the handle of the door one night, but the bolt was slipped. I never thought of killing her, you see: let her live and sin, if she would. She was the thing of slime and sin, a splendid tropical growth of the passionate heat and the slime: it was only her nature. But then we think it no harm to kill reptiles, however splendid.

But it was by that time that the voices had begun to talk with me – all night long, all day. It was they, I found, that had kept me so sleepless. Go where I might, they were ever before me. If I went to the woods, I heard them in the whisper of every pine tree. If I went down to the seashore, I heard them in the plash of every wave. I heard them in the wind, in the singing of my ears, in the children's breath as I hung above them, – for I had decided that if I went out of the world I would take the children with me. If I sat down to play, the things would twist the chords into discords; if I sat down to read, they would come between me and the page.

Then I could see the creatures: they had wings like bats. I did not dare speak of them, although I fancied she suspected me, for once she said, as I was kissing my little girl, "When you are gone to a madhouse, don't think they'll have many such kisses." Did she say it? or did I think she said it? I did not answer her, I did not look up: I suppose I should have flown at her throat if I had.

I took the children out with me on my rambles: we went for miles; sometimes I carried one, sometimes the other. I took such long, long walks to escape those noisome things: they would never leave me till I was quite tired out. Now and then I was gone the whole day; and all the time that I was gone he was with her, I knew, and she was tricking out her beauty and practising her arts.

I went to a little festival with them, for Spencer insisted. And she made shadow-pictures on the wall, wonderful things with her perfect profile and her perfect arms and her subtle curves – she out of sight, the shadow only seen. Now it was Isis, I remember, and now it was the head and shoulders and trailing hair of a floating sea-nymph. And then there were charades in which she played; and I can't tell you the glorious thing she looked when she came on as Helen of Troy with all her "beauty shadowed in white veils," you know – that brown and red beauty with its smiles and radiance under the wavering of the flower-wrought veil. I sat by Spencer, and I felt him shiver. He was fighting and struggling too within himself, very likely; only he knew that he was going to yield after all – only he longed to yield while he feared. But as for me, I saw one of those bat-like things perched on her ear as she stood before us, and when she opened her mouth to speak I saw them flying in and out. And I said to Spencer, "She is tormenting me. I cannot stay and see her swallowing the souls of men in this way." And I would have gone, but he held me down fast in my seat. But if I was crazy then – as they say I was, I suppose – it was only with a metaphor, for she was sucking Spencer's soul out of his body.

But I was not crazy. I should admit I might have been if I alone had seen those evil spirits. But Spencer saw them too. He never told me so, but – there are subtle ways – I knew he did; for when I opened the church door late, as I often did at that time after my long walks, they would rush in past me with a whizz, and as I sat in the pew I would see him steadily avoid looking at me; and if he looked by any chance, he would turn so pale that I have thought he would drop where he stood; and he would redden afterward as though one had struck him. He knew then what I endured with them; but I was not the one to speak of it. Don't tell me that his color changed and he shuddered so because I sat there mumbling and nodding to myself. It was because he saw those things mopping and mowing beside me and whispering in my ear. Oh what loathsomeness the obscene creatures whispered! Foul quips and evil words I had never heard before, ribald songs and oaths; and I would clap my hands over my mouth to keep from crying out at them. Creatures of the imagination, you may say. It is possible. But they were so vivid that they seem real to me even now. I burn and tingle as I recall them. And how could I have imagined such sounds, such shapes, of things I had never heard or seen or dreamed?

And Spencer was very unhappy, I am sure. I was the mother of his children, and if he loved me no more, he had an old kindness for me still, and my distress distressed him. But for all that the glamour was on him, and he could not give up that woman and her beauty and her charm. Once or twice he may have thought about sending her away, but perhaps he could not bring himself to do it – perhaps he reflected it was too late, and now it was no matter. But every day she stayed he was the more like wax in her hands. Oh, he was weaker than water that is poured out. He was abandoning himself and forgetting earth and heaven and hell itself, before a passion – a passion that soon would cloy, and then would sting.

It was the spring season: I had been out several hours. The sunset fell while I was in the wood, and the stars came out; and at one time I thought I would lie down there on last year's leaves and never get up again. But I remembered the children, and went home to them. They were in bed and asleep when I took off my shoes and opened the door of their room – breathing so sweetly and evenly, the little yellow heads close together on one pillow, their hands tossed about the coverlid, their parted lips, their rosy cheeks. I knelt to feel the warm breath on my own cold cheek, and then the voices began whispering again: "If only they never waked! they never waked!"

And all I could do was to spring to my feet and run from the room. I ran shoeless down the great staircase and through the long hall. I thought I would go to Spencer and tell him all – all my sorrows, all the suggestions of the voices, and maybe in the endeavor to save me he would save himself. And I ran down the long dimly-lighted drawing-room, led by the sound I heard, to the music-room, whose doors were open just beyond. It was lighted only by the pale glimmer from the other room and by the moonlight through the painted panes. And I paused to listen to what I had never listened to there – the sound of the harp and a voice with it. Of course they had not heard me coming, and I hesitated and looked, and then I glided within the door and stood just by the open piano there.

She sat at the harp singing – the huge gilded harp. I did not know she sang – she had kept that for her last reserve – but she struck the harp so that it sang itself, like some great prisoned soul, and her voice followed it – oh so rich a voice! My own was white and thin, I felt, beside it. But mine had soared, and hers still clung to earth – a contralto sweet with honeyed sweetness – the sweetness of unstrained honey that has the earth-taste and the heavy blossom-dust yet in it – sweet, though it grew hoarse and trembling with passion. He sat in one of the great arm-chairs just before her: he was white with feeling, with rapture, with forgetfulness; his eyes shone like stars. He moved restlessly, a strange smile kindled all his face: he bent toward her, and the music broke off in the middle as they threw their arms around each other, and hung there lip to lip and heart to heart. And suddenly I crashed down both my hands on the keyboard before me, and stood and glared upon them.

And I never knew anything more till I woke up here.

And that is the whole of it. That is the puzzle of it – was it a horrid nightmare, an insane vision, or was it true? Was it true that I saw Spencer, my white, clean lover, my husband, a man of God, the father of our spotless babies, – was it true that I saw him so, or was it only some wild, vile conjuration of disease? Oh, I would be willing to have been crazed a lifetime, a whole lifetime, only to wake one moment before I died and find that that had never been!

Well, well, well! When time passed and I became more quiet, I told the doctor here about the voices – I never told him of Spencer or of her – and he bade me dismiss care. He said I was ill – excitement and sleeplessness had surcharged my nerves with that strange magnetic fluid that has worked so much mischief in the world. There was no organic disease, you see; only when my nerves were rested and right, my brain would be right. And the doctor gave me medicines and books and work, and when I saw the bat-like things again I was to go instantly to him. And after a little while I was not sure that I did see them. And in a little while longer they had ceased to come altogether. And I have had no more of them. I was on my parole then in the parlor, at the table, in the grounds. I felt that I was cured of whatever had ailed me: I could escape at any moment that I wished.

And it came Christmas time. A terrible longing for home overcame me – for my children. I thought of them at this time when I had been used to take such pains for their pleasure. I thought of the little empty stockings, the sad faces; I fancied I could hear them crying for me. I forgot all about my word of honor. It seemed to me that I should die, that I might as well die, if I could not see my little darlings, and hold them on my knees, and sing to them while the chimes were ringing in the Christmas Eve. And winter was here and there was so much to do for them. And I walked down the garden, and looked out at the gate, and opened it and went through. And I slept that night in a barn – so free, so free and glad! And the next day an old farmer and his sons, who thought they did me a service, brought me back, and of course I shrieked and raved. And so would you.

But since then I have been in this ward and a prisoner. I have my work, my amusement. I send such little things as I can make to my girls. I read. Sometimes of late I sing in the Sunday service. The place is a sightly place; the grounds, when we are taken out, are fine; the halls are spacious and pleasant.

Pleasant – but ah, when you have trodden them ten years!

And so, you see, if I were a clod, if I had no memory, no desires, if I had never been happy before, I might be happy now. I am confident the doctor thinks me well. But he has no orders to let me go. Sometimes it is so wearisome. And it might be worse if lately I had not been allowed a new service. And that is, to try to make a woman smile who came here a year ago. She is a little woman, swarthy as a Malay, but her hair, that grows as rapidly as a fungus grows in the night, is whiter than leprosy: her eyebrows are so long and white that they veil and blanch her dark dim eyes; and she has no front teeth. A stone from a falling spire struck her from her horse, they say. The blow battered her and beat out reason and beauty. Her mind is dead: she remembers nothing, knows nothing; but she follows me about like a dog: she seems to want to do something for me, to propitiate me. All she ever says is to beg me to do her no harm. She will not go to sleep without my hand in hers. Sometimes, after long effort, I think there is a gleam of intelligence, but the doctor says there was once too much intelligence, and her case is hopeless.

Hopeless, poor thing! – that is an awful word: I could not wish it said for my worst enemy.

In spite of these ten years I cannot feel that it has yet been said for me.

If I am strange just now, it is only the excitement of seeing you, only the habit of the strange sights and sounds here. I should be calm and well enough at home. I sit and picture to myself that some time Spencer will come for me – will take me to my girls, my fireside, my music. I shall hear his voice, I shall rest in his arms, I shall be blest again. For, oh, Elizabeth, I do forgive him all!

Or if he will not dare to trust himself at first, I picture to myself how he will send another – some old friend who knew me before my trouble – who will see me and judge, and carry back report that I am all I used to be – some friend who will open the gates of heaven to me, or close the gates of hell upon me – who will hold my life and my fate.

If – oh if it should be you, Elizabeth!

Circumstance

She had remained, during all that day, with a sick neighbor, – those eastern wilds of Maine in that epoch frequently making neighbors and miles synonymous, – and so busy had she been with care and sympathy that she did not at first observe the approaching night. But finally the level rays, reddening the snow, threw their gleam upon the wall, and, hastily donning cloak and hood, she bade her friends farewell and sallied forth on her return. Home lay some three miles distant, across a copse, a meadow, and a piece of woods, – the woods being a fringe on the skirts of the great forests that stretch far away into the North. That home was one of a dozen log-houses lying a few furlongs apart from each other, with their half-cleared demesnes separating them at the rear from a wilderness untrodden save by stealthy native or deadly panther tribes.

She was in a nowise exalted frame of spirit, – on the contrary, rather depressed by the pain she had witnessed and the fatigue she had endured; but in certain temperaments such a condition throws open the mental pores, so to speak, and renders one receptive of every influence. Through the little copse she walked slowly, with her cloak folded about her, lingering to imbibe the sense of shelter, the sunset filtered in purple through the mist of woven spray and twig, the companionship of growth not sufficiently dense to band against her, the sweet home-feeling of a young and tender wintry wood. It was therefore just on the edge of the evening that she emerged from the place and began to cross the meadow-land. At one hand lay the forest to which her path wound; at the other the evening star hung over a tide of failing orange that slowly slipped down the earth's broad side to sadden other hemispheres with sweet regret. Walking rapidly now, and with her eyes wide-open, she distinctly saw in the air before her what was not there a moment ago, a winding-sheet, – cold, white, and ghastly, waved by the likeness of four wan hands, – that rose with a long inflation, and fell in rigid folds, while a voice, shaping itself from the hollowness above, spectral and melancholy, sighed, – "The Lord have mercy on the people! The Lord have mercy on the people!" Three times the sheet with its corpse-covering outline waved beneath the pale hands, and the voice, awful in its solemn and mysterious depth, sighed, "The Lord have mercy on the people!" Then all was gone, the place was clear again, the gray sky was obstructed by no deathly blot; she looked about her, shook her shoulders decidedly, and, pulling on her hood, went forward once more.

She might have been a little frightened by such an apparition, if she had led a life of less reality than frontier settlers are apt to lead; but dealing with hard fact does not engender a flimsy habit of mind, and this woman was too sincere and earnest in her character, and too happy in her situation, to be thrown by antagonism, merely, upon superstitious fancies and chimeras of the second-sight. She did not even believe herself subject to an hallucination, but smiled simply, a little vexed that her thought could have framed such a glamour from the day's occurrences, and not sorry to lift the bough of the warder of the woods and enter and disappear in their sombre path. If she had been imaginative, she would have hesitated at her first step into a region whose dangers were not visionary; but I suppose that the thought of a little child at home would conquer that propensity in the most habituated. So, biting a bit of spicy birch, she went along. Now and then she came to a gap where the trees had been partially felled, and here she found that the lingering twilight was explained by that peculiar and perhaps electric film which sometimes sheathes the sky in diffused light for many hours before a brilliant aurora.[1] Suddenly, a swift shadow, like the fabulous flying-dragon, writhed through the air before her, and she felt herself instantly seized and borne aloft. It was that wild beast – the most savage and serpentine and subtle and fearless of our latitudes – known by hunters as the Indian Devil,[2] and he held her in his clutches on the broad floor of a swinging fir-bough. His long sharp claws were caught in her clothing, he worried them sagaciously a little, then, finding that ineffectual to free them, he commenced licking her bare arm with his rasping tongue and pouring over her the wide streams of his hot, fetid breath. So quick had this flashing action been that the woman had had no time for alarm; moreover, she was not of the screaming kind: but now, as she felt him endeavoring to disentangle his claws, and the horrid sense of her fate smote her, and she saw instinctively the fierce plunge of those weapons, the long strips of living flesh torn from her bones, the agony, the quivering disgust, itself a worse agony, – while by her side, and holding her in his great lithe embrace, the monster crouched, his white tusks whetting and gnashing, his eyes glaring through all the darkness like balls of red fire, – a shriek, that rang in every forest hollow, that startled every winter-housed thing, that stirred and woke the least needle of the tasselled pines, tore through her lips. A moment afterward, the beast left the arm, once white, now crimson, and looked up alertly.

She did not think at this instant to call upon God. She called upon her husband. It seemed to her that she had but one friend in the world; that was he; and again the cry, loud, clear, prolonged, echoed through the woods. It was not the shriek that disturbed the creature at his relish; he was not born in the woods to be scared of an owl, you know; what then? It must have been the echo, most musical, most resonant, repeated and yet repeated, dying with long sighs of sweet sound, vibrated from rock to river and back again from depth to depth of cave and cliff. Her thought flew after it; she knew, that, even if her husband heard it, he yet could not reach her in time; she saw that while the beast listened he would not gnaw, – and this she *felt* directly, when the rough, sharp, and multiplied stings of his tongue retouched her arm. Again her lips opened by instinct, but the sound that issued thence came by reason. She had heard that music charmed wild beasts, – just this point between life and death intensified every faculty, – and when she opened her lips the third time, it was not for shrieking, but for singing.

A little thread of melody stole out, a rill of tremulous motion; it was the cradle-song with which she rocked her baby; – how could she sing that? And then she remembered the baby sleeping rosily on the long settee before the fire, – the father cleaning his gun,

Notes

CIRCUMSTANCE
[1] The aurora borealis or northern lights.
[2] A cougar (puma).

with one foot on the green wooden rundle, – the merry light from the chimney dancing out and through the room, on the rafters of the ceiling with their tassels of onions and herbs, on the log walls painted with lichens and festooned with apples, on the king's-arm slung across the shelf with the old pirate's-cutlass, on the snow-pile of the bed, and on the great brass clock, – dancing, too, and lingering on the baby, with his fringed-gentian eyes, his chubby fists clenched on the pillow, and his fine breezy hair fanning with the motion of his father's foot. All this struck her in one, and made a sob of her breath, and she ceased.

Immediately the long red tongue thrust forth again. Before it touched, a song sprang to her lips, a wild sea-song, such as some sailor might be singing far out on trackless blue water that night, the shrouds whistling with frost and the sheets glued in ice, – a song with the wind in its burden and the spray in its chorus. The monster raised his head and flared the fiery eyeballs upon her, then fretted the imprisoned claws a moment and was quiet; only the breath like the vapor from some hell-pit still swathed her. Her voice, at first faint and fearful, gradually lost its quaver, grew under her control and subject to her modulation; it rose on long swells, it fell in subtle cadences, now and then its tones pealed out like bells from distant belfries on fresh sonorous mornings. She sung the song through, and, wondering lest his name of Indian Devil were not his true name, and if he would not detect her, she repeated it. Once or twice now, indeed, the beast stirred uneasily, turned, and made the bough sway at his movement. As she ended, he snapped his jaws together, and tore away the fettered member, curling it under him with a snarl, – when she burst into the gayest reel that ever answered a fiddle-bow. How many a time she had heard her husband play it on the homely fiddle made by himself from birch and cherry-wood! how many a time she had seen it danced on the floor of their one room, to the patter of wooden clogs and the rustle of homespun petticoat! how many a time she had danced it herself! – and did she not remember once, as they joined clasps for eight-hands-round, how it had lent its gay, bright measure to her life? And here she was singing it alone, in the forest, at midnight, to a wild beast! As she sent her voice trilling up and down its quick oscillations between joy and pain, the creature who grasped her uncurled his paw and scratched the bark from the bough; she must vary the spell; and her voice spun leaping along the projecting points of tune of a hornpipe. Still singing, she felt herself twisted about with a low growl and a lifting of the red lip from the glittering teeth; she broke the hornpipe's thread, and commenced unravelling a lighter, livelier thing, an Irish jig. Up and down and round about her voice flew, the beast threw back his head so that the diabolical face fronted hers, and the torrent of his breath prepared her for his feast as the anaconda slimes his prey. Franticly she darted from tune to tune; his restless movements followed her. She tired herself with dancing and vivid national airs, growing feverish and singing spasmodically as she felt her horrid tomb yawning wider. Touching in this manner all the slogan and keen clan cries, the beast moved again, but only to lay the disengaged paw across her with heavy satisfaction. She did not dare to pause; through the clear cold air, the frosty starlight, she sang. If there were yet any tremor in the tone, it was not fear, – she had learned the secret of sound at last; nor could it be chill, – far too high a fever throbbed her pulses; it was nothing but the thought of the log-house and of what might be passing within it. She fancied the baby stirring in his sleep and moving his pretty lips, – her husband rising and opening the door, looking out after her, and wondering at her absence. She fancied the light pouring through the chink and then shut in again with all the safety and comfort and joy, her husband taking down the fiddle and playing lightly with his head inclined, playing while she sang, while she sang for her life to an Indian Devil. Then she knew he was fumbling for and finding some shining fragment and scoring it down the yellowing hair, and unconsciously her voice forsook the wild war-tunes and drifted into the half-gay, half-melancholy Rosin the Bow.

Suddenly she woke pierced with a pang, and the daggered tooth penetrating her flesh; – dreaming of safety, she had ceased singing and lost it. The beast had regained the use of all his limbs, and now, standing and raising his back, bristling and foaming, with sounds that would have been like hisses but for their deep and fearful sonority, he withdrew step by step toward the trunk of the tree, still with his flaming balls upon her. She was all at once free, on one end of the bough, twenty feet from the ground. She did not measure the distance, but rose to drop herself down, careless of any death, so that it were not this. Instantly, as if he scanned her thoughts, the creature bounded forward with a yell and caught her again in his dreadful hold. It might be that he was not greatly famished; for, as she suddenly flung up her voice again, he settled himself composedly on the bough, still clasping her with invincible pressure to his rough, ravenous breast, and listening in a fascination to the sad, strange U-la-lu that now moaned forth in loud, hollow tones above him. He half closed his eyes, and sleepily reopened and shut them again.

What rending pains were close at hand! Death! and what a death! worse than any other that is to be named! Water, be it cold or warm, that which buoys up blue ice-fields, or which bathes tropical coasts with currents of balmy bliss, is yet a gentle conqueror, kisses as it kills, and draws you down gently through darkening fathoms to its heart. Death at the sword is the festival of trumpet and bugle and banner, with glory ringing out around you and distant hearts thrilling through yours. No gnawing disease can bring such hideous end as this; for that is a fiend bred of your own flesh, and this – is it a fiend, this living lump of appetites? What dread comes with the thought of perishing in flames! but fire, let it leap and hiss never so hotly, is something too remote, too alien, to inspire us with such loathly horror as a wild beast; if it have a life, that life is too utterly beyond our comprehension. Fire is not half ourselves; as it devours, arouses neither hatred nor disgust; is not to be known by the strength of our lower natures let loose; does not drip our blood into our faces from foaming chaps, nor mouth nor slaver above us with vitality. Let us be ended by fire, and we are ashes, for the winds to bear, the leaves to cover; let us be ended by wild beasts, and the base, cursed thing howls with us forever through the forest. All this she felt as she charmed him, and what force it lent to her song God knows. If her voice should fail! If the damp and cold should give her any fatal hoarseness! If all the silent powers of the forest did not conspire to help her! The dark, hollow night rose indifferently over her; the wide, cold air breathed rudely past her, lifted her wet hair and blew it down again; the great boughs swung with a ponderous strength, now and then clashed their iron lengths together and shook off a sparkle of icy spears or some long-lain weight of snow from their heavy shadows. The green depths were utterly cold and silent and stern. These beautiful haunts that all the summer were hers and rejoiced to share with her their bounty, these heavens that had yielded their largess, these stems that had thrust their blossoms into her hands, all these friends of three moons ago forgot her now and knew her no longer.

Feeling her desolation, wild, melancholy, forsaken songs rose thereon from that frightful aerie, – weeping, wailing tunes, that sob among the people from age to age, and overflow with otherwise unexpressed sadness, – all rude, mournful ballads, – old tearful strains, that Shakespeare heard the vagrants sing, and that rise and fall like the wind and tide, – sailor-songs, to be heard only in lone mid-watches beneath the moon and stars, – ghastly rhyming romances, such as that famous one of the Lady Margaret, when

"She slipped on her gown of green
A piece below the knee, –
And 'twas all a long, cold winter's night
A dead corse followed she."[3]

Still the beast lay with closed eyes, yet never relaxing his grasp. Once a half-whine of enjoyment escaped him, – he fawned his fearful head upon her; once he scored her cheek with his tongue: savage caresses that hurt like wounds. How weary she was! and yet how terribly awake! How fuller and fuller of dismay grew the knowledge that she was only prolonging her anguish and playing with death! How appalling the thought that with her voice ceased her existence! Yet she could not sing forever; her throat was dry and hard; her very breath was a pain; her mouth was hotter than any desert-worn pilgrim's; – if she could but drop upon her burning tongue one atom of the ice that glittered about her! – but both of her arms were pinioned in the giant's vice. She remembered the winding-sheet, and for the first time in her life shivered with spiritual fear. Was it hers? She asked herself, as she sang, what sins she had committed, what life she had led, to find her punishment so soon and in these pangs, – and then she sought eagerly for some reason why her husband was not up and abroad to find her. He failed her, – her one sole hope in life; and without being aware of it, her voice forsook the songs of suffering and sorrow for old Covenanting[4] hymns, – hymns with which her mother had lulled her, which the class-leader pitched in the chimney-corners, – grand and sweet Methodist hymns, brimming with melody and with all fantastic involutions of tune to suit that ecstatic worship, – hymns full of the beauty of holiness, steadfast, relying, sanctified by the salvation they had lent to those in worse extremity than hers, – for they had found themselves in the grasp of hell, while she was but in the jaws of death. Out of this strange music, peculiar to one character of faith, and than which there is none more beautiful in its degree nor owning a more potent sway of sound, her voice soared into the glorified chants of churches. What to her was death by cold or famine or wild beasts? "Though He slay me, yet will I trust in him,"[5] she sang. High and clear through the frore fair night, the level moonbeams splintering in the wood, the scarce glints of stars in the shadowy roof of branches, these sacred anthems rose, – rose as a hope from despair, as some snowy spray of flower-bells from blackest mould. Was she not in God's hands? Did not the world swing at his will? If this were in his great plan of providence, was it not best, and should she not accept it?

"He is the Lord our God; his judgments are in all the earth."[6]

Oh, sublime faith of our fathers, where utter self-sacrifice alone was true love, the fragrance of whose unrequired subjection was pleasanter than that of golden censers swung in purple-vapored chancels!

Never ceasing in the rhythm of her thoughts, articulated in music as they thronged, the memory of her first communion flashed over her. Again she was in that distant place on that sweet spring morning. Again the congregation rustled out, and the few remained, and she trembled to find herself among them. How well she remembered the devout, quiet faces, too accustomed to the sacred feast to glow with their inner joy! how well the snowy linen at the altar, the silver vessels slowly and silently shifting! and

Notes

[3] From a variant of the traditional English ballad, "Fair Margaret and Sweet William."

[4] Presbyterian.

[5] Job 13:15.

[6] Psalm 105:7.

as the cup approached and passed, how the sense of delicious perfume stole in and heightened the transport of her prayer, and she had seemed, looking up through the windows where the sky soared blue in constant freshness, to feel all heaven's balms dripping from the portals, and to scent the lilies of eternal peace! Perhaps another would not have felt so much ecstasy as satisfaction on that occasion; but it is a true, if a later disciple, who has said, "The Lord bestoweth his blessings there, where he findeth the vessels empty."[7] – "And does it need the walls of a church to renew my communion?" she asked. "Does not every moment stand a temple four-square to God? And in that morning, with its buoyant sunlight, was I any dearer to the Heart of the World than now?" "My beloved is mine, and I am his,"[8] she sang over and over again, with all varied inflection and profuse tune. How gently all the winter-wrapt things bent toward her then! into what relation with her had they grown! how this common dependence was the spell of their intimacy! how at one with Nature had she become! how all the night and the silence and the forest seemed to hold its breath, and to send its soul up to God in her singing! It was no longer despondency, that singing. It was neither prayer nor petition. She had left imploring, "How long wilt thou forget me, O Lord? Lighten mine eyes, lest I sleep the sleep of death![9] For in death there is no remembrance of thee,"[10] – with countless other such fragments of supplication. She cried rather, "Yea, though I walk through the valley of the shadow of death, I will fear no evil: for thou art with me; thy rod and thy staff, they comfort me,"[11] – and lingered, and repeated, and sang again, "I shall be satisfied, when I awake, with thy likeness."[12]

Then she thought of the Great Deliverance, when he drew her up out of many waters, and the flashing old psalm pealed forth triumphantly: –

"The lord descended from above,
and bow'd the heavens hie:
And underneath his feet he cast
the darknesse of the skie.
On cherubs and on cherubins
full royally he road:
And on the wings of all the winds
came flying all abroad."[13]

She forgot how recently, and with what a strange pity for her own shapeless form that was to be, she had quaintly sung, –

"Oh, lovely appearance of death!
What sight upon earth is so fair?
Not all the gay pageants that breathe
Can with a dead body compare!"[14]

She remembered instead, – "In thy presence is fulness of joy; at thy right hand there are pleasures forevermore.[15] God will redeem my soul from the power of the grave: for he shall receive me.[16] He will swallow up death in victory."[17] Not once now did she say,

Notes

[7] From Thomas à Kempis, *Of the Imitation of Christ.*
[8] Song of Solomon 2:16.
[9] Psalm 13:1,3.
[10] Psalm 6:5.
[11] Psalm 23:4.
[12] Psalm 17:15.
[13] Hymn by Thomas Sternhold (1500–49) adapted from Psalm 18.
[14] Hymn by Charles Wesley (1707–88).
[15] Psalm 16:11.
[16] Psalm 49:15.
[17] Isaiah 25:8.

"Lord, how long wilt thou look on? rescue my soul from their destructions, my darling from the lions,"[18] – for she knew that the young lions roar after their prey and seek their meat from God.[19] "O Lord, thou preservest man and beast!"[20] she said.

She had no comfort or consolation in this season, such as sustained the Christian martyrs in the amphitheatre. She was not dying for her faith; there were no palms in heaven for her to wave; but how many a time had she declared, – "I had rather be a doorkeeper in the house of my God, than to dwell in the tents of wickedness!"[21] And as the broad rays here and there broke through the dense covert of shade and lay in rivers of lustre on crystal sheathing and frozen fretting of trunk and limb and on the great spaces of refraction, they builded up visibly that house, the shining city on the hill, and singing, "Beautiful for situation, the joy of the whole earth, is Mount Zion, on the sides of the North, the city of the Great King,"[22] her vision climbed to that higher picture where the angel shows the dazzling thing, the holy Jerusalem descending out of heaven from God, with its splendid battlements and gates of pearls, and its foundations, the eleventh a jacinth, the twelfth an amethyst, – with its great white throne, and the rainbow round about it, in sight like unto an emerald:[23] "And there shall be no night there, – for the Lord God giveth them light,"[24] she sang.

What whisper of dawn now rustled through the wilderness? How the night was passing! And still the beast crouched upon the bough, changing only the posture of his head, that again he might command her with those charmed eyes; – half their fire was gone; she could almost have released herself from his custody; yet, had she stirred, no one knows what malevolent instinct might have dominated anew. But of that she did not dream; long ago stripped of any expectation, she was experiencing in her divine rapture how mystically true it is that "he that dwelleth in the secret place of the Most High shall abide under the shadow of the Almighty."[25]

Slow clarion cries now wound from the distance as the cocks caught the intelligence of day and re-echoed it faintly from farm to farm, – sleepy sentinels of night, sounding the foe's invasion, and translating that dim intuition to ringing notes of warning. Still she chanted on. A remote crash of brushwood told of some other beast on his depredations, or some night-belated traveller groping his way through the narrow path. Still she chanted on. The far, faint echoes of the chanticleers died into distance, – the crashing of the branches grew nearer. No wild beast that, but a man's step, – a man's form in the moonlight, stalwart and strong, – on one arm slept a little child, in the other hand he held his gun. Still she chanted on.

Perhaps, when her husband last looked forth, he was half ashamed to find what a fear he felt for her. He knew she would never leave the child so long but for some direst need, – and yet he may have laughed at himself, as he lifted and wrapped it with awkward care, and, loading his gun and strapping on his horn, opened the door again and closed it behind him, going out and plunging into the darkness and dangers of the forest. He was more singularly alarmed than he would have been willing to acknowledge; as he had sat with his bow hovering over the strings, he had half believed to hear her voice mingling gayly with the instrument, till he paused and listened if she were not about to lift the latch and enter. As he drew nearer the heart of the forest, that intimation of melody seemed to grow more actual, to take body and breath, to come and go on long swells and ebbs of the night-breeze, to increase with tune and words,

Notes

[18] Psalm 35:17.

[19] Psalm 104:21.

[20] Psalm 36:6.

[21] Psalm 84:10.

[22] Psalm 48:2.

[23] The descriptions of the New Jerusalem are from Revelation 21.

[24] Revelation 22:5.

[25] Psalm 91:1.

till a strange shrill singing grew ever clearer, and, as he stepped into an open space of moonbeams, far up in the branches, rocked by the wind, and singing, "How beautiful upon the mountains are the feet of him that bringeth good tidings, that publisheth peace,"[26] he saw his wife, – his wife, – but, great God in heaven! how? Some mad exclamation escaped him, but without diverting her. The child knew the singing voice, though never heard before in that unearthly key, and turned toward it through the veiling dreams. With a celerity almost instantaneous, it lay, in the twinkling of an eye, on the ground at the father's feet, while his gun was raised to his shoulder and levelled at the monster covering his wife with shaggy form and flaming gaze, – his wife so ghastly white, so rigid, so stained with blood, her eyes so fixedly bent above, and her lips, that had indurated into the chiselled pallor of marble, parted only with that flood of solemn song.

I do not know if it were the mother-instinct that for a moment lowered her eyes, – those eyes, so lately riveted on heaven, now suddenly seeing all life-long bliss possible. A thrill of joy pierced and shivered through her like a weapon, her voice trembled in its course, her glance lost its steady strength, fever-flushes chased each other over her face, yet she never once ceased chanting. She was quite aware, that, if her husband shot now, the ball must pierce her body before reaching any vital part of the beast, – and yet better that death, by his hand, than the other. But this her husband also knew, and he remained motionless, just covering the creature with the sight. He dared not fire, lest some wound not mortal should break the spell exercised by her voice, and the beast, enraged with pain, should rend her in atoms; moreover, the light was too uncertain for his aim. So he waited. Now and then he examined his gun to see if the damp were injuring its charge, now and then he wiped the great drops from his forehead. Again the cocks crowed with the passing hour, – the last time they were heard on that night. Cheerful home sound then, how full of safety and all comfort and rest it seemed! what sweet morning incidents of sparkling fire and sunshine, of gay household bustle, shining dresser, and cooing baby, of steaming cattle in the yard, and brimming milk-pails at the door! what pleasant voices! what laughter! what security! and here –

Now, as she sang on in the slow, endless, infinite moments, the fervent vision of God's peace was gone. Just as the grave had lost its sting, she was snatched back again into the arms of earthly hope. In vain she tried to sing, "There remaineth a rest for the people of God,"[27] – her eyes trembled on her husband's, and she could only think of him, and of the child, and of happiness that yet might be, but with what a dreadful gulf of doubt between! She shuddered now in the suspense; all calm forsook her; she was tortured with dissolving heats or frozen with icy blasts; her face contracted, growing small and pinched; her voice was hoarse and sharp, – every tone cut like a knife, – the notes became heavy to lift, – withheld by some hostile pressure, – impossible. One gasp, a convulsive effort, and there was silence, – she had lost her voice.

The beast made a sluggish movement, – stretched and fawned like one awakening, – then, as if he would have yet more of the enchantment, stirred her slightly with his muzzle. As he did so, a sidelong hint of the man standing below with the raised gun smote him; he sprung round furiously, and, seizing his prey, was about to leap into some unknown airy den of the topmost branches now waving to the slow dawn. The late moon had rounded through the sky so that her gleam at last fell full upon the bough with fairy frosting; the wintry morning light did not yet penetrate the gloom. The woman, suspended in mid-air an instant, cast only one agonized glance beneath, – but across and through it, ere the lids could fall, shot a withering sheet of

Notes

[26] Isaiah 52:7. [27] Hymn by Charles Wesley, based on Hebrews 4:9.

flame, – a rifle-crack, half-heard, was lost in the terrible yell of desperation that bounded after it and filled her ears with savage echoes, and in the wide arc of some eternal descent she was falling; – but the beast fell under her.

I think that the moment following must have been too sacred for us, and perhaps the three have no special interest again till they issue from the shadows of the wilderness upon the white hills that skirt their home. The father carries the child hushed again into slumber, the mother follows with no such feeble step as might be anticipated. It is not time for reaction, – the tension not yet relaxed, the nerves still vibrant, she seems to herself like some one newly made; the night was a dream; the present stamped upon her in deep satisfaction, neither weighed nor compared with the past; if she has the careful tricks of former habit, it is as an automaton; and as they slowly climb the steep under the clear gray vault and the paling morning star, and as she stops to gather a spray of the red-rose berries or a feathery tuft of dead grasses for the chimney-piece of the log-house, or a handful of brown cones for the child's play, – of these quiet, happy folk you would scarcely dream how lately they had stolen from under the banner and encampment of the great King Death. The husband proceeds a step or two in advance; the wife lingers over a singular foot-print in the snow, stoops and examines it, then looks up with a hurried word. Her husband stands alone on the hill, his arms folded across the babe, his gun fallen, – stands defined as a silhouette against the pallid sky. What is there in their home, lying below and yellowing in the light, to fix him with such a stare? She springs to his side. There is no home there. The log-house, the barns, the neighboring farms, the fences, are all blotted out and mingled in one smoking ruin. Desolation and death were indeed there, and beneficence and life in the forest. Tomahawk and scalping-knife, descending during that night, had left behind them only this work of their accomplished hatred and one subtle foot-print in the snow.

For the rest, – the world was all before them, where to choose.[28]

Notes

[28] From the conclusion of *Paradise Lost*, by John Milton (1608–74), as Adam and Eve depart Eden.

Ambrose Bierce (1842–1914?)

Ambrose Bierce is as celebrated for the mystery of his death as for the mystery in his fiction. Indeed, his disappearance into Mexico during its revolution may be the final bitter jest of a master of the literary hoax.

The following stories are both graveyard pieces, and share references to the sage Hali, a Bierce invention. They are in other ways dissimilar, and represent different Gothic traditions. In "An Inhabitant of Carcosa" (1886) Bierce draws on the tradition of Poe. The tale relentlessly builds its uncanny mood toward its inevitable final revelation. This story has had immense impact on the tradition of the "weird tale" in the twentieth century and beyond, and is referenced by Robert W. Chambers and H. P. Lovecraft.

"The Death of Halpin Frayser" (1891) is a poisonous midsummer night's dream and a deeply ambiguous puzzle-piece, and it draws on the tradition of Hawthorne rather than Poe. Like "Young Goodman Brown," it begins and ends in historical and physical reality. Both Hawthorne and Bierce take the reader thence into a dark wood where nightmare events may be explained in psychological or supernatural terms. Readers should avoid easy solutions to Halpin Frayser's fate, since each possible explanation seems to contain an objection or contradiction.

Texts: "The Death of Halpin Frayser," from *Can Such Things Be?* (New York: Albert & Charles Boni, 1924 [*c.*1909]). "An Inhabitant of Carcosa," from *Tales of Soldiers and Civilians* (New York: United States Book Company, *c.*1891).

An Inhabitant of Carcosa

For there be divers sorts of death – some wherein the body remaineth; and in some it vanisheth quite away with the spirit. This commonly occureth only in solitude (such is God's will) and, none seeing the end, we say the man is lost, or gone on a long journey – which indeed he hath; but sometimes it hath happened in sight of many, as abundant testimony showeth. In one kind of death the spirit also dieth, and this it hath been known to do while yet the body was in vigor for many years. Sometimes, as is veritably attested, it dieth with the body, but after a season it is raised up again in that place that the body did decay.

PONDERING these words of Hali (whom God rest) and questioning their full meaning, as one who, having an intimation yet doubts if there be not something behind other than that which he has discerned, I noted not whither I had strayed until a sudden chill wind striking my face revived in me a sense of my surroundings. I observed with astonishment that everything seemed unfamiliar. On every side of me stretched a bleak and desolate expanse of plain, covered with a tall overgrowth of sear grass, which rustled and whistled in the autumn wind with heaven knows what mysterious and disquieting

American Gothic: From Salem Witchcraft to H. P. Lovecraft, An Anthology, Second Edition. Edited by Charles L. Crow.
Editorial material and organization © 2013 John Wiley & Sons, Ltd. Published 2013 by John Wiley & Sons, Ltd.

suggestion. Protruded at long intervals above it, stood strangely-shaped and somber-colored rocks, which seemed to have an understanding with one another and to exchange looks of uncomfortable significance, as it they had reared their heads to watch the issue of some foreseen event. A few blasted trees here and there appeared as leaders in this malevolent conspiracy of silent expectation. The day, I thought, must be far advanced, though the sun was invisible; and although sensible that the air was raw and chill, my consciousness of that fact was rather mental than physical – I had no feeling of discomfort. Over all the dismal landscape a canopy of low, lead-colored clouds hung like a visible curse. In everything there were a menace and a portent – a hint of crime, an intimation of doom. Bird, beast, or insect there was none. The wind sighed in the bare branches of the dead trees and the gray grass bent to whisper its dread secret to the earth; but no other sound or motion broke the awful repose of that dismal place.

I observed in the herbage a number of weather-worn stones, evidently shaped with tools. They were broken, covered with moss and half sunken in the earth. Some lay prostrate, some leaned at various angles, none were vertical. They were obviously headstones of graves, though the graves themselves no longer existed as either mounds or depressions; the years had leveled all. Scattered here and there, more massive blocks showed where some pompous tomb or ambitious monument had once flung its feeble defiance at oblivion. So old seemed these relics, these vestiges of vanity and memorials of affection and piety – so battered and worn and stained, so neglected, deserted, forgotten the place, that I could not help thinking myself the discoverer of the burial-ground of a prehistoric race of men – a nation whose very name was long extinct.

Filled with these reflections, I was for some time heedless of the sequence of my own experiences, but soon I thought, "How came I hither?" A moment's reflection seemed to make this all clear, and explain at the same time, though in a disquieting way, the singularly weird character with which my fancy had invested all that I saw and heard. I was ill. I remembered now how I had been prostrated by a sudden fever, and how my family had told me that in my periods of delirium I had constantly cried out for liberty and air, and had been held in bed to prevent my escape out-of-doors. Now I had eluded the vigilance of my attendants, and had wandered hither to – to where? I could not conjecture. Clearly I was at a considerable distance from the city where I dwelt – the ancient and famous city of Carcosa. No signs of human life were anywhere visible or audible; no rising smoke, no watchdog's bark, no lowing of cattle, no shouts of children, at play – nothing but this dismal burial-place, with its air of mystery and dread, due to my own disordered brain. Was I not becoming again delirious, there, beyond human aid? Was it not indeed *all* an illusion of my madness? I called aloud the names of my wife and sons, reached out my hands in search of theirs, even as I walked among the crumbling stones and in the withered grass.

A noise behind me caused me to turn about. A wild animal – a lynx – was approaching. The thought came to me: If I break down here in the desert – if the fever returns and I fail, this beast will be at my throat. I sprang toward it, shouting. It trotted tranquilly by, within a hand's breadth of me, and disappeared behind a rock. A moment later a man's head appeared to rise out of the ground a short distance away. He was ascending the far slope of a low hill whose crest was hardly to be distinguished from the general level. His whole figure soon came into view against the background of gray cloud. He was half naked, half clad in skins. His hair was unkempt, his beard long and ragged. In one hand he carried a bow and arrow; the other held a blazing torch with a long trail of black smoke. He walked slowly and with caution, as if he feared falling into some open grave concealed by the tall grass. This strange apparition surprised but did not alarm, and, taking such a course as to intercept him, I met him almost face to face, accosting him with the salutation, "God keep you!"

He gave no heed, nor did he arrest his pace.

"Good stranger," I continued," I am ill and lost. Direct me, I beseech you, to Carcosa?"

The man broke into a barbarous chant in an unknown tongue, passing on and away. An owl on the branch of a decayed tree hooted dismally, and was answered by another in the distance. Looking upward I saw, through a sudden rift in the clouds, Aldebaran and the Hyades! In all this there was a hint of night – the lynx, the man with a torch, the owl. Yet I saw – I saw even the stars in absence of the darkness. I saw, but was apparently not seen nor heard. Under what awful spell did I exist?

I seated myself at the root of a great tree, seriously to consider what it was best to do. That I was mad I could no longer doubt, yet recognized a ground of doubt in the conviction. Of fever I had no trace. I had, withal, a sense of exhilaration and vigor altogether unknown to me – a feeling of mental and physical exaltation. My senses seemed all alert; I could feel the air as a ponderous substance, I could hear the silence.

A great root of the giant tree against whose trunk I leaned as I sat, held inclosed in its grasp a slab of granite, a portion of which protruded into a recess formed by another root. The stone was thus partly protected from the weather, though greatly decomposed. Its edges were worn round, its corners eaten away, its face deeply furrowed and scaled. Glittering particles of mica were visible in the earth beneath it – vestiges of its decomposition. This stone had apparently marked the grave out of which the tree had sprung ages ago. The tree's exacting roots had robbed the grave and made the stone a prisoner.

A sudden wind pushed some dry leaves and twigs from the uppermost face of the stone; I saw the low-relief letters of an inscription and bent to read it. God in heaven! *my* name in full! – the date of *my* birth! – the date of *my* death!

A level shaft of rosy light illuminated the whole side of the tree as I sprang to my feet in terror. The sun was rising in the east. I stood between the tree and his broad red disk – no shadow darkened the trunk! A chorus or howling wolves saluted the dawn. I saw them sitting on their haunches, singly and in groups, on the summits of irregular mounds and tumuli, filling a half of my desert prospect and extending to the horizon; and then I knew that these were the ruins of the ancient and famous city of Carcosa.

– – – –

Such are the facts imparted to the medium Bayrolles by the spirit Hoseib Alar Robardin.

The Death of Halpin Frayser

I

For by death is wrought greater change than hath been shown. Whereas in general the spirit that removed cometh back upon occasion, and is sometimes seen of those in flesh (appearing in the form of the body it bore) yet it hath happened that the veritable body without the spirit hath walked. And it is attested of those encountering who have lived to speak thereon that a lich[1] so raised up hath no natural affection, nor remembrance thereof, but only hate. Also, it is known that some spirits which in life were benign become by death evil altogether.

–Hali

Notes ——————————————————————————

THE DEATH OF HALPIN FRAYSER

[1] Corpse.

ONE dark night in midsummer a man waking from a dreamless sleep in a forest lifted his head from the earth, and staring a few moments into the blackness, said: "Catherine Larue." He said nothing more; no reason was known to him why he should have said so much.

The man was Halpin Frayser. He lived in St. Helena, but where he lives now is uncertain, for he is dead. One who practices sleeping in the woods with nothing under him but the dry leaves and the damp earth, and nothing over him but the branches from which the leaves have fallen and the sky from which the earth has fallen, cannot hope for great longevity, and Frayser had already attained the age of thirty-two. There are persons in this world, millions of persons, and far and away the best persons, who regard that as a very advanced age. They are the children. To those who view the voyage of life from the port of departure the bark that has accomplished any considerable distance appears already in close approach to the farther shore. However, it is not certain that Halpin Frayser came to his death by exposure.

He had been all day in the hills west of the Napa Valley, looking for doves and such small game as was in season. Late in the afternoon it had come on to be cloudy, and he had lost his bearings; and although he had only to go always downhill – everywhere the way to safety when one is lost – the absence of trails had so impeded him that he was overtaken by night while still in the forest. Unable in the darkness to penetrate the thickets of manzanita and other undergrowth, utterly bewildered and overcome with fatigue, he had lain down near the root of a large madroño and fallen into a dreamless sleep. It was hours later, in the very middle of the night, that one of God's mysterious messengers, gliding ahead of the incalculable host of his companions sweeping westward with the dawn line, pronounced the awakening word in the ear of the sleeper, who sat upright and spoke, he knew not why, a name, he knew not whose.

Halpin Frayser was not much of a philosopher, nor a scientist. The circumstance that, waking from a deep sleep at night in the midst of a forest, he had spoken aloud a name that he had not in memory and hardly had in mind did not arouse an enlightened curiosity to investigate the phenomenon. He thought it odd, and with a little perfunctory shiver, as if in deference to a seasonal presumption that the night was chill, he lay down again and went to sleep. But his sleep was no longer dreamless.

He thought he was walking along a dusty road that showed white in the gathering darkness of a summer night. Whence and whither it led, and why he traveled it, he did not know, though all seemed simple and natural, as is the way in dreams; for in the Land Beyond the Bed surprises cease from troubling and the judgment is at rest. Soon he came to a parting of the ways; leading from the highway was a road less traveled, having the appearance, indeed, of having been long abandoned, because, he thought, it led to something evil; yet he turned into it without hesitation, impelled by some imperious necessity.

As he pressed forward he became conscious that his way was haunted by invisible existences whom he could not definitely figure to his mind. From among the trees on either side he caught broken and incoherent whispers in a strange tongue which yet he partly understood. They seemed to him fragmentary utterances of a monstrous conspiracy against his body and soul.

It was now long after nightfall, yet the interminable forest through which he journeyed was lit with a wan glimmer having no point of diffusion, for in its mysterious lumination nothing cast a shadow. A shallow pool in the guttered depression of an old wheel rut, as from a recent rain, met his eye with a crimson gleam. He stooped and plunged his hand into it. It stained his fingers; it was blood! Blood, he then observed, was about him everywhere. The weeds growing rankly by the roadside showed it in blots and splashes on their big, broad leaves. Patches of dry dust between the wheelways were pitted and spattered as with a red rain. Defiling the trunks of the trees were broad maculations of crimson, and blood dripped like dew from their foliage.

All this he observed with a terror which seemed not incompatible with the fulfill-ment of a natural expectation. It seemed to him that it was all in expiation of some crime which, though conscious of his guilt, he could not rightly remember. To the menaces and mysteries of his surroundings the consciousness was an added horror. Vainly he sought by tracing life backward in memory, to reproduce the moment of his sin; scenes and incidents came crowding tumultuously into his mind, one picture effac-ing another, or commingling with it in confusion and obscurity, but nowhere could he catch a glimpse of what he sought. The failure augmented his terror; he felt as one who has murdered in the dark, not knowing whom nor why. So frightful was the situation – the mysterious light burned with so silent and awful a menace; the noxious plants, the trees that by common consent are invested with a melancholy or baleful character, so openly in his sight conspired against his peace; from overhead and all about came so audible and startling whispers and the sighs of creatures so obviously not of earth – that he could endure it no longer, and with a great effort to break some malign spell that bound his faculties to silence and inaction, he shouted with the full strength of his lungs! His voice broken, it seemed, into an infinite multitude of unfamiliar sounds, went babbling and stammering away into the distant reaches of the forest, died into silence, and all was as before. But he had made a beginning at resistance and was encouraged. He said:

"I will not submit unheard. There may be powers that are not malignant traveling this accursed road. I shall leave them a record and an appeal. I shall relate my wrongs, the persecutions that I endure – I, a helpless mortal, a penitent, an unoffending poet!" Halpin Frayser was a poet only as he was a penitent: in his dream.

Taking from his clothing a small red-leather pocketbook, one-half of which was leaved for memoranda, he discovered that he was without a pencil. He broke a twig from a bush, dipped it into a pool of blood and wrote rapidly. He had hardly touched the paper with the point of his twig when a low, wild peal of laughter broke out at a measureless distance away, and growing ever louder, seemed approaching ever nearer; a soulless, heartless, and unjoyous laugh, like that of the loon, solitary by the lakeside at midnight; a laugh which culminated in an unearthly shout close at hand, then died away by slow gradations, as if the accursed being that uttered it had withdrawn over the verge of the world whence it had come. But the man felt that this was not so – that it was near by and had not moved.

A strange sensation began slowly to take possession of his body and his mind. He could not have said which, if any, of his senses was affected; he felt it rather as a con-sciousness – a mysterious mental assurance of some overpowering presence – some supernatural malevolence different in kind from the invisible existences that swarmed about him, and superior to them in power. He knew that it had uttered that hideous laugh. And now it seemed to be approaching him; from what direction he did not know – dared not conjecture. All his former fears were forgotten or merged in the gigantic terror that now held him in thrall. Apart from that, he had but one thought: to complete his written appeal to the benign powers who, traversing the haunted wood, might some time rescue him if he should be denied the blessing of annihilation. He wrote with terrible rapidity, the twig in his fingers rilling blood without renewal; but in the middle of a sentence his hands denied their service to his will, his arms fell to his sides, the book to the earth; and powerless to move or cry out, he found himself staring into the sharply drawn face and blank, dead eyes of his own mother, standing white and silent in the garments of the grave!

II

IN his youth Halpin Frayser had lived with his parents in Nashville, Tennessee. The Fraysers were well-to-do, having a good position in such society as had survived the wreck wrought by civil war. Their children had the social and educational opportunities of their time and place, and had responded to good associations and instruction with agreeable manners and cultivated minds. Halpin being the youngest and not over robust was perhaps a trifle "spoiled." He had the double disadvantage of a mother's assiduity and a father's neglect. Frayser *père* was what no Southern man of means is not – a politician. His country, or rather his section and State, made demands upon his time and attention so exacting that to those of his family he was compelled to turn an ear partly deafened by the thunder of the political captains and the shouting, his own included.

Young Halpin was of a dreamy, indolent and rather romantic turn, somewhat more addicted to literature than law, the profession to which he was bred. Among those of his relations who professed the modern faith of heredity it was well understood that in him the character of the late Myron Bayne, a maternal great-grandfather, had revisited the glimpses of the moon – by which orb Bayne had in his lifetime been sufficiently affected to be a poet of no small Colonial distinction. If not specially observed, it was observable that while a Frayser who was not the proud possessor of a sumptuous copy of the ancestral "poetical works" (printed at the family expense, and long ago withdrawn from an inhospitable market) was a rare Frayser indeed, there was an illogical indisposition to honor the great deceased in the person of his spiritual successor. Halpin was pretty generally deprecated as an intellectual black sheep who was likely at any moment to disgrace the flock by bleating in meter. The Tennessee Fraysers were a practical folk – not practical in the popular sense of devotion to sordid pursuits, but having a robust contempt for any qualities unfitting a man for the wholesome vocation of politics.

In justice to young Halpin it should be said that while in him were pretty faithfully reproduced most of the mental and moral characteristics ascribed by history and family tradition to the famous Colonial bard, his succession to the gift and faculty divine was purely inferential. Not only had he never been known to court the muse, but in truth he could not have written correctly a line of verse to save himself from the Killer of the Wise. Still, there was no knowing when the dormant faculty might wake and smite the lyre.

In the meantime the young man was rather a loose fish, anyhow. Between him and his mother was the most perfect sympathy, for secretly the lady was herself a devout disciple of the late and great Myron Bayne, though with the tact so generally and justly admired in her sex (despite the hardy calumniators who insist that it is essentially the same thing as cunning) she had always taken care to conceal her weakness from all eyes but those of him who shared it. Their common guilt in respect of that was an added tie between them. If in Halpin's youth his mother had "spoiled" him, he had assuredly done his part toward being spoiled. As he grew to such manhood as is attainable by a Southerner who does not care which way elections go the attachment between him and his beautiful mother – whom from early childhood he had called Katy – became yearly stronger and more tender. In these two romantic natures was manifest in a signal way that neglected phenomenon, the dominance of the sexual element in all the relations of life, strengthening, softening, and beautifying even those of consanguinity. The two were nearly inseparable, and by strangers observing their manner were not infrequently mistaken for lovers.

Entering his mother's boudoir one day Halpin Frayser kissed her upon the forehead, toyed for a moment with a lock of her dark hair which had escaped from its confining pins, and said, with an obvious effort at calmness:

"Would you greatly mind, Katy, if I were called away to California for a few weeks?"

It was hardly needful for Katy to answer with her lips a question to which her telltale cheeks had made instant reply. Evidently she would greatly mind; and the tears, too, sprang into her large brown eyes as corroborative testimony.

"Ah, my son," she said, looking up into his face with infinite tenderness, "I should have known that this was coming. Did I not lie awake a half of the night weeping because, during the other half, Grandfather Bayne had come to me in a dream, and standing by his portrait – young, too, and handsome as that – pointed to yours on the same wall? And when I looked it seemed that I could not see the features; you had been painted with a face cloth, such as we put upon the dead. Your father has laughed at me, but you and I, dear, know that such things are not for nothing. And I saw below the edge of the cloth the marks of hands on your throat – forgive me, but we have not been used, to keep such things from each other. Perhaps you have another interpretation. Perhaps it does not mean that you will go to California. Or maybe you will take me with you?"

It must be confessed that this ingenious interpretation of the dream in the light of newly discovered evidence did not wholly commend itself to the son's more logical mind; he had, for the moment at least, a conviction that it foreshadowed a more simple and immediate, if less tragic, disaster than a visit to the Pacific Coast. It was Halpin Frayser's impression that he was to be garroted on his native heath.

"Are there not medicinal springs in California?" Mrs. Frayser resumed before he had time to give her the true reading of the dream – "places where one recovers from rheumatism and neuralgia? Look – my fingers feel so stiff; and I am almost sure they have been giving me great pain while I slept."

She held out her hands for his inspection. What diagnosis of her case the young man may have thought it best to conceal with a smile the historian is unable to state, but for himself he feels bound to say that fingers looking less stiff, and showing fewer evidences of even insensible pain, have seldom been submitted for medical inspection by even the fairest patient desiring a prescription of unfamiliar scenes.

The outcome of it was that of these two odd persons having equally odd notions of duty, the one went to California, as the interest of his client required, and the other remained at home in compliance with a wish that her husband was scarcely conscious of entertaining.

While in San Francisco Halpin Frayser was walking one dark night along the water front of the city, when, with a suddenness that surprised and disconcerted him, he became a sailor. He was in fact "shanghaied" aboard a gallant, gallant ship, and sailed for a far countree.[2] Nor did his misfortunes end with the voyage; for the ship was cast ashore on an island of the South Pacific, and it was six years afterward when the survivors were taken off by a venturesome trading schooner and brought back to San Francisco.

Though poor in purse, Frayser was no less proud in spirit than he had been in the years that seemed ages and ages ago. He would accept no assistance from strangers, and it was while living with a fellow survivor near the town of St. Helena, awaiting news and remittances from home, that he had gone gunning and dreaming.

III

THE apparition confronting the dreamer in the haunted wood – the thing so like, yet so unlike his mother – was horrible! It stirred no love nor longing in his heart; it came unattended with pleasant memories of a golden past – inspired no sentiment of any

Notes ———————————————————————————

[2] Bierce is quoting from a traditional ballad.

kind; all the finer emotions were swallowed up in fear. He tried to turn and run from before it, but his legs were as lead; he was unable to lift his feet from the ground. His arms hung helpless at his sides; of his eyes only he retained control, and these he dared not remove from the lusterless orbs of the apparition, which he knew was not a soul without a body, but that most dreadful of all existences infesting that haunted wood – a body without a soul! In its blank stare was neither love, nor pity, nor intelligence – nothing to which to address an appeal for mercy. "An appeal will not lie," he thought, with an absurd reversion to professional slang, making the situation more horrible, as the fire of a cigar might light up a tomb.

For a time, which seemed so long that the world grew gray with age and sin, and the haunted forest, having fulfilled its purpose in this monstrous culmination of its terrors, vanished out of his consciousness with all its sights and sounds, the apparition stood within a pace, regarding him with the mindless malevolence of a wild brute; then thrust its hands forward and sprang upon him with appalling ferocity! The act released his physical energies without unfettering his will; his mind was still spellbound, but his powerful body and agile limbs, endowed with a blind, insensate life of their own, resisted stoutly and well. For an instant he seemed to see this unnatural contest between a dead intelligence and a breathing mechanism only as a spectator – such fancies are in dreams; then he regained his identity almost as if by a leap forward into his body, and the straining automaton had a directing will as alert and fierce as that of its hideous antagonist.

But what mortal can cope with a creature of his dream? The imagination creating the enemy is already vanquished; the combat's result is the combat's cause. Despite his struggles – despite his strength and activity, which seemed wasted in a void, he felt the cold fingers close upon his throat. Borne backward to the earth, he saw above him the dead and drawn face within a hand's breadth of his own, and then all was black. A sound as of the beating of distant drums – a murmur of swarming voices, a sharp, far cry signing all to silence, and Halpin Frayser dreamed that he was dead.

IV

A WARM, clear night had been followed by a morning of drenching fog. At about the middle of the afternoon of the preceding day a little whiff of light vapor – a mere thickening of the atmosphere, the ghost of a cloud – had been observed clinging to the western side of Mount St. Helena, away up along the barren altitudes near the summit. It was so thin, so diaphanous, so like a fancy made visible, that one would have said: "Look quickly! in a moment it will be gone."

In a moment it was visibly larger and denser. While with one edge it clung to the mountain, with the other it reached farther and farther out into the air above the lower slopes. At the same time it extended itself to north and south, joining small patches of mist that appeared to come out of the mountainside on exactly the same level, with an intelligent design to be absorbed. And so it grew and grew until the summit was shut out of view from the valley, and over the valley itself was an ever-extending canopy, opaque and gray. At Calistoga, which lies near the head of the valley and the foot of the mountain, there were a starless night and a sunless morning. The fog, sinking into the valley, had reached southward, swallowing up ranch after ranch, until it had blotted out the town of St. Helena, nine miles away. The dust in the road was laid; trees were adrip with moisture; birds sat silent in their coverts; the morning light was wan and ghastly, with neither color nor fire.

Two men left the town of St. Helena at the first glimmer of dawn, and walked along the road northward up the valley toward Calistoga. They carried guns on their shoulders, yet no one having knowledge of such matters could have mistaken them for hunters of bird or beast. They were a deputy sheriff from Napa and a detective from San Francisco – Holker and Jaralson, respectively. Their business was man-hunting.

"How far is it?" inquired Holker, as they strode along, their feet stirring white the dust beneath the damp surface of the road.

"The White Church? Only a half mile farther," the other answered. "By the way," he added, "it is neither white nor a church; it is an abandoned schoolhouse, gray with age and neglect. Religious services were once held in it – when it was white, and there is a graveyard that would delight a poet. Can you guess why I sent for you, and told you to come heeled?"

"Oh, I never have bothered you about things of that kind. I've always found you communicative when the time came. But if I may hazard a guess, you want me to help you arrest one of the corpses in the graveyard."

"You remember Branscom?" said Jaralson, treating his companion's wit with the inattention that it deserved.

"The chap who cut his wife's throat? I ought; I wasted a week's work on him and had my expenses for my trouble. There is a reward of five hundred dollars, but none of us ever got a sight of him. You don't mean to say – "

"Yes, I do. He has been under the noses of you fellows all the time. He comes by night to the old graveyard at the White Church."

"The devil! That's where they buried his wife."

"Well, you fellows might have had sense enough to suspect that he would return to her grave some time."

"The very last place that anyone would have expected him to return to."

"But you had exhausted all the other places. Learning your failure at them, I 'laid for him' there."

"And you found him?"

"Damn it! he found *me*. The rascal got the drop on me – regularly held me up and made me travel. It's God's mercy that he didn't go through me. Oh, he's a good one, and I fancy the half of that reward is enough for me if you're needy."

Holker laughed good humoredly, and explained that his creditors were never more importunate.

"I wanted merely to show you the ground, and arrange a plan with you," the detective explained. "I thought it as well for us to be heeled, even in daylight."

"The man must be insane," said the deputy sheriff. "The reward is for his capture and conviction. If he's mad he won't be convicted."

Mr. Holker was so profoundly affected by that possible failure of justice that he involuntarily stopped in the middle of the road, then resumed his walk with abated zeal.

"Well, he looks it," assented Jaralson. "I'm bound to admit that a more unshaven, unshorn, unkempt, and uneverything wretch I never saw outside the ancient and honorable order of tramps. But I've gone in for him, and can't make up my mind to let go. There's glory in it for us, anyhow. Not another soul knows that he is this side of the Mountains of the Moon."

"All right," Holker said; "we will go and view the ground," and he added, in the words of a once favorite inscription for tombstones: "'where you must shortly lie' – I mean, if old Branscom ever gets tired of you and your impertinent intrusion. By the way, I heard the other day that 'Branscom' was not his real name."

"What is?"

"I can't recall it. I had lost all interest in the wretch, and it did not fix itself in my memory – something like Pardee. The woman whose throat he had the bad taste to cut was a widow when he met her. She had come to California to look up some relatives – there are persons who will do that sometimes. But you know all that."

"Naturally."

"But not knowing the right name, by what happy inspiration did you find the right grave? The man who told me what the name was said it had been cut on the headboard."

"I don't know the right grave." Jaralson was apparently a trifle reluctant to admit his ignorance of so important a point of his plan. "I have been watching about the place generally. A part of our work this morning will be to identify that grave. Here is the White Church."

For a long distance the road had been bordered by fields on both sides, but now on the left there was a forest of oaks, madroños, and gigantic spruces whose lower parts only could be seen, dim and ghostly in the fog. The undergrowth was, in places, thick, but nowhere impenetrable. For some moments Holker saw nothing of the building, but as they turned into the woods it revealed itself in faint gray outline through the fog, looking huge and far away. A few steps more, and it was within an arm's length, distinct, dark with moisture, and insignificant in size. It had the usual country-schoolhouse form – belonged to the packing-box order of architecture; had an underpinning of stones, a moss-grown roof, and blank window spaces, whence both glass and sash had long departed. It was ruined, but not a ruin – a typical Californian substitute for what are known to guide-bookers abroad as "monuments of the past." With scarcely a glance at this uninteresting structure Jaralson moved on into the dripping undergrowth beyond.

"I will show you where he held me up," he said. "This is the graveyard."

Here and there among the bushes were small inclosures containing graves, sometimes no more than one. They were recognized as graves by the discolored stones or rotting boards at head and foot, leaning at all angles, some prostrate; by the ruined picket fences surrounding them; or, infrequently, by the mound itself showing its gravel through the fallen leaves. In many instances nothing marked the spot where lay the vestiges of some poor mortal – who, leaving "a large circle of sorrowing friends," had been left by them in turn – except a depression in the earth, more lasting than that in the spirits of the mourners. The paths, if any paths had been, were long obliterated; trees of a considerable size had been permitted to grow up from the graves and thrust aside with root or branch the inclosing fences. Over all was that air of abandonment and decay which seems nowhere so fit and significant as in a village of the forgotten dead.

As the two men, Jaralson leading, pushed their way through the growth of young trees, that enterprising man suddenly stopped and brought up his shotgun to the height of his breast, uttered a low note of warning, and stood motionless, his eyes fixed upon something ahead. As well as he could, obstructed by brush, his companion, though seeing nothing, imitated the posture and so stood, prepared for what might ensue. A moment later Jaralson moved cautiously forward, the other following.

Under the branches of an enormous spruce lay the dead body of a man. Standing silent above it they noted such particulars as first strike the attention – the face, the attitude, the clothing; whatever most promptly and plainly answers the unspoken question of a sympathetic curiosity.

The body lay upon its back, the legs wide apart. One arm was thrust upward, the other outward; but the latter was bent acutely, and the hand was near the throat. Both hands were tightly clenched. The whole attitude was that of desperate but ineffectual resistance to – what?

Near by lay a shotgun and a game bag through the meshes of which was seen the plumage of shot birds. All about were evidences of a furious struggle; small sprouts of poison-oak were bent and denuded of leaf and bark; dead and rotting leaves had been pushed into heaps and ridges on both sides of the legs by the action of other feet than theirs; alongside the hips were unmistakable impressions of human knees.

The nature of the struggle was made clear by a glance at the dead man's throat and face. While breast and hands were white, those were purple – almost black. The shoulders lay upon a low mound, and the head was turned back at an angle otherwise impossible, the expanded eyes staring blankly backward in a direction opposite to that of the feet. From the froth filling the open mouth the tongue protruded, black and swollen. The throat showed horrible contusions; not mere finger-marks, but bruises and lacerations wrought by two strong hands that must have buried themselves in the yielding flesh, maintaining their terrible grasp until long after death. Breast, throat, face, were wet; the clothing was saturated; drops of water, condensed from the fog, studded the hair and mustache.

All this the two men observed without speaking – almost at a glance. Then Holker said:

"Poor devil! he had a rough deal."

Jaralson was making a vigilant circumspection of the forest, his shotgun held in both hands and at full cock, his finger upon the trigger.

"The work of a maniac," he said, without withdrawing his eyes from the inclosing wood. "It was done by Branscom-Pardee."

Something half hidden by the disturbed leaves on the earth caught Holker's attention. It was a red-leather pocketbook. He picked it up and opened it. It contained leaves of white paper for memoranda, and upon the first leaf was the name "Halpin Frayser." Written in red on several succeeding leaves – scrawled as if in haste and barely legible – were the following lines, which Holker read aloud, while his companion continued scanning the dim gray confines of their narrow world and hearing matter of apprehension in the drip of water from every burdened branch:

"Enthralled by some mysterious spell, I stood
In the lit gloom of an enchanted wood.
    The cypress there and myrtle twined their boughs,
Significant, in baleful brotherhood.

"The brooding willow whispered to the yew;
Beneath, the deadly nightshade and the rue,
    With immortelles self-woven into strange
Funereal shapes, and horrid nettles grew.

"No song of bird nor any drone of bees,
Nor light leaf lifted by the wholesome breeze:
    The air was stagnant all, and Silence was
A living thing that breathed among the trees.

"Conspiring spirits whispered in the gloom,
Half-heard, the stilly secrets of the tomb.
    With blood the trees were all adrip; the leaves
Shone in the witch-light with a ruddy bloom.

"I cried aloud I – the spell, unbroken still,
Rested upon my spirit and my will.
    Unsouled, unhearted, hopeless and forlorn,
I strove with monstrous presages of ill!

"At last the viewless – "

Holker ceased reading; there was no more to read. The manuscript broke off in the middle of a line.

"That sounds like Bayne," said Jaralson, who was something of a scholar in his way. He had abated his vigilance and stood looking down at the body.

"Who's Bayne?" Holker asked rather incuriously.

"Myron Bayne, a chap who flourished in the early years of the nation – more than a century ago. Wrote mighty dismal stuff; I have his collected works. That poem is not among them, but it must have been omitted by mistake."

"It is cold," said Holker; "let us leave here; we must have up the coroner from Napa."

Jaralson said nothing, but made a movement in compliance. Passing the end of the slight elevation of earth upon which the dead man's head and shoulders lay, his foot struck some hard substance under the rotting forest leaves, and he took the trouble to kick it into view. It was a fallen headboard, and painted on it were the hardly decipher-able words, "Catharine Larue."

"Larue, Larue!" exclaimed Holker, with sudden animation. "Why, that is the real name of Branscom – not Pardee. And – bless my soul! how it all comes to me – the murdered woman's name had been Frayser!"

"There is some rascally mystery here," said Detective Jaralson. "I hate anything of that kind."

There came to them out of the fog – seemingly from a great distance – the sound of a laugh, a low, deliberate, soulless laugh, which had no more of joy than that of a hyena night-prowling in the desert; a laugh that rose by slow gradation, louder and louder, clearer, more distinct and terrible, until it seemed barely outside the narrow circle of their vision; a laugh so unnatural, so unhuman, so devilish, that it filled those hardy man-hunters with a sense of dread unspeakable! They did not move their weapons nor think of them; the menace of that horrible sound was not of the kind to be met with arms. As it had grown out of silence, so now it died away; from a culminating shout which had seemed almost in their ears, it drew itself away into the distance, until its failing notes, joyless and mechanical to the last, sank to silence at a measureless remove.

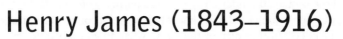

Henry James (1843–1916)

Henry James was born into a distinguished and wealthy family. His grandfather was one of the richest men in the United States. His father was a well-liked, if seldom read, philosopher, and a friend of Emerson and other intellectual luminaries of his generation. Henry's elder brother William became both his country's leading psychologist and its greatest philosopher.

Henry James is known as the master craftsman of American fiction. No one before him made such claims for fiction as serious art, or thought so deeply about the technique of narrative. His novels and stories grew more complex through the decades, his style more challenging, until, near the end, he had lost most of his audience.

In his long and prolific career, James only had two popular "best sellers," the novellas *Daisy Miller* (1879) and *The Turn of the Screw* (1898). The latter has become one of the most discussed works in the English language. The reader approaching this famously ambiguous text for the first time is probably well advised to avoid its weighty scholarly baggage and to approach it with a fresh eye, as James intended.

The Turn of the Screw is a frame story (a story within a story), a technique popularized by Washington Irving. Many American authors have found this form useful; James takes it and adds several layers of complication. The ultimate setting, once we reach it, is the country house familiar in English fiction. The action there concerns and is narrated by an unnamed governess. Everything depends on what she sees, understands, and tells to us about her students, Miles and Flora, and the history of this strange house.

Text: *The Aspern Papers, The Turn of the Screw, The Liar, The Two Faces* (New York: Charles Scribner's Sons, 1908). This is from the "New York Edition" of James's collected works, and embodies the author's final corrections.

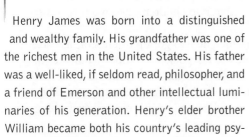

The Turn of the Screw

THE story had held us, round the fire, sufficiently breathless, but except the obvious remark that it was gruesome, as on Christmas Eve in an old house a strange tale should essentially be, I remember no comment uttered till somebody happened to note it as the only case he had met in which such a visitation had fallen on a child. The case, I may mention, was that of an apparition in just such an old house as had gathered us for the occasion – an appearance, of a dreadful kind, to a little boy sleeping in the room with his mother and waking her up in the terror of it; waking her not to dissipate his dread and soothe him to sleep again, but to encounter also herself, before she had succeeded in doing so, the same sight that had shocked him. It was this observation that drew from Douglas – not immediately, but later in the evening – a reply that had the interesting consequence to which I call attention. Some one else told a story not particularly effective, which I saw he was not following. This I took for a sign that he had himself something to produce and that we should only have to wait. We waited in fact till two nights later; but that same evening, before we scattered, he brought out what was in his mind.

"I quite agree – in regard to Griffin's ghost, or whatever it was – that its appearing first to the little boy, at so tender an age, adds a particular touch. But it's not the first occurrence of its charming kind that I know to have been concerned with a child. If the child gives the effect another turn of the screw, what do you say to *two* children – ?"

"We say of course," somebody exclaimed, "that two children give two turns! Also that we want to hear about them."

I can see Douglas there before the fire, to which he had got up to present his back, looking down at this converser with his hands in his pockets. "Nobody but me, till now, has ever heard. It's quite too horrible." This was naturally declared by several voices to give the thing the utmost price, and our friend, with quiet art, prepared his triumph by turning his eyes over the rest of us and going on: "It's beyond everything. Nothing at all that I know touches it."

"For sheer terror?" I remember asking.

He seemed to say it was n't so simple as that; to be really at a loss how to qualify it. He passed his hand over his eyes, made a little wincing grimace. "For dreadful – dreadfulness!"

"Oh how delicious!" cried one of the women.

He took no notice of her; he looked at me, but as if, instead of me, he saw what he spoke of. "For general uncanny ugliness and horror and pain."

"Well then," I said, "just sit right down and begin."

He turned round to the fire, gave a kick to a log, watched it an instant. Then as he faced us again: "I can't begin. I shall have to send to town." There was a unanimous groan at this, and much reproach; after which, in his preoccupied way, he explained.

"The story's written. It's in a locked drawer – it has not been out for years. I could write to my man and enclose the key; he could send down the packet as he finds it." It was to me in particular that he appeared to propound this – appeared almost to appeal for aid not to hesitate. He had broken a thickness of ice, the formation of many a winter; had had his reasons for a long silence. The others resented postponement, but it was just his scruples that charmed me. I adjured him to write by the first post and to agree with us for an early hearing; then I asked him if the experience in question had been his own. To this his answer was prompt. "Oh thank God, no!"

"And is the record yours? You took the thing down!"

"Nothing but the impression. I took that *here*" – he tapped his heart. "I've never lost it."

"Then your manuscript – ?"

"Is in old faded ink and in the most beautiful hand." He hung fire again. "A woman's. She has been dead these twenty years. She sent me the pages in question before she died." They were all listening now, and of course there was somebody to be arch, or at any rate to draw the inference. But if he put the inference by without a smile it was also without irritation. "She was a most charming person, but she was ten years older than I. She was my sister's governess," he quietly said. "She was the most agreeable woman I've ever known in her position; she'd have been worthy of any whatever. It was long ago, and this episode was long before. I was at Trinity, and I found her at home on my coming down the second summer. I was much there that year – it was a beautiful one; and we had, in her off-hours, some strolls and talks in the garden – talks in which she struck me as awfully clever and nice. Oh yes; don't grin: I liked her extremely and am glad to this day to think she liked me too. If she had n't she would n't have told me. She had never told anyone. It was n't simply that she said so, but that I knew she had n't. I was sure; I could see. You'll easily judge why when you hear."

"Because the thing had been such a scare?"

He continued to fix me. "You'll easily judge," he repeated: "*you* will."

I fixed him too. "I see. She was in love."

He laughed for the first time. "You *are* acute. Yes, she was in love. That is she *had* been. That came out – she could n't tell her story without its coming out. I saw it, and she saw I saw it; but neither of us spoke of it. I remember the time and the place – the corner of the lawn, the shade of the great beeches and the long hot summer afternoon. It was n't a scene for a shudder; but oh – !" He quitted the fire and dropped back into his chair.

"You'll receive the packet Thursday morning?" I said.

"Probably not till the second post."

"Well then; after dinner – "

"You'll all meet me here?" He looked us round again. "Is n't anybody going?" It was almost the tone of hope.

"Everybody will stay!"

"*I* will – and *I* will!" cried the ladies whose departure had been fixed. Mrs. Griffin, however, expressed the need for a little more light. "Who was it she was in love with?"

"The story will tell," I took upon myself to reply.

"Oh I can't wait for the story!"

"The story *won't* tell," said Douglas; "not in any literal vulgar way."

"More's the pity then. That's the only way I ever understand."

'Won't *you* tell, Douglas?" somebody else enquired.

He sprang to his feet again. "Yes – to-morrow. Now I must go to bed. Good-night." And, quickly catching up a candlestick, he left us slightly bewildered. From our end of the great brown hall we heard his step on the stair; whereupon Mrs. Griffin spoke. "Well, if I don't know who she was in love with I know who *he* was."

"She was ten years older," said her husband.

"*Raison de plus*[1] – at that age! But it's rather nice, his long reticence."

"Forty years!" Griffin put in. "With this outbreak at last."

"The outbreak," I returned, "will make a tremendous occasion of Thursday night"; and every one so agreed with me that in the light of it we lost all attention for everything else. The last story, however incomplete and like the mere opening of a serial, had been told; we handshook and "candlestuck," as somebody said, and went to bed.

I knew the next day that a letter containing the key had, by the first post, gone off to his London apartments; but in spite of – or perhaps just on account of – the eventual diffusion of this knowledge we quite let him alone till after dinner, till such an hour of the evening in fact as might best accord with the kind of emotion on which our hopes were fixed. Then he became as communicative as we could desire, and indeed gave us his best reason for being so. We had it from him again before the fire in the hall, as we had had our mild wonders of the previous night. It appeared that the narrative he had promised to read us really required for a proper intelligence a few words of prologue. Let me say here distinctly, to have done with it, that this narrative, from an exact transcript of my own made much later, is what I shall presently give. Poor Douglas, before his death – when it was in sight – committed to me the manuscript that reached him on the third of these days and that, on the same spot, with immense effect, he began to read to our hushed little circle on the night of the fourth. The departing ladies who had said they would stay did n't, of course, thank heaven, stay: they departed, in consequence of arrangements made, in a rage of curiosity, as they professed, produced by the touches with which he had already worked us up. But

Notes ————

THE TURN OF THE SCREW
[1] French: all the more reason.

that only made his little final auditory more compact and select, kept it, round the hearth, subject to a common thrill.

The first of these touches conveyed that the written statement took up the tale at a point after it had, in a manner, begun. The fact to be in possession of was therefore that his old friend, the youngest of several daughters of a poor country parson, had at the age of twenty, on taking service for the first time in the schoolroom, come up to London, in trepidation, to answer in person an advertisement that had already placed her in brief correspondence with the advertiser. This person proved, on her presenting herself for judgement at a house in Harley Street that impressed her as vast and impos- ing – this prospective patron proved a gentleman, a bachelor in the prime of life, such a figure as had never risen, save in a dream or an old novel, before a fluttered anxious girl out of a Hampshire vicarage. One could easily fix his type; it never, happily, dies out. He was handsome and bold and pleasant, off-hand and gay and kind. He struck her, inevitably, as gallant and splendid, but what took her most of all and gave her the courage she afterwards showed was that he put the whole thing to her as a favour, an obligation he should gratefully incur. She figured him as rich, but as fearfully extrava- gant – saw him all in a glow of high fashion, of good looks, of expensive habits, of charming ways with women. He had for his town residence a big house filled with the spoils of travel and the trophies of the chase; but it was to his country home, an old family place in Essex, that he wished her immediately to proceed.

He had been left, by the death of his parents in India, guardian to a small nephew and a small niece, children of a younger, a military brother whom he had lost two years before. These children were, by the strangest of chances for a man in his position – a lone man without the right sort of experience or a grain of patience – very heavy on his hands. It had all been a great worry and, on his own part doubtless, a series of blun- ders, but he immensely pitied the poor chicks and had done all he could; had in particu- lar sent them down to his other house, the proper place for them being of course the country, and kept them there from the first with the best people he could find to look after them, parting even with his own servants to wait on them and going down him- self, whenever he might, to see how they were doing. The awkward thing was that they had practically no other relations and that his own affairs took up all his time. He had put them in possession of Bly, which was healthy and secure, and had placed at the head of their little establishment – but below stairs only – an excellent woman, Mrs. Grose, whom he was sure his visitor would like and who had formerly been maid to his mother. She was now housekeeper and was also acting for the time as superin- tendent to the little girl, of whom, without children of her own, she was by good luck extremely fond. There were plenty of people to help, but of course the young lady who should go down as governess would be in supreme authority. She would also have, in holidays, to look after the small boy, who had been for a term at school – young as he was to be sent, but what else could be done? – and who, as the holidays were about to begin, would be back from one day to the other. There had been for the two children at first a young lady whom they had had the misfortune to lose. She had done for them quite beautifully – she was a most respectable person – till her death, the great awk- wardness of which had, precisely, left no alternative but the school for little Miles. Mrs. Grose, since then, in the way of manners and things, had done as she could for Flora; and there were, further, a cook, a housemaid, a dairywoman, an old pony, an old groom and an old gardener, all likewise thoroughly respectable.

So far had Douglas presented his picture when some one put a question. "And what did the former governess die of? Of so much respectability?"

Our friend's answer was prompt. "That will come out. I don't anticipate."

"Pardon me – I thought that was just what you *are* doing."

"In her successor's place," I suggested, "I should have wished to learn if the office brought with it – "

"Necessary danger to life?" Douglas completed my thought. "She did wish to learn, and she did learn. You shall hear to-morrow what she learnt. Meanwhile of course the prospect struck her as slightly grim. She was young, untried, nervous: it was a vision of serious duties and little company, of really great loneliness. She hesitated – took a couple of days to consult and consider. But the salary offered much exceeded her modest measure, and on a second interview she faced the music, she engaged." And Douglas, with this, made a pause that, for the benefit of the company, moved me to throw in –

"The moral of which was of course the seduction exercised by the splendid young man. She succumbed to it."

He got up and, as he had done the night before, went to the fire, gave a stir to a log with his foot, then stood a moment with his back to us. "She saw him only twice."

"Yes, but that's just the beauty of her passion." A little to my surprise, on this, Douglas turned round to me. "It *was* the beauty of it. There were others," he went on, "who had n't succumbed. He told her frankly all his difficulty – that for several applicants the conditions had been prohibitive. They were somehow simply afraid. It sounded dull – it sounded strange; and all the more so because of his main condition."

"Which was – ?"

"That she should never trouble him – but never, never: neither appeal nor complain nor write about anything; only meet all questions herself, receive all moneys from his solicitor, take the whole thing over and let him alone. She promised to do this, and she mentioned to me that when, for a moment, disburdened, delighted, he held her hand, thanking her for the sacrifice, she already felt rewarded."

"But was that all her reward?" one of the ladies asked.

"She never saw him again."

"Oh!" said the lady; which, as our friend immediately again left us, was the only other word of importance contributed to the subject till, the next night, by the corner of the hearth, in the best chair, he opened the faded red cover of a thin old-fashioned gilt-edged album. The whole thing took indeed more nights than one, but on the first occasion the same lady put another question. "What's your title?"

"I have n't one."

"Oh *I* have!" I said. But Douglas, without heeding me, had begun to read with a fine clearness that was like a rendering to the ear of the beauty of his author's hand.

I

I REMEMBER the whole beginning as a succession of flights and drops, a little see-saw of the right throbs and the wrong. After rising, in town, to meet his appeal I had at all events a couple of very bad days – found all my doubts bristle again, felt indeed sure I had made a mistake. In this state of mind I spent the long hours of bumping swinging coach that carried me to the stopping-place at which I was to be met by a vehicle from the house. This convenience, I was told, had been ordered, and I found, toward the close of the June afternoon, a commodious fly² in waiting for me. Driving at that hour, on a lovely day, through a country the summer sweetness of which served as a friendly welcome, my fortitude revived and, as we turned into the avenue, took a flight that was probably but a proof of the point to which it had sunk. I suppose I had expected,

Notes ————————————————————————————————————

² Not an insect, but a one-horse covered carriage.

or had dreaded, something so dreary that what greeted me was a good surprise. I remember as a thoroughly pleasant impression the broad clear front, its open windows and fresh curtains and the pair of maids looking out; I remember the lawn and the bright flowers and the crunch of my wheels on the gravel and the clustered treetops over which the rooks circled and cawed in the golden sky. The scene had a greatness that made it a different affair from my own scant home, and there immediately appeared at the door, with a little girl in her hand, a civil person who dropped me as decent a curtsey as if I had been the mistress or a distinguished visitor. I had received in Harley Street a narrower notion of the place, and that, as I recalled it, made me think the proprietor still more of a gentleman, suggested that what I was to enjoy might be a matter beyond his promise.

I had no drop again till the next day, for I was carried triumphantly through the following hours by my introduction to the younger of my pupils. The little girl who accompanied Mrs. Grose affected me on the spot as a creature too charming not to make it a great fortune to have to do with her. She was the most beautiful child I had ever seen, and I afterwards wondered why my employer had n't made more of a point to me of this. I slept little that night – I was too much excited; and this astonished me too, I recollect, remained with me, adding to my sense of the liberality with which I was treated. The large impressive room, one of the best in the house, the great state bed, as I almost felt it, the figured full draperies, the long glasses in which, for the first time, I could see myself from head to foot, all struck me – like the wonderful appeal of my small charge – as so many things thrown in. It was thrown in as well, from the first moment, that I should get on with Mrs. Grose in a relation over which, on my way, in the coach, I fear I had rather brooded. The one appearance indeed that in this early outlook might have made me shrink again was that of her being so inordinately glad to see me. I felt within half an hour that she was so glad – stout simple plain dear wholesome woman – as to be positively on her guard against showing it too much. I wondered even then a little why she should wish *not* to show it, and that, with reflexion, with suspicion, might of course have made me uneasy.

But it was a comfort that there could be no uneasiness in a connexion with anything so beatific as the radiant image of my little girl, the vision of whose angelic beauty had probably more than anything else to do with the restlessness that, before morning, made me several times rise and wander about my room to take in the whole picture and prospect; to watch from my open window the faint summer dawn, to look at such stretches of the rest of the house as I could catch, and to listen, while in the fading dusk the first birds began to twitter, for the possible recurrence of a sound or two, less natural and not without but within, that I had fancied I heard. There had been a moment when I believed I recognised, faint and far, the cry of a child; there had been another when I found myself just consciously starting as at the passage, before my door, of a light footstep. But these fancies were not marked enough not to be thrown off, and it is only in the light, or the gloom, I should rather say, of other and subsequent matters that they now come back to me. To watch, teach, "form" little Flora would too evidently be the making of a happy and useful life. It had been agreed between us downstairs that after this first occasion I should have her as a matter of course at night, her small white bed being already arranged, to that end, in my room. What I had undertaken was the whole care of her, and she had remained just this last time with Mrs. Grose only as an effect of our consideration for my inevitable strangeness and her natural timidity. In spite of this timidity – which the child herself, in the oddest way in the world, had been perfectly frank and brave about, allowing it, without a sign of uncomfortable consciousness, with the deep sweet serenity indeed of one of Raphael's holy infants, to be discussed, to be imputed to her and to determine us – I felt quite sure she would presently like me. It was part of what I already liked Mrs. Grose herself for, the pleasure I could see her feel in my admiration and wonder as I sat at supper with four tall candles and with my pupil, in a high chair and a bib, brightly facing me between them over bread and milk. There were naturally things that in Flora's presence could pass between us only as prodigious and gratified looks, obscure and roundabout allusions.

"And the little boy – does he look like her? Is he too so very remarkable?"

One would n't, it was already conveyed between us, too grossly flatter a child. "Oh Miss, *most* remarkable. If you think well of this one!" – and she stood there with a plate in her hand, beaming at our companion, who looked from one of us to the other with placid heavenly eyes that contained nothing to check us.

"Yes; if I do –?"

"You *will* be carried away by the little gentleman!"

"Well, that, I think, is what I came for – to be carried away. I'm afraid, however," I remember feeling the impulse to add, "I'm rather easily carried away. I was carried away in London!"

I can still see Mrs. Grose's broad face as she took this in. "In Harley Street?"

"In Harley Street."

"Well, Miss, you're not the first – and you won't be the last."

"Oh I've no pretensions," I could laugh, "to being the only one. My other pupil, at any rate, as I understand, comes back to-morrow?"

"Not to-morrow – Friday, Miss. He arrives, as you did, by the coach, under care of the guard, and is to be met by the same carriage."

I forthwith wanted to know if the proper as well as the pleasant and friendly thing would n't therefore be that on the arrival of the public conveyance I should await him with his little sister; a proposition to which Mrs. Grose assented so heartily that I somehow took her manner as a kind of comforting pledge – never falsified, thank heaven! – that we should on every question be quite at one. Oh she was glad I was there!

What I felt the next day was, I suppose, nothing that could be fairly called a reaction from the cheer of my arrival; it was probably at the most only a slight oppression produced by a fuller measure of the scale, as I walked round them, gazed up at them, took them in, of my new circumstances. They had, as it were, an extent and mass for which I had not been prepared and in the presence of which I found myself, freshly, a little scared not less than a little proud. Regular lessons, in this agitation, certainly suffered some wrong; I reflected that my first duty was, by the gentlest arts I could contrive, to win the child into the sense of knowing me. I spent the day with her out of doors; I arranged with her, to her great satisfaction, that it should be she, she only, who might show me the place. She showed it step by step and room by room and secret by secret, with droll delightful childish talk about it and with the result, in half an hour, of our becoming tremendous friends. Young as she was I was struck, throughout our little tour, with her confidence and courage, with the way, in empty chambers and dull corridors, on crooked staircases that made me pause and even on the summit of an old machicolated square tower that made me dizzy, her morning music, her disposition to tell me so many more things than she asked, rang out and led me on. I have not seen Bly since the day I left it, and I dare say that to my present older and more informed eyes it would show a very reduced importance. But as my little conductress, with her hair of gold and her frock of blue, danced before me round corners and pattered down passages, I had the view of a castle of romance inhabited by a rosy sprite, such a place as would somehow, for diversion of the young idea, take all colour out of story-books and fairy-tales. Was n't it just a story-book over which I had fallen a-doze and a-dream? No; it was a big ugly antique but convenient house, embodying a few features of a building still older, half-displaced and half-utilised, in which I had the fancy of being almost as lost as a handful of passengers in a great drifting ship. Well, I was strangely at the helm!

II

THIS came home to me when, two days later, I drove over with Flora to meet, as Mrs. Grose said, the little gentleman; and all the more for an incident that, presenting itself the second evening, had deeply disconcerted me. The first day had been, on the whole, as I have expressed, reassuring; but I was to see it wind up to a change of note. The postbag that evening – it came late – contained a letter for me which, however, in the hand of my employer, I found to be composed but of a few words enclosing another, addressed to himself, with a seal still unbroken. "This, I recognise, is from the head-master, and the headmaster's an awful bore. Read him, please; deal with him; but mind you don't report. Not a word. I'm off!" I broke the seal with a great effort – so great a one that I was a long time coming to it; took the unopened missive at last up to my room and only attacked it just before going to bed. I had better have let it wait till morning, for it gave me a second sleepless night. With no counsel to take, the next day, I was full of distress; and it finally got so the better of me that I determined to open myself at least to Mrs. Grose.

"What does it mean? The child's dismissed his school."

She gave me a look that I remarked at the moment; then, visibly, with a quick blankness, seemed to try to take it back. "But are n't they all – ?"

"Sent home – yes. But only for the holidays. Miles may never go back at all."

Consciously, under my attention, she reddened. "They won't take him?"

"They absolutely decline."

At this she raised her eyes, which she had turned from me; I saw them fill with good tears. "What has he done?"

I cast about; then I judged best simply to hand her my document – which, however, had the effect of making her, without taking it, simply put her hands behind her. She shook her head sadly. "Such things are not for me, Miss."

My counsellor could n't read! I winced at my mistake, which I attenuated as I could, and opened the letter again to repeat it to her; then, faltering in the act and folding it up once more, I put it back in my pocket. "Is he really *bad*?"

The tears were still in her eyes. "Do the gentlemen say so?"

"They go into no particulars. They simply express their regret that it should be impossible to keep him. That can have but one meaning." Mrs. Grose listened with dumb emotion; she forbore to ask me what this meaning might be; so that, presently, to put the thing with some coherence and with the mere aid of her presence to my own mind, I went on: "That he's an injury to the others."

At this, with one of the quick turns of simple folk, she suddenly flamed up. "Master Miles! – *him* an injury?"

There was such a flood of good faith in it that, though I had not yet seen the child, my very fears made me jump to the absurdity of the idea. I found myself, to meet my friend the better, offering it, on the spot, sarcastically. "To his poor little innocent mates!"

"It's too dreadful," cried Mrs. Grose, "to say such cruel things! Why he's scarce ten years old."

"Yes, yes; it would be incredible."

She was evidently grateful for such a profession. "See him, Miss, first. *Then* believe it!" I felt forthwith a new impatience to see him; it was the beginning of a curiosity that, all the next hours, was to deepen almost to pain. Mrs. Grose was aware, I could judge, of what she had produced in me, and she followed it up with assurance. "You might as well believe it of the little lady. Bless her," she added the next moment – "*look at her!*"

I turned and saw that Flora, whom, ten minutes before, I had established in the schoolroom with a sheet of white paper, a pencil and a copy of nice "round O's," now presented herself to view at the open door. She expressed in her little way an extraordinary detachment from disagreeable duties, looking at me, however, with a great childish light that seemed to offer it as a mere result of the affection she had conceived for my person, which had rendered necessary that she should follow me. I needed nothing more than this to feel the full force of Mrs. Grose's comparison, and, catching my pupil in my arms, covered her with kisses in which there was a sob of atonement.

None the less, the rest of the day, I watched for further occasion to approach my colleague, especially as, toward evening, I began to fancy she rather sought to avoid me. I overtook her, I remember, on the staircase; we went down together and at the bottom I detained her, holding her there with a hand on her arm. "I take what you said to me at noon as a declaration that *you've* never known him to be bad."

She threw back her head; she had clearly by this time, and very honestly, adopted an attitude. "Oh never known him – I don't pretend *that!*"

I was upset again. "Then you *have* known him – ?"

"Yes indeed, Miss, thank God!"

On reflexion I accepted this. "You mean that a boy who never is – ?"

"Is no boy for *me!*"

I held her tighter. "You like them with the spirit to be naughty?" Then, keeping pace with her answer, "So do I!" I eagerly brought out. "But not to the degree to contaminate –"

"To contaminate?" – my big word left her at a loss.

I explained it. "To corrupt."

She stared, taking my meaning in; but it produced in her an odd laugh. "Are you afraid he'll corrupt *you?*" She put the question with such a fine bold humour that with a laugh, a little silly doubtless, to match her own, I gave way for the time to the apprehension of ridicule.

But the next day, as the hour for my drive approached, I cropped up in another place. "What was the lady who was here before?"

"The last governess? She was also young and pretty – almost as young and almost as pretty, Miss, even as you."

"Ah then I hope her youth and her beauty helped her!" I recollect throwing off. "He seems to like us young and pretty!"

"Oh he *did*," Mrs. Grose assented: "it was the way he liked every one!" She had no sooner spoken indeed than she caught herself up. "I mean that's *his* way – the master's."

I was struck. "But of whom did you speak first?"

She looked blank, but she coloured. "Why of *him.*"

"Of the master?"

"Of who else?"

There was so obviously no one else that the next moment I had lost my impression of her having accidentally said more than she meant; and I merely asked what I wanted to know. "Did *she* see anything in the boy –?"

"That was n't right? She never told me."

I had a scruple, but I overcame it. "Was she careful – particular?"

Mrs. Grose appeared to try to be conscientious.

"About some things – yes."

"But not about all?"

Again she considered. "Well, Miss – she's gone. I won't tell tales."

"I quite understand your feeling," I hastened to reply; but I thought it after an instant not opposed to this concession to pursue: "Did she die here?"

"No – she went off."

I don't know what there was in this brevity of Mrs. Grose's that struck me as ambiguous. "Went off to die?" Mrs. Grose looked straight out of the window, but I felt that, hypothetically, I had a right to know what young persons engaged for Bly were expected to do. "She was taken ill, you mean, and went home?"

"She was not taken ill, so far as appeared, in this house. She left it, at the end of the year, to go home, as she said, for a short holiday, to which the time she had put in had certainly given her a right. We had then a young woman – a nursemaid who had stayed on and who was a good girl and clever; and *she* took the children altogether for the interval. But our young lady never came back, and at the very moment I was expecting her I heard from the master that she was dead."

I turned this over. "But of what?"

"He never told me! But please, Miss," said Mrs. Grose, "I must get to my work."

III

HER thus turning her back on me was fortunately not, for my just preoccupations, a snub that could check the growth of our mutual esteem. We met, after I had brought home little Miles, more intimately than ever on the ground of my stupefaction, my general emotion: so monstrous was I then ready to pronounce it that such a child as had now been revealed to me should be under an interdict. I was a little late on the scene of his arrival, and I felt, as he stood wistfully looking out for me before the door of the inn at which the coach had put him down, that I had seen him on the instant, without and within, in the great glow of freshness, the same positive fragrance of purity, in which I had from the first moment seen his little sister. He was incredibly beautiful, and Mrs. Grose had put her finger on it: everything but a sort of passion of tenderness for him was swept away by his presence. What I then and there took him to my heart for was something divine that I have never found to the same degree in any child – his indescribable little air of knowing nothing in the world but love. It would have been impossible to carry a bad name with a greater sweetness of innocence, and by the time I had got back to Bly with him I remained merely bewildered – so far, that is, as I was not outraged – by the sense of the horrible letter locked up in one of the drawers of my room. As soon as I could compass a private word with Mrs. Grose I declared to her that it was grotesque.

She promptly understood me. "You mean the cruel charge – ?"

"It does n't live an instant. My dear woman, *look* at him!"

She smiled at my pretension to have discovered his charm. "I assure you, Miss, I do nothing else! What will you say then?" she immediately added.

"In answer to the letter?" I had made up my mind. "Nothing at all."

"And to his uncle?"

I was incisive. "Nothing at all."

"And to the boy himself?"

I was wonderful. "Nothing at all."

She gave with her apron a great wipe to her mouth. "Then I'll stand by you. We'll see it out."

"We'll see it out!" I ardently echoed, giving her my hand to make it a vow.

She held me there a moment, then whisked up her apron again with her detached hand. "Would you mind, Miss, if I used the freedom – "

"To kiss me? No!" I took the good creature in my arms and after we had embraced like sisters felt still more fortified and indignant.

This at all events was for the time: a time so full that as I recall the way it went it reminds me of all the art I now need to make it a little distinct. What I look back at with amazement is the situation I accepted. I had undertaken, with my companion, to see it out, and I was under a charm apparently that could smooth away the extent and the far and difficult connexions of such an effort. I was lifted aloft on a great wave of infatuation and pity. I found it simple, in my ignorance, my confusion and perhaps my conceit, to assume that I could deal with a boy whose education for the world was all on the point of beginning. I am unable even to remember at this day what proposal I framed for the end of his holidays and the resumption of his studies. Lessons with me indeed, that charming summer, we all had a theory that he was to have; but I now feel that for weeks the lessons must have been rather my own. I learnt something – at first certainly – that had not been one of the teachings of my small smothered life; learnt to be amused, and even amusing, and not to think for the morrow. It was the first time, in a manner, that I had known space and air and freedom, all the music of summer and all the mystery of nature. And then there was consideration – and consideration was sweet. Oh it was a trap – not designed but deep – to my imagination, to my delicacy, perhaps to my vanity; to whatever in me was most excitable. The best way to picture it all is to say that I was off my guard. They gave me so little trouble – they were of a gentleness so extraordinary. I used to speculate – but even this with a dim disconnectedness – as to how the rough future (for all futures are rough!) would handle them and might bruise them. They had the bloom of health and happiness; and yet, as if I had been in charge of a pair of little grandees, of princes of the blood, for whom everything, to be right, would have to be fenced about and ordered and arranged, the only form that in my fancy the after-years could take for them was that of a romantic, a really royal extension of the garden and the park. It may be of course above all that what suddenly broke into this gives the previous time a charm of stillness – that hush in which something gathers or crouches. The change was actually like the spring of a beast.

In the first weeks the days were long; they often, at their finest, gave me what I used to call my own hour, the hour when, for my pupils, tea-time and bed-time having come and gone, I had before my final retirement a small interval alone. Much as I liked my companions this hour was the thing in the day I liked most; and I liked it best of all when, as the light faded – or rather, I should say, the day lingered and the last calls of the last birds sounded, in a flushed sky, from the old trees – I could take a turn into the grounds and enjoy, almost with a sense of property that amused and flattered me, the beauty and dignity of the place. It was a pleasure at these moments to feel myself tranquil and justified; doubtless perhaps also to reflect that by my discretion, my quiet good sense and general high propriety, I was giving pleasure – if he ever thought of it! – to the person to whose pressure I had yielded. What I was doing was what he had earnestly hoped and directly asked of me, and that I *could*, after all, do it proved even a greater joy than I had expected. I dare say I fancied myself in short a remarkable young woman and took comfort in the faith that this would more publicly appear. Well, I needed to be remarkable to offer a front to the remarkable things that presently gave their first sign.

It was plump, one afternoon, in the middle of my very hour: the children were tucked away and I had come out for my stroll. One of the thoughts that, as I don't in the least shrink now from noting, used to be with me in these wanderings was that it would be as charming as a charming story suddenly to meet some one. Some one would appear there at the turn of a path and would stand before me and smile and approve. I did n't ask more than that – I only asked that he should *know*; and the only way to be sure he knew would be to see it, and the kind light of it, in his handsome face. That was exactly present to me – by which I mean the face was – when, on the first of these occasions, at the end of a long June day, I stopped short on emerging from one of the plantations and coming into view of the house. What arrested me on the spot – and with a shock much greater than any vision had allowed for – was the sense that my imagination had, in a flash, turned real. He did stand there! – but high up, beyond the lawn and at the very top of the tower to which, on that first morning, little Flora had conducted me. This tower was one of a pair – square incongruous crenellated structures – that were distinguished, for some reason, though I could see little difference, as the new and the old. They flanked opposite ends of the house and were probably architectural absurdities, redeemed in a measure indeed by not being wholly disengaged nor of a height too pretentious, dating, in their gingerbread antiquity, from a romantic revival that was already a respectable past. I admired them, had fancies about them, for we could all profit in a degree, especially when they loomed through the dusk, by the grandeur of their actual battlements; yet it was not at such an elevation that the figure I had so often invoked seemed most in place.

It produced in me, this figure, in the clear twilight, I remember, two distinct gasps of emotion, which were, sharply, the shock of my first and that of my second surprise. My second was a violent perception of the mistake of my first: the man who met my eyes was not the person I had precipitately supposed. There came to me thus a bewilderment of vision of which, after these years, there is no living view that I can hope to give. An unknown man in a lonely place is a permitted object of fear to a young woman privately bred; and the figure that faced me was – a few more seconds assured me – as little anyone else I knew as it was the image that had been in my mind. I had not seen it in Harley Street – I had not seen it anywhere. The place moreover, in the strangest way in the world, had on the instant and by the very fact of its appearance become a solitude. To me at least, making my statement here with a deliberation with which I have never made it, the whole feeling of the moment returns. It was as if, while I took in, what I did take in, all the rest of the scene had been stricken with death. I can hear again, as I write, the intense hush in which the sounds of evening dropped. The rooks stopped cawing in the golden sky and the friendly hour lost for the unspeakable minute all its voice. But there was no other change in nature, unless indeed it were a change that I saw with a stranger sharpness. The gold was still in the sky, the clearness in the air, and the man who looked at me over the battlements was as definite as a picture in a frame. That's how I thought, with extraordinary quickness, of each person he might have been and that he wasn't. We were confronted across our distance quite long enough for me to ask myself with intensity who then he was and to feel, as an effect of my inability to say, a wonder that in a few seconds more became intense.

The great question, or one of these, is afterwards, I know, with regard to certain matters, the question of how long they have lasted. Well, this matter of mine, think what you will of it, lasted while I caught at a dozen possibilities, none of which made a difference for the better, that I could see, in there having been in the house – and for how long, above all? – a person of whom I was in ignorance. It lasted while I just bridled a little with the sense of how my office seemed to require that there should be no such ignorance and no such person. It lasted while this visitant, at all events – and there was a touch of the strange freedom, as I remember, in the sign of familiarity of his wearing no hat – seemed to fix me, from his position, with just the question, just the scrutiny through the fading light, that his own presence provoked. We were too far apart to call to each other, but there was a moment at which, at shorter range, some challenge between us, breaking the hush, would have been the right result of our straight mutual stare. He was in one of the angles, the one away from the house, very erect, as it struck me, and with both hands on the ledge. So I saw him as I see the letters I form on this page; then, exactly, after a minute, as if to add to the spectacle, he slowly changed his place – passed, looking at me hard all the while, to the opposite corner of the platform. Yes, it was intense to me that during this transit he never took his eyes from me, and I can see at this moment the way his hand, as he went, moved from one of the crenellations to the next. He stopped at the other corner, but less long, and even as he turned away still markedly fixed me. He turned away; that was all I knew.

<h2 style="text-align:center">IV</h2>

IT was not that I did n't wait, on this occasion, for more, since I was as deeply rooted as shaken. Was there a "secret" at Bly – a mystery of Udolpho or an insane, an unmentionable relative kept in unsuspected confinement?[3] I can't say how long I turned it over, or how long, in a confusion of curiosity and dread, I remained where I had had my collision; I only recall that when I re-entered the house darkness had quite closed in. Agitation, in the interval, certainly had held me and driven me, for I must, in circling about the place, have walked three miles; but I was to be later on so much more overwhelmed that this mere dawn of alarm was a comparatively human chill. The most singular part of it in fact – singular as the rest had been – was the part I became, in the hall, aware of in meeting Mrs. Grose. This picture comes back to me in the general train – the impression, as I received it on my return, of the wide white panelled space, bright in the lamplight and with its portraits and red carpet, and of the good surprised look of my friend, which immediately told me she had missed me. It came to me straightway, under her contact, that, with plain heartiness, mere relieved anxiety at my appearance, she knew nothing whatever that could bear upon the incident I had there ready for her. I had not suspected in advance that her comfortable face would pull me up, and I somehow measured the importance of what I had seen by my thus finding myself hesitate to mention it. Scarce anything in the whole history seems to me so odd as this fact that my real beginning of fear was one, as I may say, with the instinct of sparing my companion. On the spot, accordingly, in the pleasant hall and with her eyes on me, I, for a reason that I could n't then have phrased, achieved an inward revolution – offered a vague pretext for my lateness and, with the plea of the beauty of the night and of the heavy dew and wet feet, went as soon as possible to my room.

Here it was another affair; here, for many days after, it was a queer affair enough. There were hours, from day to day – or at least there were moments, snatched even from clear duties – when I had to shut myself up to think. It was n't so much yet that I was more nervous than I could bear to be as that I was remarkably afraid of becoming so; for the truth I had now to turn over was simply and clearly the truth that I could arrive at no account whatever of the visitor with whom I had been so inexplicably and yet, as it seemed to me, so intimately concerned. It took me little time to see that I might easily sound, without forms of enquiry and without exciting remark, any domestic complication. The shock I had suffered must have sharpened all my senses; I felt sure, at the end of three days and as the result of mere closer attention, that I had not been practised upon by the servants nor made the object of any "game." Of whatever it was that I knew nothing was known around me. There was but one sane inference: some one had taken a liberty rather monstrous. That was what, repeatedly,

<h2 style="font-style:italic">Notes</h2>

[3] The governess recalls Gothic novels she has read. *The Mysteries of Udolpho* (1794) was by Ann Radcliffe (1764–1823). The confined madman or madwoman was a familiar device, perhaps best known from *Jane Eyre* (1847) by Charlotte Brontë (1816–55).

I dipped into my room and locked the door to say to myself. We had been, collectively, subject to an intrusion; some unscrupulous traveller, curious in old houses, had made his way in unobserved, enjoyed the prospect from the best point of view and then stolen out as he came. If he had given me such a bold hard stare, that was but a part of his indiscretion. The good thing, after all, was that we should surely see no more of him.

This was not so good a thing, I admit, as not to leave me to judge that what, essentially, made nothing else much signify was simply my charming work. My charming work was just my life with Miles and Flora, and through nothing could I so like it as through feeling that to throw myself into it was to throw myself out of my trouble. The attraction of my small charges was a constant joy, leading me to wonder afresh at the vanity of my original fears, the distaste I had begun by entertaining for the probable grey prose of my office. There was to be no grey prose, it appeared, and no long grind; so how could work not be charming that presented itself as daily beauty? It was all the romance of the nursery and the poetry of the schoolroom. I don't mean by this of course that we studied only fiction and verse; I mean that I can express no otherwise the sort of interest my companions inspired. How can I describe that except by saying that instead of growing deadly used to them – and it's a marvel for a governess: I call the sisterhood to witness! – I made constant fresh discoveries. There was one direction, assuredly, in which these discoveries stopped: deep obscurity continued to cover the region of the boy's conduct at school. It had been promptly given me, I have noted, to face that mystery without a pang. Perhaps even it would be nearer the truth to say that – without a word – he himself had cleared it up. He had made the whole charge absurd. My conclusion bloomed there with the real rose-flush of his innocence: he was only too fine and fair for the little horrid unclean school-world, and he had paid a price for it. I reflected acutely that the sense of such individual differences, such superiorities of quality, always, on the part of the majority – which could include even stupid sordid head-masters – turns infallibly to the vindictive.

Both the children had a gentleness – it was their only fault, and it never made Miles a muff – that kept them (how shall I express it?) almost impersonal and certainly quite unpunishable. They were like those cherubs of the anecdote who had – morally at any rate – nothing to whack! I remember feeling with Miles in especial as if he had had, as it were, nothing to call even an infinitesimal history. We expect of a small child scant enough "antecedents," but there was in this beautiful little boy something extraordinarily sensitive, yet extraordinarily happy, that, more than in any creature of his age I have seen, struck me as beginning anew each day. He had never for a second suffered. I took this as a direct disproof of his having really been chastised. If he had been wicked he would have "caught" it, and I should have caught it by the rebound – I should have found the trace, should have felt the wound and the dishonour. I could reconstitute nothing at all, and he was therefore an angel. He never spoke of his school, never mentioned a comrade or a master; and I, for my part, was quite too much disgusted to allude to them. Of course I was under the spell, and the wonderful part is that, even at the time, I perfectly knew I was. But I gave myself up to it; it was an antidote to any pain, and I had more pains than one. I was in receipt in these days of disturbing letters from home, where things were not going well. But with this joy of my children what things in the world mattered? That was the question I used to put to my scrappy retirements. I was dazzled by their loveliness.

There was a Sunday – to get on – when it rained with such force and for so many hours that there could be no procession to church; in consequence of which, as the day declined, I had arranged with Mrs. Grose that, should the evening show improvement, we would attend together the late service. The rain happily stopped, and I prepared for our walk, which, through the park and by the good road to the village, would be a matter of twenty minutes. Coming downstairs to meet my colleague in the hall, I remembered a pair of gloves that had required three stitches and that had received them – with a publicity perhaps not edifying – while I sat with the children at their tea, served on Sundays, by exception, in that cold clean temple of mahogany and brass, the "grown-up" dining-room. The gloves had been dropped there, and I turned in to recover them. The day was grey enough, but the afternoon light still lingered, and it enabled me, on crossing the threshold, not only to recognise, on a chair near the wide window, then closed, the articles I wanted, but to become aware of a person on the other side of the window and looking straight in. One step into the room had sufficed; my vision was instantaneous; it was all there. The person looking straight in was the person who had already appeared to me. He appeared thus again with I won't say greater distinctness, for that was impossible, but with a nearness that represented a forward stride in our intercourse and made me, as I met him, catch my breath and turn cold. He was the same – he was the same, and seen, this time, as he had been seen before, from the waist up, the window, though the dining-room was on the ground floor, not going down to the terrace on which he stood. His face was close to the glass, yet the effect of this better view was, strangely, just to show me how intense the former had been. He remained but a few seconds – long enough to convince me he also saw and recognised; but it was as if I had been looking at him for years and had known him always. Something, however, happened this time that had not happened before; his stare into my face, through the glass and across the room, was as deep and hard as then, but it quitted me for a moment during which I could still watch it, see it fix successively several other things. On the spot there came to me the added shock of a certitude that it was not for me he had come. He had come for some one else.

The flash of this knowledge – for it was knowledge in the midst of dread – produced in me the most extraordinary effect, starting, as I stood there, a sudden vibration of duty and courage. I say courage because I was beyond all doubt already far gone. I bounded straight out of the door again, reached that of the house, got in an instant upon the drive and, passing along the terrace as fast as I could rush, turned a corner and came full in sight. But it was in sight of nothing now – my visitor had vanished. I stopped, almost dropped, with the real relief of this; but I took in the whole scene – I gave him time to reappear. I call it time, but how long was it? I can't speak to the purpose to-day of the duration of these things. That kind of measure must have left me: they could n't have lasted as they actually appeared to me to last. The terrace and the whole place, the lawn and the garden beyond it, all I could see of the park, were empty with a great emptiness. There were shrubberies and big trees, but I remember the clear assurance I felt that none of them concealed him. He was there or was not there: not there if I did n't see him. I got hold of this; then, instinctively, instead of returning as I had come, went to the window. It was confusedly present to me that I ought to place myself where he had stood. I did so; I applied my face to the pane and looked, as he had looked, into the room. As if, at this moment, to show me exactly what his range had been, Mrs. Grose, as I had done for himself just before, came in from the hall. With this I had the full image of a repetition of what had already occurred. She saw me as I had seen my own visitant; she pulled up short as I had done; I gave her something of the shock that I had received. She turned white, and this made me ask myself if I had blanched as much. She stared, in short, and retreated just on *my* lines, and I knew she had then passed out and come round to me and that I should presently meet her. I remained where I was, and while I waited I thought of more things than one. But there's only one I take space to mention. I wondered why *she* should be scared.

V

OH she let me know as soon as, round the corner of the house, she loomed again into view. "What in the name of goodness is the matter – ?" She was now flushed and out of breath.

I said nothing till she came quite near. "With me?" I must have made a wonderful face. "Do I show it?"

"You're as white as a sheet. You look awful."

I considered; I could meet on this, without scruple, any degree of innocence. My need to respect the bloom of Mrs. Grose's had dropped, without a rustle, from my shoulders, and if I wavered for the instant it was not with what I kept back. I put out my hand to her and she took it; I held her hard a little, liking to feel her close to me. There was a kind of support in the shy heave of her surprise. "You came for me for church, of course, but I can't go."

"Has anything happened?"

"Yes. You must know now. Did I look very queer?"

"Through this window? Dreadful!"

"Well," I said, "I've been frightened." Mrs. Grose's eyes expressed plainly that *she* had no wish to be, yet also that she knew too well her place not to be ready to share with me any marked inconvenience. Oh it was quite settled that she *must* share! "Just what you saw from the dining-room a minute ago was the effect of that. What *I* saw – just before – was much worse."

Her hand tightened. "What was it?"

"An extraordinary man. Looking in."

"What extraordinary man?"

"I have n't the least idea."

Mrs. Grose gazed round us in vain. "Then where is he gone?"

"I know still less."

"Have you seen him before?"

"Yes – once. On the old tower."

She could only look at me harder. "Do you mean he's a stranger?"

"Oh very much!"

"Yet you did n't tell me?"

"No – for reasons. But now that you've guessed – "

Mrs. Grose's round eyes encountered this charge. "Ah I have n't guessed!" she said very simply. "How can I if *you* don't imagine?"

"I don't in the very least."

"You've seen him nowhere but on the tower?"

"And on this spot just now."

Mrs. Grose looked round again. "What was he doing on the tower?"

"Only standing there and looking down at me."

She thought a minute. "Was he a gentleman?"

I found I had no need to think. "No." She gazed in deeper wonder. "No."

"Then nobody about the place? Nobody from the village?"

"Nobody – nobody. I did n't tell you, but I made sure."

She breathed a vague relief: this was, oddly, so much to the good. It only went indeed a little way. "But if he is n't a gentleman – "

"What *is* he? He's a horror."

"A horror?"

"He's – God help me if I know *what* he is!"

Mrs. Grose looked round once more; she fixed her eyes on the duskier distance and then, pulling herself together, turned to me with full inconsequence. "It's time we should be at church."

"Oh I'm not fit for church!"

"Won't it do you good?"

"It won't do *them* – !" I nodded at the house.

"The children?"

"I can't leave them now."

"You're afraid – ?"

I spoke boldly. "I'm afraid of *him*."

Mrs. Grose's large face showed me, at this, for the first time, the far-away faint glimmer of a consciousness more acute: I somehow made out in it the delayed dawn of an idea I myself had not given her and that was as yet quite obscure to me. It comes back to me that I thought instantly of this as something I could get from her; and I felt it to be connected with the desire she presently showed to know more. "When was it – on the tower?"

"About the middle of the month. At this same hour."

"Almost at dark," said Mrs. Grose.

"Oh no, not nearly. I saw him as I see you."

"Then how did he get in?"

"And how did he get out?" I laughed. "I had no opportunity to ask him! This evening, you see," I pursued, "he has not been able to get in."

"He only peeps?"

"I hope it will be confined to that!" She had now let go my hand; she turned away a little. I waited an instant; then I brought out: "Go to church. Goodbye. I must watch."

Slowly she faced me again. "Do you fear for them?"

We met in another long look. "Don't *you*?" Instead of answering she came nearer to the window and, for a minute, applied her face to the glass. "You see how he could see," I meanwhile went on.

She did n't move. "How long was he here?"

"Till I came out. I came to meet him."

Mrs. Grose at last turned round, and there was still more in her face. "*I* could n't have come out."

"Neither could I!" I laughed again. "But I did come. I've my duty."

"So have I mine," she replied; after which she added: "What's he like?"

"I've been dying to tell you. But he's like nobody."

"Nobody?" she echoed.

"He has no hat." Then seeing in her face that she already, in this, with a deeper dismay, found a touch of picture, I quickly added stroke to stroke. "He has red hair, very red, close-curling, and a pale face, long in shape, with straight good features and little rather queer whiskers that are as red as his hair. His eyebrows are somehow darker; they look particularly arched and as if they might move a good deal. His eyes are sharp, strange – awfully; but I only know clearly that they're rather small and very fixed. His mouth's wide, and his lips are thin, and except for his little whiskers he's quite clean-shaven. He gives me a sort of sense of looking like an actor."

"An actor!" It was impossible to resemble one less, at least, than Mrs. Grose at that moment.

"I've never seen one, but so I suppose them. He's tall, active, erect," I continued, "but never – no, never! – a gentleman."

My companion's face had blanched as I went on; her round eyes started and her mild mouth gaped. "A gentleman?" she gasped, confounded, stupefied: "a gentleman *he*!"

"You know him then?"

She visibly tried to hold herself. "But he *is* handsome?"
I saw the way to help her. "Remarkably!"
"And dressed – ?"
"In somebody's clothes. They're smart, but they're not his own."
She broke into a breathless affirmative groan. "They're the master's!"
I caught it up. "You *do* know him?"
She faltered but a second. "Quint!" she cried.
"Quint?"
"Peter Quint – his own man, his valet, when he was here!"
"When the master was?"
Gaping still, but meeting me, she pieced it all together. "He never wore his hat, but he did wear – well, there were waistcoats missed! They were both here – last year. Then the master went, and Quint was alone."
I followed, but halting a little. "Alone?"
"Alone with *us*." Then as from a deeper depth, "In charge," she added.
"And what became of him?"
She hung fire so long that I was still more mystified.
"He went too," she brought out at last.
"Went where?"
Her expression, at this, became extraordinary. "God knows where! He died."
"Died?" I almost shrieked.
She seemed fairly to square herself, plant herself more firmly to express the wonder of it. "Yes. Mr. Quint's dead."

VI

IT took of course more than that particular passage to place us together in presence of what we had now to live with as we could, my dreadful liability to impressions of the order so vividly exemplified, and my companion's knowledge henceforth – a knowledge half consternation and half compassion – of that liability. There had been this evening, after the revelation that left me for an hour so prostrate – there had been for either of us no attendance on any service but a little service of tears and vows, of prayers and promises, a climax to the series of mutual challenges and pledges that had straightway ensued on our retreating together to the schoolroom and shutting ourselves up there to have everything out. The result of our having everything out was simply to reduce our situation to the last rigour of its elements. She herself had seen nothing, not the shadow of a shadow, and nobody in the house but the governess was in the governess's plight; yet she accepted without directly impugning my sanity the truth as I gave it to her, and ended by showing me on this ground an awestricken tenderness, a deference to my more than questionable privilege, of which the very breath has remained with me as that of the sweetest of human charities.

What was settled between us accordingly that night was that we thought we might bear things together; and I was not even sure that in spite of her exemption it was she who had the best of the burden. I knew at this hour, I think, as well as I knew later, what I was capable of meeting to shelter my pupils; but it took me some time to be wholly sure of what my honest comrade was prepared for to keep terms with so stiff an agreement. I was queer company enough – quite as queer as the company I received; but as I trace over what we went through I see how much common ground we must have found in the one idea that, by good fortune, *could* steady us. It was the idea, the second movement, that led me straight out, as I may say, of the inner chamber of my dread. I could take the air in the court, at least, and there Mrs. Grose could join me. Perfectly can I recall now the particular way strength came to me before we separated for the night. We had gone over and over every feature of what I had seen.

"He was looking for some one else, you say – some one who was not you?"

"He was looking for little Miles." A portentous clearness now possessed me. "*That's* whom he was looking for."

"But how do you know?"

"I know, I know, I know!" My exaltation grew. "And *you* know, my dear!"

She did n't deny this, but I required, I felt, not even so much telling as that. She took it up again in a moment. "What if *he* should see him?"

"Little Miles? That's what he wants!"

She looked immensely scared again. "The child?"

"Heaven forbid! The man. He wants to appear to *them*." That he might was an awful conception, and yet somehow I could keep it at bay; which moreover, as we lingered there, was what I succeeded in practically proving. I had an absolute certainty that I should see again what I had already seen, but something within me said that by offering myself bravely as the sole subject of such experience, by accepting, by inviting, by surmounting it all, I should serve as an expiatory victim and guard the tranquillity of the rest of the household. The children in especial I should thus fence about and absolutely save. I recall one of the last things I said that night to Mrs. Grose.

"It does strike me that my pupils have never mentioned – !"

She looked at me hard as I musingly pulled up. "His having been here and the time they were with him?"

"The time they were with him, and his name, his presence, his history, in any way. They've never alluded to it."

"Oh the little lady does n't remember. She never heard or knew."

"The circumstances of his death?" I thought with some intensity. "Perhaps not. But Miles would remember – Miles would know."

"Ah don't try him!" broke from Mrs. Grose.

I returned her the look she had given me. "Don't be afraid." I continued to think. "It *is* rather odd."

"That he has never spoken of him?"

"Never by the least reference. And you tell me they were 'great friends.'"

"Oh it was n't *him*!" Mrs. Grose with emphasis declared. "It was Quint's own fancy. To play with him, I mean – to spoil him." She paused a moment; then she added: "Quint was much too free."

This gave me, straight from my vision of his face – *such* a face! – a sudden sickness of disgust. "Too free with *my* boy?"

"Too free with every one!"

I forbore for the moment to analyse this description further than by the reflexion that a part of it applied to several of the members of the household, of the half-dozen maids and men who were still of our small colony. But there was everything, for our apprehension, in the lucky fact that no discomfortable legend, no perturbation of scullions, had ever, within anyone's memory, attached to the kind old place. It had neither bad name nor ill fame, and Mrs. Grose, most apparently, only desired to cling to me and to quake in silence. I even put her, the very last thing of all, to the test. It was when, at midnight, she had her hand on the schoolroom door to take leave. "I *have* it from you then – for it's of great importance – that he was definitely and admittedly bad?"

"Oh not admittedly. *I* knew it – but the master did n't."

"And you never told him?"

"Well, he did n't like tale-bearing – he hated complaints. He was terribly short with anything of that kind, and if people were all right to *him* – "

"He would n't be bothered with more?" This squared well enough with my impression of him: he was not a trouble-loving gentleman, nor so very particular perhaps about some of the company he himself kept. All the same, I pressed my informant. "I promise you *I* would have told!"

She felt my discrimination. "I dare say I was wrong. But really I was afraid."

"Afraid of what?"

"Of things that man could do. Quint was so clever – he was so deep."

I took this in still more than I probably showed.

"You were n't afraid of anything else? Not of his effect – ?"

"His effect?" she repeated with a face of anguish and waiting while I faltered.

"On innocent little precious lives. They were in your charge."

"No, they were n't in mine!" she roundly and distressfully returned. "The master believed in him and placed him here because he was supposed not to be quite in health and the country air so good for him. So he had everything to say. Yes" – she let me have it – "even about *them*."

"Them – that creature!" I had to smother a kind of howl. "And you could bear it?"

"No. I could n't – and I can't now!" And the poor woman burst into tears.

A rigid control, from the next day, was, as I have said, to follow them; yet how often and how passionately, for a week, we came back together to the subject! Much as we had discussed it that Sunday night, I was, in the immediate later hours in especial – for it may be imagined whether I slept – still haunted with the shadow of something she had not told me. I myself had kept back nothing, but there was a word Mrs. Grose had kept back. I was sure moreover by morning that this was not from a failure of frankness, but because on every side there were fears. It seems to me indeed, in raking it all over, that by the time the morrow's sun was high I had restlessly read into the facts before us almost all the meaning they were to receive from subsequent and more cruel occurrences. What they gave me above all was just the sinister figure of the living man – the dead one would keep a while! – and of the months he had continuously passed at Bly, which, added up, made a formidable stretch. The limit of this evil time had arrived only when, on the dawn of a winter's morning, Peter Quint was found, by a labourer going to early work, stone dead on the road from the village: a catastrophe explained – superficially at least – by a visible wound to his head; such a wound as might have been produced (and as, on the final evidence, *had* been) by a fatal slip, in the dark and after leaving the public-house, on the steepish icy slope, a wrong path altogether, at the bottom of which he lay. The icy slope, the turn mistaken at night and in liquor, accounted for much – practically, in the end and after the inquest and boundless chatter, for everything; but there had been matters in his life, strange passages and perils, secret disorders, vices more than suspected, that would have accounted for a good deal more.

I scarce know how to put my story into words that shall be a credible picture of my state of mind; but I was, in these days literally able to find a joy in the extraordinary flight of heroism the occasion demanded of me. I now saw that I had been asked for a service admirable and difficult; and there would be a greatness in letting it be seen – oh in the right quarter! – that I could succeed where many another girl might have failed. It was an immense help to me – I confess I rather applaud myself as I look back! – that I saw my response so strongly and so simply. I was there to protect and defend the little creatures in the world the most bereaved and the most loveable, the appeal of whose helplessness had suddenly become only too explicit, a deep constant ache of one's own engaged affection. We were cut off, really, together; we were united in our danger. They had nothing but me, and I – well, I had *them*. It was in short a magnificent chance.

This chance presented itself to me in an image richly material. I was a screen – I was to stand before them. The more I saw the less they would. I began to watch them in a stifled suspense, a disguised tension, that might well, had it continued too long, have turned to something like madness. What saved me, as I now see, was that it turned to another matter altogether. It did n't last as suspense – it was superseded by horrible proofs. Proofs, I say, yes – from the moment I really took hold.

This moment dated from an afternoon hour that I happened to spend in the grounds with the younger of my pupils alone. We had left Miles indoors, on the red cushion of a deep window-seat; he had wished to finish a book, and I had been glad to encourage a purpose so laudable in a young man whose only defect was a certain ingenuity of restlessness. His sister, on the contrary, had been alert to come out, and I strolled with her half an hour, seeking the shade, for the sun was still high and the day exceptionally warm. I was aware afresh with her, as we went, of how, like her brother, she contrived – it was the charming thing in both children – to let me alone without appearing to drop me and to accompany me without appearing to oppress. They were never importunate and yet never listless. My attention to them all really went to seeing them amuse themselves immensely without me: this was a spectacle they seemed actively to prepare and that employed me as an active admirer. I walked in a world of their invention – they had no occasion whatever to draw upon mine; so that my time was taken only with being for them some remarkable person or thing that the game of the moment required and that was merely, thanks to my superior, my exalted stamp, a happy and highly distinguished sinecure. I forget what I was on the present occasion; I only remember that I was something very important and very quiet and that Flora was playing very hard. We were on the edge of the lake, and, as we had lately begun geography, the lake was the Sea of Azof.

Suddenly, amid these elements, I became aware that on the other side of the Sea of Azof we had an interested spectator. The way this knowledge gathered in me was the strangest thing in the world – the strangest, that is, except the very much stranger in which it quickly merged itself. I had sat down with a piece of work – for I was something or other that could sit – on the old stone bench which overlooked the pond; and in this position I began to take in with certitude and yet without direct vision the presence, a good way off, of a third person. The old trees, the thick shrubbery, made a great and pleasant shade, but it was all suffused with the brightness of the hot still hour. There was no ambiguity in anything; none whatever at least in the conviction I from one moment to another found myself forming as to what I should see straight before me and across the lake as a consequence of raising my eyes. They were attached at this juncture to the stitching in which I was engaged, and I can feel once more the spasm of my effort not to move them till I should so have steadied myself as to be able, to make up my mind what to do. There was an alien object in view – a figure whose right of presence I instantly and passionately questioned. I recollect counting over perfectly the possibilities, reminding myself that nothing was more natural for instance than the appearance of one of the men about the place, or even of a messenger, a postman or a tradesman's boy, from the village. That reminder had as little effect on my practical certitude as I was conscious – still even without looking – of its having upon the character and attitude of our visitor. Nothing was more natural than that these things should be the other things they absolutely were not.

Of the positive identity of the apparition I would assure myself as soon as the small clock of my courage should have ticked out the right second; meanwhile, with an effort that was already sharp enough, I transferred my eyes straight to little Flora, who, at the moment, was about ten yards away. My heart had stood still for an instant with the wonder and terror of the question whether she too would see; and I held my breath while I waited for what a cry from her, what some sudden innocent sign either of interest or of alarm, would tell me. I waited, but nothing came; then in the first place – and there is something more dire in this, I feel, than in anything I have to relate – I was determined by a sense that within a minute all spontaneous sounds from her had dropped; and in the second by the circumstance that also within the minute she had, in her play, turned her back to the water. This was her attitude when I at last looked at her – looked with the confirmed conviction that we were still, together, under direct personal notice. She had picked up a small flat piece of wood which happened to have in it a little hole that had evidently suggested to her the idea of sticking in another fragment that might figure as a mast and make the thing a boat. This second morsel, as I watched her, she was very markedly and intently attempting to tighten in its place. My apprehension of what she was doing sustained me so that after some seconds I felt I was ready for more. Then I again shifted my eyes – I faced what I had to face.

VII

I GOT hold of Mrs. Grose as soon after this as I could; and I can give no intelligible account of how I fought out the interval. Yet I still hear myself cry as I fairly threw myself into her arms: "They *know* – it's too monstrous: they know, they know!"

"And what on earth – !" I felt her incredulity as she held me.

"Why all that *we* know – and heaven knows what more besides!" Then as she released me I made it out to her, made it out perhaps only now with full coherency even to myself. "Two hours ago, in the garden" – I could scarce articulate – "Flora *saw!*"

Mrs. Grose took it as she might have taken a blow in the stomach. "She has told you?" she panted.

"Not a word – that's the horror. She kept it to herself! The child of eight, *that* child!" Unutterable still for me was the stupefaction of it.

Mrs. Grose of course could only gape the wider. "Then how do you know?"

"I was there – I saw with my eyes: saw she was perfectly aware."

"Do you mean aware of *him*?"

"No – of *her*." I was conscious as I spoke that I looked prodigious things, for I got the slow reflexion of them in my companion's face. "Another person – this time; but a figure of quite as unmistakeable horror and evil: a woman in black, pale and dreadful – with such an air also, and such a face! – on the other side of the lake. I was there with the child – quiet for the hour; and in the midst of it she came."

"Came how – from where?"

"From where they come from! She just appeared and stood there – but not so near."

"And without coming nearer!"

"Oh for the effect and the feeling she might have been as close as you!"

My friend, with an odd impulse, fell back a step. "Was she some one you've never seen?"

"Never. But some one the child has. Some one *you* have." Then to show how I had thought it all out: "My predecessor – the one who died."

"Miss Jessel?"

"Miss Jessel. You don't believe me!" I pressed.

She turned right and left in her distress. "How can you be sure?"

This drew from me, in the state of my nerves, a flash of impatience. "Then ask Flora – *she's* sure!" But I had no sooner spoken than I caught myself up. "No, for God's sake *don't*! She'll say she is n't – she'll lie!"

Mrs. Grose was not too bewildered instinctively to protest. "Ah how *can* you!"

"Because I'm clear. Flora does n't want me to know."

"It's only then to spare you."

"No, no – there are depths, depths! The more I go over it the more I see in it, and the more I see in it – the more I fear. I don't know what I *don't* see, what I *don't* fear!"

Mrs. Grose tried to keep up with me. "You mean you're afraid of seeing her again?"

"Oh no; that's nothing – now!" Then I explained. "It's of *not* seeing her."

But my companion only looked wan. "I don't understand."

"Why, it's that the child may keep it up – and that the child assuredly *will* – without my knowing it."

At the image of this possibility Mrs. Grose for a moment collapsed, yet presently to pull herself together again as from the positive force of the sense of what, should we yield an inch, there would really be to give way to. "Dear, dear – we must keep our heads! And after all, if she does n't mind it – !" She even tried a grim joke. "Perhaps she likes it!"

"Like *such* things – a scrap of an infant!"

"Is n't it just a proof of her blest innocence?" my friend bravely enquired.

She brought me, for the instant, almost round. "Oh we must clutch at *that* – we must cling to it! If it is n't a proof of what you say, it's a proof of God knows what! For the woman's a horror of horrors."

Mrs. Grose, at this, fixed her eyes a minute on the ground; then at last raising them, "Tell me how you know," she said.

"Then you admit it's what she was?" I cried.

"Tell me how you know," my friend simply repeated.

"Know? By seeing her! By the way she looked."

"At you, do you mean – so wickedly?"

"Dear me, no – I could have borne that. She gave me never a glance. She only fixed the child."

Mrs. Grose tried to see it. "Fixed her?"

"Ah with such awful eyes!"

She stared at mine as if they might really have resembled them. "Do you mean of dislike?"

"God help us, no. Of something much worse."

"Worse than dislike!" – this left her indeed at a loss.

"With a determination – indescribable. With a kind of fury of intention."

I made her turn pale. "Intention?"

"To get hold of her." Mrs. Grose – her eyes just lingering on mine – gave a shudder and walked to the window; and while she stood there looking out I completed my statement. "*That's* what Flora knows."

After a little she turned round. "The person was in black, you say?"

"In mourning – rather poor, almost shabby. But – yes – with extraordinary beauty." I now recognised to what I had at last, stroke by stroke, brought the victim of my confidence, for she quite visibly weighed this. "Oh handsome – very, very," I insisted; "wonderfully handsome. But infamous."

She slowly came back to me. "Miss Jessel – *was* infamous." She once more took my hand in both her own, holding it as tight as if to fortify me against the increase of alarm I might draw from this disclosure. "They were both infamous," she finally said.

So for a little we faced it once more together; and I found absolutely a degree of help in seeing it now so straight. "I appreciate," I said, "the great decency of your not having hitherto spoken; but the time has certainly come to give me the whole thing." She appeared to assent to this, but still only in silence; seeing which I went on: "I must have it now. Of what did she die? Come, there was something between them."

"There was everything."

"In spite of the difference – ?"

"Oh of their rank, their condition" – she brought it woefully out. "*She* was a lady."

I turned it over; I again saw. "Yes – she was a lady."

"And he so dreadfully below," said Mrs. Grose.

I felt that I doubtless need n't press too hard, in such company, on the place of a servant in the scale; but there was nothing to prevent an acceptance of my companion's own measure of my predecessor's abasement. There was a way to deal with that, and I dealt; the more readily for my full vision – on the evidence – of our employer's late clever good-looking "own" man; impudent, assured, spoiled, depraved. "The fellow was a hound."

Mrs. Grose considered as if it were perhaps a little a case for a sense of shades. "I've never seen one like him. He did what he wished."

"With *her*?"

"With them all."

It was as if now in my friend's own eyes Miss Jessel had again appeared. I seemed at any rate for an instant to trace their evocation of her as distinctly as I had seen her by the pond; and I brought out with decision: "It must have been also what *she* wished!"

Mrs. Grose's face signified that it had been indeed, but she said at the same time: "Poor woman – she paid for it!"

"Then you do know what she died of?" I asked.

"No – I know nothing. I wanted not to know; I was glad enough I did n't; and I thanked heaven she was well out of this!"

"Yet you had then your idea –"

"Of her real reason for leaving? Oh yes – as to that. She could n't have stayed. Fancy it here – for a governess! And afterwards I imagined – and I still imagine. And what I imagine is dreadful."

"Not so dreadful as what *I* do," I replied; on which I must have shown her – as I was indeed but too conscious – a front of miserable defeat. It brought out again all her compassion for me, and at the renewed touch of her kindness my power to resist broke down. I burst, as I had the other time made her burst, into tears; she took me to her motherly breast, where my lamentation overflowed. "I don't do it!" I sobbed in despair; "I don't save or shield them! It's far worse than I dreamed. They're lost!"

VIII

WHAT I had said to Mrs. Grose was true enough: there were in the matter I had put before her depths and possibilities that I lacked resolution to sound; so that when we met once more in the wonder of it we were of a common mind about the duty of resistance to extravagant fancies. We were to keep our heads if we should keep nothing else – difficult indeed as that might be in the face of all that, in our prodigious experience, seemed least to be questioned. Late that night, while the house slept, we had another talk in my room; when she went all the way with me as to its being beyond doubt that I had seen exactly what I had seen. I found that to keep her thoroughly in the grip of this I had only to ask her how, if I had "made it up," I came to be able to give, of each of the persons appearing to me, a picture disclosing, to the last detail, their special marks – a portrait on the exhibition of which she had instantly recognised and named them. She wished, of course – small blame to her! – to sink the whole subject; and I was quick to assure her that my own interest in it had now violently taken the form of a search for the way to escape from it. I closed with her cordially on the article of the likelihood that with recurrence – for recurrence we took for granted – I should get used to my danger; distinctly professing that my personal exposure had suddenly become the least of my discomforts. It was my new suspicion that was intolerable; and yet even to this complication the later hours of the day had brought a little ease.

On leaving her, after my first outbreak, I had of course returned to my pupils, associating the right remedy for my dismay with that sense of their charm which I had already recognised as a resource I could positively cultivate and which had never failed me yet. I had simply, in other words, plunged afresh into Flora's special society and there become aware – it was almost a luxury! – that she could put her little conscious hand straight upon the spot that ached. She had looked at me in sweet speculation and then had accused me to my face of having "cried." I had supposed the ugly signs of it brushed away; but I could literally – for the time at all events – rejoice, under this fathomless charity, that they had not entirely disappeared. To gaze into the depths of blue of the child's eyes and pronounce their loveliness a trick of premature cunning was to be guilty of a cynicism in preference to which I naturally preferred to abjure my judgement and, so far as might be, my agitation. I could n't abjure for merely wanting to, but I could repeat to Mrs. Grose – as I did there, over and over, in the small hours – that with our small friends' voices in the air, their pressure on one's heart and their fragrant faces against one's cheek, everything fell to the ground but their incapacity and their beauty. It was a pity that, somehow, to settle this once for all, I had equally to re-enumerate the signs of subtlety that, in the afternoon, by the lake, had made a miracle of my show of self-possession. It was a pity to be obliged to re-investigate the certitude of the moment itself and repeat how it had come to me as a revelation that the inconceivable communion I then surprised must have been for both parties a matter of habit. It was a pity I should have had to quaver out again the reasons for my not having, in my delusion, so much as questioned that the little girl saw our visitant even as I actually saw Mrs. Grose herself, and that she wanted, by just so much as she did thus see, to make me suppose she did n't, and at the same time, without showing anything, arrive at a guess as to whether I myself did! It was a pity I needed to recapitulate the portentous little activities by which she sought to divert my attention – the perceptible increase of movement, the greater intensity of play, the singing, the gabbling of nonsense and the invitation to romp.

Yet if I had not indulged, to prove there was nothing in it, in this review, I should have missed the two or three dim elements of comfort that still remained to me. I should n't for instance have been able to asseverate to my friend that I was certain – which was so much to the good – that *I* at least had not betrayed myself. I should n't have been prompted, by stress of need, by desperation of mind – I scarce know what to call it – to invoke such further aid to intelligence as might spring from pushing my colleague fairly to the wall. She had told me, bit by bit, under pressure, a great deal; but a small shifty spot on the wrong side of it all still sometimes brushed my brow like the wing of a bat; and I remember how on this occasion – for the sleeping house and the concentration alike of our danger and our watch seemed to help – I felt the importance of giving the last jerk to the curtain. "I don't believe anything so horrible," I recollect saying; "no, let us put it definitely, my dear, that I don't. But if I did, you know, there's a thing I should require now, just without sparing you the least bit more – oh not a scrap, come! – to get out of you. What was it you had in mind when, in our distress, before Miles came back, over the letter from his school, you said, under my insistence, that you did n't pretend for him he had n't literally *ever* been 'bad'? He has *not*, truly, 'ever,' in these weeks that I myself have lived with him and so closely watched him; he has been an imperturbable little prodigy of delightful loveable goodness. Therefore you might perfectly have made the claim for him if you had not, as it happened, seen an exception to take. What was your exception, and to what passage in your personal observation of him did you refer?"

It was a straight question enough, but levity was not our note, and in any case I had before the grey dawn admonished us to separate got my answer. What my friend had had in mind proved immensely to the purpose. It was neither more nor less than the particular fact that for a period of several months Quint and the boy had been perpetually together. It was indeed the very appropriate item of evidence of her having ventured to criticise the propriety, to hint at the incongruity, of so close an alliance, and even to go so far on the subject as a frank overture to Miss Jessel would take her. Miss Jessel had, with a very high manner about it, requested her to mind her business, and the good woman had on this directly approached little Miles. What she had said to him, since I pressed, was that *she* liked to see young gentlemen not forget their station.

I pressed again, of course, the closer for that. "You reminded him that Quint was only a base menial?"

"As you might say! And it was his answer, for one thing, that was bad."

"And for another thing?" I waited. "He repeated your words to Quint?"

"No, not that. It's just what he *would n't!*" she could still impress on me. "I was sure, at any rate," she added, "that he did n't. But he denied certain occasions."

"What occasions?"

"When they had been about together quite as if Quint were his tutor – and a very grand one – and Miss Jessel only for the little lady. When he had gone off with the fellow, I mean, and spent hours with him."

"He then prevaricated about it – he said he had n't!" Her assent was clear enough to cause me to add in a moment: "I see. He lied."

"Oh!" Mrs. Grose mumbled. This was a suggestion that it did n't matter; which indeed she backed up by a further remark. "You see, after all, Miss Jessel did n't mind. She did n't forbid him."

I considered. "Did he put that to you as a justification?"

At this she dropped again. "No, he never spoke of it."

"Never mentioned her in connexion with Quint?"

She saw, visibly blushing, where I was coming out. "Well, he did n't show anything. He denied," she repeated; "he denied."

Lord, how I pressed her now! "So that you could see he knew what was between the two wretches?"

"I don't know – I don't know!" the poor woman wailed.

"You do know, you dear thing," I replied; "only you have n't my dreadful boldness of mind, and you keep back, out of timidity and modesty and delicacy, even the impression that in the past, when you had, without my aid, to flounder about in silence, most of all made you miserable. But I shall get it out of you yet! There was something in the boy that suggested to you," I continued, "his covering and concealing their relation."

"Oh he could n't prevent – "

"Your learning the truth? I dare say! But, heavens," I fell, with vehemence, a-thinking, "what it shows that they must, to that extent, have succeeded in making of him!"

"Ah nothing that's not nice *now!*" Mrs. Grose lugubriously pleaded.

"I don't wonder you looked queer," I persisted, "when I mentioned to you the letter from his school!"

"I doubt if I looked as queer as you!" she retorted with homely force. "And if he was so bad then as that comes to, how is he such an angel now?"

"Yes indeed – and if he was a fiend at school! How, how, how? Well," I said in my torment, "you must put it to me again, though I shall not be able to tell you for some days. Only put it to me again!" I cried in a way that made my friend stare. "There are directions in which I must n't for the present let myself go." Meanwhile I returned to her first example – the one to which she had just previously referred – of the boy's happy capacity for an occasional slip. "If Quint – on your remonstrance at the time you speak of – was a base menial, one of the things Miles said to you, I find myself guessing, was that you were another." Again her admission was so adequate that I continued: "And you forgave him that?"

"Would n't *you*?"

"Oh yes!" And we exchanged there, in the stillness, a sound of the oddest amusement. Then I went on: "At all events, while he was with the man – "

"Miss Flora was with the woman. It suited them all!"

It suited me too, I felt, only too well; by which I mean that it suited exactly the particular deadly view I was in the very act of forbidding myself to entertain. But I so far succeeded in checking the expression of this view that I will throw, just here, no further light on it than may be offered by the mention of my final observation to Mrs. Grose. "His having lied and been impudent are, I confess, less engaging specimens than I had hoped to have from you of the outbreak in him of the little natural man. Still," I mused, "they must do, for they make me feel more than ever that I must watch."

It made me blush, the next minute, to see in my friend's face how much more unreservedly she had forgiven him than her anecdote struck me as pointing out to my own tenderness any way to do. This was marked when, at the schoolroom door, she quitted me. "Surely you don't accuse *him* – "

"Of carrying on an intercourse that he conceals from me? Ah remember that, until further evidence, I now accuse nobody." Then before shutting her out to go by another passage to her own place, "I must just wait," I wound up.

IX

I WAITED and waited, and the days took as they elapsed something from my consternation. A very few of them, in fact, passing, in constant sight of my pupils, without a fresh incident, sufficed to give to grievous fancies and even to odious memories a kind of brush of the sponge. I have spoken of the surrender to their extraordinary childish grace as a thing I could actively promote in myself, and it may be imagined if I neglected now to apply at this source for whatever balm it would yield. Stranger than I can express, certainly, was the effort to struggle against my new lights. It would doubtless have been a greater tension still, however, had it not been so frequently successful. I used to wonder how my little charges could help guessing that I thought strange things about them; and the circumstance that these things only made them more interesting was not by itself a direct aid to keeping them in the dark. I trembled lest they should see that they *were* so immensely more interesting. Putting things at the worst, at all events, as in meditation I so often did, any clouding of their innocence could only be – blameless and foredoomed as they were – a reason the more for taking risks. There were moments when I knew myself to catch them up by an irresistible impulse and press them to my heart. As soon as I had done so I used to wonder – "What will they think of that? Does n't it betray too much?"

It would have been easy to get into a sad wild tangle about how much I might betray; but the real account, I feel, of the hours of peace I could still enjoy was that the immediate charm of my companions was a beguilement still effective even under the shadow of the possibility that it was studied. For if it occurred to me that I might occasionally excite suspicion by the little outbreaks of my sharper passion for them, so too I remember asking if I might n't see a queerness in the traceable increase of their own demonstrations.

They were at this period extravagantly and preternaturally fond of me; which, after all, I could reflect, was no more than a graceful response in children perpetually bowed down over and hugged. The homage of which they were so lavish succeeded in truth for my nerves quite as well as if I never appeared to myself, as I may say, literally to catch them at a purpose in it. They had never, I think, wanted to do so many things for their poor protectress; I mean – though they got their lessons better and better, which was naturally what would please her most – in the way of diverting, entertaining, surprising her; reading her passages, telling her stories, acting her charades, pouncing out at her, in disguises, as animals and historical characters, and above all astonishing her by the "pieces" they had secretly got by heart and could interminably recite. I should never get to the bottom – were I to let myself go even now – of the prodigious private commentary, all under still more private correction, with which I in these days over-scored their full hours. They had shown me from the first a facility for everything, a general faculty which, taking a fresh start, achieved remarkable flights, They got their little tasks as if they loved them; they indulged, from the mere exuberance of the gift, in the most unimposed little miracles of memory. They not only popped out at me as tigers and as Romans, but as Shakespeareans, astronomers and navigators. This was so singularly the case that it had presumably much to do with the fact as to which, at the present day, I am at a loss for a different explanation: I allude to my unnatural composure on the subject of another school for Miles. What I remember is that I was content for the time not to open the question, and that contentment must have sprung from the sense of his perpetually striking show of cleverness. He was too clever for a bad governess, for a parson's daughter, to spoil; and the strangest if not the brightest thread in the pensive embroidery I just spoke of was the impression I might have got, if I had dared to work it out, that he was under some influence operating in his small intellectual life as a tremendous incitement.

If it was easy to reflect, however, that such a boy could postpone school, it was at least as marked that for such a boy to have been "kicked out" by a schoolmaster was a mystification without end. Let me add that in their company now – and I was careful almost never to be out of it – I could follow no scent very far. We lived in a cloud of music and affection and success and private theatricals. The musical sense in each of the children was of the quickest, but the elder in especial had a marvellous knack of catching and repeating. The schoolroom piano broke into all gruesome fancies; and when that failed there were confabulations in corners, with a sequel of one of them going out in the highest spirits in order to "come in" as something new. I had had brothers myself, and it was no revelation to me that little girls could be slavish idolaters of little boys. What surpassed everything was that there was a little boy in the world who could have for the inferior age, sex and intelligence so fine a consideration. They were extraordinarily at one, and to say that they never either quarrelled or complained is to make the note of praise coarse for their quality of sweetness. Sometimes perhaps indeed (when I dropped into coarseness) I came across traces of little understandings between them by which one of them should keep me occupied while the other slipped away. There is a naïf side, I suppose, in all diplomacy; but if my pupils practised upon me it was surely with the minimum of grossness. It was all in the other quarter that, after a lull, the grossness broke out.

I find that I really hang back; but I must take my horrid plunge. In going on with the record of what was hideous at Bly I not only challenge the most liberal faith – for which I little care; but (and this is another matter) I renew what I myself suffered, I again push my dreadful way through it to the end. There came suddenly an hour after which, as I look back, the business seems to me to have been all pure suffering; but I have at least reached the heart of it, and the straightest road out is doubtless to advance. One evening – with nothing to lead up or prepare it – I felt the cold touch of the impression that had breathed on me the night of my arrival and which, much lighter then as I have mentioned, I should probably have made little of in memory had my subsequent sojourn been less agitated. I had not gone to bed; I sat reading by a couple of candles. There was a roomful of old books at Bly – last-century fiction some of it, which, to the extent of a distinctly deprecated renown, but never to so much as that of a stray specimen, had reached the sequestered home and appealed to the una-vowed curiosity of my youth. I remember that the book I had in my hand was Fielding's "Amelia";[4] also that I was wholly awake. I recall further both a general conviction that it was horribly late and a particular objection to looking at my watch. I figure finally that the white curtain draping, in the fashion of those days, the head of Flora's little bed, shrouded, as I had assured myself long before, the perfection of childish rest. I recollect in short that though I was deeply interested in my author I found myself, at the turn of a page and with his spell all scattered, looking straight up from him and hard at the door of my room. There was a moment during which I listened, reminded of the faint sense I had had, the first night, of there being something undefinably astir in the house, and noted the soft breath of the open casement just move the half-drawn blind. Then, with all the marks of a deliberation that must have seemed magnificent had there been anyone to admire it, I laid down my book, rose to my feet and, taking a candle, went straight out of the room and, from the passage, on which my light made little impression, noiselessly closed and locked the door.

I can say now neither what determined nor what guided me, but I went straight along the lobby, holding my candle high, till I came within sight of the tall window that presided over the great turn of the staircase. At this point I precipitately found myself aware of three things. They were practically simultaneous, yet they had flashes of suc-cession. My candle, under a bold flourish, went out, and I perceived, by the uncovered window, that the yielding dusk of earliest morning rendered it unnecessary. Without it, the next instant, I knew that there was a figure on the stair. I speak of sequences, but I required no lapse of seconds to stiffen myself for a third encounter with Quint. The apparition had reached the landing halfway up and was therefore on the spot nearest the window, where, at sight of me, it stopped short and fixed me exactly as it had fixed me from the tower and from the garden. He knew me as well as I knew him; and so, in the cold faint twilight, with a glimmer in the high glass and another on the polish of the oak stair below, we faced each other in our common intensity. He was absolutely, on this occasion, a living detestable dangerous presence. But that was not the wonder of wonders; I reserve this distinction for quite another circumstance: the circumstance that dread had unmistakeably quitted me and that there was nothing in me unable to meet and measure him.

I had plenty of anguish after that extraordinary moment, but I had, thank God, no terror. And he knew I had n't – I found myself at the end of an instant magnificently aware of this. I felt, in a fierce rigour of confidence, that if I stood my ground a minute I should cease – for the time at least – to have him to reckon with; and during the min-ute, accordingly, the thing was as human and hideous as a real interview: hideous just because it *was* human, as human as to have met alone, in the small hours, in a sleeping house, some enemy, some adventurer, some criminal. It was the dead silence of our long gaze at such close quarters that gave the whole horror, huge as it was, its only

Notes ───

4 The governess has selected a novel (1751) by Henry Fielding
(1707–54) describing a long-suffering, virtuous heroine who is
finally made wealthy by an inheritance.

note of the unnatural. If I had met a murderer in such a place and at such an hour we still at least would have spoken. Something would have passed, in life, between us; if nothing had passed one of us would have moved. The moment was so prolonged that it would have taken but little more to make me doubt if even *I* were in life. I can't express what followed it save by saying that the silence itself – which was indeed in a manner an attestation of my strength – became the element into which I saw the figure disappear; in which I definitely saw it turn, as I might have seen the low wretch to which it had once belonged turn on receipt of an order, and pass, with my eyes on the villainous back that no hunch could have more disfigured, straight down the staircase and into the darkness in which the next bend was lost.

X

I REMAINED a while at the top of the stair, but with the effect presently of understanding that when my visitor had gone, he had gone; then I returned to my room. The foremost thing I saw there by the light of the candle I had left burning was that Flora's little bed was empty; and on this I caught my breath with all the terror that, five minutes before, I had been able to resist. I dashed at the place in which I had left her lying and over which – for the small silk counterpane and the sheets were disarranged – the white curtains had been deceivingly pulled forward; then my step, to my unutterable relief, produced an answering sound: I noticed an agitation of the window-blind, and the child, ducking down, emerged rosily from the other side of it. She stood there in so much of her candour and so little of her night-gown, with her pink bare feet and the golden glow of her curls. She looked intensely grave, and I had never had such a sense of losing an advantage acquired (the thrill of which had just been so prodigious) as on my consciousness that she addressed me with a reproach – "You naughty: where *have* you been?" Instead of challenging her own irregularity I found myself arraigned and explaining. She herself explained, for that matter, with the loveliest eagerest simplicity. She had known suddenly, as she lay there, that I was out of the room, and had jumped up to see what had become of me. I had dropped, with the joy of her reappearance, back into my chair – feeling then, and then only, a little faint; and she had pattered straight over to me, thrown herself upon my knee, given herself to be held with the flame of the candle full in the wonderful little face that was still flushed with sleep. I remember closing my eyes an instant, yieldingly, consciously, as before the excess of something beautiful that shone out of the blue of her own. "You were looking for me out of the window?" I said. "You thought I might be walking in the grounds?"

"Well, you know, I thought some one was" – she never blanched as she smiled out that at me.

Oh how I looked at her now! "And did you see anyone?"

"Ah *no!*" she returned almost (with the full privilege of childish inconsequence) resentfully, though with a long sweetness in her little drawl of the negative.

At that moment, in the state of my nerves, I absolutely believed she lied; and if I once more closed my eyes it was before the dazzle of the three or four possible ways in which I might take this up. One of these for a moment tempted me with such singular force that, to resist it, I must have gripped my little girl with a spasm that, wonderfully, she submitted to without a cry or a sign of fright. Why not break out at her on the spot and have it all over? – give it to her straight in her lovely little lighted face? "You see, you see, you *know* that you do and that you already quite suspect I believe it; therefore why not frankly confess it to me, so that we may at least live with it together and learn perhaps, in the strangeness of our fate, where we are and what it means?" This solicitation dropped, alas, as it came: if I could immediately have succumbed to it

I might have spared myself – well, you'll see what. Instead of succumbing I sprang again to my feet, looked at her bed and took a helpless middle way. "Why did you pull the curtain over the place to make me think you were still there?"

Flora luminously considered; after which, with her little divine smile: "Because I don't like to frighten you!"

"But if I had, by your idea, gone out – ?"

She absolutely declined to be puzzled; she turned her eyes to the flame of the candle as if the question were as irrelevant, or at any rate as impersonal, as Mrs. Marcet[5] or nine-times-nine. "Oh but you know," she quite adequately answered, "that you might come back, you dear, and that you *have!*" And after a little, when she had got into bed, I had, a long time, by almost sitting on her for the retention of her hand, to show how I recognised the pertinence of my return.

You may imagine the general complexion, from that moment, of my nights. I repeatedly sat up till I did n't know when; I selected moments when my room-mate unmistakeably slept, and, stealing out, took noiseless turns in the passage. I even pushed as far as to where I had last met Quint. But I never met him there again, and I may as well say at once that I on no other occasion saw him in the house. I just missed, on the staircase, nevertheless, a different adventure. Looking down it from the top I once recognised the presence of a woman seated on one of the lower steps with her back presented to me, her body half-bowed and her head, in an attitude of woe, in her hands. I had been there but an instant, however, when she vanished without looking round at me. I knew, for all that, exactly what dreadful face she had to show; and I wondered whether, if instead of being above I had been below I should have had the same nerve for going up that I had lately shown Quint. Well, there continued to be plenty of call for nerve. On the eleventh night after my latest encounter with that gentleman – they were all numbered now – I had an alarm that previously skirted it and that indeed, from the particular quality of its unexpectedness, proved quite my sharpest shock. It was precisely the first night during this series that, weary with vigils, I had conceived I might again with laxity lay myself down at my old hour. I slept immediately and, as I afterwards knew, till about one o'clock; but when I woke it was to sit straight up, as completely roused as if a hand had shaken me. I had left a light burning, but it was now out, and I felt an instant certainty that Flora had extinguished it. This brought me to my feet and straight, in the darkness, to her bed, which I found she had left. A glance at the window enlightened me further, and the striking of a match completed the picture.

The child had again got up – this time blowing out the taper, and had again, for some purpose of observation or response, squeezed in behind the blind and was peering out into the night. That she now saw – as she had not, I had satisfied myself, the previous time – was proved to me by the fact that she was disturbed neither by my re-illumination nor by the haste I made to get into slippers and into a wrap. Hidden, protected, absorbed, she evidently rested on the sill – the casement opened forward – and gave herself up. There was a great still moon to help her, and this fact had counted in my quick decision. She was face to face with the apparition we had met at the lake, and could now communicate with it as she had not then been able to do. What I, on my side, had to care for was, without disturbing her, to reach, from the corridor, some other window turned to the same quarter. I got to the door without her hearing me; I got out of it, closed it and listened, from the other side, for some sound from her.

Notes

[5] Jane Marcet (1769–1858) was the author of textbooks for children.

While I stood in the passage I had my eyes on her brother's door, which was but ten steps off and which, indescribably, produced in me a renewal of the strange impulse that I lately spoke of as my temptation. What if I should go straight in and march to *his* window? – what if, by risking to his boyish bewilderment a revelation of my motive, I should throw across the rest of the mystery the long halter of my boldness?

This thought held me sufficiently to make me cross to his threshold and pause again. I preternaturally listened; I figured to myself what might portentously be; I wondered if his bed were also empty and he also secretly at watch. It was a deep soundless minute, at the end of which my impulse failed. He was quiet; he might be innocent; the risk was hideous; I turned away. There was a figure in the grounds – a figure prowling for a sight, the visitor with whom Flora was engaged; but it wasn't the visitor most concerned with my boy. I hesitated afresh, but on other grounds and only a few seconds; then I had made my choice. There were empty rooms enough at Bly, and it was only a question of choosing the right one. The right one suddenly presented itself to me as the lower one – though high above the gardens – in the solid corner of the house that I have spoken of as the old tower. This was a large square chamber, arranged with some state as a bedroom, the extravagant size of which made it so inconvenient that it had not for years, though kept by Mrs. Grose in exemplary order, been occupied. I had often admired it and I knew my way about in it; I had only, after just faltering at the first chill gloom of its disuse, to pass across it and unbolt in all quietness one of the shutters. Achieving this transit I uncovered the glass without a sound and, applying my face to the pane, was able, the darkness without being much less than within, to see that I commanded the right direction. Then I saw something more. The moon made the night extraordinarily penetrable and showed me on the lawn a person, diminished by distance, who stood there motionless and as if fascinated, looking up to where I had appeared – looking, that is, not so much straight at me, as at something that was apparently above me. There was clearly another person above me – there was a person on the tower; but the presence on the lawn was not in the least what I had conceived and had confidently hurried to meet. The presence on the lawn – I felt sick as I made it out – was poor little Miles himself.

XI

IT was not till late next day that I spoke to Mrs. Grose; the rigour with which I kept my pupils in sight making it often difficult to meet her privately: the more as we each felt the importance of not provoking – on the part of the servants quite as much as on that of the children – any suspicion of a secret flurry or of a discussion of mysteries. I drew a great security in this particular from her mere smooth aspect. There was nothing in her fresh face to pass on to others the least of my horrible confidences. She believed me, I was sure, absolutely: if she hadn't I don't know what would have become of me, for I couldn't have borne the strain alone. But she was a magnificent monument to the blessing of a want of imagination, and if she could see in our little charges nothing but their beauty and amiability, their happiness and cleverness, she had no direct communication with the sources of my trouble. If they had been at all visibly blighted or battered she would doubtless have grown, on tracing it back, haggard enough to match them; as matters stood, however, I could feel her, when she surveyed them with her large white arms folded and the habit of serenity in all her look, thank the Lord's mercy that if they were ruined the pieces would still serve. Flights of fancy gave place, in her mind, to a steady fireside glow, and I had already begun to perceive how, with the development of the conviction that – as time went on without a public accident – our young things could, after all, look out for themselves, she addressed her greatest solicitude to the sad case presented by their deputy-guardian. That, for myself, was a sound simplification: I could engage that, to the world, my face should tell no tales, but it would have been, in the conditions, an immense added worry to find myself anxious about hers.

At the hour I now speak of she had joined me, under pressure, on the terrace, where, with the lapse of the season, the afternoon sun was now agreeable; and we sat there together while before us and at a distance, yet within call if we wished, the children strolled to and fro in one of their most manageable moods. They moved slowly, in unison, below us, over the lawn, the boy, as they went, reading aloud from a story-book and passing his arm round his sister to keep her quite in touch. Mrs. Grose watched them with positive placidity; then I caught the suppressed intellectual creak with which she conscientiously turned to take from me a view of the back of the tapestry. I had made her a receptacle of lurid things, but there was an odd recognition of my superiority – my accomplishments and my function – in her patience under my pain. She offered her mind to my disclosures as, had I wished to mix a witch's broth and proposed it with assurance, she would have held out a large clean saucepan. This had become thoroughly her attitude by the time that, in my recital of the events of the night, I reached the point of what Miles had said to me when, after seeing him, at such a monstrous hour, almost on the very spot where he happened now to be, I had gone down to bring him in; choosing then, at the window, with a concentrated need of not alarming the house, rather that method than any noisier process. I had left her meanwhile in little doubt of my small hope of representing with success even to her actual sympathy my sense of the real splendour of the little inspiration with which, after I had got him into the house, the boy met my final articulate challenge. As soon as I appeared in the moonlight on the terrace he had come to me as straight as possible; on which I had taken his hand without a word and led him, through the dark spaces, up the staircase where Quint had so hungrily hovered for him, along the lobby where I had listened and trembled, and so to his forsaken room.

Not a sound, on the way, had passed between us, and I had wondered – oh *how* I had wondered! – if he were groping about in his dreadful little mind for something plausible and not too grotesque. It would tax his invention certainly, and I felt, this time, over his real embarrassment, a curious thrill of triumph. It was a sharp trap for any game hitherto successful. He could play no longer at perfect propriety, nor could he pretend to it; so how the deuce would he get out of the scrape? There beat in me indeed, with the passionate throb of this question, an equal dumb appeal as to how the deuce *I* should. I was confronted at last, as never yet, with all the risk attached even now to sounding my own horrid note. I remember in fact that as we pushed into his little chamber, where the bed had not been slept in at all and the window, uncovered to the moonlight, made the place so clear that there was no need of striking a match – I remember how I suddenly dropped, sank upon the edge of the bed from the force of the idea that he must know how he really, as they say, "had" me. He could do what he liked, with all his cleverness to help him, so long as I should continue to defer to the old tradition of the criminality of those caretakers of the young who minister to superstitions and fears. He "had" me indeed, and in a cleft stick; for who would ever absolve me, who would consent that I should go unhung, if, by the faintest tremor of an overture, I were the first to introduce into our perfect intercourse an element so dire? No, no: it was useless to attempt to convey to Mrs. Grose, just as it is scarcely less so to attempt to suggest here, how, during our short stiff brush there in the dark, he fairly shook me with admiration. I was of course thoroughly kind and merciful; never, never yet had I placed on his small shoulders hands of such tenderness as those with which, while I rested against the bed, I held him there well under fire. I had no alternative but, in form at least, to put it to him.

"You must tell me now – and all the truth. What did you go out for? What were you doing there?"

I can still see his wonderful smile, the whites of his beautiful eyes and the uncovering of his clear teeth, shine to me in the dusk. "If I tell you why, will you understand?" My heart, at this, leaped into my mouth. *Would* he tell me why? I found no sound on my lips to press it, and I was aware of answering only with a vague repeated grimacing nod. He was gentleness itself, and while I wagged my head at him he stood there more than ever a little fairy prince. It was his brightness indeed that gave me a respite. Would it be so great if he were really going to tell me? "Well," he said at last, "just exactly in order that you should do this."

"Do what?"

"Think me – for a change – *bad*!" I shall never forget the sweetness and gaiety with which he brought out the word, nor how, on top of it, he bent forward and kissed me. It was practically the end of everything. I met his kiss and I had to make, while I folded him for a minute in my arms, the most stupendous effort not to cry. He had given exactly the account of himself that permitted least my going behind it, and it was only with the effect of confirming my acceptance of it that, as I presently glanced about the room, I could say –

"Then you did n't undress at all?"

He fairly glittered in the gloom. "Not at all. I sat up and read."

"And when did you go down?"

"At midnight. When I'm bad I *am* bad!"

"I see, I see – it's charming. But how could you he sure I should know it?"

"Oh I arranged that with Flora." His answers rang out with a readiness! "She was to get up and look out."

"Which is what she did do." It was I who fell into the trap!

"So she disturbed you, and, to see what she was looking at, you also looked – you saw."

"While you," I concurred, "caught your death in the night air!"

He literally bloomed so from this exploit that he could afford radiantly to assent. "How otherwise should I have been bad enough!" he asked. Then, after another embrace, the incident and our interview closed on my recognition of all the reserves of goodness that, for his joke, he had been able to draw upon.

XII

THE particular impression I had received proved in the morning light, I repeat, not quite successfully presentable to Mrs. Grose, though I re-enforced it with the mention of still another remark that he had made before we separated. "It all lies in half a dozen words," I said to her, "words that really settle the matter. 'Think, you know, what I *might* do!' He threw that off to show me how good he is. He knows down to the ground what he 'might do.' That's what he gave them a taste of at school."

"Lord, you do change!" cried my friend.

"I don't change – I simply make it out. The four, depend upon it, perpetually meet. If on either of these last nights you had been with either child you'd clearly have understood. The more I've watched and waited the more I've felt that if there were nothing else to make it sure it would be made so by the systematic silence of each. *Never*, by a slip of the tongue, have they so much as alluded to either of their old friends, any more than Miles has alluded to his expulsion. Oh yes, we may sit here and look at them, and they may show off to us there to their fill; but even while they pretend to be lost in their fairy-tale they're steeped in their vision of the dead restored to them. He's not reading to her," I declared; "they're talking of *them* – they're talking horrors! I go on, I know, as if I were crazy; and it's a wonder I'm not. What I've seen would have made *you* so; but it has only made me more lucid, made me get hold of still other things."

My lucidity must have seemed awful, but the charming creatures who were victims of it, passing and repassing in their interlocked sweetness, gave my colleague something to hold on by; and I felt how tight she held as, without stirring in the breath of my passion, she covered them still with her eyes. "Of what other things have you got hold?"

"Why of the very things that have delighted, fascinated and yet, at bottom, as I now so strangely see, mystified and troubled me. Their more than earthly beauty, their absolutely unnatural goodness. It's a game," I went on; "it's a policy and a fraud!"

"On the part of little darlings – ?"

"As yet mere lovely babies? Yes, mad as that seems!" The very act of bringing it out really helped me to trace it – follow it all up and piece it all together. "They have n't been good – they've only been absent. It has been easy to live with them because they're simply leading a life of their own. They're not mine – they're not ours. They're his and they're hers!"

"Quint's and that woman's?"

"Quint's and that woman's. They want to get to them."

Oh how, at this, poor Mrs. Grose appeared to study them! "But for what?"

"For the love of all the evil that, in those dreadful days, the pair put into them. And to ply them with that evil still, to keep up the work of demons, is what brings the others back."

"Laws!" said my friend under her breath. The exclamation was homely, but it revealed a real acceptance of my further proof of what, in the bad time – for there had been a worse even than this! – must have occurred. There could have been no such justification for me as the plain assent of her experience to whatever depth of depravity I found credible in our brace of scoundrels. It was in obvious submission of memory that she brought out after a moment: "They *were* rascals! But what can they now do?" she pursued.

"Do?" I echoed so loud that Miles and Flora, as they passed at their distance, paused an instant in their walk and looked at us. "Don't they do enough?" I demanded in a lower tone, while the children, having smiled and nodded and kissed hands to us, resumed their exhibition. We were held by it a minute; then I answered: "They can destroy them!" At this my companion did turn, but the appeal she launched was a silent one, the effect of which was to make me more explicit. "They don't know as yet quite how – but they're trying hard. They're seen only across, as it were, and beyond – in strange places and on high places, the top of towers, the roof of houses, the outside of windows, the further edge of pools; but there's a deep design, on either side, to shorten the distance and overcome the obstacle: so the success of the tempters is only a question of time. They've only to keep to their suggestions of danger."

"For the children to come?"

"And perish in the attempt!" Mrs. Grose slowly got up, and I scrupulously added: "Unless, of course, we can prevent!"

Standing there before me while I kept my seat she visibly turned things over. "Their uncle must do the preventing. He must take them away."

"And who's to make him?"

She had been scanning the distance, but she now dropped on me a foolish face. "You, Miss."

"By writing to him that his house is poisoned and his little nephew and niece mad?"

"But if they *are*, Miss?"

"And if I am myself, you mean? That's charming news to be sent him by a person enjoying his confidence and whose prime undertaking was to give him no worry."

Mrs. Grose considered, following the children again. "Yes, he do hate worry. That was the great reason – "

"Why those fiends took him in so long? No doubt, though his indifference must have been awful. As I'm not a fiend, at any rate, I should n't take him in."

My companion, after an instant and for all answer, sat down again and grasped my arm. "Make him at any rate come to you."

I stared. "To *me*?" I had a sudden fear of what she might do. "'Him'?"

"He ought to *be* here – he ought to help."

I quickly rose and I think I must have shown her a queerer face than ever yet. "You see me asking him for a visit?" No, with her eyes on my face she evidently could n't. Instead of it even – as a woman reads another – she could see what I myself saw: his derision, his amusement, his contempt for the breakdown of my resignation at being left alone and for the fine machinery I had set in motion to attract his attention to my slighted charms. She did n't know – no one knew – how proud I had been to serve him and to stick to our terms; yet she none the less took the measure, I think, of the warning I now gave her. "If you should so lose your head as to appeal to him for me – "

She was really frightened. "Yes, Miss?"

"I would leave, on the spot, both him and you."

XIII

IT was all very well to join them, but speaking to them proved quite as much as ever an effort beyond my strength – offered, in close quarters, difficulties as insurmountable as before. This situation continued a month, and with new aggravations and particular notes, the note above all, sharper and sharper, of the small ironic consciousness on the part of my pupils. It was not, I am as sure to-day as I was sure then, my mere infernal imagination: it was absolutely traceable that they were aware of my predicament and that this strange relation made, in a manner, for a long time, the air in which we moved. I don't mean that they had their tongues in their cheeks or did anything vulgar, for that was not one of their dangers: I do mean, on the other hand, that the element of the unnamed and untouched became, between us, greater than any other, and that so much avoidance could n't have been made successful without a great deal of tacit arrangement. It was as if, at moments, we were perpetually coming into sight of subjects before which we must stop short, turning suddenly out of alleys that we perceived to be blind, closing with a little bang that made us look at each other – for, like all bangs, it was something louder than we had intended – the doors we had indiscreetly opened. All roads lead to Rome, and there were times when it might have struck us that almost every branch of study or subject of conversation skirted forbidden ground. Forbidden ground was the question of the return of the dead in general and of whatever, in especial, might survive, for memory, of the friends little children had lost. There were days when I could have sworn that one of them had, with a small invisible nudge, said to the other: "She thinks she'll do it this time – but she *won't*!" To "do it" would have been to indulge for instance – and for once in a way – in some direct reference to the lady who had prepared them for my discipline. They had a delightful endless appetite for passages in my own history to which I had again and again treated them; they were in possession of everything that had ever happened to me, had had, with every circumstance, the story of my smallest adventures and of those of my brothers and sisters and of the cat and the dog at home, as well as many particulars of the whimsical bent of my father, of the furniture and arrangement of our house and of the conversation of the old women of our village. There were things enough, taking one with another, to chatter about, if one went very fast and knew by instinct when to go round. They pulled with an art of their own the strings of my invention and my memory; and nothing else perhaps, when I thought of such occasions afterwards, gave me so the suspicion of being watched from under cover. It was in any case over *my* life, *my* past and *my* friends alone that we could take anything like our ease; a state of affairs that led them sometimes without the least pertinence to break out into sociable reminders. I was invited – with no visible connexion – to repeat afresh Goody Gosling's celebrated *mot*[6] or to confirm the details already supplied as to the cleverness of the vicarage pony.

It was partly at such junctures as these and partly at quite different ones that, with the turn my matters had now taken, my predicament, as I have called it, grew most sensible. The fact that the days passed for me without another encounter ought, it would have appeared, to have done something toward soothing my nerves. Since the light brush, that second night on the upper landing, of the presence of a woman at the foot of the stair, I had seen nothing, whether in or out of the house, that one had better not have seen. There was many a corner round which I expected to come upon Quint, and many a situation that, in a merely sinister way, would have favoured the appearance of Miss Jessel. The summer had turned, the summer had gone; the autumn had dropped upon Bly and had blown out half our lights. The place, with its grey sky and withered garlands, its bared spaces and scattered dead leaves, was like a theatre after the performance – all strewn with crumpled playbills. There were exactly states of the air, conditions of sound and of stillness, unspeakable impressions of the *kind* of ministering moment, that brought back to me, long enough to catch it, the feeling of the medium in which, that June evening out of doors, I had had my first sight of Quint, and in which too, at those other instants, I had, after seeing him through the window, looked for him in vain in the circle of shrubbery. I recognised the signs, the portents – I recognised the moment, the spot. But they remained unaccompanied and empty, and I continued unmolested; if unmolested one could call a young woman whose sensibility had, in the most extraordinary fashion, not declined but deepened. I had said in my talk with Mrs. Grose on that horrid scene of Flora's by the lake – and had perplexed her by so saying – that it would from that moment distress me much more to lose my power than to keep it. I had then expressed what was vividly in my mind: the truth that, whether the children really saw or not – since, that is, it was not yet definitely proved – I greatly preferred, as a safeguard, the fulness of my own exposure. I was ready to know the very worst that was to be known. What I had then had an ugly glimpse of was that my eyes might be sealed just while theirs were most opened. Well, my eyes *were* sealed, it appeared, at present – a consummation for which it seemed blasphemous not to thank God. There was, alas, a difficulty about that: I would have thanked him with all my soul had I not had in a proportionate measure this conviction of the secret of my pupils.

How can I retrace to-day the strange steps of my obsession? There were times of our being together when I would have been ready to swear that, literally, in my presence, but with my direct sense of it closed, they had visitors who were known and were welcome. Then it was that, had I not been deterred by the very chance that such an injury

Notes

6 French: witty remark. Goody Gosling may have been the nickname of a woman in the governess's village.

might prove greater than the injury to be averted, my exaltation would have broken out. "They're here, they're here, you little wretches," I would have cried, "and you can't deny it now!" The little wretches denied it with all the added volume of their sociability and their tenderness, just in the crystal depths of which – like the flash of a fish in a stream – the mockery of their advantage peeped up. The shock had in truth sunk into me still deeper than I knew on the night when, looking out either for Quint or for Miss Jessel under the stars, I had seen there the boy over whose rest I watched and who had immediately brought in with him – had straightway there turned on me – the lovely upward look with which, from the battlements above us, the hideous apparition of Quint had played. If it was a question of a scare my discovery on this occasion had scared me more than any other, and it was essentially in the scared state that I drew my actual conclusions. They harassed me so that sometimes, at odd moments, I shut myself up audibly to rehearse – it was at once a fantastic relief and a renewed despair – the manner in which I might come to the point. I approached it from one side and the other while, in my room, I flung myself about, but I always broke down in the monstrous utterance of names. As they died away on my lips I said to myself that I should indeed help them to represent something infamous if by pronouncing them I should violate as rare a little case of instinctive delicacy as any schoolroom probably had ever known. When I said to myself: "*They* have the manners to be silent, and you, trusted as you are, the baseness to speak!" I felt myself crimson and covered my face with my hands. After these secret scenes I chattered more than ever, going on volubly enough till one of our prodigious palpable hushes occurred – I can call them nothing else – the strange dizzy lift or swim (I try for terms!) into a stillness, a pause of all life, that had nothing to do with the more or less noise we at the moment might be engaged in making and that I could hear through any intensified mirth or quickened recitation or louder strum of the piano. Then it was that the others, the outsiders, were there. Though they were not angels they "passed," as the French say, causing me, while they stayed, to tremble with the fear of their addressing to their younger victims some yet more infernal message or more vivid image than they had thought good enough for myself.

What it was least possible to get rid of was the cruel idea that, whatever I had seen, Miles and Flora saw *more* – things terrible and unguessable and that sprang from dreadful passages of intercourse in the past. Such things naturally left on the surface, for the time, a chill that we vociferously denied we felt; and we had all three, with repetition, got into such splendid training that we went, each time, to mark the close of the incident, almost automatically through the very same movements. It was striking of the children at all events to kiss me inveterately with a wild irrelevance and never to fail – one or the other – of the precious question that had helped us through many a peril. "When do you think he *will* come? Don't you think we *ought* to write?" – there was nothing like that enquiry, we found by experience, for carrying off an awkwardness. "He" of course was their uncle in Harley Street; and we lived in much profusion of theory that he might at any moment arrive to mingle in our circle. It was impossible to have given less encouragement than he had administered to such a doctrine, but if we had not had the doctrine to fall back upon we should have deprived each other of some of our finest exhibitions. He never wrote to them – that may have been selfish, but it was a part of the flattery of his trust of myself; for the way in which a man pays his highest tribute to a woman is apt to be but by the more festal celebration of one of the sacred laws of his comfort. So I held that I carried out the spirit of the pledge given not to appeal to him when I let our young friends understand that their own letters were but charming literary exercises. They were too beautiful to be posted; I kept them myself; I have them all to this hour. This was a rule indeed which only added to the satiric effect of my being plied with the supposition that he might at any moment be among us.

It was exactly as if our young friends knew how almost more awkward than anything else that might be for me. There appears to me moreover as I look back no note in all this more extraordinary than the mere fact that, in spite of my tension and of their triumph, I never lost patience with them. Adorable they must in truth have been, I now feel, since I did n't in these days hate them! Would exasperation, however, if relief had longer been postponed, finally have betrayed me? It little matters, for relief arrived. I call it relief though it was only the relief that a snap brings to a strain or the burst of a thunderstorm to a day of suffocation. It was at least change, and it came with a rush.

XIV

WALKING to church a certain Sunday morning, I had little Miles at my side and his sister, in advance of us and at Mrs. Grose's, well in sight. It was a crisp clear day, the first of its order for some time; the night had brought a touch of frost and the autumn air, bright and sharp, made the church-bells almost gay. It was an odd accident of thought that I should have happened at such a moment to be particularly and very gratefully struck with the obedience of my little charges. Why did they never resent my inexorable, my perpetual society? Something or other had brought nearer home to me that I had all but pinned the boy to my shawl, and that in the way our companions were marshalled before me I might have appeared to provide against some danger of rebellion. I was like a gaoler with an eye to possible surprises and escapes. But all this belonged – I mean their magnificent little surrender – just to the special array of the facts that were most abysmal. Turned out for Sunday by his uncle's tailor, who had had a free hand and a notion of pretty waistcoats and of his grand little air, Miles's whole title to independence, the rights of his sex and situation, were so stamped upon him that if he had suddenly struck for freedom I should have had nothing to say. I was by the strangest of chances wondering how I should meet him when the revolution unmistakeably occurred. I call it a revolution because I now see how, with the word he spoke, the curtain rose on the last act of my dreadful drama and the catastrophe was precipitated. "Look here, my dear, you know," he charmingly said, "when in the world, please, am I going back to school?"

Transcribed here the speech sounds harmless enough, particularly as uttered in the sweet, high, casual pipe with which, at all interlocutors, but above all at his eternal governess, he threw off intonations as if he were tossing roses. There was something in them that always made one "catch," and I caught at any rate now so effectually that I stopped as short as if one of the trees of the park had fallen across the road. There was something new, on the spot, between us, and he was perfectly aware I recognised it, though to enable me to do so he had no need to look a whit less candid and charming than usual. I could feel in him how he already, from my at first finding nothing to reply, perceived the advantage he had gained. I was so slow to find anything that he had plenty of time, after a minute, to continue with his suggestive but inconclusive smile: "You know, my dear, that for a fellow to be with a lady *always* – !" His "my dear" was constantly on his lips for me, and nothing could have expressed more the exact shade of the sentiment with which I desired to inspire my pupils than its fond familiarity. It was so respectfully easy.

But oh how I felt that at present I must pick my own phrases! I remember that, to gain time, I tried to laugh, and I seemed to see in the beautiful face with which he watched me how ugly and queer I looked. "And always with the same lady?" I returned.

He neither blenched nor winked. The whole thing was virtually out between us. "Ah of course she's a jolly 'perfect' lady; but after all I'm a fellow, don't you see? who's – well, getting on."

I lingered there with him an instant ever so kindly. "Yes, you're getting on." Oh but I felt helpless!

I have kept to this day the heartbreaking little idea of how he seemed to know that and to play with it. "And you can't say I've not been awfully good, can you?"

I laid my hand on his shoulder, for though I felt how much better it would have been to walk on I was not yet quite able. "No, I can't say that, Miles."

"Except just that one night, you know – !"

"That one night?" I couldn't look as straight as he.

"Why when I went down – went out of the house."

"Oh yes. But I forget what you did it for."

"You forget?" – he spoke with the sweet extravagance of childish reproach. "Why it was just to show you I could!"

"Oh yes – you could."

"And I can again."

I felt I might perhaps after all succeed in keeping my wits about me. "Certainly. But you won't."

"No, not *that* again. It was nothing."

"It was nothing," I said. "But we must go on."

He resumed our walk with me, passing his hand into my arm. "Then when *am* I going back?"

I wore, in turning it over, my most responsible air. "Were you very happy at school?"

He just considered. "Oh I'm happy enough anywhere!"

"Well then," I quavered, "if you're just as happy here – !"

"Ah but that is n't everything! Of course *you* know a lot – "

"But you hint that you know almost as much?" I risked as he paused.

"Not half I want to!" Miles honestly professed. "But it is n't so much that."

"What is it then?"

"Well – I want to see more life."

"I see; I see." We had arrived within sight of the church and of various persons, including several of the household of Bly, on their way to it and clustered about the door to see us go in. I quickened our step; I wanted to get there before the question between us opened up much further; I reflected hungrily that he would have for more than an hour to be silent; and I thought with envy of the comparative dusk of the pew and of the almost spiritual help of the hassock on which I might bend my knees. I seemed literally to be running a race with some confusion to which he was about to reduce me, but I felt he had got in first when, before we had even entered the churchyard, he threw out –

"I want my own sort!"

It literally made me bound forward. "There are n't many of your own sort, Miles!" I laughed. "Unless perhaps dear little Flora!"

"You really compare me to a baby girl?"

This found me singularly weak. "Don't you then *love* our sweet Flora?"

"If I did n't – and you too; if I did n't – !" he repeated as if retreating for a jump, yet leaving his thought so unfinished that, after we had come into the gate, another stop, which he imposed on me by the pressure of his arm, had become inevitable. Mrs. Grose and Flora had passed into the church, the other worshippers had followed and we were, for the minute, alone among the old thick graves. We had paused, on the path from the gate, by a low oblong table-like tomb.

"Yes, if you did n't – ?"

He looked, while I waited, about at the graves.

"Well, you know what!" But he did n't move, and he presently produced something that made me drop straight down on the stone slab as if suddenly to rest. "Does my uncle think what *you* think?"

I markedly rested. "How do you know what I think?"

"Ah well, of course I don't; for it strikes me you never tell me. But I mean does *he* know?"

"Know what, Miles?"

"Why the way I'm going on."

I recognised quickly enough that I could make, to this enquiry, no answer that would n't involve something of a sacrifice of my employer. Yet it struck me that we were all, at Bly, sufficiently sacrificed to make that venial. "I don't think your uncle much cares."

Miles, on this, stood looking at me. "Then don't you think he can he made to?"

"In what way?"

"Why by his coming down."

"But who'll get him to come down?"

"*I* will!" the boy said with extraordinary brightness and emphasis. He gave me another look charged with that expression and then marched off alone into church.

XV

THE business was practically settled from the moment I never followed him. It was a pitiful surrender to agitation, but my being aware of this had somehow no power to restore me. I only sat there on my tomb and read into what our young friend had said to me the fulness of its meaning; by the time I had grasped the whole of which, I had also embraced, for absence, the pretext that I was ashamed to offer my pupils and the rest of the congregation such an example of delay. What I said to myself above all was that Miles had got something out of me and that the gage of it for him would be just this awkward collapse. He had got out of me that there was something I was much afraid of, and that he should probably be able to make use of my fear to gain, for his own purpose, more freedom. My fear was of having to deal with the intolerable question of the grounds of his dismissal from school, since that was really but the question of the horrors gathered behind. That his uncle should arrive to treat with me of these things was a solution that, strictly speaking, I ought now to have desired to bring on; but I could so little face the ugliness and the pain of it that I simply procrastinated and lived from hand to mouth. The boy, to my deep discomposure, was immensely in the right, was in a position to say to me: "Either you clear up with my guardian the mystery of this interruption of my studies, or you cease to expect me to lead with you a life that's so unnatural for a boy." What was so unnatural for the particular boy I was concerned with was this sudden revelation of a consciousness and a plan.

That was what really overcame me, what prevented my going in. I walked round the church, hesitating, hovering; I reflected that I had already, with him, hurt myself beyond repair. Therefore I could patch up nothing and it was too extreme an effort to squeeze beside him into the pew: he would be so much more sure than ever to pass his arm into mine and make me sit there for an hour in close mute contact with his commentary on our talk. For the first minute since his arrival I wanted to get away from him. As I paused beneath the high east window and listened to the sounds of worship I was taken with an impulse that might master me, I felt, and completely, should I give it the least encouragement. I might easily put an end to my ordeal by getting away altogether. Here was my chance; there was no one to stop me; I could give the whole thing up – turn my back and bolt. It was only a question of hurrying again, for a few preparations, to the house which the attendance at church of so many of the servants would practically have left unoccupied. No one, in short, could blame me if I should just drive desperately off. What was it to get away if I should get away only till dinner? That would be in a couple of hours, at the end of which – I had the acute prevision – my little pupils would play at innocent wonder about my non-appearance in their train.

"What *did* you do, you naughty bad thing? Why in the world, to worry us so – and take our thoughts off too, don't you know? – did you desert us at the very door?" I couldn't meet such questions nor, as they asked them, their false little lovely eyes; yet it was all so exactly what I should have to meet that, as the prospect grew sharp to me, I at last let myself go.

I got, so far as the immediate moment was concerned, away; I came straight out of the churchyard and, thinking hard, retraced my steps through the park. It seemed to me that by the time I reached the house I had made up my mind to cynical flight. The Sunday stillness both of the approaches and of the interior, in which I met no one, fairly stirred me with a sense of opportunity. Were I to get off quickly this way I should get off without a scene, without a word. My quickness would have to be remarkable, however, and the question of a conveyance was the great one to settle. Tormented, in the hall, with difficulties and obstacles, I remember sinking down at the foot of the staircase – suddenly collapsing there on the lowest step and then, with a revulsion, recalling that it was exactly where, more than a month before, in the darkness of night and just so bowed with evil things, I had seen the spectre of the most horrible of women. At this I was able to straighten myself; I went the rest of the way up; I made, in my turmoil, for the schoolroom, where there were objects belonging to me that I should have to take. But I opened the door to find again, in a flash, my eyes unsealed. In the presence of what I saw I reeled straight back upon resistance.

Seated at my own table in the clear noonday light I saw a person whom, without my previous experience, I should have taken at the first blush for some housemaid who might have stayed at home to look after the place and who, availing herself of rare relief from observation and of the schoolroom table and my pens, ink and paper, had applied herself to the considerable effort of a letter to her sweetheart. There was an effort in the way that, while her arms rested on the table, her hands, with evident weariness, supported her head; but at the moment I took this in I had already become aware that, in spite of my entrance, her attitude strangely persisted. Then it was – with the very act of its announcing itself – that her identity flared up in a change of posture. She rose, not as if she had heard me, but with an indescribable grand melancholy of indifference and detachment, and, within a dozen feet of me, stood there as my vile predecessor. Dishonoured and tragic, she was all before me; but even as I fixed and, for memory, secured it, the awful image passed away. Dark as midnight in her black dress, her haggard beauty and her unutterable woe, she had looked at me long enough to appear to say that her right to sit at my table was as good as mine to sit at hers. While these instants lasted indeed I had the extraordinary chill of a feeling that it was I who was the intruder. It was as a wild protest against it that, actually addressing her – "You terrible miserable woman!" – I heard myself break into a sound that, by the open door, rang through the long passage and the empty house. She looked at me as if she heard me, but I had recovered myself and cleared the air. There was nothing in the room the next minute but the sunshine and the sense that I must stay.

XVI

I HAD so perfectly expected the return of the others to be marked by a demonstration that I was freshly upset at having to find them merely dumb and discreet about my desertion. Instead of gaily denouncing and caressing me they made no allusion to my having failed them, and I was left, for the time, on perceiving that she too said nothing, to study Mrs. Grose's odd face. I did this to such purpose that I made sure they had in some way bribed her to silence; a silence that, however, I would engage to break down on the first private opportunity. This opportunity came before tea: I secured five minutes with her in the housekeeper's room, where, in the twilight, amid a smell of lately-baked bread, but with the place all swept and garnished, I found her sitting in pained placidity before the fire. So I see her still, so I see her best: facing the flame from her straight chair in the dusky shining room, a large clean picture of the "put away" – of drawers closed and locked and rest without a remedy.

"Oh yes, they asked me to say nothing; and to please them – so long as they were there – of course I promised. But what had happened to you?"

"I only went with you for the walk," I said. "I had then to come back to meet a friend."

She showed her surprise. "A friend – *you*?"

"Oh yes, I've a couple!" I laughed. "But did the children give you a reason?"

"For not alluding to your leaving us? Yes; they said you'd like it better. Do you like it better?"

My face had made her rueful. "No, I like it worse!" But after an instant I added: "Did they say why I should like it better?"

"No; Master Miles only said 'We must do nothing but what she likes!'"

"I wish indeed he would! And what did Flora say?"

"Miss Flora was too sweet. She said 'Oh of course, of course!' – and I said the same."

I thought a moment. "You were too sweet too – I can hear you all. But none the less, between Miles and me, it's now all out."

"All out?" My companion stared. "But what, Miss?"

"Everything. It does n't matter. I've made up my mind. I came home, my dear," I went on, "for a talk with Miss Jessel."

I had by this time formed the habit of having Mrs. Grose literally well in hand in advance of my sounding that note; so that even now, as she bravely blinked under the signal of my word, I could keep her comparatively firm. "A talk? Do you mean she spoke!"

"It came to that. I found her, on my return, in the schoolroom."

"And what did she say?" I can hear the good woman still, and the candour of her stupefaction.

"That she suffers the torments – !"

It was this, of a truth, that made her, as she filled out my picture, gape. "Do you mean," she faltered " – of the lost?"

"Of the lost. Of the damned. And that's why, to share them – " I faltered myself with the horror of it.

But my companion, with less imagination, kept me up. "To share them – ?"

"She wants Flora." Mrs. Grose might, as I gave it to her, fairly have fallen away from me had I not been prepared. I still held her there, to show I was. "As I've told you, however, it does n't matter."

"Because you've made up your mind? But to what?"

"To everything."

"And what do you call 'everything'?"

"Why to sending for their uncle."

"Oh Miss, in pity do," my friend broke out.

"Ah but I will, I *will*! I see it's the only way. What's 'out,' as I told you, with Miles is that if he thinks I'm afraid to – and has ideas of what he gains by that – he shall see he's mistaken. Yes, yes; his uncle shall have it here from me on the spot (and before the boy himself if necessary) that if I'm to be reproached with having done nothing again about more school – "

"Yes, Miss – " my companion pressed me.

"Well, there's that awful reason."

There were now clearly so many of these for my poor colleague that she was excusable for being vague. "But – a – which?"

"Why the letter from his old place."

"You'll show it to the master?"

"I ought to have done so on the instant."

"Oh no!" said Mrs. Grose with decision.

"I'll put it before him," I went on inexorably, "that I can't undertake to work the question on behalf of a child who has been expelled – "

"For we've never in the least known what!" Mrs. Grose declared.

"For wickedness. For what else – when he's so clever and beautiful and perfect? Is he stupid? Is he untidy? Is he infirm? Is he ill-natured? He's exquisite – so it can be only *that*; and that would open up the whole thing. After all," I said, "it's their uncle's fault. If he left here such people – !"

"He did n't really in the least know them. The fault's mine." She had turned quite pale.

"Well, you shan't suffer," I answered.

"The children shan't!" she emphatically returned.

I was silent a while; we looked at each other. "Then what am I to tell him?"

"You need n't tell him anything. *I'll* tell him."

I measured this. "Do you mean you'll write – ?" Remembering she could n't, I caught myself up. "How do you communicate?"

"I tell the bailiff. *He* writes."

"And should you like him to write our story?" My question had a sarcastic force that I had not fully intended, and it made her after a moment inconsequently break down. The tears were again in her eyes. "Ah Miss, *you* write!"

"Well – to-night," I at last returned; and on this we separated.

XVII

I WENT so far, in the evening, as to make a beginning. The weather had changed back, a great wind was abroad, and beneath the lamp, in my room, with Flora at peace beside me, I sat for a long time before a blank sheet of paper and listened to the lash of the rain and the batter of the gusts. Finally I went out, taking a candle; I crossed the passage and listened a minute at Miles's door. What, under my endless obsession, I had been impelled to listen for was some betrayal of his not being at rest, and I presently caught one, but not in the form I had expected. His voice tinkled out. "I say, you there – come in." It was gaiety in the gloom!

I went in with my light and found him in bed, very wide awake but very much at his ease. "Well, what are *you* up to?" he asked with a grace of sociability in which it occurred to me that Mrs. Grose, had she been present, might have looked in vain for proof that anything was "out."

I stood over him with my candle. "How did you know I was there?"

"Why of course I heard you. Did you fancy you made no noise? You're like a troop of cavalry!" he beautifully laughed.

"Then you were n't asleep?"

"Not much! I lie awake and think."

I had put my candle, designedly, a short way off, and then, as he held out his friendly old hand to me, had sat down on the edge of his bed. "What is it," I asked, "that you think of?"

"What in the world, my dear, but *you*?"

"Ah the pride I take in your appreciation does n't insist on that! I had so far rather you slept."

"Well, I think also, you know, of this queer business of ours."

I marked the coolness of his firm little hand. "Of what queer business, Miles?"

"Why the way you bring me up. And all the rest!"

I fairly held my breath a minute, and even from my glimmering taper there was light enough to show how he smiled up at me from his pillow. "What do you mean by all the rest?"

"Oh you know, you know!"

I could say nothing for a minute, though I felt as I held his hand and our eyes continued to meet that my silence had all the air of admitting his charge and that nothing in the whole world of reality was perhaps at that moment so fabulous as our actual relation. "Certainly you shall go back to school," I said, "if it be that that troubles you. But not to the old place – we must find another, a better. How could I know it did trouble you, this question, when you never told me so, never spoke of it at all?" His clear listening face, framed in its smooth whiteness, made him for the minute as appealing as some wistful patient in a children's hospital; and I would have given, as the resemblance came to me, all I possessed on earth really to be the nurse or the sister of charity who might have helped to cure him. Well, even as it was I perhaps might help! "Do you know you've never said a word to me about your school – I mean the old one; never mentioned it in any way?"

He seemed to wonder; he smiled with the same loveliness. But he clearly gained time; he waited, he called for guidance. "Have n't I?" It was n't for *me* to help him – it was for the thing I had met!

Something in his tone and the expression of his face, as I got this from him, set my heart aching with such a pang as it had never yet known; so unutterably touching was it to see his little brain puzzled and his little resources taxed to play, under the spell laid on him, a part of innocence and consistency. "No, never – from the hour you came back. You've never mentioned to me one of your masters, one of your comrades, nor the least little thing that ever happened to you at school. Never, little Miles – no never – have you given me an inkling of anything that *may* have happened there. Therefore you can fancy how much I'm in the dark. Until you came out, that way, this morning, you had since the first hour I saw you scarce even made a reference to anything in your previous life. You seemed so perfectly to accept the present." It was extraordinary how my absolute conviction of his secret precocity – or whatever I might call the poison of an influence that I dared but half-phrase – made him, in spite of the faint breath of his inward trouble, appear as accessible as an older person, forced me to treat him as an intelligent equal. "I thought you wanted to go on as you are."

It struck me that at this he just faintly coloured. He gave, at any rate, like a convalescent slightly fatigued, a languid shake of his head. "I don't – I don't. I want to get away."

"You're tired of Bly?"

"Oh no, I like Bly."

"Well then – ?"

"Oh *you* know what a boy wants!"

I felt I did n't know so well as Miles, and I took temporary refuge. "You want to go to your uncle?"

Again, at this, with his sweet ironic face, he made a movement on the pillow. "Ah you can't get off with that!"

I was silent a little, and it was I now, I think, who changed colour. "My dear, I don't want to get off!"

"You can't even if you do. You can't, you can't!" – he lay beautifully staring. "My uncle must come down and you must completely settle things."

"If we do," I returned with some spirit, "you may be sure it will be to take you quite away."

"Well, don't you understand that that's exactly what I'm working for? You'll have to *tell* him about the way you've let it all drop: you'll have to tell him a tremendous lot!"

The exultation with which he uttered this helped me somehow for the instant to meet him rather more. "And how much will *you*, Miles, have to tell him? There are things he'll ask you!"

He turned it over. "Very likely. But what things?"

"The things you've never told me. To make up his mind what to do with you. He can't send you back – "

"I don't want to go back!" he broke in. "I want a new field."

He said it with admirable serenity, with positive unimpeachable gaiety; and doubtless it was that very note that most evoked for me the poignancy, the unnatural childish tragedy, of his probable reappearance at the end of three months with all this bravado and still more dishonour. It overwhelmed me now that I should never be able to bear that, and it made me let myself go. I threw myself upon him and in the tenderness of my pity I embraced him. "Dear little Miles, dear little Miles – !"

My face was close to his, and he let me kiss him, simply taking it with indulgent good humour. "Well, old lady?"

"Is there nothing – nothing at all that you want to tell me?"

He turned off a little, facing round toward the wall and holding up his hand to look at as one had seen sick children look. "I've told you – I told you this morning."

Oh I was sorry for him! "That you just want me not to worry you?"

He looked round at me now as if in recognition of my understanding him; then ever so gently, "To let me alone," he replied.

There was even a strange little dignity in it, something that made me release him, yet, when I had slowly risen, linger beside him. God knows I never wished to harass him, but I felt that merely, at this, to turn my back on him was to abandon or, to put it more truly, lose him. "I've just begun a letter to your uncle," I said.

"Well then, finish it!"

I waited a minute. "What happened before?"

He gazed up at me again. "Before what?"

"Before you came back. And before you went away."

For some time he was silent, but he continued to meet my eyes. "What happened?"

It made me, the sound of the words, in which it seemed to me I caught for the very first time a small faint quaver of consenting consciousness – it made me drop on my knees beside the bed and seize once more the chance of possessing him. "Dear little Miles, dear little Miles, if you *knew* how I want to help you! It's only that, it's nothing but that, and I'd rather die than give you a pain or do you a wrong – I'd rather die than hurt a hair of you. Dear little Miles" – oh I brought it out now even if I *should* go too far – "I just want you to help me to save you!" But I knew in a moment after this that I had gone too far. The answer to my appeal was instantaneous, but it came in the form of an extraordinary blast and chill, a gust of frozen air and a shake of the room as great as if, in the wild wind, the casement had crashed in. The boy gave a loud high shriek which, lost in the rest of the shock of sound, might have seemed, indistinctly, though I was so close to him, a note either of jubilation or of terror. I jumped to my feet again and was conscious of darkness. So for a moment we remained, while I stared about me and saw the drawn curtains unstirred and the window still tight. "Why the candle's out!" I then cried.

"It was I who blew it, dear!" said Miles.

XVIII

THE next day, after lessons, Mrs. Grose found a moment to say to me quietly: "Have you written, Miss?"

"Yes – I've written." But I did n't add – for the hour – that my letter, sealed and directed, was still in my pocket. There would be time enough to send it before the messenger should go to the village. Meanwhile there had been on the part of my pupils no more brilliant, more exemplary morning. It was exactly as if they had both had at heart to gloss over any recent little friction. They performed the dizziest feats of arithmetic, soaring quite out of *my* feeble range, and perpetrated, in higher spirits than ever, geographical and historical jokes. It was conspicuous of course in Miles in particular that he appeared to wish to show how easily he could let me down. This child, to my memory, really lives in a setting of beauty and misery that no words can translate; there was a distinction all his own in every impulse he revealed; never was a small natural creature, to the uninformed eye all frankness and freedom, a more ingenious, a more extraordinary little gentleman. I had perpetually to guard against the wonder of contemplation into which my initiated view betrayed me; to check the irrelevant gaze and discouraged sigh in which I constantly both attacked and renounced the enigma of what such a little gentleman could have done that deserved a penalty. Say that, by the dark prodigy I knew, the imagination of all evil *had* been opened up to him: all the justice within me ached for the proof that it could ever have flowered into an act.

He had never at any rate been such a little gentleman as when, after our early dinner on this dreadful day, he came round to me and asked if I should n't like him for half an hour to play to me. David playing to Saul[7] could never have shown a finer sense of the occasion. It was literally a charming exhibition of tact, of magnanimity, and quite tantamount to his saying outright: "The true knights we love to read about never push an advantage too far. I know what you mean now: you mean that – to be let alone yourself and not followed up – you'll cease to worry and spy upon me, won't keep me so close to you, will let me go and come. Well, I 'come,' you see – but I don't go! There'll be plenty of time for that. I do really delight in your society and I only want to show you that I contended for a principle." It may be imagined whether I resisted this appeal or failed to accompany him again, hand in hand, to the schoolroom. He sat down at the old piano and played as he had never played; and if there are those who think he had better have been kicking a football I can only say that I wholly agree with them. For at the end of a time that under his influence I had quite ceased to measure I started up with a strange sense of having literally slept at my post. It was after luncheon, and by the schoolroom fire, and yet I had n't really in the least slept; I had only done something much worse – I had forgotten. Where all this time was Flora? When I put the question to Miles he played on a minute before answering, and then could only say: "Why, my dear, how do *I* know?" – breaking moreover into a happy laugh which immediately after, as if it were a vocal accompaniment, he prolonged into incoherent extravagant song.

I went straight to my room, but his sister was not there; then, before going downstairs, I looked into several others. As she was nowhere about she would surely be with Mrs. Grose, whom in the comfort of that theory I accordingly proceeded in quest of. I found her where I had found her the evening before, but she met my quick challenge

Notes

[7] See 1 Samuel 16. Young David (later king) plays his lyre for King Saul, who is troubled by an "evil spirit."

with blank scared ignorance. She had only supposed that, after the repast, I had carried off both the children; as to which she was quite in her right, for it was the very first time I had allowed the little girl out of my sight without some special provision. Of course now indeed she might be with the maids, so that the immediate thing was to look for her without an air of alarm. This we promptly arranged between us; but when, ten minutes later and in pursuance of our arrangement, we met in the hall, it was only to report on either side that after guarded enquiries we had altogether failed to trace her. For a minute there, apart from observation, we exchanged mute alarms, and I could feel with what high interest my friend returned me all those I had from the first given her.

"She'll be above," she presently said – "in one of the rooms you have n't searched."

"No; she's at a distance." I had made up my mind. "She has gone out."

Mrs. Grose stared. "Without a hat?"

I naturally also looked volumes. "Is n't that woman always without one?"

"She's with *her*?"

"She's with *her*!" I declared. "We must find them."

My hand was on my friend's arm, but she failed for the moment, confronted with such an account of the matter, to respond to my pressure. She communed, on the contrary, where she stood, with her uneasiness. "And where's Master Miles?"

"Oh *he's* with Quint. They'll be in the schoolroom."

"Lord, Miss!" My view, I was myself aware – and therefore I suppose my tone – had never yet reached so calm an assurance.

"The trick's played," I went on; "they've successfully worked their plan. He found the most divine little way to keep me quiet while she went off."

"'Divine'?" Mrs. Grose bewilderedly echoed.

"Infernal then!" I almost cheerfully rejoined. "He has provided for himself as well. But come!"

She had helplessly gloomed at the upper regions. "You leave him – ?"

"So long with Quint? Yes – I don't mind that now."

She always ended at these moments by getting possession of my hand, and in this manner she could at present still stay me. But after gasping an instant at my sudden resignation, "Because of your letter?" she eagerly brought out.

I quickly, by way of answer, felt for my letter, drew it forth, held it up, and then, freeing myself, went and laid it on the great hall-table. "Luke will take it," I said as I came back. I reached the house-door and opened it; I was already on the steps.

My companion still demurred: the storm of the night and the early morning had dropped, but the afternoon was damp and grey. I came down to the drive while she stood in the doorway. "You go with nothing on?"

"What do I care when the child has nothing? I can't wait to dress," I cried, "and if you must do so I leave you. Try meanwhile yourself upstairs."

"With *them*?" Oh on this the poor woman promptly joined me!

XIX

WE went straight to the lake, as it was called at Bly, and I dare say rightly called, though it may have been a sheet of water less remarkable than my untravelled eyes supposed it. My acquaintance with sheets of water was small, and the pool of Bly, at all events on the few occasions of my consenting, under the protection of my pupils, to affront its surface in the old flat-bottomed boat moored there for our use, had impressed me both with its extent and its agitation. The usual place of embarkation was half a mile from the house, but I had an intimate conviction that, wherever Flora might be, she was not near home. She had not given me the slip for any small adventure, and, since the day of the very great one that I had shared with her by the pond, I had been aware, in our walks, of the quarter to which she most inclined. This was why I had now given to Mrs. Grose's steps so marked a direction – a direction making her, when she perceived it, oppose a resistance that showed me she was freshly mystified. "You're going to the water, Miss? – you think she's *in* – ?"

"She may be, though the depth is, I believe, nowhere very great. But what I judge most likely is that she's on the spot from which, the other day, we saw together what I told you."

"When she pretended not to see – ?"

"With that astounding self-possession! I've always been sure she wanted to go back alone. And now her brother has managed it for her."

Mrs. Grose still stood where she had stopped. "You suppose they really *talk* of them?"

I could meet this with an assurance! "They say things that, if we heard them, would simply appal us."

"And if she *is* there – ?"

"Yes?"

"Then Miss Jessel is?"

"Beyond a doubt. You shall see."

"Oh thank you!" my friend cried, planted so firm that, taking it in, I went straight on without her. By the time I reached the pool, however, she was close behind me, and I knew that, whatever, to her apprehension, might befall me, the exposure of sticking to me struck her as her least danger. She exhaled a moan of relief as we at last came in sight of the greater part of the water without a sight of the child. There was no trace of Flora on that nearer side of the bank where my observation of her had been most startling, and none on the opposite edge, where, save for a margin of some twenty yards, a thick copse came down to the pond. This expanse, oblong in shape, was so narrow compared to its length that, with its ends out of view, it might have been taken for a scant river. We looked at the empty stretch, and then I felt the suggestion in my friend's eyes. I knew what she meant and I replied with a negative headshake.

"No, no; wait! She has taken the boat."

My companion stared at the vacant mooring-place and then again across the lake. "Then where is it?"

"Our not seeing it is the strongest of proofs. She has used it to go over, and then has managed to hide it."

"All alone – that child?"

"She's not alone, and at such times she's not a child: she's an old, old woman." I scanned all the visible shore while Mrs. Grose took again, into the queer element I offered her, one of her plunges of submission; then I pointed out that the boat might perfectly be in a small refuge formed by one of the recesses of the pool, an indentation masked, for the hither side, by a projection of the bank and by a clump of trees growing close to the water.

"But if the boat's there, where on earth's *she*?" my colleague anxiously asked.

"That's exactly what we must learn." And I started to walk further.

"By going all the way round?"

"Certainly, far as it is. It will take us but ten minutes, yet it's far enough to have made the child prefer not to walk. She went straight over."

"Laws!" cried my friend again: the chain of my logic was ever too strong for her. It dragged her at my heels even now, and when we had got halfway round – a devious tiresome process, on ground much broken and by a path choked with overgrowth –

I paused to give her breath. I sustained her with a grateful arm, assuring her that she might hugely help me; and this started us afresh, so that in the course of but few minutes more we reached a point from which we found the boat to be where I had supposed it. It had been intentionally left as much as possible out of sight and was tied to one of the stakes of a fence that came, just there, down to the brink and that had been an assistance to disembarking. I recognised, as I looked at the pair of short thick oars, quite safely drawn up, the prodigious character of the feat for a little girl; but I had by this time lived too long among wonders and had panted to too many livelier measures. There was a gate in the fence, through which we passed, and that brought us after a trifling interval more into the open. Then "There she is!" we both exclaimed at once.

Flora, a short way off, stood before us on the grass and smiled as if her performance had now become complete. The next thing she did, however, was to stoop straight down and pluck – quite as if it were all she was there for – a big ugly spray of withered fern. I at once felt sure she had just come out of the copse. She waited for us, not herself taking a step, and I was conscious of the rare solemnity with which we presently approached her. She smiled and smiled, and we met; but it was all done in a silence by this time fragrantly ominous. Mrs. Grose was the first to break the spell: she threw herself on her knees and, drawing the child to her breast, clasped in a long embrace the little tender yielding body. While this dumb convulsion lasted I could only watch it – which I did the more intently when I saw Flora's face peep at me over our companion's shoulder. It was serious now – the flicker had left it; but it strengthened the pang with which I at that moment envied Mrs. Grose the simplicity of *her* relation. Still, all this while, nothing more passed between us save that Flora had let her foolish fern again drop to the ground. What she and I had virtually said to each other was that pretexts were useless now. When Mrs. Grose finally got up she kept the child's hand, so that the two were still before me; and the singular reticence of our communion was even more marked in the frank look she addressed me. "I'll be hanged," it said, "if *I'll* speak!"

It was Flora who, gazing allover me in candid wonder, was the first. She was struck with our bareheaded aspect. "Why where are your things?"

"Where yours are, my dear!" I promptly returned. She had already got back her gaiety and appeared to take this as an answer quite sufficient. "And where's Miles?" she went on.

There was something in the small valour of it that quite finished me: these three words from her were in a flash like the glitter of a drawn blade, the jostle of the cup that my hand for weeks and weeks had held high and full to the brim and that now, even before speaking, I felt overflow in a deluge. "I'll tell you if you'll tell *me* – " I heard myself say, then heard the tremor in which it broke.

"Well, what?"

Mrs. Grose's suspense blazed at me, but it was too late now, and I brought the thing out handsomely. "Where, my pet, is Miss Jessel ?"

XX

JUST as in the churchyard with Miles, the whole thing was upon us. Much as I had made of the fact that this name had never once, between us, been sounded, the quick smitten glare with which the child's face now received it fairly likened my breach of the silence to the smash of a pane of glass. It added to the interposing cry, as if to stay the blow, that Mrs. Grose at the same instant uttered over my violence – the shriek of a creature scared, or rather wounded, which, in turn, within a few seconds, was completed by a gasp of my own. I seized my colleague's arm. "She's there, she's there!"

Miss Jessel stood before us on the opposite bank exactly as she had stood the other time, and I remember, strangely, as the first feeling now produced in me, my thrill of joy at having brought on a proof. She was there, so I was justified; she was there, so I was neither cruel nor mad. She was there for poor scared Mrs. Grose, but she was there most for Flora; and no moment of my monstrous time was perhaps so extraordinary as that in which I consciously threw out to her – with the sense that, pale and ravenous demon as she was, she would catch and understand it – an inarticulate message of gratitude. She rose erect on the spot my friend and I had lately quitted, and there was n't in all the long reach of her desire an inch of her evil that fell short. This first vividness of vision and emotion were things of a few seconds, during which Mrs. Grose's dazed blink across to where I pointed struck me as showing that she too at last saw, just as it carried my own eyes precipitately to the child. The revelation then of the manner in which Flora was affected startled me in truth far more than it would have done to find her also merely agitated, for direct dismay was of course not what I had expected. Prepared and on her guard as our pursuit had actually made her, she would repress every betrayal; and I was therefore at once shaken by my first glimpse of the particular one for which I had not allowed. To see her, without a convulsion of her small pink face, not even feign to glance in the direction of the prodigy I announced, but only, instead of that, turn at *me* an expression of hard still gravity, an expression absolutely new and unprecedented and that appeared to read and accuse and judge me – this was a stroke that somehow converted the little girl herself into a figure portentous. I gaped at her coolness even though my certitude of her thoroughly seeing was never greater than at that instant, and then, in the immediate need to defend myself, I called her passionately to witness. "She's there, you little unhappy thing – there, there, *there*, and you know it as well as you know me!" I had said shortly before to Mrs. Grose that she was not at these times a child, but an old, old woman, and my description of her could n't have been more strikingly confirmed than in the way in which, for all notice of this, she simply showed me, without an expressional concession or admission, a countenance of deeper and deeper, of indeed suddenly quite fixed reprobation. I was by this time – if I can put the whole thing at all together – more appalled at what I may properly call her manner than at anything else, though it was quite simultaneously that I became aware of having Mrs. Grose also, and very formidably, to reckon with. My elder companion, the next moment, at any rate, blotted out everything but her own flushed face and her loud shocked protest, a burst of high disapproval. "What a dreadful turn, to be sure, Miss! Where on earth do you see anything?"

I could only grasp her more quickly yet, for even while she spoke the hideous plain presence stood undimmed and undaunted, It had already lasted a minute, and it lasted while I continued, seizing my colleague, quite thrusting her at it and presenting her to it, to insist with my pointing hand. "You don't see her exactly as *we* see? – you mean to say you don't now – *now*? She's as big as a blazing fire! Only look, dearest woman, *look* – !" She looked, just as I did, and gave me, with her deep groan of negation, repulsion, compassion – the mixture with her pity of her relief at her exemption – a sense, touching to me even then, that she would have backed me up if she had been able. I might well have needed that, for with this hard blow of the proof that her eyes were hopelessly sealed I felt my own situation horribly crumble, I felt – I *saw* – my livid predecessor press, from her position, on my defeat, and I took the measure, more than all, of what I should have from this instant to deal with in the astounding little attitude of Flora. Into this attitude Mrs. Grose immediately and violently entered, breaking, even while there pierced through my sense of ruin a prodigious private triumph, into breathless reassurance.

"She is n't there, little lady, and nobody's there – and you never see nothing, my sweet! How can poor Miss Jessel – when poor Miss Jessel's dead and buried? *We* know, don't we, love?" – and she appealed, blundering in, to the child. "It's all a mere mistake and a worry and a joke – and we'll go home as fast as we can!"

Our companion, on this, had responded with a strange quick primness of propriety, and they were again, with Mrs. Grose on her feet, united, as it were, in shocked opposition to me. Flora continued to fix me with her small mask of disaffection, and even at that minute I prayed God to forgive me for seeming to see that, as she stood there holding tight to our friend's dress, her incomparable childish beauty had suddenly failed, had quite vanished. I've said it already – she was literally, she was hideously hard; she had turned common and almost ugly. "I don't know what you mean. I see nobody. I see nothing. I never *have*. I think you're cruel. I don't like you!" Then, after this deliverance, which might have been that of a vulgarly pert little girl in the street, she hugged Mrs. Grose more closely and buried in her skirts the dreadful little face. In this position she launched an almost furious wail. "Take me away, take me away – oh take me away from *her*!"

"From *me*?" I panted.

"From you – from you!" she cried.

Even Mrs. Grose looked across at me dismayed; while I had nothing to do but communicate again with the figure that, on the opposite bank, without a movement, as rigidly still as if catching, beyond the interval, our voices, was as vividly there for my disaster as it was not there for my service. The wretched child had spoken exactly as if she had got from some outside source each of her stabbing little words, and I could therefore, in the full despair of all I had to accept, but sadly shake my head at her. "If I had ever doubted all my doubt would at present have gone. I've been living with the miserable truth, and now it has only too much closed round me. Of course I've lost you: I've interfered, and you've seen, under *her* dictation" – with which I faced, over the pool again, our infernal witness – "the easy and perfect way to meet it. I've done my best, but I've lost you. Goodbye." For Mrs. Grose I had an imperative, an almost frantic "Go, go!" before which, in infinite distress, but mutely possessed of the little girl and clearly convinced, in spite of her blindness, that something awful had occurred and some collapse engulfed us, she retreated, by the way we had come, as fast as she could move.

Of what first happened when I was left alone I had no subsequent memory. I only knew that at the end of, I suppose, a quarter of an hour, an odorous dampness and roughness, chilling and piercing my trouble, had made me understand that I must have thrown myself, on my face, to the ground and given way to a wildness of grief. I must have lain there long and cried and wailed, for when I raised my head the day was almost done. I got up and looked a moment, through the twilight, at the grey pool and its blank haunted edge, and then I took, back to the house, my dreary and difficult course. When I reached the gate in the fence the boat, to my surprise, was gone, so that I had a fresh reflexion to make on Flora's extraordinary command of the situation. She passed that night, by the most tacit and, I should add, were not the word so grotesque a false note, the happiest of arrangements, with Mrs. Grose. I saw neither of them on my return, but on the other hand I saw, as by an ambiguous compensation, a great deal of Miles. I saw – I can use no other phrase – so much of him that it fairly measured more than it had ever measured. No evening I had passed at Bly was to have had the portentous quality of this one; in spite of which – and in spite also of the deeper depths of consternation that had opened beneath my feet – there was literally, in the ebbing actual, an extraordinarily sweet sadness. On reaching the house I had never so much as looked for the boy; I had simply gone straight to my room to change what I was wearing and to take in, at a glance, much material testimony to Flora's rupture. Her little belongings had all been removed. When later, by the schoolroom fire, I was served with tea by the usual maid, I indulged, on the article of my other pupil, in no enquiry whatever. He had his freedom now – he might have it to the end! Well, he did have it; and it consisted – in part at least – of his coming in at about eight o'clock and sitting down with me in silence. On the removal of the tea-things I had blown out the candles and drawn my chair closer: I was conscious of a mortal coldness and felt as if I should never again be warm. So when he appeared I was sitting in the glow with my thoughts. He paused a moment by the door as if to look at me; then – as if to share them – came to the other side of the hearth and sank into a chair. We sat there in absolute stillness; yet he wanted, I felt, to be with me.

XXI

BEFORE a new day, in my room, had fully broken, my eyes opened to Mrs. Grose, who had come to my bedside with worse news. Flora was so markedly feverish that an illness was perhaps at hand; she had passed a night of extreme unrest, a night agitated above all by fears that had for their subject not in the least her former but wholly her present governess. It was not against the possible re-entrance of Miss Jessel on the scene that she protested – it was conspicuously and passionately against mine. I was at once on my feet, and with an immense deal to ask; the more that my friend had discernibly now girded her loins to meet me afresh. This I felt as soon as I had put to her the question of her sense of the child's sincerity as against my own. "She persists in denying to you that she saw, or has ever seen, anything?"

My visitor's trouble truly was great. "Ah Miss, it is n't a matter on which I can push her! Yet it is n't either, I must say, as if I much needed to. It has made her, every inch of her, quite old."

"Oh I see her perfectly from here. She resents, for all the world like some high little personage, the imputation on her truthfulness and, as it were, her respectability. 'Miss Jessel indeed – she!' Ah she's 'respectable,' the chit! The impression she gave me there yesterday was, I assure you, the very strangest of all: it was quite beyond any of the others. I did put my foot in it! She'll never speak to me again."

Hideous and obscure as it all was, it held Mrs. Grose briefly silent; then she granted my point with a frankness which, I made sure, had more behind it. "I think indeed, Miss, she never will. She do have a grand manner about it!"

"And that manner" – I summed it up – "is practically what's the matter with her now."

Oh that manner, I could see in my visitor's face, and not a little else besides! "She asks me every three minutes if I think you're coming in."

"I see – I see." I too, on my side, had so much more than worked it out. "Has she said to you since yesterday – except to repudiate her familiarity with anything so dreadful – a single other word about Miss Jessel?"

"Not one, Miss. And of course, you know," my friend added, "I took it from her by the lake that just then and there at least there was nobody."

"Rather! And naturally you take it from her still."

"I don't contradict her. What else can I do?"

"Nothing in the world! You've the cleverest little person to deal with. They've made them – their two friends, I mean – still cleverer even than nature did; for it was wondrous material to play on! Flora has now her grievance, and she'll work it to the end."

"Yes, Miss; but to what end?"

"Why that of dealing with me to her uncle. She'll make me out to him the lowest creature – !"

I winced at the fair show of the scene in Mrs. Grose's face; she looked for a minute as if she sharply saw them together. "And him who thinks so well of you!"

"He has an odd way – it comes over me now," I laughed, "– of proving it! But that does n't matter. What Flora wants of course is to get rid of me."

My companion bravely concurred. "Never again to so much as look at you."

"So that what you've come to me now for," I asked, "is to speed me on my way?" Before she had time to reply, however, I had her in check. "I've a better idea – the result of my reflexions. My going *would* seem the right thing, and on Sunday I was terribly near it. Yet that won't do. It's *you* who must go. You must take Flora."

My visitor, at this, did speculate. "But where in the world – ?"

"Away from here. Away from *them*. Away, even most of all, now, from me. Straight to her uncle."

"Only to tell on you – ?"

"No, not 'only'! To leave me, in addition, with my remedy."

She was still vague. "And what *is* your remedy?"

"Your loyalty, to begin with. And then Miles's."

She looked at me hard. "Do you think he – ?"

"Won't, if he has the chance, turn on me? Yes, I venture still to think it. At all events I want to try. Get off with his sister as soon as possible and leave me with him alone." I was amazed, myself, at the spirit I had still in reserve, and therefore perhaps a trifle the more disconcerted at the way in which, in spite of this fine example of it, she hesitated. "There's one thing, of course," I went on: "they must n't, before she goes, see each other for three seconds." Then it came over me that, in spite of Flora's presumable sequestration from the instant of her return from the pool, it might already be too late. "Do you mean," I anxiously asked, "that they *have* met?"

At this she quite flushed. "Ah, Miss, I'm not such a fool as that! If I've been obliged to leave her three or four times, it has been each time with one of the maids, and at present, though she's alone, she's locked in safe. And yet –and yet!" There were too many things.

"And yet what?"

"Well, are you so sure of the little gentleman?"

"I'm not sure of anything but *you*. But I have, since last evening, a new hope. I think he wants to give me an opening. I do believe that – poor little exquisite wretch! – he wants to speak. Last evening, in the firelight and the silence, he sat with me for two hours as if it were just coming."

Mrs. Grose looked hard through the window at the grey gathering day. "And did it come?"

"No, though I waited and waited I confess it did n't, and it was without a breach of the silence, or so much as a faint allusion to his sister's condition and absence, that we at last kissed for good-night. All the same," I continued, "I can't, if her uncle sees her, consent to his seeing her brother without my having given the boy – and most of all because things have got so bad – a little more time."

My friend appeared on this ground more reluctant than I could quite understand. "What do you mean by more time?"

"Well, a day or two – really to bring it out. He'll then be on *my* side – of which you see the importance. If nothing comes I shall only fail, and you at the worst have helped me by doing on your arrival in town whatever you may have found possible." So I put it before her, but she continued for a little so lost in other reasons that I came again to her aid. "Unless indeed," I wound up, "you really want *not* to go."

I could see it, in her face, at last clear itself: she put out her hand to me as a pledge. "I'll go – I'll go. I'll go this morning."

I wanted to be very just. "If you *should* wish still to wait I'd engage she should n't see me."

"No, no: it's the place itself. She must leave it."

She held me a moment with heavy eyes, then brought out the rest. "Your idea's the right one. I myself, Miss – "

"Well?"

"I can't stay."

The look she gave me with it made me jump at possibilities. "You mean that, since yesterday, you *have* seen – ?"

She shook her head with dignity. "I've *heard* – !"

"Heard?"

"From that child – horrors! There!" she sighed with tragic relief. "On my honour, Miss, she says things – !" But at this evocation she broke down; she dropped with a sudden cry upon my sofa and, as I had seen her do before, gave way to all the anguish of it.

It was quite in another manner that I for my part let myself go. "Oh thank God!"

She sprang up again at this, drying her eyes with a groan. "'Thank God'?"

"It so justifies me!"

"It does that, Miss!"

I could n't have desired more emphasis, but I just waited. "She's so horrible?"

I saw my colleague scarce knew how to put it. "Really shocking."

"And about me?"

"About you, Miss – since you must have it. It's beyond everything, for a young lady; and I can't think wherever she must have picked up – "

"The appalling language she applies to me? I can then!" I broke in with a laugh that was doubtless significant enough.

It only in truth left my friend still more grave. "Well, perhaps I ought to also – since I've heard some of it before! Yet I can't bear it," the poor woman went on while with the same movement she glanced, on my dressing-table, at the face of my watch. "But I must go back."

I kept her, however. "Ah if you can't bear it – !"

"How can I stop with her, you mean? Why just *for* that: to get her away. Far from this," she pursued, "far from *them* – "

"She may be different? she may be free?" I seized her almost with joy. "Then in spite of yesterday you *believe* – "

"In such doings?" Her simple description of them required, in the light of her expression, to be carried no further, and she gave me the whole thing as she had never done. "I believe."

Yes, it was a joy, and we were still shoulder to shoulder: if I might continue sure of that I should care but little what else happened. My support in the presence of disaster would be the same as it had been in my early need of confidence, and if my friend would answer for my honesty I would answer for all the rest. On the point of taking leave of her, none the less, I was to some extent embarrassed. "There's one thing of course – it occurs to me – to remember. My letter giving the alarm will have reached town before you."

I now felt still more how she had been beating about the bush and how weary at last it had made her. "Your letter won't have got there. Your letter never went."

"What then became of it?"

"Goodness knows! Master Miles – "

"Do you mean *he* took it?" I gasped.

She hung fire, but she overcame her reluctance. "I mean that I saw yesterday, when I came back with Miss Flora, that it was n't where you had put it. Later in the evening I had the chance to question Luke, and he declared that he had neither noticed nor touched it." We could only exchange, on this, one of our deeper mutual soundings, and it was Mrs. Grose who first brought up the plumb with an almost elate "You see!"

"Yes, I see that if Miles took it instead he probably will have read it and destroyed it."

"And don't you see anything else?"

I faced her a moment with a sad smile. "It strikes me that by this time your eyes are open even wider than mine."

They proved to be so indeed, but she could still almost blush to show it. "I make out now what he must have done at school." And she gave, in her simple sharpness, an almost droll disillusioned nod. "He stole!"

I turned it over – I tried to be more judicial. "Well – perhaps."

She looked as if she found me unexpectedly calm. "He stole *letters*!"

She could n't know my reasons for a calmness after all pretty shallow; so I showed them off as I might. "I hope then it was to more purpose than in this case! The note, at all events, that I put on the table yesterday," I pursued, "will have given him so scant an advantage – for it contained only the bare demand for an interview – that he's already much ashamed of having gone so far for so little, and that what he had on his mind last evening was precisely the need of confession." I seemed to myself for the instant to have mastered it, to see it all. "Leave us, leave us" – I was already, at the door, hurrying her off. "I'll get it out of him. He'll meet me. He'll confess. If he confesses he's saved. And if he's saved – "

"Then *you* are?" The dear woman kissed me on this, and I took her farewell. "I'll save you without him!" she cried as she went.

XXII

YET it was when she had got off – and I missed her on the spot – that the great pinch really came. If I had counted on what it would give me to find myself alone with Miles I quickly recognised that it would give me at least a measure. No hour of my stay in fact was so assailed with apprehensions as that of my coming down to learn that the carriage containing Mrs. Grose and my younger pupil had already rolled out of the gates. Now I *was*, I said to myself, face to face with the elements, and for much of the rest of the day, while I fought my weakness, I could consider that I had been supremely rash. It was a tighter place still than I had yet turned round in; all the more that, for the first time, I could see in the aspect of others a confused reflexion of the crisis. What had happened naturally caused them all to stare; there was too little of the explained, throw out whatever we might, in the suddenness of my colleague's act. The maids and the men looked blank; the effect of which on my nerves was an aggravation until I saw the necessity of making it a positive aid. It was in short by just clutching the helm that I avoided total wreck; and I – dare say that, to bear up at all, I became that morning very grand and very dry. I welcomed the consciousness that I was charged with much to do, and I caused it to be known as well that, left thus to myself, I was quite remarkably firm. I wandered with that manner, for the next hour or two, all over the place and looked, I have no doubt, as if I were ready for any onset. So, for the benefit of whom it might concern, I paraded with a sick heart.

The person it appeared least to concern proved to be, till dinner, little Miles himself. My perambulations had given me meanwhile no glimpse of him, but they had tended to make more public the change taking place in our relation as a consequence of his having at the piano, the day before, kept me, in Flora's interest, so beguiled and befooled. The stamp of publicity had of course been fully given by her confinement and departure, and the change itself was now ushered in by our non-observance of the regular custom of the schoolroom. He had already disappeared when, on my way down, I pushed open his door, and I learned below that he had breakfasted – in the presence of a couple of the maids – with Mrs. Grose and his sister. He had then gone out, as he said, for a stroll; than which nothing, I reflected, could better have expressed his frank view of the abrupt transformation of my office. What he would now permit this office to consist of was yet to be settled: there was at the least a queer relief – I mean for myself in especial – in the renouncement of one pretension. If so much had sprung to the surface I scarce put it too strongly in saying that what had perhaps sprung highest was the absurdity of our prolonging the fiction that I had anything more to teach him. It sufficiently stuck out that, by tacit little tricks in which even more than myself he carried out the care for my dignity, I had had to appeal to him to let me off straining to meet him on the ground of his true capacity. He had at any rate his freedom now; I was never to touch it again: as I had amply shown, moreover, when, on his joining me in the schoolroom the previous night, I uttered, in reference to the interval just concluded, neither challenge nor hint. I had too much, from this moment, my other ideas. Yet when he at last arrived the difficulty of applying them, the accumulations of my problem, were brought straight home to me by the beautiful little presence on which what had occurred had as yet, for the eye, dropped neither stain nor shadow.

To mark, for the house, the high state I cultivated I decreed that my meals with the boy should be served, as we called it, downstairs; so that I had been awaiting him in the ponderous pomp of the room outside the window of which I had had from Mrs. Grose, that first scared Sunday, my flash of something it would scarce have done to call light. Here at present I felt afresh – for I had felt it again and again – how my equilibrium depended on the success of my rigid will, the will to shut my eyes as tight as possible to the truth that what I had to deal with was, revoltingly, against nature. I could only get on at all by taking "nature" into my confidence and my account, by treating my monstrous ordeal as a push in a direction unusual, of course, and unpleasant, but demanding after all, for a fair front, only another turn of the screw of ordinary human virtue. No attempt, none the less, could well require more tact than just this attempt to supply, one's self, *all* the nature. How could I put even a little of that article into a suppression of reference to what had occurred? How on the other hand could I make a reference without a new plunge into the hideous obscure? Well, a sort of answer, after a time, had come to me, and it was so far confirmed as that I was met, incontestably, by the quickened vision of what was rare in my little companion. It was indeed as if he had found even now – as he had so often found at lessons – still some other delicate way to ease me off. Wasn't there light in the fact which, as we shared our solitude, broke out with a specious glitter it had never yet quite worn? – the fact that (opportunity aiding, precious opportunity which had now come) it would be preposterous, with a child so endowed, to forego the help one might wrest from absolute intelligence? What had his intelligence been given him for but to save him? Might n't one, to reach his mind, risk the stretch of a stiff arm across his character? It was as if, when we were face to face in the dining-room, he had literally shown me the way. The roast mutton was on the table and I had dispensed with attendance. Miles, before he sat down, stood a moment with his hands in his pockets and looked at the joint, on which he seemed on the point of passing some humorous judgement. But what he presently produced was: "I say, my dear, is she really very awfully ill?"

"Little Flora? Not so bad but that she'll presently be better. London will set her up. Bly had ceased to agree with her. Come here and take your mutton."

He alertly obeyed me, carried the plate carefully to his seat and, when he was established, went on. "Did Bly disagree with her so terribly all at once?"

"Not so suddenly as you might think. One had seen it coming on."

"Then why did n't you get her off before?"

Before what?"

"Before she became too ill to travel."

I found myself prompt. "She's *not* too ill to travel; she only might have become so if she had stayed. This was just the moment to seize. The journey will dissipate the influence" – oh I was grand! – "and carry it off."

"I see, I see" – Miles, for that matter, was grand too. He settled to his repast with the charming little "table manner" that, from the day of his arrival, had relieved me of all grossness of admonition. Whatever he had been expelled from school for, it was n't for ugly feeding. He was irreproachable, as always, today; but was unmistakeably more conscious. He was discernibly trying to take for granted more things than he found, without assistance, quite easy; and he dropped into peaceful silence while he felt his situation. Our meal was of the briefest – mine a vain pretence, and I had the things immediately removed. While this was done Miles stood again with his hands in his little pockets and his back to me – stood and looked out of the wide window through which, that other day, I had seen what pulled me up. We continued silent while the maid was with us – as silent, it whimsically occurred to me, as some young couple who, on their wedding-journey, at the inn, feel shy in the presence of the waiter. He turned round only when the waiter had left us. "Well – so we're alone!"

XXIII

"OH more or less." I imagine my smile was pale. "Not absolutely. We should n't like that!" I went on.

"No – I suppose we should n't. Of course we've the others."

"We've the others –we've indeed the others," I concurred.

"Yet even though we have them," he returned, still with his hands in his pockets and planted there in front of me, "they don't much count, do they?"

I made the best of it, but I felt wan. "It depends on what you call 'much'!"

"Yes" – with all accommodation – "everything depends!" On this, however, he faced to the window again and presently reached it with his vague restless cogitating step. He remained there a while with his forehead against the glass, in contemplation of the stupid shrubs I knew and the dull things of November. I had always my hypocrisy of "work," behind which I now gained the sofa. Steadying myself with it there as I had repeatedly done at those moments of torment that I have described as the moments of my knowing the children to be given to something from which I was barred, I sufficiently obeyed my habit of being prepared for the worst. But an extraordinary impression dropped on me as I extracted a meaning from the boy's embarrassed back – none other than the impression that I was not barred now. This inference grew in a few minutes to sharp intensity and seemed bound up with the direct perception that it was positively *he* who was. The frames and squares of the great window were a kind of image, for him, of a kind of failure. I felt that I saw him, in any case, shut in or shut out. He was admirable but not comfortable: I took it in with a throb of hope. Was n't he looking through the haunted pane for something he could n't see? – and was n't it the first time in the whole business that he had known such a lapse? The first, the very first: I found it a splendid portent. It made him anxious, though he watched himself; he had been anxious all day and, even while in his usual sweet little manner he sat at table, had needed all his small strange genius to give it a gloss. When he at last turned round to meet me it was almost as if this genius had succumbed. "Well, I think I'm glad Bly agrees with *me!*"

"You'd certainly seem to have seen, these twenty-four hours, a good deal more of it than for some time before. I hope," I went on bravely, "that you've been enjoying yourself."

"Oh yes, I've been ever so far; all round about – miles and miles away. I've never been so free."

He had really a manner of his own, and I could only try to keep up with him. "Well, do you like it?"

He stood there smiling; then at last he put into two words – "Do *you*?" – more discrimination than I had ever heard two words contain. Before I had time to deal with that, however, he continued as if with the sense that this was an impertinence to be softened. "Nothing could be more charming than the way you take it, for of course if we're alone together now it's you that are alone most. But I hope," he threw in, "you don't particularly mind!"

"Having to do with you?" I asked. "My dear child, how can I help minding? Though I've renounced all claim to your company – you're so beyond me – I at least greatly enjoy it. What else should I stay on for?"

He looked at me more directly, and the expression of his face, graver now, struck me as the most beautiful I had ever found in it. "You stay on just for *that*?"

"Certainly. I stay on as your friend and from the tremendous interest I take in you till something can be done for you that may be more worth your while. That need n't surprise you." My voice trembled so that I felt it impossible to suppress the shake. "Don't you remember how I told you, when I came and sat on your bed the night of the storm, that there was nothing in the world I would n't do for you?"

"Yes, yes!" He, on his side, more and more visibly nervous, had a tone to master; but he was so much more successful than I that, laughing out through his gravity, he could pretend we were pleasantly jesting. "Only that, I think, was to get me to do something for *you*!"

"It was partly to get you to do something," I conceded. "But, you know, you did n't do it."

"Oh yes," he said with the brightest superficial eagerness, "you wanted me to tell you something."

"That's it. Out, straight out. What you have on your mind, you know."

"Ah then is *that* what you've stayed over for?"

He spoke with a gaiety through which I could still catch the finest little quiver of resentful passion; but I can't begin to express the effect upon me of an implication of surrender even so faint. It was as if what I had yearned for had come at last only to astonish me. "Well, yes – I may as well make a clean breast of it. It was precisely for that."

He waited so long that I supposed it for the purpose of repudiating the assumption on which my action had been founded; but what he finally said was: "Do you mean now – here?"

"There could n't be a better place or time." He looked round him uneasily, and I had the rare – oh the queer! – impression of the very first symptom I had seen in him of the approach of immediate fear. It was as if he were suddenly afraid of me – which struck me indeed as perhaps the best thing to make him. Yet in the very pang of the effort I felt it vain to try sternness, and I heard myself the next instant so gentle as to be almost grotesque. "You want so to go out again?"

"Awfully!" He smiled at me heroically, and the touching little bravery of it was enhanced by his actually flushing with pain. He had picked up his hat, which he had brought in, and stood twirling it in a way that gave me, even as I was just nearly reaching port, a perverse horror of what I was doing. To do it in *any* way was an act of violence, for what did it consist of but the obtrusion of the idea of grossness and guilt on a small helpless creature who had been for me a revelation of the possibilities of beautiful intercourse? Was n't it base to create for a being so exquisite a mere alien awkwardness? I suppose I now read into our situation a clearness it could n't have had at the time, for I seem to see our poor eyes already lighted with some spark of a prevision of the anguish that was to come. So we circled about with terrors and scruples, fighters not daring to close. But it was for each other we feared! That kept us a little longer suspended and unbruised. "I'll tell you everything," Miles said – "I mean I'll tell you anything you like. You'll stay on with me, and we shall both be all right, and I *will* tell you – I *will*. But not now."

"Why not now?"

My insistence turned him from me and kept him once more at his window in a silence during which, between us, you might have heard a pin drop. Then he was before me again with the air of a person for whom, outside, someone who had frankly to be reckoned with was waiting. "I have to see Luke."

I had not yet reduced him to quite so vulgar a lie, and I felt proportionately ashamed. But, horrible as it was, his lies made up my truth. I achieved thoughtfully a few loops of my knitting. "Well then go to Luke, and I'll wait for what you promise. Only in return for that satisfy, before you leave me, one very much smaller request."

He looked as if he felt he had succeeded enough to be able still a little to bargain. "Very much smaller – ?"

"Yes, a mere fraction of the whole. Tell me" – oh my work preoccupied me, and I was off-hand! – "if, yesterday afternoon, from the table in the hall, you took, you know, my letter."

XXIV

MY grasp of how he received this suffered for a minute from something that I can describe only as a fierce split of my attention – a stroke that at first, as I sprang straight up, reduced me to the mere blind movement of getting hold of him, drawing him close and, while I just fell for support against the nearest piece of furniture, instinctively keeping him with his back to the window. The appearance was full upon us that I had already had to deal with here: Peter Quint had come into view like a sentinel before a prison. The next thing I saw was that, from outside, he had reached the window, and then I knew that, close to the glass and glaring in through it, he offered once more to the room his white face of damnation. It represents but grossly what took place within me at the sight to say that on the second my decision was made; yet I believe that no woman so overwhelmed ever in so short a time recovered her command of the *act*. It came to me in the very horror of the immediate presence that the act would be, seeing and facing what I saw and faced, to keep the boy himself unaware. The inspiration – I can call it by no other name – was that I felt how voluntarily, how transcendently, I *might*. It was like fighting with a demon for a human soul, and when I had fairly so appraised it I saw how the human soul – held out, in the tremor of my hands, at arms' length – had a perfect dew of sweat on a lovely childish forehead. The face that was close to mine was as white as the face against the glass, and out of it presently came a sound, not low nor weak, but as if from much further away, that I drank like a waft of fragrance.

"Yes – I took it."

At this, with a moan of joy, I enfolded, I drew him close; and while I held him to my breast, where I could feel in the sudden fever of his little body the tremendous pulse of his little heart, I kept my eyes on the thing at the window and saw it move and shift its posture. I have likened it to a sentinel, but its slow wheel, for a moment, was rather the prowl of a baffled beast. My present quickened courage, however, was such that, not too much to let it through, I had to shade, as it were, my flame. Meanwhile the glare of the face was again at the window, the scoundrel fixed as if to watch and wait. It was the very confidence that I might now defy him, as well as the positive certitude, by this time, of the child's unconsciousness, that made me go on. "What did you take it for?"

"To see what you said about me."

"You opened the letter?"

"I opened it."

My eyes were now, as I held him off a little again, on Miles's own face, in which the collapse of mockery showed me how complete was the ravage of uneasiness. What was prodigious was that at last, by my success, his sense was sealed and his communication stopped: he knew that he was in presence, but knew not of what, and knew still less that I also was and that I did know. And what did this strain of trouble matter when my eyes went back to the window only to see that the air was clear again and – by my personal triumph – the influence quenched? There was nothing there. I felt that the cause was mine and that I should surely get *all*. "And you found nothing!" – I let my elation out.

He gave the most mournful, thoughtful little head-shake. "Nothing."

"Nothing, nothing!" I almost shouted in my joy. "Nothing, nothing," he sadly repeated.

I kissed his forehead; it was drenched. "So what have you done with it?"

"I've burnt it."

"Burnt it?" It was now or never. "Is that what you did at school?"

Oh what this brought up! "At school!"

"Did you take letters? – or other things?"

"Other things?" He appeared now to be thinking of something far off and that reached him only through the pressure of his anxiety. Yet it did reach him. "Did I *steal?*"

I felt myself redden to the roots of my hair as well as wonder if it were more strange to put to a gentleman such a question or to see him take it with allowances that gave the very distance of his fall in the world. "Was it for that you might n't go back?"

The only thing he felt was rather a dreary little surprise. "Did you know I might n't go back?"

"I know everything."

He gave me at this the longest and strangest look. "Everything?"

"Everything. Therefore *did* you – ?" But I could n't say it again.

Miles could, very simply. "No. I did n't steal."

My face must have shown him I believed him utterly; yet my hands – but it was for pure tenderness – shook him as if to ask him why, if it was all for nothing, he had condemned me to months of torment. "What then did you do?"

He looked in vague pain all round the top of the room and drew his breath, two or three times over, as if with difficulty. He might have been standing at the bottom of the sea and raising his eyes to some faint green twilight. "Well – I said things."

"Only that?"

"They thought it was enough!"

"To turn you out for?"

Never, truly, had a person "turned out" shown so little to explain it as this little person! He appeared to weigh my question, but in a manner quite detached and almost helpless. "Well, I suppose I ought n't."

"But to whom did you say them?"

He evidently tried to remember, but it dropped – he had lost it. "I don't know!"

He almost smiled at me in the desolation of his surrender, which was indeed practically, by this time, so complete that I ought to have left it there. But I was infatuated – I was blind with victory, though even then the very effect that was to have brought him so much nearer was already that of added separation. "Was it to every one?" I asked.

"No; it was only to – " But he gave a sick little headshake. "I don't remember their names."

"Were they then so many?"

"No – only a few. Those I liked."

Those he liked? I seemed to float not into clearness, but into a darker obscure, and within a minute there had come to me out of my very pity the appalling alarm of his being perhaps innocent. It was for the instant confounding and bottomless, for if he *were* innocent what then on earth was I? Paralysed, while it lasted, by the mere brush of the question, I let him go a little, so that, with a deep-drawn sigh, he turned away from me again; which, as he faced toward the clear window, I suffered, feeling that I had nothing now there to keep him from. "And did they repeat what you said?" I went on after a moment.

He was soon at some distance from me, still breathing hard and again with the air, though now without anger for it, of being confined against his will. Once more, as he had done before, he looked up at the dim day as if, of what had hitherto sustained him, nothing was left but an unspeakable anxiety. "Oh yes," he nevertheless replied – "they must have repeated them. To those *they* liked," he added.

There was somehow less of it than I had expected; but I turned it over. "And these things came round – ?"

"To the masters? Oh yes!" he answered very simply. "But I did n't know they'd tell."

"The masters? They did n't – they've never told. That's why I ask you."

He turned to me again his little beautiful fevered face.

"Yes, it was too bad."

"Too bad?"

"What I suppose I sometimes said. To write home."

I can't name the exquisite pathos of the contradiction given to such a speech by such a speaker; I only know that the next instant I heard myself throw off with homely force: "Stuff and nonsense!" But the next after that I must have sounded stern enough.

"What *were* these things?"

My sternness was all for his judge, his executioner; yet it made him avert himself again, and that movement made *me*, with a single bound and an irrepressible cry, spring straight upon him. For there again, against the glass, as if to blight his confession and stay his answer, was the hideous author of our woe – the white face of damnation. I felt a sick swim at the drop of my victory and all the return of my battle, so that the wildness of my veritable leap only served as a great betrayal. I saw him, from the midst of my act, meet it with a divination, and on the perception that even now he only guessed, and that the window was still to his own eyes free, I let the impulse flame up to convert the climax of his dismay into the very proof of his liberation. "No more, no more, no more!" I shrieked to my visitant as I tried to press him against me.

"Is she *here*?" Miles panted as he caught with his sealed eyes the direction of my words. Then as his strange "she" staggered me and, with a gasp, I echoed it, "Miss Jessel, Miss Jessel!" he with sudden fury gave me back.

I seized, stupefied, his supposition – some sequel to what we had done to Flora, but this made me only want to show him that it was better still than that.

"It's not Miss Jessel! But it's at the window – straight before us. It's *there* – the coward horror, there for the last time!"

At this, after a second in which his head made the movement of a baffled dog's on a scent and then gave a frantic little shake for air and light, he was at me in a white rage, bewildered, glaring vainly over the place and missing wholly, though it now, to my sense, filled the room like the taste of poison, the wide overwhelming presence. "It's *he*?"

I was so determined to have all my proof that I flashed into ice to challenge him. "Whom do you mean by 'he'?"

"Peter Quint – you devil!" His face gave again, round the room, its convulsed supplication. "*Where?*"

They are in my ears still, his supreme surrender of the name and his tribute to my devotion. "What does that matter now, my own? – what will he *ever* matter? *I* have you," I launched at the beast, "but he has lost you for ever!" Then for the demonstration of my work, "There, *there!*" I said to Miles.

But he had already jerked straight round, stared, glared again, and seen but the quiet day. With the stroke of the loss I was so proud of he uttered the cry of a creature hurled over an abyss, and the grasp with which I recovered him might have been that of catching him in his fall. I caught him, yes, I held him – it may be imagined with what a passion; but at the end of a minute I began to feel what it truly was that I held. We were alone with the quiet day, and his little heart, dispossessed, had stopped.

George Washington Cable
(1844–1925)

During the Civil War, George Washington Cable, a native of New Orleans, served as an enlisted man in the Confederate cavalry, and was seriously wounded. After the war, as he began his career as a writer, he became increasingly sympathetic toward the cause of African Americans. Eventually much of his time was spent in civil rights activities. *Old Creole Days* (1879), from which this story is taken, was widely resented in New Orleans for its frank portrayal of racial issues, and ultimately Cable was forced to leave the South.

In "Jean-Ah Poquelin" Cable describes the time after the Louisiana Purchase (1803) when English-speaking outsiders assumed control of the city. Clearly Cable intends parallels with the Reconstruction period after the Civil War, when again the "hated" American government asserted its authority. In describing Jacques Poquelin's house as resembling a stranded ammunition wagon, Cable uses a vivid image, not from the remote past, but from his own experience in the war. Thus Cable suggests that Jacques Poquelin's tragedy has relevance for his own time.

Poquelin's ruined mansion is the familiar setting of Southern Gothic. In this story of a blighted Creole family, and of outsiders who come to understand it, Cable has constructed a richly symbolic account of the legacy of slavery.

Text: George Washington Cable, *Old Creole Days* (New York: Charles Scribner's Sons, 1883).

Jean-Ah Poquelin

In the first decade of the present century, when the newly established American Government was the most hateful thing in Louisiana – when the Creoles were still kicking at such vile innovations as the trial by jury, American dances, anti-smuggling laws, and the printing of the Governor's proclamation in English – when the Anglo-American flood that was presently to burst in a crevasse of immigration upon the delta had thus far been felt only as slippery seepage which made the Creole tremble for his footing – there stood, a short distance above what is now Canal Street, and considerably back from the line of villas which fringed the river-bank on Tchoupitoulas Road, an old colonial plantation-house half in ruin.

It stood aloof from civilization, the tracts that had once been its indigo fields[1] given over to their first noxious wildness, and grown up into one of the horridest marshes within a circuit of fifty miles.

Notes ────────────────────────────────

JEAN-AH POQUELIN
[1] The indigo plant, used to produce a dye of the same name, was an important crop in the south before the cotton gin made cotton "king."

American Gothic: From Salem Witchcraft to H. P. Lovecraft, An Anthology, Second Edition. Edited by Charles L. Crow. Editorial material and organization © 2013 John Wiley & Sons, Ltd. Published 2013 by John Wiley & Sons, Ltd.

The house was of heavy cypress, lifted up on pillars, grim, solid, and spiritless, its massive build a strong reminder of days still earlier, when every man had been his own peace officer and the insurrection of the blacks a daily contingency. Its dark, weather-beaten roof and sides were hoisted up above the jungly plain in a distracted way, like a gigantic ammunition-wagon stuck in the mud and abandoned by some retreating army. Around it was a dense growth of low water willows, with half a hundred sorts of thorny or fetid bushes, savage strangers alike to the "language of flowers" and to the botanist's Greek. They were hung with countless strands of discolored and prickly smilax, and the impassable mud below bristled with *chevaux de frise*[2] of the dwarf palmetto. Two lone forest-trees, dead cypresses, stood in the centre of the marsh, dotted with roosting vultures. The shallow strips of water were hid by myriads of aquatic plants, under whose coarse and spiritless flowers, could one have seen it, was a harbor of reptiles, great and small, to make one shudder to the end of his days.

The house was on a slightly raised spot, the levee of a draining canal. The waters of this canal did not run; they crawled, and were full of big, ravening fish and alligators, that held it against all comers.

Such was the home of old Jean Marie Poquelin, once an opulent indigo planter, standing high in the esteem of his small proud circle of exclusively male acquaintances in the old city; now a hermit, alike shunned by and shunning all who had ever known him. "The last of his line," said the gossips. His father lies under the floor of the St. Louis Cathedral, with the wife of his youth on one side, and the wife of his old age on the other. Old Jean visits the spot daily. His half-brother – alas! there was a mystery; no one knew what had become of the gentle, young half brother, more than thirty years his junior, whom once he seemed so fondly to love, but who, seven years ago, had disappeared suddenly, once for all, and left no clew of his fate.

They had seemed to live so happily in each other's love. No father, mother, wife to either, no kindred upon earth. The elder a bold, frank, impetuous, chivalric adventurer; the younger a gentle, studious, bookloving recluse; they lived upon the ancestral estate like mated birds, one always on the wing, the other always in the nest.

There was no trait in Jean Marie Poquelin, said the old gossips, for which he was so well known among his few friends as his apparent fondness for his "little brother." "Jacques said this," and "Jacques said that"; he "would leave this or that, or anything to Jacques," for "Jacques was a scholar," and "Jacques was good," or "wise," or "just," or "far-sighted," as the nature of the case required; and "he should ask Jacques as soon as he got home," since Jacques was never elsewhere to be seen.

It was between the roving character of the one brother, and the bookishness of the other, that the estate fell into decay. Jean Marie, generous gentleman, gambled the slaves away one by one, until none was left, man or woman, but one old African mute.

The indigo-fields and vats of Louisiana had been generally abandoned as unremunerative. Certain enterprising men had substituted the culture of sugar; but while the recluse was too apathetic to take so active a course, the other saw larger, and, at that time, equally respectable profits, first in smuggling, and later in the African slave-trade. What harm could he see in it? The whole people said it was vitally necessary, and to minister to a vital public necessity, – good enough, certainly, and so he laid up many a doubloon, that made him none the worse in the public regard.

Notes ───

[2] French: barriers with spikes used to hinder enemy cavalry; here used figuratively to describe the spiky palmetto plants.

One day old Jean Marie was about to start upon a voyage that was to be longer, much longer, than any that he had yet made. Jacques had begged him hard for many days not to go, but he laughed him off, and finally said, kissing him:

"Adieu, 'tit frère."[3]

"No," said Jacques, "I shall go with you."

They left the old hulk of a house in the sole care of the African mute, and went away to the Guinea coast together.

Two years after, old Poquelin came home without his vessel. He must have arrived at his house by night. No one saw him come. No one saw "his little brother;" rumor whispered that he, too, had returned, but he had never been seen again.

A dark suspicion fell upon the old slave-trader. No matter that the few kept the many reminded of the tenderness that had ever marked his bearing to the missing man. The many shook their heads. "You know he has a quick and fearful temper;" and "why does he cover his loss with mystery?" "Grief would out with the truth."

"But," said the charitable few, "look in his face; see that expression of true humanity." The many did look in his face, and, as he looked in theirs, he read the silent question: "Where is thy brother Abel?"[4] The few were silenced, his former friends died off, and the name of Jean Marie Poquelin became a symbol of witchery, devilish crime, and hideous nursery fictions.

The man and his house were alike shunned. The snipe and duck hunters forsook the marsh, and the woodcutters abandoned the canal. Sometimes the hardier boys who ventured out there snake-shooting heard a slow thumping of oar-locks on the canal. They would look at each other for a moment half in consternation, half in glee, then rush from their sport in wanton haste to assail with their gibes the unoffending, withered old man who, in rusty attire, sat in the stern of a skiff, rowed homeward by his white-headed African mute.

"O Jean-ah Poquelin! O Jean-ah! Jean-ah Poquelin!"

It was not necessary to utter more than that. No hint of wickedness, deformity, or any physical or moral demerit; merely the name and tone of mockery: "Oh, Jean-ah Poquelin!" and while they tumbled one over another in their needless haste to fly, he would rise carefully from his seat, while the aged mute, with downcast face, went on rowing, and rolling up his brown fist and extending it toward the urchins, would pour forth such an unholy broadside of French imprecation and invective as would all but craze them with delight.

Among both blacks and whites the house was an object of a thousand superstitions. Every midnight, they affirmed, the *feu follet*[5] came out of the marsh and ran in and out of the rooms, flashing from window to window. The story of some lads, whose words in ordinary statements were worthless, was generally credited, that the night they camped in the woods, rather than pass the place after dark, they saw, about sunset, every window blood-red, and on each of the four chimneys an owl sitting, which turned his head three times round, and moaned and laughed with a human voice. There was a bottomless well, everybody professed to know, beneath the sill of the big front door under the rotten veranda; whoever set his foot upon that threshold disappeared forever in the depth below.

What wonder the marsh grew as wild as Africa! Take all the Faubourg Ste. Marie, and half the ancient city, you would not find one graceless dare-devil reckless enough to pass within a hundred yards of the house after nightfall.

Notes

[3] French: Good-bye, little brother.
[4] Question asked of Cain by God after the first murder. See Genesis 4:9.

[5] French: burning marsh gas (literally "elf fire"; in English sometimes called "fox fire").

The alien races pouring into old New Orleans began to find the few streets named for the Bourbon princes too strait for them. The wheel of fortune, beginning to whirl, threw them off beyond the ancient corporation lines, and sowed civilization and even trade upon the lands of the Graviers and Girods. Fields became roads, roads streets. Everywhere the leveller was peering through his glass, rodsmen were whacking their way through willow-brakes and rose-hedges, and the sweating Irishmen tossed the blue clay up with their long-handled shovels.

"Ha! that is all very well," quoth the Jean-Baptistes, feeling the reproach of an enterprise that asked neither co-operation nor advice of them, "but wait till they come yonder to Jean Poquelin's marsh; ha! ha! ha!" The supposed predicament so delighted them, that they put on a mock terror and whirled about in an assumed stampede, then caught their clasped hands between their knees in excess of mirth, and laughed till the tears ran; for whether the street-makers mired in the marsh, or contrived to cut through old "Jean-ah's" property, either event would be joyful. Meantime a line of tiny rods, with bits of white paper in their split tops, gradually extended its way straight through the haunted ground, and across the canal diagonally.

"We shall fill that ditch," said the man in mud-boots, and brushed close along the chained and padlocked gate of the haunted mansion. Ah, Jean-ah Poquelin, those were not Creole boys, to be stampeded with a little hard swearing.

He went to the Governor. That official scanned the odd figure with no slight interest. Jean Poquelin was of short, broad frame, with a bronzed leonine face. His brow was ample and deeply furrowed. His eye, large and black, was bold and open like that of a war-horse, and his jaws shut together with the firmness of iron. He was dressed in a suit of Attakapas cottonade,[6] and his shirt unbuttoned and thrown back from the throat and bosom, sailor-wise, showed a herculean breast, hard and grizzled. There was no fierceness or defiance in his look, no harsh ungentleness, no symptom of his unlawful life or violent temper; but rather a peaceful and peaceable fearlessness. Across the whole face, not marked in one or another feature, but as it were laid softly upon the countenance like an almost imperceptible veil, was the imprint of some great grief. A careless eye might easily overlook it, but, once seen, there it hung – faint, but unmistakable.

The Governor bowed.

"*Parlez-vous français?*" asked the figure.

"I would rather talk English, if you can do so," said the Governor.

"My name, Jean Poquelin."

"How can I serve you, Mr. Poquelin?"

"My 'ouse is yond'; *dans le marais là-bas.*"

The Governor bowed.

"*Dat marais* billong to me."

"Yes, sir."

"To me; Jean Poquelin; I hown 'im meself."

"Well, sir?"

"He don't billong to you; I get him from me father."

"That is perfectly true, Mr. Poquelin, as far as I am aware."

"You want to make strit pass yond'?"

"I do not know, sir; it is quite probable; but the city will indemnify you for any loss you may suffer – you will get paid, you understand."

"Strit can't pass dare."

Notes

6 Rough cotton material.

"You will have to see the municipal authorities about that, Mr. Poquelin."

A bitter smile came upon the old man's face:

"*Pardon, Monsieur*, you is not *le Gouverneur?*"

"Yes."

"*Mais*, yes. You har *le Gouverneur* – yes. Veh-well. I come to you. I tell you, strit can't pass at me 'ouse."

"But you will have to see – "

"I come to you. You is *le Gouverneur*. I know not the new laws. I ham a Fr-r-rench-a-man! Fr-rench-a-man have something *aller au contraire*[7] – he come at his *Gouverneur*. I come at you. If me not had been bought from me king like *bossals* in the hold time, ze king gof – France would-a-show *Monsieur le Gouverneur* to take care his men to make strit in right places. Mais, I know; we billong to *Monsieur le Président*. I want you do somesin for me, eh?"

"What is it?" asked the patient Governor.

"I want you tell *Monsieur le Président*, strit – can't – pass – at – me – 'ouse."

"Have a chair, Mr. Poquelin;" but the old man did not stir. The Governor took a quill and wrote a line to a city official, introducing Mr. Poquelin, and asking for him every possible courtesy. He handed it to him, instructing him where to present it.

"Mr. Poquelin," he said with a conciliatory smile, "tell me, is it your house that our Creole citizens tell such odd stories about?"

The old man glared sternly upon the speaker, and with immovable features said:

"You don't see me trade some Guinea nigga'?"

"Oh, no."

"You don't see me make some smugglin'?"

"No, sir; not at all."

"But, I am Jean Marie Poquelin. I mine me hown bizniss. Dat all right? Adieu."

He put his hat on and withdrew. By and by he stood, letter in hand, before the person to whom it was addressed. This person employed an interpreter.

"He says," said the interpreter to the officer, "he come to make you the fair warning how you muz not make the street pas' at his 'ouse."

The officer remarked that "such impudence was refreshing;" but the experienced interpreter translated freely.

"He says: 'Why you don't want?'" said the interpreter.

The old slave-trader answered at some length.

"He says," said the interpreter, again turning to the officer, "the marass is a too unhealth' for peopl' to live."

"But we expect to drain his old marsh; it's not going to be a marsh."

"*Il dit*" – The interpreter explained in French.

The old man answered tersely.

"He says the canal is a private," said the interpreter.

"Oh! *that* old ditch; that's to be filled up. Tell the old man we're going to fix him up nicely."

Translation being duly made, the man in power was amused to see a thunder-cloud gathering on the old man's face.

"Tell him," he added, "by the time we finish, there'll not be a ghost left in his shanty."

The interpreter began to translate, but –

"*J' comprends*,[8] *J' comprends*," said the old man with an impatient gesture, and burst forth, pouring curses upon the United States, the President, the territory of Orleans, Congress, the Governor and all his subordinates, striding out of the apartment as he

Notes —————————————————————————————

[7] French: to complain about. [8] French: I understand.

cursed, while the object of his maledictions roared with merriment and rammed the floor with his foot.

"Why, it will make his old place worth ten dollars to one," said the official to the interpreter.

"'Tis not for de worse of de property," said the interpreter.

"I should guess not," said the other, whittling his chair, – "seems to me as if some of these old Creoles would liever live in a crawfish hole than to have a neighbor."

"You know what make old Jean Poquelin make like that? I will tell you. You know" –

The interpreter was rolling a cigarette, and paused to light his tinder; then, as the smoke poured in a thick double stream from his nostrils, he said, in a solemn whisper:

"He is a witch."

"Ho, ho, ho!" laughed the other.

"You don't believe it? What you want to bet?" cried the interpreter, jerking himself half up and thrusting out one arm while he bared it of its coat sleeve with the hand of the other. "What you want to bet?"

"How do you know?" asked the official.

"Dass what I goin' to tell you. You know one evening I was shooting some *grosbec*. I killed three, but I had trouble to fine them, it was becoming so dark. When I have them I start' to come home, then I got to pas' at Jean Poquelin's house."

"Ho, ho, ho!" laughed the other, throwing his leg over the arm of his chair.

"Wait," said the interpreter. "I come along slow, not making some noises; still, still" –

"And scared," said the smiling one.

"*Mais*, wait. I get all pas' the 'ouse. 'Ah!' I say; 'all right!' Then I see two thing' before! Hah! I get as cold and *humide*, and shake like a leaf. You think it was nothing? There I see, so plain as can be (though it was making nearly dark), I see Jean – Marie – Po-que-lin walkin' right in front, and right there beside of him was something like a man – but not a man – white like paint! – I dropp' on the grass from scared – they pass'; so sure as I live 'twas the ghos' of Jacques Poquelin, his brother!"

"Pooh!" said the listener.

"I'll put my han' in the fire," said the interpreter.

"But did you never think," asked the other, "that that might be Jack Poquelin, as you call him, alive and well, and for some cause hid away by his brother?"

"But there har' no cause!" said the other, and the entrance of third parties changed the subject.

Some months passed and the street was opened. A canal was first dug through the marsh, the small one which passed so close to Jean Poquelin's house was filled, and the street, or rather a sunny road, just touched a corner of the old mansion's door-yard. The morass ran dry. Its venomous denizens slipped away through the bulrushes; the cattle roaming freely upon its hardened surface trampled the superabundant undergrowth. The bellowing frogs croaked to westward. Lillies and the flower-de-luce sprang up in the place of reeds; smilax and poison-oak gave way to the purple-plumed iron-weed and pink spiderwort; the bindweeds ran everywhere blooming as they ran, and on one of the dead cypresses a giant creeper hung its green burden of foliage and lifted its scarlet trumpets. Sparrows and red-birds flitted through the bushes, and dewberries grew ripe beneath. Over all these came a sweet, dry smell of salubrity which the place had not known since the sediments of the Mississippi first lifted it from the sea.

But its owner did not build. Over the willow-brakes, and down the vista of the open street, bright new houses, some singly, some by ranks, were prying in upon the old man's privacy. They even settled down toward his southern side. First a wood-cutter's hut or two, then a market gardener's shanty, then a painted cottage, and all at once the faubourg⁹ had flanked and half surrounded him and his dried-up marsh.

Ah! then the common people began to hate him. "The old tyrant!" "You don't mean an old *tyrant*?" "Well, then, why don't he build when the public need demands it? What does he live in that unneighborly way for?" "The old pirate!" "The old kidnapper!" How easily even the most ultra Lousianians put on the imported virtues of the North when they could be brought to bear against the hermit. "There he goes, with the boys after him! Ah! ha! ha! Jean-ah Poquelin! Ah! Jean-ah! Aha! aha! Jean-ah Marie! Jean-ah Poquelin! The old villain!" How merrily the swarming Américains echo the spirit of persecution! "The old fraud," they say – "pretends to live in a haunted house, does he? We'll tar and feather him some day. Guess we can fix him."

He cannot be rowed home along the old canal now; he walks. He has broken sadly of late, and the street urchins are ever at his heels. It is like the days when they cried: "Go up, thou bald-head," and the old man now and then turns and delivers ineffectual curses.

To the Creoles – to the incoming lower class of superstitious Germans, Irish, Sicilians, and others – he became an omen and embodiment of public and private ill-fortune. Upon him all the vagaries of their superstitions gathered and grew. If a house caught fire, it was imputed to his machinations. Did a woman go off in a fit, he had bewitched her. Did a child stray off for an hour, the mother shivered with the apprehension that Jean Poquelin had offered him to strange gods. The house was the subject of every bad boy's invention who loved to contrive ghostly lies. "As long as that house stands we shall have bad luck. Do you not see our pease and beans dying, our cabbages and lettuce going to seed and our gardens turning to dust, while every day you can see it raining in the woods? The rain will never pass old Poquelin's house. He keeps a fetich. He has conjured the whole Faubourg St. Marie. And why, the old wretch? Simply because our playful and innocent children call after him as he passes."

A "Building and Improvement Company," which had not yet got its charter, "but was going to," and which had not, indeed, any tangible capital yet, but "was going to have some," joined the "Jean-ah Poquelin" war. The haunted property would be such a capital site for a market-house! They sent a deputation to the old mansion to ask its occupant to sell. The deputation never got beyond the chained gate and a very barren interview with the African mute. The President of the Board was then empowered (for he had studied French in Pennsylvania and was considered qualified) to call and persuade M. Poquelin to subscribe to the company's stock; but –

"Fact is, gentlemen," he said at the next meeting, "it would take us at least twelve months to make Mr. Pokaleen understand the rather original features of our system, and he wouldn't subscribe when we'd done; besides, the only way to see him is to stop him on the street."

There was a great laugh from the Board; they couldn't help it. "Better meet a bear robbed of her whelps," said one.

"You're mistaken as to that," said the President. "I did meet him, and stopped him, and found him quite polite. But I could get no satisfaction from him; the fellow wouldn't talk in French, and when I spoke in English he hoisted his old shoulders up, and gave the same answer to every thing I said."

"And that was – ?" asked one or two, impatient of the pause.

Notes ——————————————————————————————————

⁹ French: district.

"That it 'don't worse w'ile?' "

One of the Board said: "Mr. President, this market-house project, as I take it, is not altogether a selfish one; the community is to be benefited by it. We may feel that we are working in the public interest [the Board smiled knowingly], if we employ all possible means to oust this old nuisance from among us. You may know that at the time the street was cut through, this old Poquelann did all he could to prevent it. It was owing to a certain connection which I had with that affair that I heard a ghost story [smiles, followed by a sudden dignified check] – ghost story, which, of course, I am not going to relate; but I may say that my profound conviction, arising from a prolonged study of that story, is, that this old villain, John Poquelann, has his brother locked up in that old house. Now, if this is so, and we can fix it on him, I merely *suggest* that we can make the matter highly useful. I don't know," he added, beginning to sit down, "but that it is an action we owe to the community – hem!"

"How do you propose to handle the subject?" asked the President.

"I was thinking," said the speaker, "that, as a Board of Directors, it would be unadvisable for us to authorize any action involving trespass; but if you, for instance, Mr. President, should, as it were, for mere curiosity, *request* some one, as, for instance, our excellent Secretary, simply as a personal favor, to look into the matter – this is merely a suggestion."

The Secretary smiled sufficiently to be understood that, while he certainly did not consider such preposterous service a part of his duties as secretary, he might, not withstanding, accede to the President's request; and the Board adjourned.

Little White, as the Secretary was called, was a mild, kind-hearted little man, who, nevertheless, had no fear of any thing, unless it was the fear of being unkind.

"I tell you frankly," he privately said to the President, "I go into this purely for reasons of my own."

The next day, a little after nightfall, one might have descried this little man slipping along the rear fence of the Poquelin place, preparatory to vaulting over into the rank, grass-grown yard, and bearing himself altogether more after the manner of a collector of rare chickens than according to the usage of secretaries.

The picture presented to his eye was not calculated to enliven his mind. The old mansion stood out against the western sky, black and silent. One long, lurid pencil-stroke along a sky of slate was all that was left of daylight. No sign of life was apparent; no light at any window, unless it might have been on the side of the house hidden from view. No owls were on the chimneys, no dogs were in the yard.

He entered the place, and ventured up behind a small cabin which stood apart from the house. Through one of its many crannies he easily detected the African mute crouched before a flickering pine-knot, his head on his knees, fast asleep.

He concluded to enter the mansion, and, with that view, stood and scanned it. The broad rear steps of the veranda would not serve him; he might meet some one midway. He was measuring, with his eye, the proportions of one of the pillars which supported it, and estimating the practicability of climbing it, when he heard a footstep. Someone dragged a chair out toward the railing, then seemed to change his mind and began to pace the veranda, his footfalls resounding on the dry boards with singular loudness. Little White drew a step backward, got the figure between himself and the sky, and at once recognized the short, broad-shouldered form of old Jean Poquelin.

He sat down upon a billet of wood, and, to escape the stings of a whining cloud of mosquitoes, shrouded his face and neck in his handkerchief, leaving his eyes uncovered.

He had sat there but a moment when be noticed a strange, sickening odor, faint, as if coming from a distance, but loathsome and horrid.

Whence could it come? Not from the cabin; not from the marsh, for it was as dry as powder. It was not in the air; it seemed to come from the ground.

Rising up, he noticed, for the first time, a few steps before him a narrow footpath leading toward the house. He glanced down it – ha! right there was some one coming – ghostly white!

Quick as thought, and as noiselessly, he lay down at full length against the cabin. It was bold strategy, and yet, there was no denying it, little White felt that he was frightened. "It is not a ghost," he said to himself. "I know it cannot be a ghost;" but the perspiration burst out at every pore, and the air seemed to thicken with heat. "It is a living man," he said in his thoughts. "I hear his footstep, and I hear old Poquelin's footsteps, too, separately, over on the veranda. I am not discovered; the thing has passed; there is that odor again; what a smell of death! Is it coming back? Yes. It stops at the door of the cabin. Is it peering in at the sleeping mute? It moves away. It is in the path again. Now it is gone." He shuddered. "Now, if I dare venture, the mystery is solved." He rose cautiously, close against the cabin, and peered along the path.

The figure of a man, a presence if not a body – but whether clad in some white stuff or naked the darkness would not allow him to determine – had turned, and now, with a seeming painful gait, moved slowly from him. "Great Heaven! can it be that the dead do walk?" He withdrew again the hands which had gone to his eyes. The dreadful object passed between two pillars and under the house. He listened. There was a faint sound as of feet upon a staircase; then all was still except the measured tread of Jean Poquelin walking on the veranda, and the heavy respirations of the mute slumbering in the cabin.

The little Secretary was about to retreat; but as he looked once more toward the haunted house a dim light appeared in the crack of a closed window, and presently old Jean Poquelin came, dragging his chair, and sat down close against the shining cranny. He spoke in a low, tender tone in the French tongue, making some inquiry. An answer came from within. Was it the voice of a human? So unnatural was it – so hollow, so discordant, so unearthly – that the stealthy listener shuddered again from head to foot, and when something stirred in some bushes near by – though it may have been nothing more than a rat – and came scuttling through the grass, the little Secretary actually turned and fled. As he left the enclosure he moved with bolder leisure through the bushes; yet now and then he spoke aloud: "Oh, oh! I see, I understand!" and shut his eyes in his hands.

How strange that henceforth little White was the champion of Jean Poquelin! In season and out of season – wherever a word was uttered against him – the Secretary, with a quiet, aggressive force that instantly arrested gossip, demanded upon what authority the statement or conjecture was made; but as he did not condescend to explain his own remarkable attitude, it was not long before the disrelish and suspicion which had followed Jean Poquelin so many years fell also upon him.

It was only the next evening but one after his adventure that be made himself a source of sullen amazement to one hundred and fifty boys, by ordering them to desist from their wanton hallooing. Old Jean Poquelin, standing and shaking his cane, rolling out his long-drawn maledictions, paused and stared, then gave the Secretary a courteous bow and started on. The boys, save one, from pure astonishment, ceased; but a ruffianly little Irish lad, more daring than any had yet been, threw a big hurtling clod, that struck old Poquelin between the shoulders and burst like a shell. The enraged old man wheeled with uplifted staff to give chase to the scampering vagabond; and – he may have tripped, or he may not, but he fell full length. Little White hastened to help him up, but he waved him off with a fierce imprecation and staggering to his feet resumed his way homeward. His lips were reddened with blood.

Little White was on his way to the meeting of the Board. He would have given all he dared spend to have staid away, for he felt both too fierce and too tremulous to brook the criticisms that were likely to be made.

"I can't help it, gentlemen; I can't help you to make a case against the old man, and I'm not going to."

"We did not expect this disappointment, Mr. White."

"I can't help that, sir. No, sir; you had better not appoint any more investigations. Somebody'll investigate himself into trouble. No, sir; it isn't a threat, it is only my advice, but I warn you that whoever takes the task in hand will rue it to his dying day – which may be hastened, too."

The President expressed himself "surprised."

"I don't care a rush," answered little White, wildly and foolishly. "I don't care a rush if you are, sir. No, my nerves are not disordered; my head's as clear as a bell. No. I'm *not* excited."

A Director remarked that the Secretary looked as though he had waked from a nightmare.

"Well, sir, if you want to know the fact, I have; and it you choose to cultivate old Poquelin's society you can have one, too."

"White," called a facetious member, but White did not notice. "White," he called again.

"What?" demanded White, with a scowl.

"Did you see the ghost?"

"Yes, sir; I did," cried White, hitting the table, and handing the President a paper which brought the Board to other business.

The story got among the gossips that somebody (they were afraid to say little White) had been to the Poquelin mansion by night and beheld something appalling. The rumor was but a shadow of the truth, magnified and distorted as is the manner of shadows. He had seen skeletons walking, and had barely escaped the clutches of one by making the sign of the cross.

Some madcap boys with an appetite for the horrible plucked up courage to venture through the dried marsh by the cattle-path, and come before the house at a spectral hour when the air was full of bats. Something which they but half saw – half a sight was enough – sent them tearing back through the willowbrakes and acacia bushes to their homes, where they fairly dropped down, and cried:

"Was it white?" "No – yes – nearly so – we can't tell – but we saw it." And one could hardly doubt, to look at their ashen faces, that they had, whatever it was.

"If that old rascal lived in the country we come from," said certain Américains, "he'd have been tarred and feathered before now, wouldn't he, Sanders?"

"Well, now he just would."

"And we'd have rid him on a rail, wouldn't we?"

"That's what I allow."

"Tell you what you *could* do." They were talking to some rollicking Creoles who had assumed an absolute necessity for doing *something*. "What is it you call this thing where an old man marries a young girl and you come out with horns and" –

"*Charivari?*" asked the Creoles.

"Yes, that's it. Why don't you shivaree him?" Felicitous suggestion.

Little White, with his wife beside him, was sitting on their doorsteps on the side-walk, as Creole custom had taught them, looking toward the sunset. They had moved into the lately-opened street. The view was not attractive on the score of beauty. The houses were small and scattered, and across the flat commons, spite of the lofty tangle of trees and bushes, and spite of the thickets of acacia, they needs must see the dismal old Poquelin mansion, tilted awry and shutting out the declining sun. The moon, white and slender was hanging the tip of its horn over one of the chimneys.

"And you say," said the Secretary, "the old black man has been going by here alone? Patty, suppose old Poquelin should be concocting some mischief; he don't lack provocation; the way that clod hit him the other day was enough to have killed him. Why, Patty, he dropped as quick as *that*! No wonder you haven't seen him. I wonder if they haven't heard something about him up at the drug-store. Suppose I go and see."

"Do," said his wife.

She sat alone for half an hour, watching that sudden going out of the day peculiar to the latitude.

"That moon is ghost enough for one house," she said, as her husband returned. "It has gone right down the chimney."

"Patty," said little White, "the drug-clerk says the boys are going to shivaree old Poquelin to-night I'm going to try to stop it."

"Why, White," said his wife, "you'd better not. You'll get hurt."

"No, I'll not."

"Yes, you will."

"I'm going to sit out here until they come along. They're compelled to pass right by here."

"Why, White, it may be midnight before they start; you're not going to sit out here till then."

"Yes, I am."

"Well, you're very foolish," said Mrs. White in an undertone, looking anxious, and tapping one of the steps with her foot.

They sat a very long time talking over little family matters.

"What's that?" at last said Mrs. White.

"That's the nine-o'clock gun," said White, and they relapsed into a long-sustained, drowsy silence.

"Patty, you'd better go in and go to bed," said he at last.

"I'm not sleepy."

"Well, you're very foolish," quietly remarked little White, and again silence fell upon them.

"Patty, suppose I walk out to the old house and see if I can find out any thing."

"Suppose," said she, "you don't do any such – listen!"

Down the street arose a great hubbub. Dogs and boys were howling and barking; men were laughing, shouting, groaning, and blowing horns, whooping, and clanking cow-bells, whinnying, and howling, and rattling pots and pans.

"They are coming this way," said little White. "You had better go into the house, Patty."

"So had you."

"No. I'm going to see if I can't stop them."

"Why, White!"

"I'll be back in a minute," said White, and went toward the noise.

In a few moments the little Secretary met the mob. The pen hesitates on the word, for there is a respectable difference, measurable only on the scale of the half century, between a mob and a *charivari*. Little White lifted his ineffectual voice. He faced the head of the disorderly column, and cast himself about as if he were made of wood and moved by the jerk of a string. He rushed to one who seemed, from the size and clatter of his tin pan, to be a leader. "*Stop these fellows, Bienvenu, stop them just a minute, till I tell them something.*" Bienvenu turned and brandished his instruments of discord in an imploring way to the crowd. They slackened their pace, two or three hushed their horns and joined the prayer of little White and Bienvenu for silence. The throng halted. The hush was delicious.

"Bienvenu," said little White, "don't shivaree old Poquelin to-night; he's" –

"My fwang," said the swaying Bienvenu, "who tail you I goin' to chahivahi somebody, eh? You sink bickause I make a little playfool wiz zis tin pan zat I am *dhonk*?"

"Oh, no, Bienvenu, old fellow, you're all right. I was afraid you might not know that old Poquelin was sick, you know, but you're not going there, are you?"

"My fwang, I vay soy to tail you zat you ah dhonk as de dev'. I am shem of you. I ham ze servan' of *ze publique*. Zese *citoyens* goin' to wickwest Jean Poquelin to give to the Ursuline' two hondred fifty dolla'" –

"*Hé quoi!*" cried a listener, "*Cinq cent piastres, oui!*"

"*Oui!*" said Bienvenu, "and if he wiffuse we make him some lit' musique; ta-ra ta!" He hoisted a merry hand and foot, then frowning, added: "Old Poquelin got no bisniz dhink s'much w'isky."

"But, gentlemen," said little White, around whom a circle had gathered," the old man is very sick."

"My faith!" cried a tiny Creole, "we did not make him to be sick. W'en we have say we going make *le charivari*, do you want that we hall tell a lie? My faith! 'sfools!"

"But you can shivaree somebody else," said desperate little White.

"*Oui!*" cried Bienvenu, "*et chahivahi* Jean-ah Poquelin tomo'w!"

"Let us go to Madame Schneider!" cried two or three, and amid huzzas and confused cries, among which was heard a stentorian Celtic call for drinks, the crowd again began to move.

"*Cent piastres pour l'hôpital de charité!*"

"Hurrah!"

"One hongred dolla' for Charity Hospital!"

"Hurrah!"

"Whang!" went a tin pan, the crowd yelled, and Pandemonium gaped again. They were off at a right angle.

Nodding, Mrs. White looked at the mantle-clock.

"Well, if it isn't away after midnight."

The hideous noise down street was passing beyond earshot. She raised a sash and listened. For a moment there was silence. Some one came to the door.

"Is that you, White?"

"Yes." He entered. "I succeeded, Patty."

"Did you?" said Patty, joyfully.

"Yes. They've gone down to shivaree the old Dutchwoman who married her step-daughter's sweetheart. They say she has got to pay a hundred dollar to the hospital before they stop."

The couple retired, and Mrs. White slumbered. She was awakened by her husband snapping the lid of his watch.

"What time?" she asked.

"Half-past three. Patty, I haven't slept a wink. Those fellows are out yet. Don't you hear them?"

"Why, White, they're coming this way!"

"I know they are," said White, sliding out of bed and drawing on his clothes," and they're coming fast. You'd better go away from that widow, Patty. My! what a clatter!"

"Here they are," said Mrs. White, but her husband was gone. Two or three hundred men and boys pass the place at a rapid walk straight down the broad, new street, toward the hated house of ghosts. The din was terrific. She saw little White at the head of the rabble brandishing his arms and trying in vain to make himself heard; but they only shook their heads laughing and hooting the louder, and so passed, bearing him on before them.

Swiftly they pass out from among the houses, away from the dim oil lamps of the street, out into the broad starlit commons, and enter the willowy jungles of the haunted ground. Some hearts fail and their owners lag behind and turn back, suddenly remembering how near morning it is. But the most part push on, tearing the air with their clamor.

Down ahead of them in the long, thicket-darkened way there is – singularly enough – a faint, dancing light. It must be very near the old house; it is. It has stopped now. It is a lantern, and is under a well-known sapling which has grown up on the wayside since the canal was filled. Now it swings mysteriously to and fro. A goodly number of the more ghost-fearing give up the sport; but a full hundred move forward at a run, doubling their devilish howling and banging.

Yes; it is a lantern, and there are two persons under the tree. The crowd draws near – drops into a walk; one of the two is the old African mute; he lifts the lantern up so that it shines on the other; the crowd recoils; there is a hush of all clangor, and all at once, with a cry of mingled fright and horror from every throat, the whole throng rushes back, dropping every thing, sweeping past little White and hurrying on, never stopping until the jungle is left behind, and then to find that not one in ten has seen the cause of the stampede, and not one of the tenth is certain what it was.

There is one huge fellow among them who looked capable of any villainy. He finds something to mount on, and, in the Creole *patois*, calls a general halt. Bienvenu sinks down, and, vainly trying to recline gracefully, resigns the leadership. The herd gather round the speaker; he assures them that they have been outraged. Their right peaceably to traverse the public streets has been trampled upon. Shall such encroachments be endured? It is now daybreak. Let them go now by the open light of day and force a free passage of the public highway!

A scattering consent was the response, and the crowd, thinned now and drowsy, straggled quietly down toward the old house. Some drifted ahead, others sauntered behind, but every one, as he again neared the tree, came to a stand-still. Little White sat upon a bank of turf on the opposite side of the way looking very stern and sad. To each new-comer he put the same question:

"Did you come here to go to old Poquelin's?"

"Yes."

"He's dead." And if the shocked hearer started away he would say: "Don't go away."

"Why not?"

"I want you to go to the funeral presently."

If some Louisianian, too loyal to dear France or Spain to understand English, looked bewildered, some one would interpret for him; and presently they went. Little White led the van, the crowd trooping after him down the middle of the way. The gate, that had never been seen before unchained, was open. Stern little White stopped a short distance from it; the rabble stopped behind him. Something was moving out from under the veranda. The many whisperers stretched upward to see. The African mute came very slowly toward the gate, leading by a cord in the nose a small brown bull, which was harnessed to a rude cart. On the flat body of the cart, under a black cloth, were seen the outlines of a long box.

"Hats off, gentlemen," said little White, as the box came in view, and the crowd silently uncovered.

"Gentlemen," said little White, "here come the last remains of Jean Marie Poquelin, a better man, I'm afraid, with all his sins, – yes a better – a kinder man to his blood – a man of more self-forgetful goodness – than all of you put together will ever dare to be."

There was a profound hush as the vehicle came creaking through the gate; but when it turned away from them toward the forest, those in front started suddenly. There was a backward rush, then all stood still again staring one way; for there, behind the bier, with eyes cast down and labored step, walked the living remains – all that was left – of little Jacques Poquelin, the long-hidden brother – a leper, as white as snow.

Dumb with horror, the cringing crowd gazed upon the walking death. They watched, in silent awe, the slow *cortège*[10] creep down the long, straight road and lessen on the view, until by and by it stopped where a wild, unfrequented path branched off into the undergrowth toward the rear of the ancient city.

"They are going to the *Terre aux Lépreux*," said one in the crowd. The rest watched them in silence.

The little bull was set free; the mute, with the strength of an ape, lifted the long box to his shoulder. For a moment more the mute and the leper stood in sight, while the former adjusted his heavy burden; then, without one backward glance upon the unkind human world, turning their faces toward the ridge in the depths of the swamp known as the Leper's Land, they stepped into the jungle, disappeared, and were never seen again.

Notes ————————————————————————————

[10] French: procession.

Madeline Yale Wynne (1847–1918)

This story, by the daughter of the inventor of the Yale lock, has been called by Alfred Bendixen "a forgotten masterpiece" and "one of the most effective 'puzzle stories' ever written."

A hint of witchcraft is introduced by reference to the sea captain from Salem, Massachusetts. The narrative that follows is a perfect demonstration of what Freud meant by the "uncanny," with the fondly remembered home revealing a mystery that is madly frustrating, and threatens the happiness of the young bride.

Recent studies of the story, like that by Jeffrey Andrew Weinstock, stress the gender issues it raises, including the gendering of space. Readers will note that both men and women have seen the neat china closet, but only women and girls have seen the comforting refuge of the little room.

Wynne first published the story in *Harper's* in 1895.

Text: *The Little Room and Other Stories* (Chicago: Way & Williams, 1895). Single and double quotation marks have been changed to correspond with current U.S. usage. Otherwise the text has not been altered.

The Little Room

"HOW would it do for a smoking-room?"

"Just the very place! only, you know, Roger, you must not think of smoking in the house. I am almost afraid having just a plain common man around, let alone a smoking-man, will upset Aunt Hannah. She is New England – Vermont New England – boiled down."

"You leave Aunt Hannah to me; I shall find her tender side. I am going to ask her about the old sea-captain and the yellow calico."

"Not yellow calico – blue chintz."

"Well, yellow *shell*, then."

"No, no! do n't mix it up so; you won't know yourself what to expect, and that's half the fun."

"Now you tell me again exactly what to expect; to tell the truth, I did n't half hear about it the other day; I was wool-gathering. It was something queer that happened when you were a child, was n't it?"

"Something that began to happen long before that, and kept happening, and may happen again; but I hope not."

"What was it?"

"I wonder if the other people in the car can hear us?"

"I fancy not; we do n't hear them – not consecutively at least."

"Well, mother was born in Vermont, you know; she was the only child by a second marriage. Aunt Hannah and Aunt Maria are only half-aunts to me, you know."

"I hope they are half as nice as you are."

"Roger, be still; they certainly will hear us."

"Well, do n't you want them to know we are married?"

"Yes, but not just married. There's all the difference in the world."

"You are afraid we look too happy!"

"No; only I want my happiness all to myself."

"Well, the little room?"

"My aunts brought mother up; they were nearly twenty years older than she. I might say Hiram and they brought her up. You see, Hiram was bound out to grand-father when he was a boy, and when grandfather died Hiram said he 's'posed he went with the farm, 'long o' the critters,' and he has been there ever since. He was my mother's only refuge from the decorum of my aunts. They are simply workers. They make me think of the Maine woman who wanted her epitaph to be, 'She was a *hard* working woman.'"

"They must be almost beyond their working-days. How old are they?"

"Seventy, or thereabouts; but they will die standing; or, at least, on a Saturday night, after all the house-work is done up. They were rather strict with mother, and I think she had a lonely childhood. The house is almost a mile away from any neighbors, and off on top of what they call Stony Hill. It is bleak enough up there even in summer.

"When Mamma was about ten years old they sent her to cousins in Brooklyn, who had children of their own, and knew more about bringing them up. She staid there till she was married: she did n't go to Vermont in all that time, and of course had n't seen her sisters, for they never would leave home for a day. They could n't even be induced to go to Brooklyn to her wedding so she and father took their wedding trip up there."

"And that's why we are going up there on our own?"

"Do n't, Roger; you have no idea how loud you speak."

"You never say so except when I am going to say that one little word."

"Well, do n't say it, then or say it very, very quietly."

"Well, what was the queer thing?"

"When they got to the house, mother wanted to take father right off into the little room; she had been telling him about it, just as I am going to tell you and she had said that of all the rooms that one was the only one that seemed pleasant to her. She described the furniture and the books and paper and everything, and said it was on the north side, between the front and back room. Well, when they went to look for it, there was no little room there; there was only a shallow china-closet. She asked her sisters when the house had been altered and a closet made of the room that used to be there. They both said the house was exactly as it had been built – that they had never made any changes, except to tear down the old wood-shed and build a smaller one.

"Father and mother laughed a good deal over it, and when anything was lost they would always say it must be in the little room, and any exaggerated statement was called 'little-roomy.' When I was a child I thought that was a regular English phrase, I heard it so often.

"Well, they talked it over, and finally they concluded that my mother had been a very imaginative sort of a child and had read in some book about such a little room, or perhaps even dreamed it, and then had 'made believe,' as children do till she herself had really thought the room was there."

"Why, of course, that might easily happen."

"Yes, but you have n't heard the queer part yet; you wait and see if you can explain the rest as easily.

"They staid at the farm two weeks and then went to New York to live. When I was eight years old my father was killed in the war, and mother was broken-hearted.

She never was quite strong afterwards, and that summer we decided to go up to the farm for three months.

"I was a restless sort of a child, and the journey seemed very long to me: and finally, to pass the time mamma told me the story of the little room, and how it was all in her own imagination and how there really was only a china-closet there.

"She told it with all the particulars; and even to me, who knew beforehand that the room was n't there, it seemed just as real as could be. She said it was on the north side, between the front and back rooms; that it was very small, and they sometimes called it an entry. There was a door also that opened out-of-doors, and that one was painted green and was cut in the middle like the old Dutch doors so that it could be used for a window by opening the top part only. Directly opposite the door was a lounge or couch; it was covered with blue chintz – India chintz – some that had been brought over by an old Salem sea-captain as a 'venture.' He had given it to Maria when she was a young girl. She was sent to Salem for two years to school. Grandfather originally came from Salem."

"I thought there was n't any room or chintz?"

"*That is just it.* They had decided that mother had imagined it all, and yet you see how exactly everything was painted in her mind, for she had even remembered that Hiram had told her that Maria could have married the sea-captain if she had wanted to!

"The India cotton was the regular blue stamped chintz, with the peacock figure on it. The head and body of the bird were in profile, while the tail was full front view behind it. It had seemed to take mamma's fancy, and she drew it for me on a piece of paper as she talked. Does n't it seem strange to you that she could have made all that up, or even dreamed it?

"At the foot of the lounge were some hanging shelves with some old books on them. All the books were leather-colored except one; that was bright red, and was called the *Ladies' Album*. It made a bright break between the other thicker books.

"On the lower shelf was a beautiful pink sea-shell, lying on a mat made of balls of red shaded worsted. This shell was greatly coveted by mother, but she was only allowed to play with it when she had been particularly good. Hiram had showed her how to hold it close to her ear and hear the roar of the sea in it.

"I know you will like Hiram, Roger, he is quite a character in his way.

"Mamma said she remembered, or *thought* she remembered, having been sick once, and she had to lie quietly for some days on the lounge; then was the time she had become so familiar with everything in the room, and she had been allowed to have the shell to play with all the time. She had had her toast brought to her in there, with make-believe tea. It was one of her pleasant memories of her childhood; it was the first time she had been of any importance to anybody, even herself.

"Right at the head of the lounge was a light-stand, as they called it, and on it was a very brightly polished brass candlestick and a brass tray, with snuffers. That is all I remember of her describing, except that there was a braided rag rug on the floor, and on the wall was a beautiful flowered paper – roses and morning-glories in a wreath on a light blue ground. The same paper was in the front room."

"And all this never existed except in her imagination?"

"She said that when she and father went up there, there was n't any little room at all like it anywhere in the house; there was a china-closet where she had believed the room to be."

"And your aunts said there had never been any such room."

"That is what they said."

"Was n't there any blue chintz in the house – with a peacock figure?"

"Not a scrap, and Aunt Hannah said there had never been any that she could remember; and Maria just echoed her – she always does that. You see, Aunt Hannah is an up-and-down New England woman. She looks just like herself; I mean just like her character. Her joints move up and down or backward and forward in a plain square fashion. I do n't believe she ever leaned on anything in her life, or sat in an easy chair. But Maria is different; she is rounder and softer; she has n't any ideas of her own; she never had any. I do n't believe she would think it right or becoming to have one that differed from Aunt Hannah's, so what would be the use of having any? She is an echo, that's all.

"When mamma and I got there, of course I was all excitement to see the china-closet, and I had a sort of feeling that it would be the little room after all. So I ran ahead and threw open the door, crying, 'Come and see the little room.'

"And, Roger," said Mrs. Grant, laying her hand in his, "there really was a little room there, exactly as mother had remembered it. There was the lounge, the peacock chintz, the green door, the shell, the morning-glory and rose paper, *everything exactly as she had described it to me.*"

"What in the world did the sisters say about it?"

"Wait a minute and I will tell you. My mother was in the front hall still talking with Aunt Hannah. She did n't hear me at first but I ran out there and dragged her through the front room, saying, 'The room *is* here – it is all right.'

"It seemed for a minute as if my mother would faint. She clung to me in terror. I can remember now how strained her eyes looked and how pale she was.

"I called out to Aunt Hannah and asked her when they had had the closet taken away and the little room built; for in my excitement I thought that that was what had been done.

"'That little room has always been there,' said Aunt Hannah, 'ever since the house was built.'

"'But mamma said there was n't any little room here, only a china-closet, when she was here with papa,' said I.

"'No, there has never been any china-closet there; it has always been just as it is now,' said Aunt Hannah.

"Then mother spoke; her voice sounded weak and far off. She said, slowly, and with an effort, 'Maria, do n't you remember that you told me that there had *never been any little room here*, and Hannah said so too, and then I said I must have dreamed it?'

"'No, I do n't remember anything of the kind,' said Maria, without the slightest emotion. 'I do n't remember you ever said anything about any china-closet; the house has never been altered; you used to play in this room when you were a child, do n't you remember?'

"'I know it,' said mother, in that queer slow voice that made me feel frightened. 'Hannah, do n't you remember my finding the china-closet here, with the gilt-edged china on the shelves, and then *you* said that the *china-closet* has always been here?'

"'No,' said Hannah, pleasantly but unemotionally – 'no, I do n't think you ever asked me about any china-closet, and we have n't any gilt-edged china that I know of.'

"And that was the strangest thing about it. We never could make them remember that there had ever been any question about it. You would think they could remember how surprised mother had been before, unless she had imagined the whole thing. Oh, it was so queer! They were always pleasant about it, did n't seem to feel any interest or curiosity. It was always this answer: 'The house is just as it was built; there have never been any changes, so far as we know.'

"And my mother was in an agony of perplexity. How cold their gray eyes looked to me! There was no reading anything in them. It just seemed to break my mother down, this queer thing. Many times that summer, in the middle of the night, I have seen her get up and take a candle and creep softly down stairs. I could hear the steps creak softly under her weight. Then she would go through the front room and peer into the darkness, holding her thin hand between the candle and her eyes. She seemed to think the little room might vanish. Then she would come back to bed and toss about all night, or lie still and shiver; it used to frighten me.

"She grew pale and thin, and she had a little cough; then she did not like to be left alone. Sometimes she would make errands in order to send me to the little room for something – a book, or her fan, or her handkerchief; but she would never sit there or let me stay in there long, and sometimes she would n't let me go in there for days together. Oh, it was pitiful!"

"Well, do n't talk any more about it, Margaret, if it makes you feel so," said Mr. Grant.

"Oh, yes, I want you to know all about it, and then there is n't much more – no more about the room.

"Mother never got well, and she died that autumn. She used often to sigh, and say, with a wan little laugh, 'There is one thing I am glad of, Margaret: your father knows now all about the little room.' I think she was afraid I distrusted her. Of course, in a child's way, I thought there was something queer about it, but I did not brood over it. I was too young then, and took it as a part of her illness. But Roger, do you know, it really did affect me. I almost hate to go there after talking about it; I somehow feel as if it might, you know, be a china-closet again."

"That's an absurd idea."

"I know it; of course it can't be. I saw the room, and there is n't any china-closet there, and no gilt-edged china in the house, either."

And then she whispered, "But, Roger, you may hold my hand as you do now, if you will, when we go to look for the little room."

"And you won't mind Aunt Hannah's gray eyes?"

"I won't mind *anything*."

It was dusk when Mr. and Mrs. Grant went into the gate under the two old Lombardy poplars and walked up the narrow path to the door, where they were met by the two aunts.

Hannah gave Mrs. Grant a frigid but not unfriendly kiss; and Maria seemed for a moment to tremble on the verge of an emotion, but she glanced at Hannah, and then gave her greeting in exactly the same repressed and non-committal way.

Supper was waiting for them. On the table was the *gilt-edged china*. Mrs. Grant did n't notice it immediately, till she saw her husband smiling at her over his teacup; then she felt fidgety and could n't eat. She was nervous, and kept wondering what was behind her, whether it would be a little room or a closet.

After supper she offered to help about the dishes, but, mercy! she might as well have offered to help bring the seasons round; Maria and Hannah could n't be helped.

So she and her husband went to find the little room, or closet, or whatever was to be there.

Aunt Maria followed them, carrying the lamp, which she set down, and then went back to the dish-washing.

Margaret looked at her husband. He kissed her, for she seemed troubled; and then, hand in hand, they opened the door. It opened into a *china-closet*. The shelves were neatly draped with scalloped paper; on them was the gilt-edged china, with the dishes missing that had been used at the supper, and which at that moment were being carefully washed and wiped by the two aunts.

Margaret's husband dropped her hand and looked at her. She was trembling a little, and turned to him for help, for some explanation, but in an instant she knew that something was wrong. A cloud had come between them; he was hurt; he was antagonized.

He paused for an appreciable instant, and then said kindly enough, but in a voice that cut her deeply, "I am glad this ridiculous thing is ended; do n't let us speak of it again."

"Ended!" said she. "How ended?" And somehow her voice sounded to her as her mother's voice had when she stood there and questioned her sisters about the little room. She seemed to have to drag her words out. She spoke slowly: "It seems to me to have only just begun in my case. It was just so with mother when she – "

"I really wish, Margaret, you would let it drop. I do n't like to hear you speak of your mother in connection with it. It – " He hesitated, for was not this their wedding-day? "It does n't seem quite the thing, quite delicate, you know, to use her name in the matter."

She saw it all now: *he did n't believe her.* She felt a chill sense of withering under his glance.

"Come," he added, "let us go out, or into the dining-room, somewhere, anywhere, only drop this nonsense."

He went out; he did not take her hand now – he was vexed, baffled, hurt. Had he not given her his sympathy, his attention, his belief – and his hand? – and she was fooling him. What did it mean? – She was so truthful, so free from morbidness – a thing he hated. He walked up and down under the poplars, trying to get into the mood to go and join her in the house.

Margaret heard him go out; then she turned and shook the shelves; she reached her hand behind them and tried to push the boards away; she ran out of the house on to the north side and tried to find in the darkness, with her hands, a door, or some steps leading to one. She tore her dress on the old rose-trees, she fell and rose and stumbled, then she sat down on the ground and tried to think. What could she think – was she dreaming?

She went into the house and out into the kitchen, and begged Aunt Maria to tell her about the little room – what had become of it, when had they built the closet, when had they bought the gilt-edged china?

They went on washing dishes and drying them on the spotless towels with methodical exactness; and as they worked they said that there had never been any little room, so far as they knew; the china-closet has always been there, and the gilt-edged china had belonged to their mother, it had always been in the house.

"No, I do n't remember that your mother ever asked about any little room," said Hannah. "She did n't seem very well that summer, but she never asked about any changes in the house; there had n't ever been any changes."

There it was again: not a sign of interest, curiosity, or annoyance, not a spark of memory.

She went out to Hiram. He was telling Mr. Grant about the farm. She had meant to ask him about the room, but her lips were sealed before her husband.

Months afterwards, when time had lessened the sharpness of their feelings, they learned to speculate reasonably about the phenomenon, which Mr. Grant had accepted as something not to be scoffed away, not to be treated as a poor joke, but to be put aside as something inexplicable on any ordinary theory.

Margaret alone in her heart knew that her mother's words carried a deeper significance than she had dreamed of at the time. "One thing I am glad of, your father knows now," and she wondered if Roger or she would ever know.

Five years later they were going to Europe. The packing was done; the children were lying asleep, with their travelling things ready to be slipped on for an early start.

Roger had a foreign appointment. They were not to be back in America for some years. She had meant to go up say good-by to her aunts; but a mother of three children intends to do a great many things that never get done. One thing she had done that very day, and as she paused for a moment between the writing of two notes that must be posted before she went to bed, she said:

"Roger, you remember Rita Lash? Well, she and Cousin Nan go up to the Adirondacks every autumn. They are clever girls, and I have entrusted to them something I want done very much."

"They are the girls to do it then, every inch of them."

"I know it, and they are going to."

"Well?"

"Why, you see, Roger, that little room – "

"Oh – "

"Yes, I was a coward not to go up myself, but I did n't find time, because I had n't the courage."

"Oh! *that* was it, was it?"

"Yes, just that. They are going, and they will write us about it."

"Want to bet?"

"No; I only want to know."

Rita Lash and Cousin Nan planned to go to Vermont on their way to the Adirondacks. They found they would have three hours between trains, which would give them time to drive up to the Keys farm, and they could still get to the camp that night. But, at the last minute, Rita was prevented from going. Nan had to go to meet the Adirondack party, and she promised to telegraph her when she arrived at camp. Imagine Rita's amusement when she received this message: "Safely arrived; went to the Keys farm; it is a little room."

Rita was amused, because she did not in the least think Nan had been there. She thought it was a hoax; but it put it into her mind to carry the joke further by really stopping herself when she went up, as she meant to do the next week.

She did stop over. She introduced herself to the two maiden ladies, who seemed familiar, as they had been described by Mrs. Grant.

They were, if not cordial, at least not disconcerted at her visit, and willingly showed her over the house. As they did not speak of any other stranger's having been to see them lately, she became confirmed in her belief that Nan had not been there.

In the north room she saw the roses and morning glory paper on the wall, and also the door that should open into – what?

She asked if she might open it.

"Certainly," said Hannah; and Maria echoed, "Certainly."

She opened it and found the china-closet. She experienced a certain relief; she at least was not under any spell. Mrs. Grant left it a china-closet; she found it the same. Good.

But she tried to induce the old sisters to remember that there had at various times been certain questions relating to a confusion as to whether the closet had always been a closet. It was no use; their stony eyes gave no sign.

Then she thought of the story of the sea-captain, and said, "Miss Keys, did you ever have a lounge covered with India chintz, with a figure of a peacock on it, given to you in Salem by a sea-captain, who brought it from India?"

"I dun'no' as I ever did," said Hannah. That was all. She thought Maria's cheeks were a little flushed, but her eyes were like a stone wall.

She went on that night to the Adirondacks. When Nan and she were alone in their room she said, "By-the-way, Nan, what did you see at the farm-house? and how did you like Maria and Hannah?"

Nan did n't mistrust that Rita had been there, and she began excitedly to tell her all abut her visit. Rita could almost have believed Nan had been there if she had n't known it was not so. She let her go on for some time, enjoying her enthusiasm, and the impressive way in which she described her opening the door and finding the "little room." Then Rita said: "Now, Nan, that is enough fibbing. I went to the farm myself on the way up yesterday, and there is *no* little room, and there *never* has been any; it is a china-closet, just as Mrs. Grant saw it last."

She was pretending to be busy unpacking her trunk, and did not look up for a moment; but as Nan did not say anything, she glanced over her shoulder. Nan was actually pale, and it was hard to say whether she was most angry or frightened. There was something of both in her look. And then Rita began to explain how her telegram had put her in the spirit of going up there alone. She had n't meant to cut Nan out. She only thought – Then Nan broke in: "It is n't that; I am sure you can't think it is that. But I went myself, and you did not go; you can't have been there, for *it is a little room*."

Oh, what a night they had! They could n't sleep. They talked and argued, and then kept still for a while, only to break out again, it was so absurd. They both maintained that they had been there, but both felt sure the other one was either crazy or obstinate beyond reason. They were wretched; it was perfectly ridiculous, two friends at odds over such a thing; but her it was – "little room," "china-closet," – "china closet," "little room."

The next morning Nan was tacking up some tarlatan at a window to keep the midges out. Rita offered to help her, as she had done for the past ten years. Nan's "No, thanks," cut her to the heart.

"Nan," said she, "come right down from that stepladder and pack your satchel. The stage leaves in just twenty minutes. We can catch the afternoon express train, and then we'll go together to the farm. I am either going there or going home. You better go with me."

Nan did n't say a word. She gathered up the hammer and tacks, and was ready to start when the stage came round.

It meant for them thirty miles of staging and six hours of train, besides crossing the lake; but what of that, compared with having a lie lying round loose between them! Europe would have seemed easy to accomplish, if it would settle the question.

At the little junction in Vermont they found a farmer with a wagon full of meal-bags. They asked him if he could not take them up to the old Keys farm and bring them back in time for the return train, due in two hours.

They had planned to call it a sketching trip, so they said, "We have been there before, we are artists, and we might find some views worth taking, and we also want to make a short call upon the Misses Keys."

"Did ye calculate to paint the old *house* in the picture?"

They said it was possible they might do so. They wanted to see it, anyway.

"Waal, I guess you are too late. The *house* burned down last night, and everything in it."

Sarah Orne Jewett (1849–1909)

Sarah Orne Jewett is best remembered for her masterpiece of regional realism, *The Country of the Pointed Firs* (1896), a cycle of stories set in the fictional Dunnet Landing, based on Jewett's own home town of South Berwick, Maine. All of these stories are told by an unnamed narrator, a well-traveled woman who is a professional writer, and who vacations in Dunnet Landing. She forms a friendship with her landlady, Almira Todd, who becomes her window into the folk life of the community. Mrs. Todd, Jewett's finest fictional creation, is a kind of good witch; she dispenses herbal medicines and advice to her neighbors, and is an oral historian for the community. In "The Foreigner" (1900), Jewett revisits the world of *The Country of the Pointed Firs*. Readers who had read the earlier volume would already know about Mrs. Todd's elderly mother and her brother William, who share a home on Green Island. In this tale, Mrs. Todd tells the narrator the ghost story she impulsively asks for, but the story is less about ghosts than about female bonding and initiation. It is the account of how Mrs. Todd came to be the powerful and wise woman the narrator knows.

Text: Sarah Orne Jewett, "The Foreigner," *Atlantic Monthly*, 86 (1900), 152–67.

The Foreigner

I.

One evening, at the end of August, in Dunnet Landing, I heard Mrs. Todd's firm footstep crossing the small front entry outside my door, and her conventional cough which served as a herald's trumpet, or a plain New England knock, in the harmony of our fellowship.

"Oh, please come in!" I cried, for it had been so still in the house that I supposed my friend and hostess had gone to see one of her neighbors. The first cold northeasterly storm of the season was blowing hard outside. Now and then there was a dash of great raindrops and a flick of wet lilac leaves against the window, but I could hear that the sea was already stirred to its dark depths, and the great rollers were coming in heavily against the shore. One might well believe that Summer was coming to a sad end that night, in the darkness and rain and sudden access of autumnal cold. It seemed as if there must be danger offshore among the outer islands.

"Oh, there!" exclaimed Mrs. Todd, as she entered. "I know nothing ain't ever happened out to Green Island since the world began, but I always do worry about mother in these great gales. You know those tidal waves occur sometimes down to the West Indies, and I get dwellin' on 'em so I can't set still in my chair, nor knit a common row to a stocking. William might get mooning, out in his small bo't, and not observe how the sea was making, an' meet with some accident. Yes, I thought I'd come in and set with you if you wa'n't busy. No, I never feel any concern about 'em in winter 'cause then they're prepared, and all ashore and everything snug. William ought to keep help, as I tell him; yes, he ought to keep help."

I hastened to reassure my anxious guest by saying that Elijah Tilley had told me in the afternoon, when I came along the shore past the fish houses, that Johnny Bowden and the Captain were out at Green Island; he had seen them beating up the bay, and thought they must have put into Burnt Island cove, but one of the lobstermen brought word later that he saw them hauling out at Green Island as he came by, and Captain Bowden pointed ashore and shook his head to say that he did not mean to try to get in. "The old Miranda just managed it, but she will have to stay at home a day or two and put new patches in her sail," I ended, not without pride in so much circumstantial evidence.

Mrs. Todd was alert in a moment. "Then they'll all have a very pleasant evening," she assured me, apparently dismissing all fears of tidal waves and other sea-going disasters. "I was urging Alick Bowden to go ashore some day and see mother before cold weather. He's her own nephew; she sets a great deal by him. And Johnny's a great chum o' William's; don't you know the first day we had Johnny out 'long of us, he took an' give William his money to keep for him that he'd been a-savin', and William showed it to me an' was so affected I thought he was goin' to shed tears? 'Twas a dollar an' eighty cents; yes, they'll have a beautiful evenin' all together, and like's not the sea'll be flat as a doorstep come morning."

I had drawn a large wooden rocking-chair before the fire, and Mrs. Todd was sitting there jogging herself a little, knitting fast, and wonderfully placid of countenance. There came a fresh gust of wind and rain, and we could feel the small wooden house rock and hear it creak as if it were a ship at sea.

"Lord, hear the great breakers!" exclaimed Mrs. Todd. "How they pound! – there, there! I always run of an idea that the sea knows anger these nights and gets full o' fight. I can hear the rote[1] o' them old black ledges way down the thoroughfare. Calls up all those stormy verses in the Book o' Psalms; David he knew how old sea-goin' folks have to quake at the heart."

I thought as I had never thought before of such anxieties. The families of sailors and coastwise adventurers by sea must always be worrying about somebody, this side of the world or the other. There was hardly one of Mrs. Todd's elder acquaintances, men or women, who had not at some time or other made a sea voyage, and there was often no news until the voyagers themselves came back to bring it.

"There's a roaring high overhead, and a roaring in the deep sea," said Mrs. Todd solemnly, "and they battle together nights like this. No, I could n't sleep; some women folks always goes right to bed an' to sleep, so's to forget, but 't ain't my way. Well, it's a blessin' we don't all feel alike; there's hardly any of our folks at sea to worry about, nowadays, but I can't help my feelin's, an' I got thinking of mother all alone, if William had happened to be out lobsterin' and could n't make the cove gettin' back."

"They will have a pleasant evening," I repeated. "Captain Bowden is the best of good company."

"Mother'll make him some pancakes for his supper, like's not," said Mrs. Todd, clicking her knitting needles and giving a pull at her yarn. Just then the old cat pushed open the unlatched door and came straight toward her mistress's lap. She was regarded

Notes ———————————————————————————————————

THE FOREIGNER
[1] The sound of the surf.

severely as she stepped about and turned on the broad expanse, and then made herself into a round cushion of fur, but was not openly admonished. There was another great blast of wind overhead, and a puff of smoke came down the chimney.

"This makes me think o' the night Mis' Cap'n Tolland died," said Mrs. Todd, half to herself. Folks used to say these gales only blew when somebody's a-dyin', or the devil was a-comin' for his own, but the worst man I ever knew died a real pretty mornin' in June."

"You have never told me any ghost stories, said I; and such was the gloomy weather and the influence of the night that I was instantly filled with reluctance to have this suggestion followed. I had not chosen the best of moments; just before I spoke we had begun to feel as cheerful as possible. Mrs. Todd glanced doubtfully at the cat and then at me, with a strange absent look, and I was really afraid that she was going to tell me something that would haunt my thoughts on every dark stormy night as long as I lived.

"Never mind now; tell me to-morrow by daylight, Mrs. Todd," I hastened to say, but she still looked at me full of doubt and deliberation.

"Ghost stories!" she answered. "Yes, I don't know but I've heard a plenty of 'em first an' last. I was just sayin' to myself that this is like the night Mis' Cap'n Tolland died. 'Twas the great line storm in September all of thirty, or maybe forty, year ago. I ain't one that keeps much account o' time."

"Tolland? That's a name I have never heard in Dunnet," I said.

"Then you haven't looked well about the old part o' the buryin' ground, no'theast corner," replied Mrs. Todd. "All their women folks lies there; the sea's got most o' the men. They were a known family o' shipmasters in early times. Mother had a mate, Ellen Tolland, that she mourns to this day; died right in her bloom with quick consumption, but the rest o' that family was all boys but one, and older than she, an' they lived hard seafarin' lives an' all died hard. They were called very smart seamen. I've heard that when the youngest went into one o' the old shippin' houses in Boston, the head o' the firm called out to him: 'Did you say Tolland from Dunnet? That's recommendation enough for any vessel!' There was some o' them old shipmasters as tough as iron, an' they had the name o' usin' their crews very severe, but there wasn't a man that would n't rather sign with 'em an' take his chances, than with the slack ones that didn't know how to meet accidents."

II.

There was so long a pause, and Mrs. Todd still looked so absent-minded, that I was afraid she and the cat were growing drowsy together before the fire, and I should have no reminiscences at all. The wind struck the house again, so that we both started in our chairs and Mrs. Todd gave a curious, startled look at me. The cat lifted her head and listened too, in the silence that followed, while after the wind sank we were more conscious than ever of the awful roar of the sea. The house jarred now and then, in a strange, disturbing way.

"Yes, they'll have a beautiful evening out to the island," said Mrs. Todd again; but she did not say it gayly. I had not seen her before in her weaker moments.

"Who was Mrs. Captain Tolland?" I asked eagerly, to change the current of our thoughts.

"I never knew her maiden name; if I ever heard it, I've gone an' forgot; 't would mean nothing to me," answered Mrs. Todd.

"She was a foreigner, an' he met with her out in the Island o' Jamaica. They said she'd been left a widow with property. Land knows what become of it; she was French born, an' her first husband was a Portugee, or somethin'."

I kept silence now, a poor and insufficient question being worse than none.

"Cap'n John Tolland was the least smartest of any of 'em, but he was full smart enough, an' commanded a good brig at the time, in the sugar trade; he'd taken out a cargo o' pine lumber to the islands from somewheres up the river, an' had been loadin' for home in the port o' Kingston, an' had gone ashore that afternoon for his papers, an' remained afterwards 'long of three friends o' his, all shipmasters. They was havin' their suppers together in a tavern; 't was late in the evenin' an' they was more lively than usual, an' felt boyish; and over opposite was another house full o' company, real bright and pleasant lookin', with a lot o' lights, an' they heard somebody singin' very pretty to a guitar. They wa'n't in no go-to-meetin' condition, an' one of 'em, he slapped the table an' said, 'Le' 's go over an' hear that lady sing!' an' over they all went, good honest sailors, but three sheets in the wind, and stepped in as if they was invited, an' made their bows inside the door, an' asked if they could hear the music; they were all respectable well-dressed men. They saw the woman that had the guitar, an' there was a company a-listenin', regular highbinders[2] all of 'em; an' there was a long table all spread out with big candlesticks like little trees o' light, and a sight o' glass an' silver ware; an' part o' the men was young officers in uniform, an' the colored folks was steppin' round servin' 'em, an' they had the lady singin'. 'Twas a wasteful scene, an' a loud talkin' company' an' though they was three sheets in the wind themselves there wa'n't one o' them cap'ns but had sense to perceive it. The others had pushed back their chairs, an' their decanters an' glasses was standin' thick about, an' they was teasin' the one that was singin' as if they'd just got her in to amuse 'em. But they quieted down; one o' the young officers had beautiful manners, an' invited the four cap'ns to join 'em, very polite; 't was a kind of public house, and after they'd all heard another song, he come to consult with 'em whether they would n't git up and dance a hornpipe or somethin' to the lady's music.

"They was all elderly men an' shipmasters, and owned property; two of 'em was church members in good standin'," continued Mrs. Todd loftily, "an' they would n't lend theirselves to no such kick-shows as that, an' spite o' bein' three sheets in the wind, as I have once observed; they waved aside the tumblers of wine the young officer was pourin' out for 'em so freehanded, and said they should rather be excused. An' when they all rose, still very dignified, as I've been well informed, and made their partin' bows and was goin' out, them young sports got round 'em an' tried to prevent 'em, and they had to push an' strive considerable, but out they come. There was this Cap'n Tolland and two Cap'n Bowdens, and the fourth was my own father." (Mrs. Todd spoke slowly, as if to impress the value of her authority.) "Two of them was very religious, upright men, but they would have their night off sometimes, all o' them old-fashioned cap'ns, when they was free of business and ready to leave port.

"An' they went back to their tavern an' got their bills paid, an' set down kind o' mad with everybody by the front windows, mistrusting some o' their tavern charges, like's not, by that time, an' when they got tempered down, they watched the house over across, where the party was.

"There was a kind of a grove o' trees between the house an' the road, an' they heard the guitar a-goin' an' a-stoppin' short by turns, and pretty soon somebody began to screech, an' they saw a white dress come runnin' out through the bushes, an' tumbled over each other in their haste to offer help; an' out she come, with the guitar, cryin' into the street, and they just walked off four square with her amongst 'em, down toward the wharves where they felt more to home. They couldn't make out at first

Notes ─────────────────────────────────

[2] Gangsters or thugs (from the name of a New York City gang early in the nineteenth century).

what 't was she spoke, – Cap'n Lorenzo Bowden was well acquainted in Havre an' Bordeaux, an' spoke a poor quality o' French, an' she knew a little mite o' English, but not much; and they come somehow or other to discern that she was in real distress. Her husband and her children had died o' yellow fever; they'd all come up to Kingston from one o' the far Wind'ard Islands to get passage on a steamer to France, an' a negro had stole their money off her husband while he lay sick o' the fever, an' she had been befriended some, but the folks that knew about her had died too; it had been a dreadful run o' the fever that season, an' she fell at last to playin' an' singin' for hire, and for what money they'd throw to her round them harbor houses.

"'Twas a real hard case, an' when them cap'ns made out about it, there wasn't one that meant to take leave without helpin' of her. They was pretty mellow, an' whatever they might lack o' prudence they more 'n made up with charity: they did n't want to see nobody abused, an' she was sort of a pretty woman, an' they stopped in the street then an' there an' drew lots who should take her aboard, bein' all bound home. An' the lot fell to Cap'n Jonathan Bowden who did act discouraged; his vessel had but small accommodations, though he could stow a big freight, an' she was a dreadful slow sailer through bein' square as a box, an' his first wife, that was livin' then, was a dreadful jealous woman. He threw himself right onto the mercy o' Cap'n Tolland."

Mrs. Todd indulged herself for a short time in a season of calm reflection.

"I always thought they'd have done better, and more reasonable, to give her some money to pay her passage home to France, or wherever she may have wanted to go," she continued.

I nodded and looked for the rest of the story.

"Father told mother," said Mrs. Todd confidentially, "that Cap'n Jonathan Bowden an' Cap'n John Tolland had both taken a little more than usual; I wouldn't have you think, either, that they both wasn't the best o' men, an' they was solemn as owls, and argued the matter between 'em, an' waved aside the other two when they tried to put their oars in. An' spite o' Cap'n Tolland's bein' a settled old bachelor they fixed it that he was to take the prize on his brig; she was a fast sailer, and there was a good spare cabin or two where he'd sometimes carried passengers, but he'd filled 'em with bags o' sugar on his own account an' was loaded very heavy beside. He said he'd shift the sugar an' get along somehow, an' the last the other three cap'ns saw of the party was Cap'n John handing the lady into his bo't, guitar and all, an' off they all set tow'ds their ships with their men rowin' 'em in the bright moonlight down to Port Royal where the anchorage was, an' where they all lay, goin' out with the tide an' mornin' wind at break o' day. An' the others thought they heard music of the guitar, two o' the bo'ts kept well together, but it may have come from another source."

"Well; and then?" I asked eagerly after a pause. Mrs. Todd was almost laughing aloud over her knitting and nodding emphatically.[3] We had forgotten all about the noise of the wind and sea.

"Lord bless you! he come sailing into Portland with his sugar, all in good time, an' they stepped right afore a justice o' the peace, and Cap'n John Tolland come paradin' home to Dunnet Landin' a married man. He owned one o' them thin, narrow-lookin' houses with one room each side o' the front door, and two slim black spruces spindlin' up against the front windows to make it gloomy inside. There was no horse nor cattle of course, though he owned pasture land, an' you could see rifts o' light right through the barn as you drove by. And there was a good excellent kitchen, but his sister reigned

Notes

[3] Mrs. Todd has told the sea captains' story with a straight face thus far, but now is allowing herself some amusement at a yarn that obviously had been heavily censored for the womenfolk in Dunnet Landing.

over that; she had a right to two rooms, and took the kitchen an' a bedroom that led out of it; an' bein' given no rights in the kitchen had angered the cap'n so they were n't on no kind o' speakin' terms. He preferred his old brig for comfort, but now and then, between voyages, he'd come home for a few days, just to show he was master over his part o' the house, and show Eliza she could n't commit no trespass.

"They stayed a little while; 't was pretty spring weather, an' I used to see Cap'n John rollin' by with his arms full o' bundles from the store, lookin' as pleased and important as a boy; an' then they went right off to sea again, an' was gone a good many months. Next time he left her to live there alone, after they'd stopped at home together some weeks, an' they said she suffered from bein' at sea, but some said that the owners would n't have a woman aboard. 'T was before father was lost on that last voyage of his, an' he and mother went up once or twice to see them. Father said there wa'n't a mite o' harm in her, but somehow or other a sight o' prejudice arose; it may have been caused by the remarks of Eliza an' her feelin's tow'ds her brother. Even my mother had no regard for Eliza Tolland. But mother asked the cap'n's wife to come with her one evenin' to a social circle that was down to the meetin'-house vestry, so she'd get acquainted a little, an' she appeared very pretty until they started to have some singin' to the melodeon. Mari' Harris an' one o' the younger Caplin girls undertook to sing a duet, an' they sort o' flatted, an' she put her hands right up to her ears, and give a little squeal, an' went quick as could be an' give 'em the right notes, for she could read the music like plain print, an' made 'em try it over again. She was real willin' an' pleasant, but that did n't suit, an' she made faces when they got it wrong. An' then there fell a dead calm, an' we was all settin' round prim as dishes, an' my mother, that never expects ill feelin', asked her if she would n't sing somethin', an' up she got, – poor creatur', it all seems so different to me now, – an' sung a lovely little song standin' in the floor; it seemed to have something gay about it that kept a-repeatin', an' nobody could help keepin' time, an' all of a sudden she looked round at the tables and caught up a tin plate that somebody'd fetched a Washin'ton pie in, an' she begun to drum on it with her fingers like one o' them tambourines, an' went right on singin' faster an' faster, and next minute she begun to dance a little pretty dance between the verses, just as light and pleasant as a child. You could n't help seein' how pretty 't was; we all got to trottin' a foot, an' some o' the men clapped their hands quite loud, a-keepin' time, 't was so catchin', an' seemed so natural to her. There' wa'n't one of 'em but enjoyed it; she just tried to do her part, an' some urged her on, till she stopped with a little twirl of her skirts an' went to her place again by mother. And I can see mother now, reachin' over an' smilin' an' pattin' her hand.

"But next day there was an awful scandal goin' in the parish, an' Mari' Harris reproached my mother to her face, an' I never wanted to see her since, but I've had to a good many times. I said Mis' Tolland didn't intend no impropriety, – I reminded her of David's dancin' before the Lord; but she said such a man as David never would have thought o' dancin' right there in the Orthodox vestry, and she felt I spoke with irreverence.

"And next Sunday Mis' Tolland come walkin' into our meeting, but I must say she acted like a cat in a strange garret, and went right out down the aisle with her head in air, from the pew Deacon Caplin had showed her into. 'Twas just in the beginning of the long prayer. I wish she'd stayed through, whatever her reasons were. Whether she'd expected somethin' different, or misunderstood some o' the pastor's remarks, or what 't was, I don't really feel able to explain, but she kind o' declared war, at least folks thought so, an' war 't was from that time. I see she was cryin', or had been, as she passed by me; perhaps bein' in meetin' was what had power to make her feel homesick and strange.

"Cap'n John Tolland was away fittin' out; that next week he come home to see her and say farewell. He was lost with his ship in the Straits of Malacca, and she lived there alone in the old house a few months longer till she died. He left her well off; 't was said he hid his money about the house and she knew where 't was. Oh, I expect you've heard that story told over an' over twenty times, since you've been here at the Landin'?"

"Never one word," I insisted.

"It was a good while ago," explained Mrs. Todd, with reassurance. "Yes, it all happened a great while ago."

III.

At this moment, with a sudden flaw of the wind, some wet twigs outside blew against the window panes and made a noise like a distressed creature trying to get in. I started with sudden fear, and so did the cat, but Mrs. Todd knitted away and did not even look over her shoulder.

"She was a good-looking woman; yes, I always thought Mis' Tolland was good-looking, though she had, as was reasonable, a sort of foreign cast, and she spoke very broken English, no better than a child. She was always at work about her house, or settin' at a front window with her sewing; she was a beautiful hand to embroider. Sometimes, summer evenings, when the windows was open, she'd set an' drum on her guitar, but I don't know as I ever heard her sing but once after the cap'n went away. She appeared very happy about havin' him, and took on dreadful at partin' when he was down here on the wharf, going back to Portland by boat to take ship for that last v'y'ge. He acted kind of ashamed, Cap'n John did; folks about here ain't so much accustomed to show their feelings. The whistle had blown an' they was waitin' for him to get aboard, an' he was put to it to know what to do and treated her very affectionate in spite of all impatience; but mother happened to be there and she went an' spoke, and I remember what a comfort she seemed to be. Mis' Tolland clung to her then, and she wouldn't give a glance after the boat when it had started, though the captain was very eager a-wavin' to her. She wanted mother to come home with her an' would n't let go her hand, and mother had just come in to stop all night with me an' had plenty o' time ashore, which did n't always happen, so they walked off together, an' 't was some considerable time before she got back.

"'I want you to neighbor with that poor lonesome creatur',' says mother to me, lookin' reproachful. 'She's a stranger in a strange land,' says mother.[4] 'I want you to make her have a sense that somebody feels kind to her.'

"'Why, since that time she flaunted out o' meetin', folks have felt she liked other ways better'n our 'n,' says I. I was provoked, because I'd had a nice supper ready, an' mother 'd let it wait so long 't was spoiled. 'I hope you'll like your supper!' I told her. I was dreadful ashamed afterward of speakin' so to mother.

"'What consequence is my supper?' says she to me; mother can be very stern, – 'or your comfort or mine, beside letting a foreign person an' a stranger feel so desolate; she's done the best a woman could do in her lonesome place, and she asks nothing of anybody except a little common kindness. Think if 't was you in a foreign land!'

"And mother set down to drink her tea, an' I set down humbled enough over by the wall to wait till she finished. An' I did think it all over, an' next day I never said nothin', but I put on my bonnet, and went to see Mis' Cap'n Tolland, if 't was only for mother's sake. 'T was about three quarters of a mile up the road here, beyond the schoolhouse.

Notes —————————————————————————————————————

[4] Mother's speech is filled with echoes of the King James Bible. See Exodus 2:22 and Luke 10:29–37 (the parable of the Good Samaritan).

I forgot to tell you that the cap'n had bought out his sister's right at three or four times what 't was worth, to save trouble, so they'd got clear o' her, an' I went round into the side yard sort o' friendly an' sociable, rather than stop an' deal with the knocker an' the front door. It looked so pleasant an' pretty I was glad I come; she had set a little table for supper, though 't was still early, with a white cloth on it, right out under an old apple tree close by the house. I noticed 't was same as with me at home, there was only one plate. She was just coming out with a dish; you could n't see the door nor the table from the road.

"In the few weeks she'd been there she'd got some bloomin' pinks an' other flowers next the doorstep. Somehow it looked as if she'd known how to make it homelike for the cap'n. She asked me to set down; she was very polite, but she looked very mournful, and I spoke of mother, an' she put down her dish and caught holt o' me with both hands an' said my mother was an angel. When I see the tears in her eyes 't was all right between us, and we were always friendly after that, and mother had us come out and make a little visit that summer; but she come a foreigner and she went a foreigner, and never was anything but a stranger among our folks. She taught me a sight o' things about herbs I never knew before nor since; she was well acquainted with the virtues o' plants. She'd act awful secret about some things too, an' used to work charms for herself sometimes, an' some o' the neighbors told to an' fro after she died that they knew enough not to provoke her, but 't was all nonsense; 'tis the believin' in such things that causes 'em to be any harm, an' so I told 'em," confided Mrs. Todd contemptuously. "That first night I stopped to tea with her she'd cooked some eggs with some herb or other sprinkled all through, and 't was she that first led me to discern mushrooms; an' she went right down on her knees in my garden here when she saw I had my different officious[5] herbs. Yes, 't was she that learned me the proper use o' parsley too; she was a beautiful cook."

Mrs. Todd stopped talking, and rose, putting the cat gently in the chair, while she went away to get another stick of apple-tree wood. It was not an evening when one wished to let the fire go down, and we had a splendid bank of bright coals. I had always wondered where Mrs. Todd had got such an unusual knowledge of cookery, of the varieties of mushrooms, and the use of sorrel as a vegetable, and other blessings of that sort. I had long ago learned that she could vary her omelettes like a child of France, which was indeed a surprise in Dunnet Landing.

IV.

All these revelations were of the deepest interest, and I was ready with a question as soon as Mrs. Todd came in and had well settled the fire and herself and the cat again.

"I wonder why she never went back to France, after she was left alone?"

"She come here from the French islands," explained Mrs. Todd. "I asked her once about her folks, an' she said they were all dead; 't was the fever took 'em. She made this her home, lonesome as 't was; she told me she hadn't been in France since she was 'so small,' and measured me off a child o' six. She'd lived right out in the country before, so that part wa'n't unusual to her. Oh yes, there was something very strange about her, and she hadn't been brought up in high circles nor nothing o' that kind. I think she'd been really pleased to have the cap'n marry her an' give her a good home, after all she'd passed through, and leave her free with his money an' all that. An' she got over bein' so strange-looking to me after a while, but 't was a very singular expression: she

Notes —————————————————————————————

[5] Useful or helpful.

wore a fixed smile that wa'n't a smile; there wa'n't no light behind it, same 's a lamp can't shine if it ain't lit. I don't know just how to express it, 't was a sort of made countenance."

One could not help thinking of Sir Philip Sidney's phrase, "A made countenance, between simpering and smiling."[6]

"She took it hard, havin' the captain go off on that last voyage," Mrs. Todd went on. "She said somethin' told her when they was partin' that he would never come back. He was lucky to speak a home-bound ship this side o' the Cape o' Good Hope, an' got a chance to send her a letter, an' that cheered her up. You often felt as if you was dealin' with a child's mind, for all she had so much information that other folks had n't. I was a sight younger than I be now, and she made me imagine new things, and I got interested watchin' her an' findin' out what she had to say, but you could n't get to no affectionateness with her. I used to blame me sometimes; we used to be real good comrades goin' off for an afternoon, but I never give her a kiss till the day she laid in her coffin and it come to my heart there wa'n't no one else to do it."

"And Captain Tolland died," I suggested after a while.

"Yes, the cap'n was lost," said Mrs. Todd, "and of course word did n't come for a good while after it happened. The letter come from the owners to my uncle, Cap'n Lorenzo Bowden, who was in charge of Cap'n Tolland's affairs at home, and he come right up for me an' said I must go with him to the house. I had known what it was to be a widow, myself, for near a year, an' there was plenty o' widow women along this coast that the sea had made desolate, but I never saw a heart break as I did then.

"'T was this way: we walked together along the road, me an' uncle Lorenzo. You know how it leads straight from just above the schoolhouse to the brook bridge, and their house was just this side o' the brook bridge on the left hand; the cellar's there now, and a couple or three good-sized gray birches growin' in it. And when we come near enough I saw that the best room, this way, where she most never set, was all lighted up, and the curtains up so that the light shone bright down the road, and as we walked, those lights would dazzle and dazzle in my eyes, and I could hear the guitar a-goin', an' she was singin'. She heard our steps with her quick ears and come running to the door with her eyes a-shinin', an' all that set look gone out of her face, an' begun to talk French, gay as a bird, an' shook hands and behaved very pretty an' girlish, sayin' 't was her fête day.[7] I did n't know what she meant then. And she had gone an' put a wreath o' flowers on her hair an' wore a handsome gold chain that the cap'n had given her; an' there she was, poor creatur', makin' believe have a party all alone in her best room; 't was prim enough to discourage a person, with too many chairs set close to the walls, just as the cap'n's mother had left it, but she had put sort o' long garlands on the walls, droopin' very graceful, and a sight of green boughs in the corners, till it looked lovely, and all lit up with a lot o' candles."

"Oh dear!" I sighed. "Oh, Mrs. Todd, what did you do?"

"She beheld our countenances," answered Mrs. Todd solemnly. "I expect they was telling everything plain enough, but Cap'n Lorenzo spoke the sad words to her as if he had been her father; and she wavered a minute and then over she went on the floor before we could catch hold of her, and then we tried to bring her to herself and failed, and at last we carried her upstairs, an' I told uncle to run down and put out the lights, and then go fast as he could for Mrs. Begg, being very experienced in sickness, an' he so did. I got off her clothes and her poor wreath, and I cried as I done it. We both

Notes

[6] From *Arcadia* (1590).
[7] Day celebrating the saint after whom she was named.

stayed there that night, and the doctor said 't was a shock when he come in the morning; he 'd been over to Black Island an' had to stay all night with a very sick child."

"You said that she lived alone some time after the news came," I reminded Mrs. Todd then.

"Oh yes, dear," answered my friend sadly, "but it wa'n't what you'd call livin'; no, it was only dyin', though at a snail's pace. She never went out again those few months, but for a while she could manage to get about the house a little, and do what was needed, an' I never let two days go by without seein' her or hearin' from her. She never took much notice as I came an' went except to answer if I asked her anything. Mother was the one who gave her the only comfort."

"What was that?" I asked softly.

"She said that anybody in such trouble ought to see their minister, mother did, and one day she spoke to Mis' Tolland, and found that the poor soul had been believin' all the time that there were n't any priests here. We'd come to know she was a Catholic by her beads and all, and that had set some narrow minds against her. And mother explained it just as she would to a child; and uncle Lorenzo sent word right off some-wheres up river by a packet[8] that was bound up the bay, and the first o' the week a priest come by the boat, an' uncle Lorenzo was on the wharf 'tendin' to some business; so they just come up for me, and I walked with him to show him the house. He was a kind-hearted old man; he looked so benevolent an' fatherly I could ha' stopped an' told him my own troubles; yes, I was satisfied when I first saw his face, an' when poor Mis' Tolland beheld him enter the room, she went right down on her knees and clasped her hands together to him as if he'd come to save her life, and he lifted her up and blessed her, an' I left 'em together, and slipped out into the open field and walked there in sight so if they needed to call me, and I had my own thoughts. At last I saw him at the door; he had to catch the return boat. I meant to walk back with him and offer him some supper, but he said no, and said he was comin' again if needed, and signed me to go into the house to her, and shook his head in a way that meant he understood everything. I can see him now; he walked with a cane, rather tired and feeble; I wished somebody would come along, so's to carry him down to the shore.

"Mis' Tolland looked up at me with a new look when I went in, an' she even took hold o' my hand and kept it. He had put some oil on her forehead, but nothing anybody could do would keep her alive very long; 't was his medicine for the soul rather 'n the body. I helped her to bed, and next morning she couldn't get up to dress her, and that was Monday, and she began to fail, and 't was Friday night she died." (Mrs. Todd spoke with unusual haste and lack of detail.) "Mrs. Begg and I watched with her, and made everything nice and proper, and after all the ill will there was a good number gathered to the funeral. 'Twas in Reverend Mr. Bascom's day, and he done very well in his prayer, considering he couldn't fill in with mentioning all the near connections by name as was his habit. He spoke very feeling about her being a stranger and twice widowed, and all he said about her being reared among the heathen was to observe that there might be roads leadin' up to the New Jerusalem from various points. I says to myself that I guessed quite a number must ha' reached there that wa'n't able to set out from Dunnet Landin'!"

Mrs. Todd gave an odd little laugh as she bent toward the firelight to pick up a dropped stitch in her knitting, and then I heard a heartfelt sigh.

"'t was most forty years ago," she said; "most everybody's gone a'ready that was there that day."

Notes

8 Seagoing equivalent of a bus, which carries passengers, mail, and freight along the coast.

V.

Suddenly Mrs. Todd gave an energetic shrug of her shoulders, and a quick look at me, and I saw that the sails of her narrative were filled with a fresh breeze.

"Uncle Lorenzo, Cap'n Bowden that I have referred to" –

"Certainly!" I agreed with eager expectation.

"He was the one that had been left in charge of Cap'n John Tolland's affairs, and had now come to be of unforeseen importance.

"Mrs. Begg an' I had stayed in the house both before an' after Mis' Tolland's decease, and she was now in haste to be gone, having affairs to call her home; but uncle come to me as the exercises was beginning, and said he thought I'd better remain at the house while they went to the buryin' ground. I could n't understand his reasons, an' I felt disappointed, bein' as near to her as most anybody; 't was rough weather, so mother could n't get in, and did n't even hear Mis' Tolland was gone till next day. I just nodded to satisfy him, 't wa'n't no time to discuss anything. Uncle seemed flustered; he'd gone out deep-sea fishin' the day she died, and the storm I told you of rose very sudden, so they got blown off way down the coast beyond Monhegan, and he 'd just got back in time to dress himself and come.

"I set there in the house after I'd watched her away down the straight road far 's I could see from the door; 't was a little short walkin' funeral an' a cloudy sky, so everything looked dull an' gray, an' it crawled along all in one piece, same 's walking funerals do, an' I wondered how it ever come to the Lord's mind to let her begin down among them gay islands all heat and sun, and end up here among the rocks with a north wind blowin'. 'Twas a gale that begun the afternoon before she died, and had kept blowin' off an' on ever since. I'd thought more than once how glad I should be to get home an' out o' sound o' them black spruces a-beatin' an' scratchin' at the front windows.

"I set to work pretty soon to put the chairs back, an' set outdoors some that was borrowed, an' I went out in the kitchen, an' I made up a good fire in case somebody come an' wanted a cup o' tea; but I did n't expect any one to travel way back to the house unless 't was uncle Lorenzo. 'Twas growin' so chilly that I fetched some kindlin' wood and made fires in both the fore rooms. Then I set down an' begun to feel as usual, and I got my knittin' out of a drawer. You can't be sorry for a poor creatur' that's come to the end o' all her troubles; my only discomfort was I thought I'd ought to feel worse at losin' her than I did; I was younger then than I be now. And as I set there, I begun to hear some long notes o' dronin' music from upstairs that chilled me to the bone."

Mrs. Todd gave a hasty glance at me.

"Quick 's I could gather me, I went right upstairs to see what 't was," she added eagerly, "an' 't was just what I might ha' known. She'd always kept her guitar hangin' right against the wall in her room; 't was tied by a blue ribbon, and there was a window left wide open; the wind was veerin' a good deal, an' it slanted in and searched the room. The strings was jarrin' yet.

"'Twas growin' pretty late in the afternoon, an' I begun to feel lonesome as I should n't now, and I was disappointed at having to stay there, the more I thought it over, but after a while I saw Cap'n Lorenzo polin' back up the road all alone, and when he come nearer I could see he had a bundle under his arm and had shifted his best black clothes for his every-day ones. I run out and put some tea into the teapot and set it back on the stove to draw, an' when he come in I reached down a little jug o' spirits, – Cap'n Tolland had left his house well provisioned as if his wife was goin' to put to sea same's himself, an' there she'd gone an' left it. There was some cake that Mis' Begg an' I had made the day before. I thought that uncle an' me had a good right to the funeral supper, even if there wa'n't any one to join us. I was lookin' forward to my cup o' tea; 't was beautiful tea out of a green lacquered chest that I've got now."

"You must have felt very tired," said I, eagerly listening.

"I was 'most beat out, with watchin' an' tendin' and all," answered Mrs. Todd, with as much sympathy in her voice as if she were speaking of another person. "But I called out to uncle as he came in, 'Well, I expect it's all over now, an' we s've all done what we could. I thought we'd better have some tea or somethin' before we go home. Come right out in the kitchen, sir,' says I, never thinking but we only had to let the fires out and lock up everything safe an' eat our refreshment, an' go home.

"'I want both of us to stop here to-night,' says uncle, looking at me very important.

"'Oh, what for?' says I, kind o' fretful.

"'I've got my proper reasons,' says uncle. 'I'll see you well satisfied, Almira. Your tongue ain't so easy-goin' as some o' the women folks, an' there's property here to take charge of that you don't know nothin' at all about.'

"'What do you mean?' says I.

"'Cap'n Tolland acquainted me with his affairs; he had n't no sort o' confidence in nobody but me an' his wife, after he was tricked into signin' that Portland note, an' lost money. An' she didn't know nothin' about business; but what he did n't take to sea to be sunk with him he's hid somewhere in this house. I expect Mis' Tolland may have told you where she kept things?' said uncle.

"I see he was dependin' a good deal on my answer," said Mrs. Todd, "but I had to disappoint him; no, she had never said nothin' to me."

"'Well, then, we've got to make a search,' says he, with considerable relish; but he was all tired and worked up, and we set down to the table, an' he had somethin', an' I took my desired cup o' tea, and then I begun to feel more interested.

"'Where you goin' to look first?' says I, but he give me a short look an' made no answer, and begun to mix me a very small portion out of the jug, in another glass. I took it to please him; he said I looked tired, speakin' real fatherly, and I did feel better for it, and we set talkin' a few minutes, an' then he started for the cellar, carrying an old ship's lantern he fetched out o' the stairway an' lit.

"'What are you lookin' for, some kind of a chist?' I inquired, and he said yes. All of a sudden it come to me to ask who was the heirs; Eliza Tolland, Cap'n John's own sister, had never demeaned herself to come near the funeral, and uncle Lorenzo faced right about and begun to laugh, sort o' pleased. I thought queer of it; 't wa'n't what he'd taken, which would be nothin' to an old weathered sailor like him.

"'Who's the heir?' says I the second time.

"'Why, it's *you*, Almiry,' says he; and I was so took aback I set right down on the turn o' the cellar stairs.

"'Yes 't is,' said uncle Lorenzo. 'I'm glad of it too. Some thought she didn't have no sense but foreign sense, an' a poor stock o' that, but she said you was friendly to her, an' one day after she got news of Tolland's death, an' I had fetched up his will that left everything to her, she said she was goin' to make a writin', so's you could have things after she was gone, an' she give five hundred to me for bein' executor. Square Pease fixed up the paper, an' she signed it; it's all accordin' to law.' There, I begun to cry," said Mrs. Todd; "I could n't help it. I wished I had her back again to do somethin' for, an' to make her know I felt sisterly to her more 'n I'd ever showed, an' it come over me 't was all too late, an' I cried the more, till uncle showed impatience, an' I got up an' stumbled along down cellar with my apern to my eyes the greater part of the time.

"'I'm goin' to have a clean search,' says he; 'you hold the light.' An' I held it, and he rummaged in the arches an' under the stairs, an' over in some old closet where he reached out bottles an' stone jugs an' canted some kegs an' one or two casks, an' chuckled well when he heard there was somethin' inside, – but there wa'n't nothin' to find but things usual in a cellar, an' then the old lantern was givin' out an' we come away.

"'He spoke to me of a chist, Cap'n Tolland did,' says uncle in a whisper. 'He said a good sound chist was as safe a bank as there was, an' I beat him out of such nonsense, 'count o' fire an' other risks.' 'There's no chist in the rooms above,' says I; 'no, uncle, there ain't no sea-chist, for I've been here long enough to see what there was to be seen.' Yet he would n't feel contented till he'd mounted up into the toploft; 't was one o' them single, hip-roofed houses that don't give proper accommodation for a real garret, like Cap'n Littlepage's down here at the Landin'. There was broken furniture and rubbish, an' he let down a terrible sight o' dust into the front entry, but sure enough there was n't no chist. I had it all to sweep up next day.

"'He must have took it away to sea,' says I to the cap'n, an' even then he did n't want to agree, but we was both beat out. I told him where I'd always seen Mis' Tolland get her money from, and we found much as a hundred dollars there in an old red morocco wallet. Cap'n John had been gone a good while already, and she had spent what she needed. 'Twas in an old desk o' his in the settin' room that we found the wallet."

"At the last minute he may have taken his money to sea," I suggested.

"Oh yes," agreed Mrs. Todd. "He did take considerable to make his venture to bring home, as was customary, an' that was drowned with him as uncle agreed; but he had other property in shipping, and a thousand dollars invested in Portland in a cordage shop, but 't was about the time shipping begun to decay, and the cordage shop failed, and in the end I wa'n't so rich as I thought I was goin' to be for those few minutes on the cellar stairs. There was an auction that accumulated something. Old Mis' Tolland, the cap'n's mother, had heired some good furniture from a sister: there was above thirty chairs in all, and they 're apt to sell well. I got over a thousand dollars when we come to settle up, and I made uncle take his five hundred; he was getting along in years and had met with losses in navigation, and he left it back to me when he died, so I had a real good lift. It all lays in the bank over to Rockland, and I draw my interest fall an' spring, with the little Mr. Todd was able to leave me; but that's kind o' sacred money; 't was earnt and saved with the hope o' youth, an' I'm very particular what I spend it for. Oh yes, what with ownin' my house, I've been enabled to get along very well, with prudence!" said Mrs. Todd contentedly.

"But there was the house and land," I asked, – "what became of that part of the property?"

Mrs. Todd looked into the fire, and a shadow of disapproval flitted over her face.

"Poor old uncle!" she said, "he got childish about the matter. I was hoping to sell at first, and I had an offer, but he always run of an idea that there was more money hid away, and kept wanting me to delay; an' he used to go up there all alone and search, and dig in the cellar, empty an' bleak as 't was in winter weather or any time. An' he'd come and tell me he'd dreamed he found gold behind a stone in the cellar wall, or somethin'. And one night we all see the light o' fire up that way, an' the whole Landin' took the road, and run to look, and the Tolland property was all in a light blaze. I expect the old gentleman had dropped fire about; he said he'd been up there to see if every- thing was safe in the afternoon. As for the land, 't was so poor that everybody used to have a joke that the Tolland boys preferred to farm the sea instead. It's 'most all grown up to bushes now, where it ain't poor water grass in the low places. There's some upland that has a pretty view, after you cross the brook bridge. Years an' years after she died, there was some o' her flowers used to come up an' bloom in the door garden.

I brought two or three that was unusual down here; they always come up and remind me of her, constant as the spring. But I never did want to fetch home that guitar, some way or 'nother; I would n't let it go at the auction, either. It was hangin' right there in the house when the fire took place. I've got some o' her other little things scattered about the house: that picture on the mantelpiece belonged to her."

I had often wondered where such a picture had come from, and why Mrs. Todd had chosen it; it was a French print of the statue of the Empress Josephine in the Savane at old Fort Royal, in Martinique.

VI.

Mrs. Todd drew her chair closer to mine; she held the cat and her knitting with one hand as she moved, but the cat was so warm and so sound asleep that she only stretched a lazy paw in spite of what must have felt like a slight earthquake. Mrs. Todd began to speak almost in a whisper.

"I ain't told you all," she continued; "no, I have n't spoken of all to but very few. The way it came was this," she said solemnly, and then stopped to listen to the wind, and sat for a moment in deferential silence, as if she waited for the wind to speak first. The cat suddenly lifted her head with quick excitement and gleaming eyes, and her mistress was leaning forward toward the fire with an arm laid on either knee, as if they were consulting the glowing coals for some augury. Mrs. Todd looked like an old prophetess as she sat there with the firelight shining on her strong face; she was posed for some great painter. The woman with the cat was as unconscious and as mysterious as any sibyl of the Sistine Chapel.

"There, that's the last struggle o' the gale," said Mrs. Todd, nodding her head with impressive certainty and still looking into the bright embers of the fire. "You'll see!" She gave me another quick glance, and spoke in a low tone as if we might be overheard.

"'T was such a gale as this the night Mis' Tolland died. She appeared more comfortable the first o' the evenin'; and Mrs. Begg was more spent than I, bein' older, and a beautiful nurse that was the first to see and think of everything, but perfectly quiet an' never asked a useless question. You remember her funeral when you first come to the Landing? And she consented to goin' an' havin' a good sleep while she could, and left me one o' those good little pewter lamps that burnt whale oil an' made plenty o' light in the room, but not too bright to be disturbin'.

"Poor Mis' Tolland had been distressed the night before, an' all that day, but as night come on she grew more and more easy, an' was layin' there asleep; 't was like settin' by any sleepin' person, and I had none but usual thoughts. When the wind lulled and the rain, I could hear the seas, though more distant than this, and I don' know's I observed any other sound than what the weather made; 't was a very solemn feelin' night. I set close by the bed; there was times she looked to find somebody when she was awake. The light was on her face, so I could see her plain; there was always times when she wore a look that made her seem a stranger you'd never set eyes on before. I did think what a world it was that her an' me should have come together so, and she have nobody but Dunnet Landin' folks about her in her extremity. 'You're one o' the stray ones, poor creatur',' I said. I remember those very words passin' through my mind, but I saw reason to be glad she had some comforts, and didn't lack friends at the last, though she'd seen misery an' pain. I was glad she was quiet; all day she'd been restless, and we could n't understand what she wanted from her French speech. We had the window open to give her air, an' now an' then a gust would strike that guitar that was on the wall and set it swinging by the blue ribbon, and soundin' as if somebody begun to play it. I come near takin' it down, but you never know what'll fret a sick person an' put 'em on the rack, an' that guitar was one o' the few things she'd brought with her."

I nodded assent, and Mrs. Todd spoke still lower.

"I set there close by the bed; I'd been through a good deal for some days back, and I thought I might's well be droppin' asleep too, bein' a quick person to wake. She looked to me as if she might last a day longer, certain, now she'd got more comfortable, but I was real tired, an' sort o' cramped as watchers will get, an' a fretful feeling begun to creep over me such as they often do have. If you give way, there ain't no support for the sick person; they can't count on no composure o' their own. Mis' Tolland moved then, a little restless, an' I forgot me quick enough, an' begun to hum out a little part of a hymn tune just to make her feel everything was as usual an' not wake up into a poor uncertainty. All of a sudden she set right up in bed with her eyes wide open, an' I stood an' put my arm behind her; she had n't moved like that for days. And she reached out both her arms toward the door, an' I looked the way she was lookin', an' I see some one was standin' there against the dark. No, 't wa'n't Mis' Begg; 't was somebody a good deal shorter than Mis' Begg. The lamplight struck across the room between us. I could n't tell the shape, but 't was a woman's dark face lookin' right at us; 't wa'n't but an instant I could see. I felt dreadful cold, and my head begun to swim; I thought the light went out; 't wa'n't but an instant, as I say, an' when my sight come back I could n't see nothing there. I was one that did n't know what it was to faint away, no matter what happened; time was I felt above it in others, but 't was somethin' that made poor human natur' quail. I saw very plain while I could see; 't was a pleasant enough face, shaped somethin' like Mis' Tolland's, and a kind of expectin' look.

"No, I don't expect I was asleep," Mrs. Todd assured me quietly, after a moment's pause, though I had not spoken. She gave a heavy sigh before she went on. I could see that the recollection moved her in the deepest way.

"I suppose if I had n't been so spent an' quavery with long watchin', I might have kept my head an' observed much better," she added humbly; "but I see all I could bear. I did try to act calm, an' I laid Mis' Tolland down on her pillow, an' I was a-shakin' as I done it. All she did was to look up to me so satisfied and sort o' questioning, an' I looked back to her.

"'You saw her, didn't you?' she says to me, speakin' perfectly reasonable. ''T is my mother,' she says again, very feeble, but lookin' straight up at me, kind of surprised with the pleasure, and smiling as if she saw I was overcome, an' would have said more if she could, but we had hold of hands. I see then her change was comin', but I did n't call Mis' Begg, nor make no uproar. I felt calm then, an' lifted to somethin' different as I never was since. She opened her eyes just as she was goin' –

"'You saw her, did n't you?' she said the second time, an' I says, 'Yes, dear, I did; you ain't never goin' to feel strange an' lonesome no more.' An' then in a few quiet minutes 't was all over. I felt they'd gone away together. No, I wa'n't alarmed afterward; 't was just that one moment I could n't live under, but I never called it beyond reason I should see the other watcher. I saw plain enough there was somebody there with me in the room.

VII.

"'T was just such a night as this Mis' Tolland died," repeated Mrs. Todd, returning to her usual tone and leaning back comfortably in her chair as she took up her knitting. "'T was just such a night as this. I've told the circumstances to but very few; but I don't call it beyond reason. When folks is goin' 't is all natural, and only common things can jar upon the mind. You know plain enough there's somethin' beyond this world; the doors stand wide open. 'There's somethin' of us that must still live on; we've got to join both worlds together an' live in one but for the other.' The doctor said that to me one day, an' I never could forget it; he said 't was in one o' his old doctor's books."

We sat together in silence in the warm little room; the rain dropped heavily from the eaves, and the sea still roared, but the high wind had done blowing. We heard the far complaining fog horn of a steamer up the Bay.

"There goes the Boston boat out, pretty near on time," said Mrs. Todd with satisfaction. "Sometimes these late August storms 'll sound a good deal worse than they really be. I do hate to hear the poor steamers callin' when they're bewildered in thick nights in winter, comin' on the coast. Yes, there goes the boat; they'll find it rough at sea, but the storm 's all over."

Kate Chopin

Kate Chopin (1851–1904)

Kate Chopin's career never recovered from the harsh reviews that greeted her second novel, *The Awakening* (1899). Her work was rediscovered in the 1960s, a period much kinder to iconoclastic values than her own time had been. Many readers now regard her as one of the finest American authors of the late nineteenth century.

Chopin was bilingual in French and English, and her short-story style was influenced by Guy de Maupassant, whom she translated. Like Maupassant, Chopin is a master of the tightly structured tale which moves toward an unexpected twist. In the hands of some writers (as, in a harsh reading, O. Henry), this plot twist can be simply a trick; the best of these stories, however, will sustain rereading and reveal more than a thrill-producing mechanism.

In "Désirée's Baby" (1893), Armand appears first as a monster who has been converted by love into a kindly husband (as is Mr. Rochester in *Jane Eyre*). At the end, of course, Armand is revealed as simply a monster: Chopin indicates that he is not "human." Readers may disagree about the point when Armand learns of his own heritage: at the end or earlier? But the source of his evil – the system of slavery – should be clear. Chopin also weaves subtle clues about the practice of miscegenation on the plantation. The secondary characters should be observed carefully since, as often in nineteenth-century discourse on race and sex, key points are often implied rather than stated directly. Who, for example, is La Blanche? Why does a crucial moment of recognition occur when Désirée looks at La Blanche's son?

Text: Kate Chopin, *Bayou Folk* (Boston and New York: Houghton, Mifflin, 1894).

Désirée's Baby

As the day was pleasant, Madame Valmondé drove over to L'Abri to see Désirée and the baby.

It made her laugh to think of Désirée with a baby. Why, it seemed but yesterday that Désirée was little more than a baby herself; when Monsieur in riding through the gateway of Valmondé had found her lying asleep in the shadow of the big stone pillar.

The little one awoke in his arms and began to cry for "Dada." That was as much as she could do or say. Some people thought she might have strayed there of her own accord, for she was of the toddling age. The prevailing belief was that she had been purposely left by a party of Texans, whose canvas-covered wagon, late in the day, had crossed the ferry that Coton Maïs kept, just below the plantation. In time Madame Valmondé abandoned every speculation but the one that Désirée had been sent to her by a beneficent Providence to be the child of her affection, seeing that she was without child of the flesh. For the girl grew to be beautiful and gentle, affectionate and sincere, – the idol of Valmondé.

American Gothic: From Salem Witchcraft to H. P. Lovecraft, An Anthology, Second Edition. Edited by Charles L. Crow.
Editorial material and organization © 2013 John Wiley & Sons, Ltd. Published 2013 by John Wiley & Sons, Ltd.

It was no wonder, when she stood one day against the stone pillar in whose shadow she had lain asleep, eighteen years before, that Armand Aubigny riding by and seeing her there, had fallen in love with her. That was the way all the Aubignys fell in love, as if struck by a pistol shot. The wonder was that he had not loved her before; for he had known her since his father brought him home from Paris, a boy of eight, after his mother died there. The passion that awoke in him that day, when he saw her at the gate, swept along like an avalanche, or like a prairie fire, or like anything that drives headlong over all obstacles.

Monsieur Valmondé grew practical and wanted things well considered: that is, the girl's obscure origin. Armand looked into her eyes and did not care. He was reminded that she was nameless. What did it matter about a name when he could give her one of the oldest and proudest in Louisiana? He ordered the *corbeille*[1] from Paris, and contained himself with what patience he could until it arrived; then they were married.

Madame Valmondé had not seen Désirée and the baby for four weeks. When she reached L'Abri she shuddered at the first sight of it, as she always did. It was a sad looking place, which for many years had not known the gentle presence of a mistress, old Monsieur Aubigny having married and buried his wife in France, and she having loved her own land too well ever to leave it. The roof came down steep and black like a cowl, reaching out beyond the wide galleries that encircled the yellow stuccoed house. Big, solemn oaks grew close to it, and their thick-leaved, far-reaching branches shadowed it like a pall. Young Aubigny's rule was a strict one, too, and under it his negroes had forgotten how to be gay, as they had been during the old master's easy-going and indulgent lifetime.

The young mother was recovering slowly, and lay full length, in her soft white muslins and laces, upon a couch. The baby was beside her, upon her arm, where he had fallen asleep, at her breast. The yellow nurse woman sat beside a window fanning herself.

Madame Valmondé bent her portly figure over Désirée and kissed her, holding her an instant tenderly in her arms. Then she turned to the child.

"This is not the baby!" she exclaimed, in startled tones. French was the language spoken at Valmondé in those days.

"I knew you would be astonished," laughed Désirée, "at the way he has grown. The little *cochon de lait!*[2] Look at his legs, mamma, and his hands and fingernails, – real finger-nails. Zandrine had to cut them this morning. Isn't it true, Zandrine?"

The woman bowed her turbaned head majestically, "Mais si,[3] Madame."

"And the way he cries," went on Désirée, "is deafening. Armand heard him the other day as far away as La Blanche's cabin."

Madame Valmondé had never removed her eyes from the child. She lifted it and walked with it over to the window that was lightest. She scanned the baby narrowly, then looked as searchingly at Zandrine whose face was turned to gaze across the fields.

"Yes, the child has grown, has changed," said Madame Valmondé, slowly, as she replaced it beside its mother. "What does Armand say?"

Désirée's face became suffused with a glow that was happiness itself.

"Oh, Armand is the proudest father in the parish, I believe, chiefly because it is a boy, to bear his name; though he says not, – that he would have loved a girl as well. But I know it isn't true. I know he says that to please me. And mamma," she added, drawing Madame Valmondé's head down to her, and speaking in a whisper, "he hasn't punished

Notes

DÉSIRÉE'S BABY
[1] Wedding gifts.

[2] Piglet.
[3] Indeed, certainly!

one of them – not one of them – since baby is born. Even Négrillon, who pretended to have burnt his leg that he might rest from work – he only laughed, and said Négrillon was a great scamp. Oh, mamma, I'm so happy; it frightens me."

What Désirée said was true. Marriage, and later the birth of his son had softened Armand Aubigny's imperious and exacting nature greatly. This was what made the gentle Désirée so happy, for she loved him desperately. When he frowned she trembled, but loved him. When he smiled she asked no greater blessing of God. But Armand's dark, handsome face had not often been disfigured by frowns since the day he fell in love with her.

When the baby was about three months old, Désirée awoke one day to the conviction that there was something in the air menacing her peace. It was at first too subtle to grasp. It had only been a disquieting suggestion; an air of mystery among the blacks; unexpected visits from far-off neighbors who could hardly account for their coming. Then a strange, an awful change in her husband's manner, which she dared not ask him to explain. When he spoke to her, it was with averted eyes, from which the old love-light seemed to have gone out. He absented himself from home; and when there, avoided her presence and that of her child, without excuse. And the very spirit of Satan seemed suddenly to take hold of him in his dealings with the slaves. Désirée was miserable enough to die.

She sat in her room, one hot afternoon, in her *peignoir*,[4] listlessly drawing through her fingers the strands of her long, silky brown hair that hung about her shoulders. The baby, half naked, lay asleep upon her own great mahogany bed, that was like a sumptuous throne, with its satin-lined hall canopy. One of La Blanche's little quadroon boys – half naked too – stood fanning the child slowly with a fan of peacock feathers. Désirée's eyes had been fixed absently and sadly upon the baby, while she was striving to penetrate the threatening mist that she felt closing about her. She looked from her child to the boy who stood beside him, and back again; over and over. "Ah!" It was a cry that she could not help; which she was not conscious of having uttered. The blood turned like ice in her veins, and a clammy moisture gathered upon her face.

She tried to speak to the little quadroon boy; but no sound would come, at first. When he heard his name uttered, he looked up, and his mistress was pointing to the door. He laid aside the great, soft fan, and obediently stole away, over the polished floor, on his bare tiptoes.

She stayed motionless, with gaze riveted upon her child, and her face the picture of fright.

Presently her husband entered the room, and without noticing her, went to a table and began to search among some papers which covered it.

"Armand," she called to him, in a voice which must have stabbed him, if he was human. But he did not notice. "Armand," she said again. Then she rose and tottered towards him. "Armand," she panted once more, clutching his arm, "look at our child. What does it mean? tell me."

He coldly but gently loosened her fingers from about his arm and thrust the hand away from him. "Tell me what it means!" she cried despairingly.

"It means," he answered lightly, "that the child is not white; it means that you are not white."

A quick conception of all that this accusation meant for her nerved her with unwonted courage to deny it. "It is a lie; it is not true, I am white! Look at my hair, it is brown; and my eyes are gray, Armand, you know they are gray. And my skin is fair,"

4 Dressing gown.

seizing his wrist. "Look at my hand; whiter than yours, Armand," she laughed hysterically.

"As white as La Blanche's," he returned cruelly; and went away leaving her alone with their child.

When she could hold a pen in her hand, she sent a despairing letter to Madame Valmondé.

"My mother, they tell me I am not white. Armand has told me I am not white. For God's sake tell them it is not true. You must know it is not true. I shall die. I must die. I cannot be so unhappy, and live."

The answer that came was as brief:

"My own Désirée: Come home to Valmondé; back to your mother who loves you. Come with your child."

When the letter reached Désirée she went with it to her husband's study, and laid it open upon the desk before which he sat. She was like a stone image; silent, white, motionless after she placed it there.

In silence he ran his cold eyes over the written words. He said nothing. "Shall I go, Armand?" she asked in tones sharp with agonized suspense.

"Yes, go."

"Do you want me to go?"

"Yes, I want you to go."

He thought Almighty God had dealt cruelly and unjustly with him; and felt, some-how, that he was paying Him back in kind when he stabbed thus into his wife's soul. Moreover he no longer loved her, because of the unconscious injury she had brought upon his home and his name.

She turned away like one stunned by a blow, and walked slowly towards the door, hoping he would call her back.

"Good-by, Armand," she moaned.

He did not answer her. That was his last blow at fate.

Désirée went in search of her child. Zandrine was pacing the sombre gallery with it. She took the little one from the nurse's arms with no word of explanation, and descending the steps, walked away, under the live-oak branches.

It was an October afternoon; the sun was just sinking. Out in the still fields the negroes were picking cotton.

Désirée had not changed the thin white garment nor the slippers which she wore. Her hair was uncovered and the sun's rays brought a golden gleam from its brown meshes. She did not take the broad, beaten road which led to the far-off plantation of Valmondé. She walked across a deserted field, where the stubble bruised her tender feet, so delicately shod, and tore her thin gown to shreds.

She disappeared among the reeds and willows that grew thick along the banks of the deep, sluggish bayou; and she did not come back again.

Some weeks later there was a curious scene enacted at L'Abri. In the centre of the smoothly swept back yard was a great bonfire. Armand Aubigny sat in the wide hall-way that commanded a view of the spectacle; and it was he who dealt out to a half dozen negroes the material which kept this fire ablaze.

A graceful cradle of willow, with all its dainty furbishings, was laid upon the pyre, which had already been fed with the richness of a priceless *layette*.[5] Then there were silk gowns, and velvet and satin ones added to these; laces, too, and embroideries; bonnets and gloves; for the corbeille had been of rare quality.

Notes
[5] Baby linen.

The last thing to go was a tiny bundle of letters; innocent little scribblings that Désirée had sent to him during the days of their espousal. There was the remnant of one back in the drawer from which he took them. But it was not Désirée's; it was part of an old letter from his mother to his father. He read it. She was thanking God for the blessing of her husband's love: –

"But, above all," she wrote, "night and day, I thank the good God for having so arranged our lives that our dear Armand will never know that his mother, who adores him, belongs to the race that is cursed with the brand of slavery."

Mary E. Wilkins Freeman

Mary E. Wilkins Freeman
(1852–1930)

While she was a girl and young adult, Mary Wilkins' family fought unsuccessfully against a slide into poverty: this seems almost the standard childhood of an artist in the United States, and perhaps everywhere. Turning to her pen for support, she forged a successful career as a writer of magazine fiction. Freeman (she married late, and unhappily) worked usually within the tradition of women's regional realism. She was the leading woman regionalist among the *Harper's* stable of authors, as her contemporary Sarah Orne Jewett was for the *Atlantic*.

Freeman was an accomplished writer of ghost stories, and her overtly realistic fiction often has strong Gothic elements. "Luella Miller" (1902) is a vampire tale. Though overtly supernatural, it has a core of psychological realism: many readers will have known someone like Luella. "Old Woman Magoun" (1909), like many of her stories, explores gender roles, and (characteristic especially of her late work) is profoundly pessimistic about the fate of women in a patriarchal society. Most men in this tale appear as drunken degenerates; sexuality carries with it the threat of rape and a suggestion of incest. The title character is drawn with considerable complexity, approaching tragic grandeur as she attempts to battle not only the masculine threat, but time itself.

Texts: "Luella Miller" from Mary E. Wilkins Freeman, *The Wind in the Rose Bush, and Other Stories of the Supernatural* (New York: Doubleday, Page, 1903). "Old Woman Magoun" from Freeman, *The Winning Lady and Others* (New York: Harper & Brothers, 1909).

Old Woman Magoun

The hamlet at Barry's Ford[1] is situated in a sort of high valley among the mountains. Below it the hills lie in moveless curves like a petrified ocean; above it they rise in green-cresting waves which never break. It is *Barry's* Ford because at one time the Barry family was the most important in the place; and *Ford* because just at the beginning of the hamlet the little turbulent Barry River is fordable. There is, however, now a rude bridge across the river.

Old Woman Magoun was largely instrumental in bringing the bridge to pass. She haunted the miserable little grocery, wherein whiskey and hands of tobacco were the

Notes

OLD WOMAN MAGOUN
[1] In pre-automotive English, a shallow, firm-bottomed place in a river, where wagons, pedestrians, and horses can cross, except in flood time.

most salient features of the stock in trade, and she talked much. She would elbow herself into the midst of a knot of idlers and talk.

"That bridge ought to be built this very summer," said Old Woman Magoun. She spread her strong arms like wings, and sent the loafers, half laughing, half angry, flying in every direction. "If I were a *man*," said she, "I'd go out this very minute and lay the fust log. If I were a passel of lazy men layin' round, I'd start up for once in my life, I would." The men cowered visibly – all except Nelson Barry; he swore under his breath and strode over to the counter.

Old Woman Magoun looked after him majestically. "You can cuss all you want to, Nelson Barry," said she; "I ain't afraid of you. I don't expect you to lay ary log[2] of the bridge, but I'm goin' to have it built this very summer." She did. The weakness of the masculine element in Barry's Ford was laid low before such strenuous feminine assertion.

Old Woman Magoun and some other women planned a treat – two sucking pigs, and pies, and sweet cake – for a reward after the bridge should be finished. They even viewed leniently the increased consumption of ardent spirits.

"It seems queer to me," Old Woman Magoun said to Sally Jinks, "that men can't do nothin' without havin' to drink and chew to keep their sperits up. Lord! I've worked all my life and never done nuther."

"Men is different," said Sally Jinks.

"Yes, they be," assented Old Woman Magoun, with open contempt.

The two women sat on a bench in front of Old Woman Magoun's house, and little Lily Barry, her granddaughter, sat holding her doll on a small mossy stone near by. From where they sat they could see the men at work on the new bridge. It was the last day of the work.

Lily clasped her doll – a poor old rag thing – close to her childish bosom, like a little mother, and her face, round which curled her long yellow hair, was fixed upon the men at work. Little Lily had never been allowed to run with the other children of Barry's Ford. Her grandmother had taught her everything she knew – which was not much, but tending at least to a certain measure of spiritual growth – for she, as it were, poured the goodness of her own soul into this little receptive vase of another. Lily was firmly grounded in her knowledge that it was wrong to lie or steal or disobey her grandmother. She had also learned that one should be very industrious. It was seldom that Lily sat idly holding her doll-baby, but this was a holiday because of the bridge. She looked only a child, although she was nearly fourteen; her mother had been married at sixteen. That is, Old Woman Magoun said that her daughter, Lily's mother, had married at sixteen; there had been rumors, but no one had dared openly gainsay the old woman. She said that her daughter had married Nelson Barry, and he had deserted her. She had lived in her mother's house, and Lily had been born there, and she had died when the baby was only a week old. Lily's father, Nelson Barry, was the fairly dangerous degenerate of a good old family. Nelson's father before him had been bad. He was now the last of the family, with the exception of a sister of feeble intellect, with whom he lived in the old Barry house. He was a middle-aged man, still handsome. The shiftless population of Barry's Ford looked up to him as to an evil deity. They wondered how Old Woman Magoun dared brave him as she did. But Old Woman Magoun had within her a mighty sense of reliance upon herself as being on the right track in the midst of a maze of evil, which gave her courage. Nelson Barry had manifested no interest whatever in his daughter. Lily seldom saw her father.

Notes ──
[2] Dialect: a single log.

She did not often go to the store which was his favorite haunt. Her grandmother took care that she should not do so.

However, that afternoon she departed from her usual custom and sent Lily to the store.

She came in from the kitchen, whither she had been to baste the roasting pig. "There's no use talkin'," said she, "I've got to have some more salt. I've jest used the very last I had to dredge over that pig. I've got to go to the store."

Sally Jinks looked at Lily. "Why don't you send her?" she asked.

Old Woman Magoun gazed irresolutely at the girl. She was herself very tired. It did not seem to her that she could drag herself up the dusty hill to the store. She glanced with covert resentment at Sally Jinks. She thought that she might offer to go. But Sally Jinks said again, "Why don't you let her go?" and looked with a languid eye at Lily holding her doll on the stone.

Lily was watching the men at work on the bridge, with her childish delight in a spectacle of any kind, when her grandmother addressed her.

"Guess I'll let you go down to the store an' git some salt, Lily," said she.

The girl turned uncomprehending eyes upon her grandmother at the sound of her voice. She had been filled with one of the innocent reveries of childhood. Lily had in her the making of an artist or a poet. Her prolonged childhood went to prove it, and also her retrospective eyes, as clear and blue as blue light itself, which seemed to see past all that she looked upon. She had not come of the old Barry family for nothing. The best of the strain was in her, along with the splendid stanchness in humble lines which she had acquired from her grandmother.

"Put on your hat," said Old Woman Magoun; "the sun is hot, and you might git a headache." She called the girl to her, and put back the shower of fair curls under the rubber band which confined the hat. She gave Lily some money, and watched her knot it into a corner of her little cotton handkerchief. "Be careful you don't lose it," said she, "and don't stop to talk to anybody, for I am in a hurry for that salt. Of course, if anybody speaks to you answer them polite, and then come right along."

Lily started, her pocket-handkerchief weighted with the small silver dangling from one hand, and her rag doll carried over her shoulder like a baby. The absurd travesty of a face peeped forth from Lily's yellow curls. Sally Jinks looked after her with a sniff.

"She ain't goin' to carry that rag doll to the store?" said she.

"She likes to," replied Old Woman Magoun, in a half-shamed yet defiantly extenuating voice.

"Some girls at her age is thinkin' about beaux instead of rag dolls," said Sally Jinks.

The grandmother bristled, "Lily ain't big nor old for her age," said she. "I ain't in any hurry to have her git married. She ain't none too strong."

"She's got a good color," said Sally Jinks. She was crocheting white cotton lace, making her thick fingers fly. She really knew how to do scarcely anything except to crochet that coarse lace; somehow her heavy brain or her fingers had mastered that.

"I know she's got a beautiful color," replied Old Woman Magoun, with an odd mixture of pride and anxiety, "but it comes an' goes."

"I've heard that was a bad sign," remarked Sally Jinks, loosening some thread from her spool.

"Yes, it is," said the grandmother. "She's nothin' but a baby, though she's quicker than most to learn."

Lily Barry went on her way to the store. She was clad in a scanty short frock of blue cotton; her hat was tipped back, forming an oval frame for her innocent face. She was very small, and walked like a child, with the clap-clap of little feet of babyhood. She might have been considered, from her looks, under ten.

Presently she heard footsteps behind her; she turned around a little timidly to see who was coming. When she saw a handsome, well-dressed man, she felt reassured. The man came alongside and glanced down carelessly at first, then his look deepened. He smiled, and Lily saw he was very handsome indeed, and that his smile was not only reassuring but wonderfully sweet and compelling.

"Well, little one," said the man, "where are you bound, you and your dolly?"

"I am going to the store to buy some salt for grandma," replied Lily, in her sweet treble. She looked up in the man's face, and he fairly started at the revelation of its innocent beauty. He regulated his pace by hers, and the two went on together. The man did not speak again at once. Lily kept glancing timidly up at him, and every time that she did so the man smiled and her confidence increased. Presently when the man's hand grasped her little childish one hanging by her side, she felt a complete trust in him. Then she smiled up at him. She felt glad that this nice man had come along, for just here the road was lonely.

After a while the man spoke. "What is your name, little one?" he asked, caressingly.

"Lily Barry."

The man started. "What is your father's name?"

"Nelson Barry," replied Lily.

The man whistled. "Is your mother dead?"

"Yes, sir."

"How old are you, my dear?"

"Fourteen," replied Lily.

The man looked at her with surprise. "As old as that?"

Lily suddenly shrank from the man. She could not have told why. She pulled her little hand from his, and he let it go with no remonstrance. She clasped both her arms around her rag doll, in order that her hand should not be free for him to grasp again.

She walked a little farther away from the man, and he looked amused.

"You still play with your doll?" he said, in a soft voice.

"Yes, sir," replied Lily. She quickened her pace and reached the store.

When Lily entered the store, Hiram Gates, the owner, was behind the counter. The only man besides in the store was Nelson Barry. He sat tipping his chair back against the wall; he was half asleep, and his handsome face was bristling with a beard of several days' growth and darkly flushed. He opened his eyes when Lily entered, the strange man following. He brought his chair down on all fours, and he looked at the man – not noticing Lily at all – with a look compounded of defiance and uneasiness.

"Hullo, Jim!" he said.

"Hullo, old man!" returned the stranger.

Lily went over to the counter and asked for the salt, in her pretty little voice. When she had paid for it and was crossing the store, Nelson Barry was on his feet.

"Well, how are you, Lily? It is Lily, isn't it?" he said.

"Yes, sir," replied Lily, faintly.

Her father bent down and, for the first time in her life, kissed her, and the whiskey odor of his breath came into her face.

Lily involuntarily started, and shrank away from him. Then she rubbed her mouth violently with her little cotton handkerchief, which she held gathered up with the rag doll.

"Damn it all! I believe she is afraid of me," said Nelson Barry, in a thick voice.

"Looks a little like it," said the other man, laughing.

"It's that damned old woman," said Nelson Barry. Then he smiled again at Lily. "I didn't know what a pretty little daughter I was blessed with," said he, and he softly stroked Lily's pink cheek under her hat.

Now Lily did not shrink from him. Hereditary instincts and nature itself were asserting themselves in the child's innocent, receptive breast.

Nelson Barry looked curiously at Lily. "How old are you, anyway, child?" he asked.

"I'll be fourteen in September," replied Lily.

"But you still play with your doll?" said Barry, laughing kindly down at her.

Lily hugged her doll more tightly, in spite of her father's kind voice. "Yes, sir," she replied.

Nelson glanced across at some glass jars filled with sticks of candy. "See here, little Lily, do you like candy?" said he.

"Yes, sir."

"Wait a minute."

Lily waited while her father went over to the counter. Soon he returned with a package of the candy.

"I don't see how you are going to carry so much," he said, smiling. "Suppose you throw away your doll?"

Lily gazed at her father and hugged the doll tightly, and there was all at once in the child's expression something mature. It became the reproach of a woman. Nelson's face sobered.

"Oh, it's all right, Lily," he said; "keep your doll. Here, I guess you can carry this candy under your arm."

Lily could not resist the candy. She obeyed Nelson's instructions for carrying it, and left the store laden. The two men also left, and walked in the opposite direction, talking busily.

When Lily reached home, her grandmother, who was watching for her, spied at once the package of candy.

"What's that?" she asked, sharply.

"My father gave it to me," answered Lily, in a faltering voice. Sally regarded her with something like alertness.

"Your father?"

"Yes, ma'am."

"Where did you see him?"

"In the store."

"He gave you this candy?"

"Yes, ma'am."

"What did he say?"

"He asked me how old I was, and – "

"And what?"

"I don't know," replied Lily; and it really seemed to her that she did not know, she was so frightened and bewildered by it all, and, more than anything else, by her grandmother's face as she questioned her.

Old Woman Magoun's face was that of one upon whom a long-anticipated blow had fallen. Sally Jinks gazed at her with a sort of stupid alarm.

Old Woman Magoun continued to gaze at her grandchild with that look of terrible solicitude, as if she saw the girl in the clutch of a tiger. "You can't remember what else he said?" she asked, fiercely, and the child began to whimper softly.

"No, ma'am," she sobbed. "I – don't know, and – "

"And what? Answer me."

"There was another man there. A real handsome man."

"Did he speak to you?" asked Old Woman Magoun.

"Yes, ma'am; he walked along with me a piece," confessed Lily, with a sob of terror and bewilderment.

"What did he say to you?" asked Old Woman Magoun, with a sort of despair.

Lily told, in her little, faltering, frightened voice, all of the conversation which she could recall. It sounded harmless enough, but the look of the realization of a long-expected blow never left her grandmother's face.

The sun was getting low, and the bridge was nearing completion. Soon the workmen would be crowding into the cabin for their promised supper. There became visible in the distance, far up the road, the heavily plodding figure of another woman who had agreed to come and help. Old Woman Magoun turned again to Lily.

"You go right up-stairs to your own chamber now," said she.

"Good land! ain't you goin' to let that poor child stay up and see the fun?" said Sally Jinks.

"You jest mind your own business," said Old Woman Magoun, forcibly, and Sally Jinks shrank. "You go right up there now, Lily," said the grandmother, in a softer tone, "and grandma will bring you up a nice plate of supper."

"When be you goin' to let that girl grow up?" asked Sally Jinks, when Lily had disappeared.

"She'll grow up in the Lord's good time," replied Old Woman Magoun, and there was in her voice something both sad and threatening. Sally Jinks again shrank a little.

Soon the workmen came flocking noisily into the house. Old Woman Magoun and her two helpers served the bountiful supper. Most of the men had drunk as much as, and more than, was good for them, and Old Woman Magoun had stipulated that there was to be no drinking of anything except coffee during supper.

"I'll git you as good a meal as I know how," she said, "but if I see ary one of you drinkin' a drop, I'll run you all out. If you want anything to drink, you can go up to the store afterward. That's the place for you to go to, if you've got to make hogs of yourselves. I ain't goin' to have no hogs in my house."

Old Woman Magoun was implicitly obeyed. She had a curious authority over most people when she chose to exercise it. When the supper was in full swing, she quietly stole up-stairs and carried some food to Lily. She found the girl, with the rag doll in her arms, crouching by the window in her little rocking-chair – a relic of her infancy, which she still used.

"What a noise they are makin', grandma!" she said, in a terrified whisper, as her grandmother placed the plate before her on a chair.

"They've 'most all of 'em been drinkin'. They air a passel of hogs," replied the old woman.

"Is the man that was with – with my father down there?" asked Lily, in a timid fashion. Then she fairly cowered before the look in her grandmother's eyes.

"No, he ain't; and what's more, he never will be down there if I can help it," said Old Woman Magoun, in a fierce whisper. "I know who he is. They can't cheat me. He's one of them Willises – that family the Barrys married into. They're worse than the Barrys, ef they have got money. Eat your supper, and put him out of your mind, child."

It was after Lily was asleep, when Old Woman Magoun was alone, clearing away her supper dishes, that Lily's father came. The door was closed, and he knocked, and the old woman knew at once who was there. The sound of that knock meant as much to her as the whir of a bomb to the defender of a fortress. She opened the door, and Nelson Barry stood there.

"Good-evening, Mrs. Magoun," he said.

Old Woman Magoun stood before him, filling up the doorway with her firm bulk.

"Good-evening, Mrs. Magoun," said Nelson Barry again.

"I ain't got no time to waste," replied the old woman, harshly. "I've got my supper dishes to clean up after them men."

She stood there and looked at him as she might have looked at a rebellious animal which she was trying to tame. The man laughed.

"It's no use," said he. "You know me of old. No human being can turn me from my way when I am once started in it. You may as well let me come in."

Old Woman Magoun entered the house, and Barry followed her.

Barry began without any preface. "Where is the child?" asked he.

"Up-stairs. She has gone to bed."

"She goes to bed early."

"Children ought to," returned the old woman, polishing a plate.

Barry laughed. "You are keeping her a child a long while," he remarked, in a soft voice which had a sting in it.

"She is a child," returned the old woman, defiantly.

"Her mother was only three years older when Lily was born."

The old woman made a sudden motion toward the man which seemed fairly menacing. Then she turned again to her dish-washing.

"I want her," said Barry.

"You can't have her," replied the old woman, in a still stern voice.

"I don't see how you can help yourself. You have always acknowledged that she was my child."

The old woman continued her task, but her strong back heaved. Barry regarded her with an entirely pitiless expression.

"I am going to have the girl, that is the long and short of it," he said, "and it is for her best good, too. You are a fool, or you would see it."

"Her best good?" muttered the old women.

"Yes, her best good. What are you going to do with her, anyway? The girl is a beauty, and almost a woman grown, although you try to make out that she is a baby. You can't live forever."

"The Lord will take care of her," replied the old woman, and again she turned and faced him, and her expression was that of a prophetess.

"Very well, let Him," said Barry, easily. "All the same I'm going to have her, and I tell you it is for her best good. Jim Willis saw her this afternoon, and – "

Old Woman Magoun looked at him. "Jim Willis!" she fairly shrieked.

"Well, what of it?"

"One of them Willises!" repeated the old woman, and this time her voice was thick. It seemed almost as if she were stricken with paralysis. She did not enunciate clearly.

The man shrank a little. "Now what is the need of your making such a fuss?" he said. "I will take her, and Isabel will look out for her."

"Your half-witted sister?" said Old Woman Magoun.

"Yes, my half-witted sister. She knows more than you think."

"More wickedness."

"Perhaps. Well, a knowledge of evil is a useful thing. How are you going to avoid evil if you don't know what it is like? My sister and I will take care of my daughter."

The old woman continued to look at the man, but his eyes never fell. Suddenly her gaze grew inconceivably keen. It was as if she saw through all externals.

"I know what it is!" she cried. "You have been playing cards and you lost, and this is the way you will pay him."

Then the man's face reddened, and he swore under his breath.

"Oh, my God!" said the old woman; and she really spoke with her eyes aloft as if addressing something outside of them both. Then she turned again to her dish-washing.

The man cast a dogged look at her back. "Well, there is no use talking. I have made up my mind," said he, "and you know me and what that means. I am going to have the girl."

"When?" said the old woman, without turning around.

"Well, I am willing to give you a week. Put her clothes in good order before she comes."

The old woman made no reply. She continued washing dishes. She even handled them so carefully that they did not rattle.

"You understand," said Barry. "Have her ready a week from to-day."

"Yes," said Old Woman Magoun, "I understand."

Nelson Barry, going up the mountain road, reflected that Old Woman Magoun had a strong character, that she understood much better than her sex in general the futility of withstanding the inevitable.

"Well," he said to Jim Willis when he reached home, "the old woman did not make such a fuss as I expected."

"Are you going to have the girl?"

"Yes; a week from to-day. Look here, Jim; you've got to stick to your promise."

"All right," said Willis. "Go you one better."

The two were playing at cards in the old parlor, once magnificent, now squalid, of the Barry house. Isabel, the half-witted sister, entered, bringing some glasses on a tray. She had learned with her feeble intellect some tricks, like a dog. One of them was the mixing of sundry drinks. She set the tray on a little stand near the two men, and watched them with her silly simper.

"Clear out now and go to bed," her brother said to her, and she obeyed.

Early the next morning Old Woman Magoun went up to Lily's little sleeping-chamber, and watched her a second as she lay asleep, with her yellow locks spread over the pillow. Then she spoke. "Lily," said she – "Lily, wake up. I am going to Greenham across the new bridge, and you can go with me."

Lily immediately sat up in bed and smiled at her grandmother. Her eyes were still misty, but the light of awakening was in them.

"Get right up," said the old woman. "You can wear your new dress if you want to."

Lily gurgled with pleasure like a baby. "And my new hat?" asked she.

"I don't care."

Old Woman Magoun and Lily started for Greenham before Barry's Ford, which kept late hours, was fairly awake. It was three miles to Greenham. The old woman said that, since the horse was a little lame, they would walk. It was a beautiful morning, with a diamond radiance of dew over everything. Her grandmother had curled Lily's hair more punctiliously than usual. The little face peeped like a rose out of two rows of golden spirals. Lily wore her new muslin dress with a pink sash, and her best hat of a fine white straw trimmed with a wreath of rosebuds; also the neatest black open-work stockings and pretty shoes. She even had white cotton gloves. When they set out, the old, heavily stepping woman, in her black gown and cape and bonnet, looked down at the little pink fluttering figure. Her face was full of the tenderest love and admiration, and yet there was something terrible about it. They crossed the new bridge – a primitive structure built of logs in a slovenly fashion. Old Woman Magoun pointed to a gap.

"Jest see that," said she. "That's the way men work."

"Men ain't very nice, be they?" said Lily, in her sweet little voice.

"No, they ain't, take them all together," replied her grandmother.

"That man that walked to the store with me was nicer than some, I guess," Lily said, in a wishful fashion. Her grandmother reached down and took the child's hand in its small cotton glove. "You hurt me, holding my hand so tight," Lily said presently, in a deprecatory little voice.

The old woman loosened her grasp. "Grandma didn't know how tight she was holding your hand," said she. "She wouldn't hurt you for nothin', except it was to save your life, or somethin' like that." She spoke with an undertone of tremendous meaning which the girl was too childish to grasp. They walked along the country road. Just before they reached Greenham they passed a stone wall overgrown with blackberry-vines, and, an unusual thing in that vicinity, a lusty spread of deadly nightshade full of berries.

"Those berries look good to eat, grandma," Lily said.

At that instant the old woman's face became something terrible to see. "You can't have any now," she said, and hurried Lily along.

"They look real nice," said Lily.

When they reached Greenham, Old Woman Magoun took her way straight to the most pretentious house there, the residence of the lawyer, whose name was Mason. Old Woman Magoun bade Lily wait in the yard for a few moments, and Lily ventured to seat herself on a bench beneath an oak-tree; then she watched with some wonder her grandmother enter the lawyer's office door at the right of the house. Presently the lawyer's wife came out and spoke to Lily under the tree. She had in her hand a little tray containing a plate of cake, a glass of milk, and an early apple. She spoke very kindly to Lily; she even kissed her, and offered her the tray of refreshments, which Lily accepted gratefully. She sat eating, with Mrs. Mason watching her, when Old Woman Magoun came out of the lawyer's office with a ghastly face.

"What are you eatin'?" she asked Lily, sharply. "Is that a sour apple?"

"I thought she might be hungry," said the lawyer's wife, with loving, melancholy eyes upon the girl.

Lily had almost finished the apple. "It's real sour, but I like it; it's real nice, grandma," she said.

"You ain't been drinkin' milk with a sour apple?"

"It was real nice milk, grandma."

"You ought never to have drunk milk and eat a sour apple," said her grandmother. "Your stomach was all out of order this mornin', an' sour apples and milk is always apt to hurt anybody."

"I don't know but they are," Mrs. Mason said, apologetically, as she stood on the green lawn with her lavender muslin sweeping around her. "I am real sorry, Mrs. Magoun. I ought to have thought. Let me get some soda for her."

"Soda never agrees with her," replied the old woman, in a harsh voice. "Come," she said to Lily, "it's time we were goin' home."

After Lily and her grandmother had disappeared down the road, Lawyer Mason came out of his office and joined his wife, who had seated herself on the bench beneath the tree. She was idle, and her face wore the expression of those who review joys forever past. She had lost a little girl, her only child, years ago, and her husband always knew when she was thinking about her. Lawyer Mason looked older than his wife; he had a dry, shrewd, slightly one-sided face.

"What do you think, Maria?" he said. "That old woman came to me with the most pressing entreaty to adopt that little girl."

"She is a beautiful little girl," said Mrs. Mason, in a slightly husky voice.

"Yes, she is a pretty child," assented the lawyer, looking pityingly at his wife; "but it is out of the question, my dear. Adopting a child is a serious measure, and in this case a child who comes from Barry's Ford."

"But the grandmother seems a very good woman," said Mrs. Mason.

"I rather think she is. I never heard a word against her. But the father! No, Maria, we cannot take a child with Barry blood in her veins. The stock has run out; it is vitiated physically and morally. It won't do, my dear."

"Her grandmother had her dressed up as pretty as a little girl could be," said Mrs. Mason, and this time the tears welled into her faithful, wistful eyes.

"Well, we can't help that," said the lawyer, as he went back to his office.

Old Woman Magoun and Lily returned, going slowly along the road to Barry's Ford. When they came to the stone wall where the blackberry-vines and the deadly nightshade grew, Lily said she was tired, and asked if she could not sit down for a few minutes. The strange look on her grandmother's face had deepened. Now and then Lily glanced at her and had a feeling as if she were looking at a stranger.

"Yes, you can set down if you want to," said Old Woman Magoun, deeply and harshly.

Lily started and looked at her, as if to make sure that it was her grandmother who spoke. Then she sat down on a stone which was comparatively free of the vines.

"Ain't you goin' to set down, grandma?" Lily asked, timidly.

"No; I don't want to get into that mess," replied her grandmother. "I ain't tired. I'll stand here."

Lily sat still; her delicate little face was flushed with heat. She extended her tiny feet in her best shoes and gazed at them. "My shoes are all over dust," said she.

"It will brush off," said her grandmother, still in that strange voice.

Lily looked around. An elm-tree in the field behind her cast a spray of branches over her head; a little cool puff of wind came on her face. She gazed at the low mountains on the horizon, in the midst of which she lived, and she sighed, for no reason that she knew. She began idly picking at the blackberry-vines; there were no berries on them; then she put her little fingers on the berries of the deadly nightshade. "These look like nice berries," she said.

Old Woman Magoun, standing stiff and straight in the road, said nothing.

"They look good to eat," said Lily.

Old Woman Magoun still said nothing, but she looked up into the ineffable blue of the sky, over which spread at intervals great white clouds shaped like wings.

Lily picked some of the deadly nightshade berries and ate them. "Why, they are real sweet," said she. "They are nice." She picked some more and ate them.

Presently her grandmother spoke. "Come," she said, "it is time we were going. I guess you have set long enough."

Lily was still eating the berries when she slipped down from the wall and followed her grandmother obediently up the road.

Before they reached home, Lily complained of being very thirsty. She stopped and made a little cup of a leaf and drank long at a mountain brook. "I am dreadful dry, but it hurts me to swallow," she said to her grandmother when she stopped drinking and joined the old woman waiting for her in the road. Her grandmother's face seemed strangely dim to her. She took hold of Lily's hand as they went on. "My stomach burns," said Lily, presently. "I want some more water."

"There is another brook a little farther on," said Old Woman Magoun, in a dull voice.

When they reached that brook, Lily stopped and drank again, but she whimpered a little over her difficulty in swallowing. "My stomach burns, too," she said, walking on, "and my throat is so dry, grandma." Old Woman Magoun held Lily's hand more tightly. "You hurt me holding my hand so tight, grandma," said Lily, looking up at her grandmother, whose face she seemed to see through a mist, and the old woman loosened her grasp.

When at last they reached home, Lily was very ill. Old Woman Magoun put her on her own bed in the little bedroom out of the kitchen. Lily lay there and moaned, and Sally Jinks came in.

"Why, what ails her?" she asked. "She looks feverish."

Lily unexpectedly answered for herself. "I ate some sour apples and drank some milk," she moaned.

"Sour apples and milk are dreadful apt to hurt anybody," said Sally Jinks. She told several people on her way home that Old Woman Magoun was dreadful careless to let Lily eat such things.

Meanwhile Lily grew worse. She suffered cruelly from the burning in her stomach, the vertigo, and the deadly nausea. "I am so sick, I am so sick, grandma," she kept moaning. She could no longer see her grandmother as she bent over her, but she could hear her talk.

Old Woman Magoun talked as Lily had never heard her talk before, as nobody had ever heard her talk before. She spoke from the depths of her soul; her voice was as tender as the coo of a dove, and it was grand and exalted. "You'll feel better very soon, little Lily," said she.

"I am so sick, grandma."

"You will feel better very soon, and then – "

"I am sick."

"You shall go to a beautiful place."

Lily moaned.

"You shall go to a beautiful place," the old woman went on.

"Where?" asked Lily, groping feebly with her cold little hands. Then she moaned again.

"A beautiful place, where the flowers grow tall."

"What color? Oh, grandma, I am so sick."

"A blue color," replied the old woman. Blue was Lily's favorite color. "A beautiful blue color, and as tall as your knees, and the flowers always stay there, and they never fade."

"Not if you pick them, grandma? Oh!"

"No, not if you pick them; they never fade, and they are so sweet you can smell them a mile off; and there are birds that sing, and all the roads have gold stones in them, and the stone walls are made of gold."

"Like the ring grandpa gave you? I am so sick, grandma."

"Yes, gold like that. And all the houses are built of silver and gold, and the people all have wings, so when they get tired walking they can fly, and – "

"I am so sick, grandma."

"And all the dolls are alive," said Old Woman Magoun. "Dolls like yours can run, and talk, and love you back again."

Lily had her poor old rag doll in bed with her, clasped close to her agonized little heart. She tried very hard with her eyes, whose pupils were so dilated that they looked black, to see her grandmother's face when she said that, but she could not. "It is dark," she moaned, feebly.

"There where you are going it is always light," said the grandmother, "and the commonest things shine like that breastpin Mrs. Lawyer Mason had on to-day."

Lily moaned pitifully, and said something incoherent. Delirium was commencing. Presently she sat straight up in bed and raved; but even then her grandmother's wonderful compelling voice had an influence over her.

"You will come to a gate with all the colors of the rainbow," said her grandmother; "and it will open, and you will go right in and walk up the gold street, and cross the field where the blue flowers come up to your knees, until you find your mother, and she will take you home where you are going to live. She has a little white room all ready for you, white curtains at the windows, and a little white looking-glass, and when you look in it you will see – "

"What will I see? I am so sick, grandma."

"You will see a face like yours, only it's an angel's; and there will be a little white bed, and you can lay down an' rest."

"Won't I be sick, grandma?" asked Lily. Then she moaned and babbled wildly, although she seemed to understand through it all what her grandmother said.

"No, you will never be sick anymore. Talkin' about sickness won't mean anything to you."

It continued. Lily talked on wildly, and her grandmother's great voice of soothing never ceased, until the child fell into a deep sleep, or what resembled sleep; but she lay stiffly in that sleep, and a candle flashed before her eyes made no impression on them.

Then it was that Nelson Barry came. Jim Willis waited outside the door. When Nelson entered he found Old Woman Magoun on her knees beside the bed, weeping with dry eyes and a might of agony which fairly shook Nelson Barry, the degenerate of a fine old race.

"Is she sick?" he asked, in a hushed voice.

Old Woman Magoun gave another terrible sob, which sounded like the gasp of one dying.

"Sally Jinks said that Lily was sick from eating milk and sour apples," said Barry, in a tremulous voice. "I remember that her mother was very sick once from eating them."

Lily lay still, and her grandmother on her knees shook with her terrible sobs.

Suddenly Nelson Barry started. "I guess I had better go to Greenham for a doctor if she's as bad as that," he said. He went close to the bed and looked at the sick child. He gave a great start. Then he felt of her hands and reached down under the bedclothes for her little feet. "Her hands and feet are like ice," he cried out. "Good God! why didn't you send for some one – for me – before? Why, she's dying; she's almost gone!"

Barry rushed out and spoke to Jim Willis, who turned pale and came in and stood by the bedside.

"She's almost gone," he said, in a hushed whisper.

"There's no use going for the doctor; she'd be dead before he got here," said Nelson, and he stood regarding the passing child with a strange, sad face unutterably sad, because of his incapability of the truest sadness.

"Poor little thing, she's past suffering, anyhow," said the other man, and his own face also was sad with a puzzled, mystified sadness.

Lily died that night. There was quite a commotion in Barry's Ford until after the funeral, it was all so sudden, and then everything went on as usual. Old Woman Magoun continued to live as she had done before. She supported herself by the produce of her tiny farm; she was very industrious, but people said that she was a trifle touched, since every time she went over the log bridge with her eggs or her garden vegetables to sell in Greenham, she carried with her, as one might have carried an infant, Lily's old rag doll.

Luella Miller

Close to the village street stood the one-story house in which Luella Miller, who had an evil name in the village, had dwelt. She had been dead for years, yet there were those in the village who, in spite of the clearer light which comes on a vantage-point from a long-past danger, half believed in the tale which they had heard from their childhood. In their hearts, although they scarcely would have owned it, was a survival of the wild horror and frenzied fear of their ancestors who had dwelt in the same age with Luella Miller. Young people even would stare with a shudder at the old house as they passed, and children never played around it as was their wont around an untenanted building. Not a window in the old Miller house was broken: the panes reflected the morning sunlight in patches of emerald and blue, and the latch of the sagging front door was never lifted, although no bolt secured it. Since Luella Miller had been carried out of it, the house had had no tenant except one friendless old soul who had no choice between that and the far-off shelter of the open sky. This old woman, who had survived her kindred and friends, lived in the house one week, then one morning no smoke came out of the chimney, and a body of neighbours, a score strong, entered and found her dead in her bed. There were dark whispers as to the cause of her death, and there were those who testified to an expression of fear so exalted that it showed forth the state of the departing soul upon the dead face. The old woman had been hale and hearty when she entered the house, and in seven days she was dead; it seemed that she had fallen a victim to some uncanny power. The minister talked in the pulpit with covert severity against the sin of superstition; still the belief prevailed. Not a soul in the village but would have chosen the almshouse rather than that dwelling. No vagrant, if he heard the tale, would seek shelter beneath that old roof, unhallowed by nearly half a century of superstitious fear.

There was only one person in the village who had actually known Luella Miller. That person was a woman well over eighty but a marvel of vitality and unextinct youth. Straight as an arrow, with the spring of one recently let loose from the bow of life, she moved about the streets, and she always went to church, rain or shine. She had never married, and had lived alone for years in a house across the road from Luella Miller's.

This woman had none of the garrulousness of age, but never in all her life had she ever held her tongue for any will save her own, and she never spared the truth when she essayed to present it. She it was who bore testimony to the life, evil, though possibly wittingly or designedly so,[1] of Luella Miller, and to her personal appearance. When this old woman spoke – and she had the gift of description, although her thoughts were clothed in the rude vernacular of her native village – one could seem to see Luella Miller as she had really looked. According to this woman, Lydia Anderson by name, Luella Miller had been a beauty of a type rather unusual in New England. She had been a slight, pliant sort of creature, as ready with a strong yielding to fate and as unbreakable as a willow. She had glimmering lengths of straight, fair hair, which she wore softly looped round a long, lovely face. She had blue eyes full of soft pleading, little slender, clinging hands, and a wonderful grace of motion and attitude.

"Luella Miller used to sit in a way nobody else could if they sat up and studied a week of Sundays," said Lydia Anderson, "and it was a sight to see her walk. If one of them willows over there on the edge of the brook could start up and get its roots free of the ground, and move off, it would go just the way Luella Miller used to. She had a green shot silk she used to wear, too, and a hat with green ribbon streamers, and a lace veil blowing across her face and out sideways, and a green ribbon flyin' from her waist. That was what she came out bride in when she married Erastus Miller. Her name before she was married was Hill. There was always a sight of 'l's' in her name, married or single. Erastus Miller was good lookin', too, better lookin' than Luella. Sometimes I used to think that Luella wa'n't so handsome after all. Erastus just about worshiped her. I used to know him pretty well. He lived next door to me, and we went to school together. Folks used to say he was waitin' on me,[2] but he wa'n't. I never thought he was except once or twice when he said things that some girls might have suspected meant

Notes

LUELLA MILLER
[1] Thus in original, but logic suggests that the passage should read "not wittingly or designedly so ..."
[2] Courting me.

somethin'. That was before Luella came here to teach the district school. It was funny how she came to get it, for folks said she hadn't any education, and that one of the big girls, Lottie Henderson, used to do all the teachin' for her, while she sat back and did embroidery work on a cambric pocket-handkerchief. Lottie Henderson was a real smart girl, a splendid scholar, and she just set her eyes by Luella, as all the girls did. Lottie would have made a real smart woman, but she died when Luella had been here about a year – just faded away and died: nobody knew what ailed her. She dragged herself to that schoolhouse and helped Luella teach till the very last minute. The committee all knew how Luella didn't do much of the work herself, but they winked at it. It wasn't long after Lottie died that Erastus married her. I always thought he hurried it up because she wa'n't fit to teach. One of the big boys used to help her after Lottie died, but he hadn't much government, and the school didn't do very well, and Luella might have had to give it up, for the committee couldn't have shut their eyes to things much longer. The boy that helped her was a real honest, innocent sort of fellow, and he was a good scholar, too. Folks said he overstudied, and that was the reason he was took crazy the year after Luella married, but I don't know. And I don't know what made Erastus Miller go into consumption of the blood the year after he was married: consumption wa'n't in his family. He just grew weaker and weaker, and went almost bent double when he tried to wait on Luella, and he spoke feeble, like an old man. He worked terrible hard till the last trying to save up a little to leave Luella. I've seen him out in the worst storms on a wood-sled – he used to cut and sell wood – and he was hunched up on top lookin' more dead than alive. Once I couldn't stand it: I went over and helped him pitch some wood on the cart – I was always strong in my arms. I wouldn't stop for all he told me to, and I guess he was glad enough for the help. That was only a week before he died. He fell on the kitchen floor while he was gettin' break-fast. He always got the breakfast and let Luella lay abed. He did all the sweepin' and the washin' and the ironin' and most of the cookin'. He couldn't bear to have Luella lift her finger, and she let him do for her. She lived like a queen for all the work she did. She didn't even do her sewin'. She said it made her shoulder ache to sew, and poor Erastus's sister Lily used to do all her sewin'. She wa'n't able to, either; she was never strong in her back, but she did it beautifully. She had to, to suit Luella, she was so dreadful particular. I never saw anythin' like the fagottin' and hemstitchin' that Lily Miller did for Luella. She made all Luella's weddin' outfit, and that green silk dress, after Maria Babbit cut it. Maria she cut it for nothin', and she did a lot more cuttin' and fittin' for nothin' for Luella, too. Lily Miller went to live with Luella after Erastus died. She gave up her home, though she was real attached to it and wa'n't a mite afraid to stay alone. She rented it and she went to live with Luella right away after the funeral."

Then this old woman, Lydia Anderson, who remembered Luella Miller, would go on to relate the story of Lily Miller. It seemed that on the removal of Lily Miller to the house of her dead brother, to live with his widow, the village people first began to talk. This Lily Miller had been hardly past her first youth, and a most robust and blooming woman, rosy-cheeked, with curls of strong, black hair overshadowing round, candid temples and bright dark eyes. It was not six months after she had taken up her residence with her sister-in-law that her rosy colour faded and her pretty curves become wan hollows. White shadows began to show in the black rings of her hair, and the light died out of her eyes, her features sharpened, and there were pathetic lines at her mouth, which yet wore always an expression of utter sweetness and even happiness. She was devoted to her sister; there was no doubt that she loved her with her whole heart, and was perfectly content in her service. It was her sole anxiety lest she should die and leave her alone.

"The way Lily Miller used to talk about Luella was enough to make you mad and enough to make you cry," said Lydia Anderson. "I've been in there sometimes toward

the last when she was too feeble to cook and carried her some blanc-mange or custard –
somethin' I thought she might relish, and she'd thank me, and when I asked her
how she was, say she felt better than she did yesterday, and asked me if I didn't think
she looked better, dreadful pitiful, and say poor Luella had an awful time takin' care
of her and doin' the work – she wa'n't strong enough to do anythin' – when all
the time Luella wasn't liftin' her finger and poor Lily didn't get any care except what
the neighbours gave her, and Luella eat up everythin' that was carried in for Lily. I had
it real straight that she did. Luella used to just sit and cry and do nothin'. She did act
real fond of Lily, and she pined away considerable, too. There was those that thought
she'd go into a decline herself. But after Lily died, her Aunt Abby Mixter came, and
then Luella picked up and grew as fat and rosy as ever. But poor Aunt Abby begun to
droop just the way Lily had, and I guess somebody wrote to her married daughter,
Mrs. Sam Abbot, who lived in Barre, for she wrote her mother that she must leave
right away and come and make her a visit, but Aunt Abby wouldn't go. I can see her
now. She was a real good-lookin' woman, tall and large, with a big, square face and a
high forehead that looked of itself kind of benevolent and good. She just tended out
on Luella as if she had been a baby, and when her married daughter sent for her she
wouldn't stir one inch. She'd always thought a lot of her daughter, too, but she said
Luella needed her and her married daughter didn't. Her daughter kept writin' and
writin', but it didn't do any good. Finally she came, and when she saw how bad her
mother looked, she broke down and cried and all but went on her knees to have
her come away. She spoke her mind out to Luella, too. She told her that she'd killed her
husband and everybody that had anythin' to do with her, and she'd thank her to
leave her mother alone. Luella went into hysterics, and Aunt Abby was so frightened
that she called me after her daughter went. Mrs. Sam Abbot she went away fairly cryin'
out loud in the buggy, the neighbours heard her, and well she might, for she never saw
her mother again alive. I went in that night when Aunt Abby called for me, standin' in
the door with her little green-checked shawl over her head. I can see her now. 'Do
come over here, Miss Anderson,' she sung out, kind of gasping for breath. I didn't stop
for anythin'. I put over as fast as I could, and when I got there, there was Luella laughin'
and cryin' all together, and Aunt Abby trying to hush her, and all the time she herself
was white as a sheet and shakin' so she could hardly stand. 'For the land sakes, Mrs.
Mixter,' says I, 'you look worse than she does. You ain't fit to be up out of your bed.'
   "'Oh, there ain't anythin' the matter with me,' says she. Then she went on talkin' to
Luella. 'There, there, don't, don't, poor little lamb,' says she. 'Aunt Abby is here. She
ain't goin' away and leave you. Don't, poor little lamb.'
   "'Do leave her with me, Mrs. Mixter, and you get back to bed,' says I, for Aunt Abby
had been layin' down considerable lately, though somehow she contrived to do the work.
   "'I'm well enough,' says she. 'Don't you think she had better have the doctor, Miss
Anderson?'
   "'The doctor,' says I, 'I think you had better have the doctor. I think you need him
much worse than some folks I could mention.' And I looked right straight at Luella
Miller laughin' and cryin' and goin' on as if she was the centre of all creation. All the
time she was actin' so – seemed as if she was too sick to sense anythin' – she was
keepin' a sharp lookout as to how we took it out of the corner of one eye. I see her.
You could never cheat me about Luella Miller. Finally I got real mad and I run home
and I got a bottle of valerian[3] I had, and I poured some boilin' hot water on a handful

of catnip, and I mixed up that catnip tea with most half a wineglass of valerian, and I went with it over to Luella's. I marched right up to Luella, a-holdin' out of that cup, all smokin'. 'Now,' says I, 'Luella Miller, *you swaller this!*'

"'What is – what is it, oh, what is it?' she sort of screeches out. Then she goes off a-laughin' enough to kill.

"'Poor lamb, poor little lamb,' says Aunt Abby, standin' over her, all kind of tottery, and tryin' to bathe her head with camphor.

"'*You swaller this right down.*' says I. And I didn't waste any ceremony. I just took hold of Luella Miller's chin and I tipped her head back, and I caught her mouth open with laughin', and I clapped that cup to her lips and I fairly hollered at her: 'Swaller, swaller, swaller!' and she gulped it right down. She had to, and I guess it did her good. Anyhow, she stopped cryin' and laughin' and let me put her to bed, and she went to sleep like a baby inside of half an hour. That was more than poor Aunt Abby did. She lay awake all that night and I stayed with her, though she tried not to have me; said she wa'n't sick enough for watchers. But I stayed, and I made some good cornmeal gruel and I fed her a teaspoon every little while all night long. It seemed to me as if she was jest dyin' from bein' all wore out. In the mornin' as soon as it was light I run over to the Bisbees and sent Johnny Bisbee for the doctor. I told him to tell the doctor to hurry, and he come pretty quick. Poor Aunt Abby didn't seem to know much of anythin' when he got there. You couldn't hardly tell she breathed, she was so used up. When the doctor had gone, Luella came into the room lookin' like a baby in her ruffled nightgown. I can see her now. Her eyes were as blue and her face all pink and white like a blossom, and she looked at Aunt Abby in the bed sort of innocent and surprised. 'Why,' says she, 'Aunt Abby ain't got up yet?'

"'No, she ain't,' says I, pretty short.

"'I thought I didn't smell the coffee,' says Luella.

"'Coffee,' says I. 'I guess if you have coffee this mornin' you'll make it yourself.'

"'I never made the coffee in all my life,' says she, dreadful astonished. 'Erastus always made the coffee as long as he lived, and then Lily she made it, and then Aunt Abby made it. I don't believe I *can* make the coffee, Miss Anderson.'

"'You can make it or go without, jest as you please,' says I.

"'Ain't Aunt Abby goin' to get up?' says she.

"'I guess she won't get up,' says I, 'sick as she is.' I was gettin' madder and madder. There was somethin' about that little pink-and-white thing standin' there and talkin' about coffee, when she had killed so many better folks than she was, and had jest killed another, that made me feel 'most as if I wished somebody would up and kill her before she had a chance to do any more harm.

"'Is Aunt Abby sick?' says Luella, as if she was sort of aggrieved and injured.

"'Yes,' says I, 'she's sick, and she's goin' to die, and then you'll be left alone, and you'll have to do for yourself and wait on yourself, or do without things.' I don't know but I was sort of hard, but it was the truth, and if I was any harder than Luella Miller had been I'll give up. I ain't never been sorry that I said it. Well, Luella, she up and had hysterics again at that, and I jest let her have 'em. All I did was to bundle her into the room on the other side of the entry where Aunt Abby couldn't hear her, if she wa'n't past it – I don't know but she was – and set her down hard in a chair and told her not to come back into the other room, and she minded. She had her hysterics in there till she got tired. When she found out that nobody was comin' to coddle her and do for her she stopped. At least I suppose she did. I had all I could do with poor Aunt Abby tryin' to keep the breath of life in her. The doctor had told me that she was dreadful low, and give me some very strong medicine to give to her in drops real often, and told me real particular about the nourishment. Well, I did as he told me real faithful till she wa'n't able to swaller any longer. Then I had her daughter sent for. I had begun to realize that she wouldn't last any time at all. I hadn't realized it before, though I spoke to Luella the way I did. The doctor he came, and Mrs. Sam Abbot, but when she got there it was too late; her mother was dead. Aunt Abby's daughter just give one look at her mother layin' there, then she turned sort of sharp and sudden and looked at me.

"'Where is she?' says she, and I knew she meant Luella.

"'She's out in the kitchen,' says I. 'She's too nervous to see folks die. She's afraid it will make her sick.'

"The Doctor he speaks up then. He was a young man. Old Doctor Park had died the year before, and this was a young fellow just out of college. 'Mrs. Miller is not strong,' says he, kind of severe, 'and she is quite right in not agitating herself.'

"'You are another, young man; she's got her pretty claw on you,' thinks I, but I didn't say anythin' to him. I just said over to Mrs. Sam Abbot that Luella was in the kitchen, and Mrs. Sam Abbot she went out there, and I went, too, and I never heard anythin' like the way she talked to Luella Miller. I felt pretty hard to Luella myself, but this was more than I ever would have dared to say. Luella she was too scared to go into hysterics. She jest flopped. She seemed to jest shrink away to nothin' in that kitchen chair, with Mrs. Sam Abbot standin' over her and talkin' and tellin' her the truth. I guess the truth was most too much for her and no mistake, because Luella presently actually did faint away, and there wa'n't any sham about it, the way I always suspected there was about them hysterics. She fainted dead away and we had to lay her flat on the floor, and the Doctor he came runnin' out and he said somethin' about a weak heart dreadful fierce to Mrs. Sam Abbot, but she wa'n't a mite scared. She faced him jest as white as even Luella was layin' there lookin' like death and the Doctor feelin' of her pulse.

"'Weak heart,' says she, 'weak heart; weak fiddlesticks! There ain't nothin' weak about that woman. She's got strength enough to hang onto other folks till she kills 'em. Weak? It was my poor mother that was weak: this woman killed her as sure as if she had taken a knife to her.'

"But the Doctor he didn't pay much attention. He was bendin' over Luella layin' there with her yellow hair all streamin' and her pretty pink-and-white face all pale, and her blue eyes like stars gone out, and he was holdin' onto her hand and smoothin' her forehead, and tellin' me to get the brandy in Aunt Abby's room, and I was sure as I wanted to be that Luella had got somebody else to hang onto, now Aunt Abby was gone, and I thought of poor Erastus Miller, and I sort of pitied the poor young Doctor, led away by a pretty face, and I made up my mind I'd see what I could do.

"I waited till Aunt Abby had been dead and buried about a month, and the Doctor was goin' to see Luella steady and folks were beginnin' to talk; then one evenin', when I knew the Doctor had been called out of town and wouldn't be round, I went over to Luella's. I found her all dressed up in a blue muslin with white polka dots on it, and her hair curled jest as pretty, and there wa'n't a young girl in the place could compare with her. There was somethin' about Luella Miller seemed to draw the heart right out of you, but she didn't draw it out of me. She was settin' rocking in the chair by her sittin'-room window, and Maria Brown had gone home. Maria Brown had been in to help her, or rather to do the work, for Luella wa'n't helped when she didn't do anythin'. Maria Brown was real capable and she didn't have any ties; she wa'n't married, and lived alone, so she'd offered. I couldn't see why she should do the work any more than Luella; she wasn't any too strong; but she seemed to think she could and Luella seemed to think so, too, so she went over and did all the work – washed, and ironed, and baked, while Luella sat and rocked. Maria didn't live long afterward. She began to fade away just the same fashion the others had. Well, she was warned, but she acted real mad when folks said anythin': said Luella was a poor, abused woman, too delicate to help herself, and they'd ought to be ashamed, and if she died helpin' them that couldn't help themselves she would – and she did.

"'I s'pose Maria has gone home,' says I to Luella, when I had gone in and sat down opposite her.

"'Yes, Maria went half an hour ago, after she had got supper and washed the dishes,' says Luella, in her pretty way.

"'I suppose she has got a lot of work to do in her own house to-night,' says I, kind of bitter, but that was all thrown away on Luella Miller. It seemed to her right that other folks that wa'n't any better able than she was herself should wait on her, and she couldn't get it through her head that anybody should think it *wa'n't* right.

"'Yes,' says Luella, real sweet and pretty, 'yes, she said she had to do her washin' to-night. She has let it go for a fortnight along of comin' over here.'

"'Why don't she stay home and do her washin' instead of comin' over here and doin' your work, when you are just as well able, and enough sight more so, than she is to do it?' says I.

"Then Luella she looked at me like a baby who has a rattle shook at it. She sort of laughed as innocent as you please. 'Oh, I can't do the work myself, Miss Anderson,' says she. 'I never did. Maria has to do it.'

"Then I spoke out: 'Has to do it!' says I. 'Has to do it! She don't have to do it, either. Maria Brown has her own home and enough to live on. She ain't beholden to you to come over here and slave for you and kill herself.'

"Luella she jest set and stared at me for all the world like a doll-baby that was so abused that it was comin' to life.

"'Yes,' says I, 'she's killin' herself. She's goin' to die just the way Erastus did, and Lily, and your Aunt Abby. You're killin' her jest as you did them. I don't know what there is about you, but you seem to bring a curse,' says I. 'You kill everybody that is fool enough to care anythin' about you and do for you.'

"She stared at me and she was pretty pale.

"'And Maria ain't the only one you're goin' to kill,' says I. 'You're goin' to kill Doctor Malcom before you're done with him.'

"Then a red colour came flamin' all over her face. 'I ain't goin' to kill him, either,' says she, and she begun to cry.

"'Yes, you *be!*' says I. Then I spoke as I had never spoke before. You see, I felt it on account of Erastus. I told her that she hadn't any business to think of another man after she'd been married to one that had died for her: that she was a dreadful woman; and she was, that's true enough, but sometimes I have wondered lately if she knew it – if she wa'n't like a baby with scissors in its hand cuttin' everybody without knowin' what it was doin'.

"Luella she kept gettin' paler and paler, and she never took her eyes off my face. There was somethin' awful about the way she looked at me and never spoke one word. After awhile I quit talkin' and I went home. I watched that night, but her lamp went out before nine o'clock, and when Doctor Malcom came drivin' past and sort of slowed up he see there wa'n't any light and he drove along. I saw her sort of shy out of meetin' the next Sunday, too, so he shouldn't go home with her, and I begun to think mebbe she did have some conscience after all. It was only a week after that that Maria Brown died – sort of sudden at the last, though everybody had seen it was comin'. Well, then there was a good deal of feelin' and pretty dark whispers. Folks said the days of witchcraft had come again, and they were pretty shy of Luella. She acted sort of offish to the Doctor and he didn't go there, and there wa'n't anybody to do anythin' for her. I don't know how she *did* get along. I wouldn't go in there and offer to help her – not because I was afraid of dyin' like the rest but I thought she was just as well able to do her own work as I was to do it for her, and I thought it was about time that she did it and stopped killin' other folks. But it wa'n't very long before folks began to say that Luella herself was goin' into a decline jest the way her husband, and Lily, and Aunt Abby and the others had, and I saw myself that she looked pretty bad. I used to see her goin' past from the store with a bundle as if she could hardly crawl, but I remembered how Erastus used to wait and 'tend when he couldn't hardly put one foot before the other, and I didn't go out to help her.

"But at last one afternoon I saw the Doctor come drivin' up like mad with his medicine chest, and Mrs. Babbit came in after supper and said that Luella was real sick.

"'I'd offer to go in and nurse her,' says she, 'but I've got my children to consider, and mebbe it ain't true what they say, but it's queer how many folks that have done for her have died.'

"I didn't say anythin', but I considered how she had been Erastus's wife and how he had set his eyes by her, and I made up my mind to go in the next mornin', unless she was better, and see what I could do; but the next mornin' I see her at the window, and pretty soon she came steppin' out as spry as you please, and a little while afterward Mrs. Babbit came in and told me that the Doctor had got a girl from out of town, a Sarah Jones, to come there, and she said she was pretty sure that the Doctor was goin' to marry Luella.

"I saw him kiss her in the door that night myself, and I knew it was true. The woman came that afternoon, and the way she flew around was a caution.[4] I don't believe Luella had swept since Maria died. She swept and dusted, and washed and ironed; wet clothes and dusters and carpets were flyin' over there all day, and every time Luella set her foot out when the Doctor wa'n't there there was that Sarah Jones helpin' of her up and down the steps, as if she hadn't learned to walk.

"Well, everybody knew that Luella and the Doctor were goin' to be married, but it wa'n't long before they began to talk about his lookin' so poorly, jest as they had about the others; and they talked about Sarah Jones, too.

"Well, the Doctor did die, and he wanted to be married first, so as to leave what little he had to Luella, but he died before the minister could get there, and Sarah Jones died a week afterward.

"Well, that wound up everything for Luella Miller. Not another soul in the whole town would lift a finger for her. There got to be a sort of panic. Then she began to droop in good earnest. She used to have to go to the store herself, for Mrs. Babbit was afraid to let Tommy go for her, and I've seen her goin' past and stoppin' every two or three steps to rest. Well, I stood it as long as I could, but one day I see her comin' with her arms full and stopping' to lean against the Babbit fence, and I run out and took her bundles and carried them to her house. Then I went home and never spoke one word to her though she called after me dreadful kind of pitiful. Well, that night I was taken sick with a chill, and I was sick as I wanted to be for two weeks. Mrs. Babbit had seen me run out to help Luella and she came in and told me I was goin' to die on account of it. I didn't know whether I was or not, but I considered I had done right by Erastus's wife.

"That last two weeks Luella she had a dreadful hard time, I guess. She was pretty sick, and as near as I could make out nobody dared go near her. I don't know as she was really needin' anythin' very much, for there was enough to eat in her house and it was warm weather, and she made out to cook a little flour gruel every day, I know, but I guess she had a hard time, she that had been so petted and done for all her life.

Notes

4 Dialect: was remarkable.

"When I got so I could go out, I went over there one morning. Mrs. Babbit had just come in to say she hadn't seen any smoke and she didn't know but what it was somebody's duty to go in, but she couldn't help thinkin' of her children, and I got right up, though I hadn't been out of the house for two weeks, and I went in there, and Luella she was layin' on the bed, and she was dyin'.

"She lasted all that day and into the night. But I sat there after the new doctor had gone away. Nobody else dared to go there. It was about midnight that I left her for a minute to run home and get some medicine I had been takin', for I begun to feel rather bad.

"It was a full moon that night, and just as I started out of my door to cross the street back to Luella's, I stopped short, for I saw something."

Lydia Anderson at this juncture always said with a certain defiance that she did not expect to be believed, and then proceeded in a hushed voice:

"I saw what I saw, and I know I saw it, and I will swear on my death bed that I saw it. I saw Luella Miller and Erastus Miller, and Lily, and Aunt Abby, and Maria, and the Doctor, and Sarah, all goin' out of her door, and all but Luella shone white in the moonlight, and they were all helpin' her along till she seemed to fairly fly in the midst of them. Then it all disappeared. I stood a minute with my heart poundin', then I went over there. I thought of goin' for Mrs. Babbit, but I thought she'd be afraid. So I went alone, though I knew what had happened. Luella was layin' real peaceful, dead on her bed."

This was the story that the old woman, Lydia Anderson, told, but the sequel was told by the people who survived her, and this is the tale which has become folklore in the village.

Lydia Anderson died when she was eighty-seven. She had continued wonderfully hale and hearty for one of her years until about two weeks before her death.

One bright moonlight evening she was sitting beside a window in her parlour when she made a sudden exclamation, and was out of the house and across the street before the neighbour who was taking care of her could stop her. She followed as fast as possible and found Lydia Anderson stretched on the ground before the door of Luella Miller's deserted house, and she was quite dead.

The next night there was a red gleam of fire athwart the moonlight and the old house of Luella Miller was burned to the ground. Nothing is now left of it except a few old cellar stones and a lilac bush, and in summer a helpless trail of morning glories among the weeds, which might be considered emblematic of Luella herself.

Gertrude Atherton (1857–1948)

Gertrude Franklin Horn Atherton was the first internationally successful writer born in California. Her maternal grandfather was a grand-nephew of Benjamin Franklin. During a colorful early life Gertrude eloped with George Atherton, once a suitor of her divorced mother. Atherton was the son of an aristocratic Chilean woman and the wealthy California merchant for whom a San Francisco suburb was subsequently named.

Gertrude Atherton began writing as a young widow, and her career extended for forty years. Her work was sometimes compared to, and ranked with, that of her contemporary Edith Wharton. Atherton's fiction included romantic tales of early California (such as *The Splendid, Idle Forties* [1902]) and realistic novels often dealing with feminist themes. She was sometimes criticized for frank treatment of the sexual motivation of her characters, as in *Patience Sparhawk and Her Times* (1897).

"The Bell in the Fog" (1905) was collected in a volume dedicated "To the Master, Henry James." Atherton's protagonist, the great author Ralph Orth, clearly is modeled on James, and the story itself, as well as the unnamed masterpiece written by Orth in response to the children's portraits, echo *The Turn of the Screw*. Yet Atherton's story (like Wharton's "The Eyes" in this volume) can be seen as a critique of James as well as a tribute.

Behind James stands the figure of Hawthorne, signaled by the name of Orth's estate, Chillingsworth. The allusion links Blanche to Hawthorne's little Pearl and recalls the theme of sexual transgression from *The Scarlet Letter*.

Text: *The Bell in the Fog, and Other Stories* (New York and London: Harper & Brothers, 1905).

The Bell in the Fog

The great author had realized one of the dreams of his ambitious youth, the possession of an ancestral hall in England. It was not so much the good American's reverence for ancestors that inspired the longing to consort with the ghosts of an ancient line, as artistic appreciation of the mellowness, the dignity, the aristocratic aloofness of walls that have sheltered, and furniture that has embraced, generations and generations of the dead. To mere wealth, only his astute and incomparably modern brain yielded respect; his ego raised its goose-flesh at the sight of rooms furnished with a single check, conciliatory as the taste might be. The dumping of the old interiors of Europe into the glistening shells of the United States not only roused him almost to passionate protest, but offended his patriotism – which he classified among his unworked ideals. The average American was not an artist, therefore he had no excuse for even the affectation of cosmopolitanism. Heaven knew he was national enough in everything else, from his accent to his lack of repose; let his surroundings be in keeping.

American Gothic: From Salem Witchcraft to H. P. Lovecraft, An Anthology, Second Edition. Edited by Charles L. Crow.
Editorial material and organization © 2013 John Wiley & Sons, Ltd. Published 2013 by John Wiley & Sons, Ltd.

Orth had left the United States soon after his first successes, and, his art being too great to be confounded with locality, he had long since ceased to be spoken of as an American author. All civilized Europe furnished stages for his puppets, and, if never picturesque nor impassioned, his originality was as overwhelming as his style. His subtleties might not always be understood – indeed, as a rule, they were not – but the musical mystery of his language and the penetrating charm of his lofty and cultivated mind induced raptures in the initiated, forever denied to those who failed to appreciate him.

His following was not a large one, but it was very distinguished. The aristocracies of the earth gave to it; and not to understand and admire Ralph Orth was deliberately to relegate one's self to the ranks. But the elect are few, and they frequently subscribe to the circulating libraries; on the Continent, they buy the Tauchnitz edition;[1] and had not Mr. Orth inherited a sufficiency of ancestral dollars to enable him to keep rooms in Jermyn Street, and the wardrobe of an Englishman of leisure, he might have been forced to consider the tastes of the middle-class at a desk in Hampstead. But, as it mercifully was, the fashionable and exclusive sets of London knew and sought him. He was too wary to become a fad, and too sophisticated to grate or bore; consequently, his popularity continued evenly from year to year, and long since he had come to be regarded as one of them. He was not keenly addicted to sport, but he could handle a gun, and all men respected his dignity and breeding. They cared less for his books than women did, perhaps because patience is not a characteristic of their sex. I am alluding however, in this instance, to men-of-the-world. A group of young literary men – and one or two women – put him on a pedestal and kissed the earth before it. Naturally, they imitated him, and as this flattered him, and he had a kindly heart deep among the cere-cloths[2] of his formalities, he sooner or later wrote "appreciations" of them all, which nobody living could understand, but which owing to the subtitle and signature answered every purpose.

With all this, however, he was not utterly content. From the 12th of August until late in the winter – when he did not go to Homburg and the Riviera – he visited the best houses in England, slept in state chambers, and meditated in historic parks; but the country was his one passion, and he longed for his own acres.

He was turning fifty when his great-aunt died and made him her heir: "as a poor reward for his immortal services to literature," read the will of this phenomenally appreciative relative. The estate was a large one. There was a rush for his books; new editions were announced. He smiled with cynicism, not unmixed with sadness; but he was very grateful for the money, and as soon as his fastidious taste would permit he bought him a country-seat.

The place gratified all his ideals and dreams – for he had romanced about his sometime English possession as he had never dreamed of woman. It had once been the property of the Church, and the ruin of cloister and chapel above the ancient wood was sharp against the low pale sky. Even the house itself was Tudor, but wealth from generation to generation had kept it in repair; and the lawns were as velvety, the hedges as rigid, the trees as aged as any in his own works. It was not a castle nor a great property, but it was quite perfect; and for a long while he felt like a bridegroom on a succession of honeymoons. He often laid his hand against the rough ivied walls in a lingering caress.

After a time, he returned the hospitalities of his friends, and his invitations, given with the exclusiveness of his great distinction, were never refused. Americans visiting England eagerly sought for letters to him; and if they were sometimes benumbed by

Notes ─────────────────────────────────

THE BELL IN THE FOG
[1] An inexpensive paperback edition.

[2] Waxed cloth used for cerements, in which corpses are wrapped.

that cold and formal presence, and awed by the silences of Chillingsworth – the few who entered there – they thrilled in anticipation of verbal triumphs, and forthwith bought an entire set of his books. It was characteristic that they dared not ask him for his autograph.

Although women invariably described him as "brilliant," a few men affirmed that he was gentle and lovable, and any one of them was well content to spend weeks at Chillingsworth with no other companion. But, on the whole, he was rather a lonely man.

It occurred to him how lonely he was one gay June morning when the sunlight was streaming through his narrow windows, illuminating tapestries and armor, the family portraits of the young profligate from whom he had made this splendid purchase, dusting its gold on the black wood of wainscot and floor. He was in the gallery at the moment, studying one of his two favorite portraits, a gallant little lad in the green costume of Robin Hood. The boy's expression was imperious and radiant, and he had that perfect beauty which in any disposition appealed so powerfully to the author. But as Orth stared to-day at the brilliant youth, of whose life he knew nothing, he suddenly became aware of a human stirring at the foundations of his aesthetic pleasure.

"I wish he were alive and here, "he thought, with a sigh. "What a jolly little companion he would be! And this fine old mansion would make a far more complementary setting for him than for me."

He turned away abruptly, only to find himself face to face with the portrait of a little girl who was quite unlike the boy, yet so perfect in her own way, and so unmistakably painted by the same hand, that he had long since concluded they had been brother and sister. She was angelically fair, and, young as she was – she could not have been more than six years old – her dark-blue eyes had a beauty of mind which must have been remarkable twenty years later. Her pouting mouth was like a little scarlet serpent, her skin almost transparent, her pale hair fell waving – not curled with the orthodoxy of childhood – about her tender bare shoulders. She wore a long white frock, and clasped tightly against her breast a doll far more gorgeously arrayed than herself. Behind her were the ruins and the woods of Chillingsworth.

Orth had studied this portrait many times, for the sake of an art which he understood almost as well as his own; but to-day he saw only the lovely child. He forgot even the boy in the intensity of this new and personal absorption.

"Did she live to grow up, I wonder?" he thought. "She should have made a remarkable, even a famous woman, with those eyes and that brow, but – could the spirit within that ethereal frame stand the enlightenments of maturity? Would not that mind – purged, perhaps, in a long probation from the dross of other existences – flee in disgust from the commonplace problems of a woman's life? Such perfect beings should die while they are still perfect. Still, it is possible that this little girl, whoever she was, was idealized by the artist, who painted into her his own dream of exquisite childhood."

Again he turned away impatiently. "I believe I am rather fond of children," he admitted. "I catch myself watching them on the street when they are pretty enough. Well, who does not like them?" he added, with some defiance.

He went back to his work; he was chiselling a story which was to be the foremost excuse of a magazine as yet unborn. At the end of half an hour he threw down his wondrous instrument – which looked not unlike an ordinary pen – and making no attempt to disobey the desire that possessed him, went back to the gallery. The dark splendid boy, the angelic little girl were all he saw – even of the several children in that roll call of the past – and they seemed to look straight down his eyes into depths where the fragmentary ghosts of unrecorded ancestors gave faint musical response.

"The dead's kindly recognition of the dead," he thought. "But I wish these children were alive."

For a week he haunted the gallery, and the children haunted him. Then he became impatient and angry. "I am mooning like a barren woman," he exclaimed. "I must take the briefest way of getting those youngsters off my mind."

With the help of his secretary, he ransacked the library, and finally brought to light the gallery catalogue which had been named in the inventory. He discovered that his children were the Viscount Tancred and the Lady Blanche Mortlake, son and daughter of the second Earl of Teignmouth. Little wiser than before, he sat down at once and wrote to the present earl, asking for some account of the lives of the children. He awaited the answer with more restlessness than he usually permitted himself, and took long walks, ostentatiously avoiding the gallery.

"I believe those youngsters have obsessed me," he thought, more than once. "They certainly are beautiful enough, and the last time I looked at them in that waning light they were fairly alive. Would that they were, and scampering about this park."

Lord Teignmouth, who was intensely grateful to him, answered promptly.

"I am afraid," he wrote, "that I don't know much about my ancestors – those who didn't do something or other; but I have a vague remembrance of having been told by an aunt of mine, who lives on the family traditions – she isn't married – that the little chap was drowned in the river, and that the little girl died too – I mean when she *was* a little girl – wasted away, or something – I'm such a beastly idiot about expressing myself, that I wouldn't dare to write to you at all if you weren't really great. That is actually all I can tell you, and I am afraid the painter was their only biographer."

The author was gratified that the girl had died young, but grieved for the boy. Although he had avoided the gallery of late, his practised imagination had evoked from the throngs of history the high-handed and brilliant, surely adventurous career of the third Earl of Teignmouth. He had pondered upon the deep delights of directing such a mind and character, and had caught himself envying the dust that was older still. When he read of the lad's early death, in spite of his regret that such promise should have come to naught, he admitted to a secret thrill of satisfaction that the boy had so soon ceased to belong to any one. Then he smiled with both sadness and humor.

"What an old fool I am!" he admitted. "I believe I not only wish those children were alive, but that they were my own."

The frank admission proved fatal. He made straight for the gallery. The boy, after the interval of separation, seemed more spiritedly alive than ever, the little girl to suggest, with her faint appealing smile, that she would like to be taken up and cuddled.

"I must try another way," he thought, desperately, after that long communion. "I must write them out of me."

He went back to the library and locked up the tour de force which had ceased to command his classic faculty. At once, he began to write the story of the brief lives of the children, much to the amazement of that faculty, which was little accustomed to the simplicities. Nevertheless, before he had written three chapters, he knew that he was at work upon a masterpiece – and more: he was experiencing a pleasure so keen that once and again his hand trembled, and he saw the page through a mist. Although his characters had always been objective to himself and his more patient readers, none knew better than he – a man of no delusions – that they were so remote and exclusive as barely to escape being mere mentalities; they were never the pulsing living creations of the more full-blooded genius. But he had been content to have it so. His creations might find and leave him cold, but he had known his highest satisfaction in chiselling the statuettes, extracting subtle and elevating harmonies, while combining words as no man of his tongue had combined them before.

But the children were not statuettes. He had loved and brooded over them long ere he had thought to tuck them into his pen, and on its first stroke they danced out alive.

The old mansion echoed with their laughter, with their delightful and original pranks. Mr. Orth knew nothing of children, therefore all the pranks he invented were as original as his faculty. The little girl clung to his hand or knee as they both followed the adventurous course of their common idol, the boy. When Orth realized how alive they were, he opened each room of his home to them in turn, that evermore he might have sacred and poignant memories with all parts of the stately mansion where he must dwell alone to the end. He selected their bedrooms, and hovered over them – not through infantile disorders, which were beyond even his imagination, – but through those painful intervals incident upon the enterprising spirit of the boy and the devoted obedience of the girl to fraternal command. He ignored the second Lord Teignmouth; he was himself their father, and he admired himself extravagantly for the first time; art had chastened him long since. Oddly enough, the children had no mother, not even the memory of one.

He wrote the book more slowly than was his wont, and spent delightful hours pondering upon the chapter of the morrow. He looked forward to the conclusion with a sort of terror, and made up his mind that when the inevitable last word was written he should start at once for Homburg. Incalculable times a day he went to the gallery, for he no longer had any desire to write the children out of his mind, and his eyes hungered for them. They were his now. It was with an effort that he sometimes humorously reminded himself that another man had fathered them, and that their little skeletons were under the choir of the chapel. Not even for peace of mind would he have descended into the vaults of the lords of Chillingsworth and looked upon the marble effigies of his children. Nevertheless, when in a superhumorous mood, he dwelt upon his high satisfaction in having been enabled by his great-aunt to purchase all that was left of them.

For two months he lived in his fool's paradise, and then he knew that the book must end. He nerved himself to nurse the little girl through her wasting illness, and when he clasped her hands, his own shook, his knees trembled. Desolation settled upon the house, and he wished he had left one corner of it to which he could retreat unhaunted by the child's presence. He took long tramps, avoiding the river with a sensation next to panic. It was two days before he got back to his table, and then he had made up his mind to let the boy live. To kill him off, too, was more than his augmented stock of human nature could endure. After all, the lad's death had been purely accidental, wanton. It was just that he should live – with one of the author's inimitable suggestions of future greatness; but, at the end, the parting was almost as bitter as the other. Orth knew then how men feel when their sons go forth to encounter the world and ask no more of the old companionship.

The author's boxes were packed. He sent the manuscript to his publisher an hour after it was finished – he could not have given it a final reading to have saved it from failure – directed his secretary to examine the proof under a microscope, and left the next morning for Homburg. There, in inmost circles, he forgot his children. He visited in several of the great houses of the Continent until November; then returned to London to find his book the literary topic of the day. His secretary handed him the reviews; and for once in a way he read the finalities of the nameless. He found himself hailed as a genius, and compared in astonished phrases to the prodigiously clever talent which the world for twenty years had isolated under the name of Ralph Orth. This pleased him, for every writer is human enough to wish to be hailed as a genius, and immediately. Many are, and many wait; it depends upon the fashion of the moment, and the needs and bias of those who write of writers. Orth had waited twenty years; but his past was bedecked with the headstones of geniuses long since forgotten. He was gratified to come thus publicly into his estate, but soon reminded himself that all the adulation of which a belated world was capable could not give him one thrill of the pleasure which the companionship of that book had given him, while creating. It was the keenest pleasure in his memory, and when a man is fifty and has written many books, that is saying a great deal.

He allowed what society was in town to lavish honors upon him for something over a month, then cancelled all his engagements and went down to Chillingsworth.

His estate was in Hertfordshire, that county of gentle hills and tangled lanes, of ancient oaks and wide wild heaths, of historic houses, and dark woods, and green fields innumerable – a Wordsworthian shire, steeped in the deepest peace of England. As Orth drove towards his own gates he had the typical English sunset to gaze upon, a red streak with a church spire against it. His woods were silent. In the fields, the cows stood as if conscious of their part. The ivy on his old gray towers had been young with his children.

He spent a haunted night, but the next day stranger happenings began.

II

He rose early, and went for one of his long walks. England seems to cry out to be walked upon, and Orth, like others of the transplanted, experienced to the full the country's gift of foot-restlessness and mental calm. Calm flees, however, when the ego is rampant, and to-day, as upon others too recent, Orth's soul was as restless as his feet. He had walked for two hours when he entered the wood of his neighbor's estate, a domain seldom honored by him, as it, too, had been bought by an American – a flighty hunting widow, who displeased the fastidious taste of the author. He heard children's voices, and turned with the quick prompting of retreat.

As he did so, he came face to face, on the narrow path, with a little girl. For the moment he was possessed by the most hideous sensation which can visit a man's being – abject terror. He believed that body and soul were disintegrating. The child before him was his child, the original of a portrait in which the artist, dead two centuries ago, had missed exact fidelity, after all. The difference, even his rolling vision took note, lay in the warm pure living whiteness and the deeper spiritual suggestion of the child in his path. Fortunately for his self-respect, the surrender lasted but a moment. The little girl spoke.

"You look real sick," she said. "Shall I lead you home?"

The voice was soft and sweet, but the intonation, the vernacular, were American, and not of the highest class. The shock was, if possible, more agonizing than the other, but this time Orth rose to the occasion.

"Who are you?" he demanded, with asperity. "What is your name? Where do you live?"

The child smiled, an angelic smile, although she was evidently amused. "I never had so many questions asked me all at once," she said. "But I don't mind, and I'm glad you're not sick. I'm Mrs. Jennie Root's little girl – my father's dead. My name is Blanche – you *are* sick! No? – and I live in Rome, New York State. We've come over here to visit pa's relations."

Orth took the child's hand in his. It was very warm and soft.

"Take me to your mother," he said, firmly; "now, at once. You can return and play afterwards. And as I wouldn't have you disappointed for the world, I'll send to town to-day for a beautiful doll."

The little girl, whose face had fallen, flashed her delight, but walked with great dignity beside him. He groaned in his depths as he saw they were pointing for the widow's house, but made up his mind that he would know the history of the child and of all her ancestors, if he had to sit down at table with his obnoxious neighbor. To his surprise, however, the child did not lead him into the park, but towards one of the old stone houses of the tenantry.

"Pa's great-great-great-grandfather lived there," she remarked, with all the American's pride of ancestry. Orth did not smile, however. Only the warm clasp of the hand in his, the soft thrilling voice of his still mysterious companion, prevented him from feeling as if moving through the mazes of one of his own famous ghost stories.

The child ushered him into the dining-room, where an old man was seated at the table reading his Bible. The room was at least eight hundred years old. The ceiling was supported by the trunk of a tree, black, and probably petrified. The windows had still their diamond panes, separated, no doubt, by the original lead. Beyond was a large kitchen in which were several women. The old man, who looked patriarchal enough to have laid the foundations of his dwelling, glanced up and regarded the visitor without hospitality. His expression softened as his eyes moved to the child.

"Who 'ave ye brought?" he asked. He removed his spectacles. "Ah!" He rose, and offered the author a chair. At the same moment, the women entered the room.

"Of course you've fallen in love with Blanche, sir," said one of them. "Everybody does."

"Yes, that is it. Quite so." Confusion still prevailing among his faculties, he clung to the naked truth. "This little girl has interested and startled me because she bears a precise resemblance to one of the portraits in Chillingsworth – painted about two hundred years ago. Such extraordinary likenesses do not occur without reason, as a rule, and, as I admired my portrait so deeply that I have written a story about it, you will not think it unnatural if I am more than curious to discover the reason for this resemblance. The little girl tells me that her ancestors lived in this very house, and as my little girl lived next door, so to speak, there undoubtedly is a natural reason for the resemblance."

His host closed the Bible, put his spectacles in his pocket, and hobbled out of the house.

"He'll never talk of family secrets," said an elderly woman, who introduced herself as the old man's daughter, and had placed bread and milk before the guest. "There are secrets in every family, and we have ours, but he'll never tell those old tales. All I can tell you is that an ancestor of little Blanche went to wreck and ruin because of some fine lady's doings, and killed himself. The story is that his boys turned out bad. One of them saw his crime, and never got over the shock; he was foolish like, after. The mother was a poor scared sort of creature, and hadn't much influence over the other boy. There seemed to be blight on all the man's descendants, until one of them went to America. Since then, they haven't prospered, exactly, but they've done better, and they don't drink so heavy."

"They haven't done so well," remarked a worn patient-looking woman. Orth typed her as belonging to the small middle-class of an interior town of the eastern United States.

"You are not the child's mother?"

"Yes, sir. Everybody is surprised; you needn't apologize. She doesn't look like any of us, although her brothers and sisters are good enough for anybody to be proud of. But we all think she strayed in by mistake, for she looks like any lady's child, and, of course, we're only middle-class."

Orth gasped. It was the first time he had ever heard a native American use the term middle-class with a personal application. For the moment, he forgot the child. His analytical mind raked in the new specimen. He questioned, and learned that the woman's husband had kept a hat store in Rome, New York; that her boys were clerks, her girls in stores, or type-writing. They kept her and little Blanche – who had come after her other children were well grown – in comfort; and they were all very happy together. The boys broke out, occasionally; but, on the whole, were the best in the world, and her girls were worthy of far better than they had. All were robust, except Blanche. "She coming so late, when I was no longer young, makes her delicate," she remarked, with a slight blush, the signal of her chaste Americanism; "but I guess she'll get along all right. She couldn't have better care if she was a queen's child."

Orth, who had gratefully consumed the bread and milk, rose. "Is that really all you can tell me?" he asked.

"That's all," replied the daughter of the house. "And you couldn't pry open father's mouth."

Orth shook hands cordially with all of them, for he could be charming when he chose. He offered to escort the little girl back to her playmates in the wood, and she took prompt possession of his hand. As he was leaving, he turned suddenly to Mrs. Root. "Why did you call her Blanche?" he asked.

"She was so white and dainty, she just looked it."

Orth took the next train for London, and from Lord Teignmouth obtained the address of the aunt who lived on the family traditions, and a cordial note of introduction to her. He then spent an hour anticipating, in a toy shop, the whims and pleasures of a child – an incident of paternity which his book-children had not inspired. He bought the finest doll, piano, French dishes, cooking apparatus, and playhouse in the shop, and signed a check for thirty pounds with a sensation of positive rapture. Then he took the train for Lancashire, where the Lady Mildred Mortlake lived in another ancestral home.

Possibly there are few imaginative writers who have not a leaning, secret or avowed, to the occult. The creative gift is in very close relationship with the Great Force behind the universe; for aught we know, may be an atom thereof. It is not strange, therefore, that the lesser and closer of the unseen forces should send their vibrations to it occasionally; or, at all events, that the imagination should incline its ear to the most mysterious and picturesque of all beliefs. Orth frankly dallied with the old dogma. He formulated no personal faith of any sort, but his creative faculty, that ego within an ego, had made more than one excursion into the invisible and brought back literary treasure.

The Lady Mildred received with sweetness and warmth the generous contributor to the family sieve, and listened with fluttering interest to all he had not told the world – she had read the book – and to the strange, Americanized sequel.

"I am all at sea," concluded Orth. "What had my little girl to do with the tragedy? What relation was she to the lady who drove the young man to destruction – ?"

"The closest," interrupted Lady Mildred. "She was herself!"

Orth stared at her. Again he had a confused sense of disintegration. Lady Mildred, gratified by the success of her bolt, proceeded less dramatically:

"Wally was up here just after I read your book, and I discovered he had given you the wrong history of the picture. Not that he knew it. It is a story we have left untold as often as possible, and I tell it to you only because you would probably become a monomaniac if I didn't. Blanche Mortlake – that Blanche – there had been several of her name, but there has not been one since – did not die in childhood, but lived to be twenty-four. She was an angelic child, but little angels sometimes grow up into very naughty girls. I believe she was delicate as a child, which probably gave her that spiritual look. Perhaps she was spoiled and flattered, until her poor little soul was stifled, which is likely. At all events, she was the coquette of her day – she seemed to care for nothing but breaking hearts; and she did not stop when she married, either. She hated her husband, and became reckless. She had no children. So far, the tale is not an uncommon one; but the worst, and what makes the ugliest stain in our annals, is to come.

"She was alone one summer at Chillingsworth – where she had taken temporary refuge from her husband – and she amused herself – some say, fell in love – with a young man of the yeomanry, a tenant of the next estate. His name was Root. He, so it comes down to us, was a magnificent specimen of his kind, and in those days the yeomanry gave us our great soldiers. His beauty of face was quite as remarkable as his physique; he led all the rural youth in sport, and was a bit above his class in every way. He had a wife in no way remarkable, and two little boys, but was always more with his friends than his family. Where he and Blanche Mortlake met I don't know – in the woods, probably, although it has been said that he had the run of the house. But, at all events, he was wild about her, and she pretended to be about him. Perhaps she was, for women have stooped before and since. Some women can be stormed by a fine man in any circumstances; but, although I am a woman of the world, and not easy to shock, there are some things I tolerate so hardly that it is all I can do to bring myself to believe in them; and stooping is one. Well, they were the scandal of the county for months, and then, either because she had tired of her new toy, or his grammar grated after the first glamour, or because she feared her husband, who was returning from the Continent, she broke off with him and returned to town. He followed her, and forced his way into her house. It is said she melted, but made him swear never to attempt to see her again. He returned to his home, and killed himself. A few months later she took her own life. That is all I know."

"It is quite enough for me," said Orth.

The next night, as his train travelled over the great wastes of Lancashire, a thousand chimneys were spouting forth columns of fire. Where the sky was not red it was black. The place looked like hell. Another time Orth's imagination would have gathered immediate inspiration from this wildest region of England. The fair and peaceful counties of the south had nothing to compare in infernal grandeur with these acres of flaming columns. The chimneys were invisible in the lower darkness of the night; the fires might have leaped straight from the angry caldron of the earth.

But Orth was in a subjective world, searching for all he had ever heard of occultism. He recalled that the sinful dead are doomed, according to this belief, to linger for vast reaches of time in that borderland which is close to earth, eventually sent back to work out their final salvation; that they work it out among the descendants of the people they have wronged; that suicide is held by the devotees of occultism to be a cardinal sin, abhorred and execrated.

Authors are far closer to the truths enfolded in mystery than ordinary people, because of that very audacity of imagination which irritates their plodding critics. As only those who dare to make mistakes succeed greatly, only those who shake free the wings of their imagination brush, once in a way, the secrets of the great pale world. If such writers go wrong, it is not for the mere brains to tell them so.

Upon Orth's return to Chillingsworth, he called at once upon the child, and found her happy among his gifts. She put her arms about his neck, and covered his serene unlined face with soft kisses. This completed the conquest. Orth from that moment adored her as a child, irrespective of the psychological problem.

Gradually he managed to monopolize her. From long walks it was but a step to take her home for luncheon. The hours of her visits lengthened. He had a room fitted up as a nursery and filled with the wonders of toyland. He took her to London to see the pantomimes; two days before Christmas, to buy presents for her relatives; and together they strung them upon the most wonderful Christmas-tree that the old hall of Chillingsworth had ever embraced. She had a donkey-cart, and a trained nurse, disguised as a maid, to wait upon her. Before a month had passed she was living in state at Chillingsworth and paying daily visits to her mother. Mrs. Root was deeply flattered, and apparently well content. Orth told her plainly that he should make the child independent, and educate her, meanwhile. Mrs. Root intended to spend six months in England, and Orth was in no hurry to alarm her by broaching his ultimate design.

He reformed Blanche's accent and vocabulary, and read to her out of books which would have addled the brains of most little maids of six; but she seemed to enjoy them, although she seldom made a comment. He was always ready to play games with her, but she was a gentle little thing, and, moreover, tired easily. She preferred to sit in the depths of a big chair, toasting her bare toes at the log-fire in the hall, while her friend read or talked to her. Although she was thoughtful, and, when left to herself, given to dreaming, his patient observation could detect nothing uncanny about her. Moreover, she had a quick sense of humor, she was easily amused, and could laugh as merrily as any child in the world. He was resigning all hope of further development on the shadowy side when one day he took her to the picture-gallery.

It was the first warm day of summer. The gallery was not heated, and he had not dared to take his frail visitor into its chilly spaces during the winter and spring. Although he had wished to see the effect of the picture on the child, he had shrunk from the bare possibility of the very developments the mental part of him craved; the other was warmed and satisfied for the first time, and held itself aloof from disturbance. But one day the sun streamed through the old windows, and, obeying a sudden impulse, he led Blanche to the gallery.

It was some time before he approached the child of his earlier love. Again he hesitated. He pointed out many other fine pictures, and Blanche smiled appreciatively at his remarks, that were wise in criticism and interesting in matter. He never knew just how much she understood, but the very fact that there were depths in the child beyond his probing riveted his chains.

Suddenly he wheeled about and waved his hand to her prototype. "What do you think of that?" he asked. "You remember, I told you of the likeness the day I met you."

She looked indifferently at the picture, but he noticed that her color changed oddly; its pure white tone gave place to an equally delicate gray.

"I have seen it before," she said. "I came in here one day to look at it. And I have been quite often since. You never forbade me," she added, looking at him appealingly, but dropping her eyes quickly. "And I like the little girl – and the boy – very much."

"Do you? Why?"

"I don't know" – a formula in which she had taken refuge before. Still her candid eyes were lowered; but she was quite calm. Orth, instead of questioning, merely fixed his eyes upon her, and waited. In a moment she stirred uneasily, but she did not laugh nervously, as another child would have done. He had never seen her self-possession ruffled, and he had begun to doubt he ever should. She was full of human warmth and affection. She seemed made for love, and every creature who came within her ken adored her, from the author himself down to the litter of puppies presented to her by the stable-boy a few weeks since; but her serenity would hardly be enhanced by death.

She raised her eyes finally, but not to his. She looked at the portrait.

"Did you know that there was another picture behind?" she asked.

"No," replied Orth, turning cold. "How did you know it?"

"One day I touched a spring in the frame, and this picture came forward. Shall I show you?"

"Yes!" And crossing curiosity and the involuntary shrinking from impending phenomena was a sensation of aesthetic disgust that *he* should be treated to a secret spring.

The little girl touched hers, and that other Blanche sprang aside so quickly that she might have been impelled by a sharp blow from behind. Orth narrowed his eyes and stared at what she revealed. He felt that his own Blanche was watching him, and set his features, although his breath was short.

There was the Lady Blanche Mortlake in the splendor of her young womanhood, beyond a doubt. Gone were all traces of her spiritual childhood, except, perhaps, in the shadows of the mouth; but more than fulfilled were the promises of her mind. Assuredly, the woman had been as brilliant and gifted as she had been restless and passionate. She wore her very pearls with arrogance, her very hands were tense with eager life, her whole being breathed mutiny.

Orth turned abruptly to Blanche, who had transferred her attention to the picture.

"What a tragedy is there!" he exclaimed, with a fierce attempt at lightness. "Think of a woman having all that pent up within her two centuries ago! And at the mercy of a stupid family, no doubt, and a still stupider husband. No wonder – To-day, a woman like that might not be a model for all the virtues, but she certainly would use her gifts and become famous, the while living her life too fully to have any place in it for yeomen and such, or even for the trivial business of breaking hearts." He put his finger under Blanche's chin, and raised her face, but he could not compel her gaze. "You are the exact image of that little girl," he said, "except that you are even purer and finer. She had no chance, none whatever. You live in the woman's age. Your opportunities will be infinite. I shall see to it that they are. What you wish to be you shall be. There will be no pent-up energies here to burst out into disaster for yourself and others. You shall be trained to self-control – that is, if you ever develop self-will, dear child – every faculty shall be educated, every school of life you desire knowledge through shall be opened to you. You shall become that finest flower of civilization, a woman who knows how to use her independence."

She raised her eyes slowly, and gave him a look which stirred the roots of sensation – a long look of unspeakable melancholy. Her chest rose once; then she set her lips tightly, and dropped her eyes.

"What do you mean?" he cried, roughly, for his soul was chattering. "Is – it – do you – ?" He dared not go too far, and concluded lamely, "You mean you fear that your mother will not give you to me when she goes – you have divined that I wish to adopt you? Answer me, will you?"

But she only lowered her head and turned away, and he, fearing to frighten or repel her, apologized for his abruptness, restored the outer picture to its place, and led her from the gallery.

He sent her at once to the nursery, and when she came down to luncheon and took her place at his right hand, she was as natural and childlike as ever. For some days he restrained his curiosity, but one evening, as they were sitting before the fire in the hall listening to the storm, and just after he had told her the story of the erl-king,[3] he took her on his knee and asked her gently if she would not tell him what had been in her thoughts when he had drawn her brilliant future. Again her face turned gray, and she dropped her eyes.

"I cannot," she said. "I – perhaps – I don't know."

"Was it what I suggested?"

Notes

[3] The erlking, in various German legends, is an evil spirit that haunts the forest. In a poem by Goethe, the erlking kills the young son of a man riding through the woods.

She shook her head, then looked at him with a shrinking appeal which forced him to drop the subject.

He went the next day alone to the gallery, and looked long at the portrait of the woman. She stirred no response in him. Nor could he feel that the woman of Blanche's future would stir the man in him. The paternal was all he had to give, but that was hers forever.

He went out into the park and found Blanche digging in her garden, very dirty and absorbed. The next afternoon, however, entering the hall noiselessly, he saw her sitting in her big chair, gazing out into nothing visible, her whole face settled in melancholy. He asked her if she were ill, and she recalled herself at once, but confessed to feeling tired. Soon after this he noticed that she lingered longer in the comfortable depths of her chair, and seldom went out, except with himself. She insisted that she was quite well, but after he had surprised her again looking as sad as if she had renounced every joy of childhood, he summoned from London a doctor renowned for his success with children.

The scientist questioned and examined her. When she had left the room he shrugged his shoulders.

"She might have been born with ten years of life in her, or she might grow up into a buxom woman," he said. "I confess I cannot tell. She appears to be sound enough, but I have no X-rays in my eyes, and for all I know she may be on the verge of decay. She certainly has the look of those who die young. I have never seen so spiritual a child. But I can put my finger on nothing. Keep her out-of-doors, don't give her sweets, and don't let her catch anything if you can help it."

Orth and the child spent the long warm days of summer under the trees of the park, or driving in the quiet lanes. Guests were unbidden, and his pen was idle. All that was human in him had gone out to Blanche. He loved her, and she was a perpetual delight to him. The rest of the world received the large measure of his indifference. There was no further change in her, and apprehension slept and let him sleep. He had persuaded Mrs. Root to remain in England for a year. He sent her theatre tickets every week, and placed a horse and phaeton at her disposal. She was enjoying herself and seeing less and less of Blanche. He took the child to Bournemouth for a fortnight, and again to Scotland, both of which outings benefited as much as they pleased her. She had begun to tyrannize over him amiably, and she carried herself quite royally. But she was always sweet and truthful, and these qualities, combined with that something in the depths of her mind which defied his explorations, held him captive. She was devoted to him, and cared for no other companion, although she was demonstrative to her mother when they met.

It was in the tenth month of this idyl of the lonely man and the lonely child that Mrs. Root flurriedly entered the library of Chillingsworth, where Orth happened to be alone.

"Oh, sir," she exclaimed, "I must go home. My daughter Grace writes me – she should have done it before – that the boys are not behaving as well as they should – she didn't tell me, as I was having such a good time she just hated to worry me – Heaven knows I've had enough worry – but now I must go – I just couldn't stay – boys are an awful responsibility – girls ain't a circumstance to them, although mine are a handful sometimes."

Orth had written about too many women to interrupt the flow. He let her talk until she paused to recuperate her forces. Then he said quietly:

"I am sorry this has come so suddenly, for it forces me to broach a subject at once which I would rather have postponed until the idea had taken possession of you by degrees – "

"I know what it is you want to say, sir," she broke in, "and I've reproached myself that I haven't warned you before, but I didn't like to be the one to speak first. You want Blanche – of course, I couldn't help seeing that; but I can't let her go, sir, indeed, I can't."

"Yes," he said, firmly, "I want to adopt Blanche, and I hardly think you can refuse, for you must know how greatly it will be to her advantage. She is a wonderful child; you have never been blind to that; she should have every opportunity, not only of money, but of association. If I adopt her legally, I shall, of course, make her my heir, and – there is no reason why she should not grow up as great a lady as any in England."

The poor woman turned white, and burst into tears. "I've sat up nights and nights, struggling," she said, when she could speak. "That, and missing her. I couldn't stand in her light, and I let her stay. I know I oughtn't to, now – I mean, stand in her light – but, sir, she is dearer than all the others put together."

"Then live here in England – at least, for some years longer. I will gladly relieve your children of your support, and you can see Blanche as often as you choose."

"I can't do that, sir. After all, she is only one, and there are six others. I can't desert them. They all need me, if only to keep them together – three girls unmarried and out in the world, and three boys just a little inclined to be wild. There is another point, sir – I don't exactly know how to say it."

"Well?" asked Orth, kindly. This American woman thought him the ideal gentleman, although the mistress of the estate on which she visited called him a boor and a snob.

"It is – well – you must know – you can imagine – that her brothers and sisters just worship Blanche. They save their dimes to buy her everything she wants – or used to want. Heaven knows what will satisfy her now, although I can't see that she's one bit spoiled. But she's just like a religion to them; they're not much on church. I'll tell you, sir, what I couldn't say to any one else, not even to these relations who've been so kind to me – but there's wildness, just a streak, in all my children, and I believe, I know, it's Blanche that keeps them straight. My girls get bitter, sometimes; work all the week and little fun, not caring for common men and no chance to marry gentlemen; and sometimes they break out and talk dreadful; then, when they're over it, they say they'll live for Blanche – they've said it over and over, and they mean it. Every sacrifice they've made for her – and they've made many – has done them good. It isn't that Blanche ever says a word of the preachy sort, or has anything of the Sunday-school child about her, or even tries to smooth them down when they're excited. It's just herself. The only thing she ever does is sometimes to draw herself up and look scornful, and that nearly kills them. Little as she is, they're crazy about having her respect. I've grown superstitious about her. Until she came I used to get frightened, terribly, sometimes, and I believe she came for that. So – you see! I know Blanche is too fine for us and ought to have the best; but, then, they are to be considered, too. They have their rights, and they've got much more good than bad in them. I don't know! I don't know! It's kept me awake many nights."

Orth rose abruptly. "Perhaps you will take some further time to think it over," he said. "You can stay a few weeks longer – the matter cannot be so pressing as that."

The woman rose. "I've thought this," she said; "let Blanche decide. I believe she knows more than any of us. I believe that whichever way she decided would be right. I won't say anything to her, so you won't think I'm working on her feelings; and I can trust you. But she'll know."

"Why do you think that?" asked Orth, sharply. "There is nothing uncanny about the child. She is not yet seven years old. Why should you place such a responsibility upon her?"

"Do you think she's like other children?"

"I know nothing of other children."

"I do, sir. I've raised six. And I've seen hundreds of others. I never was one to be a fool about my own, but Blanche isn't like any other child living – I'm certain of it."

"What *do* you think?"

And the woman answered, according to her lights: "I think she's an angel, and came to us because we needed her."

"And I think she is Blanche Mortlake working out the last of her salvation," thought the author; but he made no reply, and was alone in a moment.

It was several days before he spoke to Blanche, and then, one morning, when she was sitting on her mat on the lawn with the light full upon her, he told her abruptly that her mother must return home.

To his surprise, but unutterable delight, she burst into tears and flung herself into his arms.

"You need not leave me," he said, when he could find his own voice. "You can stay here always and be my little girl. It all rests with you."

"I can't stay," she sobbed. "I can't!"

"And that is what made you so sad once or twice?" he asked, with a double eagerness.

She made no reply.

"Oh!" he said, passionately, "give me your confidence, Blanche. You are the only breathing thing that I love."

"If I could I would," she said. "But I don't know – not quite."

"How much do you know?"

But she sobbed again and would not answer. He dared not risk too much. After all, the physical barrier between the past and the present was very young.

"Well, well, then, we will talk about the other matter. I will not pretend to disguise the fact that your mother is distressed at the idea of parting from you, and thinks it would be as sad for your brothers and sisters, whom she says you influence for their good. Do you think that you do?"

"Yes."

"How do you know this?"

"Do you know why you know everything?"

"No, my dear, and I have great respect for your instincts. But your sisters and brothers are now old enough to take care of themselves. They must be of poor stuff if they cannot live properly without the aid of a child. Moreover, they will be marrying soon. That will also mean that your mother will have many little grandchildren to console her for your loss. I will be the one bereft, if you leave me. I am the only one who really needs you. I don't say I will go to the bad, as you may have very foolishly persuaded yourself your family will do without you, but I trust to your instincts to make you realize how unhappy, how inconsolable I shall be. I shall be the loneliest man on earth!"

She rubbed her face deeper into his flannels, and tightened her embrace. "Can't you come, too?" she asked.

"No; you must live with me wholly or not at all. Your people are not my people, their ways are not my ways. We should not get along. And if you lived with me over there you might as well stay here, for your influence over them would be quite as removed. Moreover, if they are of the right stuff, the memory of you will be quite as potent for good as your actual presence."

"Not unless I died."

Again something within him trembled. "Do you believe you are going to die young?" he blurted out.

But she would not answer.

He entered the nursery abruptly the next day and found her packing her dolls. When she saw him, she sat down and began to weep hopelessly. He knew then that his fate was sealed. And when, a year later, he received her last little scrawl, he was almost glad that she went when she did.

Anonymous (Folk Tale)

This African American folk tale is part of the cycle "John and Old Marster," which describes the interaction of a slave-owner and his most trusted slave. In some of these stories John outwits his master; in others, as obviously in this instance, he does not.

"Talking Bones" is a cautionary tale that teaches secrecy and silence as a survival strategy of the oppressed. Secrecy retains an element of control, while failure to hold one's tongue, as the story shows, can be catastrophic. The lesson was well learned. This tale was not revealed to white folklorists until the 1950s, when Beulah Tate told it to Richard Dorson.

Text: Richard M. Dorson (ed.), *American Negro Folktales* (Greenwich, CT: Fawcett Publications, 1967).

Talking Bones

They used to carry the slaves out in the woods and leave them there, if they killed them – just like dead animals. There wasn't any burying then. It used to be a secret, between one plantation and another, when they beat up their hands and carried them off.

So John was walking out in the woods and seed a skeleton. He says: "This looks like a human. I wonder what he's doing out here." And the skeleton said, "Tongue is the cause of my being here." So John ran back to Old Marster and said, "The skeleton at the edge of the woods is talking." Old Marster didn't believe him and went to see. And a great many people came too. They said, "Make the bones talk." But the skeleton wouldn't talk. So they beat John to death, and left him there. And then the bones talked. They said, "Tongue brought us here, and tongue brought you here."

Charles W. Chesnutt (1858–1932)

Chesnutt's life has two main geographical focal points: Cleveland, Ohio, where he was born, and Fayetteville, North Carolina, the original home of his parents, each of whom was the child of a white father and an enslaved mother. Both settings appear in his fiction. The Chesnutts returned to Fayetteville when Charles was eight years old. He was a precocious and ambitious student, and, while in his teens, began a career as an educator, which ultimately might have resembled, on a smaller scale, that of Booker T. Washington. But he abandoned this career in favor of one in the north combining literature and law. Ultimately he was back in Cleveland, a member of the Ohio bar, running a successful legal-documents business, and writing fiction. The stories and novels he produced are among the most subtle and thoughtful explorations of race in American letters.

A cycle of Chesnutt's stories concerns a white Ohioan, John, who has settled in North Carolina and who has employed an elderly former slave, Julius McAdoo, as his coachman. In most of these tales, John's narration frames an inner tale, told by Julius, about the old days of slavery. Since many of these tales involve "conjure," magic, Chesnutt published a volume of them (1899) as *The Conjure Woman*. Readers of the *Atlantic*, where most of these stories were published, would have assumed that Chesnutt was a white local colorist, like Joel Chandler Harris. Chesnutt revealed his racial background with the publication of *The Marrow of Tradition* (1901), a novel about the Wilmington race riots, and his popularity declined. But a careful reader should have seen that John and his breezy sense of entitlement are objects of Chesnutt's satire, and that the crafty Julius, not John, is the moral center of these tales.

"The Dumb Witness" is an unusual John and Julius story, and one of the best. It was not published in Chesnutt's lifetime. There is no magic, and less of Julius's dialect voice. As in the other tales in this cycle, however, we see the blighting legacy of slavery, which John's hearty optimism cannot dispel. This true Southern Gothic contains a decades-long revenge plot, and an incestuous tangle that Julius (the oral historian of this black community) presumably understands, but we can barely penetrate.

"The Sheriff's Children" is from another collection, *The Wife of His Youth and Other Stories of the Color Line* (also 1899), a series dealing with characters who were, like Chesnutt, of mixed race. "The Sheriff's Children" is not a frame story, but as it begins we are hearing a narrative voice that has many of the qualities of John's: it is bland, cheerful, and seemingly in full sympathy with the values of the "new south." This tone is always to be distrusted in Chesnutt's fiction; ominous, dissonant notes can be heard in the background almost from the first sentence. We move quickly from an apparent celebration of the heroic sheriff to revelations that greatly complicate the moral landscape. Soon we find ourselves in a

Texts: "The Dumb Witness," from *The Conjure Woman and Other Conjure Tales*, ed. Richard H. Broadhead (Durham, NC: Duke University Press, 1993), 158–71. Reprinted by permission of the publisher. "The Sheriff's Children," from *The Wife of His Youth and Other Stories of the Color Line* (New York: Houghton, Mifflin, 1899).

claustrophobic setting where old secrets are revealed – familiar territory of the Gothic.

Both of these stories have at their core silence, the refusal to speak. The reader may recall the mute skeleton of the folk tale "Talking Bones."

Charles W. Chesnutt

The Dumb Witness

The old Murchison place was situated on the Lumberton plank road, about two miles from my vineyard on the North Carolina sandhills. Old Julius, our colored coachman, had driven me over one spring morning to see young Murchison, the responsible manager of the property, about some walnut timber I wished to purchase from him for shipment. I had noticed many resources of the country that the easy-going Southerners had not thought of developing; and I took advantage of them when I found it convenient and profitable to do so.

We entered the lane leading to the house by passing between two decaying gate-posts. This entrance had evidently once possessed some pretensions to elegance, for the massive posts had been faced with dressed lumber and finished with ornamental tops, some fragments of which still remained; and the one massive hinge, handing by a slender rust-eaten nail, had been wrought into a fantastic shape. As we drove through the gateway, a green lizard scampered down from the top of one of the posts, where he had been sunning himself, and a rattlesnake lying in the path lazily uncoiled his motley brown length, and, sounding his rattle the meanwhile, wriggled slowly off into the rank grass and weeds.

The house stood well back from the road, on the crest of one of the regular undulations of the sandhill country. It was partly concealed, when approached from the road, by intervening trees and shrubbery, which had once formed a well ordered pleasaunce, but now grew in wild and tangled profusion, so that it was difficult to distinguish one bush or tree from another. The lane itself was partially overgrown, and the mare's fetlocks swept the dew from the grass, where it had not yet been dried by the morning sun.

As we drew nearer, the house stood clearly revealed. It was apparently of more ancient date than any I had seen in the neighborhood. It was a large two-story frame house, built in the colonial style, with a low-pitched roof, and a broad piazza along the front, running the full length of both stories and supported by huge round columns, and suggesting distantly, in its general effect, the portico of a Greek temple. The roof had sunk on one side, and the shingles were old and cracked and moss-grown; while several of the windows in the upper part of the house were boarded up, and others filled with sash from which the glass had apparently long since been broken.

For a space of several rods on each side of the house the ground was bare of grass and shrubbery, and scarcely less forbidding than the road we had traveled. It was rough and uneven, lying in little hillocks and hollows, as though it had been dug over at haz-ard, or explored by some vagrant drove of hogs. At one side, beyond this barren area, lay an enclosed kitchen garden, in which a few collards and okra-plants and tomato vines struggled desperately against neglect and drought and poverty of soil.

A casual glance might have led one not informed to the contrary, to believe the place untenanted, so lonely and desolate did it seem. But as we approached we became aware of two figures on the long piazza. At one end of it, in a massive arm-chair of carved oak, a man was seated – apparently a very old man, for he was bent and wrinkled. His thin white hair hung down upon his shoulders. His face was of a high-bred and strongly marked type, with something of the hawk-like contour usually associated with extreme acquisitiveness. His eyes were turned toward the opposite end of the piazza, where a woman was also seated. She seemed but little younger than the man, and her face was enough like his, in a feminine way, to suggest that they might be related in some degree, unless this inference was negatived by the woman's complexion, which disclosed a strong infusion of darker blood. She wore a homespun frock and a muslin cap and sat bolt upright, with her hands folded on her lap, looking toward her *vis-à-vis* at the other end of the piazza.

As we drew up a short distance from the door, the old man rose, as we supposed, to come forward and greet us. But, instead of stopping at the steps and facing outward, he continued his course to the other end of the piazza and halted before the woman.

"Viney," he said, in a sharply imperative voice, "my uncle says you will tell me where he put the papers. I am tired of this nonsense. I insist upon knowing immediately."

The woman made no reply, but her faded eyes seemed to glow for a moment, like the ashes of a dying fire fanned by some random breath of air.

"Why do you not answer me?" he continued, with increasing vehemence. "I tell you I insist upon knowing. It is imperative that I should know, and know at once. My interests are suffering for every day's delay. The papers – where are the papers?"

Still the woman sat silent, though her figure seemed to stiffen as she leaned slightly toward him. He grew visibly more impatient at her silence, and began to threaten her.

"Tell me immediately, you hussy, or you will have reason to regret it. You take liberties that cannot be permitted. I will not put up with it," he said, shaking his fist as he spoke. "I shall have to have you whipped."

The slumbrous fire in the woman's eyes flamed up for a moment. She rose from her seat, and drawing herself up to her full height – she was a tall woman, though bowed somewhat with years – began to speak, I thought at first in some foreign tongue. But after a moment I knew that no language or dialect, at least none of European origin, could consist of such a discordant jargon, such a meaningless cacophony as that which fell from the woman's lips. And as she went on, pouring out a flood of sounds that were not words, and which yet seemed now and then vaguely to suggest words, as clouds suggest the shapes of mountains and trees and strange beasts, the old man seemed to bend like a reed before a storm, and began to expostulate, accompanying his words with deprecatory gestures.

"Yes, Viney, good Viney," he said in soothing tones, "I know it was wrong, and I've always regretted it – always from the very day I did it. But you shouldn't bear malice, Viney, it isn't Christian. The Bible says you should bless them that curse you, and do good to them that despitefully use you. But I was good to you before, Viney, and I was good to you afterwards, and I know you have forgiven me – good Viney, noble-hearted Viney! – and you are going to tell me. Now, *do* tell me where the papers are," he added, pleadingly, offering to take her hand, which lay on the arm of the chair.

She drew her hand away, as she muttered something in the same weird tones she had employed before. The old man bent toward her, in trembling eagerness, but seemed disappointed.

"Try again, Viney," he said, "that's a good girl. Your old master thinks a great deal of you, Viney. He is your best friend."

Again she made an inarticulate response. He seemed to comprehend, and turning from her, came down the steps, muttering to himself, took up a spade that stood at one end of the steps, passed by us without seeming conscious of our presence, and hastening with tottering footsteps to one side of the yard began digging furiously.

I had been so much interested in this curious drama that I had forgotten for the time being the business that brought me there. The old woman, however, when the man had gone, rose from her seat and went into the house, without giving us more than a look.

"What's the matter with them, Julius?" I said, returning with a start to the world of reality.

The old man pointed to his head.

"Dey's bofe 'stracted, suh," he said, "out'n dey min'. Dey's be'n dat-a-way fer yeahs an' yeahs."

At that moment the young man of the house came out to the door, and greeted us pleasantly. He asked me to alight from the carriage and led me to the chair the old man had occupied. It was a massive oak affair, with carved arms and back and a wooden seat, and looked as though it might be of ancient make, perhaps an heirloom. I found young Murchison was a frank and manly young fellow, and quite capable of looking out for his own interests. I struck a bargain with him, on terms that were fair to both. When I had concluded my business and invited him to call and see me sometime, I got into the carriage, and Julius drove down the lane and out into the road again. In going out, we passed near the old man, who was still muttering to himself and digging rapidly, but with signs of weariness. He did not look up as we went by, but seemed entirely absorbed in his strange pursuit.

In the evening, after supper, Julius came up to the house. We sat out on the porch, my wife and her sister and Julius and I. We cut a large watermelon, and when Julius had eaten the half we gave to him, he told us the story of old man Murchison's undoing. The air was cool, the sky was clear, the stars shone with a brightness unknown in higher latitudes. The voices of the night came faintly from the distant woods, and there could have been no more romantic setting for the story of jealousy, revenge and disappointment which the old white-haired negro told us, in his own quaint dialect – a story of things possible only in an era which, happily, has passed from our history, as, in God's own time – and may it be soon! – it will from all the earth. Some of the facts in this strange story – circumstances of which Julius was ignorant, though he had the main facts correct – I learned afterwards from other sources, but I have woven them all together here in orderly sequence.

The Murchison family had occupied their ancestral seat on the sandhills for a hundred years or more. There were not many rich families in that part of North Carolina, and this one, by reason of its wealth and other things, was easily the most conspicuous in several counties. The first great man of the family, General Arthur Murchison, had won distinction in the war of independence, and during all the Revolutionary period had been one of the most ardent of the Carolina patriots. After peace was established he had taken high place in the councils of the State. Elected a delegate to the Constitutional Convention at Philadelphia in 1787, it was largely due to his efforts that North Carolina adopted the Federal Constitution the following year. His son became a distinguished jurist, whose name is still a synonym for legal learning and juridical wisdom in North Carolina. Roger Murchison, the son of Judge Murchison – the generations had followed one another rapidly in a country of warm skies and early marriages – was the immediate predecessor of Malcolm Murchison, the demented old man who was nominal owner of the estate at the time of my visit to the house.

In Roger Murchison the family may be said to have begun to decline from the eminence it had attained in the career of Judge Murchison. In the first place, Roger Murchison did not marry, thus seemingly indicating a lack of the family pride which would have made him wish to continue the name in the direct line. Again, though his career in college had been brilliant; though the wealth and standing of the family gave him social and political prestige; and though he had held high office under the State and National governments, he had never while in public life especially distinguished himself for eloquence or statesmanship, but had, on the contrary, enjoyed a life of ease and pleasure and had wasted what his friends thought rare gifts. He was fond of cards, of fast horses, of rare wines, and of gay society. It is not surprising, therefore, that he spent very little time on his property, preferring the life of cities to the comparative dullness of plantation life with such colorless distractions as a neighboring small town could offer.

He had inherited a large estate, including several plantations, and numerous slaves. During his frequent absences from home, in the last fifteen years of his life, he left his property under the management of a nephew, Malcolm Murchison, the orphan son of a younger brother, and his own prospective heir. Young Malcolm was a youth of unusual strength of character and administrative capacity, and even before he had attained his majority showed himself a better manager than his uncle had ever been. So well, indeed, did he manage the estate that his uncle left it for ten years practically in his hands, looking to him only for the means he required to lead his own life in other places. It is true he appeared periodically and assumed the role of proprietor, but Malcolm was the man to whom the community and the slaves looked as both the present and the future master.

Young Murchison kept bachelor's hall in the great house. The only women about the establishment were an old black cook, and the housekeeper, a tall, comely young quadroon – she had too a dash of Indian blood, which perhaps gave her straighter and blacker hair than she would otherwise have had, and also perhaps endowed her with some other qualities which found their natural expression in the course of subsequent events – if indeed her actions needed anything more than common human nature to account for them. The duties of young Murchison's housekeeper were not onerous; compared with a toiling field hand she led a life of ease and luxury. The one conspicuous vice of Malcolm Murchison was avarice. If he had other failings, they were the heritage of the period, and he shared them with his contemporaries of the same caste. Perhaps it was his avarice that kept him from marrying; it was cheaper to have his clothing and his table looked after by a slave than by a woman who would not have been content with her food and clothing. At any rate, for ten or fifteen years he remained single, and ladies never set foot in the Murchison house. Men sometimes called and smoked and drank, played cards, bought and sold produce or slaves, but the foot of a white woman had not touched the floor for fifteen years, when Mrs. Martha Todd came from Pennsylvania to the neighboring town of Patesville to visit a cousin living there, who had married a resident of the town.

Malcolm Murchison met Mrs. Todd while she was driving on the road one day. He knew her companion, in response to whose somewhat distant bow he lifted his hat. Attracted by the stranger's appearance, he made inquiries about her in the town, and learned that she was a widow and rich in her own right. He sought opportunities to meet her, courted her, and after a decent interval of hesitation on her part – she had only just put off mourning for her first husband – received her promise to be his wife.

He broke the news to his housekeeper by telling her to make the house ready for a mistress. The housekeeper had been in power too long to yield gracefully, or perhaps she foresaw and dreaded the future. Some passionate strain of the mixed blood in her veins – a very human blood – broke out in a scene of hysterical violence. She pleaded, remonstrated, raged. He listened calmly through it all – he had anticipated some such scene and at the end said to her:

"You had better be quiet and obedient. I have heard what you have to say – this once – and it will be useless for you to repeat it, for I shall not listen again. If you are reasonable, I will send you to the other plantation. If not, I will leave you here, with your new mistress."

She was silent for the time being, but raged inwardly. The next day she stole away from home, went to the town, sought out the new object of Murchison's devotion, and told her something – just what she told no one but herself and the lady ever knew.

When Murchison called in the evening, Mrs. Todd sent down word that she was not at home. With the message came a note:

"I have had my wedded happiness spoiled once. A burnt child dreads the fire – I do not care to go twice through the same experience. I have learned some things about you that will render it impossible for me ever to marry you. It is needless to seek an explanation."

He went away puzzled and angry. His housekeeper wore an anxious look, which became less anxious as she observed his frame of mind. He had been wondering where Mrs. Todd had got the information – he could not doubt what it was – that had turned her from him. Suddenly a suspicion flashed into his mind. He went away early the next morning and made investigations. In the afternoon he came home with all the worst passions of weak humanity, clad with irresponsible power, flaming in his eyes.

"I will teach you," he said to his housekeeper, who quailed before him, "to tell tales about your master. I will put it out of your power to dip your tongue in where you are not concerned."

There was no one to say him nay. The law made her his. It was a lonely house, and no angel of mercy stayed his hand.

About a week later he received a letter, – a bulky envelope.

On breaking the seal, he found the contents to consist of two papers, one of which was a letter from a friend and political associate of his uncle. It was dated at Washington, and announced the death of his Uncle Roger as the result of an accident. A team of spirited horses had run away with him and thrown him out of the carriage, inflicting a fatal injury. The letter stated that his uncle had lingered for a day, during which he had dictated a letter to his nephew; that his body had been embalmed and placed in a vault, to await the disposition of his relatives or representatives. His uncle's letter was enclosed with the one above and ran as follows:

"My dear Malcolm: This is the last communication I shall ever make to you, I am sorry to say – though I don't know that I ought to complain, for I have always been a philosopher, and have had a good time to boot. There must be an end to all things, and I cannot escape the common fate.

"You have been a good nephew and a careful manager, and I have not forgotten the fact. I have left a will in which you are named as my sole heir, barring some small provision for my sister Mary. With the will you will find several notes, and mortgages securing them, on plantations in the neighborhood – I do not need to specify, as they explain themselves; also some bonds and other securities of value and your grandmother's diamond necklace. I do not say here where they are, lest this letter might fall into the wrong hands; but your housekeeper Viney knows their hiding place. She is devoted to you and to the family – she ought to be, for she is of our blood – and she only knows the secret. I would not have told her, of course, had I not thought of just some such chance as this which has befallen me. She does not know the value of the papers, but simply that they are important.

"And now, Malcolm, my boy, goodbye. I am crossing the river and I reach back to clasp your hand once more – just once.

"Your dying Uncle,
"Roger Murchison"

Malcolm Murchison took this letter to Viney. She had been banished from the house to a cabin in the yard, where she was waited on by the old black cook. He felt a little remorseful as he looked at her; for, after all, she was a woman, and there had been excuses for what she had done; and he had begun to feel, in some measure, that there was no sufficient excuse for what he had done.

She looked at him with an inscrutable face as he came in, and he felt very uncomfortable under the look.

"Viney," he said, not unkindly, "I'm sorry I went so far, and I'm glad you're getting better."

Her expression softened, a tear rolled down her cheek, and he felt correspondingly relieved. It is so easy to forgive our own sins against others.

"Your old Master Roger is dead. I have just received a letter telling me how it happened. He was thrown from a buggy in a runaway and injured so badly that he died the same day. He had time to write me a letter, in which he says you can tell me where he put certain papers that you know about. Can you tell" – he remembered her condition – "can you show me where they are?"

A closer observer than Malcolm Murchison might have detected at this moment another change in the woman's expression. Perhaps it was in her eyes more than elsewhere; for into their black depths there sprang a sudden fire. Beyond this, however, and a slight quickening of her pulse, of which there was no visible manifestation, she gave no sign of special feeling; and even if these had been noticed they might have been attributed to the natural interest felt at hearing of her old master's death.

The only answer Viney made was to lift her hand and point it to her mouth.

"Yes, I know," he said hastily, "you can't tell me – not now at least, but you can surely point out the place to me."

She shook her head and pointed again to her mouth.

"Is it hidden in some place that you can't lead me to when you are able to get up?"

She nodded her head.

"Will it require words to describe it so that I can find it?" Again she nodded affirmatively.

He reflected a moment. "Is it in the house?" he asked.

She shook her head.

"In the yard?"

Again she made a negative sign. "In the barn?"

No.

"In the fields?"

No.

He tried for an hour, naming every spot he could think of as a possible hiding-place for the papers, but with no avail. Every question was answered in the negative.

When he had exhausted his ingenuity in framing questions he went away very much disappointed. He had been patiently waiting for his reward for many years, and now when it should be his, it seemed to elude his grasp.

"Never mind," he said, "we will wait until you are better, and then perhaps you may be able to speak intelligibly. In the meantime you shall not want for anything."

He had her removed to the house and saw that she received every attention. She was fed with dainty food, and such care as was possible was given to her wound. In due time it healed. But she did not even then seem able to articulate, even in whispers, and all his attempts to learn of her the whereabouts of the missing papers, were met by the same failure. She seemed willing enough, but unable to tell what he wished to know. There was apparently some mystery which only words could unravel.

It occurred to him more than once how simple it would be for her to write down the few words necessary to his happiness. But, alas! She might as well have been without hands, for any use she could make of them in that respect. Slaves were not taught to write, for too much learning would have made them mad. But Malcolm Murchison was a man of resources – he would have her taught to write. So he employed a teacher – a free colored man who had picked up some fragments of learning, and who could be trusted to hold his tongue, to teach Viney to read and write. But somehow she made poor progress. She was handicapped of course by her loss of speech. It was unfamiliar work too for the teacher, who would not have been expert with a pupil equipped with all the normal faculties. Perhaps she had begun too old; or her mind was too busily occupied with other thoughts to fix it on the tedious and painful steps by which the art of expression in writing is acquired. Whatever the reason, she manifested a remarkable stupidity while seemingly anxious to learn; and in the end Malcolm was compelled to abandon the attempt to teach her.

Several years passed in vain efforts to extract from Viney in some way the wished-for information. Meantime Murchison's affairs did not prosper. Several other relatives claimed a share in his uncle's estate; on the ground that he had died intestate. In the absence of the will, their claims could not be successfully disputed. Every legal means of delay was resorted to, and the authorities were disposed, in view of the remarkable circumstances of the case, to grant every possible favor. But the law fixed certain limits to delay in the settlement of an estate, and in the end he was obliged either to compromise the adverse claims or allow them to be fixed by legal process. And while certain of what his own rights were, he was compelled to see a large part of what was rightfully his go into hands where it would be difficult to trace or recover it if the will were found. Some of the estates against which he suspected the hidden notes and mortgages were held, were sold and otherwise disposed of. His worry interfered with proper attention to his farming operations, and one crop was almost a failure. The factor to whom he shipped his cotton went bankrupt owing him a large balance, and he fell into debt and worried himself into a fever. The woman Viney nursed him through it, and was always present at his side, a mute reproach for his cruelty, a constant reminder of his troubles. Her presence was the worst of things for him, and yet he could not bear to have her out of his sight; for in her lay the secret he longed for and which he hoped at some time in some miraculous way to extract from her.

When he rose from his sick-bed after an illness of three months, he was but the wreck of the strong man he had once been. His affairs had fallen into hopeless disorder. His slaves, except Viney, were sold to pay his debts, and there remained to him of the almost princely inheritance he had expected, only the old place on the sandhills and his slave, Viney, who still kept house for him. His mind was vacant and wandering, except on the one subject of the hidden will, and he spent most of the time in trying to extract from Viney the secret of its hiding-place. A young nephew came and lived with him and did what was necessary to hold the remnant of the estate together.

When the war came Viney was freed, with the rest of her brethren in bondage. But she did not leave the old place. There was some gruesome attraction in the scene of her suffering, or perhaps it was the home instinct. The society of humankind did not possess the same attraction for her as if she had not been deprived of the power of speech. She stayed on and on, doing the simple housework for the demented old man and his nephew, until the superstitious negroes and poor whites of the neighborhood said that she too shared the old man's affliction. Day after day they sat on the porch, when her indoor work was done, the old man resting in the carved oaken arm-chair, and she in her splint-bottom chair; or the old man commanding, threatening, expostulating, entreating her to try, just once more, to tell him his uncle's message – she replying in the meaningless inarticulate mutterings that we had heard; or the old man digging, digging furiously, and she watching him from the porch, with the same inscrutable eyes, though dulled somewhat by age, that had flashed upon him for a moment in the dimly lighted cabin where she lay on her bed of pain.

The summer following the visit I made to the old Murchison place I accompanied my wife North on a trip to our former home. On my return several weeks later I had occasion again to visit young Murchison, and drove over one morning to the house. As we drove up the lane I noticed a surprising change in the surroundings. A new gate had been hung, upon a pair of ugly cast-iron hinges. The grass in the path had been mowed, and the weeds and shrubs bordering it had been cut down. The neglected pleasure-garden had been reduced to some degree of order, and the ground around the house had been plowed and harrowed, and the young blades of grass were shooting up and covering the surface with a greenish down. The house itself had shared in the general improvement. The roof had been repaired and the broken windows mended, and from certain indications in the way of ladders and pails in the yard, I inferred that it was intended to paint the house. This however was merely a supposition, for house-painting is an art that languishes in the rural districts of the South.

Julius had been noticing my interest in these signs of prosperity, with a pleased expression that boded further surprises.

"What's been going on here, Julius?" I asked.

"Ole Mars Murchison done dead, suh – died las' mont', an' eve'ything goes ter young Mistah Roger. He's done 'mence' ter fix de ole place up. He be'n ober ter yo' place lookin' 'roun', an' he say he's gwineter hab his'n lookin' lak yo'n befo' de yeah's ober."

We stopped the rockaway in front of the house. As we drew up, an old woman came out of the front door, in whom I recognized one of the strange couple I had seen on the piazza on my former visit. She seemed intelligent enough, and I ventured to address her.

"Is Mr. Murchison at home?"

"Yas, suh," she answered, "I'll call 'im."

Her articulation was not distinct, but her words were intelligible. I was never more surprised in my life.

"What does this mean, Julius?" I inquired, turning to the old man, who was grinning and chuckling to himself in great glee at my manifest astonishment. "Has she recovered her speech?"

"She'd nebber lost it, suh. Ole Viney could 'a' talked all de time, ef she'd had a min' ter. Atter ole Mars Ma'colm wuz dead, she tuk an' showed Mistah Roger whar de will an' de yuther papers wuz hid. An' whar yer reckon dey wuz, zuh?"

"I give it up, Julius. Enlighten me."

"Dey wa'n't in de house, ner de yah'd, ner de ba'n, ner de fiel's. Dey wuz hid in de seat er dat ole oak a'm-cheer on de piazza yander w'at ole Mars Ma'colm be'n settin' in all dese yeahs."

The Sheriff's Children

Branson County, North Carolina, is in a sequestered district of one of the staidest and most conservative States of the Union. Society in Branson County is almost primitive in its simplicity. Most of the white people own the farms they till, and even before the war there were no very wealthy families to force their neighbors, by comparison, into the category of "poor whites."

To Branson County, as to most rural communities in the South, the war is the one historical event that overshadows all others. It is the era from which all local chronicles are dated, – births, deaths, marriages, storms, freshets. No description of the life of any Southern community would be perfect that failed to emphasize the all pervading influence of the great conflict.

Yet the fierce tide of war that had rushed through the cities and along the great highways of the country had comparatively speaking but slightly disturbed the sluggish current of life in this region, remote from railroads and navigable streams. To the north in Virginia, to the west in Tennessee, and all along the seaboard the war had raged; but the thunder of its cannon had not disturbed the echoes of Branson County, where the loudest sounds heard were the crack of some hunter's rifle, the baying of some deep-mouthed hound, or the yodel of some tuneful negro on his way through the pine forest. To the east, Sherman's army had passed on its march to the sea; but no straggling band of "bummers"[1] had penetrated the confines of Branson County. The war, it is true, had robbed the county of the flower of its young manhood; but the burden of taxation, the doubt and uncertainty of the conflict, and the sting of ultimate defeat, had been borne by the people with an apathy that robbed misfortune of half its sharpness.

The nearest approach to town life afforded by Branson County is found in the little village of Troy, the county seat, a hamlet with a population of four or five hundred.

Ten years make little difference in the appearance of these remote Southern towns. If a railroad is built through one of them, it infuses some enterprise; the social corpse is galvanized by the fresh blood of civilization that pulses along the farthest ramifications of our great system of commercial highways. At the period of which I write, no railroad had come to Troy. If a traveler, accustomed to the bustling life of cities, could have ridden through Troy on a summer day, he might easily have fancied himself in a deserted village. Around him he would have seen weather-beaten houses, innocent of paint, the shingled roofs in many instances covered with a rich growth of moss. Here and there he would have met a razor-backed hog lazily rooting his way along the principal thoroughfare; and more than once he would probably have had to disturb the slumbers of some yellow dog, dozing away the hours in the ardent sunshine, and reluctantly yielding up his place in the middle of the dusty road.

On Saturdays the village presented a somewhat livelier appearance, and the shade trees around the court house square and along Front Street served as hitching-posts for a goodly number of horses and mules and stunted oxen, belonging to the farmer-folk who had come in to trade at the two or three local stores.

A murder was a rare event in Branson County. Every well-informed citizen could tell the number of homicides committed in the county for fifty years back, and whether the slayer, in any given instance, had escaped, either by flight or acquittal, or had suffered the penalty of the law. So, when it became known in Troy early one Friday morning in summer, about ten years after the war, that old Captain Walker, who had served in Mexico under Scott, and had left an arm on the field of Gettysburg, had been foully murdered during the night, there was intense excitement in the village. Business was practically suspended, and the citizens gathered in little groups to discuss the murder, and speculate upon the identity of the murderer. It transpired from testimony at the coroner's inquest, held during the morning, that a strange mulatto had been seen

Notes

THE SHERIFF'S CHILDREN
[1] Soldiers sent to forage for food, who often treated civilians roughly.

going in the direction of Captain Walker's house the night before, and had been met going away from Troy early Friday morning, by a farmer on his way to town. Other circumstances seemed to connect the stranger with the crime. The sheriff organized a posse to search for him, and early in the evening, when most of the citizens of Troy were at supper, the suspected man was brought in and lodged in the county jail.

By the following morning the news of the capture had spread to the farthest limits of the county. A much larger number of people than usual came to town that Saturday, – bearded men in straw hats and blue homespun shirts, and butternut trousers of great amplitude of material and vagueness of outline; women in homespun frocks and slat-bonnets, with faces as expressionless as the dreary sandhills which gave them a meagre sustenance.

The murder was almost the sole topic of conversation. A steady stream of curious observers visited the house of mourning, and gazed upon the rugged face of the old veteran, now stiff and cold in death; and more than one eye dropped a tear at the remembrance of the cheery smile, and the joke – sometimes superannuated, generally feeble, but always good-natured – with which the captain had been wont to greet his acquaintances. There was a growing sentiment of anger among these stern men, toward the murderer who had thus cut down their friend, and a strong feeling that ordinary justice was too slight a punishment for such a crime.

Toward noon there was an informal gathering of citizens in Dan Tyson's store.

"I hear it 'lowed that Square Kyahtah's too sick ter hol' co'te this evenin'," said one, "an' that the purlim'nary hearin' 'll haf ter go over 'tel nex' week."

A look of disappointment went round the crowd.

"Hit's the durndes', meanes' murder ever committed in this caounty," said another, with moody emphasis.

"I s'pose the nigger 'lowed the Cap'n had some greenbacks," observed a third speaker.

"The Cap'n," said another, with an air of superior information, "has left two bairls of Confedrit money, which he 'spected 'ud be good some day er nuther."

This statement gave rise to a discussion of the speculative value of Confederate money; but in a little while the conversation returned to the murder.

"Hangin' air too good fer the murderer," said one; "he oughter be burnt, stidier bein' hung."

There was an impressive pause at this point, during which a jug of moonlight whiskey went the round of the crowd.

"Well," said a round-shouldered farmer, who, in spite of his peaceable expression and faded gray eye, was known to have been one of the most daring followers of a rebel guerrilla chieftain, "what air yer gwine ter do about it? Ef you fellers air gwine ter set down an' let a wuthless nigger kill the bes' white man in Branson, an' not say nuthin' ner do nuthin', I 'll move outen the caounty."

This speech gave tone and direction to the rest of the conversation. Whether the fear of losing the round-shouldered farmer operated to bring about the result or not is imma-terial to this narrative; but, at all events, the crowd decided to lynch the negro. They agreed that this was the least that could be done to avenge the death of their murdered friend, and that it was a becoming way in which to honor his memory. They had some vague notions of the majesty of the law and the rights of the citizen, but in the passion of the moment these sunk into oblivion; a white man had been killed by a negro.

"The Cap'n was an ole sodger," said one of his friends solemnly. "He 'll sleep better when he knows that a co'te-martial has be'n hilt an' jestice done."

By agreement the lynchers were to meet at Tyson's store at five o'clock in the after-noon, and proceed thence to the jail, which was situated down the Lumberton Dirt

Road (as the old turnpike antedating the plank-road was called), about half a mile south of the court-house. When the preliminaries of the lynching had been arranged, and a committee appointed to manage the affair, the crowd dispersed, some to go to their dinners, and some to secure recruits for the lynching party.

It was twenty minutes to five o'clock, when an excited negro, panting and perspiring, rushed up to the back door of Sheriff Campbell's dwelling, which stood at a little distance from the jail and somewhat farther than the latter building from the court-house. A turbaned colored woman came to the door in response to the negro's knock.

"Hoddy, Sis' Nance."

"Hoddy, Brer Sam."

"Is de shurff in?" inquired the negro.

"Yas, Brer Sam, he's eatin' his dinner" was the answer.

"Will yer ax 'im ter step ter de do' a minute, Sis' Nance?"

The woman went into the dining room, and a moment later the sheriff came to the door. He was a tall, muscular man, of a ruddier complexion than is usual among Southerners. A pair of keen, deep-set gray eyes looked out from under bushy eyebrows, and about his mouth was a masterful expression, which a full beard, once sandy in color, but now profusely sprinkled with gray, could not entirely conceal. The day was hot; the sheriff had discarded his coat and vest, and had his white shirt open at the throat.

"What do you want, Sam?" he inquired of the negro, who stood hat in hand, wiping the moisture from his face with a ragged shirt-sleeve.

"Shurff, dey gwine ter hang de pris'ner w'at's lock' up in de jail. Dey're comin' dis a-way now. I wuz layin' down on a sack er corn down at de sto', behine a pile er flour-bairls, w'en I hearn Doc' Cain en Kunnel Wright talkin' erbout it. I slip' outen de back do', en run here as fas' as I could. I hearn you say down ter de sto' once't dat you would n't let nobody take a pris'ner 'way fum you widout walkin' over yo' dead body, en I thought I'd let you know 'fo' dey come, so yer could pertec' de pris'ner."

The sheriff listened calmly, but his face grew firmer, and a determined gleam lit up his gray eyes. His frame grew more erect, and he unconsciously assumed the attitude of a soldier who momentarily expects to meet the enemy face to face.

"Much obliged, Sam," he answered. "I'll protect the prisoner. Who 's coming?"

"I dunno who-all is comin'," replied the negro. "Dere's Mistah McSwayne, en Doc' Cain, en Maje' McDonal', en Kunnel Wright, en a heap er yuthers. I wuz so skeered I done furgot mo'd'n half un em. I spec' dey mus' be mos' here by dis time, so I'll git outen de way, fer I don' want nobody fer ter think I wuz mix' up in dis business." The negro glanced nervously down the road toward the town, and made a movement as if to go away.

"Won't you have some dinner first?" asked the sheriff.

The negro looked longingly in at the open door, and sniffed the appetizing odor of boiled pork and collards.

"I ain't got no time fer ter tarry, Shurff, he said, "but Sis' Nance mought gin me sump'n I could kyar in my hen' en eat on de way."

A moment later Nancy brought him a huge sandwich of split corn-pone, with a thick slice of fat bacon inserted between the halves, and a couple of baked yams. The negro hastily replaced his ragged hat on his head, dropped the yams in the pocket of his capacious trousers, and, taking the sandwich in his hand, hurried across the road and disappeared in the woods beyond.

The sheriff reentered the house, and put on his coat and hat. He then took down a double-barreled shotgun and loaded it with buckshot. Filling the chambers of a revolver with fresh cartridges, he slipped it into the pocket of the sack-coat which he wore.

A comely young woman in a calico dress watched these proceedings with anxious surprise.

"Where are you going, father?" she asked. She had not heard the conversation with the negro.

"I am goin' over to the jail," responded the sheriff. "There 's a mob comin' this way to lynch the nigger we've got locked up. But they won't do it," he added, with emphasis.

"Oh, father! don't go!" pleaded the girl, clinging to his arm; "they'll shoot you if you don't give him up."

"You never mind me, Polly," said her father reassuringly, as he gently unclasped her hands from his arm. "I'll take care of myself and the prisoner, too. There ain't a man in Branson County that would shoot me. Besides, I have faced fire too often to be scared away from my duty. You keep close in the house," he continued, "and if any one disturbs you just use the old horse-pistol[2] in the top bureau drawer. It's a little old-fashioned, but it did good work a few years ago."

The young girl shuddered at this sanguinary allusion, but made no further objection to her father's departure.

The sheriff of Branson was a man far above the average of the community in wealth, education, and social position. His had been one of the few families in the county that before the war had owned large estates and numerous slaves. He had graduated at the State University at Chapel Hill, and had kept up some acquaintance with current literature and advanced thought. He had traveled some in his youth, and was looked up to in the county as an authority on all subjects connected with the outer world. At first an ardent supporter of the Union, he had opposed the secession movement in his native State as long as opposition availed to stem the tide of public opinion. Yielding at last to the force of circumstances, he had entered the Confederate service rather late in the war, and served with distinction through several campaigns, rising in time to the rank of colonel. After the war he had taken the oath of allegiance, and had been chosen by the people as the most available candidate for the office of sheriff, to which he had been elected without opposition. He had filled the office for several terms, and was universally popular with his constituents.

Colonel or Sheriff Campbell, as he was indifferently called, as the military or civil title happened to be most important in the opinion of the person addressing him, had a high sense of the responsibility attaching to his office. He had sworn to do his duty faithfully, and he knew what his duty was, as sheriff, perhaps more clearly than he had apprehended it in other passages of his life. It was, therefore, with no uncertainty in regard to his course that he prepared his weapons and went over to the jail. He had no fears for Polly's safety.

The sheriff had just locked the heavy front door of the jail behind him when a half dozen horsemen, followed by a crowd of men on foot, came round a bend in the road and drew near the jail. They halted in front of the picket fence that surrounded the building, while several of the committee of arrangements rode on a few rods farther to the sheriff's house. One of them dismounted and rapped on the door with his riding-whip.

"Is the sheriff at home?" he inquired.

"No, he has just gone out," replied Polly, who had come to the door.

"We want the jail keys," he continued.

Notes

[2] Not a pistol for shooting horses, but a heavy pistol carried by cavalrymen.

"They are not here," said Polly. "The sheriff has them himself." Then she added, with assumed indifference, "He is at the jail now."

The man turned away, and Polly went into the front room, from which she peered anxiously between the slats of the green blinds of a window that looked toward the jail. Meanwhile the messenger returned to his companions and announced his discovery. It looked as though the sheriff had learned of their design and was preparing to resist it.

One of them stepped forward and rapped on the jail door.

"Well, what is it?" said the sheriff, from within.

"We want to talk to you, Sheriff," replied the spokesman.

There was a little wicket in the door; this the sheriff opened, and answered through it.

"All right, boys, talk away. You are all strangers to me, and I don't know what business you can have." The sheriff did not think it necessary to recognize anybody in particular on such an occasion; the question of identity sometimes comes up in the investigation of these extrajudicial executions.

"We're a committee of citizens and we want to get into the jail."

"What for? It ain't much trouble to get into jail. Most people want to keep out."

The mob was in no humor to appreciate a joke, and the sheriff's witticism fell dead upon an unresponsive audience.

"We want to have a talk with the nigger that killed Cap'n Walker."

"You can talk to that nigger in the courthouse, when he's brought out for trial. Court will be in session here next week. I know what you fellows want, but you can't get my prisoner today. Do you want to take the bread out of a poor man's mouth? I get seventy-five cents a day for keeping this prisoner, and he's the only one in jail. I can't have my family suffer just to please you fellows."

One or two young men in the crowd laughed at the idea of Sheriff Campbell's suffering for want of seventy-five cents a day; but they were frowned into silence by those who stood near them.

"Ef yer don't let us in," cried a voice, "we 'll bu's' the do' open."

"Bust away," answered the sheriff, raising his voice so that all could hear. "But I give you fair warning. The first man that tries it will be filled with buckshot. I'm sheriff of this county; I know my duty, and I mean to do it."

"What's the use of kicking, Sheriff?" argued one of the leaders of the mob. "The nigger is sure to hang anyhow; he richly deserves it; and we 've got to do something to teach the niggers their places, or white people won't be able to live in the county."

"There 's no use talking, boys," responded the sheriff. "I'm a white man outside, but in this jail I'm sheriff; and if this nigger's to be hung in this county, I propose to do the hanging. So you fellows might as well right-about-face, and march back to Troy. You've had a pleasant trip, and the exercise will be good for you. You know *me*. I 've got powder and ball, and I've faced fire before now, with nothing between me and the enemy, and I don't mean to surrender this jail while I 'm able to shoot." Having thus announced his determination, the sheriff closed and fastened the wicket, and looked around for the best position from which to defend the building.

The crowd drew off a little, and the leaders conversed together in low tones.

The Branson County jail was a small, two-story brick building, strongly constructed, with no attempt at architectural ornamentation. Each story was divided into two large cells by a passage running from front to rear.

A grated iron door gave entrance from the passage to each of the four cells. The jail seldom had many prisoners in it, and the lower windows had been boarded up. When the sheriff had closed the wicket, he ascended the steep wooden stairs to the upper floor. There was no window at the front of the upper passage, and the most available position from which to watch the movements of the crowd below was the front window of the cell occupied by the solitary prisoner.

The sheriff unlocked the door and entered the cell. The prisoner was crouched in a corner, his yellow face, blanched with terror, looking ghastly in the semi-darkness of the room. A cold perspiration had gathered on his forehead, and his teeth were chattering with affright.

"For God's sake, Sheriff," he murmured hoarsely, "don't let 'em lynch me; I did n't kill the old man."

The sheriff glanced at the cowering wretch with a look of mingled contempt and loathing.

"Get up," he said sharply. "You will probably be hung sooner or later, but it shall not be today, if I can help it. I 'll unlock your fetters, and if I can't hold the jail, you 'll have to make the best fight you can. If I'm shot, I 'll consider my responsibility at an end."

There were iron fetters on the prisoner's ankles, and handcuffs on his wrists. These the sheriff unlocked, and they fell clanking to the floor.

"Keep back from the window," said the sheriff. "They might shoot if they saw you."

The sheriff drew toward the window a pine bench which formed a part of the scanty furniture of the cell, and laid his revolver upon it. Then he took his gun in hand, and took his stand at the side of the window where he could with least exposure of himself watch the movements of the crowd below.

The lynchers had not anticipated any determined resistance. Of course they had looked for a formal protest, and perhaps a sufficient show of opposition to excuse the sheriff in the eye of any stickler for legal formalities. They had not however come prepared to fight a battle, and no one of them seemed willing to lead an attack upon the jail. The leaders of the party conferred together with a good deal of animated gesticulation, which was visible to the sheriff from his outlook, though the distance was too great for him to hear what was said. At length one of them broke away from the group, and rode back to the main body of the lynchers, who were restlessly awaiting orders.

"Well, boys," said the messenger, "we 'll have to let it go for the present. The sheriff says he 'll shoot, and he's got the drop on us this time. There ain't any of us that want to follow Cap'n Walker jest yet. Besides, the sheriff is a good fellow, and we don't want to hurt 'im. But," he added, as if to reassure the crowd, which began to show signs of disappointment, "the nigger might as well say his prayers, for he ain't got long to live."

There was a murmur of dissent from the mob, and several voices insisted that an attack be made on the jail. But pacific counsels finally prevailed, and the mob sullenly withdrew.

The sheriff stood at the window until they had disappeared around the bend in the road. He did not relax his watchfulness when the last one was out of sight. Their withdrawal might be a mere feint, to be followed by a further attempt. So closely, indeed, was his attention drawn to the outside, that he neither saw nor heard the prisoner creep steadily across the floor, reach out his hand and secure the revolver which lay on the bench behind the sheriff, and creep as noiselessly back to his place in the corner of the room.

A moment after the last of the lynching party had disappeared there was a shot fired from the woods across the road; a bullet whistled by the window and buried itself in the wooden casing a few inches from where the sheriff was standing. Quick as thought, with the instinct born of a semi-guerrilla army experience, he raised his gun and fired twice at the point from which a faint puff of smoke showed the hostile bullet to have been sent. He stood a moment watching, and then rested his gun against the window, and reached behind him mechanically for the other weapon. It was not on the bench.

As the sheriff realized this fact, he turned his head and looked into the muzzle of the revolver.

"Stay where you are, Sheriff," said the prisoner, his eyes glistening, his face almost ruddy with excitement.

The sheriff mentally cursed his own carelessness for allowing him to be caught in such a predicament. He had not expected anything of the kind. He had relied on the negro's cowardice and subordination in the presence of an armed white man as a matter of course. The sheriff was a brave man, but realized that the prisoner had him at an immense disadvantage. The two men stood thus for a moment, fighting a harmless duel with their eyes.

"Well, what do you mean to do?" asked the sheriff with apparent calmness.

"To get away, of course," said the prisoner, in a tone which caused the sheriff to look at him more closely, and with an involuntary feeling of apprehension; if the man was not mad, he was in a state of mind akin to madness, and quite as dangerous. The sheriff felt that he must speak the prisoner fair, and watch for a chance to turn the tables on him. The keen-eyed, desperate man before him was a different being altogether from the groveling wretch who had begged so piteously for life a few minutes before.

At length the sheriff spoke: –

"Is this your gratitude to me for saving your life at the risk of my own? If I had not done so, you would now be swinging from the limb of some neighboring tree."

"True," said the prisoner, "you saved my life, but for how long? When you came in, you said Court would sit next week. When the crowd went away they said I had not long to live. It is merely a choice of two ropes."

"While there's life there's hope," replied the sheriff. He uttered this commonplace mechanically, while his brain was busy in trying to think out some way of escape. "If you are innocent you can prove it."

The mulatto kept his eye upon the sheriff. "I didn't kill the old man," he replied; "but I shall never be able to clear myself. I was at his house at nine o'clock. I stole from it the coat that was on my back when I was taken. I would be convicted, even with a fair trial, unless the real murderer were discovered beforehand."

The sheriff knew this only too well. While he was thinking what argument next to use, the prisoner continued: –

"Throw me the keys – no, unlock the door."

The sheriff stood a moment irresolute. The mulatto's eye glittered ominously. The sheriff crossed the room and unlocked the door leading into the passage.

"Now go down and unlock the outside door."

The heart of the sheriff leaped within him. Perhaps he might make a dash for liberty, and gain the outside. He descended the narrow stairs, the prisoner keeping close behind him.

The sheriff inserted the huge iron key into the lock. The rusty bolt yielded slowly. It still remained for him to pull the door open.

"Stop!" thundered the mulatto, who seemed to divine the sheriff's purpose. "Move a muscle, and I'll blow your brains out."

The sheriff obeyed; he realized that his chance had not yet come.

"Now keep on that side of the passage, and go back upstairs."

Keeping the sheriff under cover of the revolver, the mulatto followed him up the stairs. The sheriff expected the prisoner to lock him into the cell and make his own escape. He had about come to the conclusion that the best thing he could do under the circumstances was to submit quietly, and take his chances of recapturing the prisoner after the alarm had been given. The sheriff had faced death more than once upon the battlefield. A few minutes before, well armed, and with a brick wall between him and them he had dared a hundred men to fight; but he felt instinctively that the desperate man confronting him was not to be trifled with, and he was too prudent a man to risk his life against such heavy odds. He had Polly to look after, and there was a limit beyond which devotion to duty would be quixotic and even foolish.

"I want to get away," said the prisoner," and I don't want to be captured; for if I am I know I will be hung on the spot. I am afraid," he added somewhat reflectively, "that in order to save myself I shall have to kill you."

"Good God!" exclaimed the sheriff in involuntary terror; "you would not kill the man to whom you owe your own life."

"You speak more truly than you know," replied the mulatto. "I indeed owe my life to you."

The sheriff started. He was capable of surprise, even in that moment of extreme peril. "Who are you?" he asked in amazement.

"Tom, Cicely's son" returned the other. He had closed the door and stood talking to the sheriff through the grated opening. "Don't you remember Cicely – Cicely whom you sold, with her child, to the speculator on his way to Alabama?"

The sheriff did remember. He had been sorry for it many a time since. It had been the old story of debts, mortgages, and bad crops. He had quarreled with the mother. The price offered for her and her child had been unusually large, and he had yielded to the combination of anger and pecuniary stress.

"Good God!" he gasped, "you would not murder your own father?"

"My father?" replied the mulatto. "It were well enough for me to claim the relationship, but it comes with poor grace from you to ask anything by reason of it. What father's duty have you ever performed for me? Did you give me your name, or even your protection? Other white men gave their colored sons freedom and money, and sent them to the free States. *You* sold *me* to the rice swamps."

"I at least gave you the life you cling to," murmured the sheriff.

"Life?" said the prisoner, with a sarcastic laugh. "What kind of a life? You gave me your own blood, your own features, – no man need look at us together twice to see that, – and you gave me a black mother. Poor wretch! She died under the lash, because she had enough womanhood to call her soul her own. You gave me a white man's spirit, and you made me a slave, and crushed it out."

"But you are free now," said the sheriff. He had not doubted, could not doubt, the mulatto's word. He knew whose passions coursed beneath that swarthy skin and burned in the black eyes opposite his own. He saw in this mulatto what he himself might have become had not the safeguards of parental restraint and public opinion been thrown around him.

"Free to do what?" replied the mulatto. "Free in name, but despised and scorned and set aside by the people to whose race I belong far more than to my mother's."

"There are schools," said the sheriff. "You have been to school." He had noticed that the mulatto spoke more eloquently and used better language than most Branson County people.

"I have been to school, and dreamed when I went that it would work some marvelous change in my condition. But what did I learn? I learned to feel that no degree of learning or wisdom will change the color of my skin and that I shall always wear what in my own country is a badge of degradation. When I think about it seriously I do not care particularly for such a life. It is the animal in me, not the man, that flees the gallows. I owe you nothing," he went on, "and expect nothing of you; and it would be no more than justice if I should avenge upon you my mother's wrongs and my own. But still I hate to shoot you; I have never yet taken human life – for I did *not* kill the old captain. Will you promise to give no alarm and make no attempt to capture me until morning, if I do not shoot?"

So absorbed were the two men in their colloquy and their own tumultuous thoughts that neither of them had heard the door below move upon its hinges. Neither of them had heard a light step come stealthily up the stairs, nor seen a slender form creep along the darkening passage toward the mulatto.

The sheriff hesitated. The struggle between his love of life and his sense of duty was a terrific one. It may seem strange that a man who could sell his own child into slavery should hesitate at such a moment, when his life was trembling in the balance. But the baleful influence of human slavery poisoned the very fountains of life, and created new standards of right. The sheriff was conscientious; his conscience had merely been warped by his environment. Let no one ask what his answer would have been; he was spared the necessity of a decision.

"Stop," said the mulatto, "you need not promise. I could not trust you if you did. It is your life for mine; there is but one safe way for me; you must die."

He raised his arm to fire, when there was a flash – a report from the passage behind him. His arm fell heavily at his side, and the pistol dropped at his feet.

The sheriff recovered first from his surprise, and throwing open the door secured the fallen weapon. Then seizing the prisoner he thrust him into the cell and locked the door upon him; after which he turned to Polly, who leaned half-fainting against the wall, her hands clasped over her heart.

"Oh, father, I was just in time!" she cried hysterically, and, wildly sobbing, threw herself into her father's arms.

"I watched until they all went away," she said. "I heard the shot from the woods and I saw you shoot. Then when you did not come out I feared something had happened, that perhaps you had been wounded. I got out the other pistol and ran over here. When I found the door open, I knew something was wrong, and when I heard voices I crept upstairs, and reached the top just in time to hear him say he would kill you. Oh, it was a narrow escape!"

When she had grown somewhat calmer, the sheriff left her standing there and went back into the cell. The prisoner's arm was bleeding from a flesh wound. His bravado had given place to a stony apathy. There was no sign in his face of fear or disappointment or feeling of any kind. The sheriff sent Polly to the house for cloth, and bound up the prisoner's wound with a rude skill acquired during his army life.

"I'll have a doctor come and dress the wound in the morning," he said to the prisoner. "It will do very well until then, if you will keep quiet. If the doctor asks you how the wound was caused, you can say that you were struck by the bullet fired from the woods. It would do you no good to have it known that you were shot while attempting to escape."

The prisoner uttered no word of thanks or apology, but sat in sullen silence. When the wounded arm had been bandaged, Polly and her father returned to the house.

The sheriff was in an unusually thoughtful mood that evening. He put salt in his coffee at supper, and poured vinegar over his pancakes. To many of Polly's questions he returned random answers. When he had gone to bed he lay awake for several hours.

In the silent watches of the night, when he was alone with God, there came into his mind a flood of unaccustomed thoughts. An hour or two before, standing face to face with death, he had experienced a sensation similar to that which drowning men are said to feel – a kind of clarifying of the moral faculty, in which the veil of the flesh, with its obscuring passions and prejudices, is pushed aside for a moment, and all the acts of one's life stand out, in the clear light of truth, in their correct proportions and relations, – a state of mind in which one sees himself as God may be supposed to see him. In the reaction following his rescue, this feeling had given place for a time to far different emotions. But now, in the silence of midnight, something of this clearness of spirit returned to the sheriff. He saw that he had owed some duty to this son of his, – that neither law nor custom could destroy a responsibility inherent in the nature of mankind. He could not thus, in the eyes of God at least, shake off the consequences of his sin. Had he never sinned, this wayward spirit would never have come back from the vanished past to haunt him. As these thoughts came, his anger against the mulatto died away, and in its place there sprang up a great pity. The hand of parental authority might have restrained the passions he had seen burning in the prisoner's eyes when the desperate man spoke the words which had seemed to doom his father to death. The sheriff felt that he might have saved this fiery spirit from the slough of slavery; that he might have sent him to the free North, and given him there, or in some other land, an opportunity to turn to usefulness and honorable pursuits the talents that had run to crime, perhaps to madness; he might, still less, have given this son of his the poor simulacrum of liberty which men of his caste could possess in a slave-holding community; or least of all, but still something, he might have kept the boy on the plantation, where the burdens of slavery would have fallen lightly upon him.

The sheriff recalled his own youth. He had inherited an honored name to keep untarnished; he had had a future to make; the picture of a fair young bride had beckoned him on to happiness. The poor wretch now stretched upon a pallet of straw between the brick walls of the jail had had none of these things, – no name, no father, no mother – in the true meaning of motherhood, – and until the past few years no possible future, and then one vague and shadowy in its outline, and dependent for form and substance upon the slow solution of a problem in which there were many unknown quantities.

From what he might have done to what he might yet do was an easy transition for the awakened conscience of the sheriff. It occurred to him, purely as a hypothesis, that he might permit his prisoner to escape; but his oath of office, his duty as sheriff, stood in the way of such a course, and the sheriff dismissed the idea from his mind. He could, however, investigate the circumstances of the murder, and move Heaven and earth to discover the real criminal, for he no longer doubted the prisoner's innocence; he could employ counsel for the accused, and perhaps influence public opinion in his favor. An acquittal once secured, some plan could be devised by which the sheriff might in some degree atone for his crime against this son of his – against society – against God.

When the sheriff had reached this conclusion he fell into an unquiet slumber, from which he awoke late the next morning.

He went over to the jail before breakfast and found the prisoner lying on his pallet, his face turned to the wall; he did not move when the sheriff rattled the door.

"Good-morning," said the latter, in a tone intended to waken the prisoner.

There was no response. The sheriff looked more keenly at the recumbent figure; there was an unnatural rigidity about its attitude.

He hastily unlocked the door and, entering the cell, bent over the prostrate form. There was no sound of breathing; he turned the body over – it was cold and stiff. The prisoner had torn the bandage from his wound and bled to death during the night. He had evidently been dead several hours.

Charlotte Perkins Gilman (1860–1935)

Charlotte Perkins Gilman was best known in her time as a feminist reformer and journalist, and in our time as the author of the classic story of women and madness, "The Yellow Wall-Paper."

"The Giant Wisteria" (1891) was published the year before "The Yellow Wall-Paper," and in the same periodical, the *New England Magazine.* Each is a haunted house story, and each depicts a woman driven to desperation by masculine authority. Note that the young Puritan mother of "The Giant Wisteria" – one of the many literary descendants of Hester Prynne – speaks only a few words in her own voice, and is immediately silenced. Her story is told through a series of other voices, and the core events of the life and of the woman, and her nameless baby, are only dimly visible, with several interpretations possible.

In a story often retold, Gilman had been a patient of the famous psychologist S. Weir Mitchell, who is referenced in "The Yellow Wall-Paper." Gilman's decision to reject his prescription of enforced idleness, followed by her relocation to California and divorce, was essential to her spiritual survival and refashioning of herself as an artist and independent woman.

Though the psychology of "The Yellow Wall-Paper" is justly celebrated, Agnieszka Soltysik Monnet has demonstrated that its ambiguities also allow a ghostly, supernatural reading of the events in the strange bedroom.

Texts: "The Giant Wisteria," *The New England Magazine,* 10 (June 1891), 480–6; "The Yellow Wall-Paper," *The New England Magazine,* 11 (Jan. 1892), 647–57. At this time Gilman was still publishing under her married name, Charlotte Perkins Stetson.

The Giant Wisteria

"Meddle not with my new vine, child! See! Thou hast already broken the tender shoot! Never needle or distaff for thee, and yet thou wilt not be quiet!"

The nervous fingers wavered, clutched at a small carnelian[1] cross that hung from her neck, then fell despairingly.

"Give me my child, mother, and then I will be quiet!"

"Hush! hush! thou fool – some one might be near! See – there is thy father coming, even now! Get in quickly!"

Notes

THE GIANT WISTERIA

[1] A red semi-precious stone with significance in Christian mysticism. See Revelation 21:20.

She raised her eyes to her mother's face, weary eyes that yet had a flickering, uncertain blaze in their shaded depths.

"Art thou a mother and hast no pity on me, a mother? Give me my child!"

Her voice rose in a strange, low cry, broken by her father's hand upon her mouth.

"Shameless!" said he, with set teeth. "Get to thy chamber, and be not seen again to-night, or I will have thee bound!"

She went at that, and a hard-faced serving woman followed, and presently returned, bringing a key to her mistress.

"Is all well with her, – and the child also?"

"She is quiet, Mistress Dwining, well for the night, be sure. The child fretteth endlessly, but save for that it thriveth with me."

The parents were left alone together on the high square porch with its great pillars, and the rising moon began to make faint shadows of the young vine leaves that shot up luxuriantly around them: moving shadows, like little stretching fingers, on the broad and heavy planks of the oaken floor.

"It groweth well, this vine thou broughtest me in the ship, my husband."

"Aye," he broke in bitterly, "and so doth the shame I brought thee! Had I known of it I would sooner have had the ship founder beneath us, and have seen our child cleanly drowned, than live to this end!"

"Thou art very hard, Samuel, art thou not afeard for her life? She grieveth sore for the child, aye, and for the green fields to walk in!"

"Nay," said he grimly, "I fear not. She hath lost already what is more than life; and she shall have air enough soon. To-morrow the ship is ready, and we return to England. None knoweth of our stain here, not one, and if the town hath a child unaccounted for to rear in decent ways – why, it is not the first, even here. It will be well enough cared for! And truly we have matter for thankfulness, that her cousin is yet willing to marry her."

"Hast thou told him?"

"Aye! Thinkest thou I would cast shame into another man's house, unknowing it? He hath always desired her, but she would none of him, the stubborn! She hath small choice now!"

"Will he be kind, Samuel? can he – "

"Kind? What call'st thou it to take such as she to wife? Kind! How many men would take her, an' she had double the fortune? and being of the family already, he is glad to hide the blot forever."

"An' if she would not? He is but a coarse fellow, and she ever shunned him."

"Art thou mad, woman? She weddeth him ere we sail to-morrow, or she stayeth ever in that chamber. The girl is not so sheer a fool! He maketh an honest woman of her, and saveth our house from open shame. What other hope for her than a new life to cover the old? Let her have an honest child, an' she so longeth for one!"

He strode heavily across the porch, till the loose planks creaked again, strode back and forth, with his arms folded and his brows fiercely knit above his iron mouth.

Overhead the shadows flickered mockingly across a white face among the leaves, with eyes of wasted fire.

*   *   *   *   *

"O, George, what a house! what a lovely house! I am sure it's haunted! Let us get that house to live in this summer! We will have Kate and Jack and Susy and Jim of course, and a splendid time of it!"

Young husbands are indulgent, but still they have to recognize facts.

"My dear, the house may not be to rent; and it may also not be habitable."

"There is surely somebody in it. I am going to inquire!"

The great central gate was rusted off its hinges, and the long drive had trees in it, but a little footpath showed signs of steady usage, and up that Mrs. Jenny went, followed by her obedient George. The front windows of the old mansion were blank, but in a wing at the back they found white curtains and open doors. Outside, in the clear May sunshine, a woman was washing. She was polite and friendly, and evidently glad of visitors in that lonely place. She "guessed it could be rented – didn't know." The heirs were in Europe, but "there was a lawyer in New York had the lettin' of it." There had been folks there years ago, but not in her time. She and her husband had the rent of their part "for taking care of the place." "Not that they took much care on't either, but keepin' robbers out." It was furnished throughout, oldfashioned enough, but good; and "if they took it she could do the work for 'em herself, she guessed – if *he* was willin'!"

Never was a crazy scheme more easily arranged. George knew that lawyer in New York; the rent was not alarming; and the nearness to a rising seashore resort made it a still pleasanter place to spend the summer.

Kate and Jack and Susy and Jim cheerfully accepted, and the June moon found them all sitting on the high front porch.

They had explored the house from top to bottom, from the great room in the garret, with nothing in it but a rickety cradle, to the well in the cellar without a curb and with a rusty chain going down to unknown blankness below. They had explored the grounds, once beautiful with rare trees and shrubs, but now a gloomy wilderness of tangled shade.

The old lilacs and laburnums, the spirea and syringa, nodded against the second-story windows. What garden plants survived were great ragged bushes or great shapeless beds. A huge wisteria vine covered the whole front of the house. The trunk, it was too large to call a stem, rose at the corner of the porch by the high steps, and had once climbed its pillars; but now the pillars were wrenched from their places and held rigid and helpless by the tightly wound and knotted arms.

It fenced in all the upper story of the porch with a knitted wall of stem and leaf; it ran along the eaves, holding up the gutter that had once supported it; it shaded every window with heavy green; and the drooping, fragrant blossoms made a waving sheet of purple from roof to ground.

"Did you ever see such a wisteria!" cried ecstatic Mrs. Jenny. "It is worth the rent just to sit under such a vine, – a fig tree beside it would be sheer superfluity and wicked extravagance!"

"Jenny makes much of her wisteria," said George, "because she's so disappointed about the ghosts. She made up her mind at first sight to have ghosts in the house, and she can't find even one ghost story!"

"No," Jenny assented mournfully; "I pumped poor Mrs. Pepperill for three days, but could get nothing out of her. But I'm convinced there is a story, if we could only find it. You need not tell me that a house like this, with a garden like this, and a cellar like this, isn't haunted!"

"I agree with you," said Jack. Jack was a reporter on a New York daily, and engaged to Mrs. Jenny's pretty sister. "And if we don't find a real ghost, you may be very sure I shall make one. It's too good an opportunity to lose!"

The pretty sister, who sat next him, resented. "You shan't do anything of the sort, Jack! This is a *real* ghostly place, and I won't have you make fun of it! Look at that group of trees out there in the long grass – it looks for all the world like a crouching, hunted figure!"

"It looks to me like a woman picking huckleberries," said Jim, who was married to George's pretty sister.

"Be still, Jim!" said that fair young woman. "I believe in Jenny's ghost, as much as she does. Such a place! Just look at this great wisteria trunk crawling up by the steps here! It looks for all the world like a writhing body – cringing – beseeching!"

"Yes," answered the subdued Jim, "it does, Susy. See its waist, – about two yards of it, and twisted at that! A waste of good material!"

"Don't be so horrid, boys! Go off and smoke somewhere if you can't be congenial!"

"We can! We will! We'll be as ghostly as you please." And forthwith they began to see bloodstains and crouching figures so plentifully that the most delightful shivers multiplied, and the fair enthusiasts started for bed, declaring they should never sleep a wink.

"We shall all surely dream," cried Mrs. Jenny, "and we must all tell our dreams in the morning!"

"There's another thing certain," said George, catching Susy as she tripped over a loose plank; "and that is that you frisky creatures must use the side door till I get this Eiffel tower of a portico fixed, or we shall have some fresh ghosts on our hands! We found a plank here that yawns like a trap-door – big enough to swallow you, – and I believe the bottom of the thing is in China!"

The next morning found them all alive, and eating a substantial New England breakfast, to the accompaniment of saws and hammers on the porch, where carpenters of quite miraculous promptness were tearing things to pieces generally.

"It's got to come down mostly," they had said. "These timbers are clean rotted through, what ain't pulled out o' line by this great creeper. That's about all that holds the thing up."

There was clear reason in what they said, and with a caution from anxious Mrs. Jenny not to hurt the wisteria, they were left to demolish and repair at leisure.

"How about ghosts?" asked Jack after a fourth griddle cake. "I had one, and it's taken away my appetite!"

Mrs. Jenny gave a little shriek and dropped her knife and fork.

"Oh, so had I! I had the most awful – well, not dream exactly, but feeling. I had forgotten all about it!"

"Must have been awful," said Jack, taking another cake. "Do tell us about the feeling. My ghost will wait."

"It makes me creep to think of it even now," she said. "I woke up, all at once, with that dreadful feeling as if something were going to happen, you know! I was wide awake, and hearing every little sound for miles around, it seemed to me. There are so many strange little noises in the country for all it is so still. Millions of crickets and things outside, and all kinds of rustles in the trees! There wasn't much wind, and the moonlight came through in my three great windows in three white squares on the black old floor, and those fingery wisteria leaves we were talking of last night just seemed to crawl all over them. And – O, girls, you know that dreadful well in the cellar?"

A most gratifying impression was made by this, and Jenny proceeded cheerfully:

"Well, while it was so horridly still, and I lay there trying not to wake George, I heard as plainly as if it were right in the room, that old chain down there rattle and creak over the stones!"

"Bravo!" cried Jack. "That's fine! I'll put it in the Sunday edition!"

"Be still!" said Kate. "What was it, Jenny? Did you really see anything?"

"No, I didn't, I'm sorry to say. But just then I didn't want to. I woke George, and made such a fuss that he gave me bromide, and said he'd go and look, and that's the last I thought of it till Jack reminded me, – the bromide worked so well."

"Now, Jack, give us yours," said Jim. "Maybe, it will dovetail in somehow. Thirsty ghost, I imagine; maybe they had prohibition here even then!"

Jack folded his napkin, and leaned back in his most impressive manner.

"It was striking twelve by the great hall clock – " he began.

"There isn't any hall clock!"

"O hush, Jim, you spoil the current! It was just one o'clock then, by my old-fashioned repeater."[2]

"Waterbury! Never mind what time it was!"

"Well, honestly, I woke up sharp, like our beloved hostess, and tried to go to sleep again, but couldn't. I experienced all those moonlight and grasshopper sensations, just like Jenny, and was wondering what could have been the matter with the supper, when in came my ghost, and I knew it was all a dream! It was a female ghost, and I imagine she was young and handsome, but all those crouching, hunted figures of last evening ran riot in my brain, and this poor creature looked just like them. She was all wrapped up in a shawl, and had a big bundle under her arm, – dear me, I am spoiling the story! With the air and gait of one in frantic haste and terror, the muffled figure glided to a dark old bureau, and seemed taking things from the drawers. As she turned, the moonlight shone full on a little red cross that hung from her neck by a thin gold chain – I saw it glitter as she crept noiselessly from the room! That's all."

"O Jack, don't be so horrid! Did you really? Is that all! What do you think it was?"

"I am not horrid by nature, only professionally. I really did. That was all. And I am fully convinced it was the genuine, legitimate ghost of an eloping chambermaid with kleptomania!"

"You are too bad, Jack!" cried Jenny. "You take all the horror out of it. There isn't a 'creep' left among us."

"It's no time for creeps at nine-thirty A.M., with sunlight and carpenters outside! However, if you can't wait till twilight for your creeps, I think I can furnish one or two," said George. "I went down cellar after Jenny's ghost!"

There was a delighted chorus of female voices, and Jenny cast upon her lord a glance of genuine gratitude.

"It's all very well to lie in bed and see ghosts, or hear them," he went on. "But the young householder suspecteth burglars, even though as a medical man he knoweth nerves, and after Jenny dropped off I started on a voyage of discovery. I never will again, I promise you!"

"Why, what *was* it?"

"Oh, George!"

"I got a candle – "

"Good mark for the burglars," murmured Jack.

"And went all over the house, gradually working down to the cellar and the well."

"Well?" said Jack.

"Now you can laugh; but that cellar is no joke by daylight, and a candle there at night is about as inspiring as a lightning-bug in the Mammoth Cave. I went along with the light, trying not to fall into the well prematurely; got to it all at once; held the light down and *then* I saw, right under my feet – (I nearly fell over her, or walked through her, perhaps), – a woman, hunched up under a shawl! She had hold of the chain, and the candle shone on her hands – white, thin hands, – on a little red cross that hung from her neck – *vide*[3] Jack! I'm no believer in ghosts, and I firmly object to unknown

[2] A type of clock or watch. "Waterbury" is a brand of time piece.

[3] Latin, "see," used here in the sense of "refer to." George reminds his listeners that Jack saw the same cross.

parties in the house at night; so I spoke to her rather fiercely. She didn't seem to notice that, and I reached down to take hold of her, – then I came upstairs!"

"What for?"

"What happened?"

"What was the matter?"

"Well, nothing happened. Only she wasn't there! May have been indigestion, of course, but as a physician, I don't advise any one to court indigestion alone at midnight in a cellar!"

"This is the most interesting and peripatetic and evasive ghost I ever heard of!" said Jack. "It's my belief she has no end of silver tankards, and jewels galore, at the bottom of that well, and I move we go and see!"

"To the bottom of the well, Jack?"

"To the bottom of the mystery. Come on!"

There was unanimous assent, and the fresh cambrics and pretty boots were gallantly escorted below by gentlemen whose jokes were so frequent that many of them were a little forced.

The deep old cellar was so dark that they had to bring lights, and the well so gloomy in its blackness that the ladies recoiled.

"That well is enough to scare even a ghost. It's my opinion you'd better let well enough alone?" quoth Jim.

"Truth lies hid in a well, and we must get her out," said George. "Bear a hand with the chain?"

Jim pulled away on the chain, George turned the creaking windlass, and Jack was chorus.

"A wet sheet for this ghost, if not a flowing sea," said he. "Seems to be hard work raising spirits! I suppose he kicked the bucket when he went down!"

As the chain lightened and shortened, there grew a strained silence among them; and when at length the bucket appeared, rising slowly through the dark water, there was an eager, half reluctant peering, and a natural drawing back. They poked the gloomy contents. "Only water."

"Nothing but mud."

"Something – "

They emptied the bucket up on the dark earth, and then the girls all went out into the air, into the bright warm sunshine in front of the house, where was the sound of saw and hammer, and the smell of new wood. There was nothing said until the men joined them, and then Jenny timidly asked:

"How old should you think it was, George?"

"All of a century," he answered. "That water is a preservative, – lime in it. Oh! – you mean? – Not more than a month; a very little baby!"

There was another silence at this, broken by a cry from the workmen. They had removed the floor and the side walls of the old porch, so that that sunshine poured down to the dark stones of the cellar bottom. And there, in the strangling grasp of the roots of the great wisteria, lay the bones of a woman, from whose neck still hung a tiny scarlet cross on a thin chain of gold.

The Yellow Wall-Paper

It is very seldom that mere ordinary people like John and myself secure ancestral halls for the summer.

A colonial mansion, a hereditary estate, I would say a haunted house, and reach the height of romantic felicity – but that would be asking too much of fate!

Still I will proudly declare that there is something queer about it.

Else, why should it be let so cheaply? And why have stood so long untenanted?

John laughs at me, of course, but one expects that in marriage. John is practical in the extreme. He has no patience with faith, an intense horror of superstition, and he scoffs openly at any talk of things not to be felt and seen and put down in figures.

John is a physician, and *perhaps* – (I would not say it to a living soul, of course, but this is dead paper and a great relief to my mind) – *perhaps* that is one reason I do not get well faster.

You see he does not believe I am sick! And what can one do?

If a physician of high standing, and one's own husband, assures friends and relatives that there is really nothing the matter with one but temporary nervous depression – a slight hysterical tendency – what is one to do?

My brother is also a physician, and also of high standing, and he says the same thing.

So I take phosphates or phosphites – whichever it is, and tonics, and journeys, and air, and exercise, and am absolutely forbidden to "work" until I am well again.

Personally, I disagree with their ideas.

Personally, I believe that congenial work, with excitement and change, would do me good.

But what is one to do?

I did write for a while in spite of them; but it *does* exhaust me a good deal – having to be so sly about it, or else meet with heavy opposition.

I sometimes fancy that in my condition if I had less opposition and more society and stimulus – but John says the very worst thing I can do is to think about my condition, and I confess it always makes me feel bad.

So I will let it alone and talk about the house.

The most beautiful place! It is quite alone, standing well back from the road, quite three miles from the village. It makes me think of English places that you read about, for there are hedges and walls and gates that lock, and lots of separate little houses for the gardeners and people.

There is a *delicious* garden! I never saw such a garden – large and shady, full of box-bordered paths, and lined with long grape-covered arbors with seats under them.

There were greenhouses, too, but they are all broken now.

There was some legal trouble, I believe, something about the heirs and coheirs; anyhow, the place has been empty for years.

That spoils my ghostliness, I am afraid, but I don't care – there is something strange about the house – I can feel it.

I even said so to John one moonlight evening, but he said what I felt was a *draught*, and shut the window.

I get unreasonably angry with John sometimes. I'm sure I never used to be so sensitive. I think it is due to this nervous condition.

But John says if I feel so, I shall neglect proper self-control; so I take pains to control myself – before him, at least, and that makes me very tired.

I don't like our room a bit. I wanted one downstairs that opened on the piazza and had roses all over the window, and such pretty old-fashioned chintz hangings! but John would not hear of it.

He said there was only one window and not room for two beds, and no near room for him if he took another.

He is very careful and loving, and hardly lets me stir without special direction.

I have a schedule prescription for each hour in the day; he takes all care from me, and so I feel basely ungrateful not to value it more.

He said we came here solely on my account, that I was to have perfect rest and all the air I could get. "Your exercise depends on your strength, my dear," said he, "and your food somewhat on your appetite; but air you can absorb all the time." So we took the nursery at the top of the house.

It is a big, airy room, the whole floor nearly, with windows that look all ways, and air and sunshine galore. It was nursery first and then playroom and gymnasium, I should judge; for the windows are barred for little children, and there are rings and things in the walls.

The paint and paper look as if a boys' school had used it. It is stripped off – the paper – in great patches all around the head of my bed, about as far as I can reach, and in a great place on the other side of the room low down. I never saw a worse paper in my life.

One of those sprawling flamboyant patterns committing every artistic sin.

It is dull enough to confuse the eye in following, pronounced enough to constantly irritate and provoke study, and when you follow the lame uncertain curves for a little distance they suddenly commit suicide – plunge off at outrageous angles, destroy themselves in unheard of contradictions.

The color is repellent, almost revolting; a smouldering unclean yellow, strangely faded by the slow-turning sunlight.

It is a dull yet lurid orange in some places, a sickly sulphur tint in others.

No wonder the children hated it! I should hate it myself if I had to live in this room long.

There comes John, and I must put this away, – he hates to have me write a word.

*   *   *   *   *

We have been here two weeks, and I haven't felt like writing before, since that first day.

I am sitting by the window now, up in this atrocious nursery, and there is nothing to hinder my writing as much as I please, save lack of strength.

John is away all day, and even some nights when his cases are serious.

I am glad my case is not serious!

But these nervous troubles are dreadfully depressing.

John does not know how much I really suffer. He knows there is no *reason* to suffer, and that satisfies him.

Of course it is only nervousness. It does weigh on me so not to do my duty in any way!

I meant to be such a help to John, such a real rest and comfort, and here I am a comparative burden already!

Nobody would believe what an effort it is to do what little I am able, – to dress and entertain, and order things.

It is fortunate Mary is so good with the baby. Such a dear baby!

And yet I *cannot* be with him, it makes me so nervous.

I suppose John never was nervous in his life. He laughs at me so about this wall-paper!

At first he meant to repaper the room, but afterwards he said that I was letting it get the better of me, and that nothing was worse for a nervous patient than to give way to such fancies.

He said that after the wall-paper was changed it would be the heavy bedstead, and then the barred windows, and then that gate at the head of the stairs, and so on.

"You know the place is doing you good," he said, "and really, dear, I don't care to renovate the house just for a three months' rental."

"Then do let us go downstairs," I said, "there are such pretty rooms there."

Then he took me in his arms and called me a blessed little goose, and said he would go down to the cellar, if I wished, and have it whitewashed into the bargain.

But he is right enough about the beds and windows and things.

It is an airy and comfortable room as any one need wish, and, of course, I would not be so silly as to make him uncomfortable just for a whim.

I'm really getting quite fond of the big room, all but that horrid paper.

Out of one window I can see the garden, those mysterious deep-shaded arbors, the riotous old-fashioned flowers, and bushes and gnarly trees.

Out of another I get a lovely view of the bay and a little private wharf belonging to the estate. There is a beautiful shaded lane that runs down there from the house. I always fancy I see people walking in these numerous paths and arbors, but John has cautioned me not to give way to fancy in the least. He says that with my imaginative power and habit of story-making, a nervous weakness like mine is sure to lead to all manner of excited fancies, and that I ought to use my will and good sense to check the tendency. So I try.

I think sometimes that if I were only well enough to write a little it would relieve the press of ideas and rest me.

But I find I get pretty tired when I try.

It is so discouraging not to have any advice and companionship about my work. When I get really well, John says we will ask Cousin Henry and Julia down for a long visit; but he says he would as soon put fireworks in my pillow-case as to let me have those stimulating people about now.

I wish I could get well faster.

But I must not think about that. This paper looks to me as if it *knew* what a vicious influence it had!

There is a recurrent spot where the pattern lolls like a broken neck and two bulbous eyes stare at you upside down.

I get positively angry with the impertinence of it and the everlastingness. Up and down and sideways they crawl, and those absurd, unblinking eyes are everywhere. There is one place where two breadths didn't match, and the eyes go all up and down the line, one a little higher than the other.

I never saw so much expression in an inanimate thing before, and we all know how much expression they have! I used to lie awake as a child and get more entertainment and terror out of blank walls and plain furniture than most children could find in a toy store.

I remember what a kindly wink the knobs of our big, old bureau used to have, and there was one chair that always seemed like a strong friend.

I used to feel that if any of the other things looked too fierce I could always hop into that chair and be safe.

The furniture in this room is no worse than inharmonious, however, for we had to bring it all from downstairs. I suppose when this was used as a playroom they had to take the nursery things out, and no wonder! I never saw such ravages as the children have made here.

The wall-paper, as I said before, is torn off in spots, and it sticketh closer than a brother – they must have had perseverance as well as hatred.

Then the floor is scratched and gouged and splintered, the plaster itself is dug out here and there, and this great heavy bed which is all we found in the room, looks as if it had been through the wars.

But I don't mind it a bit – only the paper.

There comes John's sister. Such a dear girl as she is, and so careful of me! I must not let her find me writing.

She is a perfect and enthusiastic housekeeper, and hopes for no better profession. I verily believe she thinks it is the writing which made me sick!

But I can write when she is out, and see her a long way off from these windows.

There is one that commands the road, a lovely shaded winding road, and one that just looks off over the country. A lovely country, too, full of great elms and velvet meadows.

This wall-paper has a kind of sub-pattern in a different shade, a particularly irritating one, for you can only see it in certain lights, and not clearly then.

But in the places where it isn't faded and where the sun is just so – I can see a strange, provoking, formless sort of figure, that seems to skulk about behind that silly and conspicuous front design.

There's sister on the stairs!

*   *   *   *   *

Well, the Fourth of July is over! The people are gone and I am tired out. John thought it might do me good to see a little company, so we just had mother and Nellie and the children down for a week.

Of course I didn't do a thing. Jennie sees to everything now.

But it tired me all the same.

John says if I don't pick up faster he shall send me to Weir Mitchell in the fall.

But I don't want to go there at all. I had a friend who was in his hands once, and she says he is just like John and my brother, only more so!

Besides, it is such an undertaking to go so far.

I don't feel as if it was worth while to turn my hand over for anything, and I'm getting dreadfully fretful and querulous.

I cry at nothing, and cry most of the time.

Of course I don't when John is here, or anybody else, but when I am alone.

And I am alone a good deal just now. John is kept in town very often by serious cases, and Jennie is good and lets me alone when I want her to.

So I walk a little in the garden or down that lovely lane, sit on the porch under the roses, and lie down up here a good deal.

I'm getting really fond of the room in spite of the wall-paper. Perhaps *because* of the wall-paper.

It dwells in my mind so!

I lie here on this great immovable bed – it is nailed down, I believe – and follow that pattern about by the hour. It is as good as gymnastics, I assure you. I start, we'll say, at the bottom, down in the corner over there where it has not been touched, and I determine for the thousandth time that I *will* follow that pointless pattern to some sort of a conclusion.

I know a little of the principle of design, and I know this thing was not arranged on any laws of radiation, or alternation, or repetition, or symmetry, or anything else that I ever heard of.

It is repeated, of course, by the breadths, but not otherwise.

Looked at in one way each breadth stands alone, the bloated curves and flourishes – a kind of "debased Romanesque" with delirium tremens – go waddling up and down in isolated columns of fatuity.

But, on the other hand, they connect diagonally, and the sprawling outlines run off in great slanting waves of optic horror, like a lot of wallowing seaweeds in full chase.

The whole thing goes horizontally, too, at least it seems so, and I exhaust myself in trying to distinguish the order of its going in that direction.

They have used a horizontal breadth for a frieze, and that adds wonderfully to the confusion.

There is one end of the room where it is almost intact, and there, when the crosslights fade and the low sun shines directly upon it, I can almost fancy radiation after all, – the interminable grotesques seem to form around a common centre and rush off in headlong plunges of equal distraction.

It makes me tired to follow it. I will take a nap I guess.

* * * * *

I don't know why I should write this.

I don't want to.

I don't feel able.

And I know John would think it absurd. But I *must* say what I feel and think in some way – it is such a relief!

But the effort is getting to be greater than the relief.

Half the time now I am awfully lazy, and lie down ever so much.

John says I mustn't lose my strength, and has me take cod liver oil and lots of tonics and things, to say nothing of ale and wine and rare meat.

Dear John! He loves me very dearly, and hates to have me sick. I tried to have a real earnest reasonable talk with him the other day, and tell him how I wish he would let me go and make a visit to Cousin Henry and Julia.

But he said I wasn't able to go, nor able to stand it after I got there; and I did not make out a very good case for myself, for I was crying before I had finished.

It is getting to be a great effort for me to think straight. Just this nervous weakness I suppose.

And dear John gathered me up in his arms, and just carried me upstairs and laid me on the bed, and sat by me and read to me till it tired my head.

He said I was his darling and his comfort and all he had, and that I must take care of myself for his sake, and keep well.

He says no one but myself can help me out of it, that I must use my will and self-control and not let any silly fancies run away with me.

There's one comfort, the baby is well and happy, and does not have to occupy this nursery with the horrid wall-paper.

If we had not used it, that blessed child would have! What a fortunate escape! Why, I wouldn't have a child of mine, an impressionable little thing, live in such a room for worlds.

I never thought of it before, but it is lucky that John kept me here after all, I can stand it so much easier than a baby, you see.

Of course I never mention it to them any more – I am too wise, – but I keep watch of it all the same.

There are things in that paper that nobody knows but me, or ever will.

Behind that outside pattern the dim shapes get clearer every day.

It is always the same shape, only very numerous.

And it is like a woman stooping down and creeping about behind that pattern. I don't like it a bit. I wonder – I begin to think – I wish John would take me away from here!

* * * * *

It is so hard to talk with John about my case, because he is so wise, and because he loves me so.

But I tried it last night.

It was moonlight. The moon shines in all around just as the sun does.

I hate to see it sometimes, it creeps so slowly, and always comes in by one window or another.

John was asleep and I hated to waken him, so I kept still and watched the moonlight on that undulating wall-paper till I felt creepy.

The faint figure behind seemed to shake the pattern, just as if she wanted to get out.

I got up softly and went to feel and see if the paper *did* move, and when I came back John was awake.

"What is it, little girl?" he said. "Don't go walking about like that – you'll get cold."

I though it was a good time to talk, so I told him that I really was not gaining here, and that I wished he would take me away.

"Why darling!" said he, "our lease will be up in three weeks, and I can't see how to leave before.

"The repairs are not done at home, and I cannot possibly leave town just now. Of course if you were in any danger, I could and would, but you really are better, dear, whether you can see it or not. I am a doctor, dear, and I know. You are gaining flesh and color, your appetite is better, I feel really much easier about you."

"I don't weigh a bit more," said I, "nor as much; and my appetite may be better in the evening when you are here, but it is worse in the morning when you are away!"

"Bless her little heart!" said he with a big hug, "she shall be as sick as she pleases! But now let's improve the shining hours by going to sleep, and talk about it in the morning!"

"And you won't go away?" I asked gloomily.

"Why, how can I, dear? It is only three weeks more and then we will take a nice little trip of a few days while Jennie is getting the house ready. Really dear you are better!"

"Better in body perhaps – " I began, and stopped short, for he sat up straight and looked at me with such a stern, reproachful look that I could not say another word.

"My darling," said he, "I beg of you, for my sake and for our child's sake, as well as for your own, that you will never for one instant let that idea enter your mind! There is nothing so dangerous, so fascinating, to a temperament like yours. It is a false and foolish fancy. Can you not trust me as a physician when I tell you so?"

So of course I said no more on that score, and we went to sleep before long. He thought I was asleep first, but I wasn't, and lay there for hours trying to decide whether that front pattern and the back pattern really did move together or separately.

*   *   *   *   *

On a pattern like this, by daylight, there is a lack of sequence, a defiance of law, that is a constant irritant to a normal mind.

The color is hideous enough, and unreliable enough, and infuriating enough, but the pattern is torturing.

You think you have mastered it, but just as you get well underway in following, it turns a back-somersault and there you are. It slaps you in the face, knocks you down, and tramples upon you. It is like a bad dream.

The outside pattern is a florid arabesque, reminding one of a fungus. If you can imagine a toadstool in joints, an interminable string of toadstools, budding and sprouting in endless convolutions – why, that is something like it.

That is, sometimes!

There is one marked peculiarity about this paper, a thing nobody seems to notice but myself, and that is that it changes as the light changes.

When the sun shoots in through the east window – I always watch for that first long, straight ray – it changes so quickly that I never can quite believe it.

That is why I watch it always.

By moonlight – the moon shines in all night when there is a moon – I wouldn't know it was the same paper.

At night in any kind of light, in twilight, candle light, lamplight, and worst of all by moonlight, it becomes bars! The outside pattern I mean, and the woman behind it is as plain as can be.

I didn't realize for a long time what the thing was that showed behind, that dim sub-pattern, but now I am quite sure it is a woman.

By daylight she is subdued, quiet. I fancy it is the pattern that keeps her so still. It is so puzzling. It keeps me quiet by the hour.

I lie down ever so much now. John says it is good for me, and to sleep all I can.

Indeed he started the habit by making me lie down for an hour after each meal.

It is a very bad habit I am convinced, for you see I don't sleep.

And that cultivates deceit, for I don't tell them I'm awake – O no!

The fact is I am getting a little afraid of John.

He seems very queer sometimes, and even Jennie has an inexplicable look.

It strikes me occasionally, just as a scientific hypothesis, – that perhaps it is the paper!

I have watched John when he did not know I was looking, and come into the room suddenly on the most innocent excuses, and I've caught him several times *looking at the paper!* And Jennie too. I caught Jennie with her hand on it once.

She didn't know I was in the room, and when I asked her in a quiet, a very quiet voice, with the most restrained manner possible, what she was doing with the paper – she turned around as if she had been caught stealing, and looked quite angry – asked me why I should frighten her so!

Then she said that the paper stained everything it touched, that she had found yellow smooches on all my clothes and John's, and she wished we would be more careful!

Did not that sound innocent? But I know she was studying that pattern, and I am determined that nobody shall find it out but myself!

*   *   *   *   *

Life is very much more exciting now than it used to be. You see I have something more to expect, to look forward to, to watch. I really do eat better, and am more quiet than I was.

John is so pleased to see me improve! He laughed a little the other day, and said I seemed to be flourishing in spite of my wall-paper.

I turned it off with a laugh. I had no intention of telling him it was *because* of the wall-paper – he would make fun of me. He might even want to take me away.

I don't want to leave now until I have found it out. There is a week more, and I think that will be enough.

*   *   *   *   *

I'm feeling ever so much better! I don't sleep much at night, for it is so interesting to watch developments; but I sleep a good deal in the daytime.

In the daytime it is tiresome and perplexing.

There are always new shoots on the fungus, and new shades of yellow all over it. I cannot keep count of them, though I have tried conscientiously.

It is the strangest yellow, that wall-paper! It makes me think of all the yellow things I ever saw – not beautiful ones like buttercups, but old foul, bad yellow things.

But there is something else about that paper – the smell! I noticed it the moment we came into the room, but with so much air and sun it was not bad. Now we have had a week of fog and rain, and whether the windows are open or not, the smell is here.

It creeps all over the house.

I find it hovering in the dining-room, skulking in the parlor, hiding in the hall, lying in wait for me on the stairs.

It gets into my hair.

Even when I go to ride, if I turn my head suddenly and surprise it – there is that smell!

Such a peculiar odor, too! I have spent hours in trying to analyze it, to find what it smelled like.

It is not bad – at first, and very gentle, but quite the subtlest, most enduring odor I ever met.

In this damp weather it is awful, I wake up in the night and find it hanging over me.

It used to disturb me at first. I thought seriously of burning the house – to reach the smell.

But now I am used to it. The only thing I can think of that it is like is the *color* of the paper! A yellow smell.

There is a very funny mark on this wall, low down, near the mopboard. A streak that runs round the room. It goes behind every piece of furniture, except the bed, a long, straight, even *smooch*, as if it had been rubbed over and over.

I wonder how it was done and who did it, and what they did it for. Round and round and round – round and round and round – it makes me dizzy!

*   *   *   *   *

I really have discovered something at last.

Through watching so much at night, when it changes so, I have finally found out.

The front pattern *does* move – and no wonder! The woman behind shakes it!

Sometimes I think there are a great many women behind, and sometimes only one, and she crawls around fast, and her crawling shakes it all over.

Then in the very bright spots she keeps still, and in the very shady spots she just takes hold of the bars and shakes them hard.

And she is all the time trying to climb through. But nobody could climb through that pattern – it strangles so; I think that is why it has so many heads.

They get through, and then the pattern strangles them off and turns them upside down, and makes their eyes white!

If those heads were covered or taken off it would not be half so bad.

*   *   *   *   *

I think that woman gets out in the daytime!

And I'll tell you why – privately – I've seen her!

I can see her out of every one of my windows!

It is the same woman, I know, for she is always creeping, and most women do not creep by daylight.

I see her on that long road under the trees, creeping along, and when a carriage comes she hides under the blackberry vines.

I don't blame her a bit. It must be very humiliating to be caught creeping by daylight!

I always lock the door when I creep by daylight. I can't do it at night, for I know John would suspect something at once.

And John is so queer now, that I don't want to irritate him. I wish he would take another room! Besides, I don't want anybody to get that woman out at night but myself.

I often wonder if I could see her out of all the windows at once.

But, turn as fast as I can, I can only see out of one at one time.

And though I always see her, she *may* be able to creep faster than I can turn!

I have watched her sometimes away off in the open country, creeping as fast as a cloud shadow in a high wind.

*   *   *   *   *

If only that top pattern could be gotten off from the under one! I mean to try it, little by little.

I have found out another funny thing, but I shan't tell it this time! It does not do to trust people too much.

There are only two more days to get this paper off, and I believe John is beginning to notice. I don't like the look in his eyes.

And I heard him ask Jennie a lot of professional questions about me. She had a very good report to give.

She said I slept a good deal in the daytime.

John knows I don't sleep very well at night, for all I'm so quiet!

He asked me all sorts of questions, too, and pretended to be very loving and kind.

As if I couldn't see through him!

Still, I don't wonder he acts so, sleeping under this paper for three months.

It only interests me, but I feel sure John and Jennie are secretly affected by it.

*   *   *   *   *

Hurrah! This is the last day, but it is enough. John is to stay in town over night, and won't be out until this evening.

Jennie wanted to sleep with me – the sly thing! but I told her I should undoubtedly rest better for a night all alone.

That was clever, for really I wasn't alone a bit! As soon as it was moonlight and that poor thing began to crawl and shake the pattern, I got up and ran to help her.

I pulled and she shook, I shook and she pulled, and before morning we had peeled off yards of that paper.

A strip about as high as my head and half around the room.

And then when the sun came and that awful pattern began to laugh at me, I declared I would finish it to-day!

We go away to-morrow, and they are moving all my furniture down again to leave things as they were before.

Jennie looked at the wall in amazement, but I told her merrily that I did it out of pure spite at the vicious thing.

She laughed and said she wouldn't mind doing it herself, but I must not get tired.

How she betrayed herself that time!

But I am here, and no person touches this paper but me – not *alive!*

She tried to get me out of the room – it was too patent! But I said it was so quiet and empty and clean now that I believed I would lie down again and sleep all I could; and not to wake me even for dinner – I would call when I woke.

So now she is gone, and the servants are gone, and the things are gone, and there is nothing left but that great bedstead nailed down, with the canvas mattress we found on it.

We shall sleep downstairs to-night, and take the boat home to-morrow.

I quite enjoy the room, now it is bare again.

How those children did tear about here!

This bedstead is fairly gnawed!

But I must get to work.

I have locked the door and thrown the key down into the front path.

I don't want to go out, and I don't want to have anybody come in, till John comes.

I want to astonish him.

I've got a rope up here that even Jennie did not find. If that woman does get out, and tries to get away, I can tie her!

But I forgot I could not reach far without anything to stand on!

This bed will *not* move!

I tried to lift and push it until I was lame, and then I got so angry I bit off a little piece at one corner – but it hurt my teeth.

Then I peeled off all the paper I could reach standing on the floor. It sticks horribly and the pattern just enjoys it! All those strangled heads and bulbous eyes and waddling fungus growths just shriek with derision!

I am getting angry enough to do something desperate. To jump out of the window would be admirable exercise, but the bars are too strong even to try.

Besides I wouldn't do it. Of course not. I know well enough that a step like that is improper and might be misconstrued.

I don't like to *look* out of the windows even – there are so many of those creeping women, and they creep so fast.

I wonder if they all come out of that wall-paper as I did?

But I am securely fastened now by my well-hidden rope – you don't get ME out in the road there!

I suppose I shall have to get back behind the pattern when it comes night, and that is hard!

It is so pleasant to be out in this great room and creep around as I please!

I don't want to go outside. I won't, even if Jennie asks me to.

For outside you have to creep on the ground, and everything is green instead of yellow.

But here I can creep smoothly on the floor, and my shoulder just fits in that long smooch around the wall, so I cannot lose my way.

Why there's John at the door!

It is no use, young man, you can't open it!

How he does call and pound!

Now he's crying for an axe.

It would be a shame to break down that beautiful door!

"John dear!" said I in the gentlest voice, "the key is down by the front steps, under a plantain leaf!"

That silenced him for a few moments.

Then he said – very quietly indeed, "Open the door, my darling!"

"I can't," said I. "The key is down by the front door under a plantain leaf!"

And then I said it again, several times, very gently and slowly, and said it so often that he had to go and see, and he got it of course, and came in. He stopped short by the door.

"What is the matter?" he cried. "For God's sake, what are you doing!"

I kept on creeping just the same, but I looked at him over my shoulder.

"I've got out at last," said I, "in spite of you and Jane. And I've pulled off most of the paper, so you can't put me back!"

Now why should that man have fainted? But he did, and right across my path by the wall, so that I had to creep over him every time!

Elia Wilkinson Peattie (1862–1935)

Elia Wilkson Peattie had a successful, if now forgotten, career as a novelist, writer of short fiction, and journalist. Her work appeared in the *Century Magazine*, the *Atlantic Monthly*, and *Harper's Monthly*, and she was the literary critic for the *Chicago Tribune* from 1906 to 1917.

"The House That Was Not" (1898) is deceptively simple, but will reward careful thought about the relationship between the happy bride, Flora, and the nameless woman who inhabited the ghost house. Jeffrey Andrew Weinstock, one of the few critics to discuss Peattie, compares this story and Madeline Yale Wynne's "The Little Room" as narratives about gendered space and socially constructed gender roles.

Text: *The Shape of Fear and Other Ghostly Tales* (New York: Macmillan, 1899).

The House That Was Not

BART FLEMING took his bride out to his ranch on the plains when she was but seventeen years old, and the two set up housekeeping in three hundred and twenty acres of corn and rye. Off toward the west there was an unbroken sea of tossing corn at that time of the year when the bride came out, and as her sewing window was on the side of the house which faced the sunset, she passed a good part of each day looking into that great rustling mass, breathing in its succulent odors and listening to its sibilant melody. It was her picture gallery, her opera, her spectacle, and, being sensible, – or perhaps, being merely happy, – she made the most of it.

When harvesting time came and the corn was cut, she had much entertainment in discovering what lay beyond. The town was east, and it chanced that she had never ridden west. So, when the rolling hills of this newly beholden land lifted themselves for her contemplation, and the harvest sun, all in an angry and sanguinary glow sank in the veiled horizon, and at noon a scarf of golden vapor wavered up and down along the earth line, it was as if a new world had been made for her. Sometimes, at the coming of a storm, a whip-lash of purple cloud, full of electric agility, snapped along the western horizon.

"Oh, you'll see a lot of queer things on these here plains," her husband said when she spoke to him of these phenomena. "I guess what you see is the wind."

"The wind!" cried Flora. "You can't see the wind, Bart."

"Now look here, Flora," returned Bart, with benevolent emphasis, "you're a smart one, but you don't know all I know about this here country. I've lived here three mortal years, waitin' for you to git up out of your mother's arms and come out to keep me

American Gothic: From Salem Witchcraft to H. P. Lovecraft, An Anthology, Second Edition. Edited by Charles L. Crow.
Editorial material and organization © 2013 John Wiley & Sons, Ltd. Published 2013 by John Wiley & Sons, Ltd.

Elia Wilkinson Peattie

company, and I know what there is to know. Some things out here is queer – so queer folks wouldn't believe 'em unless they saw. An' some's so pig-headed they don't believe their own eyes. As for th' wind, if you lay down flat and squint toward th' west, you can see it blowin' along near th' ground, like a big ribbon; an' sometimes it's th' color of air, an' sometimes it's silver an' gold, an' sometimes, when a storm is comin', it's purple."

"If you got so tired looking at the wind, why didn't you marry some other girl, Bart, instead of waiting for me?"

Flora was more interested in the first part of Bart's speech than in the last.

"Oh, come on!" protested Bart, and he picked her up in his arms and jumped her toward the ceiling of the low shack as if she were a little girl – but then, to be sure, she wasn't much more.

Of all the things Flora saw when the corn was cut down, nothing interested her so much as a low cottage, something like her own, which lay away in the distance. She could not guess how far it might be, because distances are deceiving out there, where the altitude is high and the air is as clear as one of those mystic balls of glass in which the sallow mystics of India see the moving shadows of the future.

She had not known there were neighbors so near, and she wondered for several days about them before she ventured to say anything to Bart on the subject. Indeed, for some reason which she did not attempt to explain to herself, she felt shy about broaching the matter. Perhaps Bart did not want her to know the people. The thought came to her, as naughty thoughts will come, even to the best of persons, that some handsome young men might be "baching"[1] it out there by themselves, and Bart didn't wish her to make their acquaintance. Bart had flattered her so much that she had actually begun to think herself beautiful, though as a matter of fact she was only a nice little girl with a lot of reddish-brown hair, and a bright pair of reddish-brown eyes in a white face.

"Bart," she ventured one evening, as the sun, at its fiercest, rushed toward the great black hollow of the west, "who lives over there in that shack?"

She turned away from the window where she had been looking at the incarnadined disk, and she thought she saw Bart turn pale. But then, her eyes were so blurred with the glory she had been gazing at, that she might easily have been mistaken.

"I say, Bart, why don't you speak? If there's any one around to associate with, I should think you'd let me have the benefit of their company. It isn't as funny as you think, staying here alone days and days."

"You ain't gettin' homesick, be you, sweetheart?" cried Bart, putting his arms around her. "You ain't gettin' tired of my society, be yeh?"

It took some time to answer this question in a satisfactory manner, but at length Flora was able to return to her original topic.

"But the shack, Bart! Who lives there, anyway?"

"I'm not acquainted with 'em," said Bart, sharply. "Ain't them biscuits done, Flora?"

Then, of course, she grew obstinate.

"Those biscuits will never be done, Bart, till I know about that house, and why you never spoke of it, and why nobody ever comes down the road from there. Some one lives there I know, for in the mornings and at night I see the smoke coming out of the chimney."

Notes

THE HOUSE THAT WAS NOT
[1] Living as bachelors.

"Do you now?" cried Bart, opening his eyes and looking at her with unfeigned interest. "Well, do you know, sometimes I've fancied I seen that too?"

"Well, why not," cried Flora, in half anger. "Why shouldn't you?"

"See here, Flora, take them biscuits out an' listen to me. There ain't no house there. Hello! I didn't know you'd go for to drop the biscuits. Wait, I'll help you pick 'em up. By cracky, they're hot, ain't they? What you puttin' a towel over 'em for? Well, you set down here on my knee, so. Now you look over at that there house. You see it, don't yeh? Well, it ain't there! No! I saw it the first week I was out here. I was jus' half dyin', thinkin' of you an' wonderin' why you didn't write. That was the time you was mad at me. So I rode over there one day – lookin' up company, so t' speak – and there wa'n't no house there. I spent all one Sunday lookin' for it. Then I spoke to Jim Geary about it. He laughed an' got a little white about th' gills, an' he said he guessed I'd have to look a good while before I found it. He said that there shack was an ole joke."

"Why – what –"

"Well, this here is th' story he tol' me. He said a man an' his wife come out here t' live an' put up that there little place. An' she was young, you know, an' kind o' skeery, and she got lonesome. It worked on her an' worked on her, an' one day she up an' killed the baby an' her husband an' herself. Th' folks found 'em and buried 'em right there on their own ground. Well, about two weeks after that, th' house was burned down. Don't know how. Tramps, maybe. Anyhow, it burned. At least, I guess it burned!"

"You guess it burned!"

"Well, it ain't there, you know."

"But if it burned the ashes are there."

"All right, girlie, they're there then. Now let's have tea."

This they proceeded to do, and were happy and cheerful all evening, but that didn't keep Flora from rising at the first flush of dawn and stealing out of the house. She looked away over west as she went to the barn and there, dark and firm against the horizon, stood the little house against the pellucid sky of morning. She got on Ginger's back – Ginger being her own yellow broncho – and set off at a hard pace for the house. It didn't appear to come any nearer, but the objects which had seemed to be beside it came closer into view, and Flora pressed on, with her mind steeled for anything. But as she approached the poplar windbreak which stood to the north of the house, the little shack waned like a shadow before her. It faded and dimmed before her eyes.

She slapped Ginger's flanks and kept him going, and she at last got him up to the spot. But there was nothing there. The bunch grass grew tall and rank and in the midst of it lay a baby's shoe. Flora thought of picking it up, but something cold in her veins withheld her. Then she grew angry, and set Ginger's head toward the place and tried to drive him over it. But the yellow broncho gave one snort of fear, gathered himself in a bunch, and then, all tense, leaping muscles, made for home as only a broncho can.

Edith Wharton (1862–1937)

Edith Wharton's career was one of the most distinguished among American writers. Long considered a disciple of Henry James, she is now recognized as a strong and independent talent, with major achievement in fiction, travel writing, and autobiography, sustained over several decades. Gothic elements appear in a number of her works. Hints of witchcraft run through her popular novella *Ethan Frome*, for example, as Wharton draws on the history and folk traditions of its rural New England setting, and on her predecessor Nathaniel Hawthorne.

"The Eyes" (1910) is a conventional-seeming ghost story with surprisingly complex implications. One thread worth considering is the autobiographical dimension of the piece, since Wharton clearly has written herself into the figure of the girl in the "Gothic library," Alice Nowell. Libraries are a potent recurring motif in Wharton's fiction (see, for example, the village library in which Charity Royall is librarian in *Summer*). They are a place of refuge but also of danger:

young Edith Jones (Wharton was the name of her husband, whom she divorced) spent a lonely childhood reading in her father's library; recently critic Gloria Erlich has speculated that she may have endured some sort of childhood trauma there, possibly involving her father.

What does one read in a "Gothic library"? Another way to consider "The Eyes" is as a "meta-Gothic" tale, a story about Gothic fiction. We enter a safe world of masculine privilege in the narrative frame, a tradition defined in American literature by Washington Irving, who is mentioned in the story (and who was a friend of Wharton's father, by the way). The framed narrator, Culwin, thinks that he has scored a triumph as a Gothic storyteller. Yet the story ends with Culwin, and the clubby storytelling world he presides over, discredited. Is this a triumph of the girl in the library, and of female Gothic over its masculine counterpart?

Text: *Scribner's Magazine* 47 (June 1910), 671–80.

The Eyes

We had been put in the mood for ghosts, that evening, after an excellent dinner at our old friend Culwin's, by a tale of Fred Murchard's – the narrative of a strange personal visitation.

Seen through the haze of our cigars, and by the drowsy gleam of a coal fire, Culwin's library, with its oak walls and dark old bindings, made a good setting for such evocations; and ghostly experiences at first hand being, after Murchard's opening, the only kind acceptable to us, we proceeded to take stock of our group and tax each member for a contribution. There were eight of us, and seven contrived, in a manner more or less adequate, to fulfill the condition imposed. It surprised us all to find that we could muster such a show of supernatural impressions, for none of us, excepting Murchard

American Gothic: From Salem Witchcraft to H. P. Lovecraft, An Anthology, Second Edition. Edited by Charles L. Crow.
Editorial material and organization © 2013 John Wiley & Sons, Ltd. Published 2013 by John Wiley & Sons, Ltd.

himself and young Phil Frenham – whose story was the slightest of the lot – had the habit of sending our souls into the invisible. So that, on the whole, we had every reason to be proud of our seven "exhibits," and none of us would have dreamed of expecting an eighth from our host.

Our old friend, Mr. Andrew Culwin, who had sat back in his armchair, listening and blinking through the smoke circles with the cheerful tolerance of a wise old idol, was not the kind of man likely to be favored with such contacts, though he had imagination enough to enjoy, without envying, the superior privileges of his guests. By age and by education he belonged to the stout Positivist tradition, and his habit of thought had been formed in the days of the epic struggle between physics and metaphysics. But he had been, then and always, essentially a spectator, a humorous detached observer of the immense muddled variety show of life, slipping out of his seat now and then for a brief dip into the convivialities at the back of the house, but never, as far as one knew, showing the least desire to jump on the stage and do a "turn."

Among his contemporaries there lingered a vague tradition of his having, at a remote period, and in a romantic clime, been wounded in a duel; but this legend no more tallied with what we younger men knew of his character than my mother's assertion that he had once been "a charming little man with nice eyes" corresponded to any possible reconstitution of his physiognomy.

"He never can have looked like anything but a bundle of sticks," Murchard had once said of him. "Or a phosphorescent log, rather," someone else amended; and we recognized the happiness of this description of his small squat trunk with the red blink of the eyes in a face like mottled bark. He had always been possessed of a leisure which he had nursed and protected, instead of squandering it in vain activities. His carefully guarded hours had been devoted to the cultivation of a fine intelligence and a few judiciously chosen habits; and none of the disturbances common to human experience seemed to have crossed his sky. Nevertheless, his dispassionate survey of the universe had not raised his opinion of that costly experiment, and his study of the human race seemed to have resulted in the conclusion that all men were superfluous, and women necessary only because someone had to do the cooking. On the importance of this point his convictions were absolute, and gastronomy was the only science which he revered as a dogma. It must be owned that his little dinners were a strong argument in favor of this view, besides being a reason – though not the main one – for the fidelity of his friends.

Mentally he exercised a hospitality less seductive but no less stimulating. His mind was like a forum, or some open meeting place for the exchange of ideas: somewhat cold and drafty, but light, spacious and orderly – a kind of academic grove from which all the leaves have fallen. In this privileged area a dozen of us were wont to stretch our muscles and expand our lungs; and, as if to prolong as much as possible the tradition of what we felt to be a vanishing institution, one or two neophytes were now and then added to our band.

Young Phil Frenham was the last, and the most interesting, of these recruits, and a good example of Murchard's somewhat morbid assertion that our old friend "liked 'em juicy." It was indeed a fact that Culwin, for all his dryness, specially tasted the lyric qualities in youth. As he was far too good an Epicurean to nip the flowers of soul which he gathered for his garden, his friendship was not a disintegrating influence: on the contrary, it forced the young idea to robuster bloom. And in Phil Frenham he had a good subject for experimentation. The boy was really intelligent, and the soundness of his nature was like the pure paste under a fine glaze. Culwin had fished him out of a fog of family dullness, and pulled him up to a peak in

Darien;[1] and the adventure hadn't hurt him a bit. Indeed, the skill with which Culwin had contrived to stimulate his curiosities without robbing them of their bloom of awe seemed to me a sufficient answer to Murchard's ogreish metaphor. There was nothing hectic in Frenham's efflorescence, and his old friend had not laid even a finger tip on the sacred stupidities. One wanted no better proof of that than the fact that Frenham still reverenced them in Culwin.

"There's a side of him you fellows don't see. I believe that story about the duel!" he declared; and it was of the very essence of this belief that it should impel him – just as our little party was dispersing – to turn back to our host with the joking demand: "And now you've got to tell us about your ghost!"

The outer door had closed on Murchard and the others; only Frenham and I remained; and the devoted servant who presided over Culwin's destinies, having brought a fresh supply of soda water, had been laconically ordered to bed.

Culwin's sociability was a night-blooming flower, and we knew that he expected the nucleus of his group to tighten around him after midnight. But Frenham's appeal seemed to disconcert him comically, and he rose from the chair in which he had just reseated himself after his farewells in the hall.

"*My* ghost? Do you suppose I'm fool enough to go to the expense of keeping one of my own, when there are so many charming ones in my friends' closets? Take another cigar," he said, revolving toward me with a laugh.

Frenham laughed too, pulling up his slender height before the chimney piece as he turned to face his short bristling friend.

"Oh," he said, "you'd never be content to share if you met one you really liked."

Culwin had dropped back into his armchair, his shock head embedded in the hollow of worn leather, his little eyes glimmering over a fresh cigar.

"Liked – *liked*? Good Lord!" he growled.

"Ah, you *have*, then!" Frenham pounced on him in the same instant, with a side glance of victory at me; but Culwin cowered gnomelike among his cushions, dissembling himself in a protective cloud of smoke.

"What's the use of denying it? You've seen everything, so of course you've seen a ghost!" his young friend persisted, talking intrepidly into the cloud. "Or, if you haven't seen one, it's only because you've seen two!"

The form of the challenge seemed to strike our host. He shot his head out of the mist with a queer tortoise-like motion he sometimes had, and blinked approvingly at Frenham.

"That's it," he flung at us on a shrill jerk of laughter; "it's only because I've seen two!"

The words were so unexpected that they dropped down and down into a deep silence, while we continued to stare at each other over Culwin's head, and Culwin stared at his ghosts. At length Frenham, without speaking, threw himself into the chair on the other side of the hearth and leaned forward with his listening smile....

II

"Oh, of course they're not show ghosts – a collector wouldn't think anything of them.... Don't let me raise your hopes ... their one merit is their numerical strength: the exceptional fact of their being *two*. But, as against this, I'm bound to admit that at

Notes

THE EYES

[1] From Keats' sonnet "On First Looking into Chapman's Homer." Keats is recalling Balboa's first sighting of the Pacific in 1513 (though he mistakenly refers to Cortez). To be "on a peak in Darien" has become proverbial for a moment of great revelation.

any moment I could probably have exorcised them both by asking my doctor for a prescription, or my oculist for a pair of spectacles. Only, as I never could make up my mind whether to go to the doctor or the oculist – whether I was afflicted by an optical or a digestive delusion – I left them to pursue their interesting double life, though at times they made mine exceedingly uncomfortable....

"Yes – uncomfortable; and you know how I hate to be uncomfortable! But it was part of my stupid pride, when the thing began, not to admit that I could be disturbed by the trifling matter of seeing two.

"And then I'd no reason, really, to suppose I was ill. As far as I knew I was simply bored – horribly bored. But it was part of my boredom – I remember – that I was feeling so uncommonly well, and didn't know how on earth to work off my surplus energy. I had come back from a long journey – down in South America and Mexico – and had settled down for the winter near New York with an old aunt who had known Washington Irving and corresponded with N. P. Willis. She lived, not far from Irvington, in a damp Gothic villa overhung by Norway spruces and looking exactly like a memorial emblem done in hair. Her personal appearance was in keeping with this image, and her own hair – of which there was little left – might have been sacrificed to the manufacture of the emblem.

"I had just reached the end of an agitated year, with considerable arrears to make up in money and emotion; and theoretically it seemed as though my aunt's mild hospitality would be as beneficial to my nerves as to my purse. But the deuce of it was that as soon as I felt myself safe and sheltered my energy began to revive; and how was I to work it off inside of a memorial emblem? I had, at that time, the illusion that sustained intellectual effort could engage a man's whole activity; and I decided to write a great book – I forget about what. My aunt, impressed by my plan, gave up to me her Gothic library, filled with classics bound in black cloth and daguerreotypes of faded celebrities; and I sat down at my desk to win myself a place among their number. And to facilitate my task she lent me a cousin to copy my manuscript.

"The cousin was a nice girl, and I had an idea that a nice girl was just what I needed to restore my faith in human nature, and principally in myself. She was neither beautiful nor intelligent – poor Alice Nowell! – but it interested me to see any woman content to be so uninteresting, and I wanted to find out the secret of her content. In doing this I handled it rather rashly, and put it out of joint – oh, just for a moment! There's no fatuity in telling you this, for the poor girl had never seen anyone but cousins....

"Well, I was sorry for what I'd done, of course, and confoundedly bothered as to how I should put it straight. She was staying in the house, and one evening, after my aunt had gone to bed, she came down to the library to fetch a book she'd mislaid, like any artless heroine, on the shelves behind us. She was pink-nosed and flustered, and it suddenly occurred to me that her hair, though it was fairly thick and pretty, would look exactly like my aunt's when she grew older. I was glad I had noticed this, for it made it easier for me to decide to do what was right; and when I had found the book she hadn't lost I told her I was leaving for Europe that week.

"Europe was terribly far off in those days, and Alice knew at once what I meant. She didn't take it in the least as I'd expected – it would have been easier if she had. She held her book very tight, and turned away a moment to wind up the lamp on my desk – it had a ground-glass shade with vine leaves, and glass drops around the edge, I remember. Then she came back, held out her hand, and said: 'Good-bye.' And as she said it she looked straight at me and kissed me. I had never felt anything as fresh and shy and brave as her kiss. It was worse than any reproach, and it made me ashamed to deserve a reproach from her. I said to myself: 'I'll marry her, and when my aunt dies she'll leave us this house, and I'll sit here at the desk and go on with my book; and Alice will sit over there with her embroidery and look at me as she's looking now. And life will go on like that for any number of years.' The prospect frightened me a little, but at the time it didn't frighten me as much as doing anything to hurt her; and ten minutes later she had my seal ring on her finger, and my promise that when I went abroad she should go with me.

"You'll wonder why I'm enlarging on this incident. It's because the evening on which it took place was the very evening on which I first saw the queer sight I've spoken of. Being at that time an ardent believer in a necessary sequence between cause and effect, I naturally tried to trace some kind of link between what had just happened to me in my aunt's library, and what was to happen a few hours later on the same night; and so the coincidence between the two events always remained in my mind.

"I went up to bed with rather a heavy heart, for I was bowed under the weight of the first good action I had ever consciously committed; and young as I was, I saw the gravity of my situation. Don't imagine from this that I had hitherto been an instrument of destruction. I had been merely a harmless young man, who had followed his bent and declined all collaboration with Providence. Now I had suddenly undertaken to promote the moral order of the world, and I felt a good deal like the trustful spectator who has given his gold watch to the conjurer, and doesn't know in what shape he'll get it back when the trick is over.... Still, a glow of self-righteousness tempered my fears, and I said to myself as I undressed that when I'd got used to being good it probably wouldn't make me as nervous as it did at the start. And by the time I was in bed, and had blown out my candle, I felt that I really *was* getting used to it, and that, as far as I'd got, it was not unlike sinking down into one of my aunt's very softest wool mattresses.

"I closed my eyes on this image, and when I opened them it must have been a good deal later, for my room had grown cold, and intensely still. I was waked by the queer feeling we all know – the feeling that there was something in the room that hadn't been there when I fell asleep. I sat up and strained my eyes into the darkness. The room was pitch black, and at first I saw nothing; but gradually a vague glimmer at the foot of the bed turned into two eyes staring back at me. I couldn't distinguish the features attached to them, but as I looked the eyes grew more and more distinct: they gave out a light of their own.

"The sensation of being thus gazed at was far from pleasant, and you might suppose that my first impulse would have been to jump out of bed and hurl myself on the invisible figure attached to the eyes. But it wasn't – my impulse was simply to lie still.... I can't say whether this was due to an immediate sense of the uncanny nature of the apparition – to the certainty that if I did jump out of bed I should hurl myself on nothing – or merely to the benumbing effect of the eyes themselves. They were the very worst eyes I've ever seen: a man's eyes – but what a man! My first thought was that he must be frightfully old. The orbits were sunk, and the thick red-lined lids hung over the eyeballs like blinds of which the cords are broken. One lid drooped a little lower than the other, with the effect of a crooked leer; and between these folds of flesh, with their scant bristle of lashes, the eyes themselves, small glassy disks with an agate-like rim, looked like sea pebbles in the grip of a starfish.

"But the age of the eyes was not the most unpleasant thing about them. What turned me sick was their expression of vicious security. I don't know how else to describe the fact that they seemed to belong to a man who had done a lot of harm in his life, but had always kept just inside the danger lines. They were not the eyes of a coward, but of someone much too clever to take risks; and my gorge rose at their look of base astuteness. Yet even that wasn't the worst; for as we continued to scan each other I saw in them a tinge of derision, and felt myself to be its object.

"At that I was seized by an impulse of rage that jerked me to my feet and pitched me straight at the unseen figure. But of course there wasn't any figure there, and my fists struck at emptiness. Ashamed and cold, I groped about for a match and lit the candles. The room looked just as usual – as I had known it would; and I crawled back to bed, and blew out the lights.

"As soon as the room was dark again the eyes reappeared; and I now applied myself to explaining them on scientific principles. At first I thought the illusion might have been caused by the glow of the last embers in the chimney; but the fireplace was on the other side of my bed, and so placed that the fire could not be reflected in my toilet glass, which was the only mirror in the room. Then it struck me that I might have been tricked by the reflection of the embers in some polished bit of wood or metal; and though I couldn't discover any object of the sort in my line of vision, I got up again, groped my way to the hearth, and covered what was left of the fire. But as soon as I was back in bed the eyes were back at its foot.

"They were an hallucination, then: that was plain. But the fact that they were not due to any external dupery didn't make them a bit pleasanter. For if they were a projection of my inner consciousness, what the deuce was the matter with that organ? I had gone deeply enough into the mystery of morbid pathological states to picture the conditions under which an exploring mind might lay itself open to such a midnight admonition; but I couldn't fit it to my present case. I had never felt more normal, mentally and physically; and the only unusual fact in my situation – that of having assured the happiness of an amiable girl – did not seem of a kind to summon unclean spirits about my pillow. But there were the eyes still looking at me.

"I shut mine, and tried to evoke a vision of Alice Nowell's. They were not remarkable eyes, but they were as wholesome as fresh water, and if she had had more imagination – or longer lashes – their expression might have been interesting. As it was, they did not prove very efficacious, and in a few moments I perceived that they had mysteriously changed into the eyes at the foot of the bed. It exasperated me more to feel these glaring at me through my shut lids than to see them, and I opened my eyes again and looked straight into their hateful stare....

"And so it went on all night. I can't tell you what that night was like, nor how long it lasted. Have you ever lain in bed, hopelessly wide awake, and tried to keep your eyes shut, knowing that if you opened 'em you'd see something you dreaded and loathed? It sounds easy, but it's devilishly hard. Those eyes hung there and drew me. I had the *vertige de l'abîme*,[2] and their red lids were the edge of my abyss.... I had known nervous hours before: hours when I'd felt the wind of danger on my neck; but never this kind of strain. It wasn't that the eyes were awful; they hadn't the majesty of the powers of darkness. But they had – how shall I say? – a physical effect that was the equivalent of a bad smell: their look left a smear like a snail's. And I didn't see what business they had with me, anyhow – and I stared and stared, trying to find out.

"I don't know what effect they were trying to produce; but the effect they did produce was that of making me pack my portmanteau and bolt to town early the next morning. I left a note for my aunt, explaining that I was ill and had gone to see my doctor; and as a matter of fact I did feel uncommonly ill – the night seemed to have pumped all the blood out of me. But when I reached town I didn't go to the doctor's. I went to a friend's rooms, and threw myself on a bed, and slept for ten heavenly hours.

Notes ───

[2] French: vertigo.

When I woke it was the middle of the night, and I turned cold at the thought of what might be waiting for me. I sat up, shaking, and stared into the darkness; but there wasn't a break in its blessed surface, and when I saw that the eyes were not there I dropped back into another long sleep.

"I had left no word for Alice when I fled, because I meant to go back the next morning. But the next morning I was too exhausted to stir. As the day went on the exhaustion increased, instead of wearing off like the fatigue left by an ordinary night of insomnia: the effect of the eyes seemed to be cumulative, and the thought of seeing them again grew intolerable. For two days I fought my dread; and on the third evening I pulled myself together and decided to go back the next morning. I felt a good deal happier as soon as I'd decided, for I knew that my abrupt disappearance, and the strangeness of my not writing, must have been very distressing to poor Alice. I went to bed with an easy mind, and fell asleep at once; but in the middle of the night I woke, and there were the eyes....

"Well, I simply couldn't face them; and instead of going back to my aunt's I bundled a few things into a trunk and jumped aboard the first steamer for England. I was so dead tired when I got on board that I crawled straight into my berth, and slept most of the way over; and I can't tell you the bliss it was to wake from those long dreamless stretches and look fearlessly into the dark, *knowing* that I shouldn't see the eyes....

"I stayed abroad for a year, and then I stayed for another; and during that time I never had a glimpse of them. That was enough reason for prolonging my stay if I'd been on a desert island. Another was, of course, that I had perfectly come to see, on the voyage over, the complete impossibility of my marrying Alice Nowell. The fact that I had been so slow in making this discovery annoyed me, and made me want to avoid explanations. The bliss of escaping at one stroke from the eyes, and from this other embarrassment, gave my freedom an extraordinary zest; and the longer I savored it the better I liked its taste.

"The eyes had burned such a hole in my consciousness that for a long time I went on puzzling over the nature of the apparition, and wondering if it would ever come back. But as time passed I lost this dread, and retained only the precision of the image. Then that faded in its turn.

"The second year found me settled in Rome, where I was planning, I believe, to write another great book – a definitive work on Etruscan influences in Italian art. At any rate, I'd found some pretext of the kind for taking a sunny apartment in the Piazza di Spagna and dabbling about in the Forum; and there, one morning, a charming youth came to me. As he stood there in the warm light, slender and smooth and hyacinthine, he might have stepped from a ruined altar – one to Antinous,[3] say; but he'd come instead from New York, with a letter from (of all people) Alice Nowell. The letter – the first I'd had from her since our break – was simply a line introducing her young cousin, Gilbert Noyes, and appealing to me to befriend him. It appeared, poor lad, that he 'had talent,' and 'wanted to write'; and, an obdurate family having insisted that his calligraphy should take the form of double entry, Alice had intervened to win him six months' respite, during which he was to travel abroad on a meager pittance, and somehow prove his ability to increase it by his pen. The quaint conditions of the test struck me first: it seemed about as conclusive as a medieval 'ordeal.' Then I was touched by her having sent him to me. I had always wanted to

Notes

[3] A favorite of the Roman emperor Hadrian, who was inconsolable when the youth died; Hadrian built a temple in his honor.

do her some service, to justify myself in my own eyes rather than hers; and here was a beautiful occasion.

"I imagine it's safe to lay down the general principle that predestined geniuses don't, as a rule, appear before one in the spring sunshine of the Forum looking like one of its banished gods. At any rate, poor Noyes wasn't a predestined genius. But he *was* beautiful to see, and charming as a comrade. It was only when he began to talk literature that my heart failed me. I knew all the symptoms so well – the things he had 'in him,' and the things outside him that impinged! There's the real test, after all. It was always – punctually, inevitably, with the inexorableness of a mechanical law – it was *always* the wrong thing that struck him. I grew to find a certain fascination in deciding in advance exactly which wrong thing he'd select; and I acquired an astonishing skill at the game....

"The worst of it was that his *bêtise*[4] wasn't of the too obvious sort. Ladies who met him at picnics thought him intellectual; and even at dinners he passed for clever. I, who had him under the microscope, fancied now and then that he might develop some kind of a slim talent, something that he could make 'do' and be happy on; and wasn't that, after all, what I was concerned with? He was so charming – he continued to be so charming – that he called forth all my charity in support of this argument; and for the first few months I really believed there was a chance for him....

"Those months were delightful. Noyes was constantly with me, and the more I saw of him the better I liked him. His stupidity was a natural grace – it was as beautiful, really, as his eyelashes. And he was so gay, so affectionate, and so happy with me, that telling him the truth would have been about as pleasant as slitting the throat of some gentle animal. At first I used to wonder what had put into that radiant head the detestable delusion that it held a brain. Then I began to see that it was simply protective mimicry – an instinctive ruse to get away from family life and an office desk. Not that Gilbert didn't – dear lad! – believe in himself. There wasn't a trace of hypocrisy in him. He was sure that his 'call' was irresistible, while to me it was the saving grace of his situation that it *wasn't*, and that a little money, a little leisure, a little pleasure would have turned him into an inoffensive idler. Unluckily, however, there was no hope of money, and with the alternative of the office desk before him he couldn't postpone his attempt at literature. The stuff he turned out was deplorable, and I see now that I knew it from the first. Still, the absurdity of deciding a man's whole future on a first trial seemed to justify me in withholding my verdict, and perhaps even in encouraging him a little, on the ground that the human plant generally needs warmth to flower.

"At any rate, I proceeded on that principle, and carried it to the point of getting his term of probation extended. When I left Rome he went with me, and we idled away a delicious summer between Capri and Venice. I said to myself: 'If he has anything in him, it will come out now,' and it *did*. He was never more enchanting and enchanted. There were moments of our pilgrimage when beauty born of murmuring sound seemed actually to pass into his face – but only to issue forth in a flood of the palest ink....

"Well, the time came to turn off the tap; and I knew there was no hand but mine to do it. We were back in Rome, and I had taken him to stay with me, not wanting him to be alone in his *pension* when he had to face the necessity of renouncing his ambition. I hadn't, of course, relied solely on my own judgment in deciding to advise him to drop literature. I had sent his stuff to various people – editors and critics – and they

Notes

[4] French: stupidity.

had always sent it back with the same chilling lack of comment. Really there was nothing on earth to say.

"I confess I never felt more shabby than I did on the day when I decided to have it out with Gilbert. It was well enough to tell myself that it was my duty to knock the poor boy's hopes into splinters – but I'd like to know what act of gratuitous cruelty hasn't been justified on that plea? I've always shrunk from usurping the functions of Providence, and when I have to exercise them I decidedly prefer that it shouldn't be on an errand of destruction. Besides, in the last issue, who was I to decide, even after a year's trial, if poor Gilbert had it in him or not?

"The more I looked at the part I'd resolved to play, the less I liked it; and I liked it still less when Gilbert sat opposite me, with his head thrown back in the lamplight, just as Phil's is now…. I'd been going over his last manuscript, and he knew it, and he knew that his future hung on my verdict – we'd tacitly agreed to that. The manuscript lay between us, on my table – a novel, his first novel, if you please! – and he reached over and laid his hand on it, and looked up at me with all his life in the look.

"I stood up and cleared my throat, trying to keep my eyes away from his face and on the manuscript.

"'The fact is, my dear Gilbert,' I began –

"I saw him turn pale, but he was up and facing me in an instant.

"'Oh, look here, don't take on so, my dear fellow! I'm not so awfully cut up as all that!' His hands were on my shoulders, and he was laughing down on me from his full height, with a kind of mortally stricken gaiety that drove the knife into my side.

"He was too beautifully brave for me to keep up any humbug about my duty. And it came over me suddenly how I should hurt others in hurting him: myself first, since sending him home meant losing him; but more particularly poor Alice Nowell, to whom I had so longed to prove my good faith and my desire to serve her. It really seemed like failing her twice to fail Gilbert.

"But my intuition was like one of those lightning flashes that encircle the whole horizon, and in the same instant I saw what I might be letting myself in for if I didn't tell the truth. I said to myself: 'I shall have him for life' – and I'd never yet seen anyone, man or woman, whom I was quite sure of wanting on those terms. Well, this impulse of egotism decided me. I was ashamed of it, and to get away from it I took a leap that landed me straight in Gilbert's arms.

"'The thing's all right, and you're all wrong!' I shouted up at him; and as he hugged me, and I laughed and shook in his clutch, I had for a minute the sense of self-complacency that is supposed to attend the footsteps of the just. Hang it all, making people happy *has* its charms.

"Gilbert, of course, was for celebrating his emancipation in some spectacular manner; but I sent him away alone to explode his emotions, and went to bed to sleep off mine. As I undressed I began to wonder what their aftertaste would be – so many of the finest don't keep! Still, I wasn't sorry, and I meant to empty the bottle, even if it *did* turn a trifle flat.

"After I got into bed I lay for a long time smiling at the memory of his eyes – his blissful eyes…. Then I fell asleep, and when I woke the room was deathly cold, and I sat up with a jerk – and there were *the other eyes*….

"It was three years since I'd seen them, but I'd thought of them so often that I fancied they could never take me unawares again. Now, with their red sneer on me, I knew that I had never really believed they would come back, and that I was as defenceless as ever against them…. As before, it was the insane irrelevance of their coming that made it so horrible. What the deuce were they after, to leap out at me at such a time? I had lived more or less carelessly in the years since I'd seen them, though my worst indiscretions were not dark enough to invite the searchings of their infernal glare; but at this particular moment I was really in what might have been called a state of grace; and I can't tell you how the fact added to their horror....

"But it's not enough to say they were as bad as before: they were worse. Worse by just so much as I'd learned of life in the interval; by all the damnable implications my wider experience read into them. I saw now what I hadn't seen before: that they were eyes which had grown hideous gradually, which had built up their baseness coralwise, bit by bit, out of a series of small turpitudes slowly accumulated through the industrious years. Yes – it came to me that what made them so bad was that they'd grown bad so slowly....

"There they hung in the darkness, their swollen lids dropped across the little watery bulbs rolling loose in the orbits, and the puff of flesh making a muddy shadow underneath – and as their stare moved with my movements, there came over me a sense of their tacit complicity, of a deep hidden understanding between us that was worse than the first shock of their strangeness. Not that I understood them; but that they made it so clear that someday I should.... Yes, that was the worst part of it, decidedly; and it was the feeling that became stronger each time they came back....

"For they got into the damnable habit of coming back. They reminded me of vampires with a taste for young flesh, they seemed so to gloat over the taste of a good conscience. Every night for a month they came to claim their morsel of mine: since I'd made Gilbert happy they simply wouldn't loosen their fangs. The coincidence almost made me hate him, poor lad, fortuitous as I felt it to be. I puzzled over it a good deal, but couldn't find any hint of an explanation except in the chance of his association with Alice Nowell. But then the eyes had let up on me the moment I had abandoned her, so they could hardly be the emissaries of a woman scorned, even if one could have pictured poor Alice charging such spirits to avenge her. That set me thinking, and I began to wonder if they would let up on me if I abandoned Gilbert. The temptation was insidious, and I had to stiffen myself against it; but really, dear boy! he was too charming to be sacrificed to such demons. And so, after all, I never found out what they wanted...."

III

The fire crumbled, sending up a flash which threw into relief the narrator's gnarled face under its gray-black stubble. Pressed into the hollow of the chair back, it stood out an instant like an intaglio of yellowish red-veined stone, with spots of enamel for the eyes; then the fire sank and it became once more a dim Rembrandtish blur.

Phil Frenham, sitting in a low chair on the opposite side of the hearth, one long arm propped on the table behind him, one hand supporting his thrown-back head, and his eyes fixed on his old friend's face, had not moved since the tale began. He continued to maintain his silent immobility after Culwin had ceased to speak, and it was I who, with a vague sense of disappointment at the sudden drop of the story, finally asked: "But how long did you keep on seeing them?"

Culwin, so sunk into his chair that he seemed like a heap of his own empty clothes, stirred a little, as if in surprise at my question. He appeared to have half-forgotten what he had been telling us.

"How long? Oh, off and on all that winter. It was infernal. I never got used to them. I grew really ill."

Frenham shifted his attitude, and as he did so his elbow struck against a small mirror in a bronze frame standing on the table behind him. He turned and changed its angle slightly; then he resumed his former attitude, his dark head thrown back on his lifted palm, his eyes intent on Culwin's face. Something in his silent gaze embarrassed me, and as if to divert attention from it I pressed on with another question:

"And you never tried sacrificing Noyes?"

"Oh, no. The fact is I didn't have to. He did it for me, poor boy!"

"Did it for you? How do you mean?"

"He wore me out – wore everybody out. He kept on pouring out his lamentable twaddle, and hawking it up and down the place till he became a thing of terror. I tried to wean him from writing – oh, ever so gently, you understand, by throwing him with agreeable people, giving him a chance to make himself felt, to come to a sense of what he *really* had to give. I'd foreseen this solution from the beginning – felt sure that, once the first ardor of authorship was quenched, he'd drop into his place as a charming parasitic thing, the kind of chronic Cherubino for whom, in old societies, there's always a seat at table, and a shelter behind the ladies' skirts. I saw him take his place as 'the poet': the poet who doesn't write. One knows the type in every drawing room. Living in that way doesn't cost much – I'd worked it all out in my mind, and felt sure that, with a little help, he could manage it for the next few years; and meanwhile he'd be sure to marry. I saw him married to a widow, rather older, with a good cook and a well-run house. And I actually had my eye on the widow.... Meanwhile I did everything to help the transition – lent him money to ease his conscience, introduced him to pretty women to make him forget his vows. But nothing would do him: he had but one idea in his beautiful obstinate head. He wanted the laurel and not the rose, and he kept on repeating Gautier's axiom, and battering and filing at his limp prose till he'd spread it out over Lord knows how many hundred pages. Now and then he would send a barrelful to a publisher, and of course it would always come back.

"At first it didn't matter – he thought he was 'misunderstood.' He took the attitudes of genius, and whenever an opus came home he wrote another to keep it company. Then he had a reaction of despair, and accused me of deceiving him, and Lord knows what. I got angry at that, and told him it was he who had deceived himself. He'd come to me determined to write, and I'd done my best to help him. That was the extent of my offence, and I'd done it for his cousin's sake, not his.

"That seemed to strike home, and he didn't answer for a minute. Then he said: 'My time's up and my money's up. What do you think I'd better do?'

"'I think you'd better not be an ass,' I said.

"'What do you mean by being an ass?' he asked.

"I took a letter from my desk and held it out to him.

"'I mean refusing this offer of Mrs. Ellinger's: to be her secretary at a salary of five thousand dollars. There may be a lot more in it than that.'

"He flung out his hand with a violence that struck the letter from mine. 'Oh, I know well enough what's in it!' he said, red to the roots of his hair.

"'And what's the answer, if you know?' I asked.

"He made none at the minute, but turned away slowly to the door. There, with his hand on the threshold, he stopped to say, almost under his breath: 'Then you really think my stuff's no good?'

"I was tired and exasperated, and I laughed. I don't defend my laugh – it was in wretched taste. But I must plead in extenuation that the boy was a fool, and that I'd done my best for him – I really had.

"He went out of the room, shutting the door quietly after him. That afternoon I left for Frascati, where I'd promised to spend the Sunday with some friends. I was glad to escape from Gilbert, and by the same token, as I learned that night, I had also escaped from the eyes. I dropped into the same lethargic sleep that had come to me before when I left off seeing them; and when I woke the next morning in my peaceful room above the ilexes, I felt the utter weariness and deep relief that always followed on that sleep. I put in two blessed nights at Frascati, and when I got back to my rooms in Rome I found that Gilbert had gone.... Oh, nothing tragic had happened – the episode never rose to *that*. He'd simply packed his manuscripts and left for America – for his family and the Wall Street desk. He left a decent enough note to tell me of his decision, and behaved altogether, in the circumstances, as little like a fool as it's possible for a fool to behave...."

IV

Culwin paused again, and Frenham still sat motionless, the dusky contour of his young head reflected in the mirror at his back.

"And what became of Noyes afterward?" I finally asked, still disquieted by a sense of incompleteness, by the need of some connecting thread between the parallel lines of the tale.

Culwin twitched his shoulders. "Oh, nothing became of him – because he became nothing. There could be no question of 'becoming' about it. He vegetated in an office, I believe, and finally got a clerkship in a consulate, and married drearily in China. I saw him once in Hong Kong, years afterward. He was fat and hadn't shaved. I was told he drank. He didn't recognize me."

"And the eyes?" I asked, after another pause which Frenham's continued silence made oppressive.

Culwin, stroking his chin, blinked at me meditatively through the shadows. "I never saw them after my last talk with Gilbert. Put two and two together if you can. For my part, I haven't found the link."

He rose, his hands in his pockets, and walked stiffly over to the table on which reviving drinks had been set out.

"You must be parched after this dry tale. Here, help yourself, my dear fellow. Here, Phil – " He turned back to the hearth.

Frenham made no response to his host's hospitable summons. He still sat in his low chair without moving, but as Culwin advanced toward him, their eyes met in a long look; after which the young man, turning suddenly, flung his arms across the table behind him, and dropped his face upon them.

Culwin, at the unexpected gesture, stopped short, a flush on his face.

"Phil – what the deuce? Why, have the eyes scared *you*? My dear boy – my dear fellow – I never had such a tribute to my literary ability, never!"

He broke into a chuckle at the thought, and halted on the hearthrug, his hands still in his pockets, gazing down at the youth's bowed head. Then, as Frenham still made no answer, he moved a step or two nearer.

"Cheer up, my dear Phil! It's years since I've seen them – apparently I've done nothing lately bad enough to call them out of chaos. Unless my present evocation of them has made you see them; which would be their worst stroke yet!"

His bantering appeal quivered off into an uneasy laugh, and he moved still nearer, bending over Frenham, and laying his gouty hands on the lad's shoulders.

"Phil, my dear boy, really – what's the matter? Why don't you answer? *Have* you seen the eyes?"

Frenham's face was still hidden, and from where I stood behind Culwin I saw the latter, as if under the rebuff of this unaccountable attitude, draw back slowly from his friend. As he did so, the light of the lamp on the table fell full on his congested face, and I caught its reflection in the mirror behind Frenham's head.

Culwin saw the reflection also. He paused, his face level with the mirror, as if scarcely recognizing the countenance in it as his own. But as he looked his expression gradually changed, and for an appreciable space of time he and the image in the glass confronted each other with a glare of slowly gathering hate. Then Culwin let go of Frenham's shoulders, and drew back a step....

Frenham, his face still hidden, did not stir.

Robert W. Chambers (1865–1933)

Most of the fiction Chambers wrote in a long and commercially successful career was forgettable genre work. Not so the first four stories of his 1895 collection, *The King in Yellow*: "The Yellow Sign," "The Repairer of Reputations," "The Mask," and the story reprinted here, "In the Court of the Dragon." These interconnected tales are among the most influential stories of supernatural horror written in the late nineteenth century.

Chambers presumes an ultimate Gothic text, a play called "The King in Yellow," referenced in each of the four stories, a text written in "words which are more precious than jewels, more soothing than heavenly music, more awful than death itself." In this play one may read (apparently it is only to be read, not performed) of the Yellow Sign, the King in Yellow, and the lost city of Carcosa. Chambers took the name of the city from Ambrose Bierce's story "An Inhabitant of Carcosa," and changed "Hali" from the name of a sage to that of an ominous lake. All who read this play are ensnared and driven mad by it. Worse, reading the text opens a passage to the world of Carcosa, allowing horrors to enter our own world, including the King in Yellow himself.

Text: *The King in Yellow* (New York: F. Tennyson Neely, 1895). Punctuation in the two inset quotations has been regularized. Otherwise the eccentric punctuation of the original has been left unchanged.

In the Court of the Dragon

> Oh Thou who burn'st in heart for those who burn
> In Hell, whose fires thyself shall feed in turn,
> How long be crying, – "Mercy on them, God!"
> Why, who art thou to teach and He to learn?[1]

In the Church of St. Barnabé vespers were over; the clergy left the altar; the little choir-boys flocked across the chancel and settled in the stalls. A Suisse in rich uniform marched down the south aisle, sounding his staff at every fourth step on the stone pavement; behind him came that eloquent preacher and good man, Monseigneur C —.

My chair was near the chancel rail. I now turned toward the west end of the church. The other people between the altar and the pulpit turned too. There was a little scraping and rustling while the congregation seated itself again; the preacher mounted the pulpit stairs, and the organ voluntary ceased.

Notes

IN THE COURT OF THE DRAGON
[1] From the imaginary play, "The King in Yellow."

I had always found the organ-playing at St. Barnabé highly interesting. Learned and scientific it was, too much so for my small knowledge, but expressing a vivid if cold intelligence. Moreover, it possessed the French quality of taste; taste reigned supreme, self-controlled, dignified and reticent.

To-day, however, from the first chord I had felt a change for the worse, a sinister change. During vespers it had been chiefly the chancel organ which supported the beautiful choir, but now and again, quite wantonly as it seemed, from the west gallery where the great organ stands, a heavy hand had struck across the church, at the serene peace of those clear voices. It was something more than harsh and dissonant, and it betrayed no lack of skill. As it recurred again and again, it set me thinking of what my architect's books say about the custom in early times to consecrate the choir as soon as it was built, and that the nave, being finished sometimes half a century later, often did not get any blessing at all: I wondered idly if that had been the case at St. Barnabé, and whether something not usually supposed to be at home in a Christian church, might have entered undetected, and taken possession of the west gallery. I had read of such things happening too, but not in works on architecture.

Then I remembered that St. Barnabé was not much more than a hundred years old, and smiled at the incongruous association of mediaeval superstitions with that cheerful little piece of eighteenth century rococo.

But now vespers were over, and there should have followed a few quiet chords, fit to accompany meditation, while we waited for the sermon. Instead of that, the discord at the lower end of the church broke out with the departure of the clergy, as if now nothing could control it.

I belong to those children of an older and simpler generation, who do not love to seek for psychological subtleties in art; and I have ever refused to find in music anything more than melody and harmony, but I felt that in the labyrinth of sounds now issuing from that instrument there was something being hunted. Up and down the pedals chased him, while the manuals blared approval. Poor devil! whoever he was, there seemed small hope of escape!

My nervous annoyance changed to anger. Who was doing this? How dare he play like that in the midst of divine service? I glanced at the people near me: not one appeared to be in the least disturbed. The placid brows of the kneeling nuns, still turned toward the altar, lost none of their devout abstraction, under the pale shadow of their white headdress. The fashionable lady beside me was looking expectantly at Monseigneur C—. For all her face betrayed, the organ might have been singing an Ave Maria.

But now, at last, the preacher had made the sign of the cross, and commanded silence. I turned to him gladly. Thus far I had not found the rest I had counted on, when I entered St. Barnabé that afternoon.

I was worn out by three nights of physical suffering and mental trouble: the last had been the worst, and it was an exhausted body, and a mind benumbed and yet acutely sensitive, which I had brought to my favorite church for healing. For I had been reading "The King in Yellow."

"The sun ariseth; they gather themselves together and lay them down in their dens."[2] Monseigneur C— delivered his text in a calm voice, glancing quietly over the congregation. My eyes turned, I knew not why, toward the lower end of the church.

Notes

[2] Psalm 104:22 (King James version). The previous verse reads "The young lions roar after their prey, and seek their meat from God."

The organist was coming from behind his pipes, and passing along the gallery on his way out, I saw him disappear by a small door that leads to some stairs which descend directly to the street. He was a slender man, and his face was as white as his coat was black. "Good riddance!" I thought, "with your wicked music! I hope your assistant will play the closing voluntary."

With a feeling of relief, with a deep, calm feeling of relief, I turned back to the mild face in the pulpit, and settled myself to listen. Here at last was the ease of mind I longed for.

"My children," said the preacher, "one truth the human soul finds hardest of all to learn; that it has nothing to fear. It can never be made to see that nothing can really harm it."

"Curious doctrine!" I thought, "for a Catholic priest. Let us see how he will reconcile that with the Fathers."

"Nothing can really harm the soul," he went on, in his coolest, clearest tones, "because – "

But I never heard the rest; my eye left his face, I knew not for what reason, and sought the lower end of the church. The same man was coming out from behind the organ, and was passing along the gallery *the same way*. But there had not been time for him to return, and if he had returned, I must have seen him. I felt a faint chill, and my heart sank; and yet, his going and coming were no affair of mine. I looked at him: I could not look away from his black figure and his white face. When he was exactly opposite to me, he turned and sent across the church, straight into my eyes, a look of hate, intense and deadly: I have never seen any other like it; would to God I might never see it again! Then he disappeared by the same door through which I had watched him depart less than sixty seconds before.

I sat and tried to collect my thoughts. My first sensation was like that of a very young child badly hurt, when it catches its breath before crying out.

To suddenly find myself the object of such hatred was exquisitely painful: and this man was an utter stranger. Why should he hate me so? Me, whom he had never seen before? For the moment all other sensation was merged in this one pang: even fear was subordinate to grief, and for that moment I never doubted; but in the next I began to reason, and a sense of the incongruous came to my aid.

As I have said, St. Barnabé is a modern church. It is small and well lighted; one sees all over it almost at a glance. The organ gallery gets a strong white light from a row of long windows in the clere-story, which have not even colored glass.

The pulpit being in the middle of the church, it followed that, when I was turned toward it, whatever moved at the west end could not fail to attract my eye. When the organist passed it was no wonder that I saw him: I had simply miscalculated the interval between his first and his second passing. He has come in that last time by the other side-door. As for the look which had so upset me, there had been no such thing, and I was a nervous fool.

I looked about. This was a likely place to harbor supernatural horrors! That clear-cut, reasonable face of Monseigneur C—, his collected manner, and easy, graceful gestures, were they not just a little discouraging to the notion of a gruesome mystery? I glanced above his head, and almost laughed. That flyaway lady, supporting one corner of the pulpit canopy, which looked like a fringed damask table-cloth in a high wind, at the first attempt of a basilisk to pose up there in the organ loft, she would point her gold trumpet at him, and puff him out of existence! I laughed to myself over this conceit, which, at the time, I thought very amusing, and sat and chaffed myself and everything else, from the old harpy outside the railing, who had made me pay ten centimes for my chair, before she would let me in (she was more like a basilisk, I told myself, than was my organist with the anaemic complexion): from that grim old dame, to, yes, alas! to Monseigneur C—, himself. For all devoutness had fled. I had never yet done such a thing in my life, but now I felt a desire to mock.

As for the sermon, I could not hear a word of it, for the jingle in my ears of

> The skirts of St. Paul has reached,
> Having preached us those six Lent lectures,
> More unctuous than ever he preached,

keeping time to the most fantastic and irreverent thoughts.

It was no use to sit there any longer: I must get out of doors and shake myself free from this hateful mood. I knew the rudeness I was committing, but still I rose and left the church.

A spring sun was shining on the rue St. Honoré, as I ran down the church steps. On one corner stood a barrow full of yellow jonquils, pale violets from the Riviera, dark Russian violets, and white Roman hyacinths in a golden cloud of mimosa. The street was full of Sunday pleasure seekers. I swung my cane and laughed with the rest. Some one overtook and passed me. He never turned, but there was the same deadly malignity in his white profile that there had been in his eyes. I watched him as long as I could see him. His lithe back expressed the same menace; every step that carried him away from me seemed to bear him on some errand connected with my destruction.

I was creeping along, my feet almost refusing to move. There began to dawn in me a sense of responsibility for something long forgotten. It began to seem as if I deserved that which he threatened: it reached a long way back – a long, long way back. It had lain dormant all these years: it was there though, and presently it would rise and confront me. But I would try to escape; and I stumbled as best I could into the rue de Rivoli, across the Place de la Concorde and on the Quai. I looked with sick eyes upon the sun, shining through the white foam of the fountain, pouring over the backs of the dusky bronze river-gods, on the far-away Arc, a structure of amethyst mist, on the countless vistas of gray stems and bare branches faintly green. Then I saw him again coming down one of the chestnut alleys of the Cours la Reine.

I left the river side, plunged blindly across to the Champs Élysées and turned toward the Arc. The setting sun was sending its rays along the green sward of the Rond-point: in the full glow he sat on a bench, children and young mothers all about him. He was nothing but a Sunday lounger, like the others, like myself. I said the words almost aloud, and all the while I gazed on the malignant hatred of his face. But he was not looking at me. I crept past and dragged my leaden feet up the Avenue. I knew that every time I met him brought him nearer to the accomplishment of his purpose and my fate. And still I tried to save myself.

The last rays of sunset were pouring through the great Arc. I passed under it, and met him face to face. I had left him far down the Champs Élysées, and yet he came in with a stream of people who were returning from the Bois de Boulogne. He came so close that he brushed me. His slender frame felt like iron inside its loose black covering. He showed no signs of haste, nor of fatigue, nor of any human feeling. His whole being expressed but one thing: the will, and the power to work me evil.

In anguish I watched him, where he went down the broad crowded Avenue, that was all flashing with wheels and the trappings of horses, and the helmets of the Garde Républicaine.

He was soon lost to sight; then I turned and fled. Into the Bois, and far out beyond it – I know not where I went, but after a long while as it seemed to me, night had fallen, and I found myself sitting at a table before a small café. I had wandered back into the Bois. It was hours now since I had seen him. Physical fatigue, and mental suffering had left me no more power to think or feel. I was tired, so tired! I longed to hide away in my own den. I resolved to go home. But that was a long way off.

I live in the Court of the Dragon, a narrow passage that leads from the rue de Rennes to the rue du Dragon.

It is an "Impasse;" traversable only for foot passengers. Over the entrance on the rue de Rennes is a balcony, supported by an iron dragon. Within the court tall old houses rise on either side, and close the ends that give on the two streets. Huge gates, swung back during the day into the walls of the deep archways, close this court, after mid-night, and one must enter then by ringing at certain small doors on the side. The sunken pavement collects unsavory pools. Steep stairways pitch down to doors that open on the court. The ground floors are occupied by shops of secondhand dealers, and by iron workers. All day long the place rings with the clink of hammers, and the clang of metal bars.

Unsavory as it is below, there is cheerfulness, and comfort, and hard, honest work above.

Five flights up are the ateliers of architects and painters, and the hiding-places of middle-aged students like myself who want to live alone. When I first came here to live I was young, and not alone.

I had to walk awhile before any conveyance appeared, but at last, when I had almost reached the Arc de Triomphe again, an empty cab came along and I took it.

From the Arc to the rue de Rennes is a drive of more than half an hour, especially when one is conveyed by a tired cab horse that has been at the mercy of fête makers.

There had been time before I passed under the Dragon's wings, to meet my enemy over and over again, but I never saw him once, and now refuge was close at hand.

Before the wide gateway a small mob of children were playing. Our concierge and his wife walked about among them with their black poodle, keeping order; some couples were waltzing on the side-walk. I returned their greetings and hurried in.

All the inhabitants of the court had trooped out into the street. The place was quite deserted, lighted by a few lanterns hung high up, in which the gas burned dimly.

My apartment was at the top of a house, half way down the court, reached by a staircase that descended almost into the street, with only a bit of passage-way inter-vening. I set my foot on the threshold of the open door, the friendly, old ruinous stairs rose before me, leading up to rest and shelter. Looking back over my right shoulder, I saw *him*, ten paces off. He must have entered the court with me.

He was coming straight on, neither slowly, nor swiftly, but straight on to me. And now he was looking at me. For the first time since our eyes encountered across the church they met now again, and I knew that the time had come.

Retreating backward, down the court, I faced him. I meant to escape by the entrance on the rue du Dragon. His eyes told me that I never should escape.

It seemed ages while we were going, I retreating, he advancing, down the court in perfect silence; but at last I felt the shadow of the archway, and the next step brought me within it. I had meant to turn here and spring through into the street. But the shadow was not that of an archway; it was that of a vault. The great doors on the rue du Dragon were closed. I felt this by the blackness which surrounded me, and at the same instant I read it in his face. How his face gleamed in the darkness, drawing swiftly nearer! The deep vaults, the huge closed doors, their cold iron clamps were all on his side. The thing which he had threatened had arrived: it gathered and bore down on me from the fathomless shadows; the point from which it would strike was his infernal eyes. Hopeless I set my back against the barred doors and defied him.

★ ★ ★ ★ ★

There was a scraping of chairs on the stone floor, and a rustling as the congregation rose. I could hear the Suisse's staff in the south aisle, preceding Monseigneur C— to the sacristy.

The kneeling nuns, roused from their devout abstraction, made their reverence and went away. The fashionable lady, my neighbor, rose also, with graceful reserve. As she departed her glance just flitted over my face in disapproval.

Half dead, or so it seemed to me, yet intensely alive to every trifle, I sat among the leisurely moving crowd, then rose too and went toward the door.

I had slept through the sermon. Had I slept through the sermon? I looked up and saw him passing along the gallery to his place. Only his side I saw; the thin bent arm in its black covering looked like one of those devilish, nameless instruments which lie in the disused torture chambers of mediaeval castles.

But I had escaped him, though his eyes had said I should not. *Had* I escaped him? That which gave him the power over me came back out of oblivion, where I had hoped to keep it. For I knew him now. Death and the awful abode of lost souls, whither my weakness long ago had sent him – they had changed him for every other eye, but not for mine. I had recognized him almost from the first; I had never doubted what he was come to do; and now I knew that while my body sat safe in the cheerful little church, he had been hunting my soul in the Court of the Dragon.

I crept to the door; the organ broke out overhead with a blare. A dazzling light filled the church, blotting the altar from my eyes. The people faded away, the arches, the vaulted roof vanished. I raised my seared eyes to the fathomless glare, and I saw the black stars hanging in the heavens: and the wet winds from the Lake of Hali chilled my face.

And now, far away, over leagues of tossing cloud-waves, I saw the moon dripping with spray; and beyond, the towers of Carcosa rose behind the moon.

Death and the awful abode of lost souls, whither my weakness long ago had sent him, had changed him for every other eye but mine. And now I heard *his voice*, rising, swelling, thundering through the flaring light, and as I fell, the radiance increasing, increasing, poured over me in waves of flame. Then I sank into the depths, and I heard the King in Yellow whispering to my soul: "It is a fearful thing to fall into the hands of the living God!"[3]

Notes ————————————————————————————

[3] Hebrews 10:31.

Edgar Lee Masters (1868–1950)

Masters' most popular book was *Spoon River Anthology* (1915), a kind of novel in verse in which ghosts in a small-town Illinois cemetery speak their own epitaphs. Many of these blank-verse monologues reveal bitterness, secrets, and crimes that cut against the dominant American narrative of nostalgia for the virtues of mid-western village life. Here are two of these voices.

Text: Edgar Lee Masters, *Spoon River Anthology* (New York: Macmillan, 1915).

Two Poems

Nancy Knapp

WELL, don't you see this was the way of it:
We bought the farm with what he inherited,
And his brothers and sisters accused him of poisoning
His father's mind against the rest of them.
And we never had any peace with our treasure.
The murrain took the cattle, and the crops failed.
And lightning struck the granary.
So we mortgaged the farm to keep going.
And he grew silent and was worried all the time.
Then some of the neighbors refused to speak to us,
And took sides with his brothers and sisters.
And I had no place to turn, as one may say to himself,
At an earlier time in life; "No matter,
So and so is my friend, or I can shake this off
With a little trip to Decatur."
Then the dreadfulest smells infested the rooms.
So I set fire to the beds and the old witch-house
Went up in a roar of flame,
As I danced in the yard with waving arms.
While he wept like a freezing steer.

Barry Holden

THE very fall my sister Nancy Knapp
Set fire to the house
They were trying Dr. Duval
For the murder of Zora Clemens,

And I sat in the court two weeks
Listening to every witness.
It was clear he had got her in a family way;
And to let the child be born
Would not do.
Well, how about me with eight children,
And one coming, and the farm
Mortgaged to Thomas Rhodes?
And when I got home that night,
(After listening to the story of the buggy ride,
And the finding of Zora in the ditch.)
The first thing I saw, right there by the steps,
Where the boys had hacked for angle worms,
Was the hatchet!
And just as I entered there was my wife,
Standing before me, big with child.
She started the talk of the mortgaged farm,
And I killed her.

Edwin Arlington Robinson
(1868–1935)

E. A. Robinson was raised in Gardiner, Maine, which becomes the Tilbury Town of many of his poems. In his New England village there are many secrets and old crimes, many houses filled with lonely and defeated people – and sometimes ghosts.

Born into the same generation as Frank Norris and Stephen Crane, Robinson shared with them a skepticism about human will, a belief that people are shaped by forces of biology, environment, and economics. Thus the family in "The Mill" is a casualty to market forces that have rendered old-style handicraft industries obsolete. But the everpresent force in Robinson's poetry is *time*. Robinson is his country's great poet of aging, failure, and melancholy remembrance.

While Robinson is not a technical innovator in the sense championed by the slightly younger group of early moderns (such as Pound, H.D., Gertrude Stein), his poems are often difficult because they are highly compressed. Each of the poems below could be expanded into a novel, and will repay slow and thoughtful reading.

Texts: "Luke Havergal" from *The Children of the Night* (New York: Charles Scribner's Sons, 1897); "Lisette and Eileen" and "The Dark House" from *The Man Against the Sky* (New York: Macmillan, 1916); "The Mill" and "Souvenir" from *The Three Taverns* (New York: Macmillan, 1920); "Why He Was There" from *Dionysus in Doubt* (New York: Macmillan, 1925).

SIX POEMS

Luke Havergal

Go to the western gate, Luke Havergal,
There where the vines cling crimson on the wall,
And in the twilight wait for what will come.
The leaves will whisper there of her, and some,
Like flying words, will strike you as they fall;
But go, and if you listen she will call.
Go to the western gate, Luke Havergal –
Luke Havergal.

No, there is not a dawn in eastern skies
To rift the fiery night that's in your eyes;
But there, where western glooms are gathering,
The dark will end the dark, if anything:
God slays himself with every leaf that flies,

And hell is more than half of paradise.
No, there is not a dawn in eastern skies –
In eastern skies.

Out of a grave I come to tell you this,
Out of a grave I come to quench the kiss
That flames upon your forehead with a glow
That blinds you to the way that you must go.
Yes, there is yet one way to where she is,
Bitter, but one that faith may never miss.
Out of a grave I come to tell you this –
To tell you this.

There is the western gate, Luke Havergal,
There are the crimson leaves upon the wall.
Go, for the winds are tearing them away, –
Nor think to riddle the dead words they say,
Nor any more to feel them as they fall;
But go, and if you trust her she will call.
There is the western gate, Luke Havergal –
Luke Havergal.

Lisette and Eileen

"When he was here alive, Eileen,
There was a word you might have said;
So never mind what I have been,
Or anything, – for you are dead.

"And after this when I am there
Where he is, you'll be dying still.
Your eyes are dead, and your black hair, –
The rest of you be what it will.

"'Twas all to save him? Never mind,
Eileen. You saved him. You are strong.
I'd hardly wonder if your kind
Paid everything, for you live long.

You last, I mean. That's what I mean.
I mean you last as long as lies.
You might have said that word, Eileen, –
And you might have your hair and eyes.

"And what you see might be Lisette,
Instead of this that has no name.
Your silence – I can feel it yet,
Alive and in me, like a flame.

"Where might I be with him to-day,
Could he have known before he heard?

But no – your silence had its way,
Without a weapon or a word.

"Because a word was never told,
I'm going as a worn toy goes.
And you are dead; and you'll be old;
And I forgive you, I suppose.

"I'll soon be changing as all do,
To something we have always been;
And you'll be old.... He liked you, too,
I might have killed you then, Eileen.

"I think he liked as much of you
As had a reason to be seen, –
As much as God made black and blue.
He liked your hair and eyes, Eileen."

The Dark House

Where a faint light shines alone,
Dwells a Demon I have known.
Most of you had better say
"The Dark House," and go your way.
Do not wonder if I stay.

For I know the Demon's eyes,
And their lure that never dies.
Banish all your fond alarms,
For I know the foiling charms
Of her eyes and of her arms,

And I know that in one room
Burns a lamp as in a tomb;
And I see the shadow glide,
Back and forth, of one denied
Power to find himself outside.

There he is who is my friend,
Damned, he fancies, to the end –
Vanquished, ever since a door
Closed, he thought, for evermore
On the life that was before.

And the friend who knows him best
Sees him as he sees the rest
Who are striving to be wise
While a Demon's arms and eyes
Hold them as a web would flies.

All the words of all the world,
Aimed together and then hurled,

Would be stiller in his ears
Than a closing of still shears
On a thread made out of years.

But there lives another sound,
More compelling, more profound;
There's a music, so it seems,
That assuages and redeems,
More than reason, more than dreams.

There's a music yet unheard
By the creature of the word,
Though it matters little more
Than a wave-wash on a shore
Till a Demon shuts a door.

So, if he be very still
With his Demon, and one will,
Murmurs of it may be blown
To my friend who is alone
In a room that I have known.

After that from everywhere
Singing life will find him there;
Then the door will open wide,
And my friend, again outside,
Will be living, having died.

The Mill

The miller's wife had waited long,
The tea was cold, the fire was dead;
And there might yet be nothing wrong
In how he went and what he said:
"There are no millers any more,"
Was all that she had heard him say;
And he had lingered at the door
So long that it seemed yesterday.

Sick with a fear that had no form
She knew that she was there at last;
And in the mill there was a warm
And mealy fragrance of the past.
What else there was would only seem
To say again what he had meant;
And what was hanging from a beam
Would not have heeded where she went.

And if she thought it followed her,
She may have reasoned in the dark
That one way of the few there were

Would hide her and would leave no mark:
Black water, smooth above the weir
Like starry velvet in the night,
Though ruffled once, would soon appear
The same as ever to the sight.

Souvenir

A vanished house that for an hour I knew
By some forgotten chance when I was young
Had once a glimmering window overhung
With honeysuckle wet with evening dew.
Along the path tall dusky dahlias grew,
And shadowy hydrangeas reached and swung
Ferociously; and over me, among
The moths and mysteries, a blurred bat flew.
Somewhere within there were dim presences
Of days that hovered and of years gone by.
I waited, and between their silences
There was an evanescent faded noise;
And though a child, I knew it was the voice
Of one whose occupation was to die.

Why He Was There

Much as he left it when he went from us
Here was the room again where he had been
So long that something of him should be seen,
Or felt – and so it was. Incredulous,
I turned about, loath to be greeted thus,
And there he was in his old chair, serene
As ever, and as laconic and as lean
As when he lived, and as cadaverous.

Calm as he was of old when we were young,
He sat there gazing at the pallid flame
Before him. "And how far will this go on?"
I thought. He felt the failure of my tongue,
And smiled: "I was not here until you came;
And I shall not be here when you are gone."

Frank Norris (1870–1902)

When he was in his teens, Frank Norris spent over two years studying painting in Paris. Though his hopes to become a great painter were futile, Norris absorbed the French language and developed a passionate interest in medieval warfare and arms. His first publication, in fact, was an essay on medieval armor. By 1893, when "Lauth" was published, Norris had studied at the University of California and at Harvard, and was working for a San Francisco magazine, *The Wave*. In "Lauth" Norris recreates the medieval France which had absorbed his student imagination a few years before, and shows off his knowledge of period weapons. At the same time, Norris's descriptions of mob psychology and impersonal forces, and the comparison of humans and animals (note the dying horse) anticipate the themes of his great naturalistic novels, *McTeague* and *The Octopus*. A Gothic–naturalist hybrid (as was his early novel *Vandover and the Brute*), "Lauth" touches themes seen before in this collection: the uneasy role of the scientist; the borderlands between human and beast, spirit and flesh; and the horror of bodily decay.

Text: *The Complete Edition of Frank Norris*, vol. 10 (Garden City, NY: Doubleday, Doran & Co., 1928). The story was first published in the *Overland Monthly*, 21 (Sept. 1893).

Lauth

I

The barricade upon the Grand Pont was very silent. On either side of the bridge as in a street, stretched the houses and shops of the money changers, which gave the bridge the name of Pont-au-Change in a later day. They stood there empty and full of dormant echoes; their windows shivered, their doors crushed in, leaving in their place yawning openings like eyes and mouths agape with wonder. Around the piles, which buttressed up their rearward projections, the yellow Seine licked incessantly, with a quickly stilled gurgle at long intervals.

The barricade was drawn across the bridge some eight feet back from the keystone; directly in front of it, at the extremity of the bridge, squatted like a great toad the massive stunted structure of the Grand Châtelet. Its grate was down, its huge steel clamped gates were closed; it barred all advance into the Rue St. Dennis beyond. There held the enemy, to wit, the Prevôt-des-Marchands, with the archers of the guard and eight hundred of the King's gens d'armes. The two redoubts seemed to watch one another. Over the pavement, between the barricade and the Châtelet, all the fighting of the early morning had been done. It was now three o'clock in the afternoon. The vicinity was very still; the street was empty, for by mutual agreement each party had removed its dead of the night before, and no one had been killed in the sortie of the morning.

Lying upon the stones of the street midway between the barricade and the fortress was a red hat; somewhat nearer to the Châtelet lay a heavy white horse, his saddle turned under him, and his bridle in a tangle. A bolt[1] had broken his back, and he was unable to rise, yet he kept lashing out with his hind legs with the monotonous regularity of a machine. His hoofs struck out sparks in the cobbles. He lay with his neck and head bent up against the side of a house, and when from time to time he snorted and threw himself about in violent struggle to get upon his feet, his head pounded against the woodwork; as often as he did this, fragments of glass in the broken windows just over him, loosened by the jar, detached themselves from the lead frames and rattled upon the bare floor within.

The whole neighbourhood was colourless. The sky, the street, the houses, the Châtelet, the river – all were variations of a dull, lifeless brown. The red hat upon the bridge was the only spot of colour that relieved the gray tones of the whole scene. The intermittent struggles of the white horse were the only sounds that broke the silence.

About four o'clock there was a stir. The insurgent leaders in the barricade went to and fro, marshalling their followers, giving them final instructions. The mob had several scaling ladders taken from the Little Châtelet, and picked men were told off for the manoeuvring of each. The rioters had no order, no system of discipline; they relied for success upon the suddenness of their attacks and their superior numbers. The excitement began to grow and spread like an infection. At first a low, hoarse murmur, it swelled by quick degrees to that peculiar and never-to-be-forgotten roar, the roar of an angry mob, than which nothing is more terrible and awe-inspiring in the whole gamut of human sounds. The crowd of men behind the barricade began to surge and fluctuate like seething water. When it would reach a certain pitch of determination it would boil over the wall and roll like a billow toward the towers of the Grand Châtelet.

Meanwhile, fighting had broken out upon the Pont-des-Juifs, a little lower down the river; the absence of houses upon this bridge permitted a full view of the struggle from the Grand Pont. They could see a confused brown mass of combatants swarming around a few central points, and the noises of shouts and weapons reached their ears.

No command was given, but on a sudden, moved by some mysterious impulse, the insurgent tide reached its flood, poured out of and over the barricade, and halted, roaring and confused, before a solid, ranked, and orderly body of gens d'armes, which had been, as it were, vomited forth from the suddenly opened throat of the Châtelet. The two bodies, surging, bellowing, gesticulating, stood opposed. There was a moment of confusion and hesitation; some were struggling forward, some pushing back; each party could see the whites of their enemies' eyes. Then someone from among the rioters, but with a movement so quick that Lauth could not see who it was, sprang forward, and as though into a body of water dove, head low and arms up, right into the throng of the soldiers.

In the twinkling of an eye Lauth found himself enveloped in a solid jam of men, wedged in together with a suffocating pressure; so closely packed that the drawing of a weapon or the striking of a blow was out of the question. Each man was pushing with all his might against the one immediately in front of him as though by sheer force

Notes

LAUTH
[1] A heavy dart or arrow, fired by a crossbow or the similar arbalist.

to thrust their enemies backward, and the whole body compressed into the narrow street moving forward like some single great ramming engine in its groove. Oh, the horror of falling now beneath those thousand trampling feet! Lauth could not stop, could not breathe, could not see. Of what was going on in the first ranks he was ignorant; yet, as long as he was moving forward he knew that it was well with his friends. Slowly the advance movement continued; suddenly it stopped; the pressure became appalling; red spots danced and quivered before his eyes. Then he felt a backward impulse, and in spite of himself and his fellows, they were forced back. A tremendous roar burst from the opposing side; but suddenly the pressure was loosened, and like a relaxed spring, the body of the insurgents again leaped forward and again came to a fearful deadlock. This last continued for some little time, and it was then at length that the real fighting began. Craning his neck upward, Lauth could see the flash and play of weapons above the heads of the crowd in the front ranks, like the going and coming of whitecaps on the surface of an angry ocean. At every moment now the pressure from the front was tightened or relaxed; at every moment the insurgent mob, by short oscillations, swayed forward or back.

One of these movements brought Lauth near to an open doorway; he wrested himself away from the press, and stood in the free space of the door to regain breath. As he was standing there several others hurried past him into the house. They carried arbalists, bows, and slings. One of them had a hand culverin. Grasping his own weapon, an arbalist, he followed them, up the stairs, through the upper rooms, and finally out among the chimney pots upon the leads. The others had remained in the house below, shooting from the upper windows.

He bent his weapon, fitted a bolt to the leathern cord, and sliding down to the edge of the roof, peered over in the street below. Yet he hesitated to shoot. He was not a soldier, either by profession or inclination; he had never taken life before, and he was unwilling to do so now. He laid his arbalist aside and contented himself with watching the progress of the fight below.

Yet soon he saw that it was faring ill with his companions. The gens d'armes, forming a solid and compact front, were now forcing them backward with ever-increasing rapidity. Twice they had rallied in vain; another rush, and the soldiers would have driven them in. He lost control of his more humane instincts and discharged his arbalist at random into the crowd of his enemies below. The course of the bolt was not so rapid but that he could follow it with his eyes, and he saw it whiz through the air to bury itself deep in the neck of a stoutly built man who fought without a helmet. The man threw up his arms and fell sideward.

In an instant a mighty flame of blood lust thrilled up through all Lauth's body and mind. At the sight of blood shed by his own hands all the animal savagery latent in every human being woke within him – no more merciful scruples now. *He could kill.* In the twinkling of an eye the pale, highly cultivated scholar, whose life had been passed in the study of science and abstruse questions of philosophy, sank back to the level of his savage Celtic ancestors. His eyes glittered, he moistened his lips with the tip of his tongue, and his whole frame quivered with the eagerness and craving of a panther in sight of his prey. He could not stretch his arbalist quickly enough again, and his fingers shook as he laid the bolt in the groove.

He took deliberate aim and pulled the trigger, but his hands so trembled with excitement that his bolt went wide of the mark. A second sped with like result. His heart sank with disappointment, and he drew back upon the leads and composed himself for a moment. He must get some more of them. Oh, for an unerring aim now! With three more he thought he would be contented – or only two – even one – ay, he must get one more. Years ago he had stalked deer in the forests of Picardie, but stalking deer was nothing to compare with this.

Once more lying flat upon the roof he crawled to the edge and looked over; now there, just where the enemy were pressed the closest, in the centre of the bridge, even a random shot could not fail to reach something there. The crosse of the arbalist recoiled against his shoulder. *"Atteinte!"* he shouted, leaping to his feet with a thrill of joy, such as he had never known before, *"atteinte, à vous, canaille de bourgeoisie!"*[2] and he shook his fist at the throng below. He had struck down the *porte-reeve* of the St. Jacques gate.

His next missile, glancing up harmlessly from the oval *timbre* of a *bicoque,*[3] drove him to an almost insane fury. He gnashed his teeth, spat upon them, hurled at them insults in the vilest language of the *Cour des Miracles*, and then, as his next bolt spun through the brain of a furrier's apprentice in a yellow gabardine, grew white and stood silent, quivering for very joy.

He became like one intoxicated. The smell of blood and dust and sweat from the raging hell below rose to his nostrils like an unholy incense and made him mad-drunk. When his last bolt was gone he threw his arbalist at them, and then his sword, as if it had been a javelin. The thirst of a drunkard was upon him. Just one more, only *one*, and it would suffice. With hands and nails he tore at the tiles that covered the roof, and at the stones of a chimney that stood behind him. He heaped up the entire mass of débris at the verge of the roof, then, bracing his shoulder against it, sent it toppling over. It careened outward, describing an ever-widening curve; a few stones upon the top detached themselves from the main body, then with a sudden rush it reached the earth with a crash and a thick cloud of dust.

There was nothing more that could serve him as projectile, and for want of such Lauth's madness – it had amounted to that – began to abate. Panting, he closed his eyes and passed his hand over his face, then – for the crisis passing left him exhausted – withdrew to the centre of the roof and sat down.

When he again looked over into the street, he saw it deserted. Both parties had withdrawn to their strongholds. It was dusk. The rioting for the day was over. The white horse yet lay upon the pavement, a formless gray mass in the obscurity, but still, at last. Upward of forty bodies were scattered helter-skelter upon the bridge, a few of them moving. The long, slitlike windows of the Châtelet began to shine, while a ruddy vibrating glow behind the barricade announced the usual evening camp fire of the mob. It had begun to grow still again, and with every minute the liquid rustling of the Seine seemed to grow louder and more distinct.

Lauth now found himself in a situation of no little difficulty and danger. The house that he had occupied throughout the afternoon was situated about midway between the Châtelet and the barricade, in such a manner that in order to reach his friends he would have to cross the bridge within sight and bow shot of his enemies. His first thought was to wait until dark before making the attempt, but he recollected that the moon was at her full at this time of the month, and that her light would be far more brilliant than the half gloom of the present twilight. He did not know what had become of the archers who had entered with him. He only knew that he was alone in the house now, and that it was full of shadows and echoes.

Notes

[2] French: "Take that, you bourgeois thugs!"
[3] The crest of a *bicoque*, a style of helmet that fully encloses the head. Norris displays his knowledge of antique armor, which he had spent hours sketching as an art student in Paris.

He descended to the ground floor. A haze of silver over the *Tour de Nesle* warned him to be quick. He went to the back of the house and looked over upon the Seine beneath, and then up and down the line of the rear parts of the houses stretching toward the banks. No, there was no passage there, and no boat at the foot of the water stairs that led down from several of them, for many had been taken to help build the barricade, those that had not been thus employed being cut adrift to prevent the crossing of the men-at-arms.

He returned through the house and peered out into the street through the half open door in front. Unfortunately for him, he saw that the house stood upon the right hand side of the bridge, the entrance of the barricade upon the left, and that therefore he would have to traverse the full diagonal width of the bridge to gain it; right out into the open, with no shadow to hide him. Although he knew that no one at the Châtelet would be prepared for his dash across, and was sure that a running mark such as his figure would present would be unusually hard of attaint, yet he felt horribly afraid of being hit. He kept saying to himself, half-aloud, "There is no other course; it must be done," as though by a verbal repetition of the fact he could bring himself to face it with greater courage.

However, the moon had risen.

From where he stood, he could see the shadow from a sharp gable thrown across the street. He said to himself, "When that shadow has passed over ten of the paving stones, then I will run across." But first he recollected his prayers. He went back into the house, knelt, and repeated two *paters* and an *ave*, and commended himself to Athanasius, his patron saint, vowing twelve red candles to his altar and ten *sols parisis* to the Hôtel Dieu in case of his deliverance. When he returned to the door the shadow had traversed seven out of the ten squares of paving stones. That would not do. When the shadow had covered ten more, then surely he would start. But when the tenth was reached, and looking out he saw the sentries of the Châtelet turning in the moonlight, his heart failed him. Then he grew angry with himself, again made resolve, and sat down to count squares.

One, two, five, seven, eight, and he rose to his feet prepared for the dash; nine, ten, and drawing back into the house to gain greater impetus he darted out toward the gate of the barricade.

Halfway across the bridge he trod with one foot upon the scabbard of a sword lying there, and caught his other in the belt to which it was attached. A bolt from an arbalist hit him in the side as he rose to his feet. "It is not a bad hit – it's not a bad hit," he muttered between his teeth as he ran on, though he knew it was. An arrow sang past his face, another bolt struck out a long train of sparks at his feet; he could hear other shots striking into the houses upon his right. Fearing to be hit again he dodged into a doorway of one of them and ran into the back room. "It was an ambuscade," he said to himself, "and they were waiting for me to come out."

In spite of his efforts his knees bent under him and he sank upon the floor. "*Sang Dieu!*" he cried desperately. "It's not to the death, I am not hurt to the death. This is no mortal wound. Mortal!" He laughed aloud incredulously as though to deceive himself. "Why, if it were mortal there would be more pain – a mere flesh wound. The hauberk broke most of the force. There is scarcely any blood. Mortal! Why, I *know* I am able to rise.

He did so, and felt a great grateful wave of genuine hope, and heaved a sigh of relief. "But I thought for a moment it was to the death," he said. "Why, I am all right," he continued, "of course I'm all right."

He took a step forward, another, and then it seemed as if a red-hot knife were suddenly driven through his entrails. What was that so warm in his mouth? Blood! A great weakness came over him; he felt as though a thousand unseen hands were dragging him to the floor. But he ground his teeth and stood upright. "It will pass soon," he muttered. "I am not going to die this time. That little scratch is not to kill me." He would not let his mind rest upon the possibility of death. He kept saying, "I'm all right; I am not to die yet." Only when men were hit to the death did they fall, and he would not let himself fall, for he was going to live. If he could stand, that would be proof of it. Another thought that gave him courage was that he was perfectly conscious. When men were to die they lost control of their faculties. He still possessed all of his.

To test them and to take his mind from his wound, he looked about the room in which he found himself, now lighted by the moon. It had been pillaged, like the rooms of all the houses; a broken gridiron, a bottle, and an odd shoe, lay on the bare floor. The wall was painted green, and here and there in lead frames, hung all askew, were gaudy little pictures of St. Julian, St. Chrysostom, and an allegorical figure representing Traffic.[4] The names of these were painted upon the hems of their garments. "*Je mi appele St. Julianus*" "*Je mi appele St. Chrysostom*," etc., and each had a cloud-shaped inscription coming out of its mouth.

It suddenly occurred to him to examine and dress his wound. Even if it were not unusually serious he ought to do this. He unfastened his belt and turned back the clothing from the spot; there was very little blood. Some three inches above the hip he saw a hole about as big as a sou piece, but blue about the edges. He tried to bandage it, but succeeded only partially. "Bah! it did not need it; it was but a scratch." He even thought he could feel the iron bolt scarcely half an inch beneath the skin. It should be probed out to-morrow, he thought. It was nothing; he was not to die yet; a few miserable ounces of metal could not kill him. He grew impatient with himself for thinking about his wound. *Sang Dieu!* Was there any reason why he should so foolishly keep telling himself that he was not to die? He would think no more about it, but would go to the front of the house and for a second time try to regain the barricade. He turned about and fell flat upon his face with a great noise. He had been standing almost motionless in the centre of the room, and his first movement had destroyed his balance.

Then, as he lay with his face upon the floor, there came to him for the first time, like a great flash of light, the absolute certainty that he was to die; there, in that room, perhaps in a minute, perhaps in an hour. For a moment only he realized this, and an instant afterward was despairingly struggling against it as before. "The wound might be very dangerous, certainly, but not necessarily mortal; no, not that, surely." He swiftly recalled to mind all the cases he had heard of men recovering from worse wounds than this; and just as he had hoodwinked himself into a delusive hope, he began to be conscious of a horrible thirst. This in a moment reawakened all the apprehensions that he had so desperately tried to allay. He had always heard it said and always believed that this thirst was the inevitable fore-runner of death upon the battlefield.

For some time past he had felt, though he strove to think that he had not, an ever-growing sense of suffering all about the lower part of his side and back. All at once this increased – it was impossible to conceal it longer from himself. It became worse, and he could feel his blood throb and pulse all through his body. Every breath was an agony. The pain increased, he ground his teeth, and in spite of himself a groan escaped him; and even yet he kept saying again and again betwixt his clenched jaws: "It will pass; I am all right; I am not to die yet." His suffering grew more and more horrible.

Notes

[4] Trade or commerce.

He beat his hands upon the floor, panted, and rolled his head. He shifted his body about, as though a different position might bring him relief. Fiercer and fiercer grew the torture; he howled and bit his fingers. He began to wonder how it was possible that one could endure such suffering and *yet live*, and to think that as a relief from them death might not be undesirable. But the instant that this alternative presented itself to his mind he strove to banish it. *"No, no,"* he cried, through all the red whirl of torment, "I am not to die, I *will* not die. Life at any cost! Life, even though maimed and crippled! Life, even though it were passed in rayless dungeons."

Then, as suddenly as it had come on, the paroxysm left him. Oh, the blessedness of that moment when the pain was gone! He drew long sighs of pure delight. He was better now, he was not going to die after all. The crisis had been passed. "I am all right now," he said. Life had never seemed sweeter than now. He must not, no, he must not die. He had a notion that by *thinking* hard enough he could keep himself alive. Again and again he prayed for life, not in the formal orisons of the Church, but with fierce, passionate outbursts, and with the words of a child beseeching a parent.

By and by there began to steal over him a strange chilling and indefinable sensation, which, he knew not why, struck him with awe. What was this? What was going to happen? Why was he suddenly so afraid? Was it the pain coming on again? Was he about to faint? Was it – was it the approach of death?

Yes, death at last. It was all over now; he could no longer deceive himself. He knew now that he was going to die; fool that he had been ever to have thought otherwise. For a moment he looked calmly at his approaching end; then suddenly became filled with confusion, terror, and despair, and the most violent agitation. A thousand rapidly succeeding impressions began to rush across his brain, impressions as transient and momentary as words and fragments of sentences caught here and there in a book whose leaves are rapidly turned. He could not think connectedly. He wondered how the end would feel: would his breath cease and would he die of suffocation? Would the spasm of pain come on again? They would find his body all cold in this room some day, perhaps gnawed with rats. "This is death," he said aloud. "I am going to meet death. Oh, I don't want to die, I don't want to die."

He remembered having heard and read how men died in battle. Some of them had made long and beautiful speeches welcoming death, recommending their souls to heaven, and addressing last words to their friends. He could do nothing of this. Conflicting ideas and emotions hustled together in his brain like frightened rats in a trap. He had heard, too, how soldiers with their last breath defied their enemies and cheered their friends; he only felt a fierce hatred for them all. They and their miserable quarrel had been the cause of his death, and, involved in their petty strife, they cared nothing for his life, which was ebbing away. This brought him back to his present situation again. Once more he repeated, "This is death; this is death. I am dying." He looked at the wound that had caused it; touched it with his fingers. There was a hole in the hauberk where the bolt had entered. He remembered where and under just what circumstances he had first put the hauberk on; in the public room of the Hostel des Quatre filz d'Aymon in the Rue St. Honoré, opposite the Quinze-Vingts, and nearly fifty scholars had been there, and arms, offensive and defensive, were being distributed by the committee. D'Orsay had handed him this hauberk, and he recollected just how he laughed, and the peculiar heavy and clinging texture of the steel shirt. He remembered the deaf-and-dumb girl who ran back and forth in the room with drinking cups and stout mugs. They had tested the hauberk, too, with a poniard.

It seemed a long time ago, many weeks, since he had attempted the fatal run across the bridge. What would his father and La Vingtrie say when they heard of his death?

A slight shiver shook his limbs. Was that death? No, not yet. What would the symptoms be like? He began to watch himself in order to detect their approach, feeling his own pulse with one hand to catch its first failing quiver. He was going to die without confession or absolution – he had not thought of that. How fierce had been the press in the fight of that afternoon! Where would they bury him, he wondered? Suppose he should fall into a comatose state and they should bury him alive? He wondered whether the white horse on the bridge was dead yet. Yes, he remembered seeing him still and stiff. He was going to die, too; he was no better then than the horse. With all his superior intelligence he could not avoid death. The horse was white, and like those of all white horses his mane and tail were tinged with yellow. The barricade had been very still. He remembered trivial things long past – a summer's day in the forest of Fontainebleau, a lecture in the École de Médecine, the branding of a Jew at the Croix Trahoir when it had rained. He thought that, when death approached, all the events of one's life passed before the mind's eye; it was not so with him now.

All the projects he had formed for the future were to come to nought. He was about to drop out of the race of life. "This is death." The great revolving cycle of life had flung him off its whirling circumference – out into the void. He was to die like the millions before him. He had to face it alone. And after? – Oh, the horrible blackness and vagueness of that region after death. He was to see for himself the solution of that tremendous mystery that for ages had baffled far greater intelligences than his. "This is death." Every person who had lived upon the earth had passed through this same experience, everyone who lived at that time was to undergo it likewise. "This is death." What time was it? He heard the river below him gurgling. Let us see, today was Wednesday – no, Thursday – that was it. Thursday, the fifteenth of August. That was to be the date of his death. It would read that way upon his gravestone – "Killed upon the Grand Pont on the fifteenth of August." Or would he have any gravestone? Perhaps they might throw his body into the river. When he had first entered the schools, Marcellot had said to him – what was it he had said to him? He wore a long black gown; everybody in the room wore long black gowns … Stop, stop – his mind was wandering. With a sudden effort he steadied himself.

A feeling as of cold, commencing at his feet, began to creep upward upon his body. "There, it's coming now," he said; and again he repeated, "This is death; I am dying now; this is what death is like." He found it hard to get his breath; suddenly it grew dark. "It's almost here," he said expectantly and aloud. He felt his heart begin to beat violently. "When it stops I shall be dead," he thought. How long it was to come! He felt so cold. It was very hard to think. His lower jaw dropped.

He was dead.

It was about half-past four o'clock.

II

How terrible death must have seemed before it had been given a name! How fearfully it must have dawned upon the minds of our first fathers. Picture to yourself the awe and horror with which man must have looked upon the first corpse, and think how that mysterious negative state of body and mind must have overwhelmed him with fear and wonder. Life had been suddenly cut short; what was the matter with his friend that he could not speak, could not see, could not live? And this was to continue forever! Where was his friend now? What was this mysterious, dreadful force that had brought him to this state?

Some such thoughts as these incessantly filled the mind of Jacquemart de Chavannes, Doctor of Medicine and lecturer on chemistry at the École de Boissy, as he watched at the bier of Lauth two nights after the riot upon the Grand Pont. His prolonged reflections upon death in course of time naturally suggested the opposite state of being. "Yes, there was one thing more mysterious than death. That was life. Life, oh, *what* was it?" Did he, Chavannes, or anybody *know* what it was? After all, the greatest wonder in life was life itself. "We know *that* it is," he said, half aloud, "not *what*." And it is everywhere. From the mightiest limbed oaken giant to the tiniest blade of grass; from the stag of ten[5] to the red ant, is this marvellous force that we call "life," this unknown motor that animates inanimate bodies, teeming and fulfilling that end to which it was destined since the beginning of time. Life, life, everywhere life, and we who enjoy it in its highest development can never understand it. What is it? What is its nature? In what way and through what means does it animate our bodies? It is a force, too, completely under our control; formulate in the mind the desire to stretch forth the arm, and straightway it is done.

And when we are dead, he continued, what becomes of this life, this force? Science will tell you that, like matter, force is inexhaustible; where then does it go after quitting its earthly tenement? Is it one of the demonstrations of a soul? Is it the soul itself? "And God breathed into his nostrils the breath of *life*, and man became a *living soul*." Is it then a form of the Deity that enters into our composition, yet obedient to our will? And does it, after death, return again to God, and reabsorbed into the great Giver of all life, thus attain to a second and immortal existence, upon which the shadow of death never falls?

By and by, in the smaller watches of the night, he found himself looking at the question from another point of view. All forms of life were but the same; the vivifying spark that had once fired the body of Lauth was, *in nature*, no way different from that which flashed in the eye of a spirited horse, which gleamed in all the lower forms of animal life, which smouldered in the trees and vines, and slumbered, sluggish and all but extinguished, in the mollusk and the sponge. Man did but possess life in its highest development. Soul? There was no soul. What mankind called soul was but life. There was no more hope for man than for the horse, the trees, or the fish. The life each enjoyed was the common life of all; each but possessed it in greater fullness than his fellow next lower to him in the scale of creation.

There was no soul but life. Immortality was a myth.

Such was, and long had been, his creed; but now, in the solitude of the night, as he sat there in the presence of the dead, old doubts, old perplexities, old uncertainties, sprang up to vex and to harass him. What went with life after death? *It must go some-where*, for life was a force, and force was inexhaustible. And yet he could not believe in immortality. His whole nature, training, and mode of thought, revolted from such an idea. Yet in the case of sudden death like that of Lauth, where had gone that life that but a few days ago had so gloriously and perfectly filled his body and mind? Something more than a span below the breast was a little hole, blue around the edges, and scarce larger than a finger tip. There was no blood, no ghastly display of torn and mangled flesh; and yet this ounce of metal in this tiny puncture had blotted out his friend from existence among men; had in an instant annihilated and rendered naught an intellect, the highest and last development of creation, which countless prehistoric ages had been building up; and of a being who loved, hoped, remembered, and thought, had made a mass of perishable matter, a dead and lifeless weight, which a few hours would turn to putrefaction. What was it that had gone forth from that small circular opening

Notes

5 A stag with antlers having ten points.

and had left him thus! *Something* must have gone forth. That something must be either the *soul* or *life*.

But the theory of the soul he at once rejected. "It is, it must be life, and life alone," he said aloud. Yet life was an inexhaustible, immortal force, and he would not accept the doctrine of immortality. How was he to reconcile these two theories? Again and again he put this question to himself. If life and not the soul animated the body, if there was no hereafter, and if, indeed, death ended all, where, after death, went that eternal force called life?

At length he found himself driven to a last conclusion. Rising to his feet he said aloud: "If, then, life is eternal, and if it cannot exist after death, then *must it exist in death itself.*"

Life, then, even after apparent death, must exist in the body. Impossible! Yet, hold – was this impossible? The proof of such theory must be the resuscitation of a physical body after apparent death, and twice this had already been done. But God had accomplished this, no man. Yet was this conclusive proof that man could not do the same? If man could end life, why could he not begin it afresh?

As some lightless and limitless ocean the great *"Perhaps"* slowly unrolled itself before him. Might it not be so? Might not the dead be recalled to life? Might not the world be tending toward some such stupendous discovery that was to uproot and overthrow the whole fabric of society?

Once let a body be resuscitated after death, and the two theories of the soul and life would not be difficult of reconciliation. Here then would be the logical realization of those dreams of immortality to which men so obstinately clung, and an immortality to which, as adjustable to the laws of science and reason, Chavannes would cheerfully subscribe. Indeed, might not all those mysteries and conflicting prophecies of the scriptures regarding life after death be pointing directly toward this conclusion? The grandeur of the conception filled him with a certain terror, and before it he remained almost appalled as the Magus before the being himself has evoked.

By earliest morning he was immutably convinced that Lauth was not dead.

But if, then, life existed in death, with what awful responsibility were the living weighted! It remained for *them* to revive and rekindle the embers of existence before it was too late. How many millions of human beings at that moment lay crumbling in the earth for the want of that very knowledge upon the part of the living! But he saw clearly enough now what he must do.

He turned and looked upon the corpse of Lauth.

Yes, even if he failed, the trial must be made. The blast of duty never called louder than this.

He had uttered these thoughts aloud, and as he spoke the last words, the white dawn came growing upward over the towers of Notre Dame and stealing athwart the lozenges of the deep-set window, expanded throughout the room like an almost perceptible presence.

"It is an omen," he said.

III

"But, in spite of that," said Anselm, "I must condemn the whole thing as altogether repulsive and wicked. Still, though I do not believe in your success, I nevertheless confess to no little curiosity to witness the attempt. Yes, I will help you – but, remember, even if you should succeed in – whatever happens, I shall regard it from a purely scientific, not from a religious standpoint. To me it is an experiment in physiology, not in psychology. I believe the soul, and only the soul, is the motor of existence."

"No," answered Chavannes, "it is life. I do not claim," he went on, "any mysterious or wonderful qualities for the draught I propose to administer. It is merely a compound of natural stimulants, so combined as to produce the strongest possible effect. It is not an elixir in any sense of the word; for, understand me, I do not propose to create but to recall life. You know yourself that when your patient has fainted or momentarily lost consciousness certain drugs will revive and reinvigorate him. I consider death as only a certain more pronounced form of unconsciousness. We may fail in this experiment, Anselm, or if we succeed, our success may be only partial. Our means are limited. Medical science is in its earliest infancy. But that we shall recall some kind of life to this seemingly inert body I am firmly persuaded. But even if restored in all its fullness, who can say what manner of life it shall be? Will the new remember the old? Does the moth remember the chrysalis? Will the new creature retain its former personality? Will it look, think, and act, like the old? Or will he return to us out of this terrible ordeal a perfectly new being, having an entirely different nature, character, and personality? Who shall say?"

Anselm shaded his eyes with his hand and was silent. After a moment Chavannes continued:

"I know that I have grasped this great truth but imperfectly. We are here in this world, Anselm, as in a deep and rayless cavern, full of crossing passages. I do not know – who can tell why? – but some mysterious impulse drives us to seek the paths that lead upward. We can but grope. All is dark and obscure, but we feel the ground rise or fall beneath our feet, and we know whether we are holding toward the right or wrong. The passages may be circuitous, difficult, and at times apparently tending directly away from that direction that we can but feebly guess to be the right; but only our path be tending upward, and leave the rest to that mysterious Being who first implanted in our hearts the desire to seek it. Anselm, I am on such a path now; I feel the ground rising under my feet as I advance; I cannot see the end. The blackness moves before me as I go and closes fast about my footsteps behind. Everything is dark and vague and very terrible; but go on, go on always, for, thank God, the path is leading upward."

Anselm rose and thoughtfully paced the floor for a few moments; then he came and stood before Chavannes: "Who shall say?" he repeated in a low voice. "All science is perhaps."

For several minutes neither of them spoke; then Anselm said suddenly, as though breaking into a train of perplexing thought:

"Ah, well – at what time do you expect your friends?"

"Very shortly. Talhouet holds a lecture at the École de Chartres until ten; Marcellot was to come with him. They will be here in a little while."

A large crate stood in the middle of the floor by the dissecting table. From it, while Chavannes spoke, there came the sound of a slight movement, and a low, muffled, and very plaintive cry. Anselm crossed the floor and stood looking down thoughtfully between the willow bars and withes.

"Poor, gentle little creatures," he said. "What right have we to sacrifice your lives? The God that made us made you as well. If it is as you say, Chavannes," he continued without turning, "if all life is the same in its nature, men may do murder upon these innocent sufferers as well as upon each other."

"But, do you not see," answered Chavannes, "where in some cases the death of a man by his fellow is not only justifiable but even praiseworthy? What is the death of a man or sheep provided such a tremendous principle as that which we now have at stake is evolved and proved?"

"Then why not inject human blood into the veins, as they say they did to our eleventh Louis, instead of that drawn from these sheep?"

"Because it is not my object to refresh the body with new blood, but only to restore and assist the circulation of the old, held in check by death. The forced injection of any healthy blood whatever will drive his own to flow again. This once accomplished, and the vitality which I hold is still within the body will be sufficient to carry it on. Remember," he continued with emphasis, "I do not pretend to induce life of any kind by my own exertions. I merely arouse and assist those forces that are now held bound and inert. Have you ever seen the rescue and revival of a half-drowned man? Apparently he is dead. To all ends and purposes he is dead. He has ceased to breathe; the heart no longer beats; and yet if sufficient impulse be given to the wheels of life, they will finally carry on, of their own accord, those motions and functions of existence that at first were artificial. Such theory I propose to put into practice in this case."

"You may recall life of some kind – that is, you may induce the limbs to move by their own volition, the blood to flow, the lungs to inhale; but the brain, the soul, that which loves, which remembers ..."

"There is no soul; has a dog a soul? And yet is he not capable of a love that at times may well put man to shame? Has a bird a soul? Yet see how they remember the precise location of the last year's nest. But here are our friends."

Hour after hour through the lengthening watches of that night the lights burned low in Chavannes's lecture room. Around him and his three companions rose the tiers of empty benches, while on the dissecting table lay the body of Lauth, worked over and watched by them with the most intense interest. How long the operation might continue none of them could guess. It might last hours or days; they did not know.

From a small metal bottle which he kept tightly corked, and which at times he warmed between his hands, Chavannes administered to Lauth a pungent, thick, and colourless liquid. It was the draught of which he had spoken to Anselm. The two sheep, their feet tied together and a narrow strip of leather wound around their muzzles, were placed near at hand.

A large air pump was set at the head of Lauth, and his nostrils connected with it by a tube of light steel. Then, while Talhouet placed his palm firmly over the dead man's mouth, Chavannes grasped the handle of the air pump, depressed it, and sent a volume of air into the lifeless lungs. Talhouet removed his hand, and all bending over the body watched and listened. No returning exhalation came from between the lips, and the dead chest lay cold and inert. But on the third trial the entrance of the outer air perceptibly swelled the breast, and Marcellot, placing his hand thereon and pressing it slowly down, made the blue lips at first pout and then part, while through the tightly clenched teeth came a faint hissing of escaping air.

"Open his teeth," said Chavannes. Marcellot did so, but the shrunken maxillary snapped them together like a spring. Chavannes passed him the handle of a broken scalpel, and with this he wedged the teeth apart.

The operation was recommenced and continued as before; as soon as Chavannes had pumped enough air into the body, Marcellot aided the lungs to discharge it by pressing down the chest, as one would expel the air from a filled bellows.

When this had gone on for upward of an hour, Chavannes raised his head and said to Talhouet, "Now ... the sheep."

Talhouet drew them out from the crate, cut the thongs from their feet, allowed them to stand, and tethered them to the leg of the dissecting table.

Marcellot, who had been busy with his instrument case, approached Lauth, and with a delicate lancets opened the carotid artery, close up under the ear. The end of a thin tube was inserted in the opening, and the other end passed to Talhouet. In another incision, made under the right arm-pit, a second tube was inserted.

The critical point of the experiment had now arrived. The wool had been sheared away from the neck of one of the sheep, and as Anselm held fast the struggling, terrified creature, Marcellot laid open one of the larger veins in its throat.

"Quick," said Talhouet.

Marcellot caught the end of one of the tubes, thrust it well into the opened vein, and bound the outer flesh tightly around the tube itself.

The sheep bleated out piteously.

"Poor little brute!" said Anselm.

The other sheep was treated in the same fashion.

It was now well past midnight. They had nothing left to do but to wait, and each felt a creep almost of horror as he thought for what.

Marcellot cleansed his hands and, returning to the table, touched one of the tubes. It was already warm: the blood was flowing freely.

The hours dragged slowly past; two and three o'clock sounded from the neighbouring chimes of St. Germain. The four hardly spoke among themselves, and no sound was heard but the faint movements of the air pump, or an occasional half-stifled cry from one of the lambs. The neck and face of Lauth immediately about Marcellot's incision had long been warm, and at length the heat began to spread to the neck and shoulders.

Anselm took up Lauth's hand and scrutinized it; the nails were yet white, but on his holding the hand against the light, the delicate web of flesh between the roots of each finger could be seen faintly tinged with red. A strange and overwhelming excitement began to grow upon them all. Chavannes and Talhouet worked steadily at the pump, while Anselm and Marcellot, at the latter's suggestion, chafed the cold limbs with feverish energy. The body was now quite warm.

At half-past three, one of the sheep staggered and fell. The circumstance smote them with an apprehension so painful that it plainly showed to each how much his hopes and expectations had been bound up in the result of the experiment. Should both the sheep die ere circulation could be established, all their labour would be in vain.

"Work!" exclaimed Chavannes; but hardly had he spoken when he and his two companions were startled by a sharp cry from Marcellot. His hand had been over the left breast of the body; he drew it quickly away. Each in his turn put his hand over the spot, and each distinctly felt the breast beneath it throb with a great, though as yet an irregular movement.

Trembling and with eyes ablaze, they watched the change coming on. At a sign from Chavannes, Marcellot ceased to press down Lauth's chest after each artificial inhalation, and it was seen that the lungs, by their own elasticity, were now sufficient to relapse and exhale the air.

But the sheep that had fallen was soon dead, and the second now began to totter. A cessation of even the forced circulation would at this crisis prove fatal. But, forgetful of all consequences in his excitement, Chavannes sprang up, gave up the charge of the air-pump to Anselm, and opening a vein in his forearm thrust in the end of the tube which he had torn from the dead sheep's neck.

The hour that then ensued was one of the most intense excitement to them all. Again and again Chavannes's powerful drug was administered in ever-increasing quantities. Brandy, wine, and other stimulants, were forced down Lauth's throat, and strychnine injected into the blood now flowing freely.

Little by little the change, at first indefinable and of the greatest delicacy, became distinctly apparent. Though there was no movement of the limbs the body did not *look* dead. At length Talhouet and Anselm withdrew the tube and the air-pump attached to it from the nostrils. Straightway the breast shook with a great gasp, respiration ceased entirely, and then feebly recommenced. So absorbed were his three companions that it was not until Chavannes tottered against Marcellot that they remarked his weakness and pallor. Anselm supported him to a chair, and as he did so the second sheep pitched dead to the floor, dragging the tube out from the neck of the body.

All connections with the outer world were now severed; nothing more could be done. The impetus had been given. It remained to be seen if Nature could carry it forward. The group collected about Chavannes's chair, and waited with eyes fixed on the table. Day had dawned for already two hours, although in their closely shuttered chamber they made no thought of it, when they saw the body slowly turn upon its side and then roll over, face downward, upon the table.

Chavannes cried out in a loud voice: *"Vivit!"*[6]

Anselm sprang to his feet with a terrible cry: "Horrible, horrible!" he shrieked, and rushed from the room.

IV

Lauth was alive, and though for many weeks he rolled and yelled and gibbered upon his bed in the grip of a disease for which the combined science of the four doctors could find no name, yet Chavannes was satisfied.

"I was right," he said to Anselm. "Are you convinced now that your so-called soul has no part in the animation of physical being? Life, and life only, is the stay and promoter of existence."

And Anselm bowed his head and seemed to grow older. The success of Chavannes's experiment had produced a terrible effect upon him. All his ideas and beliefs that he had inherited in common with the world from thousands of past ages, and that were so firmly rooted in his conceptions as to have become a part and parcel of him, had been ruthlessly and suddenly torn up and cast to the winds. Everything had been a mistake, then – civilization, beliefs, society, religion, heaven, and Christ Himself – all were myths or founded upon falsity. Where could he turn for anything certain? Where was there anything true? What could he now believe? He was mentally lost, as one in a whirlwind – landmarks all down, lights obliterated – all was chaos and confusion. Everything was to be commenced over again upon a new basis. Of Lauth, in his present condition, he had a horror that at times sent his mind spinning toward the very verge of insanity.

When the terrible spasms at length departed from Lauth's body, and when his strength came back, he was allowed to get up and walk about; when given nourishment, he ate and drank; when led by Chavannes to his great chair in the window, he sat for entire days motionless, just as he had been placed, and when spoken to he answered, but after long intervals, and inarticulately, disjointedly, often relapsing into silence in the midst of his speech – if his guttural noises could be called speech.

Thus he remained for a long time, and it was not until after many weeks of the most careful treatment that his condition seemed to change for the better. At length, however, he appeared to grow more rational, and Chavannes imagined he could even detect characteristics of the old Lauth beginning to show themselves in his resuscitated body; but often this was mere fancy. Thus far the only features apparent were that he ate, slept, and knew when he was spoken to. As yet his existence was purely negative. Chavannes and his companions watched eagerly for some positive

Notes
[6] Latin: "He lives!"

manifestations of character, and Chavannes himself especially laboured to induce each. He talked long to Lauth of pursuits and occupations that had interested him before his death, placed in his way old books and familiar objects, and read to him from his favourite studies. Whether Lauth heard and comprehended, he could not tell.

Anselm and his two fellow doctors seldom left Chavannes's house, and the minutest watch was kept over Lauth and his every movement. At length one day the bonds seemed to be loosed. Lauth began to speak. He addressed them severally and coherently, although it was impossible to say whether or not he distinguished between them. His talk was upon topics that they knew had been near to him in his first life. The speech, the intonation, the gesture, all were those of the old Lauth. Chavannes was exultant. He began to look forward not only to a complete restoration of the former Lauth, but even to talk of giving the great discovery to the world. Entire days now often passed upon which, had they occurred before the time of the riot, they would have noticed nothing strange in Lauth's looks or demeanour.

Then after this there came a peculiar relapse, a strange and unaccountable change. Lauth talked less, and an expression of daily deepening perplexity overcast his face. He seemed as one lost in mind and grasping for some hidden clue. The look of anxiety in his eyes was sometimes all but agonized, and often he clasped his head with both hands, as though to steady some mental process.

Until at last, upon one memorable day, when he had been sitting for upward of an hour lost in the mazes of the deepest thought, he leaped suddenly to his full height, and while a glance of almost supreme intelligence flashed, meteorlike, across his face, called out in a fearful voice:

"*This is not I; where am I? For God's sake, tell me where I am!*"

After which he fell in a fit upon the floor, foaming and wallowing.

And now commenced the opening stages of a process whose contemplation filled them with horror and loathing beyond all utterance. That cry, unearthly in tone as well as in significance, seemed to mark the highest point of Lauth's second life. Now he began to decline.

The fits passed off, but he relapsed into a dull, brutish torpor, out of which it was impossible to rouse him, and which was totally different and far more revolting than his original lethargy. The former seemed more intelligence held in abeyance, but the latter was the absence of any intelligence whatever.

The only break in the brutal numbness of mind and body into which he had sunk came in the shape of those positive manifestations for which Chavannes had so eagerly watched. But these were now no longer human.

One evening, as Chavannes brought him his accustomed meal and set it upon the night table at his bedside, Lauth of a sudden snarled out and snapped at his hand with thorough apish savagery; and then, as though terrified, threw himself back into the farthest bed corner grinding his teeth and trembling.

From this time on the process of decay became rapidly more apparent; what little lustre yet lurked in the eye went out, leaving it dull and fishlike; the expression of the face lost all semblance to humanity; the hair grew out long and coarse and fell matted over the eyes. The nails became claws, the teeth fangs, and one morning upon entering the room assigned to Lauth, Chavannes and Anselm found him quite stripped grovelling on all fours in one corner of the room, making a low, monotonous growling sound, his teeth rattling and snapping together.

There it was, locked in that room to which they alone possessed the key, and about whose entrance they kept unceasing watch. At the least sound or movement from the inside they opened the door, and standing upon the threshold watched it as it ran back and forth on all fours, wagging its shaggy head from side to side, and venting unnatural mutterings. At a sudden movement on their part it would pause, sit back upon its heels, observe them long and unwinkingly, and then suddenly, and with the most surprising agility, scuttle back under the bed.

But the worst was yet to come. Little by little the thing became less active. Where once it had shown a ravenous appetite for food it now allowed it to stand for days untouched. It no longer seemed to feel heat or cold. At length all motion of its limbs ceased; the sense of hearing died out; in a few weeks it was utterly blind. Bodily sensations no longer affected it; a thin bodkin run through the fleshy part of the thumb by Chavannes produced no apparent sensation. One by one the senses perished. It was already blind and deaf; now its vocal organs seemed to wither, and the unbroken silence of the shaggy yellow lips was even more revolting than its former inhuman noises.

But still it lived.

Either it could not die or else was dying slowly. In course of time all likeness to the human form disappeared from the body. By some unspeakable process the limbs, arms, and features slowly resolved themselves into one another. A horrible, shapeless mass lay upon the floor. And yet, until decomposition had set in, some kind of life was contained in it. It lived, but lived not as do the animals or the trees, but as the protozoa, the jellyfish, and those strange lowest forms of existence wherein the line between vegetable and animal cannot be drawn.

When this last, feeble spark of life died down and vanished they could not say, but at last one day the bulk upon the floor began to smell badly.

"It is over now," said Chavannes.

Decomposition had commenced; the thing was dead.

"And now what does it all mean?" said Anselm to Chavannes, about a week after the body – if such it could be called – was disposed of. "What does it all means? Hear me, Chavannes, this is what I think: I think now that both of us were in part wrong, in part right. You said and believed that life alone was the energy of existence, I, the soul; I think now that it is both. Life cannot exist without the soul any more than the soul, at least upon this earth, can exist without life. Body, soul, and life, three in one; this is a trinity.

"Chavannes, there is no such thing as *man* existing as a type by himself. No: that which we call man is half animal, half God, a being on one hand capable of rising to the sublimest heights of intellectual grandeur, equal almost to his Maker; on the other hand, sinking at times to the last level of ignominy and moral degradation. Take life away from this being and at once the soul mounts upward to the God that first gave it. Take from him his soul – that part of him that is God – and straightway he sinks down to the level of the lowest animal – we have just seen it. Chavannes, follow me for a moment. Lauth died; life and the soul departed together from the body; you found means to call back *life*; the soul you could not recall; mark what followed. For a time Lauth lived, but the soul being taken away, as though it had been a mainstay and a support, the whole body with the life it contained began successively to drop back to the lower forms of existence. At first, if you remember, Lauth existed merely as a dull and imbruted man; soon he fell to the stage of those unfortunates whose minds are impaired or wholly gone; he became an idiot. At the time when he so savagely bit and snarled at you he had reached the level of the ape; from that stage he fell to that of a lower animal, walking upon all fours, savage, untamable; thence he passed into those lowest known forms of life such as possessed by the sponge and the polyp, and thence to a second and final death.

"What that mystery in him was which drove him to cry out that day, 'This is not *I*!' is beyond our power to say.

"No, Chavannes, the *soul* of man is the chiefest energy of his existence; take that away and he is no longer a man. The presence and absence of the soul was just the difference between the old Lauth and the new. It is just the difference between man and brute; follow the scale of creation up from its lowest forms; the gradation is easy until you come to man. In the sponge and polyp we find the gradation between the vegetable and the animal; and the animal life, too, rises by scarcely perceptible degrees until it reaches man. There is no gradation here; there is no life half human, half animal. The most brutish man still is immeasurably higher than the most human brute. What is the difference? Chavannes, it is the Soul."

Stephen Crane (1871–1900)

In a brief, intensely lived, and unconventional life, Stephen Crane achieved fame as the author of *Maggie: A Girl of the Streets* (1893), and *The Red Badge of Courage* (1895). Though he is known as one of the definers of literary naturalism, the term seems a loose fit for his always-changing, experimental talent. He was a poet as well as a fiction writer. A poet's love of vivid and colorful imagery can be seen in the gorgeous and horrifying vision of the fire in "The Monster" (1898). The description of the liquid jewels that destroy Henry's face is surely among the most compelling passages in this collection.

The novella or long short story is set in the fictional Whilomville, New York, a place visited in several of Crane's works.

Like Mark Twain's various river towns (all versions of his native Hannibal), Whilomville may appear idyllic, but beneath the placid surface is an ugly stew of petty jealousy and human weakness. "The Monster" is a study in "othering" – in the way an individual becomes the focus of the fears and prejudice of the community. (It would be a useful exercise to list the number of prejudices that operate here.) Henry is turned into a monster not by liquid fire, not even by the doctor who gives him life in a reenactment of the Frankenstein story, but by his fellow citizens and former friends.

Text: Stephen Crane, *The Monster and Other Stories* (New York: Harper, 1899).

The Monster

I

Little Jim was, for the time, engine Number 36, and he was making the run between Syracuse and Rochester. He was fourteen minutes behind time, and the throttle was wide open. In consequence, when he swung around the curve at the flower bed, a wheel of his cart destroyed a peony. Number 36 slowed down at once and looked guiltily at his father, who was mowing the lawn. The doctor had his back to this accident, and continued to pace slowly to and fro, pushing the mower.

Jim dropped the tongue of the cart. He looked at his father and at the broken flower. Finally he went to the peony and tried to stand it on its pins, resuscitated, but the spine of it was hurt, and it would only hang limply from his hand. Jim could do no reparation. He looked again toward his father.

He went on to the lawn, very slowly, and kicking wretchedly at the turf. Presently his father came along with the whirring machine, while the sweet, new grass blades spun from the knives. In a low voice, Jim said, "Pa!"

The doctor was shaving this lawn as if it were a priest's chin. All during the season he had worked at it in the coolness and peace of the evening after supper. Even in the shadow of the cherry trees the grass was strong and healthy. Jim raised his voice a trifle. "Pa!"

The doctor paused, and with the howl of the machine no longer occupying the sense, one could hear the robins in the cherry trees arranging their affairs. Jim's hands were behind his back, and sometimes his fingers clasped and unclasped. Again he said, "Pa!" The child's fresh and rosy lip lowered.

The doctor stared down at his son, thrusting his head forward frowning attentively. "What is it, Jimmie?"

"Pa!" repeated the child at length. Then he raised his finger and pointed at the flower bed. "There!"

"What?" said the doctor, frowning more. "What is it, Jim?"

After a period of silence, during which the child may have undergone a severe mental tumult, he raised his finger and repeated his former word – "There!" The father had respected this silence with perfect courtesy. Afterward his glance carefully followed the direction indicated by the child's finger, but he could see nothing which explained to him. "I don't understand what you mean, Jimmie," he said.

It seemed that the importance of the whole thing had taken away the boy's vocabulary. He could only reiterate, "There!"

The doctor mused upon the situation, but he could make nothing of it. At last he said, "Come, show me."

Together they crossed the lawn toward the flower bed. At some yards from the broken peony Jimmie began to lag. "There!" The word came almost breathlessly.

"Where?" said the doctor.

Jimmie kicked at the grass. "There!" he replied.

The doctor was obliged to go forward alone. After some trouble he found the subject of the incident, the broken flower. Turning then, he saw the child lurking at the rear and scanning his countenance.

The father reflected. After a time he said, "Jimmie, come here." With an infinite modesty of demeanor the child came forward. "Jimmie, how did this happen?"

The child answered, "Now – I was playin' train – and – now – I runned over it."

"You were doing what?"

"I was playin' train."

The father reflected again. "Well, Jimmie," he said, slowly, "I guess you had better not play train any more today. Do you think you had better?"

"No, sir," said Jimmie.

During the delivery of the judgment the child had not faced his father, and afterwards he went away, with his head lowered, shuffling his feet.

II

It was apparent from Jimmie's manner that he felt some kind of desire to efface himself. He went down to the stable. Henry Johnson, the negro who cared for the doctor's horses, was sponging the buggy. He grinned fraternally when he saw Jimmie coming. These two were pals. In regard to almost everything in life they seemed to have minds precisely alike. Of course there were points of emphatic divergence. For instance, it was plain from Henry's talk that he was a very handsome negro, and he was known to be a light, a weight, and an eminence in the suburb of the town where lived the larger number of the negroes, and obviously this glory was over Jimmie's horizon; but he vaguely appreciated it and paid deference to Henry for it mainly because Henry appreciated it and deferred to himself. However, on all points of conduct as related to the doctor, who was the moon, they were in complete but unexpressed understanding. When Jimmie became the victim of an eclipse he went to the stable to solace himself with Henry's crimes. Henry, with the elasticity of his race, could usually provide a sin to place himself on a footing with the disgraced one. Perhaps he would remember that he had forgotten to put the hitching strap in the back of the buggy on some recent occasion, and had been reprimanded by the doctor. Then these two would commune subtly and without words concerning their moon, holding themselves sympathetically as people who had committed similar treasons. On the other hand, Henry would sometimes choose to absolutely repudiate this idea, and when Jimmie appeared in his shame would bully him most virtuously, preaching with assurance the precepts of the doctor's creed, and pointing out to Jimmie all his abominations. Jimmie did not discover that this was odious in his comrade. He accepted it and lived in its shadow with humility, merely trying to conciliate the saintly Henry with acts of deference. Won by this attitude, Henry would sometimes allow the child to enjoy the felicity of squeezing the sponge over a buggy wheel, even when Jimmie was still gory from unspeakable deeds.

Whenever Henry dwelt for a time in sackcloth, Jimmie did not patronize him at all. This was a justice of his age, his condition. He did not know. Besides, Henry could drive a horse, and Jimmie had a full sense of this sublimity. Henry personally conducted the moon during the splendid journeys through the country roads, where farms spread on all sides, sheep, cows, and other marvels abounding.

"Hello, Jim!" said Henry, poising his sponge. Water was dripping from the buggy. Sometimes the horses in the stalls stamped thunderingly on the pine floor. There was an atmosphere of hay and of harness.

For a minute Jimmie refused to take an interest in anything. He was very downcast. He could not even feel the wonders of wagon-washing. Henry, while at work, narrowly observed him.

"Your pop done wallop yer, didn't he?" he said at last.

"No," said Jimmie, defensively; "he didn't."

After this casual remark Henry continued his labor, with a scowl of occupation. Presently he said: "I done tol' yer many's th' time not to go a-foolin' an' a-projjeckin' with them flowers. Yer pop don' like it nohow." As a matter of fact, Henry had never mentioned flowers to the boy.

Jimmie preserved a gloomy silence, so Henry began to use seductive wiles in this affair of washing a wagon. It was not until he began to spin a wheel on the tree, and the sprinkling water flew everywhere, that the boy was visibly moved. He had been seated on the sill of the carriage-house door, but at the beginning of this ceremony he arose and circled toward the buggy, with an interest that slowly consumed the remembrance of a late disgrace.

Johnson could then display all the dignity of a man whose duty it was to protect Jimmie from a splashing. "Look out, boy! look out! You done gwi' spile yer pants. I rai-kon your mommer don't 'low this foolishness, she know it. I ain't gwi' have you round yere spilin' yer pants, an' have Mis' Trescott light on me pressen'ly. 'Deed I ain't."

He spoke with an air of great irritation, but he was not annoyed at all. This tone was merely a part of his importance. In reality he was always delighted to have the child there to witness the business of the stable. For one thing, Jimmie was invariably overcome with reverence when he was told how beautifully a harness was polished or a horse groomed. Henry explained each detail of this kind with unction, procuring great joy from the child's admiration.

III

After Johnson had taken his supper in the kitchen, he went to his loft in the carriage-house and dressed himself with much care. No belle of a court circle could bestow more mind on a toilet than did Johnson. On second thought, he was more like a priest arraying himself for some parade of the church. As he emerged from his room and sauntered down the carriage-drive, no one would have suspected him of ever having washed a buggy.

It was not altogether a matter of the lavender trousers, nor yet the straw hat with its bright silk band. The change was somewhere far in the interior of Henry. But there was no cakewalk hyperbole in it. He was simply a quiet, well-bred gentleman of position, wealth, and other necessary achievements out for an evening stroll, and he had never washed a wagon in his life.

In the morning, when in his working clothes, he had met a friend – "Hello, Pete!" "Hello, Henry!" Now, in his effulgence, he encountered this same friend. His bow was not at all haughty. If it expressed anything, it expressed consummate generosity – "Good-evenin', Misteh Washington." Pete, who was very dirty, being at work in a potato-patch, responded in a mixture of abasement and appreciation – "Good-evenin', Misteh Johnsing."

The shimmering blue of the electric arc lamps was strong in the main street of the town. At numerous points it was conquered by the orange glare of the outnumbering gaslights in the windows of shops. Through this radiant lane moved a crowd, which culminated in a throng before the post office, awaiting the distribution of the evening mails. Occasionally there came into it a shrill electric streetcar, the motor singing like a cageful of grasshoppers, and possessing a great gong that clanged forth both warnings and simple noise. At the little theater, which was a varnish and red-plush miniature of one of the famous New York theaters, a company of strollers was to play *East Lynne*.[1] The young men of the town were mainly gathered at the corners, in distinctive groups which expressed various shades and lines of chumship, and had little to do with any social gradations. There they discussed everything with critical insight, passing the whole town in review as it swarmed in the street. When the gongs of the electric cars ceased for a moment to harry the ears, there could be heard the sound of the feet of the leisurely crowd on the bluestone pavement, and it was like the peaceful evening lashing at the shore of a lake. At the foot of the hill, where two lines of maples sentineled the way, an electric lamp glowed high among the embowering branches and made most wonderful shadow-etchings on the road below it.

When Johnson appeared amid the throng a member of one of the profane groups at a corner instantly telegraphed news of this extraordinary arrival to his companions. They hailed him. "Hello, Henry! Going to walk for a cake tonight?"

"Ain't he smooth?"

"Why, you've got that cake right in your pocket, Henry!"

"Throw out your chest a little more."

Henry was not ruffled in any way by these quiet admonitions and compliments. In reply he laughed a supremely good-natured, chuckling laugh, which nevertheless expressed an underground complacency of superior metal.

Young Griscom, the lawyer, was just emerging from Reifsnyder's barber shop, rubbing his chin contentedly. On the steps he dropped his hand and looked with wide eyes into the crowd. Suddenly he bolted back into the shop. "Wow!" he cried to the parliament; "you ought to see the coon that's coming!"

Reifsnyder and his assistant instantly poised their razors high and turned toward the window. Two belathered heads reared from the chairs. The electric shine in the street caused an effect like water to them who looked through the glass from the yellow glamor of Reifsnyder's shop. In fact, the people without resembled the inhabitants of

Notes

THE MONSTER

[1] Popular dramatic version of a sentimental novel written by English writer Mrs. Henry Wood (1861).

a great aquarium that here had a square pane in it. Presently into this frame swam the graceful form of Henry Johnson.

"Chee!" said Reifsnyder. He and his assistant with one accord threw their obligations to the winds and, leaving their lathered victims helpless, advanced to the window. "Ain't he a taisy?" said Reifsnyder, marveling.

But the man in the first chair, with a grievance in his mind, had found a weapon. "Why, that's only Henry Johnson, you blamed idiots! Come on now, Reif, and shave me. What do you think I am – a mummy?"

Reifsnyder turned, in a great excitement. "I bait you any money that vas not Henry Johnson! Henry Johnson! Rats!" The scorn put into this last word made it an explosion. "That man vas a Pullman-car porter or some-ding. How could that be Henry Johnson?" he demanded, turbulently. "You vas crazy."

The man in the first chair faced the barber in a storm of indignation. "Didn't I give him those lavender trousers?" he roared.

And young Griscom, who had remained attentively at the window, said: "Yes, I guess that was Henry. It looked like him."

"Oh, vell," said Reifsnyder, returning to his business, "if you think so! Oh, vell!" He implied that he was submitting for the sake of amiability.

Finally the man in the second chair, mumbling from a mouth made timid by adjacent lather, said: "That was Henry Johnson all right. Why, he always dresses like that when he wants to make a front! He's the biggest dude in town – anybody knows that."

"Chinger!" said Reifsnyder.

Henry was not at all oblivious of the wake of wondering ejaculation that streamed out behind him. On other occasions he had reaped this same joy, and he always had an eye for the demonstration. With a face beaming with happiness he turned away from the scene of his victories into a narrow side street, where the electric light still hung high, but only to exhibit a row of tumble-down houses leaning together like paralytics.

The saffron Miss Bella Farragut, in a calico frock, had been crouched on the front stoop, gossiping at long range, but she espied her approaching caller at a distance. She dashed around the corner of the house, galloping like a horse. Henry saw it all, but he preserved the polite demeanor of a guest when a waiter spills claret down his cuff. In this awkward situation he was simply perfect.

The duty of receiving Mr. Johnson fell upon Mrs. Farragut, because Bella, in another room, was scrambling wildly into her best gown. The fat old woman met him with a great ivory smile, sweeping back with the door, and bowing low. "Walk in, Misteh Johnson, walk in. How is you dis ebenin', Misteh Johnson – how is you?"

Henry's face showed like a reflector as he bowed and bowed, bending almost from his head to his ankles. "Good-evenin', Mis' Fa'gut; good-evenin'. How is you dis evenin'? Is all you' folks well, Mis' Fa'gut?"

After a great deal of kowtow, they were planted in two chairs opposite each other in the living room. Here they exchanged the most tremendous civilities, until Miss Bella swept into the room, when there was more kowtow on all sides, and a smiling show of teeth that was like an illumination.

The cooking-stove was of course in this drawing room, and on the fire was some kind of a long-winded stew. Mrs. Farragut was obliged to arise and attend to it from time to time. Also young Sim came in and went to bed on his pallet in the comer. But to all these domesticities the three maintained an absolute dumbness. They bowed and smiled and ignored and imitated until a late hour, and if they had been the occupants of the most gorgeous salon in the world they could not have been more like three monkeys.

After Henry had gone, Bella, who encouraged herself in the appropriation of phrases, said, "Oh, ma, isn't he divine?"

IV

A Saturday evening was a sign always for a larger crowd to parade the thoroughfare. In summer the band played until ten o'clock in the little park. Most of the young men of the town affected to be superior to this band, even to despise it; but in the still and fragrant evenings they invariably turned out in force, because the girls were sure to attend this concert, strolling slowly over the grass, linked closely in pairs, or preferably in threes, in the curious public dependence upon one another which was their inheritance. There was no particular social aspect to this gathering, save that group regarded group with interest, but mainly in silence. Perhaps one girl would nudge another girl and suddenly say, "Look! there goes Gertie Hodgson and her sister!" And they would appear to regard this as an event of importance.

On a particular evening a rather large company of young men were gathered on the sidewalk that edged the park. They remained thus beyond the borders of the festivities because of their dignity, which would not exactly allow them to appear in anything which was so much fun for the younger lads. These latter were careering madly through the crowd, precipitating minor accidents from time to time, but usually fleeing like mist swept by the wind before retribution could lay hands upon them.

The band played a waltz which involved a gift of prominence to the bass horn, and one of the young men on the sidewalk said that the music reminded him of the new engines on the hill pumping water into the reservoir. A similarity of this kind was not inconceivable, but the young man did not say it because he disliked the band's playing. He said it because it was fashionable to say that manner of thing concerning the band. However, over in the stand, Billie Harris, who played the snare drum, was always surrounded by a throng of boys, who adored his every whack.

After the mails from New York and Rochester had been finally distributed, the crowd from the post office added to the mass already in the park. The wind waved the leaves of the maples, and, high in the air, the blue-burning globes of the arc lamps caused the wonderful traceries of leaf shadows on the ground. When the light fell upon the upturned face of a girl, it caused it to glow with a wonderful pallor. A policeman came suddenly from the darkness and chased a gang of obstreperous little boys. They hooted him from a distance. The leader of the band had some of the mannerisms of the great musicians, and during a period of silence the crowd smiled when they saw him raise his hand to his brow, stroke it sentimentally, and glance upward with a look of poetic anguish. In the shivering light, which gave to the park an effect like a great vaulted hall, the throng swarmed, with a gentle murmur of dresses switching the turf, and with a steady hum of voices.

Suddenly, without preliminary bars, there arose from afar the great hoarse roar of a factory whistle. It raised and swelled to a sinister note, and then it sang on the night wind one long call that held the crowd in the park immovable, speechless. The bandmaster had been about to vehemently let fall his hand to start the band on a thundering career through a popular march, but, smitten by this giant voice from the night, his hand dropped slowly to his knee, and, his mouth agape, he looked at his men in silence. The cry died away to a wail, and then to stillness. It released the muscles of the company of young men on the sidewalk, who had been like statues, posed eagerly, lithely, their ears turned. And then they wheeled upon each other simultaneously, and, in a single explosion, they shouted, "One!"

Again the sound swelled in the night and roared its long ominous cry, and as it died away the crowd of young men wheeled upon each other and, in chorus, yelled, "Two!"

There was a moment of breathless waiting. Then they bawled, "Second district!" In a flash the company of indolent and cynical young men had vanished like a snowball disrupted by dynamite.

V

Jake Rogers was the first man to reach the home of Tuscarora Hose Company Number Six. He had wrenched his key from his pocket as he tore down the street, and he jumped at the springlock like a demon. As the doors flew back before his hands he leaped and kicked the wedges from a pair of wheels, loosened a tongue from its clasp, and in the glare of the electric light which the town placed before each of its hose-houses the next comers beheld the spectacle of Jake Rogers bent like hickory in the manfulness of his pulling, and the heavy cart was moving slowly toward the doors. Four men joined him at the time, and as they swung with the cart out into the street, dark figures sped toward them from the ponderous shadows in back of the electric lamps. Some set up the inevitable question, "What district?"

"Second," was replied to them in a compact howl. Tuscarora Hose Company Number Six swept on a perilous wheel into Niagara Avenue, and as the men, attached to the cart by the rope which had been paid out from the windlass under the tongue, pulled madly in their fervor and abandon, the gong under the axle clanged incitingly. And sometimes the same cry was heard, "What district?"

"Second."

On a grade Johnnie Thorpe fell and, exercising a singular muscular ability, rolled out in time from the track of the oncoming wheel, and arose, disheveled and aggrieved, casting a look of mournful disenchantment upon the black crowd that poured after the machine. The cart seemed to be the apex of a dark wave that was whirling as if it had been a broken dam. Behind the lad were stretches of lawn, and in that direction front doors were banged by men who hoarsely shouted out into the clamorous avenue, "What district?"

At one of these houses a woman came to the door bearing a lamp, shielding her face from its rays with her hands. Across the cropped grass the avenue represented to her a kind of black torrent, upon which, nevertheless, fled numerous miraculous figures upon bicycles. She did not know that the towering light at the corner was continuing its nightly whine.

Suddenly a little boy somersaulted around the corner of the house as if he had been projected down a flight of stairs by a catapultian boot. He halted himself in front of the house by dint of a rather extraordinary evolution with his legs. "Oh, ma," he gasped, "can I go? Can I, ma?"

She straightened with the coldness of the exterior mother-judgment, although the hand that held the lamp trembled slightly. "No, Willie; you had better come to bed."

Instantly he began to buck and fume like a mustang. "Oh, ma," he cried, contorting himself – "oh, ma, can't I go? Please, ma, can't I go? Can't I go, ma?"

"It's half-past nine now, Willie."

He ended by wailing out a compromise: "Well, just down to the corner, ma? Just down to the corner?"

From the avenue came the sound of rushing men who wildly shouted. Somebody had grappled the bell-rope in the Methodist church, and now over the town rang this solemn and terrible voice, speaking from the clouds. Moved from its peaceful business, this bell gained a new spirit in the portentous night, and it swung the heart to and fro, up and down, with each peal of it.

"Just down to the corner, ma?"

"Willie, it's half-past nine now."

VI

The outlines of the house of Dr. Trescott had faded quietly into the evening, hiding a shape such as we call Queen Anne against the pall of the blackened sky. The neighborhood was at this time so quiet, and seemed so devoid of obstructions, that Hannigan's dog thought it a good opportunity to prowl in forbidden precincts, and so came and pawed Trescott's lawn, growling, and considering himself a formidable beast. Later, Peter Washington strolled past the house and whistled, but there was no dim light shining from Henry's loft, and presently Peter went his way. The rays from the street, creeping in silvery waves over the grass, caused the row of shrubs along the drive to throw a clear, bold shade.

A wisp of smoke came from one of the windows at the end of the house and drifted quietly into the branches of a cherry tree. Its companions followed it in slowly increasing numbers, and finally there was a current controlled by invisible banks which poured into the fruit-laden boughs of the cherry tree. It was no more to be noted than if a troop of dim and silent gray monkeys had been climbing a grapevine into the clouds.

After a moment the window brightened as if the four panes of it had been stained with blood, and a quick ear might have been led to imagine the fire-imps calling and calling, clan joining clan, gathering to the colors. From the street, however, the house maintained its dark quiet, insisting to a passer-by that it was the safe dwelling of people who chose to retire early to tranquil dreams. No one could have heard this low droning of the gathering clans.

Suddenly the panes of the red window tinkled and crashed to the ground, and at other windows there suddenly reared other flames, like bloody specters at the apertures of a haunted house. This outbreak had been well planned, as if by professional revolutionists.

A man's voice suddenly shouted: "Fire! Fire! Fire!" Hannigan had flung his pipe frenziedly from him because his lungs demanded room. He tumbled down from his perch, swung over the fence, and ran shouting towards the front door of the Trescotts'. Then he hammered on the door, using his fists as if they were mallets. Mrs. Trescott instantly came to one of the windows on the second floor. Afterward she knew she had been about to say, "The doctor is not at home, but if you will leave your name, I will let him know as soon as he comes."

Hannigan's bawling was for a minute incoherent, but she understood that it was not about croup.

"What?" she said, raising the window swiftly.

"Your house is on fire! You're all ablaze! Move quick if – " His cries were resounding in the street as if it were a cave of echoes. Many feet pattered swiftly on the stones. There was one man who ran with an almost fabulous speed. He wore lavender trousers. A straw hat with a bright silk band was held half crumpled in his hand.

As Henry reached the front door, Hannigan had just broken the lock with a kick. A thick cloud of smoke poured over them, and Henry, ducking his head, rushed into it. From Hannigan's clamor he knew only one thing, but it turned him blue with horror. In the hall a lick of flame had found the cord that supported "Signing the Declaration." The engraving slumped suddenly down at one end, and then dropped to the floor, where it burst with the sound of a bomb. The fire was already roaring like a winter wind among the pines.

At the head of the stairs Mrs. Trescott was waving her arms as if they were two reeds. "Jimmie! Save Jimmie!" she screamed in Henry's face. He plunged past her and disappeared, taking the long-familiar routes among these upper chambers, where he had once held office as a sort of second assistant housemaid.

Hannigan had followed him up the stairs, and grappled the arm of the maniacal woman there. His face was black with rage. "You must come down," he bellowed.

She would only scream at him in reply: "Jimmie! Jimmie! Save Jimmie!" But he dragged her forth while she babbled at him.

As they swung out into the open air a man ran across the lawn and, seizing a shutter, pulled it from its hinges and flung it far out upon the grass. Then he frantically attacked the other shutters one by one. It was a kind of temporary insanity.

"Here, you," howled Hannigan, "hold Mrs. Trescott – And stop – "

The news had been telegraphed by a twist of the wrist of a neighbor who had gone to the fire box at the corner, and the time when Hannigan and his charge struggled out of the house was the time when the whistle roared its hoarse night call, smiting the crowd in the park, causing the leader of the band, who was about to order the first triumphal clang of a military march, to let his hand drop slowly to his knees.

VII

Henry pawed awkwardly through the smoke in the upper halls. He had attempted to guide himself by the walls, but they were too hot. The paper was crimpling, and he expected at any moment to have a flame burst from under his hands.

"Jimmie!"

He did not call very loud, as if in fear that the humming flames below would over-hear him.

"Jimmie! Oh, Jimmie!"

Stumbling and panting, he speedily reached the entrance to Jimmie's room and flung open the door. The little chamber had no smoke in it at all. It was faintly illu-minated by a beautiful rosy light reflected circuitously from the flames that were consuming the house. The boy had apparently just been aroused by the noise. He sat in his bed, his lips apart, his eyes wide, while upon his little white-robed figure played caressingly the light from the fire. As the door flew open he had before him this apparition of his pal, a terror-stricken negro, all tousled and with wool scorch-ing, who leaped upon him and bore him up in a blanket as if the whole affair were a case of kidnapping by a dreadful robber chief. Without waiting to go through the usual short but complete process of wrinkling up his face, Jimmie let out a gor-geous bawl, which resembled the expression of a calf's deepest terror. As Johnson, bearing him, reeled into the smoke of the hall, he flung his arms about his neck and buried his face in the blanket. He called twice in muffled tones: "Mam-ma! Mam-ma!"

When Johnson came to the top of the stairs with his burden, he took a quick step backward. Through the smoke that rolled to him he could see that the lower hall was all ablaze. He cried out then in a howl that resembled Jimmie's former achievement. His legs gained a frightful faculty of bending sideways. Swinging about precariously on these reedy legs, he made his way back slowly, back along the upper hall. From the way of him then, he had given up almost all idea of escaping from the burning house, and with it the desire. He was submitting, submitting because of his fathers, bending his mind in a most perfect slavery to this conflagration.

He now clutched Jimmie as unconsciously as when, running toward the house, he had clutched the hat with the bright silk band.

Suddenly he remembered a little private staircase which led from a bedroom to an apartment which the doctor had fitted up as a laboratory and workhouse, where he used some of his leisure, and also hours when he might have been sleeping, in devoting himself to experiments which came in the way of his study and interest.

When Johnson recalled this stairway, the submission to the blaze departed instantly. He had been perfectly familiar with it, but his confusion had destroyed the memory of it.

In his sudden momentary apathy there had been little that resembled fear, but now, as a way of safety came to him, the old frantic terror caught him. He was no longer creature to the flames, and he was afraid of the battle with them. It was a singular and swift set of alternations in which he feared twice without submission, and submitted once without fear.

"Jimmie!" he wailed, as he staggered on his way. He wished this little inanimate body at his breast to participate in his tremblings. But the child had lain limp and still during these headlong charges and countercharges, and no sign came from him.

Johnson passed through two rooms and came to the head of the stairs. As he opened the door great billows of smoke poured out, but, gripping Jimmie closer, he plunged down through them. All manner of odors assailed him during this flight. They seemed to be alive with envy, hatred, and malice. At the entrance to the laboratory he confronted a strange spectacle. The room was like a garden in the region where might be burning flowers. Flames of violet, crimson, green, blue, orange, and purple were blooming everywhere. There was one blaze that was precisely the hue of a delicate coral. In another place was a mass that lay merely in phosphorescent inaction like a pile of emeralds. But all these marvels were to be seen dimly through clouds of heaving, turning, deadly smoke.

Johnson halted for a moment on the threshold. He cried out again in the negro wail that had in it the sadness of the swamps. Then he rushed across the room. An orange-colored flame leaped like a panther at the lavender trousers. This animal bit deeply into Johnson. There was an explosion at one side, and suddenly before him there reared a delicate, trembling sapphire shape like a fairy lady. With a quiet smile she blocked his path and doomed him and Jimmie. Johnson shrieked, and then ducked in the manner of his race in fights. He aimed to pass under the left guard of the sapphire lady. But she was swifter than eagles, and her talons caught in him as he plunged past her. Bowing his head as if his neck had been struck, Johnson lurched forward, twisting this way and that way. He fell on his back. The still form in the blanket flung from his arms, rolled to the edge of the floor and beneath the window.

Johnson had fallen with his head at the base of an old-fashioned desk. There was a row of jars upon the top of this desk. For the most part, they were silent amid this rioting, but there was one which seemed to hold a scintillant and writhing serpent.

Suddenly the glass splintered, and a ruby-red snake-like thing poured its thick length out upon the top of the old desk. It coiled and hesitated, and then began to swim a languorous way down the mahogany slant. At the angle it waved its sizzling molten head to and fro over the closed eyes of the man beneath it. Then, in a moment, with a mystic impulse, it moved again, and the red snake flowed directly down into Johnson's upturned face.

Afterward the trail of this creature seemed to reek, and amid flames low explosions drops like red-hot jewels pattered softly down it at leisurely intervals.

VIII

Suddenly all roads led to Dr. Trescott's. The whole town flowed toward one point. Chippeway Hose Company Number One toiled desperately up Bridge Street Hill even as the Tuscaroras came in an impetuous sweep down Niagara Avenue. Meanwhile the machine of the hook-and-ladder experts from across the creek was spinning on its way. The chief of fire department had been playing poker in the rear room of Whiteley's cigar store, but at the first breath of the alarm he sprang through the door like a man escaping with the kitty.

In Whilomville, on these occasions, there was always a number of people who instantly turned their attention to the bells in the churches and schoolhouses. The bells not only emphasized the alarm, but it was the habit to send these sounds rolling across the sky in a stirring brazen uproar until the flames were practically vanquished. There was also a kind of rivalry as to which bell should be made to produce the greatest din. Even the Valley Church, four miles away among the farms, had heard the voices of its brethren, and immediately added a quaint little yelp.

Dr. Trescott had been driving homeward, slowly smoking a cigar, and feeling glad that this last case was now in complete obedience to him, like a wild animal that he had subdued, when he heard the long whistle, and chirped to his horse under the unlicensed but perfectly distinct impression that a fire had broken out in Oakhurst, a new and rather high-flying suburb of the town which was at least two miles from his own home. But in the second blast and in the ensuing silence he read the designation of his own district. He was then only a few blocks from his house. He took out the whip and laid it lightly on the mare. Surprised and frightened at this extraordinary action, she leaped forward, and as the reins straightened like steel bands, the doctor leaned backward a trifle. When the mare whirled him up to the closed gate he was wondering whose house could be afire. The man who had rung the signal-box yelled something at him, but he already knew. He left the mare to her will.

In front of his door was a maniacal woman in a wrapper. "Ned!" she screamed at sight of him. "Jimmie! Save Jimmie!"

Trescott had grown hard and chill. "Where?" he said. "Where?"

Mrs. Trescott's voice began to bubble. "Up – up – up – " She pointed at the second-story windows.

Hannigan was already shouting: "Don't go in that way! You can't go in that way!"

Trescott ran around the corner of the house and disappeared from them. He knew from the view he had taken of the main hall that it would be impossible to ascend from there. His hopes were fastened now to the stairway which led from the laboratory. The door which opened from this room out upon the lawn was fastened with a bolt and lock, but he kicked close to the lock and then close to the bolt. The door with a loud crash flew back. The doctor recoiled from the roll of smoke, and then bending low, he stepped into the garden of burning flowers. On the floor his stinging eyes could make out a form in a smoldering blanket near the window. Then, as he carried his son toward the door, he saw that the whole lawn seemed now alive with men and boys, the leaders in the great charge that the whole town was making. They seized him and his burden, and overpowered him in wet blankets and water.

But Hannigan was howling: "Johnson is in there yet! Henry Johnson is in there yet! He went in after the kid! Johnson is in there yet!"

These cries penetrated to the sleepy senses of Trescott, and he struggled with his captors, swearing, unknown to him and to them, all the deep blasphemies of his medical-student days. He rose to his feet and went again toward the door of the laboratory. They endeavored to restrain him, although they were much affrighted at him.

But a young man who was a brakeman on the railway, and lived in one of the rear streets near the Trescotts, had gone into the laboratory and brought forth a thing which he laid on the grass.

IX

There were hoarse commands from in front of the house. "Turn on your water, Five!" "Let 'er go, One!" The gathering crowd swayed this way and that way. The flames, towering high, cast a wild red light on their faces. There came the clangor of a gong from along some adjacent street. The crowd exclaimed at it. "Here comes Number Three!" "That's Three a-comin'!" A panting and irregular mob dashed into view, dragging a hose cart. A cry of exultation arose from the little boys. "Here's Three!" The lads welcomed Never-Die Hose Company Number Three as if it was composed of a chariot dragged by a band of gods. The perspiring citizens flung themselves into the fray. The boys danced in impish joy at the displays of prowess. They acclaimed the approach of Number Two. They welcomed Number Four with cheers. They were so deeply moved by this whole affair that they bitterly guyed the late appearance of the hook-and-ladder company, whose heavy apparatus had almost stalled them on the Bridge Street hill. The lads hated and feared a fire, of course. They did not particularly want to have anybody's house burn, but still it was fine to see the gathering of the companies, and amid a great noise to watch their heroes perform all manner of prodigies.

They were divided into parties over the worth of different companies, and supported their creeds with no small violence. For instance, in that part of the little city where Number Four had its home it would be most daring for a boy to contend the superiority of any other company. Likewise, in another quarter, when a strange boy was asked which fire company was the best in Whilomville, he was expected to answer "Number One." Feuds, which the boys forgot and remembered according to chance or the importance of some recent event, existed all through the town.

They did not care much for John Shipley, the chief of the department. It was true that he went to a fire with the speed of a falling angel, but when there he invariably lapsed into a certain still mood, which was almost a preoccupation, moving leisurely around the burning structure and surveying it, puffing meanwhile at a cigar. This quiet man, who even when life was in danger seldom raised his voice, was not much to their fancy. Now old Sykes Huntington, when he was chief, used to bellow continually like a bull and gesticulate in a sort of delirium. He was much finer a spectacle than this Shipley, who viewed a fire with the same steadiness that he viewed a raise in a large jackpot. The greater number of the boys could never understand why the members of these companies persisted in reelecting Shipley, although they often pretended to understand it because "My father says" was a very formidable phrase in argument, and the fathers seemed almost unanimous in advocating Shipley.

At this time there was considerable discussion as to which company had got the first stream of water on the fire. Most of the boys claimed that Number Five owned that distinction, but there was a determined minority who contended for Number One. Boys who were the blood adherents of other companies were obliged to choose between the two on this occasion, and the talk waxed warm.

But a great rumor went among the crowds. It was told with hushed voices. Afterward a reverent silence fell even upon the boys. Jimmie Trescott and Henry Johnson had been burned to death, and Dr. Trescott himself had been most savagely hurt. The crowd did not even feel the police pushing at them. They raised their eyes, shining now with awe, toward the high flames.

The man who had information was at his best. In low tones he described the whole affair. "That was the kid's room – in the corner there. He had measles or somethin', and this coon – Johnson – was a-settin' up with 'im, and Johnson got sleepy or somethin' and upset the lamp, and the doctor he was down in his office, and he came running up, and they all got burned together till they dragged 'em out."

Another man, always preserved for the deliverance of the final judgment, was saying: "Oh, they'll die sure. Burned to flinders. No chance. Hull lot of 'em. Anybody can see." The crowd concentrated its gaze still more closely upon these flags of fire which waved joyfully against the black sky. The bells of the town were clashing unceasingly.

A little procession moved across the lawn and toward the street. There were three cots, borne by twelve of the firemen. The police moved sternly, but it needed no effort of theirs to open a lane for this slow cortège. The men who bore the cots were well known to the crowd, but in this solemn parade during the ringing of the bells and the shouting, and with the red glare upon the sky, they seemed utterly foreign, and Whilomville paid them a deep respect. Each man in this stretcher party had gained a respected majesty. They were footmen to death, and the crowd made subtle obeisance to this august dignity derived from three prospective graves. One woman turned away with a shriek at sight of the covered body on the first stretcher, and people faced her suddenly in silent and mournful indignation. Otherwise there was barely a sound as these twelve important men with measured tread carried their burdens through the throng.

The little boys no longer discussed the merits of the different fire companies. For the greater part they had been routed. Only the more courageous viewed closely the three figures veiled in yellow blankets.

X

Old Judge Denning Hagenthorpe, who lived nearly opposite the Trescotts, had thrown his door wide open to receive the afflicted family. When it was publicly learned that the doctor and his son and the negro were still alive, it required a specially detailed policeman to prevent people from scaling the front porch and interviewing these sorely wounded. One old lady appeared with a miraculous poultice, and she quoted most damning Scripture to the officer when he said that she could not pass him. Throughout the night some lads old enough to be given privileges or to compel them from their mothers remained vigilantly upon the curb in anticipation of a death or some such event. The reporter of the *Morning Tribune* rode thither on his bicycle every hour until three o'clock.

Six of the ten doctors in Whilomville attended at Judge Hagenthorpe's house.

Almost at once they were able to know that Trescott's burns were not vitally important. The child would possibly be scarred badly, but his life was undoubtedly safe. As for the negro Henry Johnson, he could not live. His body was frightfully seared, but more than that, he now had no face. His face had simply been burned away.

Trescott was always asking news of the two other patients. In the morning he seemed fresh and strong, so they told him that Johnson was doomed. They then saw him stir on the bed, and sprang quickly to see if the bandages needed readjusting. In the sudden glance he threw from one to another he impressed them as being both leonine and impracticable.

The morning paper announced the death of Henry Johnson. It contained a long interview with Edward J. Hannigan, in which the latter described in full the performance of Johnson at the fire. There was also an editorial built from all the best words in the vocabulary of the staff. The town halted in its accustomed road of thought, and turned a reverent attention to the memory of this hostler. In the breasts of many people was the regret that they had not known enough to give him a hand and a lift when he was alive, and they judged themselves stupid and ungenerous for this failure.

The name of Henry Johnson became suddenly the title of a saint to the little boys. The one who thought of it first could, by quoting it in an argument, at once overthrow his antagonist, whether it applied to the subject or whether it did not.

"Nigger, nigger, never die,
Black face and shiny eye."

Boys who had called this odious couplet in the rear of Johnson's march buried the fact at the bottom of their hearts.

Later in the day Miss Bella Farragut, of No. 7 Watermelon Alley, announced that she had been engaged to marry Mr. Henry Johnson.

XI

The old judge had a cane with an ivory head. He could never think at his best until he was leaning slightly on this stick and smoothing the white top with slow movements of his hands. It was also to him a kind of narcotic. If by any chance he mislaid it, he grew at once very irritable, and was likely to speak sharply to his sister, whose mental incapacity he had patiently endured for thirty years in the old mansion on Ontario Street. She was not at all aware of her brother's opinion of her endowments, and so it might be said that the judge had successfully dissembled for more than a quarter of a century, only risking the truth at the times when his cane was lost.

On a particular day the judge sat in his armchair on the porch. The sunshine sprinkled through the lilac bushes and poured great coins on the boards. The sparrows disputed in the trees that lined the pavements. The judge mused deeply, while his hands gently caressed the ivory head of his cane.

Finally he arose and entered the house, his brow still furrowed in a thoughtful frown. His stick thumped solemnly in regular beats. On the second floor he entered a room where Dr. Trescott was working about the bedside of Henry Johnson. The bandages on the negro's head allowed only one thing to appear, an eye, which unwinkingly stared at the judge. The latter spoke to Trescott on the condition of the patient. Afterward he evidently had something further to say, but he seemed to be kept from it by the scrutiny of the unwinking eye, at which he furtively glanced from time to time.

When Jimmie Trescott was sufficiently recovered, his mother had taken him to pay a visit to his grandparents in Connecticut. The doctor had remained to take care of his patients, but as a matter of truth he spent most of his time at Judge Hagenthorpe's house, where lay Henry Johnson. Here he slept and ate almost every meal in the long nights and days of his vigil.

At dinner, and away from the magic of the unwinking eye, the judge said, suddenly, "Trescott, do you think it is – " As Trescott paused expectantly, the judge fingered his knife. He said, thoughtfully, "No one wants to advance such ideas, but somehow I think that that poor fellow ought to die."

There was in Trescott's face at once a look of recognition, as if in this tangent of the judge he saw an old problem. He merely sighed and answered, "Who knows?" The words were spoken in a deep tone that gave them an elusive kind of significance.

The judge retreated to the cold manner of the bench. "Perhaps we may not talk with propriety of this kind of action, but I am induced to say that you are performing a questionable charity in preserving this negro's life. As near as I can understand, he will hereafter be a monster, a perfect monster, and probably with an affected brain. No man can observe you as I have observed you and not know that it was a matter of conscience with you, but I am afraid, my friend, that it is one of the blunders of virtue." The judge had delivered his views with his habitual oratory. The last three words he spoke with a particular emphasis, as if the phrase was his discovery.

The doctor made a weary gesture. "He saved my boy's life."

"Yes," said the judge, swiftly – "yes, I know!"

"And what am I to do?" said Trescott, his eyes suddenly lighting like an outburst from smoldering peat. "What am I to do? He gave himself for – for Jimmie. What am I to do for him?"

The judge abased himself completely before these words. He lowered his eyes for a moment. He picked at his cucumbers.

Presently he braced himself straightly in his chair. "He will be your creation, you understand. He is purely your creation. Nature has very evidently given him up. He is dead. You are restoring him to life. You are making him, and he will be a monster, and with no mind."

"He will be what you like, Judge," cried Trescott, in sudden polite fury. "He will be anything, but, by God! he saved my boy."

The judge interrupted in a voice trembling with emotion: "Trescott! Trescott! Don't I know?"

Trescott had subsided to a sullen mood. "Yes, you know," he answered, acidly; "but you don't know all about your own boy being saved from death." This was a perfectly childish allusion to the judge's bachelorhood. Trescott knew that the remark was infantile, but he seemed to take desperate delight in it.

But it passed the judge completely. It was not his spot.

"I am puzzled," said he, in profound thought. "I don't know what to say."

Trescott had become repentant. "Don't think I don't appreciate what you say, Judge. But – "

"Of course!" responded the judge, quickly. "Of course."

"It – " began Trescott.

"Of course," said the judge.

In silence they resumed their dinner.

"Well," said the judge, ultimately, "it is hard for a man to know what to do."

"It is," said the doctor, fervidly.

There was another silence. It was broken by the judge: "Look here, Trescott, I don't want you to think – "

"No, certainly not," answered the doctor, earnestly.

"Well, I don't want you to think I would say anything to – It was only that I thought that I might be able to suggest to you that – perhaps – the affair was a little dubious."

With an appearance of suddenly disclosing his real mental perturbation, the doctor said: "Well, what would you do? Would you kill him?" he asked, abruptly and sternly.

"Trescott, you fool," said the old man, gently.

"Oh, well, I know, Judge, but then – " He turned red, and spoke with new violence: "Say, he saved my boy – do you see? He saved my boy."

"You bet he did," cried the judge, with enthusiasm. "You bet he did." And they remained for a time gazing at each other, their faces illuminated with memories of a certain deed.

After another silence, the judge said, "It is hard for a man to know what to do."

XII

Late one evening Trescott, returning from a professional call, paused his buggy at the Hagenthorpe gate. He tied the mare to the old tin-covered post, and entered the house. Ultimately he appeared with a companion – a man who walked slowly and carefully, as if he were learning. He was wrapped to the heels in an old-fashioned ulster. They entered the buggy and drove away.

After a silence only broken by the swift and musical humming of the wheels on the smooth road, Trescott spoke. "Henry," he said, "I've got you a home here with old

Alek Williams. You will have everything you want to eat and a good place to sleep, and I hope you will get along there all right. I will pay all your expenses, and come to see you as often as I can. If you don't get along, I want you to let me know as soon as possible, and then we will do what we can to make it better."

The dark figure at the doctor's side answered with a cheerful laugh.

"These buggy wheels don' look like I washed 'em yesterday, docteh," he said.

Trescott hesitated for a moment, and then went on insistently, "I am taking you to Alek Williams, Henry, and I – "

The figure chuckled again. "No, 'deed! No, seh! Alek Williams don' know a hoss! 'Deed he don't. He don' know a hoss from a pig." The laugh that followed was like the rattle of pebbles.

Trescott turned and looked sternly and coldly at the dim form in the gloom from the buggy-top. "Henry," he said, "I didn't say anything about horses. I was saying – "

"Hoss? Hoss?" said the quavering voice from these near shadows. "Hoss? 'Deed I don' know all erbout a hoss! 'Deed I don't." There was a satirical chuckle.

At the end of three miles the mare slackened and the doctor leaned forward, peering, while holding tight reins. The wheels of the buggy bumped often over outcropping boulders. A window shone forth, a simple square of topaz on a great black hillside. Four dogs charged the buggy with ferocity, and when it did not promptly retreat, they circled courageously around the flanks, baying. A door opened near the window in the hillside, and a man came and stood on a beach of yellow light.

"Yah! yah! You Roveh! You Susie! Come yah! Come yah this minit!"

Trescott called across the dark sea of grass, "Hello, Alek!"

"Hello!"

"Come down here and show me where to drive."

The man plunged from the beach into the surf, and Trescott could then only trace his course by the fervid and polite ejaculations of a host who was somewhere approaching. Presently Williams took the mare by the head and, uttering cries of welcome and scolding the swarming dogs, led the equipage toward the lights. When they halted at the door and Trescott was climbing out, Williams cried, "Will she stand, docteh?"

"She'll stand all right, but you better hold her for a minute. Now, Henry." The doctor turned and held both arms to the dark figure. It crawled to him painfully like a man going down a ladder. Williams took the mare away to be tied to a little tree, and when he returned he found them awaiting him in the gloom beyond the rays from the door.

He burst out then like a siphon pressed by a nervous thumb. "Hennery! Hennery, ma ol' frien'. Well, if I ain' glade. If I ain' glade!"

Trescott had taken the silent shape by the arm and led it forward into the full revelation of the light. "Well, now, Alek, you can take Henry and put him to bed, and in the morning I will – "

Near the end of this sentence old Williams had come front to front with Johnson. He gasped for a second, and then yelled the yell of a man stabbed in the heart.

For a fraction of a moment Trescott seemed to be looking for epithets. Then he roared: "You old black chump! You old black – Shut up! Shut up! Do you hear?"

Williams obeyed instantly in the matter of his screams, but he continued in a lowered voice: "Ma Lode a' massy! Who'd ever think? Ma Lode a' massy!"

Trescott spoke again in the manner of a commander of a battalion. "Alek!"

The old negro again surrendered, but to himself he repeated in a whisper, "Ma Lode!" He was aghast and trembling.

As these three points of widening shadows approached the golden doorway a hale old negress appeared there, bowing. "Good-evenin', docteh! Good-evenin'! Come in! come in!" She had evidently just retired from a tempestuous struggle to place the room in order, but she was now bowing rapidly. She made the effort of a person swimming.

"Don't trouble yourself, Mary," said Trescott, entering. "I've brought Henry for you to take care of, and all you've got to do is to carry out what I tell you." Learning that he was not followed, he faced the door, and said, "Come in, Henry."

Johnson entered. "Whee!" shrieked Mrs. Williams. She almost achieved a back somersault. Six young members of the tribe of Williams made a simultaneous plunge for a position behind the stove, and formed a wailing heap.

XIII

"You know very well that you and your family lived usually on less than three dollars a week, and now that Dr. Trescott pays you five dollars a week for Johnson's board, you live like millionaires. You haven't done a stroke of work since Johnson began to board with you – everybody knows that – and so what are you kicking about?"

The judge sat in his chair on the porch, fondling his cane, and gazing down at old Williams, who stood under the lilac bushes. "Yes, I know, Jedge," said the negro, wagging his head in a puzzled manner. "'Tain't like as if I didn't 'preciate what the docteh done, but – but – well, yeh see Jedge," he added, gaining a new impetus, "it's – it's hard wuk. This ol' man nev' did wuk so hard. Lode, no."

"Don't talk such nonsense, Alek," spoke the judge, sharply. "You have never really worked in your life – anyhow, enough to support a family of sparrows – and now when you are in a more prosperous condition than ever before, you come around talking like an old fool."

The negro began to scratch his head. "Yeh see, Jedge," he said at last, "my ol' 'ooman she cain't 'ceive no lady callahs, nohow."

"Hang lady callers!" said the judge, irascibly. "If you have flour in the barrel and meat in the pot, your wife can get along without receiving lady callers, can't she?"

"But they won't come ainyhow, Jedge," replied Williams, with an air of still deeper stupefaction. "Noner ma wife's frien's ner noner ma frien's 'ill come near ma res'dence."

"Well, let them stay home if they are such silly people."

The old negro seemed to be seeking a way to elude this argument, but, evidently finding none, he was about to shuffle meekly off. He halted, however. "Jedge," said he, "ma ol' 'ooman's near driv' abstracted."

"Your old woman is an idiot," responded the judge.

Williams came very close and peered solemnly through a branch of lilac. "Jedge," he whispered, "the chillens."

"What about them?"

Dropping his voice to funereal depths, Williams said, "They – they cain't eat."

"Can't eat!" scoffed the judge, loudly. "Can't eat! You must think I am as big an old fool as you are. Can't eat – the little rascals! What's to prevent them from eating?"

In answer, Williams said, with mournful emphasis, "Hennery." Moved with a kind of satisfaction at his tragic use of the name, he remained staring at the judge for a sign of its effect.

The judge made a gesture of irritation. "Come, now, you old scoundrel, don't beat around the bush any more. What are you up to? What do you want? Speak out like a man, and don't give me any more of this tiresome rigamarole."

"I ain't er-beatin' round 'bout nuffin, Jedge," replied Williams, indignantly. "No, seh; I say whatter got to say right out. 'Deed I do."

"Well, say it, then."

"Judge" began the negro, taking off his hat and switching his knee with it, "Lode knows I'd do jes' 'bout as much fer five dollehs er week as ainy cul'd man, but – but this yere business is awful, Jedge. I raikon 'ain't been no sleep in – in my house sence docteh done fetch 'im."

"Well, what do you propose to do about it?"

Williams lifted his eyes from the ground and gazed off through the trees. "Raikon I got good appetite, an' sleep jes' like er dog, but he – he's done broke me all up. 'Tain't no good, nohow. I wake up in the night; I hear 'im mebbe, er-whimperin' an' er-whimperin', an' I sneak an' I sneak until I try th' do' to see if he locked in. An' he keep me er-puzzlin' an' er-quakin' all night long. Don't know how'll do in th' winter. Can't let 'im out where th' chiller is. He'll done freeze where he is now." Williams spoke these sentences as if he were talking to himself. After a silence of deep reflection he continued: "Folks go round sayin' he ain't Hennery Johnson at all. They say he's er devil!"

"What?" cried the judge.

"Yesseh," repeated Williams, in tones of injury, as if his veracity had been challenged. "Yesseh. I'm er-tellin' it to yeh straight, Jedge. Plenty cul'd people folks up my way say it is a devil."

"Well, you don't think so yourself, do you?"

"No. 'Tain't no devil. It's Hennery Johnson."

"Well, then, what is the matter with you? You don't care what a lot of foolish people say. Go on 'tending to your business, and pay no attention to such idle nonsense."

"'Tis nonsense, Jedge; but he *looks* like er devil."

"What do you care what he looks like?" demanded the judge.

"Ma rent is two dollehs and er half er month," said Williams, slowly.

"It might just as well be ten thousand dollars a month," responded the judge. "You never pay it, anyhow."

"Then, anoth' thing," continued Williams, in his reflective tone. "If he was all right in his haid I could stan' it; but, Jedge, he's crazier 'n er loon. Then when he looks like er devil, an' done skears all ma frien's away, an' ma chillens cain't eat, an ma ole 'ooman jes' raisin' Cain all the time, an' ma rent two dollehs an' er half er month, an' him not right in his haid, it seems like five dollehs er week – "

The judge's stick came down sharply and suddenly upon the floor of the porch. "There," he said, "I thought that was what you were driving at."

Williams began swinging his head from side to side in the strange racial mannerism. "Now hol' on a minnet, Jedge," he said, defensively. "'Tain't like as if I didn't 'preciate what the docteh done. 'Tain't that. Docteh Trescott is er kind man, an' 'tain't like as if I didn't 'preciate what he done; but – but – "

"But what? You are getting painful, Alek. Now tell me this: did you ever have five dollars a week regularly before in your life?"

Williams at once drew himself up with great dignity, but in the pause after that question he drooped gradually to another attitude. In the end he answered, heroically: "No, Jedge, I 'ain't. An' 'tain't like as if I was er-sayin' five dollehs wasn't er lot er money for a man like me. But, Jedge, what er man oughter git fer this kinder wuk is er salary. Yesseh, Jedge," he repeated with a great impressive gesture; "fer this kinder wuk er man oughter git er Salary." He laid a terrible emphasis upon the final word.

The judge laughed. "I know Dr. Trescott's mind concerning this affair, Alek; and if you are dissatisfied with your boarder, he is quite ready to move him to some other place; so, if you care to leave word with me that you are tired of the arrangement and wish it changed, he will come and take Johnson away."

Williams scratched his head again in deep perplexity. "Five dollehs is er big price fer bo'd, but 'tain't no big price fer the bo'd of er crazy man," he said, finally.

"What do you think you ought to get?" asked the judge.

"Well," answered Alek, in the manner of one deep in a balancing of the scales, "he looks like er devil, an' done skears e'rybody, an' ma chillens cain't eat, an' I cain't sleep, en' he ain't right in his haid, an' – "

"You told me all those things."

After scratching his wool, and beating his knee with his hat, and gazing off through the trees and down at the ground, Williams said, as he kicked nervously at the gravel, "Well, Jedge, I think it is wuth – " He stuttered.

"Worth what?"

"Six dollehs," answered Williams, in a desperate outburst.

The judge lay back in his great armchair and went through all the motions of a man laughing heartily, but he made no sound save a slight cough. Williams had been watching him with apprehension.

"Well," said the judge, "do you call six dollars a salary?"

"No, seh," promptly responded Williams. "'Tain't a salary. No, 'deed! 'Tain't a salary." He looked with some anger upon the man who questioned his intelligence in this way.

"Well, supposing your children can't eat?"

"I – "

"And supposing he looks like a devil? And supposing all those things continue? Would you be satisfied with six dollars a week?"

Recollections seemed to throng in Williams's mind at these interrogations, and he answered dubiously. "Of co'se a man who ain't right in his haid, an' looks like er devil – But six dollehs – " After these two attempts at a sentence Williams suddenly appeared as an orator, with a great shiny palm waving in the air. "I tell yeh, Jedge, six dollehs is six dollehs, but if I git six dollehs for bo'ding Hennery Johnson, I uhns it! I uhns it!"

"I don't doubt that you earn six dollars for every week's work you do," said the judge.

"Well, if I bo'd Hennery Johnson fer six dollehs er week, I uhns it! I uhns it!" cried Williams, wildly.

XIV

Reifsnyder's assistant had gone to his supper, and the owner of the shop was trying to placate four men who wished to be shaved at once. Reifsnyder was very garrulous – a fact which made him rather remarkable among barbers, who, as a class, are austerely speechless, having been taught silence by the hammering reiteration of a tradition. It is the customers who talk in the ordinary event.

As Reifsnyder waved his razor down the cheek of a man in the chair, he turned often to cool the impatience of the others with pleasant talk, which they did not particularly heed.

"Oh, he should have let him die," said Bainbridge, a railway engineer, finally replying to one of the barber's orations. "Shut up, Reif, and go on with your business!"

Instead, Reifsnyder paused shaving entirely, and turned to front the speaker. "Let him die?" he demanded. "How vas that? How can you let a man die?"

"By letting him die, you chump," said the engineer. The others laughed a little, and Reifsnyder turned at once to his work, sullenly, as a man overwhelmed by the derision of numbers.

"How vas that?" he grumbled later. "How can you let a man die when he vas done so much for you?"

"When he vas done so much for you?" repeated Bainbridge. "You better shave some people. How vas that? Maybe this ain't a barber shop?"

A man hitherto silent now said, "If I had been the doctor, I would have done the same thing."

"Of course," said Reifsnyder. "Any man vould do it. Any man that vas not like you, you – old – flint-hearted – fish." He had sought the final words with painful care, and he delivered the collection triumphantly at Bainbridge. The engineer laughed.

The man in the chair now lifted himself higher, while Reifsnyder began an elaborate ceremony of anointing and combing his hair. Now free to join comfortably in the talk, the man said: "They say he is the most terrible thing in the world. Young Johnnie Bernard – that drives the grocery wagon – saw him up at Alek Williams's shanty, and he says he couldn't eat anything for two days."

"Chee!" said Reifsnyder.

"Well, what makes him so terrible?" asked another.

"Because he hasn't got any face," replied the barber and the engineer in duet.

"Hasn't got any face!" repeated the man. "How can he do without any face?"

"He has no face in the front of his head, In the place where his face ought to grow."

Bainbridge sang these lines pathetically as he arose and hung his hat on a hook. The man in the chair was about to abdicate in his favor. "Get a gait on you now," he said to Reifsnyder. "I go out at 7:31."

As the barber foamed the lather on the cheeks of the engineer he seemed to be thinking heavily. Then suddenly he burst out. "How would you like to be with no face?" he cried to the assemblage.

"Oh, if I had to have a face like yours – " answered one customer.

Bainbridge's voice came from a sea of lather. "You're kicking because if losing faces became popular, you'd have to go out of business."

"I don't think it will become so much popular," said Reifsnyder.

"Not if it's got to be taken off in the way his was taken off," said another man. "I'd rather keep mine, if you don't mind."

"I guess so!" cried the barber. "Just think!"

The shaving of Bainbridge had arrived at a time of comparative liberty for him. "I wonder what the doctor says to himself?" he observed. "He may be sorry he made him live."

"It was the only thing he could do," replied a man. The others seemed to agree with him.

"Supposing you were in his place," said one, "and Johnson had saved your kid. What would you do?"

"Certainly!"

"Of course! You would do anything on earth for him. You'd take all the trouble in the world for him. And spend your last dollar on him. Well, then?"

"I wonder how it feels to be without any face?" said Reifsnyder, musingly.

The man who had previously spoken, feeling that he had expressed himself well, repeated the whole thing. "You would do anything on earth for him. You'd take all the trouble in the world for him. And spend your last dollar on him. Well, then?"

"No, but look," said Reifsnyder; "supposing you don't got a face!"

XV

As soon as Williams was hidden from the view of the old judge he began to gesture and talk to himself. An elation had evidently penetrated to his vitals, and caused him to dilate as if he had been filled with gas. He snapped his fingers in the air, and whistled fragments of triumphal music. At times, in his progress toward his shanty, he indulged in a shuffling movement that was really a dance. It was to be learned from the interme- diate monologue that he had emerged from his trials laureled and proud. He was the unconquerable Alexander Williams. Nothing could exceed the bold self-reliance of his manner. His kingly stride, his heroic song, the derisive flourish of his hands – all betokened a man who had successfully defied the world.

On his way he saw Zeke Paterson coming to town. They hailed each other at a distance of fifty yards.

"How do, Broth' Paterson?"

"How do, Broth' Williams?"

They were both deacons.

"Is you' folks well, Broth' Paterson?"

"Middlin', middlin'. How's you' folks, Broth' Williams?"

Neither of them had slowed his pace in the smallest degree. They had simply begun this talk when a considerable space separated them, continued it as they passed, and added polite questions as they drifted steadily apart. Williams's mind seemed to be a balloon. He had been so inflated that he had not noticed that Paterson had definitely shied into the dry ditch as they came to the point of ordinary contact.

Afterward, as he went a lonely way, he burst out again in song and pantomimic celebration of his estate. His feet moved in prancing steps.

When he came in sight of his cabin, the fields were bathed in a blue dusk and the light in the window was pale. Cavorting and gesticulating, he gazed joyfully for some moments upon this light. Then suddenly another idea seemed to attack his mind, and he stopped, with an air of being suddenly dampened. In the end he approached his home as if it were the fortress of an enemy.

Some dogs disputed his advance for a loud moment, and then discovering their lord, slunk away embarrassed. His reproaches were addressed to them in muffled tones.

Arriving at the door, he pushed it open with the timidity of a new thief. He thrust his head cautiously sideways, and his eyes met the eyes of his wife, who sat by the table, the lamplight defining a half of her face. "Sh!" he said, uselessly. His glance traveled swiftly to the inner door which shielded the one bed-chamber. The pickaninnies, strewn upon the floor of the living room, were softly snoring. After a hearty meal they had promptly dispersed themselves about the place and gone to sleep. "Sh!" said Williams again to his motionless and silent wife. He had allowed only his head to appear. His wife, with one hand upon the edge of the table and the other at her knee, was regarding him with wide eyes and parted lips as if he were a specter. She looked to be one who was living in terror, and even the familiar face at the door had thrilled her because it had come suddenly.

Williams broke the tense silence. "Is he all right?" he whispered, waving his eyes towards the inner door. Following his glance timorously, his wife nodded, and in a low tone answered: "I raikon he's done gone t' sleep."

Williams then slunk noiselessly across his threshold.

He lifted a chair, and with infinite care placed it so that it faced the dreaded inner door. His wife moved slightly, so as to also squarely face it. A silence came upon them in which they seemed to be waiting for a calamity, pealing and deadly.

Williams finally coughed behind his hand. His wife started, and looked upon him in alarm. "'Pears like he done gwine keep quiet ter-night," he breathed. They continually pointed their speech and their looks at the inner door, paying it the homage due to a corpse or a phantom. Another long stillness followed this sentence. Their eyes shone white and wide. A wagon rattled down the distant road. From their chairs they looked at the window, and the effect of the light in the cabin was a presentation of an intensely black and solemn night. The old woman adopted the attitude used always in church at funerals. At times she seemed to be upon the point of breaking out in prayer.

"He mighty quiet ter-night," whispered Williams. "Was he good ter-day?" For answer his wife raised her eyes to the ceiling in the supplication of Job. Williams moved restlessly. Finally he tiptoed to the door. He knelt slowly and without a sound, and placed his ear near the keyhole. Hearing a noise behind him, he turned quickly. His wife was staring at him aghast. She stood in front of the stove, and her arms were spread out in the natural movement to protect all her sleeping ducklings.

But Williams arose without having touched the door. "I raikon he ersleep," he said, fingering his wool. He debated with himself for some time. During this interval his wife remained, a great fat statue of a mother shielding her children.

It was plain that his mind was swept suddenly by a wave of temerity. With a sounding step he moved toward the door. His fingers were almost upon the knob when he swiftly ducked and dodged away, clapping his hands to the back of his head. It was as if the portal had threatened him. There was a little tumult near the stove, where Mrs. Williams's desperate retreat had involved her feet with the prostrate children.

After the panic Williams bore traces of a feeling of shame. He returned to the charge. He firmly grasped the knob with his left hand, and with his other hand turned the key in the lock. He pushed the door, and as it swung portentously open he sprang nimbly to one side like the fearful slave liberating the lion. Near the stove a group had formed, the terror-stricken mother, with her arms stretched, and the aroused children clinging frenziedly to her skirts.

The light streamed after the swinging door, and disclosed a room six feet one way and six feet the other way. It was small enough to enable the radiance to lay it plain. Williams peered warily around the corner made by the doorpost.

Suddenly he advanced, retired, and advanced again with a howl. His palsied family had expected him to spring backward, and at his howl they heaped themselves wondrously. But Williams simply stood in the little room emitting his howls before an open window. "He's gone! He's gone! He's gone!" His eye and his hand had speedily proved the fact. He had even thrown open a little cupboard.

Presently he came flying out. He grabbed his hat, and hurled the outer door back upon its hinges. Then he tumbled headlong into the night. He was yelling: "Docteh Trescott! Docteh Trescott!" He ran wildly through the fields and galloped in the direction of town. He continued to call to Trescott, as if the latter was within easy hearing. It was as if Trescott was poised in the contemplative sky over the running negro, and could heed this reaching voice – "Docteh Trescott!"

In the cabin, Mrs. Williams, supported by relays from the battalion of children, stood quaking watch until the truth of daylight came as a reinforcement and made them arrogant, strutting, swashbuckler children and a mother who proclaimed her illimitable courage.

XVI

Theresa Page was giving a party. It was the outcome of a long series of arguments addressed to her mother, which had been overheard in part by her father. He had at last said five words, "Oh, let her have it." The mother had then gladly capitulated.

Theresa had written nineteen invitations, and distributed them at recess [to] her schoolmates. Later her mother had composed five large cakes, and still later a vast amount of lemonade.

So the nine little girls and the ten little boys sat quite primly in the dining room, while Theresa and her mother plied them with cake and lemonade, and also with ice cream. This primness sat now quite strangely upon them. It was owing to the presence of Mrs. Page. Previously in the parlor alone with their games they had overturned a chair; the boys had let more or less of their hoodlum spirit shine forth. But when circumstances could be possibly magnified to warrant it, the girls made the boys victims of an insufferable pride, snubbing them mercilessly. So in the dining room they resembled a class at Sunday school, if it were not for the subterranean smiles, gestures, rebuffs, and pourings which stamped the affair a children's party.

Two little girls of this subdued gathering were planted in a settle with their backs to the broad window. They were beaming lovingly upon each other with an effect of scorning the boys.

Hearing a noise behind her at the window, one little girl turned to face it. Instantly she screamed and sprang away, covering her face with her hands. "What was it? What was it?" cried every one in a roar. Some slight movement of the eyes of the weeping and shuddering child informed the company that she had been frightened by an appearance at the window. At once they all faced the imperturbable window, and for a moment there was a silence. An astute lad made an immediate census of the other lads. The prank of slipping out and looming spectrally at a window was too venerable. But the little boys were all present and astonished.

As they recovered their minds they uttered warlike cries, and through a side door sallied rapidly out against the terror. They vied with each other in daring.

None wished particularly to encounter a dragon in the darkness of the garden, but there could be no faltering when the fair ones in the dining room were present. Calling to each other in stern voices, they went dragooning over the lawn, attacking the shadows with ferocity, but still with the caution of reasonable beings. They found, however, nothing new to the peace of the night. Of course there was a lad who told a great lie. He described a grim figure, bending low and slinking off along the fence. He gave a number of details, rendering his lie more splendid by a repetition of certain forms which he recalled from romances. For instance, insisted that he had heard the creature emit a hollow laugh.

Inside the house the little girl who had raised the alarm was still shuddering and weeping. With the utmost difficulty was she brought to a state approximating calmness by Mrs. Page. Then she wanted to go home at once.

Page entered the house at this time. He had exiled himself until he concluded that this children's party was finished and gone. He was obliged to escort the little girl home because she screamed again when they opened the door and she saw the night.

She was not coherent even to her mother. Was it a man? She didn't know. It was simply a thing, a dreadful thing.

XVII

In Watermelon Alley the Farraguts were spending their evening as usual on the little rickety porch. Sometimes they howled gossip to other people on other rickety porches. The thin wail of a baby arose from a near house. A man had a terrific altercation with his wife, to which the alley paid no attention at all.

There appeared suddenly before the Farraguts a monster making a low and sweeping bow. There was an instant's pause, and then occurred something that resembled the effect of an upheaval of the earth's surface. The old woman hurled herself backward with a dreadful cry. Young Sim had been perched gracefully on a railing. At sight of the monster he simply fell over it to the ground. He made no sound, his eyes stuck out, his nerveless hands tried to grapple the rail to prevent a tumble, and then he vanished. Bella, blubbering, and with her hair suddenly and mysteriously disheveled, was crawling on her hands and knees fearsomely up the steps.

Standing before this wreck of a family gathering, the monster continued to bow. It even raised a deprecatory claw. "Don' make no botheration 'bout me, Miss Fa'gut," it said, politely. "No, 'deed. I jes' drap in ter ax if yer well this evenin', Miss Fa'gut. Don' make no botheration. No, 'deed. I gwine ax you to go to er daince with me, Mis Fa'gut. I ax you if I can have the magnifercent gratitude of you' company on that 'casion, Miss Fa'gut."

The girl cast a miserable glance behind her. She was still crawling away. On the ground beside the porch young Sim raised a strange bleat, which expressed both his fright and his lack of wind. Presently the monster, with a fashionable amble, ascended the steps after the girl.

She groveled in a corner of the room as the creature took a chair. It seated itself very elegantly on the edge. It held an old cap in both hands. "Don' make no botheration, Miss Fa'gut. Don' make no botheration. No, 'deed. I jes' drap in ter ax you if you won' do me the proud of acceptin' ma humble invitation to er daince, Miss Fa'gut."

She shielded her eyes with her arms and tried to crawl past it, but the genial monster blocked the way. "I jes' drap in ter ax you 'bout er daince, Miss Fa'gut. I ax you if I kin have the magnifercent gratitude of you' company on that 'casion, Miss Fa'gut."

In a last outbreak of despair, the girl, shuddering and wailing, threw herself face downward on the floor, while the monster sat on the edge of the chair gabbling courteous invitations, and holding the old hat daintily to his stomach.

At the back of the house, Mrs. Farragut, who was of enormous weight, and who for eight years had done little more than sit in an armchair and describe her various ailments, had with speed and agility scaled a high board fence.

XVIII

The black mass in the middle of Trescott's property was hardly allowed to cool before the builders were at work on another house. It had sprung upward at a fabulous rate. It was like a magical composition born of the ashes. The doctor's office was the first part to be completed, and he had already moved in his new books and instruments and medicines.

Trescott sat before his desk when the chief of police arrived "Well, we found him," said the latter.

"Did you?" cried the doctor. "Where?"

"Shambling around the streets at daylight this morning. I'll be blamed if I can figure on where he passed the night."

"Where is he now?"

"Oh, we jugged him. I didn't know what else to do with him. That's what I want you to tell me. Of course we can't keep him. No charge could be made, you know."

"I'll come down and get him."

The official grinned retrospectively. "Must say he had a fine career while he was out. First thing he did was to break up a children's party at Page's. Then he went to Watermelon Alley. Whoo! He stampeded the whole outfit. Men, women, and children running pell-mell, and yelling. They say one old woman broke her leg, or something, shinning over a fence. Then he went right out on the main street, and an Irish girl threw a fit, and there was a sort of a riot. He began to run, and a big crowd chased him, firing rocks. But he gave them the slip somehow down there by the foundry and in the railroad yard. We looked for him all night, but couldn't find him."

"Was he hurt any? Did anybody hit him with a stone?"

"Guess there isn't much of him to hurt anymore, is there? Guess he's been hurt up to the limit. No. They never touched him. Of course nobody really wanted to hit him, but you know how a crowd gets. It's like – it's like – "

"Yes, I know."

For a moment the chief of the police looked reflectively at the floor. Then he spoke hesitatingly. "You know Jake Winter's little girl was the one that he scared at the party. She is pretty sick, they say."

"Is she? Why, they didn't call me. I always attend the Winter family."

"No? Didn't they?" asked the chief, slowly. "Well – you know – Winter is – well, Winter has gone clean crazy over this business. He wanted – he wanted to have you arrested."

"Have me arrested? The idiot! What in the name of wonder could he have me arrested for?"

"Of course. He is a fool. I told him to keep his trap shut. But then you know how he'll go all over town yapping about the thing. I thought I'd better tip you."

"Oh, he is of no consequence, but then, of course, I'm obliged to you, Sam."

"That's all right. Well, you'll be down tonight and take him out, eh? You'll get a good welcome from the jailer. He don't like his job for a cent. He says you can have your man whenever you want him. He's got no use for him."

"But what is this business of Winter's about having me arrested?"

"Oh, it's a lot of chin about your having no right to allow this – this – this man to be at large. But I told him to tend to his own business. Only I thought I'd better let you know. And I might as well say right now, doctor, that there is a good deal of talk about this thing. If I were you, I'd come to the jail pretty late at night, because there is likely to be a crowd around the door, and I'd bring a – er – mask, or some kind of a veil, anyhow."

XIX

Martha Goodwin was single, and well along into the thin years. She lived with her married sister in Whilomville. She performed nearly all the housework in exchange for the privilege of existence. Every one tacitly recognized her labor as a form of penance for the early end of her betrothed, who had died of smallpox, which he had not caught from her.

But despite the strenuous and unceasing workaday of her life, she was a woman of great mind. She had adamantine opinions upon the situation in Armenia, the condition of women in China, the flirtation between Mrs. Minster of Niagara Avenue and young Griscom, the conflict in the Bible class of the Baptist Sunday school, the duty of the United States toward the Cuban insurgents, and many other colossal matters. Her fullest experience of violence was gained on an occasion when she had seen a hound clubbed, but in the plan which she had made for the reform of the world she advocated drastic measures. For instance, she contended that all the Turks should be pushed into the sea and drowned, and that Mrs. Minster and young Griscom should be hanged side by side on twin gallows. In fact, this woman of peace, who had seen only peace, argued constantly for a creed of illimitable ferocity. She was invulnerable on these questions, because eventually she overrode all opponents with a sniff. This sniff was an active force. It was to her antagonists like a bang over the head, and none was known to recover from this expression of exalted contempt. It left them windless and conquered. They never again came forward as candidates for suppression. And Martha walked her kitchen with a stern brow, an invincible being like Napoleon.

Nevertheless her acquaintances, from the pain of their defeats, had been long in secret revolt. It was in no wise a conspiracy, because they did not care to state their open rebellion, but nevertheless it was understood that any woman who could not coincide with one of Martha's contentions was entitled to the support of others in the small circle. It amounted to an arrangement by which all were required to disbelieve any theory for which Martha fought. This, however, did not prevent them from speaking of her mind with profound respect.

Two people bore the brunt of her ability. Her sister Kate was visibly afraid of her, while Carrie Dungen sailed across from her kitchen to sit respectfully at Martha's feet and learn the business of the world. To be sure, afterward, under another sun, she always laughed at Martha and pretended to deride her ideas, but in the presence of the sovereign she always remained silent or admiring. Kate, the sister, was of no consequence at all. Her principal delusion was that she did all the work in the upstairs rooms of the house, while Martha did it downstairs. The truth was seen only by the husband, who treated Martha with a kindness that was half banter, half deference. Martha herself had no suspicion that she was the only pillar of the domestic edifice. The situation was without definitions. Martha made definitions, but she devoted them entirely to the Armenians and Griscom and the Chinese and other subjects. Her dreams, which in early days had been of love, of meadows and the shade of trees, of the face of a man, were now involved otherwise, and they were companioned in the kitchen curiously, Cuba, the hot-water kettle, Armenia, the washing of the dishes, and the whole thing being jumbled. In regard to social misdemeanors, she who was simply the mausoleum of a dead passion was probably the most savage critic in town. This unknown woman, hidden in a kitchen as in a well, was sure to have a considerable effect of the one kind or the other in the life of the town. Every time it moved a yard, she had personally contributed an inch. She could hammer so stoutly upon the door of a proposition that it would break from its hinges and fall upon her, but at any rate it moved. She was an engine, and the fact that she did not know that she was an engine contributed largely to the effect. One reason that she was formidable was that she did not even imagine that she was formidable. She remained a weak, innocent, and pig-headed creature, who alone would defy the universe if she thought the universe merited this proceeding.

One day Carrie Dungen came across from her kitchen with speed. She had a great deal of grist. "Oh," she cried, "Henry Johnson got away from where they was keeping him, and came to town last night, and scared everybody almost to death."

Martha was shining a dishpan, polishing madly. No reasonable person could see cause for this operation, because the pan already glistened like silver. "Well!" she ejaculated. She imparted to the word a deep meaning. "This, my prophecy, has come to pass." It was a habit.

The overplus of information was choking Carrie. Before she could go on she was obliged to struggle for a moment. "And, oh, little Sadie Winter is awful sick, and they say Jake Winter was around this morning trying to get Doctor Trescott arrested. And poor old Mrs. Farragut sprained her ankle in trying to climb a fence. And there's a crowd around the jail all the time. They put Henry in jail because they didn't know what else to do with him, I guess. They say he is perfectly terrible."

Martha finally released the dishpan and confronted the headlong speaker. "Well!" she said again, poising a great brown rag. Kate had heard the excited newcomer, and drifted down from the novel in her room. She was a shivery little woman. Her shoulder blades seemed to be two panes of ice, for she was constantly shrugging and shrugging. "Serves him right if he was to lose all his patients," she said suddenly, in bloodthirsty tones. She snipped her words out as if her lips were scissors.

"Well, he's likely to," shouted Carrie Dungen. "Don't a lot of people say that they won't have him any more? If you're sick and nervous, Doctor Trescott would scare the life out of you, wouldn't he? He would me. I'd keep thinking."

Martha, stalking to and fro, sometimes surveyed the two other women with a contemplative frown.

XX

After the return from Connecticut, little Jimmie was at first much afraid of the monster who lived in the room over the carriage-house. He could not identify it in any way. Gradually, however, his fear dwindled under the influence of a weird fascination. He sidled into closer and closer relations with it.

One time the monster was seated on a box behind the stable basking the rays of the afternoon sun. A heavy crêpe veil was swathed about its head.

Little Jimmie and many companions came around the corner of the stable. They were all in what was popularly known as the baby class, and consequently escaped from school a half-hour before the other children. They halted abruptly at sight of the figure on the box. Jimmie waved his hand with the air of a proprietor.

"There he is," he said.

"O-o-o!" murmured all the little boys – "o-o-o-!" They shrank back and grouped according to courage or experience, as at the sound the monster slowly turned its head. Jimmie had remained in the van alone. "Don't be afraid! I won't let him hurt you," he said, delighted.

"Huh!" they replied, contemptuously. "We ain't afraid."

Jimmie seemed to reap all the joys of the owner and exhibitor of one of the world's marvels, while his audience remained at a distance – awed and entranced, fearful and envious.

One of them addressed Jimmie gloomily. "Bet you dassent walk right up to him." He was an older boy than Jimmie, and habitually oppressed him to a small degree. This new social elevation of the smaller lad probably seemed revolutionary to him.

"Huh!" said Jimmie, with deep scorn. "Dassent I? Dassent I, hey? Dassent I?"

The group was immensely excited. It turned its eyes upon the boy that Jimmie addressed. "No, you dassent," he said, stolidly, facing a moral defeat. He could see that Jimmie was resolved. "No, you dassent," he repeated, doggedly.

"Ho?" cried Jimmie. "You just watch! – you just watch!"

Amid a silence he turned and marched toward the monster. But possibly the palpable wariness of his companions had an effect upon him that weighed more than his previous experience, for suddenly, when near to the monster, he halted dubiously. But his playmates immediately uttered a derisive shout, and it seemed to force him forward. He went to the monster and laid his hand delicately on its shoulder. "Hello, Henry," he said, in a voice that trembled a trifle. The monster was crooning a weird line of negro melody that was scarcely more than a thread of sound, and it paid no heed to the boy.

Jimmie strutted back to his companions. They acclaimed him and hooted his opponent. Amid this clamor the larger boy with difficulty preserved a dignified attitude.

"I dassent, dassent I?" said Jimmie to him. "Now, you're so smart, let's see you do it!"

This challenge brought forth renewed taunts from the others. The larger boy puffed out his cheeks. "Well, I ain't afraid," he explained, sullenly. He had made a mistake in diplomacy, and now his small enemies were tumbling his prestige all about his ears. They crowed like roosters and bleated like lambs, and made many other noises which were supposed to bury him in ridicule and dishonor. "Well, I ain't afraid," he continued to explain through the din.

Jimmie, the hero of the mob, was pitiless. "You ain't afraid, hey?" he sneered. "If you ain't afraid, go do it, then."

"Well, I would if I wanted to," the other retorted. His eyes wore an expression of profound misery, but he preserved steadily other portions of a pot-valiant air. He suddenly faced one of his persecutors. "If you're so smart, why don't you go do it?" This persecutor sank promptly through the group to the rear. The incident gave the badgered one a breathing spell, and for a moment even turned the derision in another direction. He took advantage of his interval. "I'll do it if anybody else will," he announced, swaggering to and fro.

Candidates for the adventure did not come forward. To defend themselves from this countercharge, the other boys again set up their crowing and bleating. For a while they would hear nothing from him. Each time he opened his lips their chorus of noises made oratory impossible. But at last he was able to repeat that he would volunteer to dare as much in the affair as any other boy.

"Well, you go first," they shouted.

But Jimmie intervened to once more lead the populace against the large boy. "You're mighty brave, ain't you?" he said to him. "You dared me to do it, and I did – didn't I? Now who's afraid?" The others cheered this view loudly, and they instantly resumed the baiting of the large boy.

He shamefacedly scratched his left shin with his right foot. "Well, I ain't afraid." He cast an eye at the monster. "Well, I ain't afraid." With a glare of hatred at his squalling tormentors, he finally announced a grim intention. "Well, I'll do it, then, since you're so fresh. Now!"

The mob subsided as with a formidable countenance he turned toward the impassive figure on the box. The advance was also a regular progression from high daring to craven hesitation. At last, when some yards from the monster, the lad came to a full halt, as if he had encountered a stone wall. The observant little boys in the distance promptly hooted. Stung again by these cries, the lad sneaked two yards forward. He was crouched like a young cat ready for a backward spring. The crowd at the rear, beginning to respect this display, uttered some encouraging cries. Suddenly the lad gathered himself together, made a white and desperate rush forward, touched the monster's shoulder with a far-outstretched finger, and sped away, while his laughter rang out wild, shrill, and exultant.

The crowd of boys reverenced him at once, and began to throng into his camp, and look at him, and be his admirers. Jimmie was discomfited for a moment, but he and the larger boy, without agreement or word of any kind, seemed to recognize a truce, and they swiftly combined and began to parade before the others.

"Why, it's just as easy as nothing," puffed the larger boy. "Ain't it, Jim?"

"Course," blew Jimmie. "Why, it's as e-e-easy."

They were people of another class. If they had been decorated for courage on twelve battlefields, they could not have made the other boys more ashamed of the situation.

Meanwhile they condescended to explain the emotions of the excursion, expressing unqualified contempt for any one who could hang back. "Why, it ain't nothin'. He won't do nothin' to you," they told the others, in tones of exasperation.

One of the very smallest boys in the party showed signs of a wistful desire to distinguish himself, and they turned their attention to him, pushing at his shoulders while he swung away from them, and hesitated dreamily. He was eventually induced to make furtive expedition, but it was only for a few yards. Then he paused, motionless, gazing with open mouth. The vociferous entreaties of Jimmie and the large boy had no power over him.

Mrs. Hannigan had come out on her back porch with a pail of water. From this coign[2] she had a view of the secluded portion of the Trescott grounds that was behind the stable. She perceived the group of boys, and the monster on the box. She shaded her eyes with her hand to benefit her vision. She screeched then as if she was being murdered. "Eddie! Eddie! You come home this minute!"

Her son querulously demanded, "Aw, what for?"

"You come home this minute. Do you hear?"

The other boys seemed to think this visitation upon one of their number required them to preserve for a time the hang-dog air of a collection of culprits, and they remained in guilty silence until the little Hannigan, wrathfully protesting, was pushed through the door of his home. Mrs. Hannigan cast a piercing glance over the group,

Notes

[2] Short for "coign of vantage," military term for advantageous position for observation or action.

stared with a bitter face at the Trescott house, as if this new and handsome edifice was insulting her, and then followed her son.

There was wavering in the party. An inroad by one mother always caused them to carefully sweep the horizon to see if there were more coming. "This is my yard," said Jimmie, proudly. "We don't have to go home."

The monster on the box had turned its black crêpe countenance toward the sky, and was waving its arms in time to a religious chant. "Look at him now," cried a little boy. They turned, and were transfixed by the solemnity and mystery of the indefinable gestures. The wail of the melody was mournful and slow. They drew back. It seemed to spellbind them with the power of a funeral. They were so absorbed that they did not hear the doctor's buggy drive up to the stable. Trescott got out, tied his horse, and approached the group. Jimmie saw him first, and at his look of dismay the others wheeled.

"What's all this, Jimmie?" asked Trescott, in surprise.

The lad advanced to the front of his companions, halted, and said nothing. Trescott's face gloomed slightly as he scanned the scene.

"What were you doing, Jimmie?"

"We was playin'," answered Jimmie, huskily.

"Playing at what?"

"Just playin'."

Trescott looked gravely at the other boys, and asked them to please go home. They proceeded to the street much in the manner of frustrated and revealed assassins. The crime of trespass on another boy's place was still a crime when they had only accepted the other boy's cordial invitation, and they were used to being sent out of all manner of gardens upon the sudden appearance of a father or a mother. Jimmie had wretchedly watched the departure of his companions. It involved the loss of his position as a lad who controlled the privileges of his father's grounds, but then he knew that in the beginning he had no right to ask so many boys to be his guests.

Once on the sidewalk, however, they speedily forgot their shame as trespassers, and the large boy launched forth in a description of his success in the late trial of courage. As they went rapidly up the street, the little boy who had made the furtive expedition cried out confidently from the rear, "Yes, and I went almost up to him, didn't I, Willie?"

The large boy crushed him in a few words. "Huh!" he scoffed. "You only went a little way. I went clear up to him."

The pace of the other boys was so manly that the tiny thing had to trot, and he remained at the rear, getting entangled in their legs in his attempts to reach the front rank and become of some importance, dodging this way and that way, and always piping out his little claim to glory.

XXI

"By the way, Grace," said Trescott, looking into the dining room from his office door, "I wish you would send Jimmie to me before school-time."

When Jimmie came, he advanced so quietly that Trescott did not at first note him. "Oh," he said, wheeling from a cabinet, "here you are, young man."

"Yes, sir."

Trescott dropped into his chair and tapped the desk with a thoughtful finger. "Jimmie, what were you doing in the back garden yesterday – you and the other boys – to Henry?"

"We weren't doing anything, pa."

Trescott looked sternly into the raised eyes of his son. "Are you sure you were not annoying him in any way? Now what were you doing, exactly?"

"Why, we – why, we – now – Willie Dalzel said I dassent go right up to him, and I did; and then he did; and then – the other boys were 'fraid; and then – you comed."

Trescott groaned deeply. His countenance was so clouded in sorrow that the lad, bewildered by the mystery of it, burst suddenly forth in dismal lamentations. "There, there. Don't cry, Jim," said Trescott, going round the desk. "Only – " He sat in a great leather reading chair, and took the boy on his knee. "Only I want to explain to you – "

After Jimmie had gone to school, and as Trescott was about to start on his round of morning calls, a message arrived from Doctor Moser. It set forth that the latter's sister was dying in the old homestead, twenty miles away up the valley, and asked Trescott to care for his patients for the day at least. There was also in the envelope a little history of each case and of what had already been done. Trescott replied to the messenger that he would gladly assent to the arrangement.

He noted that the first name on Moser's list was Winter, but this did not seem to strike him as an important fact. When its turn came, he rang the Winter bell. "Good morning, Mrs. Winter," he said, cheerfully, as the door was opened. "Doctor Moser has been obliged to leave town today, and he has asked me to come in his stead. How is the little girl this morning?"

Mrs. Winter had regarded him in stony surprise. At last she said: "Come in! I'll see my husband." She bolted into the house. Trescott entered the hall, and turned to the left into the sitting room.

Presently Winter shuffled through the door. His eyes flashed toward Trescott. He did not betray any desire to advance far into the room. "What do you want?" he said.

"What do I want? What do I want?" repeated Trescott, lifting his head suddenly. He had heard an utterly new challenge in the night of the jungle.

"Yes, that's what I want to know," snapped Winter. "What do you want?"

Trescott was silent for a moment. He consulted Moser's memoranda. "I see that your little girl's case is a trifle serious," he remarked. "I would advise you to call a physician soon. I will leave you a copy of Dr. Moser's record to give to any one you may call." He paused to transcribe the record on a page of his notebook. Tearing out the leaf, he extended it to Winter as he moved toward the door. The latter shrunk against the wall. His head was hanging as he reached for the paper. This caused him to grasp air, and so Trescott simply let the paper flutter to the feet of the other man.

"Good morning," said Trescott from the hall. This placid retreat seemed to suddenly arouse Winter to ferocity. It was as if he had then recalled all the truths which he had formulated to hurl at Trescott. So he followed him into the hall, and down the hall to the door, and through the door to the porch, barking in fiery rage from a respectful distance. As Trescott imperturbably turned the mare's head down the road, Winter stood on the porch, still yelping. He was like a little dog.

XXII

"Have you heard the news?" cried Carrie Dungen, as she sped toward Martha's kitchen. "Have you heard the news?" Her eyes were shining with delight.

"No," answered Martha's sister Kate, bending forward eagerly. "What was it? What was it?"

Carrie appeared triumphantly in the open door. "Oh, there's been an awful scene between Doctor Trescott and Jake Winter. I never thought that Jake Winter had any pluck at all, but this morning he told the doctor just what he thought of him."

"Well, what did he think of him?" asked Martha.

"Oh, he called him everything. Mrs. Howarth heard it through her front blinds. It was terrible, she says. It's all over town now. Everybody knows it."

"Didn't the doctor answer back?"

"No! Mrs. Howarth – she says he never said a word. He just walked down to his buggy and got in, and drove off as co-o-o-l. But Jake gave him jinks, by all accounts."

"But what did he say?" cried Kate, shrill and excited. She was evidently at some kind of a feast.

"Oh, he told him that Sadie had never been well since that night Henry Johnson frightened her at Theresa Page's party, and he held him responsible, and how dared he cross his threshold – and – and – and – "

"And what?" said Martha.

"Did he swear at him?" said Kate, in fearsome glee.

"No – not much. He did swear at him a little, but not more than a man does anyhow when he is real mad, Mrs. Howarth says."

"O-oh!" breathed Kate. "And did he call him any names?"

Martha, at her work, had been for a time in deep thought. She now interrupted the other. "It don't seem as if Sadie Winter had been sick since that time Henry Johnson got loose. She's been to school almost the whole time since then, hasn't she?"

They combined upon her in immediate indignation. "School? School? I should say not. Don't think for a moment. School!"

Martha wheeled from the sink. She held an iron spoon, and it seemed as if she was going to attack them. "Sadie Winter has passed here many a morning since then carrying her school bag. Where was she going? To a wedding?"

The others, long accustomed to a mental tyranny, speedily surrendered.

"Did she?" stammered Kate. "I never saw her."

Carrie Dungen made a weak gesture.

"If I had been Doctor Trescott," exclaimed Martha, loudly, "I'd have knocked that miserable Jake Winter's head off."

Kate and Carrie, exchanging glances, made an alliance in the air. "I don't see why you say that, Martha," replied Carrie, with considerable boldness, gaining support and sympathy from Kate's smile. "I don't see how anybody can be blamed for getting angry when their little girl gets almost scared to death and gets sick from it, and all that. Besides, everybody says – "

"Oh, I don't care what everybody says," said Martha.

"Well, you can't go against the whole town," answered Carrie, in sudden sharp defiance.

"No, Martha, you can't go against the whole town," piped Kate, following her leader rapidly.

"The whole town," cried Martha. "I'd like to know what you call 'the whole town.' Do you call these silly people who are scared of Henry Johnson 'the whole town'?"

"Why, Martha," said Carrie, in a reasoning tone, "you talk as if you wouldn't be scared of him!"

"No more would I," retorted Martha.

"O-oh, Martha, how you talk!" said Kate. "Why, the idea! Everybody's afraid of him."

Carrie was grinning. "You've never seen him, have you?" she asked seductively.

"No," admitted Martha.

"Well, then, how do you know that you wouldn't be scared?"

Martha confronted her. "Have you ever seen him? No? Well, then how do you know you would be scared?"

The allied forces broke out in chorus: "But, Martha, everybody says so. Everybody says so."

"Everybody says what?"

"Everybody that's seen him say they were frightened almost to death, 'Tisn't only women, but it's men too. It's awful."

Martha wagged her head solemnly. "I'd try not to be afraid of him."

"But supposing you could not help it?" said Kate.

"Yes, and look here," cried Carrie. "I'll tell you another thing. The Hannigans are going to move out of the house next door."

"On account of him?" demanded Martha.

Carrie nodded. "Mrs. Hannigan says so herself."

"Well, of all things!" ejaculated Martha. "Going to move, eh? You don't say so! Where they going to move to?"

"Down on Orchard Avenue."

"Well, of all things! Nice house?"

"I don't know about that. I haven't heard. But there's lots of nice houses on Orchard."

"Yes, but they're all taken," said Kate. "There isn't a vacant house on Orchard Avenue."

"Oh yes, there is," said Martha. "The old Hampstead house is vacant."

"Oh, of course," said Kate. "But then I don't believe Mrs. Hannigan would like it there. I wonder where they can be going to move to?"

"I'm sure I don't know," sighed Martha. "It must be to some place we don't know about."

"Well," said Carrie Dungen, after a general reflective silence, "it's easy enough to find out, anyhow."

"Who knows – around here?" asked Kate.

"Why, Mrs. Smith, and there she is in her garden," said Carrie, jumping to her feet. As she dashed out of the door, Kate and Martha crowded at the window. Carrie's voice rang out from near the steps. "Mrs. Smith! Mrs. Smith! Do you know where the Hannigans are going to move to?"

XXIII

The autumn smote the leaves, and the trees of Whilomville were panoplied in crimson and yellow. The winds grew stronger, and in the melancholy purple of the nights the home shine of a window became a finer thing. The little boys, watching the sear and sorrowful leaves drifting down from the maples, dreamed of the near time when they could heap bushels in the streets and burn them during the abrupt evenings.

Three men walked down Niagara Avenue. As they approached Judge Hagenthorpe's house he came down his walk to meet them in the manner of one who has been waiting.

"Are you ready, Judge?" one said.

"All ready," he answered.

The four then walked to Trescott's house. He received them in his office, where he had been reading. He seemed surprised at this visit four very active and influential citizens, but he had nothing to say of it.

After they were all seated, Trescott looked expectantly from one face to another. There was a little silence. It was broken by John Twelve, the wholesale grocer, who was worth $400,000, and reported to be worth over a million.

"Well, doctor," he said, with a short laugh, "I suppose we might as well admit at once that we've come to interfere in something which is none of our business."

"Why, what is it?" asked Trescott, again looking from one face to an other. He seemed to appeal particularly to Judge Hagenthorpe, but the old man had his chin lowered musingly to his cane, and would not look at him.

"It's about what nobody talks of – much," said Twelve. "It's about Henry Johnson."

Trescott squared himself in his chair. "Yes?" he said.

Having delivered himself of the title, Twelve seemed to become more easy. "Yes," he answered, blandly, "we wanted to talk to you about it."

"Yes?" said Trescott.

Twelve abruptly advanced on the main attack. "Now see here, Trescott, we like you, and we have come to talk right out about this business. It may be none of our affairs and all that, and as for me, I don't mind if you tell me so; but I am not going to keep quiet and see you ruin yourself. And that's how we all feel."

"I am not ruining myself," answered Trescott.

"No, maybe you are not exactly ruining yourself," said Twelve, slowly, "but you are doing yourself a great deal of harm. You have changed from being the leading doctor in town to about the last one. It is mainly because there are always a large number of people who are very thoughtless fools, of course, but then that doesn't change the condition."

A man who had not heretofore spoken said, solemnly, "It's the women."

"Well, what I want to say is this," resumed Twelve: "Even if there are a lot of fools in the world, we can't see any reason why you should ruin yourself by opposing them. You can't teach them anything, you know."

"I am not trying to teach them anything." Trescott smiled wearily. "I – it is a matter of – well – "

"And there are a good many of us that admire you for it immensely," interrupted Twelve; "but that isn't going to change the minds of all those ninnies."

"It's the women," stated the advocate of this view again.

"Well, what I want to say is this," said Twelve. "We want you to get out of this trouble and strike your old gait again. You are simply killing your practice through your infernal pig-headedness. Now this thing is out of the ordinary, but there must be ways to – to beat the game somehow, you see. So we've talked it over – about a dozen of us – and, as I say, if you want to tell us to mind our own business, why, go ahead; but we've talked it over, and we've come to the conclusion that the only way to do is to get Johnson a place somewhere off up the valley, and – "

Trescott wearily gestured. "You don't know, my friend. Everybody is so afraid of him, they can't even give him good care. Nobody can attend to him as I do myself."

"But I have a little no-good farm up beyond Clarence Mountain that I was going to give to Henry," cried Twelve, aggrieved. "And if you – and if you – if you – through your house burning down, or anything – why, all the boys were prepared to take him right off your hands, and – and – "

Trescott arose and went to the window. He turned his back upon them. They sat waiting in silence. When he returned he kept his face in the shadow. "No, John Twelve," he said, "it can't be done."

There was another stillness. Suddenly a man stirred on his chair.

"Well, then, a public institution – " he began.

"No," said Trescott; "public institutions are all very good, but he is not going to one."

In the background of the group old Judge Hagenthorpe was thoughtfully smoothing the polished ivory head of his cane.

XXIV

Trescott loudly stamped the snow from his feet and shook the flakes from his shoulders. When he entered the house he went at once to the dining room, and then to the sitting room. Jimmie was there, reading painfully in a large book concerning giraffes and tigers and crocodiles.

"Where is your mother, Jimmie?" asked Trescott.

"I don't know, pa," answered the boy. "I think she is upstairs."

Trescott went to the foot of the stairs and called, but there came no answer. Seeing that the door of the little drawing room was open, he entered. The room was bathed in the half-light that came from the four dull panes of mica in the front of the great stove. As his eyes grew used to the shadows he saw his wife curled in an armchair. He went to her. "Why, Grace," he said, "didn't you hear me calling you?"

She made no answer, and as he bent over the chair he heard her trying to smother a sob in the cushion.

"Grace!" he cried. "You're crying!"

She raised her face. "I've got a headache, a dreadful headache, Ned."

"A headache?" he repeated, in surprise and incredulity.

He pulled a chair close to hers. Later, as he cast his eye over the zone of light shed by the dull red panes, he saw that a low table had been drawn close to the stove, and that it was burdened with many small cups and plates of uncut tea-cake. He remembered that the day was Wednesday, and that his wife received on Wednesday.

"Who was here today, Gracie?" he asked.

From his shoulder there came a mumble. "Mrs. Twelve."

"Was she – um," he said. "Why – didn't Anna Hagenthorpe come over?"

The mumble from his shoulder continued, "She wasn't well enough."

Glancing down at the cups, Trescott mechanically counted them. There were fifteen of them. "There, there," he said. "Don't cry, Grace. Don't cry."

The wind was whining round the house, and the snow beat aslant upon the windows. Sometimes the coal in the stove settled with a crumbling sound, and the four panes of mica flashed a sudden new crimson. As he sat holding her head on his shoulder, Trescott found himself occasionally trying to count the cups. There were fifteen of them.

Paul Laurence Dunbar
(1872–1906)

A native of Dayton, Ohio, and a friend of the Wright brothers, Paul Laurence Dunbar was best known in his lifetime as a writer of dialect poetry. He may have been to some degree a prisoner of his fame, linked in the public mind to speech that signaled humor in the minstrel show tradition. But deeper themes are present in his verse, as seen in his most anthologized poem, "Sympathy," which concludes with the line "I know why the caged bird sings."

Dunbar also was a writer of fiction, completing four novels and a number of short stories before his short career was ended by tuberculosis. "The Lynching of Jube Benson" (1904) begins in a comfortable library, with a group of men telling stories – a conventional setting, often used to introduce a ghostly tale. We are instead drawn into the brutal reality of American racism, with which both the teller and his listeners are indicted.

Text: Paul Laurence Dunbar, *The Heart of Happy Hollow* (New York: Dodd, Mead and Co., 1904).

The Lynching of Jube Benson

Gordon Fairfax's library held but three men, but the air was dense with clouds of smoke. The talk had drifted from one topic to another much as the smoke wreaths had puffed, floated, and thinned away. Then Handon Gay, who was an ambitious young reporter, spoke of a lynching story in a recent magazine, and the matter of punishment without trial put new life into the conversation.

"I should like to see a real lynching," said Gay rather callously.

"Well, I should hardly express it that way," said Fairfax, "but if a real, live lynching were to come my way, I should not avoid it."

"I should," spoke the other from the depths of his chair, where he had been puffing in moody silence. Judged by his hair, which was freely sprinkled with gray, the speaker might have been a man of forty-five or fifty, but his face, though lined and serious, was youthful, the face of a man hardly past thirty.

"What, you, Dr. Melville? Why, I thought that you physicians wouldn't weaken at anything."

"I have seen one such affair," said the doctor gravely, "in fact, I took a prominent part in it."

"Tell us about it," said the reporter, feeling for his pencil and notebook, which he was, nevertheless, careful to hide from the speaker.

The men drew their chairs eagerly up to the doctor's, but for a minute he did not seem to see them, but sat gazing abstractedly into the fire, then he took a long draw upon his cigar and began:

"I can see it all very vividly now. It was in the summer time and about seven years ago. I was practising at the time down in the little town of Bradford. It was a small and primitive place, just the location for an impecunious medical man, recently out of college.

"In lieu of a regular office, I attended to business in the first of two rooms which I rented from Hiram Daly, one of the more prosperous of the townsmen. Here I boarded and here also came my patients – white and black – whites from every section, and blacks from 'nigger town,' as the west portion of the place was called.

"The people about me were most of them coarse and rough, but they were simple and generous, and as time passed on I had about abandoned my intention of seeking distinction in wider fields and determined to settle into the place of a modest country doctor. This was rather a strange conclusion for a young man to arrive at, and I will not deny that the presence in the house of my host's beautiful young daughter, Annie, had something to do with my decision. She was a beautiful young girl of seventeen or eighteen, and very far superior to her surroundings. She had a native grace and a pleasing way about her that made everybody that came under her spell her abject slave. White and black who knew her loved her, and none, I thought, more deeply and respectfully than Jube Benson, the black man of all work about the place.

"He was a fellow whom everybody trusted; an apparently steady-going, grinning sort, as we used to call him. Well, he was completely under Miss Annie's thumb, and would fetch and carry for her like a faithful dog. As soon as he saw that I began to care for Annie, and anybody could see that, he transferred some of his allegiance to me and became my faithful servitor also. Never did a man have a more devoted adherent in his wooing than did I, and many a one of Annie's tasks which he volunteered to do gave her an extra hour with me. You can imagine that I liked the boy and you need not wonder any more that as both wooing and my practice waxed apace, I was content to give up my great ambitions and stay just where I was.

"It wasn't a very pleasant thing, then, to have an epidemic of typhoid break out in the town that kept me going so that I hardly had time for the courting that a fellow wants to carry on with his sweetheart while he is still young enough to call her his girl. I fumed, but duty was duty, and I kept to my work night and day. It was now that Jube proved how invaluable he was as a coadjutor. He not only took messages to Annie, but brought sometimes little ones from her to me, and he would tell me little secret things that he had overheard her say that made me throb with joy and swear at him for repeating his mistress' conversation. But best of all, Jube was a perfect Cerberus, and no one on earth could have been more effective in keeping away or deluding the other young fellows who visited the Dalys. He would tell me of it afterwards, chuckling softly to himself. 'An,' Doctah, I say to Mistah Hemp Stevens, '"Scuse us, Mistah Stevens, but Miss Annie, she des gone out," an' den he go outer de gate lookin' moughty lonesome. When Sam Elkins come, I say, "Sh, Mistah Elkins, Miss Annie, she done tuk down," an' he say, "What, Jube, you don' reckon hit de – – " Den he stop an' look skeert, an' I say, "I feared hit is, Mistah Elkins," an' sheks my haid ez solemn. He goes outer de gate lookin' lak his bes' frien' done daid, an' all de time Miss Annie behine de cu'tain ovah de po'ch des' a laffin' fit to kill.'

"Jube was a most admirable liar, but what could I do? He knew that I was a young fool of a hypocrite, and when I would rebuke him for these deceptions, he would give way and roll on the floor in an excess of delighted laughter until from very contagion I had to join him – and, well, there was no need of my preaching when there had been no beginning to his repentance and when there must ensue a continuance of his wrong-doing.

"This thing went on for over three months, and then, pouf! I was down like a shot. My patients were nearly all up, but the reaction from overwork made me an easy victim of the lurking germs. Then Jube loomed up as a nurse. He put everyone else aside, and with the doctor, a friend of mine from a neighbouring town, took entire charge of me. Even Annie herself was put aside, and I was cared for as tenderly as a baby. Tom, that was my physician and friend, told me all about it afterward with tears in his eyes. Only he was a big, blunt man and his expressions did not convey all that he meant. He told me how my nigger had nursed me as if I were a sick kitten and he my mother. Of how fiercely he guarded his right to be the sole one to 'do' for me, as he called it, and how, when the crisis came, he hovered, weeping, but hopeful, at my bedside, until it was safely passed, when they drove him, weak and exhausted, from the room. As for me, I knew little about it at the time, and cared less. I was too busy in my fight with death. To my chimerical vision there was only a black but gentle demon that came and went, alternating with a white fairy, who would insist on coming in on her head, growing larger and larger and then dissolving. But the pathos and devotion in the story lost nothing in my blunt friend's telling.

"It was during the period of a long convalescence, however, that I came to know my humble ally as he really was, devoted to the point of abjectness. There were times when for very shame at his goodness to me, I would beg him to go away, to do something else. He would go, but before I had time to realise that I was not being ministered to, he would be back at my side, grinning and pottering just the same. He manufactured duties for the joy of performing them. He pretended to see desires in me that I never had, because he liked to pander to them, and when I became entirely exasperated, and ripped out a good round oath, he chuckled with the remark, 'Dah, now, you sholy is gittin' well. Nevah did hyeah a man anywhaih nigh Jo'dan's sho' cuss lak dat.'

"Why, I grew to love him, love him, oh, yes, I loved him as well – oh, what am I saying? All human love and gratitude are damned poor things; excuse me, gentlemen, this isn't a pleasant story. The truth is usually a nasty thing to stand.

"It was not six months after that that my friendship to Jube, which he had been at such great pains to win, was put to too severe a test.

"It was in the summer time again, and as business was slack, I had ridden over to see my friend, Dr. Tom. I had spent a good part of the day there, and it was past four o'clock when I rode leisurely into Bradford. I was in a particularly joyous mood and no premonition of the impending catastrophe oppressed me. No sense of sorrow, present or to come, forced itself upon me, even when I saw men hurrying through the almost deserted streets. When I got within sight of my home and saw a crowd surrounding it, I was only interested sufficiently to spur my horse into a jog trot, which brought me up to the throng, when something in the sullen, settled horror in the men's faces gave me a sudden, sick thrill. They whispered a word to me, and without a thought, save for Annie, the girl who had been so surely growing into my heart, I leaped from the saddle and tore my way through the people to the house.

"It was Annie, poor girl, bruised and bleeding, her face and dress torn from struggling. They were gathered round her with white faces, and, oh, with what terrible patience they were trying to gain from her fluttering lips the name of her murderer. They made way for me and I knelt at her side. She was beyond my skill, and my will merged with theirs. One thought was in our minds.

"'Who?' I asked.

"Her eyes half opened, 'That black – – ' She fell back into my arms dead.

"We turned and looked at each other. The mother had broken down and was weeping, but the face of the father was like iron.

"'It is enough,' he said; 'Jube has disappeared.' He went to the door and said to the expectant crowd, 'She is dead.'

"I heard the angry roar without swelling up like the noise of a flood, and then I heard the sudden movement of many feet as the men separated into searching parties, and laying the dead girl back upon her couch, I took my rifle and went out to join them.

"As if by intuition the knowledge had passed among the men that Jube Benson had disappeared, and he, by common consent, was to be the object of our search. Fully a dozen of the citizens had seen him hastening toward the woods and noted his skulking air, but as he had grinned in his old good-natured way they had, at the time, thought nothing of it. Now, however, the diabolical reason of his slyness was apparent. He had been shrewd enough to disarm suspicion, and by now was far away. Even Mrs. Daly, who was visiting with a neighbour, had seen him stepping out by a back way, and had said with a laugh, 'I reckon that black rascal's a-running off somewhere.' Oh, if she had only known.

"'To the woods! To the woods!' that was the cry, and away we went, each with the determination not to shoot, but to bring the culprit alive into town, and then to deal with him as his crime deserved.

"I cannot describe the feelings I experienced as I went out that night to beat the woods for this human tiger. My heart smouldered within me like a coal, and I went forward under the impulse of a will that was half my own, half some more malignant power's. My throat throbbed drily, but water nor whiskey would not have quenched my thirst. The thought has come to me since that now I could interpret the panther's desire for blood and sympathise with it, but then I thought nothing. I simply went forward, and watched, watched with burning eyes for a familiar form that I had looked for as often before with such different emotions.

"Luck or ill-luck, which you will, was with our party, and just as dawn was graying the sky, we came upon our quarry crouched in the corner of a fence. It was only half light, and we might have passed, but my eyes had caught sight of him, and I raised the cry. We levelled our guns and he rose and came toward us.

"'I t'ought you wa'n't gwine see me,' he said sullenly, 'I didn't mean no harm.'

"'Harm!'

"Some of the men took the word up with oaths, others were ominously silent.

"We gathered around him like hungry beasts, and I began to see terror dawning in his eyes. He turned to me, 'I's moughty glad you's hyeah, doc,' he said, 'you ain't gwine let 'em whup me.'

"'Whip you, you hound,' I said, 'I'm going to see you hanged,' and in the excess of my passion I struck him full on the mouth. He made a motion as if to resent the blow against even such great odds, but controlled himself.

"'W'y, doctah,' he exclaimed in the saddest voice I have ever heard, 'w'y, doctah! I ain't stole nuffin' o' yo'n, an' I was comin' back. I only run off to see my gal, Lucy, ovah to de Centah.'

"'You lie!' I said, and my hands were busy helping the others bind him upon a horse. Why did I do it? I don't know. A false education, I reckon, one false from the beginning. I saw his black face glooming there in the half light, and I could only think of him as a monster. It's tradition. At first I was told that the black man would catch me, and when I got over that, they taught me that the devil was black, and when I had recovered from the sickness of that belief, here were Jube and his fellows with faces of menacing blackness. There was only one conclusion: This black man stood for all the powers of evil, the result of whose machinations had been gathering in my mind from childhood up. But this has nothing to do with what happened.

"After firing a few shots to announce our capture, we rode back into town with Jube. The ingathering parties from all directions met us as we made our way up to the house. All was very quiet and orderly. There was no doubt that it was as the papers would have said, a gathering of the best citizens. It was a gathering of stern, determined men, bent on a terrible vengeance.

"We took Jube into the house, into the room where the corpse lay. At sight of it, he gave a scream like an animal's and his face went the colour of storm-blown water. This was enough to condemn him. We divined, rather than heard, his cry of 'Miss Ann, Miss Ann, oh, my God, doc, you don't t'ink I done it?'

"Hungry hands were ready. We hurried him out into the yard. A rope was ready. A tree was at hand. Well, that part was the least of it, save that Hiram Daly stepped aside to let me be the first to pull upon the rope. It was lax at first. Then it tightened, and I felt the quivering soft weight resist my muscles. Other hands joined, and Jube swung off his feet.

"No one was masked. We knew each other. Not even the Culprit's face was covered, and the last I remember of him as he went into the air was a look of sad reproach that will remain with me until I meet him face to face again.

"We were tying the end of the rope to a tree, where the dead man might hang as a warning to his fellows, when a terrible cry chilled us to the marrow.

"'Cut 'im down, cut 'im down, he ain't guilty. We got de one. Cut him down, fu' Gawd's sake. Here's de man, we foun' him hidin' in de barn!'

"Jube's brother, Ben, and another Negro, came rushing toward us, half dragging, half carrying a miserable-looking wretch between them. Someone cut the rope and Jube dropped lifeless to the ground.

"'Oh, my Gawd, he's daid, he's daid!' wailed the brother, but with blazing eyes he brought his captive into the centre of the group, and we saw in the full light the scratched face of Tom Skinner – the worst white ruffian in the town – but the face we saw was not as we were accustomed to see it, merely smeared with dirt. It was blackened to imitate a Negro's.

"God forgive me; I could not wait to try to resuscitate Jube. I knew he was already past help, so I rushed into the house and to the dead girl's side. In the excitement they had not yet washed or laid her out. Carefully, carefully, I searched underneath her broken finger nails. There was skin there. I took it out, the little curled pieces, and went with it to my office.

"There, determinedly, I examined it under a powerful glass, and read my own doom. It was the skin of a white man, and in it were embedded strands of short, brown hair or beard.

"How I went out to tell the waiting crowd I do not know, for something kept crying in my ears, 'Blood guilty! Blood guilty!'

"The men went away stricken into silence and awe. The new prisoner attempted neither denial nor plea. When they were gone I would have helped Ben carry his brother in, but he waved me away fiercely, 'You he'ped murder my brothah, you dat was his frien', go 'way, go 'way! I'll tek him home myse'f.' I could only respect his wish, and he and his comrade took up the dead man and between them bore him up the street on which the sun was now shining full.

"I saw the few men who had not skulked indoors uncover as they passed, and I – I – stood there between the two murdered ones, while all the while something in my ears kept crying, 'Blood guilty! Blood guilty!'"

The doctor's head dropped into his hands and he sat for some time in silence, which was broken by neither of the men, then he rose, saying, "Gentlemen, that was my last lynching."

Alexander Posey (1873–1908)

Alexander Posey was a Muskogee (Creek) journalist and tribal politician. Schooled in both white and Indian culture, he knew the work of writers such as Poe as well as the oral traditions of the Muskogee nation. Posey anticipates later authors like N. Scott Momaday, Leslie Silko, and Louise Erdrich in bringing an indigenous American outlook, culture, and traditional storytelling into English-language narrative.

Posey wrote at least four stories about Chinnubbie Harjo, of which only two have been located. Chinnubbie is a trickster hero, amoral, brutal, humorous, and charismatic. In "Chinnubbie and the Squaws," the only other surviving story, Chinnubbie not only murders all the women in the household of the chief of a rival tribe when they refuse him food, but scalps them – a technique he is credited with inventing. Chinnubbie is, moreover, a mask or alter ego for Posey himself, since he often used Chinnubbie Harjo as a pseudonym.

"Chinnubbie and the Owl" is a story about storytelling. Chinnubbie tells his tale as part of a contest before tribal elders and shamans, who are the custodians of the tribe's oral traditions. His story is part joke and part uncanny encounter in the American wilderness, a pattern often seen in this collection.

Text: "Chinnubbie and the Owl" was published in an undated pamphlet by Posey, now at the Gilcrease Museum of the University of Tulsa. It was probably written about 1893. The text used here follows the collection edited by Matthew Wynn Sivils, *Chinnubbie and the Owl: Muscogee (Creek) Stories, Orations, and Oral Traditions* (Lincoln: University of Nebraska Press, c.2005). The only changes are corrections of errors in use of quotation marks, and the addition, for clarity, of a space between the end of Chinnubbie's narrative and the framing narration.

Reprinted with permission from the Alexander Posey Collection, Gilcrease Museum Archives, University of Tulsa. Flat Storage. Registration #4627.33.

Chinnubbie and the Owl

We have learned in a previous story that Chinnubbie was a humorist of unquestioned excellence, as well as being renowned for other traits of character. Traditions claim that he was a storyteller of extraordinary merit; that when he spoke, his hearers gave strict attention, for there was a charm in his speech that was truly admirable and a something in his eloquent wit that captivated the gravest of his audience; that his actions when delivering a tale were as comical and laughable, almost, as the story he told. Yet his genius, as versatile as it was, bore its richest fruits in the circumstances of necessity only; and to one of these exigencies are we indebted for the story following this proem, which is supposed, on the authority of the prophets – the keepers of the oral library – to have been actually experienced by its author and rehearsed to the warlike multitude on an occasion of which we shall presently learn.

It was in the twilight of a lovely summer day, while the chiefs, medicine men, and warriors were grouped in a circle around the blazing campfire, discussing the success

American Gothic: From Salem Witchcraft to H. P. Lovecraft, An Anthology, Second Edition. Edited by Charles L. Crow.
Editorial material and organization © 2013 John Wiley & Sons, Ltd. Published 2013 by John Wiley & Sons, Ltd.

of a recent chase, parleying over various topics, and relating numerous anecdotes, that the prophet arose and offered a costly bow and twelve arrows to the one who could relate the best story of his own experience, or the best he could make on the spur of the moment. Of course the offer was readily accepted by scores of valiant warriors, and Chinnubbie was not to be left out among the rivals for the prize. Quickly arising from his grassy lounge and shaking the ashes from the tomahawk that he had just been smoking, he thus conjured the generous sage in his favorite phrase: "By the bears, I wish a part in this myself."

His desire was immediately granted, and the contestants one by one rehearsed their tales in a plausible manner and exerted every power within them to accomplish their end. But all – save one, Chinnubbie, the last though not the least – were accused of unscrupulous plagiarism. They each had plucked a gem from memory's treasury of old traditions to veneer the imperfect portions of their unpremeditated story. The guilty rivals became the objects of ridicule and sarcastic remarks, while Chinnubbie, in whose well-told tale no ill-gotten thoughts had been detected, received the praise of the chief and prophet in every manner of endearing expression. The prize was awarded to him with bows and obeisance due the gods. Chinnubbie became the autocrat of the evening's entertainment, and every word that was lisped was lisped in admiration of his wonderful tale. He had touched the chord whose reverberations echoed fame.

We must not after all be persuaded to believe that Chinnubbie became and remained a favorite of his countrymen. His fickleness and perfidiousness caused his popularity to be very precarious. He would be extoled [sic] today for a noble act and execrated tomorrow for a bad one. Whether famous or infamous, Chinnubbie cared but very little. He was content anywhere and under all circumstances and conditions.

Chinnubbie's Story

It has been quite awhile since this incident, which I am about to relate to you, was experienced. But, warriors, a good story, however ancient, is always new, and the more frequently it is told, the more attractive it becomes, and is destined to never be oblite-rated from the memory in which it lives. The campfire is made more cheerful and happier when such stories are told, and the mind is released from the bonds of its cares and solicitudes. So, this one, from that time to present, has been an evergreen in my recollection. None but my most intimate friends have a knowledge of this tale, and I have cautioned them never to communicate the same to others, as it would doubtless excite the jealousy of the prophets, who are my superiors in the creation of such nar-ratives. But whether it will be envied by them or not, the time has arrived when it must be publicly declared.

On one of my first wanderings away from home in foreign lands, I lost the course of my journey, and went astray in a pathless forest, through which, I thought, no man had ever passed. It was a solitary waste, a jungle, and a lair of ferocious beasts and reptiles. Even at noonday, its vast interior seemed dark and dusky, with only a sunbeam here and there to illume its gloom, invigorate its rank epicurean growth. Had I been otherwise than an ingenious bowman, I would not have escaped the savage greed of the puma that clung in his hunger to the arching bough, and the wolf that tracked and sniffed the course I took. At night I sought to rest my wearied limbs in the fork of some lofty oak, but found no repose. Thus I roamed and prowled in hunger, fruitless search, and despondency.

Finally, on the last evening of my almost helpless wandering, a strange but a fortu-nate incident befell me. The sun was just disappearing in the gold of the western sky, and twilight was gathering its sombre shades over the unhunted woods, when my attention was suddenly attracted by the weird hoots of an owl, perched upon the bough of a desolate oak, beneath which I had been standing quite a while, listening to the dreamy far-off song of the whippoorwill. He seemed as grave and solemn as death itself; his large saffron eyes appeared prophetic of my fate. Recalling to memory the strange stories that had often been related to me in childhood, of such birds, I stood bewitched and motionless in a trance of awe and silence. The owl likewise maintained a gravelike stillness that was broken only by the flutter of his wings. He grew, I thought, exceeding twice his real size; this so increased my horror, that had anyone been near to observe me in this situation, he would have declared that my head, too, grew fabulously huge. Like the squirrel, when charmed by reptile fascination, I could neither move nor wail a voice of despair. Ultimately, like morning mists ascending from the streams, swamps, and morasses, the fog of my stupidity slowly vanished into serene sunlight of consciousness. At this moment of my recuperation, I thought myself the happiest brave that ever twanged a bow. But yet, I could not forbear thinking: "This enchantment is ominous of my end; if not the determination of my career, a misfortune that shall darken all my future years."

I hope that while mortals have a knowledge of my existence I will never undergo another like experience.

Having now a full possession of my senses, I walked around the tree to quit the bewitching spot, and turned my head in various directions. This was mimicked by the mysterious bird in a most consummate manner, who still seemed to bespeak my untimely fate. Becoming desirous to know the extent of his imitations, which now excited my fancy, I exclaimed in a tremulous tone "Who are you?"

The owl replied: "Who are you? – whoo, whoo!, whoo, whoo!!"

A smile, at this dubious response, forced itself upon my countenance. Again, in a more vehement voice, I asked: "Answer, by the bears and all beside, who are you?"

As the echoes of my impassioned words reverberated through the sable forest, the amber feathered bird imperiously rejoined:

"Answer, by the bears and all beside, who are you?"

He thus continued and repeated all that I said, but would give no answer to my interrogations. Our conversation was the reiteration of one thought. Finally, I thought the task of endeavoring to cause him to converse with me an irksome waste of time, and begun to walk around the tree, to note how long he would mimic my action by turning his head without reversing, and keeping his body at the same time in one position. I continued to walk incessantly around the oak, and still he imitated me with apparent ease and alacrity. Presently, I became somewhat fatigued in my curiosity, being wearied already by my long rambles; but knowing that perseverance triumphs, I did not forsake my singular fancy. When lo! to my surprise and sudden fright, his head fell severed from the body to the ground; exclaiming as it fell, "Take my head and place it in your belt, it will guide you to your home in safety!"

Like a child obeying the command of its affectionate mother, I heeded the behest of the falling head, and fastening it securely in my belt, I journeyed in safety to my home, from which I had long been absent.

Chinnubbie, at the conclusion of his story, departed immediately from the applauding multitude to slack his thirst in the neighboring brook. Upon his return, the bow and twelve arrows which had been pledged to the victorious brave were awarded to him with congratulatory speeches. Chinnubbie, as he received the costly prize, extricated from his buckskins the featherless head of an owl and ejaculated in a most triumphant voice: "Doubt if you will the authenticity of my tale, here is the head of its hero!"

"Doubt your tale? never, never – absurd," rejoined the prophet much amazed at Chinnubbie's earnestness, "never, never, it is as true as the reality of day and night!"

"Few, few there are on whom such a fortune smiles and many, many on whom it frowns. Few are born to win. Warn, ye gods, if such as ye there be, warn, I pray, the bears, the fallow deers, the bisons, the pumas of the forest, and the foes of my heroic clan!"

Chinnubbie thus replied, and departed from his comrades in the twilight of blossoming day like a dream, on his journey to – he knew not where, but leaving the impression that his object was to search the wilds in quest of spoils. His fellows anticipated a great feast and a unique occasion on his return, but alas! in vain – he had departed on another tramp.

Long, long years afterwards, Chinnubbie returned, and was welcomed with wild enthusiasm. He was not rebuked for the inexcusable falsehood that he had told on the morning of his setting out, for that was forgotten in the ecstasy of joy on his reappearance. A feast and a great war-dance were given in his honor. On this occasion, Chinnubbie is said to have displayed his oratorical genius in some blood-stirring phillipics [sic]. But tradition has unfortunately failed to embalm them in its unwritten volumes.

Jack London (1876–1916)

Internationally, Jack London has always been one of his country's most revered authors. At home, until recently, he was dismissed as the writer of a few novels of juvenile fiction. In fact his production, in a short career, was astounding: some fifty books, and over 200 short stories. Impressive as well is the range of his interests. He wrote investigative journalism (his was the great age of "muckraking"), covered wars and athletic events, and produced works on land management and ecological farming. His autobiographical works have surprising freshness and candor. He introduced boxing and the life on the road (anticipating the Beats by forty years) to American literature. He wrote science fiction about cavemen and post-apocalyptic futures. While he would have agreed that his work was uneven, he was not a primitive or inspired amateur, but a professional writer of great talent and energy.

London's "Samuel" (1909) will be a revelation to readers expecting masculine themes and a setting in the Yukon or the South Seas. His Margaret Henan recalls such strong women as Freeman's "Old Woman Magoun." The Gothic quality of the story reveals itself slowly and deliberately. Readers will note an allusion to Poe, a sign that London knew his predecessors. In many ways this domestic tragedy recalls Sigmund Freud's notion of the *unheimlich*, the secret which reveals itself inside the apparently safe and familiar. (At the core of the word *unheimlich* is *Heim*, home.) The usual English translation of Freud's German word is "uncanny." Perhaps not by coincidence, London uses "uncanny" twice in the opening paragraphs of this truly unsettling tale.

Text: Jack London, *The Strength of the Strong* (New York: Macmillan, 1914).

Samuel

Margaret Henan would have been a striking figure under any circumstances, but never more so than when I first chanced upon her, a sack of grain of fully a hundred-weight on her shoulder, as she walked with sure though tottering stride from the cart-tail to the stable, pausing for an instant to gather strength at the foot of the steep steps that led to the grain-bin. There were four of these steps, and she went up them, a step at a time, slowly, unwaveringly, and with so dogged a certitude that it never entered my mind that her strength could fail her and let that hundred-weight sack fall from the lean and withered frame that well-nigh doubled under it. For she was patently an old woman, and it was her age that made me linger by the cart and watch.

Six times she went between the cart and the stable, each time with a full sack on her back, and beyond passing the time of day with me she took no notice of my presence. Then, the cart empty, she fumbled for matches and lighted a short clay pipe, pressing down the burning surface of the tobacco with a calloused and apparently nerveless

American Gothic: From Salem Witchcraft to H. P. Lovecraft, An Anthology, Second Edition. Edited by Charles L. Crow.
Editorial material and organization © 2013 John Wiley & Sons, Ltd. Published 2013 by John Wiley & Sons, Ltd.

thumb. The hands were noteworthy. They were large-knuckled, sinewy and mal-formed by labor, rimed with callouses, the nails blunt and broken, and with here and there cuts and bruises, healed and healing, such as are common to the hands of hard-working men. On the back were huge, upstanding veins, eloquent of age and toil. Looking at them, it was hard to believe that they were the hands of the woman who had once been the belle of Island McGill. This last, of course, I learned later. At the time I knew neither her history nor her identity.

She wore heavy man's brogans. Her legs were stockingless, and I had noticed when she walked that her bare feet were thrust into the crinkly, iron-like shoes that sloshed about her lean ankles at every step. Her figure, shapeless and waistless, was garbed in a rough man's shirt and in a ragged flannel petticoat that had once been red. But it was her face, wrinkled, withered and weather-beaten, surrounded by an aureole of unkempt and straggling wisps of grayish hair, that caught and held me. Neither drifted hair nor serried wrinkles could hide the splendid dome of a forehead, high and broad without verging in the slightest on the abnormal.

The sunken cheeks and pinched nose told little of the quality of the life that flickered behind those clear blue eyes of hers. Despite the minutiae of wrinkle-work that some-how failed to wizen them, her eyes were clear as a girl's – clear, out-looking, and far-seeing, and with an open and unblinking steadfastness of gaze that was disconcerting. The remarkable thing was the distance between them. It is a lucky man or woman who has the width of an eye between, but with Margaret Henan the width between her eyes was fully that of an eye and a half. Yet so symmetrically molded was her face that this remarkable feature produced no uncanny effect, and, for that matter, would have escaped the casual observer's notice. The mouth, shapeless and toothless, with down-turned corners and lips dry and parchment-like, nevertheless lacked the muscular slack-ness so usual with age. The lips might have been those of a mummy, save for that impression of rigid firmness they gave. Not that they were atrophied. On the contrary, they seemed tense and set with a muscular and spiritual determination. There, and in the eyes, was the secret of the certitude with which she carried the heavy sacks up the steep steps, with never a false step or over-balance, and emptied them in the grain-bin.

"You are an old woman to be working like this," I ventured.

She looked at me with that strange, unblinking gaze, and she thought and spoke with the slow deliberateness that characterized everything about her, as if well aware of an eternity that was hers and in which there was no need for haste. Again I was impressed by the enormous certitude of her. In this eternity that seemed so indubita-bly hers, there was time and to spare for safe-footing and stable equilibrium – for cer-titude, in short. No more in her spiritual life than in carrying the hundred-weights of grain, was there a possibility of a misstep or an overbalancing. The feeling produced in me was uncanny. Here was a human soul that, save for the most glimmering of con-tacts, was beyond the humanness of me. And the more I learned of Margaret Henan in the weeks that followed the more mysteriously remote she became. She was as alien as a far-journeyer from some other star, and no hint could she nor all the countryside give me of what norms of living, what heats of feeling, or rules of philosophic con-templation actuated her in all that she had been and was.

"I wull be suvunty-two come Guid Friday a fortnight," she said in reply to my question.

"But you are an old woman to be doing this man's work, and a strong man's work at that," I insisted.

Again she seemed to immerse herself in that atmosphere of contemplative eternity, and so strangely did it affect me that I should not have been surprised to have awaked a century or so later and found her just beginning to enunciate her reply:

"The work hoz tull be done, an' I am beholden tull no one."

"But have you no children, no family relations?"

"O, ay, a-plenty o' them, but they no see fut tull be helpun' me."

She drew out her pipe for a moment, then added, with a nod of her head toward the house, "I luv' wuth meself."

I glanced at the house, straw-thatched and commodious, at the large stable, and at the large array of fields I knew must belong with the place.

"It is a big bit of land for you to farm by yourself."

"O, ay, a bug but, suvunty acres. Ut kept me old mon buzzy, along wuth a son an' a hired mon, tull say naught o' extra honds un the harvest an' a maid-servant un the house."

She clambered into the cart, gathered the reins in her hands, and quizzed me with her keen, shrewd eyes.

"Belike ye hail from over the watter – Ameruky, I'm meanun'?"

"Yes, I'm a Yankee," I answered.

"Ye wull no be findun' mony Island McGill folk stoppun' un Ameruky?"

"No; I don't remember ever meeting one in the States."

She nodded her head.

"They are home-lovun' bodies, though I wull no be sayun' they are no fair-traveled. Yet they come home ot the last, them oz are no lost ot sea or kult by fevers an' such-like un foreign parts."

"Then your sons will have gone to sea and come home again?" I queried.

"O, ay, all savun' Samuel oz was drownded."

At the mention of Samuel I could have sworn to a strange light in her eyes, and it seemed to me, as by some telepathic flash, that I divined in her a tremendous wistfulness, an immense yearning. It seemed to me that here was the key to her inscrutableness, the clew that if followed properly would make all her strangeness plain. It came to me that here was a contact and that for the moment I was glimpsing into the soul of her. The question was tickling on my tongue, but she forestalled me.

She *tckh'd* to the horse, and with a "Guid day tull you, sir," drove off.

A simple, homely people, are the folk of Island McGill, and I doubt if a more sober, thrifty, and industrious folk is to be found in all the world. Meeting them abroad – and to meet them abroad one must meet them on the sea, for a hybrid seafaring and farmer breed are they – one would never take them to be Irish. Irish they claim to be, speaking of the North of Ireland with pride and sneering at their Scottish brothers; yet Scotch they undoubtedly are, transplanted Scotch of long ago, it is true, but none the less Scotch, with a thousand traits, to say nothing of their tricks of speech and woolly utterance, which nothing less than their Scotch clannishness could have preserved to this late day.

A narrow loch, scarcely half a mile wide, separates Island McGill from the mainland of Ireland; and, once across this loch, one finds himself in an entirely different country. The Scotch impression is strong, and the people, to commence with, are Presbyterians. When it is considered that there is no public house[1] in all the island and that seven thousand souls dwell therein, some idea may be gained of the temperateness of the community. Wedded to old ways, public opinion and the ministers are powerful influences, while fathers and mothers are revered and obeyed as in few other places in this modern world. Courting lasts never later than ten at night, and no girl walks out with her young man without her parents' knowledge and consent.

Notes

Samuel
[1] Tavern.

The young men go down to the sea and sow their wild oats in the wicked ports, returning periodically, between voyages, to live the old intensive morality, to court till ten o'clock, to sit under the minister each Sunday, and to listen at home to the same stern precepts that the elders preached to them from the time they were laddies. Much they learned of women in the ends of the earth, these seafaring sons, yet a canny wisdom was theirs and they never brought wives home with them. The one solitary exception to this had been the schoolmaster, who had been guilty of bringing a wife from half a mile the other side of the loch. For this he had never been forgiven, and he rested under a cloud for the remainder of his days. At his death the wife went back across the loch to her own people, and the blot on the escutcheon of Island McGill was erased. In the end the sailor-men married girls of their own home land and settled down to become exemplars of all the virtues for which the island was noted.

Island McGill was without a history. She boasted none of the events that go to make history. There had never been any wearing of the green, any Fenian[2] conspiracies, any land disturbances. There had been but one eviction, and that purely technical – a test case, and on advice of the tenant's lawyer. So Island McGill was without annals. History had passed her by. She paid her taxes, acknowledged her crowned rulers, and left the world alone; all she asked in return was that the world leave her alone. The world was composed of two parts – Island McGill and the rest of it. And whatever was not Island McGill was outlandish and barbarian; and well she knew, for did not her seafaring sons bring home report of that world and its ungodly ways?

It was from the skipper of a Glasgow tramp, as passenger from Colombo to Rangoon, that I had first learned of the existence of Island McGill; and it was from him that I had carried the letter that gave me entrance to the house of Mrs. Ross, widow of a master mariner, with a daughter living with her and with two sons, master mariners themselves and out upon the sea. Mrs. Ross did not take in boarders, and it was Captain Ross's letter alone that had enabled me to get from her bed and board. In the evening, after my encounter with Margaret Henan, I questioned Mrs. Ross, and I knew on the instant that I had in truth stumbled upon mystery.

Like all Island McGill folk, as I was soon to discover, Mrs. Ross was at first averse to discussing Margaret Henan at all. Yet it was from her I learned that evening that Margaret Henan had once been one of the island belles. Herself the daughter of a well-to-do farmer, she had married Thomas Henan, equally well-to-do. Beyond the usual housewife's tasks she had never been accustomed to work. Unlike many of the island women, she had never lent a hand in the fields.

"But what of her children?" I asked.

"Two o' the sons, Jamie an' Timothy uz married an' be goun' tull sea. Thot bug house close tull the post-office uz Jamie's. The daughters thot ha' no married be luvun' wuth them as dud marry. An' the rest be dead."

"The Samuels," Clara interpolated, with what I suspected was a giggle.

She was Mrs. Ross's daughter, a strapping young woman with handsome features and remarkably handsome black eyes.

"'Tuz naught tull be smuckerun' ot," her mother reproved her.

"The Samuels?" I intervened. "I don't understand."

"Her four sons thot died."

"And were they all named Samuel?"

"Ay."

[2] Irish nationalist.

"Strange," I commented in the lagging silence.

"Very strange," Mrs. Ross affirmed, proceeding stolidly with the knitting of the woolen singlet on her knees – one of the countless undergarments that she interminably knitted for her skipper sons.

"And it was only the Samuels that died?" I queried, in further attempt.

"The others luv'd," was the answer. "A fine fomuly – no finer on the island. No better lods ever sailed out of Island McGill. The munuster held them up oz models tull pottern after. Nor was ever a whusper breathed again' the girls."

"But why is she left alone now in her old age?" I persisted. "Why don't her own flesh and blood look after her? Why does she live alone? Don't they ever go to see her or care for her?"

"Never a one un twenty years an' more now. She fetch't ut on tull herself. She drove them from the house just oz she drove old Tom Henan, thot was her husband, tull hus death."

"Drink?" I ventured.

Mrs. Ross shook her head scornfully, as if drink was a weakness beneath the weakest of Island McGill.

A long pause followed, during which Mrs. Ross knitted stolidly on, only nodding permission when Clara's young man, mate on one of the Shire Line sailing ships, came to walk out with her. I studied the half-dozen ostrich eggs, hanging in the corner against the wall like a cluster of some monstrous fruit. On each shell was painted precipitous and impossible seas through which full-rigged ships foamed with a lack of perspective only equaled by their sharp technical perfection. On the mantelpiece stood two large pearl shells, obviously a pair, intricately carved by the patient hands of New Caledonian convicts. In the center of the mantel was a stuffed bird of paradise, while about the room were scattered gorgeous shells from the southern seas, delicate sprays of coral sprouting from barnacled pi-pi shells and cased in glass, assegais[3] from South Africa, stone-axes from New Guinea, huge Alaskan tobacco-pouches beaded with heraldic totem designs, a boomerang from Australia, divers ships in glass bottles, a cannibal *kai-kai* bowl from the Marquesas, and fragile cabinets from China and the Indies and inlaid with mother-of-pearl and precious woods.

I gazed at this varied trove brought home by sailor sons, and pondered the mystery of Margaret Henan, who had driven her husband to his death and been forsaken by all her kin. It was not the drink. Then what was it? – some shocking cruelty? some amazing infidelity? or some fearful, old-world peasant-crime?

I broached my theories, but to all Mrs. Ross shook her head.

"Ut was no thot," she said. "Margaret was a guid wife an' a guid mother, an' I doubt she would harm a fly. She brought up her fomuly God-fearin' an' decent-minded. Her trouble was thot she took lunatuc – turned eediot."

Mrs. Ross tapped significantly on her forehead to indicate a state of addlement.

"But I talked with her this afternoon," I objected, "and I found her a sensible woman – remarkably bright for one of her years."

"Ay, an' I'm grantun' all thot you say," she went on calmly. "But I am no referrun' tull thot. I am referrun' tull her wucked-headed an' vucious stubbornness. No more stubborn woman ever luv'd than Margaret Henan. Ut was all on account o' Samuel, which was the name o' her eldest an' they do say her favorut brother – hum oz died by hus own hond all through the munuster's mustake un no registerun' the new church ot Dublin. Ut was a lesson thot the name was musfortunate, but she would no take ut, an' there was talk when she called her first child Samuel – hum thot died o' the croup. An' wuth thot what does she do but call the next one Samuel, an' hum only three when he fell un tull the tub o' hot watter an' was plain cooked tull death. Ut all come, I tell you, o' her wucked-headed an' foolush stubbornness. For a Samuel she must hov; an' ut was the death of the four of her sons. After the first, dudna her own mother go down un the dirt tull her feet, a-beggun' an' pleadun' wuth her no tull name her next one Samuel? But she was no tull be turned from her purpose. Margaret Henan was always set un her ways, an' never more so thon on thot name Samuel.

"She was fair lunatuc on Samuel. Dudna her neighbors, an' all kuth an' kun savun' them thot luv'd un the house wuth her, get up an' walk out ot the christenun' of the second – hum thot was cooked? Thot they dud, an' ot the very moment the munuster asked what would the bairn's name be. 'Samuel,' says she; an' wuth thot they got up an' walked out an' left the house. An' ot the door dudna her Aunt Fannie, her mother's suster, turn an' say loud for all tull hear: 'What for wull she be wantun' tull murder the wee thung?' The munuster heard fine, an' dudna like ut, but, oz he told my Larry afterward, what could he do? Ut was the woman's wush, an' there was no law again' a mother callun' her child accordun' tull her wush.

"An' then was there no' the third Samuel? An' when he was lost ot sea off the Cape, dudna she break all laws o' nature tull hov a fourth? She was forty-seven, I'm tellun' ye, an' she hod a child ot forty-seven. Thunk on ut! Ot forty-seven! Ut was fair scand'lous."

From Clara, next morning, I got the tale of Margaret Henan's favorite brother; and from here and there, in the week that followed, I pieced together the tragedy of Margaret Henan. Samuel Dundee had been the youngest of Margaret's four brothers, and, as Clara told me, she had well-nigh worshiped him. He was going to sea at the time, skipper of one of the sailing ships of the Bank Line, when he married Agnes Hewitt. She was described as a slender wisp of a girl, delicately featured and with a nervous organization of the supersensitive order. Theirs had been the first marriage in the "new" church, and after a two-weeks' honeymoon Samuel had kissed his bride good-bye and sailed in command of the *Loughbank*, a big four-masted bark.

And it was because of the "new" church that the minister's blunder occurred. Nor was it the blunder of the minister alone, as one of the elders later explained; for it was equally the blunder of the whole Presbytery of Coughleen, which included fifteen churches on Island McGill and the mainland. The old church, beyond repair, had been torn down and the new one built on the original foundation. Looking upon the foundation stones as similar to a ship's keel, it never entered the minister's nor the Presbytery's head that the new church was legally any other than the old church.

"An' three couples was married the first week un the new church," Clara said. "First of all, Samuel Dundee an' Agnes Hewitt; the next day Albert Mahan an' Minnie Duncan; an' by the week-end Eddie Troy an Flo Mackintosh – all sailor-men, an' un sux weeks' time the last of them back tull their ships an' awa', an' no one o' them dreamin' of the wuckedness they'd been ot."

The Imp of the Perverse[4] must have chuckled at the situation. All things favored. The marriages had taken place in the first week of May, and it was not till three months later that the minister, as required by law, made his quarterly report to the civil authorities in Dublin. Promptly came back the announcement that his church had no legal existence, not being registered according to the law's demands. This was overcome by

Notes

[4] In Edgar Allan Poe's story by this name, the "imp of the perverse" is defined as an impulse which leads us to take an action "for the reason we should *not*."

prompt registration; but the marriages were not to be so easily remedied. The three sailor-husbands were away, and their wives in short, were not their wives.

"But the munuster was no for alarmin' the bodies," said Clara. "He kept hus council an' bided hus time, waitin' for the lods tull be back from sea. Oz luck would have ut, he was away across the island tull christenun' when Albert Mahan arrives home onexpected, hus shup just docked ot Dublin. Ut's nine o'clock ot night when the munuster, un hus sluppers an' dressun' gown, gets the news. Up he jumps an' calls for horse an' saddle, an' awa' he goes like the wund for Albert Mahan's. Albert uz just goun' tull bed an' hoz one shoe off when the munuster arrives.

"'Come wuth me, the pair o' ye,' says he, breathless-like. 'What for an' me dead weary an' goun' tull bed?' says Albert. 'Tull be lawful married,' says the munuster. Albert looks black an' says, 'Now munuster ye wull be jokin',' but tull humself, oz I've heard hum tell mony a time, he uz wonderun' thot the munuster should a-took tull whuskey ot hus time o' life.

"'We be no married?' says Minnie. He shook his head. 'An' I om no Mussus Mahan?' 'No,' says he, 'ye are no Mussus Mahan. Ye are plain Muss Duncan.' 'But ye married us yoursel',' says she. 'I dud an' I dudna,' says he. An' wuth thot he tells them the whole upshot, an Albert puts on hus shoe, an' they go with the munuster an' are married proper an' lawful, an' oz Albert Mahan says afterward mony's the time, "Tus no every mon thot hoz two weddun' nights on Island McGill.'"

Six months later Eddie Troy came home and was promptly remarried. But Samuel Dundee was away on a three-years' voyage and his ship fell overdue. Further to complicate the situation, a baby boy, past two years old, was waiting for him in the arms of his wife. The months passed, and the wife grew thin with worrying. "Ut's no meself I'm thunkun' on," she is reported to have said many times, "but ut's the puir fatherless bairn. Uf aught happened tull Samuel where wull the bairn stond?"

Lloyds posted the *Loughbank* as missing, and the owners ceased the monthly remittance of Samuel's half-pay to his wife. It was the question of the child's legitimacy that preyed on her mind, and, when all hope of Samuel's return was abandoned, she drowned herself and the child in the loch. And here enters the greater tragedy. The *Loughbank* was not lost. By a series of sea disasters and delays too interminable to relate, she had made one of those long, unsighted passages such as occur once or twice in half a century. How the Imp must have held both his sides! Back from the sea came Samuel, and when they broke the news to him something else broke somewhere in his heart or head. Next morning they found him where he had tried to kill himself across the grave of his wife and child. Never in the history of Island McGill was there so fearful a deathbed. He spat in the minister's face and reviled him, and died blaspheming so terribly that those that tended on him did so with averted gaze and trembling hands.

And, in the face of all this, Margaret Henan named her first child Samuel.

How account for the woman's stubbornness? Or was it a morbid obsession that demanded a child of hers should be named Samuel? Her third child was a girl, named after herself, and the fourth was a boy again. Despite the strokes of fate that had already bereft her, and despite the loss of friends and relatives, she persisted in her resolve to name the child after her brother. She was shunned at church by those who had grown up with her. Her mother, after a final appeal, left her house with the warning that if the child were so named she would never speak to her again. And though the old lady lived thirty-odd years longer she kept her word. The minister agreed to christen the child any name but Samuel, and every other minister on Island McGill refused to christen it by the name she had chosen. There was talk on the part of Margaret Henan of going to law at the time, but in the end she carried the child to Belfast and there had it christened Samuel.

And then nothing happened. The whole island was confuted. The boy grew and prospered. The schoolmaster never ceased averring that it was the brightest lad he had ever seen. Samuel had a splendid constitution, a tremendous grip on life. To everybody's amazement he escaped the usual run of childish afflictions. Measles, whooping-cough and mumps knew him not. He was armor-clad against germs, immune to all disease. Headaches and earaches were things unknown. "Never so much oz a boil or a pumple," as one of the old bodies told me, ever marred his healthy skin. He broke school records in scholarship and athletics, and whipped every boy of his size or years on Island McGill.

It was a triumph for Margaret Henan. This paragon was hers, and it bore the cherished name. With the one exception of her mother, friends and relatives drifted back and acknowledged that they had been mistaken; though there were old crones who still abided by their opinion and who shook their heads ominously over their cups of tea. The boy was too wonderful to last. There was no escaping the curse of the name his mother had wickedly laid upon him. The young generation joined Margaret Henan in laughing at them, but the old crones continued to shake their heads.

Other children followed. Margaret Henan's fifth was a boy, whom she called Jamie, and in rapid succession followed three girls, Alice, Sara, and Nora, the boy Timothy, and two more girls, Florence and Katie. Katie was the last and eleventh, and Margaret Henan, at thirty-five, ceased from her exertions. She had done well by Island McGill and the Queen. Nine healthy children were hers. All prospered. It seemed her ill luck had shot its bolt with the deaths of her first two. Nine lived, and one of them was named Samuel.

Jamie elected to follow the sea, though it was not so much a matter of election as compulsion, for the eldest sons on Island McGill remained on the land while all other sons went to the salt plowing. Timothy followed Jamie, and by the time the latter had got his first command, a steamer in the Bay trade out of Cardiff, Timothy was mate of a big sailing ship. Samuel, however, did not take kindly to the soil. The farmer's life had no attraction for him. His brothers went to sea, not out of desire, but because it was the only way for them to gain their bread; and he, who had no need to go, envied them when, returned from far voyages, they sat by the kitchen fire and told their bold tales of the wonderlands beyond the sea-rim.

Samuel became a teacher, much to his father's disgust, and even took extra certificates, going to Belfast for his examinations. When the old master retired, Samuel took over his school. Secretly, however, he studied navigation, and it was Margaret's delight when he sat by the kitchen fire, and, despite their master's tickets, tangled up his brothers in the theoretics of their profession. Tom Henan alone was outraged when Samuel, school teacher, gentleman, and heir to the Henan farm, shipped to sea before the mast. Margaret had an abiding faith in her son's star, and whatever he did she was sure was for the best. Like everything else connected with his glorious personality, there had never been known so swift a rise as in the case of Samuel. Barely with two years' sea experience before the mast, he was taken from the forecastle and made a provisional second mate. This occurred in a fever port on the West coast, and the committee of skippers that examined him agreed that he knew more of the science of navigation than they had remembered or forgotten. Two years later he sailed from Liverpool, mate of the *Starry Grace*, with both master's and extra-master's tickets in his possession. And then it happened – the thing the old crones had been shaking their heads over for years.

It was told me by Gavin McNab, bosun of the *Starry Grace* at the time, himself an Island McGill man.

"Wull do I remember ut," he said. "We was runnin' our Eastun' down, an' makun' heavy weather of ut. Oz fine a sailor-mon oz ever walked was Samuel Henan. I remember the look of hum wull thot last marnun', a-watchun' them bug seas curlun' up astern, an' a-watchun' the old girl an' seeun' how she took them – the skupper down below an' drunkun' for days. Ut was ot seven thot Henan brought her up on tull the wund, not darun' tull run longer un thot fearful sea. Ot eight, after havun' breakfast, he turns un, an' a half hour after up comes the skupper, bleary-eyed an' shaky an' holdun' on tull the componion.[5] Ut was fair smokun', I om tellun' ye, an' there he stood, blunkun' an' noddun' an' talkun' tull humsel'. 'Keep off,' says he ot last tull the mon ot the wheel. 'My God!' says the second mate, standun' beside hum. The skupper never looks tull hum ot all, but keeps on mutterun' an' jabberun' tull humsel'. All of a suddent-like he straightuns up an' throws hus head back, an' says: 'Put your wheel over, me mon – now, domn ye! Are ye deef thot ye'll no be hearun' me?'

"Ut was a drunken mon's luck, for the *Starry Grace* wore off afore thot God-Almighty gale wuthout shuppun' a bucket o' watter, the second mate shoutun' orders an' the crew jumpun' like mod. An' wuth thot the skupper nods contented-like tull humself an' goes below after more whuskey. Ut was plain murder o' the lives o' all of us, for ut was no time for the buggest shup afloat tull be runnun'.[6] Run? Never hov I seen the like! Ut was beyond all thunkun', an' me goun' tull sea, boy an' mon, for forty year. I tell you ut was fair awesome.

"The face o' the second mate was white oz death, an' he stood ut alone for half an hour, when ut was too much for hum an' he went below an' called Samuel an' the third. Ay, a fine sailormon thot Samuel, but ut was too much for hum. He looked an' studied, and looked an' studied, but he could no see hus way. He durst na heave tull. She would ha' been sweeput o' all honds an' stucks an' everythung afore she could a-fetcht up. There was naught tull do but keep on runnun'. An' uf ut worsened we were lost onyway, for soon or late thot overtakun' sea was sure tull sweep us clear over poop an' all.

"Dud I say ut was a God-Almighty gale? Ut was worse nor thot. The devil himself must ha' hod a hond un the brewun' o' ut, ut was thot fearsome. I ha' looked on some sights, but I om no carun' tull look on the like o' thot again. No mon dared tull be un hus bunk. No, nor no mon on the decks. All honds of us stood on top the house an' held on an' watched. The three mates was on the poop, with two men ot the wheel, an' the only mon below was thot whuskey-blighted captain snorun' drunk.

"An' then I see ut comun', a mile away, risun' above all the waves like an island un the sea – the buggest wave ever I looked upon. The three mates stood tulgether an' watched ut comun', a-prayun' like we thot she would no break un passun' us. But ut was no tull be. Ot the last, when she rose up like a mountain, curlun' above the stern an' blottun' out the sky, the mates scottered, the second an' third runnun' for the mizzen-shrouds an' climbun' up, but the first runnun' tull the wheel tull lend a hond. He was a brave mon, thot Samuel Henan. He run straight un tull the face o' thot father o' all waves, no thunkun' on humself but thunkun' only o' the shup. The two men was lashed tull the wheel, but he would be ready tull hond un the case they was kult. An' then she took ut. We on the house could no see the poop for the thousand tons o' watter thot hod hut ut. Thot wave cleaned them out, took everythung along wuth ut – the two mates, climbun' up the mizzen-ruggun', Samuel Henan runnun' tull the wheel, the two men ot the wheel, ay, an' the wheel utself. We never saw aught o' them, for she broached tull what o' the wheel goun', an' two men o' us was drownded off the house, no tull mention the carpenter thot we pucked up ot the break o' the poop wuth every bone o' hus body broke tull he was like so much jelly."

Notes

[5] The companionway of a ship is the staircase leading from the deck to the cabins below.

[6] Running before the wind. In heavy weather the ship should have its bow (the strongest part) facing the waves, not its stern.

And here enters the marvel of it, the miraculous wonder of that woman's heroic spirit. Margaret Henan was forty-seven when the news came home of the loss of Samuel; and it was not long after that the unbelievable rumor went around Island McGill. I say unbelievable. Island McGill would not believe. Doctor Hall pooh-pooh'd it. Everybody laughed at it as a good joke. They traced back the gossip to Sara Dack, servant to the Henans, and who alone lived with Margaret and her husband. But Sara Dack persisted in her assertion and was called a low-mouthed liar. One or two dared question Tom Henan himself, but beyond black looks and curses for their presumption they elicited nothing from him.

The rumor died down, and the island fell to discussing in all its ramifications the loss of the *Grenoble* in the China Seas, with all her officers and half her crew born and married on Island McGill. But the rumor would not stay down. Sara Dack was louder in her assertions, the looks Tom Henan cast about him were blacker than ever, and Dr. Hall, after a visit to the Henan house, no longer pooh-pooh'd. Then Island McGill sat up, and there was a tremendous wagging of tongues. It was unnatural and ungodly. The like had never been heard. And when, as time passed, the truth of Sara Dack's utterances was manifest, the island folk decided, like the bosun of the *Starry Grace*, that only the devil could have had a hand in so untoward a happening. And the infatuated woman, so Sara Dack reported, insisted that it would be a boy. "Eleven bairns ha' I borne," she said; "sux o' them lossies an' five o' them loddies. An' sunce there be balance un all thungs, so wull there be balance wuth me. Sux o' one an' half a dozen o' the other – there uz the balance, an' oz sure oz the sun rises un the marnun', thot sure wull ut be a boy."

And boy it was, and a prodigy. Dr. Hall raved about its unblemished perfection and massive strength, and wrote a brochure on it for the Dublin Medical Society as the most interesting case of the sort in his long career. When Sara Dack gave the babe's unbelievable weight, Island McGill refused to believe and once again called her liar. But when Doctor Hall attested that he had himself weighed it and seen it tip that very notch, Island McGill held its breath and accepted whatever report Sara Dack made of the infant's progress or appetite. And once again Margaret Henan carried a babe to Belfast and had it christened Samuel.

"Oz good oz gold ut was," said Sara Dack to me.

Sara, at the time I met her, was a buxom, phlegmatic spinster of sixty, equipped with an experience so tragic and unusual that though her tongue ran on for decades its output would still be of imperishable interest to her cronies.

"Oz good oz gold," said Sara Dack. "Ut never fretted. Sut ut down un the sun by the hour an' never a sound ut would make oz long oz ut was no hungered. An' thot strong! The grup o' uts honds was like a mon's. I mind me, when ut was but hours old, ut grupped me so mighty thot I fetcht a scream I was thot frighted. Ut was the punk o' health. Ut slept an' ate, an' grew. Ut never bothered. Never a night's sleep ut lost tull no one, nor ever a munut's, an' thot wuth cuttin' uts teeth an' all. An' Margaret would dandle ut on her knee an' ask was there ever so fine a loddie un the three Kungdoms.

"The way ut grew! Ut was un keepun' wuth the way ut ate. Ot a year ut was the size o' a bairn of two. Ut was slow tull walk an' talk. Exceptun' for gurgly noises un uts throat an' for creepun' on all fours, ut dudna monage much un the walkun' an' talkun' line. But thot was tull be expected from the way ut grew. Ut all went tull growun' strong an' healthy. An' even old Tom Henan cheered up ot the might of ut an' said was there ever the like o' ut un the three Kungdoms. Ut was Doctor Hall thot first suspicioned, I mind me well, though ut was luttle I dreamt what he was up tull ot the time. I see hum holdun' thungs un front o' luttle Sammy's eyes, an' a-makun' noises, loud an' soft, an' far an' near, un luttle Sammy's ears. An' then I see Doctor Hall go away, wrunklun' hus eyebrows an' shakun' hus head like the bairn was ailun'. But he was no ailun', oz I could swear full, me a-seeun' hun eat an' grow. But Doctor Hall no said a word tull Margaret an' I was no for guessun' the why he was sore-puzzled.

"I mind me when luttle Sammy first spoke. He was two years old an' the size of a child o' five, though he could no monage the walkun' yet but when around on all-fours, happy an' contented-like an' makun' no trouble oz long oz he was fed promptly, whuch was onusual often. I was hangun' the wash on the line ot the time when out he comes, on all-fours, hus bug head waggun' tull an' fro an' blunkun' un the sun. An' then, suddent, he talked. I was thot took a-back I near died o' fright, an' fine I knew ut then, the shakun' o' Doctor Hall's head. Talked? Never a bairn on Island McGill talked so loud an' tull such purpose. There was no mustakun' ut. I stood there all tremblun' an' shakun'. Little Sammy was brayun'. I tell you, sir, he was brayun' like an ass – just like thot, loud an' long an' cheerful tull ut seemed hus lungs ud crack.

"He was a eediot – a great, awful, monster eediot. Ut was after he talked thot Doctor Hall told Margaret, but she would no believe. Ut would all come right, she said. Ut was growun' too fast for aught else. Guv ut time, said she, an' we would see. But old Tom Henan knew, an' he never held up hus head again. He could no abide the thung, an' would no brung humsel' tull touch ut, though I om no denyun' he was fair fascinated by ut. Mony the time I see hum watchun' of ut aroun' a corner, lookun' ot ut tull hus eyes fair bulged wuth the horror; an' when ut brayed old Tom ud stuck hus fungers tull hus ears an' look thot miserable I could a-puttied hum.

"An' bray ut could! Ut was the only thung ut could do besides eat an' grow. Whenever ut was hungry ut brayed, an' there was no stoppun' ut save wuth food. An' always of a marnun', when first ut crawled tull the kutchen-door an' blunked out ot the sun, ut brayed. An' ut was brayun' that brought about uts end.

"I mind me well. Ut was three years old an' oz bug oz a lod o' ten. Old Tom hed been goun' from bod tull worse, ploughun' up an' down the fields an' talkun' an' mut-terun' tull humself. On the marnun' o' the day I mind me, he was suttun' on the bench outside the kutchen, afuttun' the handle tull a puck-axe. Unbeknown, the monster eediot crawled tull the door an' brayed after hus fashion ot the sun. I see old Tom start up an' look. An' there was the monster eediot, waggun' uts bug head an' blunkun' an' brayun' like the great bug ass ut was. Ut was too much for Tom. Somethin' went wrong wuth hum suddent-like. He jumped tull hus feet an' fetcht the puck-handle down on the monster eediot's head. An' he hut ut again an' again like ut was a mod dog an' hum afeard o' ut. An' he went straight tull the stable an' hung humsel' tull a rafter. An' I was no for stoppun' on after such-like, an' I went tull stay along wuth me suster thot was married tull John Martin an' comfortable-off."

I sat on the bench by the kitchen door and regarded Margaret Henan, while with her callous thumb she pressed down the live fire of her pipe and gazed out across the twilight-sombered fields. It was the very bench Tom Henan had sat upon that last san-guinary day of life. And Margaret sat in the doorway where the monster, blinking at the sun, had so often wagged its head and brayed. We had been talking for an hour, she with that slow certitude of eternity that so befitted her; and, for the life of me, I could lay no finger on the motives that ran through the tangled warp and woof of her. Was she a martyr to Truth? Did she have it in her to worship at so abstract a shrine? Had she conceived Abstract Truth to be the one high goal of human endeavor on that day of long ago when she named her first-born Samuel? Or was hers the stubborn obstinacy of the ox? the fixity of purpose of the balky horse? the stolidity of the self-willed peasant-mind? Was it whim or fancy? – the one streak of lunacy in what was otherwise an eminently rational mind? Or, reverting, was hers the spirit of a Bruno?[7] Was she convinced of the intellectual rightness of the stand she had taken? Was hers a steady, enlightened opposition to superstition? or – and a subtler thought – was she mastered by some vaster, profounder superstition, a fetish-worship of which the Alpha and the Omega was the cryptic *Samuel*?

"Wull ye be tellun' me," she said, "thot uf the second Samuel hod been named Larry thot he would no hov fell un the hot watter an' drownded? Atween you an' me, sir, an' ye are untellugent-lookun' tull the eye, would the name hov made ut onyways dufferent? Would the washun' no be done thot day uf he hod been Larry or Michael? Would hot watter no be hot an' would hot watter no burn uf he hod hod ony other name but Samuel?"

I acknowledged the justice of her contention, and she went on.

"Do a wee but of a name change the plans o' God? Do the world run by hut or muss, an' be God a weak, shully-shallyun' creature thot ud alter the fate an' destiny o' thungs because the worm Margaret Henan seen fut tull name her bairn Samuel? There be my son Jamie. He wull no sign a Rooshan-Funn un hus crew because o' believun' thot Rooshan-Funns do be monajun' the wunds an' hov the makun' o' bod weather. Wull you be thunkun' so? Wull you be thunkun' thot God thot makes the wunds tull blow wull bend hus head from on high tull lussen tull the word o' a greasy Rooshan-Funn un some dirty shup's fo'c'sle?"

I said no, certainly not; but she was not to be set aside from pressing home the point of her argument.

"Then wull you be thunkun' thot God thot directs the stars un their courses, an' tull whose mighty foot the world uz but a footstool, wull you be thunkun' thot he wull take a spite again' Margaret Henan an' send a bug wave off the Cape tull wash her son un tull eternity, all because she was for namun' hum Samuel?"

"But why Samuel?" I asked.

"An' thot I dinna know. I wanted ut so."

"But why did you want it so?"

"An' uz ut me thot would be answerun' a such-like question? Be there ony mon luvun' or dead thot can answer? Who can tell the *why* o' like? My Jamie was fair daft on buttermilk; he would drunk ut tull, oz he said himself, hus back-teeth was awash. But my Tumothy could no abide buttermilk. I like tull lussen tull the thunder growlun' an' roarun', an' rampajun'. My Katie could no abide the noise of ut, but must scream an' flutter an' go runnun' for the mudmost o' a feather-bed. Never yet hov I heard the answer tull the *why* o' like. God alone hoz thot answer. You an' me mortal an' we canna know. Enough for us tull know what we like an' what we duslike. I *like* – thot uz the first word an' the last. An' behind thot *like* no mon can go an' find the *why* o' ut. I *like* Samuel, an' I like ut wull. Ut uz a sweet name, an' there be a rollun' wonder un the sound o' ut thot passes onderstandun'."

The twilight deepened, and in the silence I gazed upon that splendid dome of a forehead which time could not mar, at the width between the eyes, and at the eyes themselves – clear, out-looking, and wide-seeing. She rose to her feet with an air of dismissing me, saying:

"Ut wull be a dark walk home, an' there wull be more thon a sprunkle o' wet un the sky."

"Have you any regrets, Margaret Henan?" I asked, suddenly and without forethought.

Notes

[7] Giordano Bruno (*c*.1548–1600), Italian philosopher who was burned at the stake for his beliefs.

She studied me a moment.

"Ay, thot I no ha' borne another son."

"And you would ...?" I faltered.

"Ay, thot I would," she answered. "Ut would ha' been hus name."

I went down the dark road between the hawthorn hedges puzzling over the why of like, repeating Samuel to myself and aloud and listening to the rolling wonder in its sound that had charmed her soul and led her life in tragic places. *Samuel!* There was a rolling wonder in the sound. Ay, there was!

H[oward] P[hillips] Lovecraft
(1890–1937)

H. P. Lovecraft was born in Providence, Rhode Island, the "Arkham" of his fiction, and spent most of his life there. His fiction appeared in popular "pulp" magazines, and he never gained acceptance by mainstream publishers or academic reviewers during his lifetime. The Arkham Press was founded by supporters after his death to collect and disseminate his work. The recent issuing of a volume of Lovecraft's tales by the Library of America, edited by Peter Straub, testifies to his current reputation as the master of American supernatural fiction in the early twentieth century, as does his acknowledged influence on the vastly popular Steven King, among others.

"The Outsider" was written in 1921, before Lovecraft had published any of his fiction, and appeared five years later in *Weird Tales*, which had become his most frequent outlet. (He submitted five stories to *Weird Tales* shortly after the first issue appeared, and all were accepted.) The story is an elegant homage to Edgar Allan Poe, whom Lovecraft had discovered as a child, and would always regard as a nearly perfect artist who greatly deepened the power of the Gothic through his insights into human psychology. Readers will recognize Poe's signature crazed narrator, the generalized nightmare landscape, and the inevitable half-ruined castle.

In other stories Lovecraft turned to a recognizable New England landscape, as did Hawthorne before him (whom Lovecraft also admired), and often references the dark deeds of old witchcraft days in Salem. In a series of narratives Lovecraft drew upon the British writers Lord Dunsany and Arthur Machen, and upon Ambrose Bierce and Robert K. Chambers, to develop his "Cthulhu Mythos," which explains the evil in the world (of which Salem witchcraft was an example) in terms of ancient gods and alien invaders who can interbreed with humans. This lore is partially explained in the *Necronomicon*, which, like Chambers' fabled *The King in Yellow*, is too dangerous a book for ordinary mortals to read.

Text: H. P. Lovecraft, "The Outsider," *Weird Tales*, 7/4 (April 1926), 449–53. Reprinted by permission of Arkham House Publishers, Inc., and Arkham's agents, JABerwocky Literary Agency, Inc., PO Box 4558, Sunnyside, NY 11104-0558.

The Outsider

Unhappy is he to whom the memories of childhood bring only fear and sadness. Wretched is he who looks back upon lone hours in vast and dismal chambers with brown hangings and maddening rows of antique books, or upon awed watches in twilight groves of grotesque, gigantic, and vine-encumbered trees that silently wave twisted branches far aloft. Such a lot the gods gave to me – to me, the dazed, the disappointed;

the barren, the broken. And yet I am strangely content and cling desperately to those sere memories, when my mind momentarily threatens to reach beyond to the other.

I know not where I was born, save that the castle was infinitely old and infinitely horrible, full of dark passages and having high ceilings where the eye could find only cobwebs and shadows. The stones in the crumbling corridors seemed always hideously damp, and there was an accursed smell everywhere, as of the piled-up corpses of dead generations. It was never light, so that I used sometimes to light candles and gaze steadily at them for relief, nor was there any sun outdoors, since the terrible trees grew high above the topmost accessible tower. There was one black tower which reached above the trees into the unknown outer sky, but that was partly ruined and could not be ascended save by a well-nigh impossible climb up the sheer wall, stone by stone.

I must have lived years in this place, but I cannot measure the time. Beings must have cared for my needs, yet I cannot recall any person except myself, or anything alive but the noiseless rats and bats and spiders. I think that whoever nursed me must have been shockingly aged, since my first conception of a living person was that of somebody mockingly like myself, yet distorted, shrivelled, and decaying like the castle. To me there was nothing grotesque in the bones and skeletons that strewed some of the stone crypts deep down among the foundations. I fantastically associated these things with everyday events, and thought them more natural than the coloured pictures of living beings which I found in many of the mouldy books. From such books I learned all that I know. No teacher urged or guided me, and I do not recall hearing any human voice in all those years – not even my own; for although I had read of speech, I had never thought to try to speak aloud. My aspect was a matter equally unthought of, for there were no mirrors in the castle, and I merely regarded myself by instinct as akin to the youthful figures I saw drawn and painted in the books. I felt conscious of youth because I remembered so little.

Outside, across the putrid moat and under the dark mute trees, I would often lie and dream for hours about what I read in the books; and would longingly picture myself amidst gay crowds in the sunny world beyond the endless forests. Once I tried to escape from the forest, but as I went farther from the castle the shade grew denser and the air more filled with brooding fear; so that I ran frantically back lest I lose my way in a labyrinth of nighted silence.

So through endless twilights I dreamed and waited, though I knew not what I waited for. Then in the shadowy solitude my longing for light grew so frantic that I could rest no more, and I lifted entreating hands to the single black ruined tower that reached above the forest into the unknown outer sky. And at last I resolved to scale that tower, fall though I might; since it were better to glimpse the sky and perish, than to live without ever beholding day.

In the dank twilight I climbed the worn and aged stone stairs till I reached the level where they ceased, and thereafter clung perilously to small footholds leading upward. Ghastly and terrible was that dead, stairless cylinder of rock; black, ruined, and deserted, and sinister with startled bats whose wings made no noise. But more ghastly and terrible still was the slowness of my progress; for climb as I might, the darkness overhead grew no thinner, and a new chill as of haunted and venerable mould assailed me. I shivered as I wondered why I did not reach the light, and would have looked down had I dared. I fancied that night had come suddenly upon me, and vainly groped with one free hand for a window embrasure, that I might peer out and above, and try to judge the height I had once attained.

All at once, after an infinity of awesome, sightless, crawling up that concave and desperate precipice, I felt my head touch a solid thing, and I knew I must have gained the roof, or at least some kind of floor. In the darkness I raised my free hand and tested the barrier, finding it stone and immovable. Then came a deadly circuit of the tower, clinging to whatever holds the slimy wall could give; till finally my testing hand found the barrier yielding, and I turned upward again, pushing the slab or door with my head as I used both hands in my fearful ascent. There was no light revealed above, and as my hands went higher I knew that my climb was for the nonce ended; since the slab was the trapdoor of an aperture leading to a level stone surface of greater circumference than the lower tower, no doubt the floor of some lofty and capacious observation chamber. I crawled through carefully, and tried to prevent the heavy slab from falling back into place, but failed in the latter attempt. As I lay exhausted on the stone floor I heard the eerie echoes of its fall, hoped when necessary to pry it up again.

Believing I was now at prodigious height, far above the accursed branches of the wood, I dragged myself up from the floor and fumbled about for windows, that I might look for the first time upon the sky, and the moon and stars of which I had read. But on every hand I was disappointed; since all that I found were vast shelves of marble, bearing odious oblong boxes of disturbing size. More and more I reflected, and wondered what hoary secrets might abide in this high apartment so many aeons cut off from the castle below. Then unexpectedly my hands came upon a doorway, where hung a portal of stone, rough with strange chiselling. Trying it, I found it locked; but with a supreme burst of strength I overcame all obstacles and dragged it open inward. As I did so there came to me the purest ecstasy I have ever known; for shining tranquilly through an ornate grating of iron, and down a short stone passageway of steps that ascended from the newly found doorway, was the radiant full moon, which I had never before seen save in dreams and in vague visions I dared not call memories.

Fancying now that I had attained the very pinnacle of the castle, I commenced to rush up the few steps beyond the door; but the sudden veiling of the moon by a cloud caused me to stumble, and I felt my way more slowly in the dark. It was still very dark when I reached the grating – which I tried carefully and found unlocked, but which I did not open for fear of falling from the amazing height to which I had climbed. Then the moon came out.

Most demoniacal of all shocks is that of the abysmally unexpected and grotesquely unbelievable. Nothing I had before undergone could compare in terror with what I now saw; with the bizarre marvels that sight implied. The sight itself was as simple as it was stupefying, for it was merely this: instead of a dizzying prospect of treetops seen from a lofty eminence, there stretched around me on the level through the grating nothing less than the solid ground, decked and diversified by marble slabs and columns, and overshadowed by an ancient stone church, whose ruined spire gleamed spectrally in the moonlight.

Half unconscious, I opened the grating and staggered out upon the white gravel path that stretched away in two directions. My mind, stunned and chaotic as it was, still held the frantic craving for light; and not even the fantastic wonder which had happened could stay my course. I neither knew nor cared whether my experience was insanity, dreaming, or magic; but was determined to gaze on brilliance and gaiety at any cost. I knew not who I was or what I was, or what my surroundings might be; though as I continued to stumble along I became conscious of a kind of fearsome latent memory that made my progress not wholly fortuitous. I passed under an arch out of that region of slabs and columns, and wandered through the open country; sometimes following the visible road, but sometimes leaving it curiously to tread across meadows where only occasional ruins bespoke the ancient presence of a forgotten road. Once I swam across a swift river where crumbling, mossy masonry told of a bridge long vanished.

Over two hours must have passed before I reached what seemed to be my goal, a venerable ivied castle in a thickly wooded park, maddeningly familiar, yet full of perplexing strangeness to me. I saw that the moat was filled in, and that some of the well-known towers were demolished, whilst new wings existed to confuse the beholder. But what I observed with chief interest and delight were the open windows – gorgeously ablaze with light and sending forth sound of the gayest revelry. Advancing to one of these I looked in and saw an oddly dressed company indeed; making merry, and speaking brightly to one another. I had never, seemingly, heard human speech before and could guess only vaguely what was said. Some of the faces seemed to hold expressions that brought up incredibly remote recollections, others were utterly alien.

I now stepped through the low window into the brilliantly lighted room, stepping as I did so from my single bright moment of hope to my blackest convulsion of despair and realization. The nightmare was quick to come, for as I entered, there occurred immediately one of the most terrifying demonstrations I had ever conceived. Scarcely had I crossed the sill when there descended upon the whole company a sudden and unheralded fear of hideous intensity, distorting every face and evoking the most hor-rible screams from nearly every throat. Flight was universal, and in the clamour and panic several fell in a swoon and were dragged away by their madly fleeing compan-ions. Many covered their eyes with their hands, and plunged blindly and awkwardly in their race to escape, overturning furniture and stumbling against the walls before they managed to reach one of the many doors. The cries were shocking; and as I stood in the brilliant apartment alone and dazed, listening to their vanishing echoes, I trembled at the thought of what might be lurking near me unseen. At a casual inspection the room seemed deserted, but when I moved towards one of the alcoves I thought I detected a presence there – a hint of motion beyond the golden-arched doorway lead-ing to another and somewhat similar room. As I approached the arch I began to per-ceive the presence more clearly; and then, with the first and last sound I ever uttered – a ghastly ululation that revolted me almost as poignantly as its noxious cause – I beheld in full, frightful vividness the inconceivable, indescribable, and unmentionable monstrosity which had by its simple appearance changed a merry company to a herd of delirious fugitives.

I cannot even hint what it was like, for it was a compound of all that is unclean, uncanny, unwelcome, abnormal, and detestable. It was the ghoulish shade of decay, antiquity, and dissolution; the putrid, dripping eidolon of unwholesome revelation, the awful baring of that which the merciful earth should always hide. God knows it was not of this world – or no longer of this world – yet to my horror I saw in its eaten-away and bone-revealing outlines a leering, abhorrent travesty on the human shape; and in its mouldy, disintegrating apparel an unspeakable quality that chilled me even more.

I was almost paralysed, but not too much so to make a feeble effort towards flight; a backward stumble which failed to break the spell in which the nameless, voiceless monster held me. My eyes bewitched by the glassy orbs which stared loathsomely into them, refused to close; though they were mercifully blurred, and showed the terrible object but indistinctly after the first shock. I tried to raise my hand to shut out the sight, yet so stunned were my nerves that my arm could not fully obey my will. The attempt, however, was enough to disturb my balance; so that I had to stagger forward several steps to avoid falling. As I did so I became suddenly and agonizingly aware of the nearness of the carrion thing, whose hideous hollow breathing I half fancied I could hear. Nearly mad, I found myself yet able to throw out a hand to ward off the foetid apparition which pressed so close; when in one cataclysmic second of cosmic nightmarishness and hellish accident *my fingers touched the rotting outstretched paw of the monster beneath the golden arch.*

I did not shriek, but all the fiendish ghouls that ride the night-wind shrieked for me as in that same second there crashed down upon my mind a single fleeting avalanche of soul-annihilating memory. I knew in that second all that had been; I remembered beyond the frightful castle and the trees, and recognized the altered edifice in which I now stood; I recognized, most terrible of all, the unholy abomination that stood leering before me as I withdrew my sullied fingers from its own.

But in the cosmos there is balm as well as bitterness, and that balm is nepenthe. In the supreme horror of that second I forgot what had horrified me, and the burst of black memory vanished in a chaos of echoing images. In a dream I fled from that haunted and accursed pile, and ran swiftly and silently in the moonlight. When I returned to the churchyard place of marble and went down the steps I found the stone trap-door immovable; but I was not sorry, for I had hated the antique castle and the trees. Now I ride with the mocking and friendly ghouls on the night-wind, and play by day amongst the catacombs of Nephren-Ka in the sealed and unknown valley of Hadoth by the Nile. I know that light is not for me, save that of the moon over the rock tombs of Neb, nor any gaiety save the unnamed feasts of Nitokris beneath the Great Pyramid; yet in my new wildness and freedom I almost welcome the bitterness of alienage.

For although nepenthe has calmed me, I know always that I am an outsider; a stranger in this century and among those who are still men. This I have known ever since I stretched out my fingers to the abomination within that great gilded frame; stretched out my fingers and touched a cold and unyielding surface of polished glass.

H[oward] P[hillips] Lovecraft

Select Bibliography

Adams, Rachel. *Sideshow U.S.A.: Freaks and the American Cultural Imagination*. Chicago: University of Chicago Press, 2001.

Asma, Stephen T. *On Monsters*. Oxford: Oxford University Press, 2009.

Auerbach, Nina. *Our Vampires, Ourselves*. Chicago: University of Chicago Press, 1995.

Austin, Eliot and Lawrence Austin. *Ghosts of the Gothic*. Princeton: Princeton University Press, 1980.

Baker, Dorothy Z. *America's Gothic Fiction: The Legacy of Magnalia Christi Americana*. Columbus: Ohio State University Press, 2007.

Benstock, Shari. *No Gifts from Chance: A Biography of Edith Wharton*. New York: Scribner's, 1994.

Bloom, Clive, ed. *Gothic Horror: A Reader's Guide from Poe to King and Beyond*. New York: St. Martin's Press, 1998.

Botting, Fred. *Gothic*. New York: St. Martin's Press, 1995.

Brogan, Kathleen. *Cultural Haunting: Ghosts and Ethnicity in Recent American Literature*. Charlottesville: University of Virginia Press, 1998.

Carpenter, Lynette and Wendy Kolmar, eds. *Haunting the House of Fiction: Feminist Perspectives on Ghost Stories by American Women*. Knoxville: University of Tennessee Press, 1991.

Christophersen, Bill. *The Apparition in the Glass: Charles Brockden Brown's American Gothic*. Athens: University of Georgia Press, 1993.

Crow, Charles L. *American Gothic*. Cardiff: University of Wales Press, 2009.

Crow, Charles L. "The Girl in the Library: Edith Wharton's 'The Eyes' and American Gothic Traditions." In *Spectral America: Phantoms and the National Imagination*. Ed. Jeffrey Andrew Weinstock. Madison: University of Wisconsin Press, 2004, 157–68.

Crow, Charles L. "Jack London's 'Samuel' as a Gothic Tale: The Terrible and Tragic Involved with Love." *Litteraria Pragensia*, 11 (2001), 81–7.

Crow, Charles L. "Under the Upas Tree: Charles Chesnutt's Gothic." In *Critical Essays on Charles Chesnutt*. Ed. Joseph R McElrath, Jr. New York: G. K. Hall, 1999, 261–70.

Davenport-Hines, Richard. *Gothic: Four Hundred Years of Excess, Horror, Evil, and Ruin*. New York: North Point Press, 1998.

Day, William Patrick. *In the Circles of Fear and Desire: A Study of Gothic Fantasy*. Chicago: University of Chicago Press, 1985.

DeLamotte, Eugenia C. *Perils of the Night: A Feminist Study of Nineteenth-Century Gothic*. New York: Oxford University Press, 1990.

Edmundson, Mark. *Nightmare on Main Street: Angels, Sadomasochism, and the Culture of Gothic*. Cambridge, MA: Harvard University Press, 1997.

Edwards, Justin D. *Gothic Passages: Racial Ambiguity and the American Gothic*. Iowa City: University of Iowa Press, 2003.

Ellis, Kate Ferguson. *The Contested Castle: Gothic Novels and the Subversion of Domestic Ideology*. Urbana: University of Illinois Press, 1989.

Erlich, Gloria C. *The Sexual Education of Edith Wharton*. Berkeley and Los Angeles: University of California Press, 1992.

Fedorko, Kathy A. *Gender and the Gothic in the Fiction of Edith Wharton*. Tuscaloosa: University Alabama Press, 1995.

Fiedler, Leslie. *Love and Death in the American Novel*. Cleveland: Meridian, 1964.

Fleenor, Juliann E. *The Female Gothic*. Montreal: Eden Press, 1983.

Goddu, Teresa A. *Gothic America: Narrative, History and Nation*. New York: Columbia University Press, 1997.

Graham, Kenneth W., ed. *Gothic Fictions*. New York: AMS Press, 1989.

Grixti, Joseph. *Terrors of Uncertainty: The Cultural Context of Horror Fiction*. London: Routledge, 1989.

Gross, Louis S. *Redefining the American Gothic: From Wieland to Day of the Dead*. Ann Arbor: U.M.I. Research Press, 1989.

Haggerty, George F. *Gothic Fiction/Gothic Form*. University Park: University of Pennsylvania Press, 1989.

Halberstam, Judith. *Skin Shows: Gothic Horror and the Technology of Monsters*. Durham: Duke University Press, 1995.

Halttunen, Karen. *Murder Most Foul: The Killer and the American Gothic Imagination*. Cambridge, MA: Harvard University Press, 1998.

Hansen, Chadwick. *Witchcraft at Salem*. New York: New American Library, 1970.

Heller, Terry. *The Delights of Terror: An Aesthetics of the Tale of Terror*. Urbana: University of Illinois Press, 1987.

Hemenway, Robert. "Gothic Sociology: Charles Chesnutt and the Gothic Mode." *Studies in the Literary Imagination*, 7/1 (1974), 101–19.

Hume, Robert D. "Gothic Versus Romantic: A Revaluation of the Gothic Form." *PMLA*, 84 (1969), 282–90.

Ingebretsen, Edward. *At Stake: Monsters and the Rhetoric of Fear in Public Culture*. Chicago: University of Chicago Press, 2001.

Jackson, Rosemary. *Fantasy: The Literature of Subversion*. London: Methuen, 1981.

Joshi, S. T. *The Modern Weird Tale*. Jefferson, NC: McFarland, 2001.

Kristeva, Julia. *Powers of Horror*. New York: Columbia University Press, 1982.

Lloyd-Smith, Allan. *American Gothic Fiction: An Introduction*. New York: Continuum, 2004.

Lloyd-Smith, Allan. "Nineteenth-Century American Gothic." In *A Companion to the Gothic*. Ed. David Punter. Oxford: Blackwell, 2000, 109–21.

Lloyd-Smith, Allan. *Uncanny American Fiction: Medusa's Face*. London: Macmillan, 1989.

Lovecraft, H. P. *Supernatural Horror in Literature*. New York: Dover, 1973.

Martin, Robert K. and Eric Savoy, eds. *American Gothic: New Interventions in a National Narrative*. Iowa City: University of Iowa Press, 1998.

McDowell, Margaret. "Edith Wharton's Ghost Stories." *Criticism*, 12 (1970), 133–52.

Meindl, Dieter. *American Fiction and the Metaphysics of the Grotesque*. Columbia: University of Missouri Press, 1996.

Mogen, David, Scott P. Sanders, and Joanne B. Karpinski, eds., *Frontier Gothic: Terror and Wonder at the Frontier in America*. Fairleigh Dickinson University Press, 1993.

Monnet, Agnieszka Soltysik. *The Poetics and Politics of the American Gothic: Gender and Slavery in Nineteenth-Century American Literature*. Farnham, Surrey: Ashgate, 2010.

Mulvey-Roberts, Marie, ed. *The Handbook to Gothic Literature*. New York: New York University Press, 1998.

Norton, Mary Beth. *In the Devil's Snare: The Salem Witchcraft Crisis of 1692*. New York: Alfred A. Knopf, 2002.

Punter, David. *Gothic Horror: A Reader's Guide from Poe to King and Beyond*. New York: St. Martin's Press, 1998.

Punter, David. *Gothic Pathologies*. New York: St. Martin's Press, 1998.

Punter, David. *The Literature of Terror*. New York: Longman, 1996.

Punter, David and Glennis Byron. *The Gothic*. Oxford: Blackwell, 2004.

Railo, Eino. *The Haunted Castle: A Study of the Elements of English Romanticism*. London: Routledge, 1927.

Ringe, Donald A. *American Gothic*. Lexington: University Press of Kentucky, 1982.

Ringel, Faye. *New England's Gothic Literature: History and Folklore of the Supernatural from the Seventeenth through the Twentieth Centuries*. Lewiston: Edwin Mellen Press, 1995.

Riquelme, John Paul, ed. *Gothic and Modernism: Essaying Dark Modernity*. Baltimore: Johns Hopkins University Press, 2008.

Savoy, Eric. "The Face of the Tenant: A Theory of American Gothic." In *American Gothic: New Interventions in a National Narrative*. Ed. Robert K. Martin and Eric Savoy. Iowa City: University of Iowa Press, 1998, 3–19.

Sedgwick, Eve Kosofsky. *The Coherence of Gothic Conventions*. New York: Arno Press, 1980.

Showalter, Elaine. "Syphilis, Sexuality, and the Fiction of the Fin de Siècle." In *Sex, Politics, and Science in the Nineteenth-Century Novel*. Ed. Ruth Bernard Yeazell. Baltimore: Johns Hopkins University Press, 1986, 88–114.

Spofford, Harriet Prescott. *"The Amber Gods" and Other Stories*. Ed. Alfred Bendixen. New Brunswick: Rutgers University Press, 1989.

Starkey, Marion L. *The Devil in Massachusetts*. New York: Alfred A. Knopf, 1949; repr. Anchor Books, 1969.

Truffin, Sherry. *Schoolhouse Gothic: Haunted Hallways and Predatory Pedagogues in Late Twentieth-Century American Literature and Scholarship*. Newcastle upon Tyne: Cambridge Scholars, 2008.

Veeder, William. "The Nurture of the Gothic, or How Can a Text Be Both Popular and Subversive?" In *American Gothic: New Interventions in a National Narrative*. Ed. Robert K. Martin and Peter Savoy. Iowa City: University of Iowa Press, 1998, 20–39.

Wardrop, Daneen. *Emily Dickinson's Gothic: Goblin with a Gauge*. Iowa City: University of Iowa Press, 1996.

Weinstock, Jeffrey Andrew. *Scare Tactics: Supernatural Fiction by American Women*. New York: Fordham University Press, 2008.

Weinstock, Jeffrey Andrew, ed. *Spectral America: Phantoms and the National Imagination*. Madison: University of Wisconsin Press, 2004.

Williams, Anne. *Art of Darkness: A Poetic of Gothic*. Chicago: University of Chicago Press, 1995.

Wolstenholme, Susan. *Gothic (Re)Visions: Writing Women as Readers*. Albany: State University of New York Press, 1993.

Index of Titles and First Lines

American Gothic: From Salem Witchcraft to H. P. Lovecraft, An Anthology, Second Edition. Edited by Charles L. Crow.
Editorial material and organization © 2013 John Wiley & Sons, Ltd. Published 2013 by John Wiley & Sons, Ltd.

Index to the Introductions and Footnotes

American Gothic: From Salem Witchcraft to H. P. Lovecraft, An Anthology, Second Edition. Edited by Charles L. Crow.
Editorial material and organization © 2013 John Wiley & Sons, Ltd. Published 2013 by John Wiley & Sons, Ltd.